Exploring Inequality

Exploring Inequality

A Sociological Approach

Jenny Stuber

University of North Florida

New York   Oxford

OXFORD UNIVERSITY PRESS

Oxford University Press is a department of the University of Oxford.
It furthers the University's objective of excellence in research,
scholarship, and education by publishing worldwide.

Oxford   New York

Auckland   Cape Town   Dar es Salaam   Hong Kong   Karachi
Kuala Lumpur   Madrid   Melbourne   Mexico City   Nairobi
New Delhi   Shanghai   Taipei   Toronto

With offices in

Argentina   Austria   Brazil   Chile   Czech Republic   France   Greece
Guatemala   Hungary   Italy   Japan   Poland   Portugal   Singapore
South Korea   Switzerland   Thailand   Turkey   Ukraine   Vietnam

For titles covered by Section 112 of the US Higher Education
Opportunity Act, please visit www.oup.com/us/he for the
latest information about pricing and alternate formats.

Published by Oxford University Press
198 Madison Avenue, New York, New York 10016
http://www.oup.com

Oxford is a registered trademark of Oxford University Press.

Library of Congress Cataloging-in-Publication Data
Stuber, Jenny.
    Exploring inequality : a sociological approach / Jenny Stuber,
University of North Florida.
        pages cm
    Includes bibliographical references and index.
    ISBN 978-0-19-933112-3
    1. Equality. I. Title.
    HM821.S767 2016
    305.8—dc23

                                                          2015005867

Printing number: 9 8 7 6 5 4 3 2 1

Printed in the United States of America
on acid-free paper

Contents

Do we really need another sociology textbook? With the market seemingly saturated, and with more formats moving to online editions, it may seem like an odd time to publish yet another traditional textbook. But after teaching an introductory course on diversity and inequality for many years, I believe a new textbook is needed. I know of no existing textbook on the topic of diversity and inequality that truly catches students' attention and provides them a solid sociological foundation on the topic. This book is written for a broad audience. It is designed to capture the imagination of students who are "natural-born sociologists" and those who do not yet have a well-honed sociological imagination. This text is written so that budding sociologists can become further committed to the field and so that one-time sociologists come away with a strong framework for understanding diversity and inequality. It pulls readers in by engaging personally relevant questions; it helps readers understand how their various identities were formed and how their social experiences are structured by those identities.

By giving equal attention to forces at the micro- and macro-levels—a core attribute of the sociological perspective—this text provides a unique and much-needed perspective. When applied to the topics of diversity and inequality, the sociological imagination demonstrates that *identities*—like sex, gender, sexuality, race and ethnicity, social class, and disability status—are social constructed: they are molded by face-to-face interactions and through socialization. These identities, however, are molded within specific historical and cultural milieu. This text also focuses on *social inequality*, illustrating how individual forces at the micro-level, along with structural factors on the macro-level, perpetuate inequality. This text shows that power and privilege operating at the macro-level, along with cultural meanings and face-to-face interactions, shape the unequal worlds in which we live.

What makes this text unique are the clever and engaging metaphors used throughout, as well as the theoretical and thematic organization of each unit. Within the first half of the text I focus on the socially constructed nature of our identities and the processes by which we acquire them. This means, in part, using an historical perspective. I use the metaphor of the "time machine" to show that much of what we take for granted in the realm of social identities and social categories has varied over time. Taking a cross-cultural perspective further illustrates the socially constructed nature of our worlds. I use the metaphor of the "study abroad trip" to show how social identities and social categories vary from place to place. Together, these metaphors constitute a core feature of the sociological perspective, showing that the identities and inequalities we take for granted are never static but are, in fact, always changing.

A key sociological assumption is that virtually any social phenomenon—including how long we live, how much money we earn, whether we marry and later divorce—can best be understood by examining the issue from both the micro- and macro-levels. As I show in the second half of the text, unequal outcomes of this sort are also structured by our social identities. By exploring social inequalities at the micro-level, I give the reader an understanding of how individual-level factors, including motivations, talents, and behaviors, contribute to social inequality. By exploring social inequalities at the macro-level, I show that the broader social context—in terms of institutional dynamics, social policies, and neighborhood/environmental forces—structures social inequality. I use the metaphors of "the player" and "the game" to show how social inequalities are the result of equally important and intricately intertwined forces operating at the individual and structural levels.

While this text is written with a clear and comprehensive sociological perspective, I have also deliberately left some things unsaid. These intentional gaps allow each instructor to craft their own take on these issues. Should an instructor wish to emphasize power and domination more fully, this text allows for it; if the instructor favors a symbolic interactionist take or wants to highlight "functional" aspects of inequality and diversity, there is space for that as well. With respect to "evidence," this text combines both classic and contemporary sociological research, and draws on research in anthropology, economics, and psychology. This is done to show the unique value of the sociological perspective and how scholarship from other disciplines can be used to illustrate that perspective.

Finally, while sociology is a vital and immediately relevant field of study, students sometimes feel overwhelmed by the constant attention to social problems. As instructors, we may not do enough to show how the sociological perspective can empower people to work against social inequality and engage in social change. Throughout this book, I include examples of social activism aimed at reducing social inequality and enhancing the dignity and opportunities of diverse people. In many cases, I use examples of activism taking place on college campuses featuring college students as activists engaged in issues relevant to a collegiate population. Although more can always be done to spark our engagement with social issues and injustice, these examples show that ordinary college students and citizens can powerfully affect the worlds around them.

ACKNOWLEDGMENTS

I would first like to thank Sherith Pankratz and the wonderful team at Oxford University Press. Sherith's enthusiasm for this project was a constant motivator. She understood my vision for this textbook from the beginning and championed my voice in a way that made writing it a true pleasure. Second, I would like to thank the thousands of students who sat through my classes as I honed the ideas and metaphors used in *Exploring Inequality*. Their continual feedback helped me understand which examples and concepts resonate with an undergraduate audience and which should be jettisoned. The anonymous reviewers of this manuscript have provided a similarly valuable service. These reviewers include:

Patricia Campion, Saint Leo University

Laurie Chancey, Asnuntuck Community College

Daniel K. Cortese, Governors State University

Michelle Dietert, Texas A&M University - Central Texas

Mary L. Donaghy, Arkansas State University

Heather Downs, Jacksonville University

Omari Jackson, Colby-Sawyer College

Steve Jacobs, Piedmont College

Kimberly E. Fox, Bridgewater State University

Melissa Gosdin, Albany State University

George Guay, American Public University

John C. Kilburn Jr., Texas A&M International University

Julie A. Kmec, Washington State University

Katherine Lineberger, Florida International University

Yvonne M. Luna, Northern Arizona University

Barbara C. Medley, University of Tennessee – Chattanooga

Kristin D. Mickelson, Arizona State University

Milan Zafirovski, University of North Texas

Lisa K. Zottarelli, San Antonio College

This project has been a labor of love, and I thank all of those who contributed to it, directly and indirectly.

Can't We All Just Get Along?

A Sociological Approach to Diversity

Since the late 1700s, Irish Americans living in New York City have put on a St. Patrick's Day parade. Marching down a 1.5-mile parade route through Manhattan's Midtown, the event features an exuberant collection of firefighters, military and police groups, bands, and social and cultural clubs. With approximately 150,000 formal participants, it is now the largest St. Patrick's Day parade in the world. While the occasion began as a way to honor the homeland, it has morphed into an "all-American" affair, with celebrants raising a glass of beer and proclaiming that at least for one day of the year, "Everyone's a Little Irish." The entire city of Chicago celebrates the day with the bold gesture of dyeing the Chicago River green. Down in Savannah, Georgia—where many Irish immigrants arrived as indentured servants— the event resembles Mardi Gras, with much of the city transformed into an open-air party.

Three months later, down in lower Manhattan, a similarly exuberant parade takes place. Dating back to the early-1970s, the annual "Pride March" commemorates the starting point of the gay civil rights movement. Initially a way to remind people of the police aggression that took place at the Stonewall Inn in Greenwich Village on June 28, 1969, the event has grown larger and more celebratory over time. In addition to brightly colored floats featuring dance music and scantily clad revelers, the parade routinely features an assemblage of politicians, entertainers, religious organizations, and ordinary families—all in a public effort to normalize the presence of sexual diversity in our society.

Given the celebratory nature of both parades, it is perhaps ironic that one group that is excluded from New York City's St. Patrick's Day parade is that of those who wish to march as *gay* Irish Americans. While gay Irish Americans are welcome to march in the parade generally speaking, they are banned from doing so in a way that explicitly proclaims their *gay* Irish pride. During the spring of 2014, discontent with the ban intensified. Guinness and Heineken brewers, major sponsors of the event,

Everyone is a little bit Irish on St. Patrick's Day. Once discriminated against, Irish Americans are now celebrated.

In some communities, gay pride parades are a popular occasion. Still, they sometimes are criticized or opposed for being too "out there."

pulled their support for the parade and Mayor Bill de Blasio opted to march in the Queens St. Patrick's Day parade instead—which has no restrictions on public declarations of being both gay and Irish.

What these modern celebrations generally lack, and what the fervor surrounding the 2014 St. Patrick's Day Parade in New York City tended to obscure, is a historical perspective. For much of the nineteenth and early twentieth centuries, Irish Americans were a much-maligned social group. In the context of an overwhelmingly Protestant nation, waves of Irish Catholic immigrants were treated with suspicion. Depicted in newspapers and magazines as animals and uncivilized pagans, Irish Catholics experienced discrimination and exclusion for many decades. Historically, St. Patrick's Day parades were a way to publicly voice an opposition to nativist movements in the United States that stigmatized immigrant groups like the Irish, while also making a statement against British oppression in the homeland. The political flavor of the St. Patrick's Day parade, and the underlying theme of pride in the face of stigma and oppression, is now echoed in gay pride parades across the country. Despite these similarities, many Americans remain deeply uncomfortable with public declarations of "gay pride"—which they see as overly hedonistic and uncomfortably "in-your-face."

This "tale of two parades" highlights many themes woven throughout this book. The goal of this chapter is to provide an overview of the sociological perspective and a vocabulary for talking about two issues that are at the heart of sociology: diversity and inequality. While sociologists and others embrace diversity and believe that it enriches society, the presence of diversity also seems to go hand in hand with inequality. When groups are different from one another—whether in terms of culture, religion, race, or ethnicity—these *differences* are often transformed into *deficiencies*. This theme will re-emerge in the second half of the chapter. For now, we turn to a discussion of *sociological perspective*, and two of the major themes that characterize it; we then turn to a more focused discussion of how sociologists look at diversity and inequality.

ILLUSTRATING THE SOCIOLOGICAL PERSPECTIVE

In the simplest terms, **sociology** can be defined as the systematic study of human society. Referring to it as "systematic" means that sociology is an academic field that uses the scientific method and other rigorous techniques to develop its theories and knowledge. Yet describing to it as the study of "human society" is quite vague, given that psychology, anthropology, and history also study aspects of society. In fact, the same social phenomena might be studied in each of these fields—alcohol consumption, for example, or marriage and the family, just to name a few—yet how each field approaches these topics differs considerably. Considering the many ways in which human behavior and social arrangements can be studied, there are several unique and powerful aspects of the sociological perspective. This section highlights two consistent themes running through the field of sociology: the notion that much of our social world is *socially constructed* and that many social phenomena can be understood best by looking at them from both a *micro-* and a *macro-level* perspective. Let me illustrate.

IS IT SPIT OR SALIVA? THE SOCIALLY CONSTRUCTED NATURE OF OUR SOCIAL WORLDS

Take a moment and think about what is right now going on in your mouth. While we rarely stop to do so, there is a fascinating phenomenon happening all the time, right now, in our mouths. Permit me, for a moment, to direct your attention to the saliva that is currently coating the inside of your mouth, minding its own business. It lives there every day, all day long, not bothering anyone. In fact, it has an important job to do, helping with digestion and protecting teeth from decay. Although you may feel a twinge of awkwardness now that I have asked you to become more aware of its existence, the fact of the matter is that a substance we call saliva is a very ordinary, unquestioned resident of your mouth.

Consider now, what happens when that saliva exits your mouth. If you are consuming a beverage, it becomes the forbidden substance known as "backwash." If you feel an excess of saliva building up in your mouth and you expel it on the ground, it becomes "spit." While there are some instances when the saliva that leaves our mouths may carry infection or chewing tobacco residue, it is generally the case that the substance that leaves our mouth—what we call *spit*—is no different from the substance that is currently lining your mouth—what we call *saliva*. Indeed, if I were to spit into a spoon, and then immediately re-ingest that exact same substance, it is quite likely that onlookers would be utterly disgusted. The nature of this disgust raises interesting questions, given that these two substances have the same chemical composition: the substance is essentially the same, the only difference being whether it is located inside or outside the mouth.

To understand how saliva becomes spit, one needs to understand the sociological perspective, in this case the idea that much of our social world is socially constructed. To say that something is **socially constructed** is to draw attention to the fact that it is humans who *give meaning* to their worlds. We give meaning to things as seemingly trivial as the distinction between spit and saliva. The distinction between these two substances—one considered normal and the other considered disgusting—is simply a matter of human definition. Humans give meaning to many other concepts, such as what it means to be an alcoholic or have a mental illness. These definitions are created out of human understanding, and the implications of being labeled an alcoholic or schizophrenic are also a matter of human labeling and definition. For the purposes of this text, much of our attention will be focused on the ways in which gender, sexuality, race, and social class are *socially constructed*.

There are two components to the process by which our worlds are "socially constructed." First, humans give meaning to their worlds through face-to-face communication. The unique power of the human brain is that our species can interact symbolically; that means that we can think in abstract terms, give objects and phenomena disparate meanings. The important idea is that we do this together, rather than individually or idiosyncratically. The meanings we give to our social worlds—whether in naming spit or saliva, or gender and sexuality—are co-constructions built out of human interaction. Children learn these definitions through *socialization*—the process by which we learn our society's cultural rules and expectations. Later in life, they either perpetuate these definitions by continuing to act on them or they challenge them and propose new meanings. When enough people jointly agree that what it means to be an ideal woman should be modified, or that the line between forbidden and acceptable sexual acts needs to be redrawn, a new social construction emerges.

Yet humans do not create these definitions out of thin air. Thus, the second thing to know about our worlds being socially constructed is that these meanings arise from the social structure. The **social structure** generally refers to the large-scale social institutions that make up society. These institutions include the family, religious authorities and organizations, economic arrangements, the political order, mass media and communications, and more. To take a concrete example, we know that definitions of gender have changed over time and vary across cultures: what it means to be a man and what it means to be a woman are historically and cross-culturally variable. We can explain these variations, or the fact that gender is socially constructed, by pointing to the fact that religious and economic arrangements were very different in the 1700s than they are today. As society has become more secular, and as society has moved from an industrial economy that needs physical strength to an information-based economy built upon service skills and intellectual knowledge, women's (and men's) roles have changed. These broad social transformations have given new opportunities to men and women, thereby socially reconstructing gender roles. These changing conceptions of masculinity and femininity did not happen overnight, nor did they emerge out of nowhere: they arose out of transformations in the social structure (and through social movements aimed at explicitly changing dynamics of power and privilege).

By adopting the social constructionist perspective, sociologists reject the notion that social phenomena are rooted in an inherent reality. In this sense, the social constructionist perspective stands in opposition to the essentialist perspective. The **essentialist perspective** generally views a social phenomena as fixed, universal, and transhistorical—that is, true, regardless of a social or historical context. A common theme within the essentialist perspective is the assumption that social phenomena are rooted in underlying biological realities. In the case of gender differences, the assumption is that men and women are different due to biological differences in brain structure, hormones, and so forth. Applied to race, an essentialist perspective might argue that there are distinct racial groups and that social differences between these groups— in terms of talents and traits—are rooted in biological differences between the races.

The social constructionist perspective, however, challenges these assumptions. It derives its analytic power from examining the world from a historical and cross-cultural perspective. When we take the time to examine all of the human variations that exist cross-culturally and that have existed historically, it is almost impossible to identify any social phenomenon that is universally true. What it means to be a man or woman—ideal manifestations of masculinity and femininity—exhibits tremendous variation. Consider, for example, the fact that men in Arab cultures have considerable social dominance and that homosexuality is highly stigmatized, but that men have intimate relationships with one another and may be seen walking arm-in-arm down the street. This version of masculinity is different from the one seen in northern Europe, which is different still from the *machismo* (intense masculine power that strongly differentiates male and female roles) that characterizes many Latin American cultures. Using an entirely different example—in this case men involved in an intimate sex act—we will see in this text that the same physical act that is considered forbidden in one society (spit) is seen as an ideal form of male sexuality in another (saliva).

Throughout this text, I use the metaphors of the *study abroad trip* and *traveling through time* to illustrate the social constructionist perspective; these metaphors take us on a journey that draws our attention to cross-cultural and historical variations in social phenomena. In doing so, we see both the incredible creativity and variation that humans bring to their lived experiences as well as the role that social structures play in shaping those experiences.

THE PLAYER AND THE GAME: BRINGING TOGETHER THE MICRO- AND MACRO-LEVEL PERSPECTIVES

"Anyone can make it if they try." This is one of the core beliefs in American life. This belief emphasizes individualism and agency above all else. It expresses limitless faith in human potential and recognizes no external barriers to one's success or well-being. This statement suggests that in the game of life, the talents, desires, and motivations of the player—or individual—are of primary importance. So how would a sociologist evaluate this claim? To answer that question, we turn to the work of Malcolm Gladwell, an award-winning journalist who has been recognized for bringing sociological ideas to the public's attention in his best-selling books, *The Tipping Point*, *Blink*, and *Outliers*.

Will this little guy end up in the big leagues? For sociologists, the player's skills matter, but so do the rules of the game.

In his book *Outliers: The Story of Success*, Malcolm Gladwell examines the lives of especially successful people—like Microsoft founder Bill Gates and the Beatles—and looks for common themes in their achievements. These were immensely talented people who without doubt worked hard and made it. One example from his book, drawn from the work of Canadian psychologist Roger Barnsley, illustrates the sociological perspective. In his analysis of elite Canadian hockey players, Barnsley observed a unique pattern: 40 percent of the players on elite junior teams were born in the first three months of the year, while only 10 percent were born in the last three months of the year. Gladwell reports similar patterns in Swedish and Czech hockey teams. What is it about being born in the first three months of the year that makes those players four times more likely to "make it," in this case playing hockey at the elite level?

If only the will and talent of the player mattered, it is unlikely that the data would display this pattern. Indeed, there is little reason to believe players born early in the year have special endowments of talent or motivation. In fact, neither Barnsley nor Gladwell attributed these players' success to their individual traits. Instead, the authors focused on the nature of the game. In this instance, I do not mean the game of hockey itself; I mean **"the game"** in terms of the structure and rules that govern this particular phenomenon. When it comes to how competitive hockey is structured in Canada, Gladwell wrote: "It's simply that in Canada the eligibility cutoff for age-class hockey is January 1. A boy who turns ten on January 2, then, could be playing alongside someone who doesn't turn ten until the end of the year—and at that age, in pre-adolescence, a twelve-month gap in age represents an enormous difference in physical maturity." Once their talent emerges—which Gladwell partially sees as the luck of the birth-month lottery—the player gets better coaching, practices more frequently, and has better teammates to play with. By the age of 13, these "cumulative advantages" add up, so that the initially small advantage of being born early in the year later appears as exceptional talent and motivation.

So what does this seemingly obscure example have to do with the sociological perspective? It helps illustrate the dual importance of the micro- and macro-level forces. The **micro-level** refers to the level of the individual. It focuses on the ways

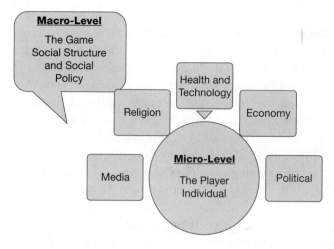

Figure 1.1 Illustrating the Sociological Perspective: Micro- and Macro-Level Processes

that social phenomena reflect the circumstances of the individual. In this instance, playing competitive hockey was used as an example. The focus on the individual would examine whether the individual was born with the physical qualities commensurate with the task at hand (height, for example), as well as the talent and motivation (or even financial ability to compete) needed for success. Elsewhere in this book we focus on how micro-level factors impact a person's educational outcomes, how much money they earn, and how long they may live. Indeed, sociologists believe that individual factors—like how hard we try in school, the careers that we independently select, and the health-related choices we all make—matter. Throughout this book, I use the metaphor of **"the player"** to illustrate the micro-level perspective.

What the player brings to the game clearly matters, but the player does not have the independent authority to construct the rules of the game. Sociologists acknowledge, then, that macro-level factors also matter for our social experiences. The **macro-level** refers to the structural level of society and, especially, the social institutions that comprise it. The macro-level is characterized by rules and policies, as well as historical and cultural realities that exist *outside* of the

A proponent of the "sociological imagination," C. Wright Mills encourages us to analyze social phenomena through the lenses of history, biography, and social structure.

individual. In the example of competitive hockey, the player does not get to choose when the season begins or what rule is used to establish the cutoff for playing in a particular age group. Players are subject to those rules, and it is evident that these rules benefit some players more than others. Beyond the hockey example, sociologists focus on how the structure of public school funding—which relies on local property taxes—benefits some "players" more than others in terms of the resources their schools are able to acquire. In terms of how long a person may live, the game is structured in such a way that some groups are systematically exposed to more toxins and environmental health threats than others. While individuals can elect to move to a new location, or can lobby for a new set of "rules" and arrangements, it is likely that these macro-level conditions will continue to impact the lives of many, many people. Figure 1.1 provides a graphic illustration of these concepts.

Throughout this book, I use the metaphor of "the player" and the "the game" to draw attention to how individuals are embedded in a particular social context. In 1959, the sociologist C. Wright Mills coined the term "**the sociological imagination**" to describe sociology's unique emphasis on the macro- and micro-level dimensions of society. For Mills, the power of sociology is that it identifies the interconnections between an individual's biography, on the one hand, and the historical evolution of society and the social structural constraints, on the other. Mills argued, and I agree, that the uniqueness of the sociological perspective is that it provides a tool for comprehensively understanding social phenomena. In many cases, what initially appear as *personal troubles*—such as being unemployed, getting divorced, or being diagnosed with a chronic illness—can better be understood as a *public issue*. While an individual couple may be incompatible and have poor communication skills, when the divorce rate rises precipitously—as it did during the early 1970s—there is likely more going on than simply a spike in individual couples who cannot communicate. When divorce laws changed in the early 1970s, many underlying personal troubles transformed into a broader public issue: the introduction of no-fault divorce laws made divorce far more accessible, thereby altering the macro-level context in which individual couples sought to resolve their differences. By bringing these two components together, we can better understand social issues like why some people earn more than others and some people live long healthy lives and others do not.

THE ROLE OF POWER IN SOCIOLOGICAL THINKING

Issues of social constructionism and the role of macro- and micro-level dynamics cannot be discussed without discussing the issue of power. For sociologists, power—and its unequal distribution—stands at the heart of most social issues. With respect to social constructionism, sociologists believe that not everyone has the same amount of power to have their view of reality become the dominant view of reality. Although our socially constructed realities emerge out of shared meanings and human interactions, it is often difficult for stigmatized or minority groups to gain recognition for their understandings of reality. For example, gay or transgender people may work hard to have their identities and realities accepted as normal sexual orientations or gender expressions, but their voices are often drowned out by majority voices who assert that same-sex love is deviant or that there must be something psychologically wrong with someone who claims a transgender identity.

Power is also evident in terms of how the social structure and "the game" are organized. Here, not everyone has the same level of influence over the social institutions and policies that make up the macro-level of society. As mentioned above, one central aspect of how the educational system is structured in the United States is that public schools are funded by taxes collected at the local level; accordingly, school districts with a strong property tax base will have more resources than those with a weak property tax base. Historically, this "rule" was put in place to ensure local control over public schools. Today, this rule remains in place in part because it benefits people with privilege, who have the power to defend it; meanwhile, those who are disadvantaged by this rule have limited power and resources to try to alter this aspect of the educational "game." As you move through this text, keep these issues in mind as you think about who has the power to decide what is saliva (normal and socially acceptable) and what is spit (abnormal and deviant), and who has the power to mold the social institutions—the schools, workplaces, neighborhoods, medical systems, media outlets—that structure our lived experiences.

THINKING ABOUT DIVERSITY: SOCIAL IDENTITIES AS A MATTER OF DIFFERENCE OR DEFICIENCIES?

What is diversity? Is it something that enriches society, where different religions, racial and ethnic groups, and gender and sexual identities, come together and each contributes something unique and valuable to the overall culture? Or is it something that potentially fragments and fractures society, where differences are seen as something that undermines a strong, collective identity? The "tale of two parades" addresses these questions and others. How is it that an Irish St. Patrick's Day parade is considered a positive expression of ethnic pride and a reason to celebrate, while a structurally similar Gay Pride parade is considered by many to be inappropriate, and possibly even an affront to core social values?

Diversity refers to social variations in identity and cultures, including how they interact with each other, especially in terms of religion, sexual expression, gender identity, social class background, and racial and ethnic identity. Diversity is a reflection of our unique social identities. From a sociological perspective, **social identity** refers to those group memberships by which we define ourselves in relation to other social groups. This contrasts with a person's *individual identity*, which refers to the personal traits (hobbies, interests, abilities, personality) by which we define ourselves in relation to other individuals. Sociology is primarily the study of social identities. Sociologists assume that it *matters* whether we are male or female, white or nonwhite, poor or wealthy, Christian or Muslim. It matters to our sense of self, as well as our day-to-day life experiences and opportunities. All of us, moreover, have multiple social identities: I, for example, am a white, heterosexual female, who grew up lower income but now occupy a solidly middle-class position. Each of these identities *intersects* with the others to form a more complicated, yet comprehensive, social identity.

This more complex identity is called one's **social location**. Sociologically, this term refers to one's position in the social structure. My social location is very different from a lower-income black male who identifies as bisexual; or a wealthy Cuban American woman who has a physical disability. Our social locations differ in the degree of power or privilege associated with them. Sociologists believe, for example, that men have more social privilege than women; and that heterosexuality is often considered the invisible "norm" in society, so that it too is associated with social privilege. These various facets of our identities, then, come together as a complex social location where most of us have some form of social privilege (based on our sex, sexual identity, religion, race or ethnicity, social class, or ability status), and may also lack privilege. In short, our social location is both an identity and a position that we occupy in an unequal, stratified social order. The first half of this book focuses on our social identities (how they are defined, how we acquire them), while the second half examines the social inequalities associated with these identities.

SOCIAL IDENTITIES: LABELING OTHERS AND LABELING OURSELVES

"Cream puffs" and "cake-eaters": when I was in high school, these were the names many of us at Southwest High used to describe the students at neighboring Edina High. These terms reflected the stereotype we had of these affluent students: soft, pampered, and overly indulged. Despite the fact that I had only ever met one person who had attended Edina—my aunt's boyfriend, Brent—I had a clear stereotype of its students. To a person, they were snobby, privileged "preps."

When it comes to social identities, humans have a tendency to apply labels to others. There is an almost immediate tendency to categorize the people we come in contact with, quickly sizing them up as a "white male," "black female," "Arab American," "woman with a disability," or even "cream puff." But why do we do this and what are the consequences? One reason humans are so quick to categorize and label is that our human brains *demand* it. Imagine what life would be like if every situation we encountered was a new one? This would lead to chaos, as we sought to define every person, place, or interaction from the ground up. Instead, the human brain creates schemas to facilitate social interaction. **Schemas** are mental structures or organized patterns of thought or behavior. It is likely that we all possess gender schemas, for example. These schemas provide a mental framework to guide our behaviors and interactions. When we size someone up as female, we are able to act in accordance with that schema. The old *Saturday Night Live* skit (and later movie) about "Pat" illustrates this point: because those around Pat could never figure out Pat's gender, their social interactions were awkward, undefined, and characterized by an ongoing quest to figure out whether Pat is *he* or *she*. Only when we label our social worlds can we effectively operate in the world.

Sometimes the labels and categories we use become more elaborated stereotypes. A **stereotype** is an overgeneralized belief that describes an entire group of people. There are many stereotypes that circulate in the United States, such as:

- "Jews are cheap."
- "Native Americans are strong, proud people."
- "Black men are skilled lovers."
- "Gay men are feminine and act like 'queens.'"
- "Poor people are lazy and dependent on the government."

The fact that stereotypes are "overgeneralized beliefs" is evident in the use of the word *are* in each statement above. I sometimes hear my students say that a stereotype wouldn't exist if it didn't contain some grain of truth. But "some grain of truth" is very different from the assumption that everyone in a particular category shares a particular trait. Therefore, another thing that makes a stereotype a stereotype is that it is typically based on partial or incomplete evidence. Take, for example, the statement, "Gay men are feminine and act like 'queens.'" This statement may be correct if one's only piece of evidence is the television program *RuPaul's Drag Race*. Yet it would be incorrect if one had wider exposure to gay men, who clearly exhibit many personality traits and many different ways of being masculine.

Even if a person did take greater notice of the diversity among gay men, that person's brain may have difficulty thinking about gay men in more complicated terms. This leads to another characteristic of stereotypes: they are difficult to change or eradicate. One reason for this is confirmation bias. **Confirmation bias** is the tendency for people to notice and retain information that confirms existing beliefs while ignoring or rejecting information that challenges these beliefs. Take this stereotype: "Women are terrible drivers." Imagine you are driving down the highway and become frustrated with the driver in front of you; perhaps he or she is driving too slow or using the passing lane instead of the center lane. As you pass that person, you look with frustration into the other car and think to yourself, "Yep, another woman driver." Through this experience, you have confirmed a belief you have long held. Yet on your commute to work, you failed to take note of the women on the highway who were driving just fine, as well as the male driver two miles earlier who drove slowly down the center lane while talking on a cell phone. Stereotypes are resistant to change, then, because they are built out of mental schemas—schemas that can become deeply embedded and resistant to new information.

This brings us to an interesting question: Are stereotypes only negative in tone and harmful in their effects? Is there such a thing as a positive stereotype? Many stereotypes, including several above, give praise and seem to have positive connotations. Yet sociologists are critical of all stereotypes, even those that appear to be positive. Take the notion that Asian Americans are intelligent and hardworking, with special talents in math and technical fields. Although this stereotype has a positive connotation, it has some negative ramifications. First, it places a large population inside a fairly narrow box. For an Asian American child who grows up hearing this stereotype,

Chief Illiniwek, the much-celebrated mascot for the University of Illinois, is considered offensive by many Native Americans.

Positive stereotypes of Native Americans, which label them as strong and proud, conceal a complicated history of systematic destruction and denigration.

he or she may feel pressured to pursue particular academic subjects and careers; he or she may also fail to gain recognition for being a skilled illustrator or creative writer. Accordingly, such stereotypes may actually limit a person's potential.

Second, positive stereotypes can often conceal unpleasant historical realities. Take the notion that "Native Americans are strong, proud people." For many decades, people have defended athletic team mascots like the Indians and the Redskins by asserting that these mascots honor Native American people. These current statements of honoring Native Americans may effectively conceal the brutal treatment Native Americans have been subjected to throughout U.S. history. Since the time that Europeans settled in North America, the Native population has declined dramatically. Hundreds of thousands of Native Americans have died as a result of infection, forced removals and resettlements (e.g., the Trail of Tears), and warfare. The history of Native–European contact is not one of respect or honor. My point is not to accuse supporters of the Florida State Seminoles or Washington Redskins of committing these atrocities. Rather, my point is that stereotypes sometimes mask inequality, brutality, and the historical context out of which particular beliefs take shape. In this regard, and in the way they box people in and limit their potential, stereotypes become mechanisms of power, shaping our sense of history and our ideas of how diverse groups fit into society.

While sociologists are not fans of stereotypes, they do use a lot of generalizations. **Generalizations** are statements that describe a general pattern or tendency of a particular group. The following statements are generalizations:

- On average, Latinos earn less money than whites.
- Asian Americans tend to score higher on standardized math tests compared to other racial groups.
- Females are more likely than males to be nurses and teachers.
- African Americans have higher rates of incarceration than other racial/ethnic groups.

Compared to stereotypes, generalizations are not intended to apply to *all* members of a particular group. Instead, they describe statistical rates or tendencies. Whereas stereotypes use the word "are" to describe an entire group, generalizations use words like *on average*, *tend to*, or *more/less likely*. These words illustrate another key difference between stereotypes and generalizations: the latter are based on reliable evidence. "Reliable" in this case means that a sufficient number of cases have been assessed (hundreds, rather than a handful), so that they have the power of statistics, and that the source of these statistics is considered trustworthy. If, for example, I wanted to test the hypothesis that "Women are terrible drivers," I would have to *operationalize*, or define my terms (What *is* a terrible driver?), gather data from hundreds of cases, and make sure my source of data was sound (and relevant factors were controlled for). Within the social sciences, we generally consider public opinion data from organizations like Pew and Gallup to be good data, as well as data from the federal governmental (Bureau of Labor Statistics, the U.S. Census Bureau) and big data sets with names like the General Social Survey (GSS), National Election Studies (NES), and the National Longitudinal Survey of Youth (NLSY).

If stereotypes can be used to rationalize inequality, can generalizations be considered harmful? In one sense, the answer should be no: given that they are facts, generalizations are neither harmful nor helpful; they simply *are*. The statement that African Americans have higher rates of incarceration is simply a statistical reality. Yet moving from the academic level to the personal level, some students have told me they do feel hurt or harmed by such statements. Even if they are factual, black students may feel a steady erosion of their confidence and well-being after sitting in a sociology (or criminal justice) class where the statistics presented continually portray their group in a negative light. Similarly, Asian American students may feel excluded by the fact that many racial comparisons and studies of racial inequality often exclude their group altogether, offering no generalizations about their group's experience in the United States. Sociological studies of racial and ethnic inequality remain incomplete, so that some students may feel that their realities are being erased or ignored. In this way, simple generalizations or facts become more complex—and possibly even harmful—depending on who is hearing these facts and the broader context of their presentation.

That said, one key feature of the sociological perspective is the use of generalizations. The sociological perspective is founded on the assumption that the social world is patterned and that systematic differences exist across groups. How much education a person receives, how much money they earn, or how long they live is not a random occurrence. Rather, there are tendencies and patterns across groups. Even something as seemingly private and biologically based as how often a person has sex and how satisfied that person is with the experience can be linked to one's social location. One's sexual experiences are statistically predicted by gender, education, and religious identification. "Statistically predicted by" means that there is a significant relationship between variables, so that conservative Protestant women generally express greater sexual satisfaction compared to female atheists. Yet sociologists know that these patterns do not apply to every one in a particular group; they are merely statistical tendencies. And while there may be significant variation *among* women and *among* men, sociologists generally focus on the patterned differences between them. Finally, sociologists acknowledge that outliers and exceptions exist for every generalization; these are, after all, merely tendencies. Therefore, sociologists also strive to understand why someone may defy expectations or "beat the odds" associated with his or her particular group.

PLURALISM OR ASSIMILATION: HOW SOCIETIES RESPOND TO DIVERSITY

It is not simply that groups are labeled socially through stereotypes and categorizations or by sociologists and their use of generalizations. Indeed, many people make independent, public declarations of their group affinities. Some people hang flags from their car's rearview mirror proclaiming their country of origin. Some years ago, the retailer Urban Outfitters sold T-shirts declaring "Everyone loves a Jewish [or Irish or Catholic] Girl." Across the southern United States, T-shirts and bumper stickers use Confederate flags to assert "Dixie Pride." In more subtle ways, wearing a necklace decorated with a Star of David or cross can be interpreted as a public statement of one's religious beliefs and group membership. In addition to the individual declarations of group memberships, there are within the United States many examples of public celebrations or memorials—like St. Patrick's Day or Gay Pride parades—that allow people to identify as members of a particular group. While St. Patrick's Day parades have become mainstream, Gay Pride parades are still met in some communities with discomfort, if not opposition—as the opening vignette illustrated. In other contexts, wearing a cross necklace may be considered a normal and subtle (saliva) expression of one's religious beliefs, while wearing a headscarf—denoting one's Muslim faith—may be regarded as strange (spit). These examples raise the question: How do societies respond to the presence of such diversity?

The question of diversity is increasingly important in our interconnected world. In the current era of globalization, people, jobs, ideas, and culture fluidly move across national boundaries. Although many have grown up thinking the United States is especially unique in terms of its diversity, many countries have similarly high or even higher levels of diversity. Like the United States, Canada, Mexico, and Australia all had substantial native populations before being colonized by Europeans. Subsequent waves of colonization brought Europeans to many corners of the globe; in many cases, Europeans captured slaves from Africa and brought these populations to South America, North America, and the Caribbean. In the United States and Canada, workers from China and Japan were brought in to work on expanding railroad lines and growing port cities. During the 1800s, Europeans from countries like Ireland, Greece, and Italy left their homelands seeking better economic opportunities. In more recent decades, refugees have fled countries around the globe, seeking economic, political, and social freedom. Today, within European countries and North America, the percentage of the population that is foreign-born ranges from 9 to 28 (Table 1.1). Because of these global population flows, many people live in societies that are diverse in terms of culture, language, and religion.

While it would be wonderful to believe that diverse groups can peacefully coexist, that is less often the case. **Pluralism** occurs when smaller cultural groups are able to maintain their cultural uniqueness within the context of the wider society. Under pluralism, diverse groups' values and cultural practices are accepted, if not appreciated, in society as a whole. Pluralism can apply to many different forms of cultural difference, including religion, ethnicity, language, and sexual expression. A pluralistic society would not, for example, legally establish one official language; instead, it would allow multiple languages to be used in schools and for official governmental purposes (election ballots, drivers' license manuals, etc.). Pluralistic societies do not require citizens to pay taxes to an official state religion (as is done in Iceland). Instead, such countries provide freedom of religious expression and have no formal mechanisms requiring people to support financially the state religion. In truly pluralistic societies, cultural differences are not considered threatening. They are not perceived as a threat to tradition or social cohesion. In a truly pluralistic society, a Gay Pride parade would be as accepted as a St. Patrick's Day parade.

Table 1.1 **Percentage of Foreign-Born in Different Countries**

Australia	26.8%
Canada	21.3%
Sweden	16.8%
Germany	16.4%
Ireland	15.5%
United States	13.1%
The United Kingdom	12.9%
France	12.65%
Italy	8.8%

Source: United Nations 2013.
OECD (2013), *OECD Factbook 2013: Economic, Environmental and Social Statistics*, OECD Publishing, Paris. DOI: http://dx.doi.org/10.1787/factbook-2013-en

Can one be both Muslim and a citizen of France? This protestor of France's headscarf ban thinks so.

Many societies, including the United States, struggle to be truly pluralistic. One country that has gained attention in recent years for its response to diversity is France. Historically, much emphasis has been placed in France on the notion of the *citoyen*, or citizen. Since the French Revolution ended in 1799, great effort has been made to create a unified French society. Rather than be divided by religion, language, or nationality, France has strived to create a cohesive civic body, one composed of people who identify as *French* above all else. Waves of recent immigrants, many arriving from France's former colonies in Africa with large Muslim populations (Algeria, Morocco, and Tunisia), have prompted new questions of how to balance pluralism and citizenship. Tensions surrounding these issues erupted in the Spring of 2015, when the offices of "Charlie Hebdo," a satirical publication, were subject to a terror attack for printing images that were considered offensive to some in the local Muslim community.

Since 1905, France has had a law declaring a separation between church and state; as part of this law, schools and governments are prohibited from endorsing any religious teachings or practices. In 2004, this law was strengthened by then-President Jacques Chirac, who passed a law banning the conspicuous (i.e., visible) display of religious symbolism within educational settings. Technically, the law applies to all forms of religious expression; therefore, a student who visibly displays a cross necklace is prohibited from doing so, as would be a Sikh student wearing a turban, a Jewish student wearing a yarmulke, and a Muslim student wearing a headscarf. Although all religious groups are covered by the law, many commentators believe it was sparked by the influx of Muslim immigrants from Africa. According to reports, many feared that religious expressions within public schools would distract students from learning and from focusing on their collective (French) identity. In making public declarations of one's religious beliefs, some worried that the values of secularism and citizenship—values that emphasize the collective identity and well-being—would be compromised.

Because diversity is often perceived as threatening to the collective well-being, many societies tend toward assimilation rather than pluralism. **Assimilation** is the process by which cultural differences are incorporated into existing cultural patterns. It is a process that typically includes changes to a group's language use (abandonment of their native language), residential location (movement out of ethnic enclaves and into the "wider community"), and higher rates of intermarriage. Less a blending of cultures, assimilation often means that newcomers are pressured to leave their culture behind and adopt the cultural norms, values, language, or religious beliefs of the majority society. In France, for example, it was expected that immigrant newcomers would leave behind some of their religious practices—especially those visible in public—and adopt the French value of secularism.

Illustrating these terms with a metaphor, pluralism can be compared to a delicious stir-fry or tossed salad. In both dishes, additional ingredients can be added into the mix, but each ingredient retains its character and adds something valuable to the whole. A tossed salad is made delicious by a rich and creamy cheese, the flavorful crunch of a crouton, and the freshness of the vegetables. With assimilation, the metaphor of the "melting pot" is often used. This suggests a soup pot where ingredients are added and individual flavors break down and blend into the whole. Yet with assimilation, it is unclear whether each new ingredient naturally blends into the existing flavors or the existing flavors retain their dominance, despite the addition of an occasional carrot or potato.

Beyond the metaphor of the melting pot, the process of assimilation raises questions of power and of whose culture counts. In many cases, whose culture counts is the group with the largest population, which typically translates to those with the greatest political or social power. Today, these dynamics are evident in battles over **English-only laws**, which strive to make English the official language of the United States. While the United States does not have an official language at the federal level, more than half of the states within the United States have passed laws making English the official language. Support for these laws generally rests on three basic arguments: first, learning English is the key to upward mobility; second, learning English shows allegiance to the United States and its culture; and third, having a single language promotes government efficiency and a cohesive social or national identity. Embedded in arguments for official English language laws is the concern that those who use another language or retain their cultural traditions are disloyal or threatening to society as a whole. Echoing this sentiment, the website for ProEnglish, an advocacy group for English-only policies, states that "in pluralistic nations such as ours, the function of government should be to foster and support the similarities that unite us, rather than institutionalize the differences that divide us."

Like many issues that sociologists focus on, the significance of today's English-only laws can better be understood by adding historical perspective. Struggles over diversity and how to incorporate newcomers are not new to the United States. When my grandmother asked me some years ago why her Mexican co-workers at a fast-food restaurant "don't want to learn English," she was echoing a centuries-old sentiment. What she didn't realize was the irony—maybe even hypocrisy—of her question. One hundred and fifty years ago, the same questions were asked of German immigrants who wanted German to be the official language of instruction in their public schools in Chicago, Milwaukee, Cincinnati, and St. Louis. As a woman who proudly proclaimed her Irish heritage, my grandmother seemed unaware of the fact that 150 years earlier, Irish immigrants were similarly stigmatized, and many wondered why the Irish wouldn't give up their "primitive" Catholic religion and assimilate into the preferred Protestant faith. My points here are twofold: while the United States has long struggled with questions of diversity, what has changed is which groups are considered outsiders, and the existing culture is typically considered the normal and preferred culture, so that newcomers are expected to adapt to it rather than retain their own cultural patterns.

While the United States strives, in many ways, to be a pluralistic society, issues like English-only laws show that pressures to assimilate remain. Instead of regarding cultural differences as enriching to society, differences of culture, language, and religion are often treated as deficiencies—something that makes the person in question *less than*. Wearing a headscarf may be seen as strange, if not deviant or oppressive. It is forgotten that many women in the United States wear veils on their wedding days, and that the Virgin Mary and many Catholic nuns also wear headscarves. Instead of recognizing points of connection across religions, humans in diverse societies tend to treat one set of religious beliefs as saliva (normal) and others as spit (abnormal or deviant).

Even when it comes to gender differences, men's cultural practices are often defined as normative. **Normative behaviors** are those social behaviors and cultural practices that are defined as normal and expected; other behaviors are judged in relation to this standard. When Hilary Clinton ran to be the Democratic nominee for president of the United States in 2008, she was criticized for tearing up on the campaign trail. Commentators wondered whether someone who cries has the emotional strength needed to be president. When winning an award or a championship, recipients sometimes say, "I told myself I wasn't going to cry." When stressed-out students cry in my office, apologies for their behavior are typical. These examples suggest that crying in our society is defined as a sign of weakness. But is this necessarily the case? Crying could also be viewed as evidence of passion and commitment, or a functional way to process emotions. A sociologist might argue that crying is stigmatized not for any inherent reason but because such emotional expressions are associated with women. Men's behaviors are considered the norm, and any deviation from that norm is regarded with some skepticism. Therefore, crying is bad.

The examples in this chapter lead to another sociological observation: the presence of cultural differences often translates into the establishment of a cultural hierarchy. The notion of a cultural hierarchy suggests that some cultural practices are better than others. In some cases, *better* does means superior: the average American—who is statistically likely to identify as Christian—may believe women are treated better in Christianity than they are in the Islamic and Mormon faiths. Here, Christianity may be considered superior, not just different, from the standpoint of women's rights. Returning to the example of gender differences, being emotionally restrained and of rational mind—stereotypically male traits—may be defined as preferable to being emotionally expressive and guided by emotional principles.

In other cases, notions of cultural hierarchy and superiority are more subtle: some cultural practices are simply considered typical and others "weird." As discussed later in this book, job résumés with "black names" like Lakisha and Jamal are less likely to receive a call-back compared to those with "white names" like Brendan and Emily (Bertrand and Mullainathan 2004), suggesting racial discrimination based on names and their cultural associations. Although it would be difficult to argue that Emily is a "better" name than Lakisha, some of my students advise parents to give their kids "normal names"—like Emily and Brendan—in order to protect them from discrimination. The presumption is that names like John, Michael, Andrew, Kristin, and Sarah are not just more common than names like Malik, Tyrone, Latoya, and Ebony, but that they are normal and the standard by which other names are judged. While the expression of superiority is less explicit or overt in the case of names than it is in the case of evaluating religious practices, the consequences are similar. Once something is considered different, even in the most mild or subtle sense, it sets up the possibility that those in power or those whose culture is considered normal will negatively evaluate those who are seen as different. This sense of difference *as* deviance may translate into discrimination when it comes to jobs, housing, or other opportunities.

Immigrants to the United States have understood this reality for hundreds of years. As waves of immigrants have come to the United States since the early 1800s, many have Anglicized or Americanized their last names. **Americanized**, in this sense, refers to the process by which cultural traditions like family names, language, food, and religion lose some of their original "flavor" and take on characteristics of American culture. Within the United States, this is part of assimilation; abroad, it is a form of cultural diffusion. For the last two centuries, many immigrants to the United States *Anglicized* (made them sound more English) their names as a way to downplay their ethnic origins. The German piano maker Heinrich Engelhard Steinweg, for example, became Henry E. Steinway when he founded his company in America. Hundreds of Irish and Scottish immigrants dropped the O's and Mc/Macs from their names (O'Sullivan Sullivan), while Polish "-skis" and Greek "opolous(es)" did the same. More recent research shows that current waves of immigrants are more likely to hold on to their names. This is one indicator that the United States is becoming a more pluralistic society.

MOVING FORWARD

As a sociologist, I often find that "the more things change, the more they stay the same." This suggests that while the United States shows signs of increased pluralism, there may be lingering pressures to assimilate. The sweep of the last 200 years appears to be one of greater tolerance, social integration, and equality. Yet examples of enduring inequalities and social exclusion remain. While fewer immigrants are changing their names now compared to previous generations and higher percentages of Americans are marrying across racial and ethnic boundaries, occasional incidents remind us that hierarchies and inequalities remain in our diverse society. During the television broadcast of football's Super Bowl in 2014, this lesson was brought home. Social media sites and the Internet buzzed with commentary after Coca-Cola aired a commercial where "America the Beautiful" was sung in a variety of languages. Using the twitter hashtag #f***coke, users posted comments like, "I'm sorry but you can't sing about America in other languages. That's just un-American," and "F*** you coke for trying to diversify my country tis of them f***ing speak English and be normal." Such comments reflect the belief that America itself is synonymous with its English history, that English is not just the most commonly spoken language but considered the normal mode of communication, and that cultural differences can threaten our unity.

The sociological perspective can contribute much toward understanding controversies such as these. First, it can help us understand how our identities, and the social inequalities that often accompany them, are a matter of social construction. This means that it is humans who have decided what various languages, religions, and cultural practices mean and which of these forms of diversity are considered saliva (normal and preferred) and which are considered spit (abnormal and deviant). Yet the notion that our social world is socially constructed also allows for social change and transformations in these differences. Over time, the Irish moved from a position of deviance and stigma in society to being considered normal and typical. Even more, one day of the year, many Americans jump on the Irish bandwagon.

Second, the sociological perspective helps us understand how our identities and inequalities are constituted at both the micro- and macro-levels. As we will see throughout this book, there are dynamics at the individual level that perpetuate our understandings of difference and diversity as well as our life circumstances and positions in the social structure. At the same time, there are larger institutional forces at play. Emphasis on the macro-level more clearly demonstrates the role of power in structuring social inequality and shows that, at the micro-level, not everyone has the same ability to influence social inequality or the socially constructed nature of our worlds.

As you read this book, I hope to leave you with many broader lessons. First, I hope to share with you how wonderfully creative and powerful human beings are. We have tremendous power to shape our social realities; our historical and cross-cultural understandings show that we do so in remarkably different ways. Second, I hope to convince you that human beings are powerful agents of social change. While inequality appears to be a nearly universal feature of human societies, so is social change. In conjunction with our creativity and power, many humans today are engaged in efforts to transform society and erode differences and inequalities that often appear all too enduring. In fact, by the fall of 2014, organizers of New York City's St. Patrick's Day parade agreed to lift the ban on openly gay marchers. Even Cardinal Timothy M. Dolan, leader of the city's Catholic faith community and grand marshal of the 2015 parade, said: "I have no trouble with the decision at all. I think the decision is a wise one."

CHAPTER 1: REVIEW OF KEY POINTS

- Sociology is the systematic, or scientific, study of human society.
- The sociological perspective sees much of the world as "socially constructed"—composed of phenomena that humans define and to which they give meaning.
- The sociological perspective is distinct from the essentialist perspective, which sees social phenomena as shaped by underlying biological forces.
- The sociological perspective blends the micro- (player, individual) and macro-level (game, structural) perspectives; sociologists believe that focusing on these two dimensions provides a comprehensive understanding of social phenomena.
- The "sociological imagination" is C. Wright Mills's term for the perspective that blends the emphasis on the individual and the social; this perspective seeks to differentiate *personal troubles* and *public issues*.
- The sociological perspective can be used to study concepts related to diversity.
- It is natural to pay attention to differences between social groups. When we use stereotypes, however, we see differences as universal and totalizing; when we use generalizations we see variations and patterns, most of which are drawn from systematic data.
- *Pluralism* and *assimilation* are two strategies that societies use to manage diversity; one emphasizes the acknowledgment and appreciation of differences, while the other emphasizes the blending of differences into a more homogeneous culture.

CHAPTER 1: QUESTIONS FOR REVIEW

1. What does it mean to say that something is socially constructed? How might this concept apply to a social phenomenon like homosexuality or same-sex attraction?
2. How does the essentialist perspective compare to the social constructionist perspective? How would the essentialist perspective explain a social phenomenon like homosexuality or same-sex attraction?
3. When you think about social phenomena like differences between men and women, or the fact that some humans demonstrate attraction to the same sex while others are attracted to the other sex, are you more compelled by the social constructionist explanation or the essentialist explanation?
4. The sociological perspective explains social phenomena by bringing together micro- and macro-level understandings. What are these two components, and what does each contribute to a broader understanding of the social world?

5. According to the sociological perspective, why is labeling such an important part of the human experience?

6. What is confirmation bias, and what role does it play in the perpetuation of stereotypes?

7. Pluralism and assimilation are two ways in which societies tend to incorporate diversity. What are these two approaches, and how do they differ?

8. In what ways do you see the United States as a pluralistic society? In what ways is it assimilationist? Of these two approaches, which do you think provides the most strength to a society?

KEY TERMS

Americanized

assimilation

confirmation bias

diversity

English-only laws

essentialist perspective

"the game"

generalization

macro-level

micro-level

normative behaviors

"the player"

pluralism

schemas

sociology

social identity

social location

social structure

socially constructed

sociological imagination

stereotype

REFERENCES

Bertrand, Marianne and Sendhil Mullainathan. 2004. "Are Emily and Greg More Employable Than Lakisha and Jamal? A Field Experiment on Labor Market Discrimination." *American Economic Review* 94(4):991–1013.

OECD. 2013. *OECD Factbook 2013: Economic, Environmental and Social Statistics.* Paris, France: OECD Publishing. DOI: http://dx.doi.org/10.1787/factbook-2013-en

The Social Construction of Identity

In 1977, when Susie Guillory Phipps went to obtain a copy of her birth certificate so that she could apply for a passport, she discovered something shocking: according to the state of Louisiana's official records, she was black. This was a shock because Phipps had only ever considered herself white. In terms of phenotype—or outward appearance—it is likely that those with whom she came into contact would also consider her white. Yet according to law, the fact that she had 2/32 black ancestry made her black under Louisiana state law. The question of Ms. Guillory Phipps's race becomes even more confusing when you consider the fact that if she had been born in any other state, her race would have been classified as white. And if she had been born 100 years earlier, her racial classification may have been something else, entirely. After all, Americans of Irish descent were once considered "colored."

The case of Susie Guillory Phipps illustrates the fact that many of our social identities—including sex, gender, sexuality, race, and social class—are socially constructed. Sociologists emphasize the socially constructed nature of our worlds as a counterpoint to the assumption that our social world has an inherent reality—whether from a biological or a social perspective. In the case of Phipps, an analysis of her DNA would have revealed considerable European heritage; just looking at her, she would likely have been classified as white. When classifying her race legally, neither of these "realities" was as powerful as local conventions.

Over the next four chapters we explore the socially constructed nature of our social identities. To do so, we compare the sociological perspective to the essentialist perspective. The essentialist perspective sees many human differences—whether in terms of sex, gender, sexuality, or race—as rooted in underlying biological differences. While sociologists engage with the essentialist perspective, they do not fully embrace it. Instead, they embrace the notion that these identities are socially constructed. To make this point, I use the metaphors of the "time machine" and "study abroad trip" to show how many of the identities and social differences that we take for granted—and sometimes assume to be rooted in biology—vary across historical periods and cross-cultural locations. It is when we begin to acknowledge the amazing historical and cross-cultural variation in these social identities that we begin to see the creativity and adaptability that is central to the human experience.

Is Biology Destiny? Understanding Sex and Gender

In the summer of 2009, Caster Semenya of South Africa took the World Championships of track and field by storm. With a time of 1:55.45, Semenya won gold in the 800-meter race, recording the fastest time of the year. Yet what should have been a joyous celebration quickly turned sour, as the International Association of Athletics Federations (IAAF) asked Semenya to submit to a gender verification test. Her rapid improvement in time, margin of victory, and masculine appearance raised doubts about whether Semenya was qualified to compete as a female. The IAAF convened a panel of experts made up of an endocrinologist, gynecologist, internal medicine specialist, and psychologist to verify her gender. Pending the results of their investigation, Semenya was barred from competition.

During the spring of 2010, Caster Semenya returned to international competition, where once again she began posting dominant results. A cloud, however, still hung over her. According to its official statement, "The IAAF accepts the conclusion of a panel of medical experts that she can compete with immediate effect." It added that "the medical details of the case remain confidential and the IAAF will make no further comment on the matter." The panel declined to reveal the results of their investigation.

The vagueness and secrecy of Semenya's ordeal conceals more about the concepts of sex and gender than it reveals. While some argue that the results of the IAAF investigation were never revealed out of respect for the runner's privacy, the lack of results may simply reflect the problems of "sex verification." What, precisely, were the experts looking for? If it's not as simple as identifying chromosomes or locating a vagina or ovaries, what does the process involve? All of this begs the question: How do we "really" know if someone is male or female?

The case of Caster Semenya speaks directly to the sociological perspective. Our exploration begins with the notion that even seemingly simple terms such as "sex" and "gender" are socially constructed—that is, defined and shaped by humans. The goal of this chapter is to show the clever and contradictory meanings that humans give to our most basic identities—and the social forces that play a part in this process.

With a record-breaking performance, the International Association of Athletics Federations raised questions about Caster Semenya's classification as female.

DEFINING SEX: WHAT IS IT AND HOW MANY ARE THERE?

When it comes to the concept of *sex*, how many are there? Generally speaking, our society treats sex as a **dichotomy** or **binary**—something that can be divided into two mutually exclusive categories. Indeed, in legal documents, such as birth certificates, the identification of one's sex is required, and only two options are accepted. But is it possible there are more than two sexes?

To figure out how many sexes there are, we first need to understand what *determines* a person's sex? Whether there are two or five or some other number of sexes, we need to know what criteria can be used to label people with their proper identity. According to many of my students, it is "what's in your pants"—that is, having a penis or vagina—that determines a person's sex. If only it were that easy.

The term **sex** can be defined as the *set* of biological distinctions that differentiate males and females. This definition has three points of emphasis. First, when it comes to sex, the appropriate terminology is "male" and "female." (Later, I will show that the terms "men" and "women" apply to the concept of gender.) Second, sex is a trait that humans are born with. Again, this point will gain greater clarity when comparing it to the notion of gender. Third and finally, this definition asserts that sex is a *set* of characteristics that differentiate females and males. This means that there is no single trait that determines a person's sex. Rather, a person's sex reflects a constellation of traits—namely chromosomes, gonads, hormones, and genitalia. It is this "constellation" that gave the International Association of Athletics Federations so much trouble in the case of Caster Semenya.

Although sex determination begins with chromosomes, it does not end there. If it were that easy, the IAAF could simply examine the 23rd chromosome pair and look for the typical pattern of **XX** for female and **XY** for male. Six weeks after fertilization, when the egg always contributes an X chromosome and the sperm contributes either an X or a Y, the plot thickens. According to current understandings of sex differentiation, sex chromosomes soon lead to the development of gonads—that is, testes or ovaries. By the 8th week, as the gonads mature, the fetus begins to produce sex hormones. Male fetuses produce higher levels of androgens, the most familiar being testosterone. In the absence of "male" sex hormones, female Müllerian ducts kick into gear and eventually produce a uterus and ovaries. It is only in the final stages of fetal development that humans develop the signature traits of males and females: the penis and vagina (genitalia). It is this typical story of fetal development, where chromosomes produce the gonads, hormones, and eventually genitalia, which that allows doctors to declare, "You have a beautiful baby boy (or girl)." In most births the criteria used to label a newborn's sex (and the number of options that doctors have) are fairly straightforward.

The case of **intersexuality** makes the question of how many sexes there are and what determines a person's sex more biologically *and* sociologically interesting. Intersexuality refers to a congenital anomaly of the sexual or reproductive system. Previously known as hermaphrodism, intersexuality describes individuals whose sex is ambiguous or who have atypical combinations of male and female sex characteristics.

The term "hermaphrodite" dates back to the mythological story of a creature that possessed the physical traits of both father (Hermes) and mother (Aphrodite). Within academic circles Anne Fausto-Sterling, professor of biology and women's studies, brought renewed interest to the topic. In *Sexing the Body: Gender Policies and the Construction of Sexuality* (1993), Fausto-Sterling argued that there were at least five sexes. There are, of course, men and women. In addition, Fausto-Sterling identified a group called *herms*—those who possess both an ovary and a testis. Another group she called *merms*—those who have testes and some female genitalia, but no ovaries. Finally, she used the term *ferms* to refer to those who have ovaries and some male genitalia but no testes. While identifying these five categories, Fausto-Sterling speculated that "sex is a vast, infinitely malleable continuum that defies the constraints of even five categories" (p. 21).

Indeed, the range of conditions falling under the intersexual umbrella is incredibly diverse. This diversity includes chromosomal, hormonal, and morphological (in terms of physical structures) variations. While the "typical" chromosomal structures of males and females are XY and XX, respectively, some infants are born with atypical chromosomal structures, including XXY (Klinefelter syndrome), XYY (sometimes called Superman syndrome), and XO (Turner syndrome). In addition, there are hormonal anomalies. These conditions include congenital adrenal hyperplasia, androgen

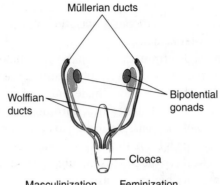

Müllerian ducts

Wolffian ducts

Bipotential gonads

Cloaca

Masculinization   Feminization

Müllerian ducts
degrade

Wolffian ducts
degrade

Wolffian ducts
become epididymis and
ductus (vas) deferens

Müllerian ducts
become uterine tubes
and uterus

Up until the 8th
week of gestation,
humans are sexually
"bipotential." At
that point,
hormonal processes
typically kick in and
result in male or
female sexual
development.

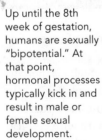

Urinary
bladder

Urethra

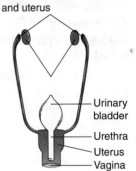

Urinary
bladder

Urethra
Uterus
Vagina

insensitivity syndrome, and 5-alpha reductase deficiency. Finally, to add another layer to the conversation, there are morphological variations. These are conditions that affect the structure—and sometimes functioning—of the genitals and/or gonads. Perhaps some examples will help illustrate this topic.

Chromosomal abnormalities occur when cell meiosis (division) fails or is incomplete. The term "abnormality" is used here in a statistical sense, meaning rare. In Klinefelter syndrome, the X and Y sex chromosomes of the sperm fail to separate as they fertilize an (X) egg, thereby producing an XXY offspring. How those with Klinefelter syndrome are affected differs from person to person. With a male appearance, those with Klinefelter typically have less muscle development and greater fatty tissue than the "typical" male—especially in hips and breasts (gynecomastia). Due to lower levels of testosterone, individuals with Kleinfelter's may have less than average facial and body hair, contributing to a more youthful appearance. The lack of "masculinizing" hormones may cause infertility. These physical manifestations may cause anxiety and depression, especially for those with noticeable breast tissue. Accordingly, testosterone therapy is sometimes advised. Because those with Klinefelter syndrome are often without symptoms, have vague symptoms, or never seek a diagnosis, it is difficult to estimate its prevalence. Estimates of its incidence range from 1:500 to 1:1000 in the male population.

Intersexuality also involves "hormonal abnormalities," or variations in the composition or functioning of one's sex hormones. These conditions often result from imbalances in the "hormone bath" during fetal development. This imbalance may alter the effect of masculinizing and feminizing hormones on gonads and genitalia. One example is androgen insensitivity syndrome, or AIS; this condition also highlights the challenge of determining a person's sex. A person with androgen insensitivity syndrome is chromosomally male (XY) and produces male sex hormones, yet the individual's body is "insensitive" to these hormones. Accordingly, the body does not respond to the testosterone flowing through it. This causes the genetic male to develop some female sex characteristics, including breasts and a vaginal opening. The condition may be discovered when an adolescent or young adult does not begin to menstruate and consequently seeks medical advice. Medical imaging may show that despite having female sex characteristics, there are no ovaries or fetus; in fact, testes may be embedded in the abdomen. Further karyotype testing may reveal male sex chromosomes (XY).

What makes AIS especially perplexing from a sex determination standpoint is that the person with AIS is chromosomally and hormonally male but, due to a genetic anomaly, the body does not virilize—that is, become "manly." Consequently, this individual may appear female in terms of genitals and gonads. It raises the question as to what "counts" when it comes to sex determination—underlying chromosomes or the appearance of genitalia? In the case of androgen insensitivity syndrome—a condition for which the Intersex Society of North America reports an incidence of 1:13,000 births—the underlying, invisible biology takes a backseat to the more visible, external

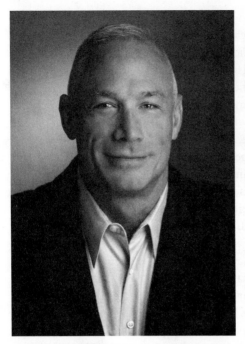

Activist and intersexual Tiger Devore opposes sex reassignment surgeries to "normalize" the sex characteristics of those born intersex.

Cheryl Chase, also known as Bo Laurent, founded the Intersex Society of North America to educate and advocate on behalf of those born intersex.

manifestations. Because of these external manifestations, the individual typically appears and identifies as a woman.

Sociologically and biologically, the topic of intersexuality raises questions about what determines a person's sex and how many sexes there are. According to Anne Fausto-Sterling (1993: 21), sex can be looked at as an "infinitely malleable continuum." This reflects the fact that sex is determined by a set of biological distinctions rather than a single characteristic. In the majority of humans, this "set of biological distinctions" are correlated; that is, if a person has XX chromosomes, it is likely that she also has a higher proportion of female sex hormones and a vagina and ovaries. Yet in some portion of the population these criteria do not form a coherent bundle; some may have, for example, a vagina and XY chromosomes. This confounds the notion of the sex dichotomy.

Because some sex characteristics show morphological variations, it is also possible to argue for a continuum. It is sometimes difficult to differentiate a large clitoris from a "micropenis" (one that is 2.5 standard deviations below the median length of the erect human penis). Because the size of this structure varies from human to human, it can be mapped along a continuum rather than easily labeled "penis" or "not penis." This morphological variation makes more sense once you recognize that humans are "sexually bipotential": the tissues comprising male and female gonads and genitalia are essentially the same; in fact, developing fetuses have the capacity to become male *or* female. It is during the 8th week of gestation that the fetal hormonal environment nudges these structures in the direction of testes or ovaries, penis or vagina.

One could also argue that sex is a continuum, rather than a dichotomy, by focusing on hormones. In so doing, we find that each human has a unique combination of sex hormones—including androgens, testosterone, estrogen, and progesterone—flowing through its body. Therefore, on a hormonal level, every individual is a unique combination of male and female, falling somewhere along that continuum. Figure 2.1 shows how *sex* can be conceptualized as both a dichotomy (binary) and a continuum.

Returning to the question of how many sexes there are, Alice Dreger (1998)—a historian and medical ethicist—argues the answer is a social construction, rather than a biological truth. Calling something a "social construction" means it is made by humans, rather than a natural fact. In her book *Hermaphrodites and the Medical Invention of Sex,* Dreger shows that doctors in the 1800s invented the notion that there are two and only two sexes (a dichotomy). At this time, with new methods of gynecological examination, doctors discovered confusing and contradictory evidence on the question of "sex," forcing doctors to grapple with the existence of "hermaphrodites." Most medical professionals took the biologically simplistic path of declaring there to be two and only two sexes. According to Dreger, the decision could have been different; there was nothing automatic about this decision. She argues that growing social anxieties about homosexuality and women's position in society prompted medical professionals to reduce all of this biological messiness by drawing a clean line between two opposite sexes. Dreger asserts that there is no such line—certainly not in terms of the biology that characterizes male and female. Instead, it is humans who drew this line and, therefore, humans who determined that there are only two sexes.

The question of whether sex can be viewed as a continuum is not merely an intellectual exercise. For some, it is a basic question of identity; for others, a question of life and death. In the United States, for example, those born with ambiguous genitalia routinely undergo medical intervention. In extreme cases, infants undergo **sex reassignment surgery** (SRS)—a set of procedures designed to alter the appearance of external genitalia and other secondary sex characteristics. Take the condition called

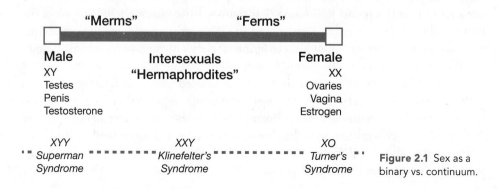

Figure 2.1 Sex as a binary vs. continuum.

partial androgen insensitivity syndrome, or PAIS. Individuals with PAIS are born with ambiguous genitalia—having either an enlarged clitoris or a small penis; despite advances in diagnostic procedures, it is not always possible to determine which is which. These infants may undergo vaginoplasty or a phalloplasty to normalize the appearance of their genitalia. Vaginoplasty typically uses the patient's own tissue to build a vagina and/or create a vaginal opening; the goal of a phalloplasty is to create a structure that looks like a penis, even if it may not function as one (in terms of sexual response and/or urination).

Sometimes repeated surgeries are needed. Sex therapist and intersex activist Tiger Devore, PhD, has had 22 genital surgeries, the first at three months and the last at age 52. Doctors prescribed these surgeries to repair his 3rd degree hypospadias—an opening in the urethra on the underside of his penis. This surgery has a high rate of complications and unsatisfactory outcomes, including scarring that makes erections and urination uncomfortable (Glassberg 1999). Thus, while these procedures aim to normalize the appearance of the genitalia, they create scarring, which alters the goal of a normal appearance and reduces sexual functioning.

Intersexuality may also involve hormonal therapies. For example, men with Klinefelter syndrome (XXY) and women with Turner syndrome (XO) may receive lifelong hormone replacement to help their bodies develop—or suppress—secondary sex characteristics, like breast tissue, facial hair, and Adam's apples.

In recent years, sex reassignment surgery has become a controversial issue. The Intersex Society of North America (ISNA) has criticized doctors' efforts to "normalize" intersex individuals. The goal of these surgeries is to make the body recognizably male or female so that the child could be assigned a gender role. Once assigned a gender role, it is believed, the child would experience relatively normal gender development. The ISNA objects to these procedures for many reasons. Primarily, they believe the bodies of intersex individuals are already physiologically normal and do not need fixing and that the message that their bodies need fixing may cause psychological harm to children.

For historian and medical ethicist Alice Dreger and social psychologist Suzanne Kessler (1998), the medical treatment of intersexuality reflects not so much the fact that intersexuality threatens the individual but that it threatens society at large. As a society, we are not equipped to deal with sex or gender ambiguity. Because much of our society is built around the notion that there are two sexes, there is no place for those who don't fit in. Dreger, Kessler, and the ISNA criticize the medical establishment for altering intersex individuals to fit into society's dichotomous organization of sex; they prefer that society be altered to accommodate intersex individuals.

Admittedly, there are some medical risks associated with intersexuality. Women with AIS may need surgery if they have testicular tissue embedded in their abdomens, as that tissue may become cancerous. Hormone therapies may be necessary to prevent or minimize osteoporosis, given that low levels of estrogen are linked to low bone density and fractures. Ultimately, the Intersex Society of North America recommends that doctors treat conditions that present a legitimate physical risk. Otherwise, the

Society recommends assigning the child a gender role in order to facilitate healthy development, while waiting to perform surgeries until the individual can make an informed choice.

Finally, our journey through the social construction of sex takes us to a remote village in the Dominican Republic to see what we can learn from the *guevedoces*. First documented to an audience in the United States by endocrinologist Julianne Imperato-McGinley and her colleagues (1974), *guevedoces* translates as "penis at 12"; the medical term is 5-alpha reductase deficiency. At her research site, Imperato-McGinley documented 18 children who were raised unambiguously as little girls. At birth and through their first 10 years of life (or so), they displayed no signs that they were anything but biological females. At puberty, however, hormones kicked in, resulting in deepening voices, growing muscles, and lengthening of what was previously thought to be a clitoris. Of the 18 cases documented, 17 made a relatively seamless shift to the male gender role. Perhaps due to the frequency of these conditions—with estimates as high as 2 percent of the population—some experience relief, if not normalcy, when the *guevedoces* cut their hair, abandon little girls' clothes, and take on male interests and responsibilities.

Our trip to the Dominican Republic provides several lessons. First, the same human body may be interpreted differently across cultures; the notion of "sex" itself is a human creation. Second, and by extension, what is threatening in the United States and in need of medical intervention ("spit") may be considered normal elsewhere ("saliva"). Had they been born in the United States, these *guevedoces* would have undergone surgery. In fact, Imperato-McGinley provides a case study of eight children born in the United States with 5-alpha reductase deficiency who were castrated to prevent masculinization and preserve their female sex characteristics. Later in life, most experienced psychological struggles. While their bodies continued to send chemical impulses that told them they were male, they were assigned a female gender identity. While medical interventions may "fix" the outsides, they seem to be less successful in "fixing" the individual's insides (with many questioning whether these are conditions that need fixing).

DEFINING GENDER: WHAT IS IT AND HOW MANY ARE THERE?

While sex and gender are often used interchangeably, there are some important differences in these terms. **Gender** refers to the set of social distinctions that differentiate women and men. Additionally, we can use the terms masculine and feminine to describe the behavioral expectations of men and women. Because we generally assume there are two and only two sexes, we also assume there are two and only two genders. This shows that the concepts of sex and gender are tightly and causally linked. But while sex is a biological category, gender is a social category: sex is something we are born with, but gender is learned.

Like sex, a person's gender cannot be determined by any one thing. The *set* of social distinctions that differentiate men and women (and girls and boys), includes one's appearance, personality, hobbies, preferences, and behaviors. A person's gender may be evident in their hair, given the current pattern in the United States for men to have shorter hair and women to have longer hair. It is also evident in one's body: how much space we take up and whether and how we cross our legs can also be tied to gender. Gender may be evident in color-coded clothes or accessories that declare one's interests—a skateboard, for example, or a glittery pink cell phone cover. Would I be wrong to assume that every short-haired individual with a skateboard was a guy? Yes, I would, but it's likely I would be right more often than wrong.

Although gender schemas can be relatively predictable, not every facet of our personhood is gendered. If I asked my classroom of 200 students to write the same phrase on a notecard (e.g., "My favorite class this semester is sociology"), I might be able to predict the writer's gender about 85 percent of the time. There is something about most people's writing—large and neat versus small and messy—that reveals their gender. If I asked this same group to type out their favorite movie, I might be able to predict their gender about 65 percent of the time. Many female students favor "chick flicks" like *The Notebook*, *The Vow*, *Titanic*, and *Love, Actually*, but some prefer "bro-mances" like *The Hangover* and action movies like *Fast and Furious*. If I asked students to identify their majors, I would probably have success in labeling aspiring teachers as women and aspiring engineers as men; at times, I would be wrong, and those studying biology and marketing would surely confuse me. Finally, if I asked students their favorite ice cream flavor, it would be nearly impossible to predict their gender. To my knowledge, there is nothing gendered about ice cream. What's the point? That many aspects of our everyday lives are gendered, while others are not.

During the 1970s, psychologist Sandra Bem developed a tool to measure gender distinctions called the **Bem Gender Roles Inventory** (BGRI). Comprised of 60 questions, the BGRI allows individuals to rate themselves on an array of personality traits, including aggressive, loyal, friendly, dominant, and sympathetic. Rather than answering yes or no, the individual selects a score ranging from 1 to 7 ("almost always" or "almost never") to describe oneself. After tallying scores, the individual receives a score labeled Feminine, Nearly Feminine, Androgynous, Nearly Masculine, or Masculine. **Androgyny** refers to a combination of male and female combining the Greek word origins for men (andro) and woman (gyn).

Sandra Bem (1981) developed this tool based on the theory that people process behaviors based on sex-linked associations, what she called a "gender schema." In developing this theory, her goal was not to identify an essential list of traits that describe masculinity and femininity; her goal was to develop a model of how categories like gender become internalized and acted upon. By calling gender a "schema," Bem captured the notion that gender operates as a mental device for processing social cues. By creating a simplified construct called gender and dividing the social world into two broad categories, gender becomes a tool for organizing our social world. Her theory asserts that we become boys and girls, and later men and women, due to the fact that dividing tasks and identities up into two complementary camps makes life easy.

While researchers have questioned the notion that gender can be captured by a number and have questioned the specific traits used in the BGRI, it is still a useful tool. When my students take the inventory, their results consistently show differences in the mean scores of males and females. The BGRI also allows us to think about gender as a continuum. Although we conventionally use the terms masculinity and femininity to describe the gender role expectations associated with males or females, in reality we all blend elements of masculinity and femininity. Someone may choose a career in retail or fashion—traditionally feminine pursuits—but may execute their job with a high level of assertiveness—a traditionally masculine trait. The same person may manifest different traits across different settings, showing a high degree of empathy in one and little in another. Similarly, young girls may identify as "tomboys" during childhood but transition into "girly-girls" as young adults. These examples show the fluidity of gender within an individual's life experiences.

The number of individuals identifying as **transgender** has increased in recent decades. Transgender people are those whose gender identities deviate from the traditional gender binary, or whose gender identity does not correspond to their biological sex. This identity is represented by Laverne Cox, the transgender actress who portrays the transgender inmate, Sophia, on the groundbreaking Netflix series *Orange Is the New Black* (her pretransition self is portrayed in flashbacks by her real-life twin brother). Another version of identifying as transgender is represented by those who reject the notion that there are two and only two genders and instead create their own unique gender expression (sometimes called "genderqueer"). It is unclear whether transgender identities are rooted in underlying biological processes or if there is a direct relationship between being born intersex and identifying as transgender. While some transgender people opt for surgical or hormonal treatments to better express their gender identities, others do not; instead, they simply alter their exterior gender expression to align better with their personal gender identity. As a group, transgender people further highlight the notion of the continuum, especially when they "play" with gender and disrupt conventional or rigid notions of masculinity and femininity. Some transpeople further reject the way that the gender binary is inscribed in our language, and use them/their/theirs as preferred gender pronouns.

Figure 2.2 illustrates the possibility of thinking of *gender* as both a dichotomy (binary) and a continuum. When thinking about gender as continuum, we can ask which sex has an easier time navigating the continuum. Do men and women have equal freedom to blend so-called masculine and feminine traits? Evidence from the popular culture suggests that females have greater latitude traversing the gender continuum. During the spring of 2011, a dust-up occurred in the American media over an image from retailer J. Crew's webpage. The photo that caused the stir featured the company's creative director, Jenna Lyons, painting the toenails (neon pink!) of her 5-year-old son. While this example may be trivial, what it reveals about gender

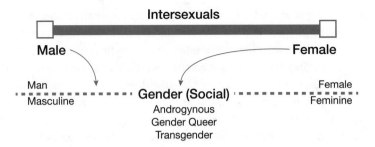

Figure 2.2 Gender as a binary vs. continuum.

expectations is profound. What the company intended to portray as an instance of mother–child bonding was interpreted by some as a threat to conventional notions of gender and her son's psychological well-being. In an on-line editorial, Fox News's Dr. Keith Ablow (2011) commented: "It may be fun and games now, Jenna, but at least put some money aside for psychotherapy for the kid—and maybe a little for others who'll be affected by your 'innocent' pleasure." For Ablow, engaging in gender-atypical activities may derail a child's gender development, pushing him into transgender or homosexual territory.

But what if the J. Crew image featured a father and a 5-year-old daughter fishing off the end of a dock? Would Dr. Ablow have suggested that Jenna Lyons put money away for her daughter's psychotherapy sessions? I doubt that such an ad would have caused a second look, much less a media firestorm. There are countless examples where young girls and women are encouraged to participate in typically masculine activities. During the summer of 2014, Mo-ne Davis appeared on the cover of Sports Illustrated, celebrated for pitching a historic shutout at the Little League World Series. Young women can go to the mall and purchase "boyfriend jeans"—relaxed and sexy at the same time. And while I have never seen an ad for cologne where a man is wearing his girlfriend's negligee, I have seen numerous ads implying that a woman wearing her boyfriend's oversized shirt (and nothing else!) is wildly appealing.

Scholarly research also illustrates the notion that boys experience stricter gender policing. Sociologist Emily Kane (2006, 2012) shows that parents encourage daughters who express "gender nonconformity" but fear gender nonconformity among sons. Worried he might turn out to be gay, or just perceived as such, Kane found that fathers react negatively to sons' requests for tea sets, ballet lessons, etc.; they saw it as their duty to ensure their sons become sufficiently masculine. As boys grow older, they become their own gender police, teasing boys who associate with girls, marking boundaries between themselves and "cootie-ridden" girls (Thorne 1993), and heaping the epithet "fag" on those who are inadequately crude, athletic, and reckless (Kimmel 2008; Pascoe 2007).

In a society where women have fought for greater rights, it is ironic that gender expression is one area where women have greater freedom. Women, after all, can wear skirts, dresses, and pants—usually without fear of reprisal! Conversely, men cannot even drink diet soda without worrying about being too girly, hence products like

"Dr. Pepper 10," whose tag lines declare it has "10 manly calories" and that "It's not for women." What does it mean when something as benign as diet soda can threaten one's masculinity?

According to cultural theorist R. W. Connell (1995), efforts to police men's gender expression are efforts to protect male power. In many societies, that which is masculine is defined as good and valuable and that which is feminine as less valuable. The things men do are celebrated—or simply treated as the norm against which other behaviors are compared. The heralding of all things masculine is highlighted by the feminist Gloria Steinem, who once suggested that if men menstruated, it would become a "boast-worthy event," with men bragging about how much and how long ("I'm a three-pad man!"); no longer would this monthly event be treated as a secret shame. Women are applauded when they do "masculine" things, yet when men stray too far toward the feminine end of the gender continuum, they are punished. These sanctions and admonitions ("Don't be such a sissy," "Little boys don't play with Barbie") reinforce the gender hierarchy by rewarding boys when they act like real men and devaluing things associated with femininity.

Speaking of continuum makes even more sense once we acknowledge there is considerable overlap between the genders. When it comes to traits like aggression and empathy, abilities like mathematics and motor skills, or even social attitudes, we speak of men and women as the "opposite sex." Sociologist Michael Kimmel (2010) calls this the "interplanetary theory of gender difference," because it implies that men and women hail from different worlds. Yet research frequently fails to find statistically significant differences between men and women. Psychologist Janet Shibley-Hyde (2005) found that when examining cognitive skills, communication styles, and personality traits, differences between men and women were either small or nonexistent. Gender differences were found in only 22 percent of measured traits, including attitudes regarding sexuality and incidents of physical aggression (see Figure 2.3). In nearly 75 percent of the traits she measured, there were no differences between men and women. So much for the notion of "opposite sexes"!

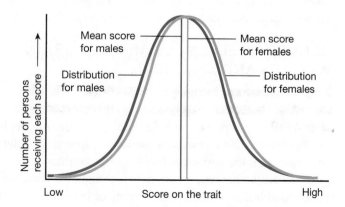

Figure 2.3 Male/female aggressiveness bell curve. (Source: Shibley-Hyde 2005)

Rather than emphasize differences between men and women, we should acknowledge that there is more variation *among* women and men and few differences between the "average" man and woman. Where differences arise is *within* the categories of woman and man. The most nurturing female and the least nurturing female are more different from one another than the "typical man" and "typical woman." Ultimately, men and women have more in common with one another than they have differences.

NATURE VS. NURTURE: EXPLAINING THE SOCIAL DIFFERENCES BETWEEN MEN AND WOMEN

While men and women are in many ways similar, natural and social scientists are trying to understand the differences that do exist. This section outlines two ways of explaining these differences: the **essentialist** and **social constructionist** perspectives. The assumption, from both theoretical camps, is that there exist some very real gender differences; where they diverge is in how they explain these differences.

This question about gender is echoed across other human differences (like race), and efforts to explain why such differences exist across individuals and groups. Discussed by natural and social scientists, as well as philosophers, this is referred to as the **nature vs. nurture debate**. The goal of the debate is to determine the degree to which differences between humans reflect biological forces (nature), on the one hand, and social influences (nurture), on the other. This is not merely an academic debate. As I demonstrate, explanations favoring the "nature" perspective have sometimes been used to justify social inequality.

NATURE AND THE ESSENTIALIST PERSPECTIVE

The essentialist perspective captures the "nature" side of the debate, arguing that human differences are rooted in biology. When applied to the question of gender, this perspective asserts that biological factors cause men and women to behave differently. These biological factors include the structure and functioning of the brain, hormones, and genetics (DNA). Another term for this perspective, *biological determinism*, captures the basic idea that human behavior is *determined* by underlying biological forces.

GENDER DIFFERENCES AND THE BRAIN: WAFFLES AND SPAGHETTI?

Within popular psychology and academic research, the notion persists that men and women have different brains—and that this explains why men and women act differently. While it was previously believed that the men's larger brains gave them superior intelligence, current research focuses on the structural differences in men's and women's brains and the hormones flowing through them. To explore the brain and social behavior, researchers use a variety of techniques: analysis of living rodents, autopsies of deceased humans, and brain imaging of living humans (e.g., functional magnetic resonance imaging, or fMRI).

Neuroscientists see the brain divided into two hemispheres—or halves—each with its own functions. The pioneering work of Nobel Prize winner Roger Sperry (1961) and the ongoing research of Michael Gazzaniga (2005, 2011) show that the brain is *lateralized*, with linear reasoning ("X causes Y") and some language functions taking place on the left side, and holistic reasoning ("Y is a complicated reality, influenced by a number of things, connected to a number of other things") taking place on the right. This leads to the popularized believe that the left side of the brain is "in charge" of logic and verbal reasoning while the right side is "in charge" of emotional and artistic expression.

Although cognitive neuroscientists challenge this simplistic view, they generally agree that women have a denser *corpus collosum* than men. The corpus collosum is the structure of nerve fibers that connects the brain's two hemispheres. With a denser corpus collosum, it is believed that women can communicate more efficiently across the brain's two halves. They can unite emotion and reason, linear processing and holistic thinking. MRI studies show that when given an array of verbal tasks, both halves of women's brains "glow," while men's brains show activity on only one side of the brain. This structural difference may help explain why women tend to be more emotionally expressive than men (Blum 1997). Within the popular culture, men's brains have been compared to waffles and women's brains to spaghetti. The image of the waffle brain evokes the idea that men compartmentalize their thoughts in the same way that syrup slides into different compartments of a waffle; as a result, men have a hard time switching gears between, say, work, home, and other domains of life. Conversely, the image of women's spaghetti brain suggests that everything blends together, so that they are more adept at multitasking and seeing the connections between various domains—all due, perhaps, to the corpus collosum.

The notion that structural differences in the brain can explain social differences between men and women has been popularly articulated by neuropsychiatrist Louann Brizendine, author of *The Female Brain* and *The Male Brain* (2006 and 2011, respectively). Popular in the mainstream media, but less respected by her scholarly peers, Brizendine has graced the morning talk shows and has been reviewed positively in media outlets including *Elle Magazine* and CNN and by Oprah herself. Her research suggests that gender differences in behavior—ranging from emotional expression to sexual desire to depression and well-being to the nature of friendships—are hardwired into men's and women's brains. Her image of the female brain is that of a tangled telephone cord; the male brain is represented by a sticky role of tape.

The essentialist perspective can be found in a comedy skit called "Mind Ninja" by Dane Cook. In this skit, Cook describes women as "mental terrorists" who push men's buttons with their uncanny ability to weave together emotions and logic; meanwhile, men get tongue-tied and become completely paralyzed, unable to reply with a witty retort to their girlfriends' verbal prodding. Although he does not explicitly invoke cognitive neuroscience, Dane Cook humorously shows that men get stuck on the emotional side of their brains while women dance verbal circles around them—perhaps because of the structure of their brains.

THE SOCIOLOGICAL RESPONSE TO BRAIN RESEARCH

Sociologists caution against the conclusion that social differences between men and women can be traced back to underlying biological differences. The critique of the essentialist perspective begins with the observation that the brain is a "plastic" organ. Through repetition from external stimuli, the brain may change in much the same way that pull-ups change arms, back, and shoulders. Researchers do not know whether gender differences in the corpus collosum exist at birth. Autopsies on infants' brains, after all, are met with resistance. According to the sociological critique, the greater density in women's corpus collosum may reflect different social experiences rather than innate structural differences. Perhaps the denser brain tissue emerges through socialization and the frequent use of emotional reasoning among women, rather than being present from birth.

A second shortcoming is that some of this research seems based more on ideology than rigorous science. While fellow neuroscientists have criticized research like Louann Brizendine's as shoddy, based on small sample sizes, and quick to draw grand conclusions based on small measured differences, others argue that the misuse of science is simply par for the course. Sociologists like Michael Kimmel (2010) and Judith Lorber (1993) and psychologist Cordelia Fine (2010) argue that many use science as a tool to help them find the gender differences they seek. When it was discovered men's larger brains did not mean they were more intelligent, researchers began looking for other evidence to show men's superiority. When it was shown that women's brains showed more lateral connectivity than men's, some said this proved women are "flighty" and have fragmented thought processes. A problem, then, with the essentialist perspective is that it has been sloppily used to justify a cultural perspective that seeks easy explanations for why men and women are different.

"ARE YOU PMS'ING, OR SOMETHING?": HORMONES AND BEHAVIOR

Another focus of the essentialist perspective is the impact of hormones on behavior, the theory being that the hormonal differences between males and females account for their social differences. According to this perspective, men are more aggressive and more sexual than women because they have higher levels of testosterone, while female sex hormones make women more nurturing and empathetic.

Some of the most cutting-edge research on testosterone's effects on behavior derives from studies involving castration. Lab animals that have been castrated, and therefore lack the testosterone produced in their testes, demonstrate lower levels of aggressive behavior. While research involving humans similarly concludes that high levels of circulating testosterone can be linked to aggression, many questions remain regarding the link between testosterone and behavior (Kuepper et al. 2010; Simpson 2001). These questions, moreover, may have practical application: research on the link between testosterone and antisocial behaviors has inspired suggestions on how to fight crime. A widely cited German study found that within 10 years after release from prison, sex offenders who agreed to voluntary castration had a recidivism rate of 3 percent (reoffending), compared to 46 percent among those not castrated (Wille and Beier 1989). Future offenders can breathe easy: ethical and medical concerns have prevented this from becoming a mainstream crime-fighting strategy.

If scientific evidence suggests that castration can reduce aggressive behaviors, is the converse true? Can an *increase* in testosterone cause more aggressive behaviors? On a practical level, doctor-prescribed hormone replacement therapy is used by aging men to buttress muscle mass, sex drive, and mood. For men not suffering from "Low-T," Abbott Labs' Androgel has an unofficial, "off-label" use, endorsed by some bodybuilders as a tool to "get big." Can masculinity be purchased in a tube?

On this point, researchers are skeptical. According to Robert Sapolsky (1998), a Stanford professor of biology and neurology, it would take a fourfold increase in testosterone in a human male to produce a measurable increase in his aggressive behavior. As Sapolsky notes, it is difficult to conceive of a real-life scenario where a human would experience a fourfold increase in testosterone. Instead, he urges us to focus on what happens in the real world, where testosterone levels ranging from 20 percent of normal to twice the normal range are typically associated with similar levels of aggression. This suggests that different levels of testosterone generally do not result in different levels of aggression and that moderate increases in testosterone are not associated with higher levels of aggression.

Researchers have also studied the connection between hormones and behaviors among women. This research suggests that women's nurturing capacities are partially a matter of their hormonal makeup. Oxytocin, a hormone released in high doses during childbirth, has been called the "love hormone" and the "cuddle chemical." Researchers have connected it to the maternal ability to produce milk, nurse, and bond with a newborn, along with the ability to quell anxiety and fear and increase feelings of empathy and trust (Hurlemann et al. 2010; Lee at al. 2009). This leads to the belief that there is something essential in women that makes them nurturing.

Yet women's hormonal fluctuations have also been linked to negative behaviors. Hormonal variations have, for example, been linked to women's mood swings, irritability, and forgetfulness. This bundle of behaviors has been labeled premenstrual syndrome, or PMS;

Both the medical establishment and comic artists have capitalized on portraying women's emotional states as a reflection of underlying biology.

researchers estimate that upwards of 19 percent of women experience PMS (Strine et al. 2005). Perhaps 3–8 percent of women's symptoms are so problematic that they have been labeled a disorder: premenstrual dysphoric disorder (PMDD).

As of 2013, PMDD has been listed as a psychiatric disorder in the American Psychological Association's fifth edition of the Diagnostic and Statistical Manual (DSM-V). That PMDD has been conceptualized as a "disorder" reflects older perspectives that portrayed women as fundamentally crazy. Up until 1980, *hysteria* was listed in the DSM as a uniquely female disorder. Influenced by Victorian thinking on sex and Sigmund Freud's psychoanalytic theory, hysteria was conceived as a psychological disturbance manifesting in stress, anxiety, and nervousness, thought to be caused by problems in the reproductive system (Micale 1995). *Hysterectomies* were the cure. While hysteria no longer exists as a medical diagnosis, the belief persists that women's hormonal fluctuations sometimes make them "crazy."

THE SOCIOLOGICAL RESPONSE TO RESEARCH ON HORMONES AND BEHAVIOR

How do sociologists respond to the essentialist notion that women's hormones make them alternately compassionate and crazy? First, they would critique the methods used to investigate this connection. It's easy to find negative outcomes if that's all you look for. Because few research instruments assume there could be any positive effects associated with menstruation—that women may experience an increase in creativity or mental focus—they do not ask about them; consequently, researchers can only conclude that menstruation leads to problematic conditions like PMS and PMDD (Figert 1996; Ripper 1991).

A more pointed sociological critique is the notion that PMS is "socially constructed"—that is, something made up by humans rather than a scientific fact. While "periods" are real and are accompanied by verifiable shifts in hormones, the social and cultural meaning given to this event varies across cultures. For the Kalahari women profiled in Marjorie Shostak's (1981) classic anthropological tale, *Nisa: The Life and Words of a !Kung Woman*, the notion that one's period could be difficult or traumatic was incomprehensible. While the underlying symptoms may have been present, menstruation was experienced by the !Kung women as a nonevent.

Similarly, it has been suggested that PMS and PMDD are the creation of the psychological and medical establishment, who stood to benefit by creating a set of diagnostic criteria, a reliable cadre of patients, and a market filled with products to cure these conditions (Figert 1995; Rodin 1992). Women now define and interpret their physical symptoms in particular ways because medical professionals have taught us to interpret them in these ways. Feminist scholars assert that current thinking about women, hormones, and PMS is a modern instance of male-dominated social institutions trying to control women's bodies. If scientific authorities can convince the public that women's mental states periodically break down, it may be possible to exclude women from important areas of decision making, such as politics, economics, and the military.

When it comes to the link between hormones and behavior among men, sociologists acknowledge that men's higher levels of testosterone are associated with higher levels of aggression at the group level. Yet with respect to studies drawing a link between testosterone and aggression, researchers point to the contextual nature of hormonal variations. The production and circulation of testosterone in the body is malleable, fluctuating both throughout the day and throughout the life cycle. Social context and environmental conditions have a measurable impact on hormone levels.

Accordingly, sociologists argue that higher levels of testosterone don't *cause* aggressive behavior; rather, the opportunity to experience aggression and competition may cause an increase in testosterone. Whether studying chess, tennis, or soccer, researchers find that testosterone levels spike prior to play and later rise or fall depending on whether one wins or loses the contest (Kemper 1990; Mazur and Booth 1998; Mazur, Booth, and Dabbs 1992). In fact, simply watching an athletic contest can increase testosterone levels (Carré and Putnam 2010). Testosterone levels among females also fluctuate (Hamilton et al. 2009; Jimenez et al. 2012). When female athletes engage in intense competition, their hormones rise and fall. This finding suggests a chicken-and-egg problem: Do hormones cause the aggressive behavior, or does the opportunity to engage in aggressive behaviors cause hormone levels to rise?

Finally, the environmental or contextual nature of hormones is evident in studies exploring the relationship between hormones and life events like marriage and divorce. Researchers find higher levels of testosterone among men undergoing divorce (Mazur and Michalek 1998) and lower levels among married men (Gray et al. 2002). Among recent fathers, testosterone levels are lower still (Gettler et al. 2011; Storey et al. 2000). Researchers argue that lower levels of testosterone "may facilitate paternal care in humans by decreasing the likelihood that a father will engage in competitive and/or mating behavior" (Gray et al. 2002:193) and that the hormonal response is an evolutionary adaption that facilitates male caregiving of vulnerable infants (Gettler et al. 2011).

THE DANGERS OF THE ESSENTIALIST PERSPECTIVE

While the usefulness of the essentialist perspective is ultimately a question of whether it is backed by scientific evidence, this perspective has been used to justify bad behaviors. The phrase "boys will be boys" exemplifies the dangers of embracing the essentialist perspective. This phrase suggests that behaviors ranging from boys' rough and tumble play, to their occasional violence and destruction, to their sexual misdeeds are biologically motivated. The perspective aligns with "evolutionary psychology," whose research is sometimes interpreted as suggesting that men have a biological imperative to "spread their seed," meaning they are biologically programmed to maximize their genetic potential through sex and reproduction. Consequently, cheating is to be expected.

Magazines such as *Psychology Today* and popular psychology books like Eric Anderson's (2012) *Monogamy Gap: Men, Love, and the Reality of Cheating* and *Sex at Dawn: How We Mate, Why We Stray, and What It Means for Modern Relationships* by

Christopher Ryan and Cacilda Jetha (2011) bring this perspective to the public. According to a 2009 blog-post written by Leon Seltzer of *Psychology Today*, testosterone induces "a biological urge that sooner or later demands expression, [and] literally guarantees the survival of the species." Further, he states, women are "expressly designed to alleviate men's sexual tensions." While acknowledging that men can learn to resist these urges, the lingering message is that biology is more powerful than social learning and that sexual aggression is to be expected. The testosterone "demanded" it, after all.

The essentialist perspective has also been used to justify gender inequality. Throughout the 1800s, women fought for access to higher education. An educational reformer in his day, then–Harvard President Charles Eliot refused to admit women to his esteemed university. In an 1899 speech at Wellesley College—a women's college—he proclaimed that "Women should concentrate on an education that will not injure women's bodily powers and functions." A rigorous liberal arts education was inappropriate for women, because while they may graduate as "excellent scholars," the blood flow from reproductive system to the brain meant that they would also graduate with "undeveloped ovaries" (Clarke 1873: 39). In a context where women were ultimately valued for their fertility, scholars advised that women be given a domestic form of education, lest their fundamental essence be harmed by trying to compete with the boys.

These quotes of yesteryear would be downright funny if they were not echoed in recent years. In 2005, then–president of Harvard University Lawrence Summers suggested that women's underrepresentation in math and science careers could be partially explained by their lower levels of innate mathematical and scientific ability. While admitting that women rarely receive as much mentoring in math or science and are often socialized to enter the "helping professions," Summers also suggested that women's brains may not be designed for math and science. Such a view perpetuates gender inequality by suggesting that women's underrepresentation in technical fields is biologically determined and that little can be done to change it.

Essentialist arguments have been used to limit women's roles in the military. Arguments for restricting women's combat roles have often rested on biological assumptions. It has been argued that women are not capable of serving in combat because they are too emotional and that their emotions are especially unpredictable during menstruation. Further, men may feel a biological imperative to protect the women soldiers on the front lines, thereby compromising the mission. During 2012, amid resistance and controversy, more combat roles were officially opened to women. Efforts to integrate women into combat roles reflect structural changes, namely changes in the nature of combat duties and shortages in military personnel. Resistance to these changes illustrates the tendency to attribute gender differences—and therefore limit women's opportunities—to underlying biological forces.

NURTURE AND THE SOCIAL CONSTRUCTIONIST PERSPECTIVE

An alternate way of viewing social differences—like the differences between men and women—is through the lens of nurture rather than nature. The social constructionist perspective captures the "nurture" point of view; it explains social differences as a reflection of social forces. When applied to the question of gender differences, this perspective asserts that socialization and social interaction powerfully shape gender differences. The social context in which humans are socialized provides the setting in which gender role expectations are created. By "social context," I refer to macro-level aspects of society, including the economy, religion, technology, politics, and so forth. From this perspective, gender roles do not emerge from uncontrollable biological forces but from the social circumstances in which humans live.

The social constructionist perspective views gender differences as contextual, flexible, and, therefore, variable. It gets its credibility by observing variations in gender expression over time and across cultures. If gender differences were simply the reflection of biological forces, we would expect that men and women would be essentially the same, no matter the time or place. Yet that is not the case. To explore the social constructionist perspective, we must first travel abroad and then back in time.

THE STUDY ABROAD TRIP

From a sociological perspective, much is learned by looking at what happens in other cultures. We learn, for example, that what we take for granted as normal and natural may not necessarily be so. To illustrate this point, we need to take a metaphorical study abroad trip. On this trip we will pair up with anthropologists, since they too believe that much of the world, including how we define femininity and masculinity, is socially constructed. The goal of our journey is not simply to describe the various ways in which other cultures and societies have defined their gender role expectations but to explain why these definitions emerge in the first place.

Our first stop is Papua New Guinea, a culturally and ecologically diverse island nation in the Pacific Ocean. As a nation with hundreds of indigenous ethnic groups and perhaps as many as 825 languages, there may be no other area on earth that has as much to offer in terms of lessons on cultural variations. It is, perhaps, for this reason that anthropologist Margaret Mead (2001) chose Papua New Guinea as the setting for her groundbreaking 1935 work, *Sex and Temperament in Three Primitive Societies*. After getting acclimated with some mountain hikes, sightseeing trips to volcanoes, and taking in a rugby or cricket match in the capital, our exploration of gender roles begins.

Guided by Margaret Mead, we would discover that the tribes of this island nation challenge common assumptions of what it means to be male and female. During her time with the *Arapesh* tribe, Mead found that both men and women were generally pacifists who organized social roles in an egalitarian way; men and women were both cooperative in temperament and shared duties of diplomacy, agricultural production, and childrearing. Among the *Mundugumor*, by contrast, she found that men and women both had "warlike" natures. With traditions in headhunting and cannibalism, Mead described the male and female members of this remote tribe as virile, jealous, violent, and arrogant. Rather than embrace childrearing with a "natural" tendency to nurture, Mundugumor women generally regarded motherhood as a time of stress and inconvenience. Finally, among the *Tchambuli*, gender roles were opposite of what is observed in most Western societies. Mead found that Tchambuli women took on the dominant roles and were deeply involved in the acquisition of food and trade between villages. Men, by contrast, were found to be vain and preoccupied by bodily decoration. Among these three tribes alone, Mead depicted significant variation in men's and women's social roles.

A trip around the world, guided by anthropologist George Murdoch, would yield similar lessons. In an effort to document variations across cultures, Murdoch and his colleagues developed during the 1940s the "Cross Cultural Survey" (known today as the Human Relations Area Files). The goal of this project was to develop a database of information on a wide variety of cultural traits (e.g., techniques of child socialization, food preparation, war and diplomacy, gender roles) to test hypotheses about human life. Encompassing 400 different cultures, this research tool reveals that while men act as providers and protectors in a majority of world cultures, and women generally take on domestic tasks (food preparation and childrearing), there are also noteworthy variations across the globe as to who takes on which tasks.

To amplify, while most world cultures are patriarchal in organization, some adhere to a more matriarchal model. **Patriarchy**, meaning "rule of fathers," refers to a model of social organization where men are dominant in terms of economic, cultural, and political affairs. This style of social organization reinforces the notion that men are "breadwinners" and that they are naturally inclined toward rationality and leadership. In many cases, this form of social organization produces social arrangements where men are superior and women subordinate. **Matriarchy**, by contrast, refers to a form of social organization where women play dominant roles. Although few in number, matriarchal societies—such as the Iroquois Indians of North America—are ones where women perform key roles in leadership and moral authority.

In traveling to the desert Southwest of the United States, we would learn that the Hopi and Navajo tribes have traditionally followed **matrilineal** family structures. Matrilineal societies are ones where the tracing of descent and the handing down of names, property, and affiliation occurs through the mother's line. Although the specific forms of matrilineal organization vary, and in some cases men still hold more power than women, the takeaway point is that significant cross-cultural variation exists in the social organization of gender and how authority and family ties are arranged.

Our next stop is the small southern European country of Albania. Although we would find some modern comforts in the capital city of Tirana, our journey into the mountainous rural areas would reveal a country that adheres to many traditional customs. One custom that seems to be dying out is the **sworn virgin**. A sworn virgin is a young woman who takes an oath of sexual abstinence and begins dressing and acting as a man—which means earning money, protecting the family, wearing pants, carrying weapons, and associating socially with other men. Rather than regarding "sworn virgins" with scorn or skepticism, residents in these areas either regard them with respect or fail to notice that they are not biologically male.

In some ways, the sworn virgin is similar to the Afghan *bacha posh*—which, in the Dari language, means "dressed up as a boy." Bacha posh dress like boys, take jobs outside of the home, attend school, and provide protection to female family members. Where they differ from the sworn virgins is that the role of the bacha posh is typically not permanent. Rather, around puberty, they typically transition back into a female gender role. This transition, which adolescent girls sometimes resent or find difficult, is motivated by the parents' desire to marry off their daughter.

By journeying through the exotic locales of Albania and Afghanistan, we learn an important lesson: different structural conditions give rise to different gender expectations. This is what sociologists mean when they say that the "macro-level"—or big picture—shapes many aspects of our day-to-day experiences. In both Albania and Afghanistan there have been centuries of wars and "blood feuds" (rivalries between families and clans); over time, this violence has resulted in an imbalanced sex ratio (more females than males). In addition, both are patriarchal societies—ones where women have little value and few opportunities. The ancient legal codes of Albania, known as the *Kanun*, defined the value of women as equivalent to 12 oxen. Given these conditions, gender role expectations evolved to solve a social problem: How can a society make sure that "men's work" gets done when there are not enough men for the job? Rather than redefine women's gender roles and allow them to act as providers and protectors, these societies allowed women to go "undercover" as men. This creative solution—Albanian sworn virgins and Afghani bacha posh—evolved as a way of creating more "men" in society while allowing the patriarchal order to remain in place.

The Albanian sworn virgins are disappearing. As peace and modernity have come to this small European country, new solutions have emerged to solve feuds between

In Albania (left) and Afghanistan (right), females sometimes take on the male gender role to protect and provide for their families.

families and women have gained greater respect. While the examples from our meta-phorical trips abroad may be exotic, the lesson is simple: rather than create gender role expectations out of thin air, definitions of what is appropriate for men and women emerge from the broader social and cultural environment. Further, when broader social conditions change, so do gender role expectations.

Our journey so far has yielded this lesson: in some societies women take on "men's roles" and in others men take on "women's roles." Yet what about the possibility that some societies do not construct gender in this simple, dichotomous way? By journeying to Mexico, the American Southwest, and India we learn that some societies have three gender possibilities. Whether the *muxe* of Mexico, the *berdache* of the Plains Indians, the *nadle* of the Navajo, the *hwame* of the Mohave, or the *hijra* of India, these "third gender" categories reveal how complicated the whole notion of gender is and how creative human beings are in constructing their social worlds.

Although the specific identities and social roles of third-gender people vary across cultures, some commonalities exist. Let's use the berdache of the Plains Indians as a starting point. In his book *The Spirit and the Flesh*, anthropologist Walter Williams (1992 [1986]) describes the berdache as biological males who take on the female gender role (in how they dress, how they behave, and their work roles and social responsibilities). In other Native tribes, they also take on traditional male roles, such as going to war and participating in sweat lodge ceremonies. What is common among societies with a third gender category is that the individual in question dresses and acts "as a woman," and that individual is regarded as neither male nor female; they are considered as a legitimate third-gender option.

Third-gender people, such as the hijra of India and Pakistan, are sometimes viewed as having unique spiritual powers.

Another variation among cultures with a third gender category is the role they play in sexual encounters and family relationships. Among the muxe of Mexico (Oaxaca State), partnerships with biological men and the formation of families are typical. Among the Lakota Indians of the American Plains, partnerships with men may be allowed, but primarily among widowers. In such cases, third-gender individuals may take on a maternal role, but they do not become biological parents. Finally, among the hijra of India and Pakistan, partnerships with biological men are allowed, although it is expected that the hijra will take the "passive role" in sexual relations (Agarwal 1997).

Variations also exist cross-culturally in the degree to which third-gender people are stigmatized. Lynn Stephens notes that the muxe of Oaxaca, Mexico, are sometimes targeted or ridiculed—usually by men and more so in urban areas than traditional rural communities (2002). In India and Pakistan, the category of "hijra" has been institutionalized as a legal category. There, formal documents and identity cards permit individuals to check this third option—which suggests social recognition, and possibly even acceptance. That "two-spirit people" is a preferred term for Native American berdache provides further insight into social and cultural attitudes. The notion of having "two spirits" reflects these cultures' beliefs that third-gender people possess the traits of both men and women and that they combine them in unique and powerful ways (Lang 1998); some are even thought to have special powers. That said, when they work as healers, two-spirit people may be scorned or killed for perceived bad deeds. In her book *Men as Women, Women as Men*, Sabine Lang (1998) reports that among the Mohave, two-spirit persons might be killed if they are suspected of failing to produce rain or a harvest. To be fair, medicine men or spiritual leaders of any sex or gender are sometimes killed if they are suspected of being frauds.

EXPLORING ACTIVISM:
CHALLENGING THE GENDER BINARY ON COLLEGE CAMPUSES

Virtually everywhere we go, we find a world divided into two and only two gender categories. The notion of the gender binary is evident when going to buy children's clothing and toys, where stores are neatly divided into "Boys" and Girls" sections; the lesson is reinforced in school, where children form "Girls" and "Boys" lines and are organized into friendly competitions pitting one against the other. Yet what about individuals who do not easily identify with one sex or the other? What about those who identify as transgender, in that they do not identify with the typical gender categories or their gender expression does not match their biological sex?

As young folks go off to college and experience more autonomy and more crystallized identities, some wish to throw off the gender binary. Increasingly, transgender activists are working with allies to make the college campus a comfortable place. Many campus outreach groups, for example, have broadened their names and their missions, adding a T to the mix ("Lesbian, Gay, Bi, and Transgender"). While transgender individuals have their own unique struggles—determining whether and how to physically transition to the other sex, for example—they generally share with the lesbian and gay community the fact that their gender and sexual expression lies outside of the mainstream. Clubs and resource centers on campus work to provide a safe space for such students and educate the campus as a whole about alternate gender and sexual identities.

On college campuses around the country, student activists have also lobbied for "gender-neutral housing" options. Some transgender activists see this as an issue of equal opportunity and legal recognition of their gender expression. More common in New England and on progressive campuses across the country, perhaps as many as 100 colleges and universities currently offer gender-neutral housing. According to the University of Michigan's website, the goal of gender-neutral housing is "to provide a safe, inclusive, comfortable and supportive living experience for all students living in Michigan's residential facilities." This housing is available to "students who, because of gender identity or gender expression, prefer this option. This allows transgender students the ability to choose a roommate of any gender." A student who is biologically male, but identifies as a woman, may be paired with another female student (with her consent). On other campuses, gender-neutral housing works against the notion that men and women are "opposite sexes," as university officials allow cross-gender friends, brothers, and sisters to share rooms. While some colleges have designated wings in specific units for this option, others integrate gender-neutral housing units across the housing system.

Just as campuses in more conservative states—like the University of Tennessee and the University of North Carolina, Chapel Hill—have moved to expand their housing policies, Boston University decided in 2012 to end its gender-neutral housing initiative. In conjunction with their student government body, the Center for Gender, Sexuality, and Activism formed the lobby group, "Gender Neutral BU." Mirroring the student activism of the 1960s, students marched to the president's office to present him with a petition containing 2,300 student signatures, requesting that gender-neutral housing be reinstated. In another move echoing student activism of the 1960s, the dean of students warned that if students did not evacuate the premises, they would be arrested and suspended from the university. These threats were not idle: while exiting the building, student activists passed police officers armed with batons and zip-tie handcuffs.

Elsewhere throughout the United States, campus counseling centers have begun hiring counselors to help students with issues related to sexual orientation and gender identity (students who may identify as "transgender"). On the campus where I teach, official intake forms include options that do not require students to identify as male or female. These examples show that many institutions within the United States are currently changing how they recognize and organize gender differences. Still, struggles exist over questions as basic as which bathroom trans students can or should use. The examples also show that efforts to redefine gender categories have come about through the activism of students seeking to change the climate of their campuses.

TRAVELING BACK IN TIME

The notion that gender is "socially constructed" can also be illustrated by looking at historical variations in gender role expectations. Our time machine awaits!

Entering our time machine, where would we go to find the most gender **egalitarian** society? An egalitarian society is one characterized by equality among groups or individuals. Would we go to modern Scandinavian societies, some of which require equal representation of women in political offices? Actually, we would go way, way back in time. The greatest evidence of gender equality is found in **hunter-gatherer societies**. Up until about 10,000 years ago, all humans lived in hunter-gatherer societies—ones where humans survive by hunting (or scavenging) animals and gathering plants and seeds. In such societies, the anthropological and archeological evidence suggests, both men and women hunted—with men typically hunting larger animals—and both gathered plant-based foods—although women typically gathered more. Because both men and women made significant caloric contributions to their group, and because no one was able to gather a surplus (they merely subsisted), men and women were interdependent, with little opportunity to develop a social advantage (Dahlberg 1975; Lee and Devore 1968).

The notion that men and women were relatively equal in hunter-gatherer societies may come as a surprise. The essentialist perspective and evolutionary psychology, after all, suggest that men are naturally dominant and that their muscular and testosterone-fueled bodies engineer them to provide and protect. This story has been used to explain men's social dominance: it's hardwired into their hard bodies! Yet anthropologists Donna Hart and Robert Sussman (2005) found that early humans (way before the hunters and gatherers) did not eat much meat and that their teeth were better adapted to a diet of fruit and nuts. As such, women's food gathering was central to survival. Rather than hang out at home and protect vulnerable offspring, women typically carried their babies while they foraged for food. Examples like this help us gain a more accurate idea of what is "natural" when it comes to gender.

Another hypothesis that can be tested through time travel is the notion that women are naturally nurturing. Imagine you are a social scientist trained in the twenty-first century and want to know "what it means to be a woman" throughout American history. To begin, we must time travel to Massachusetts Bay Colony, circa 1675. Settled by the English beginning in 1620, the Massachusetts Bay Colony began as a trading base in the "New World" but quickly evolved into a home for Puritans seeking religious freedom. There we would discover that women were generally not thought of as delicate, emotional, maternal creatures.

To understand this, it is necessary to explain the role of children in society. Historians Steven Mintz and Susan Kellogg (1989) show that conceptions of motherhood and femininity cannot be understood apart from conceptions of childhood. Because women and men had little control over their fertility, children in the seventeenth century arrived whether they were wanted or not. Further, the lack of medical know-how meant that somewhere between one in three and one in 10 children died in infancy. People quickly learned that infancy is precarious. In addition, children at this time were viewed more as an economic asset than an emotional asset. Children helped sustain the family's economic well-being—helping raise younger siblings and allowing mom to do more complex tasks, or working in the garden, managing livestock, washing, cooking, etc. Because it took so much work to sustain a family, children were rarely doted on, read to, or played with. Colonial-era religious views also shaped perceptions of children. Rather than regard children as innocent creatures in need of love and nurturing, Puritanical beliefs (rooted in conservative Protestantism) framed children as willful, stubborn, and filled with "original sin."

Given these views on children, it would have been almost impossible for women to take on emotional, caretaking roles. This example shows that the belief that women are nurturing is a social construction: that they give birth does not automatically make them doting mothers. It illustrates how macro-level factors shape concepts like gender. In this case, medical technology (precarious infancy) affects how children and women are viewed. Further, the level of economic development (everyone works) influences how children and women are viewed. Finally, religious ideas affect how children are viewed (evil). The conceptions began to change during the Industrial Revolution of the mid-1800s. As more men began working in factories and offices, their middle-class incomes allowed women to stay at home. Further, the growth of factories allowed women some "time-saving" conveniences in the form of premade foods and clothing. Because they no longer had to work so hard, and because middle-class children were also freed from work, they became emotional assets rather than economic assets within the family.

As our time machine returns us to the present, it is essential that we take our lessons with us. The main lesson is that notions of masculinity and femininity come from the macro-level—conditions within the economy, technology, medicine, religion, media, education, and so forth. These conditions are mutually reinforcing, so that as conditions at the macro-level change, so do gender role expectations (and vice versa). Were we to chart gender role changes over the last 200 years, we would see this lesson reinforced time and again. Whether in terms of the Victorian-era male "dandy," the 1920s flapper, Rosie the Riveter, or the "sensitive male" of the 1970s, our travels would show that gender role changes are a reflection of changes in the broader social context.

INTERROGATING INTERSECTIONALITY: RACE, GENDER, AND PRIVILEGE

In 1851, when Sojourner Truth provocatively asked, "Ain't I a woman?" she provided sociologists one of the first examples of "intersectional" thinking. The concept of intersectionality refers to the notion that it is insufficient to focus only on differences between women and men without paying attention to the other identities that gender "intersects" with. While men and women may exhibit some differences between them, it is also the case that there are profound differences in the experiences of women (and men) from differential racial and ethnic and social class backgrounds. We must examine, therefore, how our social identities and traits like race, gender, sexuality, and social class intersect. The concept of intersectionality was first defined by legal scholar Kimberlé Crenshaw in 1989. Her goal was to show that systems of power and oppression are not organized in a simple and straightforward way, but that they intersect in complicated ways. Accordingly, some people experience multiple forms of oppression (a poor, black lesbian, for example), while others have power and privilege in some domains while lacking it in others (a middle-class, white lesbian, for example).

The notion of intersectionality, specifically focusing on race and gender, was hinted at by anti-slavery icon Sojourner Truth in her 1851 speech to the Women's Convention in Akron, Ohio. During the 1800s, the dominant image of women in the United States was of delicate, frail creatures, who needed protection by males and society alike. The notion that women were frail, delicate creatures fed the dominant social and political ideology that excluded them from the workplace, voting, and education while keeping them ensconced in domestic duties. Within this rhetoric, Sojourner Truth detected a troubling contradiction: the same rhetoric that provided white women with chivalrous treatment and protected them from difficult work did not apply to black women. Instead, like the immigrant women from Ireland, Italy, and Poland who would soon arrive on these shores, black women toiled in fields and factories and were routinely denied the dignity given to middle-class white women.

I Sell the Shadow to Support the Substance.
SOJOURNER TRUTH.

In asking "Ain't I a woman?" Sojourner Truth showed that gender and race are inextricably bound. To be black and female is different from being white and female.

That man over there says that women need to be helped into carriages, and lifted over ditches, and to have the best place everywhere. Nobody ever helps me into carriages, or over mud-puddles, or gives me any best place! And ain't I a woman? Look at me! Look at my arm! I have ploughed and planted, and gathered into barns, and no man could head me! And ain't I a woman? I could work as much and eat as much as a man—when I could get it—and bear the lash as well! And ain't I a woman? I have borne thirteen children, and seen most all sold off to slavery, and when I cried out with my mother's grief, none but Jesus heard me! And ain't I a woman? – Sojourner Truth

At the time, Truth's speech represented both a condemnation of slavery—a system that provided no protection to allegedly frail women—and an indictment of patriarchal gender roles—in that women may not actually need such protection. Today, her speech reminds us how complicated gender is. Even within the same era and same social context, gender may be constructed differently depending on how it intersects with race, social class, and other sociologically relevant social identities.

WHAT DOES IT ALL MEAN? THE SOCIOLOGICAL TAKEAWAY ON GENDER

During the summer of 2012, Caster Semenya carried the flag of her native South Africa in the opening ceremonies of the London Olympic Games. She left those games with a silver medal in the 800-meter race. Weeks before the games began, the International Olympic Committee (IOC) revealed a new policy for sex verification. This policy uses hormones as the deciding factor in determining a person's sex. According to the IOC, female athletes with *hyperandrogenism*, an excessive amount of male sex hormones, will be barred from competition. The rationale behind the policy is that male sex hormones, particularly testosterone, give female athletes an unfair advantage. Within this context, chromosomes, gonads, and genitalia have been ruled imperfect, if not irrelevant, indicators of a person's sex.

The evolution of this case reveals a central theme of this chapter: sex and gender are socially constructed. Even when it comes to "sex," something that should be simple and biologically verifiable, we find that humans are *still* looking for ways to determine how many sexes there are and what determines a person's sex. There is, as it turns out, no single marker for "sex." Instead, understandings of sex shift, and lines get redrawn as the broader social environment—including the state of scientific knowledge, the political climate, and gender relations—changes.

With respect to the nature vs. nurture debate, we conclude this chapter by clarifying where sociologists stand. Ultimately, sociologists give some credence to the nature side of the debate: most sociologists *do* believe that biological differences between males and females account for some of the social differences between men and women. Ultimately, though, sociologists reject the notion that biology is destiny. While biology may provide us with some predispositions and capacities, it does not *make* us act a certain way.

One final example may clarify the sociological position: the issue of height differences between men and women. Scientists know that males have a genetic predisposition to be taller and more muscular than females. Sociologists and anthropologists accept this assertion but note that social practices *amplify* many underlying differences between men and women (Kuzawa 2007). Across the globe, there are many societies in which male children are considered more valuable than female children. Male children bring prestige and greater ability to support the family. Given this belief, male children receive more of a family's nutritional resources—they are fed more. In turn, they are more likely to survive, make favorable partnerships, and thrive.

They end up taller due to both biological predispositions and social practices. In turn, these social practices reinforce the notion that men are bigger and stronger than women and that they are more beneficial for a family's well-being.

Finally, this chapter shows just how creative and flexible humans are. It is humans who define what it means to be a man and a woman, as well as what it means to be male or female. These definitions are not automatic; they are not a given. With respect to notions of "sex," the sociological perspective shows how humans take something that is so incredibly complicated—the myriad factors that make us male and female—and make it quite simple (a dichotomy). With respect to gender, definitions of "man" and "woman" are not random; they do not emerge from the other. Instead, humans give meaning to masculinity and femininity, and make sense of gender differences, within the broader social environment. What sociologists call the macro-level provides the setting in which these meanings get made. We have seen in this chapter that economic conditions, technology, medicine, and religious beliefs all play a part in defining gender. What we know, then, is that definitions of gender and the expectations that we have of men and women will continue to evolve as social conditions evolve.

CHAPTER 2: REVIEW OF KEY POINTS

- *Sex* refers to a biological category, while *gender* refers to a social category.
- Sex and gender can be considered as categorical identities (usually binary identities) or as identities that can be plotted along a continuum.
- Intersex and transgender identities encourage us to think about sex and gender in more complex ways.
- Females typically experience greater freedom and flexibility than males in navigating the "gender continuum." This tells us something about the power and privilege associated with masculinity.
- The *essentialist perspective*—which sociologists typically critique—sees gender differences as being rooted in underlying biological differences. The essentialist perspective has also been used to justify gender inequality.
- The *social constructionist perspective*—which is embraced by sociologists—sees gender differences as historically and cross-culturally variable. They are largely created and reinforced by humans through socialization and the social structure.
- While most human societies have been male-dominated and male-centered, hunter-gatherer societies and matrilineal societies show variations in how societies have organized gender.
- An *intersectional perspective* shows that gender cannot be understood as an isolated identity; instead, it intersects in complex ways with race, social class, and other identities.

CHAPTER 2: QUESTIONS FOR REVIEW

1. What is sex? "Sex" can be viewed as both a dichotomy and as existing along a continuum—how so?
2. What is gender? "Gender" can be viewed as both a dichotomy and as existing along a continuum—how so?
3. The essentialist perspective sees the social differences between men and women as primarily rooted in biology. What evidence do they use to argue this case?

4. The social constructionist perspective sees the social differences between men and women as primarily rooted in social factors. What evidence do they use to argue this case?

5. What are some of the negative consequences associated with looking at sex and gender as biologically rooted? Do you think there are negative consequences associated with looking at differences in gender behavior as a product of human social interaction?

6. Considering your own social experiences, which perspective do you find more persuasive—the essentialist or the social constructionist? Why?

7. As gender roles and expectations continue to change, what do you see as the relative role of biological forces and social forces in these changes? Thinking, for example, about the greater visibility of transgender people, how do you think that greater insights into the science of sex and gender versus social changes account for this? As men's and women's roles change in society, do you think that these can be attributed to biological explanations or social explanations?

KEY WORDS

androgyny	matrilineal
Bem Gender Role Inventory	nature vs. nurture debate
binary	patriarchy
dichotomy	sex reassignment surgery
egalitarian	sex
essentialist	social constructionist
gender	sworn virgin
hunter-gatherer societies	transgender
intersexuality	XX
matriarchy	XY

REFERENCES

Ablow, Keith. 2011. "J.Crew Plants the Seeds for Gender Identity." Retrieved April 13, 2015 (http://www.foxnews.com/health/2011/04/11/j-crew-plants-seeds-gender-identity/).

Agrawal, Anuja. 1997. "Gendered Bodies: The Case of the 'Third Gender' in India." *Contributions to Indian Sociology* 31:273–297.

Anderson, Eric. 2012. *The Monogamy Gap: Men, Love and the Reality of Cheating.* New York: Oxford University Press.

Bem, Sandra. 1981. "Gender Schema Theory: A Cognitive Account of Sex Typing." *Psychological Review* 88:354–364.

Blum, Deborah. 1997. *Sex on the Brain: The Biological Differences between Men and Women.* New York: Penguin Books.

Brizendine, Louann. 2006. *The Female Brain.* New York: Broadway Books.

Brizendine, Louann. 2011. *The Male Brain.* New York: Three Rivers Press.

Carré, Justin M. and Susan K. Putman. 2010. "Watching a Previous Victory Produces an Increase in Testosterone among Elite Hockey Players." *Psychoneuroendocrinology* 35: 475–479.

Clarke, Edward. 1873. *Sex in Education, or a Fair Chance for Girls.* Boston: J.R. Osgood and Co.

Connell, R. W. 1995. *Masculinities.* Berkeley: University of California Press.

Dahlberg, Frances, ed. 1975. *Woman the Gatherer*. New Haven, CT: Yale University Press.

Dreger, Alice. 1998. *Hermaphrodites and the Medical Invention of Sex*. Cambridge, MA: Harvard University Press.

Fausto-Sterling, Anne. 1993. "The Five Sexes: Why Male and Female Are Not Enough." *The Sciences* March/April: 20–25.

Figert, Anne E. 1995. "The Three Faces of PMS: The Scientific, Political and Professional Structuring of a Psychiatric Disorder." *Social Problems* 42:56–73.

Figert, Anne E. 1996. *Women and the Ownership of PMS; The Structuring of a Psychiatric Disorder*. New York: Aldine-de Gruyter.

Fine, Cordelia. 2010. *Delusions of Gender: How our Minds, Society, and Neurosexism Create Difference*. New York: W.W. Norton.

Gazzaniga, Michael S. 2005. "Forty-five Years of Split-Brain Research and Still Going Strong." *Nature Reviews Neuroscience* 6:653–659.

Gazzaniga, Michael S. 2011. *Who's in Charge?: Free Will and the Science of the Brain*. New York: Ecco.

Gettler, Lee T., Thomas W. McDade, Alan B. Feranil, and Christopher W. Kuzawa. 2011. "Longitudinal Evidence that Fatherhood Decreases Testosterone in Human Males." *Proceedings of the National Academy of Sciences* 108:16194–16199.

Glassberg, Kenneth I. 1999. "Editorial: Gender Assignment and the Pediatric Urologist." *Journal of Urology* 161:1308–1310.

Gray, Peter B., Sonya M. Kahlenberg, Emily S. Barrett, Susan F. Lipson, and Peter T. Ellison. 2002. "Marriage and Fatherhood are Associated with Lower Testosterone in Males." *Evolution and Human Behavior* 23:193–201.

Hart, Donna and Robert Wald Sussman. 2005. *Man the Hunted: Primates, Predators, and Human Evolution*. New York: Basic Books.

Hamilton, Lisa, Sari M. van Anders, David N. Cox, and Neil V. Watson. 2009. "The Effects of Competition on Salivary Testosterone in Elite Female Athletes." *International Journal of Sports Physiology and Performance* 4:539–542.

Hurlemann, Rene, Alexandra Patin, Oezguer A. Onur, Michael X. Cohen, Tobias Baumgartner, Sarah Metzler, Isabel Dziobek, Juergen Gallinek, Michael Wagner, Wolfgang Maier, and Keith M. Kendrick. 2010. "Oxytocin Enhances Amygdala-Dependent Socially Reinforced Learning and Emotional Empathy in Humans." *The Journal of Neuroscience* 30: 4999–5007.

Imperato-McGinley, Julianne, Luis Guerrero, Teofilo Gautier, and Ralph Edward Peterson. 1974. "Steroid 5-Alpha-reductase Deficiency in Man: An Inherited Form of Male Pseudohermaphroditism." *Science* 186:1213–1215.

Jiménez, Manuel, Raúl Aguilar, and José R. Alvero-Cruz. 2012. "Effects of Victory and Defeat on Testosterone and Cortisol Response to Competition: Evidence for Same Response Patterns in Men and Women." *Psychoneuroendrocrinology* 37:1577–1581.

Kane, Emily W. 2006. "'No Way My Boys Are Going to Be Like That!': Parent's Responses to Children's Gender Nonconformity." *Gender & Society* 20:149–176.

Kane, Emily W. 2012. *The Gender Trap: Parents and the Pitfalls of Raising Boys and Girls*. New York: New York University Press.

Kemper, Theodore T. 1990. *Social Structure and Testosterone: Explorations in the Socio-Bio-Social Chain*. New Brunswick, NJ: Rutgers University Press.

Kessler, Suzanne. 1998. *Lessons from the Intersexed*. New Brunswick, NJ: Rutgers University Press.

Kimmel, Michael. 2008. *Guyland: The Perilous World Where Boys Become Men*. New York: HarperCollins.

Kimmel, Michael. 2010. *The Gendered Society*, 4th ed. New York: Oxford University Press.

Kuepper, Yvonne, Nina Alexander, Roman Osinsky, Eva Mueller, Anya Schmitz, Petra Netter, and Juergen Hennig. 2010. "Aggression—Interactions of Serotonin and Testosterone in Healthy Men and Women." *Behavioral Brain Research* 206:93–100.

Kuzawa, Christopher W. 2007. "Developmental Origins of Life History: Growth, Productivity, and Reproduction." *American Journal of Human Biology* 19:654–661.

Lang, Sabine. 1998. *Men as Women, Women as Men: Changing Gender in Native American Cultures*. Austin, TX: University of Texas Press.

Lee, Heon-Jin, Abbe H. Macbeth, Jerome Pagani, and W. Scott Young. 2009. "Oxytocin: The Great Facilitator of Life." *Progress in Neurobiology* 88:127–151.

Lee, Richard B. and Irven DeVore. 1968. *Man The Hunter*. Chicago: Aldine.

Lorber, Judith. 1993. "Seeing Is Believing: Biology as Ideology." *Gender and Society* 7:568–581.

Mazur, Allan and Alan Booth. 1998. "Testosterone and Dominance in Men." *Behavioral Science and the Brain* 21:353–363.

Mazur, Allan and Joel Michalek. 1998. "Marriage, Divorce, and Male Testosterone." *Social Forces* 77:315–330.

Mazur, Allan, Alan Booth, and James M. Dabbs. 1992. "Testosterone and Chess Competition." *Social Psychological Quarterly* 55:70–77.

Mead, Margaret. 2001 [1935]. *Sex and Temperament in Three Primitive Societies*. New York: Harper Perennial.

Merton, Robert K. 1948. "The Self-Fulfilling Prophesy." *The Antioch Review* 8:193–210.

Micale, Mark S. 1995. *Approaching Hysteria: Disease and Its Interpretations*. Princeton, NJ: Princeton University Press.

Mintz, Steven and Susan Kellogg. 1989. *Domestic Revolutions: A Social History of American Family Life*. New York: The Free Press.

Pascoe, C. J. 2007. *Dude, You're a Fag; Masculinity and Sexuality in High School*. Berkeley: University of California Press.

Ripper, Margie. 1991. "A Comparison of the Effect of Menstrual Cycle and the Social Week on Mood, Sexual Interest, and Self-Assessed Performance." Pp. 19–33 in *Menstruation, Health and Illness*, edited by Diana L. Taylor and Nancy F. Woods. New York: Hemisphere.

Rodin, Mari. 1992. "The Social Construction of Premenstrual Syndrome." *Social Science and Medicine* 35:49–56.

Ryan, Christopher and Cacilda Jetha. 2011. *Sex at Dawn: How We Mate, Why We Stray, and What It Means for Modern Relationships*. New York: Harper Perennial.

Sapolsky, Robert. 1998. *The Trouble with Testosterone and Other Essays on the Biology of the Human Predicament*. New York: Scribner.

Seltzer, Leon. 2009. "The Testosterone Curse (Part 1)." *Psychology Today*. Retrieved April 13, 2015 (https://www.psychologytoday.com/blog/evolution-the-self/200904/the-testosterone-curse-part-1)

Shibley-Hyde, Janet. 2005. "The Gender Similarities Hypothesis." *The American Psychologist* 60:581–592.

Shostack, Marjorie. 1981. *Nisa: The Life and Words of a !Kung Woman*. Cambridge, MA: Harvard University Press.

Simpson, Katherine. 2001. "The Role of Testosterone in Aggression." *McGill Journal of Medicine* 6:32–40.

Skolnick, Arlene. 1993. *Embattled Paradise: The American Family in an Age of Uncertainty.* New York: Basic Books.

Sperry, Roger W. 1961. "Cerebral Organization and Behavior: The Split Brain Behaves in Many Respects Like Two Separate Brains, Providing New Research Possibilities." *Science* 133:1749–1757.

Stephens, Lynn. 2002. "Sexualities and Genders in Zapotec Oaxaca." *Latin American Perspectives* 29:41–59.

Storey, Anne E., Carolyn J. Walsh, Roma L. Quinton, and Katherine E. Wynne-Edwards. 2000. "Hormonal Correlates of Paternal Responsiveness in New and Expectant Fathers." *Evolution and Human Behavior* 21:79–95.

Strine, Tara W., Daniel P. Chapman, and Indu B. Ahluwalia. 2005. "Menstrual-Related Problems and Psychological Distress among Women in the United States." *Journal of Women's Health* 14:316–323.

Thorne, Barrie. 1993. *Gender Play: Boys and Girls in School.* New Brunswick, NJ: Rutgers University Press.

Wille, Reinhard and Klaus M. Beier. 1989. "Castration in Germany." *Sexual Abuse: A Journal of Research and Treatment* 2:103–133.

Williams, Walter L. 1992 [1986]. *The Spirit and the Flesh; Sexual Diversity in Indian American Culture.* Boston: Beacon Press.

Baby, Was I Born This Way?

Understanding Sexual Orientation and Sexuality

Although controversial for many years, a counseling practice known as "conversion therapy" came under renewed attack during the fall of 2012. Also known as reparative therapy, conversion therapy is built on the premise that some individuals who struggle with "unwanted same-sex sexual attractions" can be helped to manage these homosexual urges. Through religious practice and discipline, conversion therapy aims to return homosexual individuals to a heterosexual lifestyle. Despite these claims, leading scientific and medical groups have denounced providers of conversion therapy, like JONAH International and Journey into Manhood (JiM). In September 2012, controversy erupted in California, where Governor Jerry Brown passed a law banning conversion therapy for minors; soon after, a similar ban was passed in New Jersey, where former patients charged JONAH with "deceptive practices." Additional states have since joined the cause, and in the spring of 2015, President Obama has called to ban conversion therapy.

Christian legal groups have challenged these bans, arguing that they represent an unconstitutional infringement on free speech and religion. Not only do supporters feel they have the legal right to provide conversion therapy to those who seek it, they also cite testimony from those who have successfully recovered their "God-given innate heterosexuality" (see jonahweb.org). Some former patients, however, described being subjected to "humiliating" practices, including rituals involving physical touch and nudity, and being encouraged to express rage at parents for causing their inappropriate sexual attractions.

At issue in these legal cases is whether it is lawful for counselors to provide individuals who want help in overcoming homosexual urges, or whether doing so is both dangerous, irresponsible, and at odds with the nature of homosexuality. While some individuals voluntarily pay thousands of dollars to participate in retreats and counseling sessions, the American Psychiatric Association warns that conversion therapy can cause depression, anxiety, and self-destructive behavior. It is, from their point of view, a fraudulent and exploitative medical practice. It is this testimony that has led the courts to uphold the bans on conversion therapy.

Although these cases raise complicated legal issues involving freedom of speech, freedom of religion, and protection from fraudulent promises, at their core they pose a seemingly simple question: Can you turn a gay person straight? That is, is homosexuality—or sexual orientation, more broadly—something a person is born with, or is it a condition that can be changed? This question is a focal point in this chapter on sexual orientation and sexuality. To answer this question, we must first define our terms. Our intellectual journey, thereafter, will take us across the globe, back in time, and behind closed doors, as we explore sociologically one of our most fundamental and yet most private social identities.

DEFINING SEXUAL ORIENTATION: WHAT IT IS AND HOW MANY ARE THERE?

Sometimes I fancy myself a time-traveling survey researcher. Imagine, if you will, stepping into my time machine as a research assistant. Our goal, on the surface, is simple: to document patterns of sexual attraction in Europe during the early nineteenth century. Stepping out of the time machine into the streets of Berlin, we begin asking passersby: "How do you define your sexual orientation?" Immediately it becomes clear that our question is confusing. No, it's not our shoddy German-language skills causing the confusion—the time machine is so magical that it makes passengers perfectly multilingual. It is that the term "sexual orientation" did not exist at the time.

So how would you go about defining "sexual orientation" if the term was not yet known? Would it suffice to get at this question by asking this citizen of Berlin about previous sexual experiences? For some, the connection between sexual behavior and sexual orientation seems automatic. That is, some believe that a reliable and valid approach to determining a person's sexual orientation is to take note of one's previous sexual encounters: if you are a man who has had sexual encounters exclusively with other men, you are gay; conversely, if you are a female who has had sexual encounters exclusively with men, you are straight. According to this perspective, "You are who you do."

As it turns out, sociologists don't much like the idea that "you are who you do." Although there is a great deal of **concordance** for much of the population in terms of sexual orientation and sexual behavior, for a subset of the population there is **discordance** between the two. There are, for example, "closeted" women who have had sex only with men but do not identify as heterosexual. There may also be performers in the adult film industry who have partnered with both men and women; at the end of the day, they may draw a line between the sex they have at work and the sex they have in their private lives. Finally, there are individuals who have experienced nonconsensual sexual activity; although this is part of their "sexual history," the nonconsensual nature of such encounters makes it problematic to conclude that you are who you have done.

For these reasons, sociologists and psychologists generally agree that it is useful to separate sexual behavior from sexual orientation. In doing so, they draw a distinction between activities and behaviors, on the one hand, and desire and affect, on the other. Using language borrowed from the American Psychological Association, **sexual orientation** can be defined as an enduring pattern of attraction—emotional, romantic, and/or sexual—that is directed at men, women, or both. Basing this definition on internal desires rather than actual behaviors, this explains why I knew I was heterosexual the moment Kirk R. came into my life during first grade—even though I never so much as stole a kiss off him on the playground.

With this definition, a couple of components deserve further elaboration. First, to say that sexual orientation involves an "enduring pattern of attraction" highlights the idea that our sexual identities are a core component of who we are; it also suggests that no single sexual encounter—or even subset of encounters—can reveal our fundamental sexual identities. The fact that people voluntarily "experiment" during a phase of their life or whether they were coerced into sex by someone of the same sex does not reveal their sexual orientation, given that this definition emphasizes enduring patterns rather than individual instances, and attractions rather than actions.

A second more curious component of this definition is embedded in the term itself: note that the concept is called "sexual orientation" rather than "gender orientation." By calling it "sexual orientation," this concept seems to foreground either sexual organs or sexual activity above all else. For heterosexual women, the assumption seems to be that their identity is built on a focused desire for a particular sexual organ or that they are attracted to men based exclusively on their ability to fulfill sexual desires. Perhaps I speak only for myself, but when I find myself attracted to someone, it is a stretch to think that my attraction is built either on an assumption of what is hidden beneath their clothes or on the desire to engage with them sexually. For that reason, "gender orientation" may be a more accurate term, capturing the emotional and romantic component of this term—rather than the sexual component. This term suggests that for many people, intimate desires are based on an attraction to how gender roles are expressed—masculinity, femininity, or other—and not what genitalia a person possesses. Although the term "gender orientation" is unlikely to be adopted any time soon, unpacking this term provides insight into some of the assumptions that are built into this taken-for-granted concept.

Now that we've defined "sexual orientation," our next task is to explore how many such identities there are, or how this identity is configured. If we visualize ourselves back on the streets of Berlin, imagine that instead of trying to define "sexual orientation" to our confused local, we simply read a list of options among which one could choose. How many choices should we offer? Which choices should they be? In everyday situations, we often fill out forms where we are asked about our sexual orientation. Although the question does not exist in surveys conducted by the U.S. Census Bureau, organizations ranging from the Gallup organization—which conducts public opinion polls—to online retailers, to counseling centers on college campuses routinely ask questions about sexual orientation. But what is the best way to ask this question? According to the Williams Institute at the University of California at Los Angeles School of Law, the best way of asking this question is as follows:

Do you consider yourself to be:
a) Heterosexual or straight;
b) Gay or lesbian; or
c) Bisexual?

Looking at this seemingly simple question, a number of points should be addressed. First, what results are achieved when asking this question? When phrased in this way, survey researchers across the United States find that at least 95 percent of the population identifies at heterosexual. Although there may be some debate about exact numbers (given issues with sampling error and such), organizations like the Williams Institute, Gallup, and the Family Research Report estimate that perhaps 2 percent of the population identifies as gay or lesbian and another 2 percent identifies as bisexual. Although gay and lesbian populations may make up 12 to 15 percent of the population in urban areas like San Francisco, Seattle, Minneapolis, and Atlanta, representation within the general population is considerably lower, somewhere between 3 and 5 percent.

Second, consistent with our discussion above, the Williams Institute recommends that separate questions be asked to disentangle sexual orientation from sexual behaviors. Especially for surveys that have implications for mental and physical health, the Williams Institute task force recommends that separate questions be asked about actual behaviors, as well as underlying attractions.

Finally, survey questions about sexual orientation suggest a categorical understanding of this identity. This fact does not simply reflect the tendency among survey researchers to divide most of the human experience into discrete categories. Here, the fact that survey takers are asked to check a particular box reflects the fact that sexual orientation is generally understood—as mentioned earlier—as a fixed human trait. It is, quite simply, a description of who you *are*. When most of us are given questions like this, we have little difficulty in checking that box that neatly and tidily describes us. Even so, those who study human sexuality—sometimes called sexologists—argue that sexual orientation could be understood differently: it could be understood as a continuum.

The idea that sexual orientation can be understood better as a continuum than a category has its roots in the late 1800s, as evidenced by the work of German (more accurately, Prussian) sexologist Magnus Hirschfeld. In his 1896 work *Sappho and Socrates: How Can One Explain the Love of Men and Women for Individuals of Their Own Sex?*—written while living in Berlin, home to many early sex researchers—Hirschfeld proposed two separate vectors across which sexual attraction could be measured: one being the strength of attraction, the other being the object of that attraction. According to Hirschfeld, an individual may be attracted to both males and females or neither—with attraction ranging from intense to nonexistent.

Yet it was in the early 1950s, under the pioneering work of Alfred Kinsey, that the notion of a continuum received its strongest expression. Originally trained in etymology and zoology, Kinsey stands as the first public sexologist in the United States. A controversial figure in his day, Kinsey turned his attention to human sexual behavior after losing interest in the study of gall wasps. Today, an active research institute bearing his name exists at Indiana University in Bloomington, where he published *Sexual Behavior in the Human Male* and its follow-up, *Sexual Behavior in the Human Female*, in 1948 and 1953, respectively.

While researching these topics, Kinsey and colleagues conducted in-depth life-history interviews with male and female college students and, later, residents of their picturesque college town. Their conversations—considered quite risqué in postwar America—included questions about sexual experiences (during adulthood and childhood), physical desires and attractions, emotional desires and attractions, dreams, and fantasies. Using these data, Kinsey concluded that human sexuality is a complicated affair—one that cannot be arranged into a narrow set of categories. Writing in *Sexual Behavior in the Human Male*, Kinsey (1948) and his colleagues commented: "The world is not to be divided into sheep and goats. Not all things are black nor all things white. . . . The living world is a continuum in each and every one of its aspects. The sooner we learn this concerning human sexual behavior, the sooner we shall reach a sound understanding of the realities of sex" (p. 639). This insight is captured in the **Kinsey Scale** (see Figure 3.1).

Although not a true continuum, the Kinsey Scale famously represents the fluidity of human sexuality. Comprised of 7 distinct points, from 0 to 6, Kinsey concluded that human sexuality ranges from "exclusively heterosexual" to "exclusively homosexual," with 5 points in between. It includes the possibility that the preponderance of an individual's sexual experiences and desires may involve persons of the opposite sex but that an individual may have had fantasies or "incidental contact" (Kinsey's own words) with

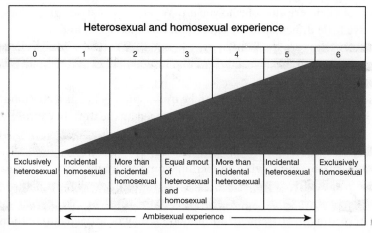

Figure 3.1 The Kinsey Scale.

persons of the same sex. Kinsey's data revealed that while 37 percent of male respondents reported having "some homosexual experience," only 4 percent fell into the "exclusively homosexual" category based on the totality of their responses. Even today, high-quality sex research finds that nearly 8 percent of adults express same-sex attractions and about 8 percent report having had some same-sex contact, yet the percentage of the population identifying as homosexual is around 3 to 5 percent (Chandra et al. 2011). It is due to these complicated realities and these distinct combinations of sexual desire, experience, and self-identification that Kinsey made famous this multi-point scale.

Subsequently, researchers have sought to bring greater flexibility into Kinsey's scale. Fritz Klein, for example, produced a 21-point scale—known as the Klein Sexual Orientation Grid (KSOG)—that added dimensions accounting for behaviors and desires across past, present, and "ideal" domains. Although his name has not become synonymous with sexual fluidity as Kinsey's has, he did make a name for himself in the study of *bisexuality*. In his groundbreaking work, *The Bisexual Option*, Klein (1978) explored the nature of bisexuality and addressed some controversies associated with it. One of the biggest controversies surrounding bisexuality is whether it exists. Some argue that virtually no one possesses *equal* attractions to both males and females. In response, Klein and others have emphasized that bisexuals are simply individuals who have some sexual experiences and erotic attractions to both males and females, even if the proportion of those attractions and experiences varies over one's lifetime. His research further makes the point that all sexual identities are fluid—even over the course of one's life.

Bisexuality has also been a topic of controversy within the LGBT community. There, it has been attacked as an identity where individuals can hold onto social privilege by virtue of their heterosexual attractions without having to claim the potentially riskier identity of "gay" or "lesbian." Indeed, during the 1970s and '80s, bisexuality was considered a threat to the "gay liberation movement," as activists questioned whether bisexuals could be counted on to champion the cause or whether they would one day retreat to a more comfortable heterosexual position. This point was emphasized by Martin Weinberg, Collin Williams, and Douglas Pryor (1995) in their book *Dual Attraction*, where some bisexuals spoke of feeling excluded and marginalized from a movement that generally seeks to promote greater tolerance for nonheterosexuals. Bisexual people have also been accused of spreading HIV/AIDS among the heterosexual population. Thus, while some people joke that being bisexual gives people access to the best of both worlds and maximizes their sexual options, researchers find that being bisexual can be a controversial and potentially stigmatizing identity.

In recent years, the debate over how to understand sexual orientation—as a set of categories or as a continuum—has become even more complicated, as researchers and activists have proposed additional understandings. Kinsey himself identified **asexuality**—where individuals experience the lack of sexual desire—as a category entirely separate from his continuum. Today, groups like the Asexual Visibility and Education Network (AVEN) promote awareness of the identity. They argue that while celibacy is a choice, asexuality is a sexual orientation where individuals typically seek intimate relationships and emotional ties but generally do not have an interest in sex.

The Asexuality Visibility and Awareness Network provides education about those who feel desire and human intimacy but do not experience sexual attraction.

Research on asexuality remains nascent; while about 1 percent of the population describe themselves as having a lack of sexual desire, the jury is out as to whether this reflects an underlying physical dysfunction (perhaps in "excitatory" response) or constitutes a legitimate sexual orientation (Bogaert 2007; Prause and Graham 2007).

A second form of sexuality that has received greater attention in recent years, as well as a fair share of confusion and controversy, is pansexuality. **Pansexuals**—also called omnisexuals—are sexually attracted to persons of *all* genders and biological sexes. If this definition sounds to you a lot like bisexuality, you are not alone. The question then is: How does pansexuality differ from bisexuality? According to academics and sex educators, what makes pansexuals different is that they explicitly reject the gender binary (Diamond and Butterworth 2008); that is, pansexuals generally do not experience their attraction to others as a pull toward masculinity or femininity. A bisexual person may alternately be attracted to masculine forms of physical and sexual expression and feminine forms of physical and sexual expression. By contrast, pansexuals are attracted simply to *individual people* and their unique energies and modes of physical and sexual expression. One controversy, then, is whether pansexuality is truly distinct from bisexuality. Second, some are uncomfortable with the all-encompassing nature of pansexuality. In a society such as the United States, where sexual imagery is everywhere, yet in many ways sexual norms are still very narrow, some are uneasy with the degree to which pansexuals seem to have such wide and voracious sexual appetites.

Two hundred years ago, the notion of "sexual orientation" was largely unknown. Today, some individuals, scholars, and activists argue for more fluid definitions of sexual orientation, ones that allow people to identify their place on a continuum—and then change that position over time, if need be. Others still adhere to a categorical model of sexual orientation, yet propose that more categories are needed, including asexual and pansexual. One reason why this issue matters is that social and political consequences are associated with these identities. To identify and check a box labeled "bisexual" is not simply to define to whom you are sexually attracted; it is also to claim an identity within a group that has varying levels of privilege. For some, to identify as bisexual is to distance one's self from the category "homosexual" and, therefore, to retain a degree of privilege within society. Thinking of the social and political consequences of these identities, some opt for the umbrella term of **queer**. The label of "queer"—as in LGBTQ—is meant to capture all of those who do not fit within the heterosexual and heteronormative gender binary, and in some cases to refer to those who do not want to be classified, period. By conceptualizing gender and sexual orientation as something closer to a continuum, the movement gains greater support by including an array of people who do not fit neatly into socially accepted categories. These terms matter, then, because they are associated with communities, with social movements, and with claims to rights and legitimacy. And, the fact remains, some of these identities experience greater legitimacy than others.

BORN THIS WAY? EXPLAINING SEXUAL ORIENTATION AND HUMAN SEXUALITY

In 2011, pop star Lady Gaga scored a Billboard number one for her anthem to individualism and self-acceptance. An ode to many identities and axes of difference, "Born This Way" most memorably intoned listeners to "rejoice and love yourself today"—regardless of sexual orientation (or gender expression)—because, baby, "you were born this way." Was Lady Gaga right? When it comes to sexual orientation, are we *born* with a particular identity and set of desires? Or, as conversion therapists claim, are sexual desires a product of nurture, shaped by our social and cultural experiences and, therefore, amenable to change? In this section we explore the **essentialist** and **social constructionist** perspectives on sexual identity and desire. First, we examine efforts to explain sexual identity as a product of nature; second, we explore the fluid, socially constructed nature of sexual identities and activities. Finally, we will see that these are not simply academic questions; rather, there are important social and political consequences associated with the answers.

THE ESSENTIALIST PERSPECTIVE: BIOLOGICAL APPROACHES TO SEXUAL ORIENTATION AND HUMAN SEXUALITY

Because the notion of "sexual orientation" is relatively recent, social and scientific efforts to explain it are also quite young. While the "essentialist perspective" strictly refers to explanations that focus on underlying biological factors, in this section we examine how science more broadly has been used to explain questions of sexual orientation. We will see that scientists increasingly conclude that we are, in fact, "born this way."

Early Scientific Understandings of Homosexuality

Scientific interest in sexual behavior, in general, and sexual orientation, in particular, can be traced back to a group of psychiatrists, doctors, and philosophers working in the region now known as Germany. During the late nineteenth and early twentieth centuries, Berlin in particular became the intellectual capital of sex research. While the concept of "sexual orientation" would not have been known there during the early nineteenth century—as our metaphorical survey researcher found out—it was there that the concept first emerged. In one of the first "coming-out stories," author and early gay rights advocate Karl Heinrich Ulrich described himself in the 1860s as an *urning*, a man who desires men—as a female psyche trapped in a man's body. In developing an early system of sexual classification, he posited that sexual desires—including same-sex desires—are natural and biological. Many early sexologists described those with same-sex attractions as **sexual inverts**: individuals who are *born* with reversed gender traits.

Indeed, the earliest understandings of same-sex desires were built on a medical model. As soon as the term **homosexual** was coined by Austrian-born writer Karl-Maria Kertbeny in 1869, consensus emerged among intellectuals that it was a trait individuals were born with. Differences of opinion emerged, however, in how this inborn trait should be viewed. There were those like Richard von Krafft-Ebing, an Austro-German psychiatrist, who viewed homosexuality as a disease. In his ground-breaking 1886 work *Sexual Psychopathy*, Krafft-Ebing wrote of homosexuality as a "cerebral neurosis" with its origins in fetal brain development. Perhaps the most enduring contribution of his work is that he moved understandings of sexual behavior from the realm of religion and morality into the realm of science. He proposed, moreover, a model of human sexuality where virtually all behaviors other than pro-creative sex should be understood as a perversion; such perversions could become pathological—a mental illness requiring treatment. While his views were relatively progressive at the time, Krafft-Ebing considered many forms of sexual expression, including homosexuality, something that should be treated by medical professionals. In fact, some people today reject the term homosexuality—given its early association with mental illness—and prefer the labels gay and lesbian.

While fellow physician and early sexologist Magnus Hirschfeld similarly viewed homosexuality as an inborn trait, he saw it as a naturally occurring biological variation rather than a mental illness. Called "the Einstein of Sex," Hirschfeld founded the Institute for Sex Research in Berlin as one of the earliest centers to develop a scientific understanding of sexual behavior. His actions, however, were as much political as they were scientific. As the founder of the Scientific Humanitarian Committee, he worked as an early gay rights advocate, especially in terms of his efforts to repeal **Paragraph 175**—the section of the German penal code that criminalized homosexual behavior. Although the committee's efforts gained considerable support among leading intellectuals, they were ultimately unsuccessful as the rise of the Nazi party increasingly viewed homosexuality as a perversion and threat. Marked with a pink triangle, homosexuals were persecuted as "degenerates" along with Jews, Catholics, and Roma people (Gypsies) in the Holocaust.

The early German sexologist Magnus Hirschfeld was an advocate for gay rights.

Originally a symbol used by Nazis to identify homosexuals, the pink triangle has since been transformed into a symbol of gay pride.

Despite the efforts of Magnus Hirschfeld, it was the pathological model of homosexuality that prevailed for most of the twentieth century. Until 1973, homosexuality was listed as a disorder in the American Psychiatric Association's *Diagnostic and Statistical Manual* (the DSM). It was, ironically, the labeling of homosexuality as a disorder that allowed it to be studied systematically with grant money from organizations like the National Institutes of Health (NIH). After decades-long accumulation of scientific evidence, the American Psychiatric Association and the American Psychological Association (Conger 1975) declared that "homosexuality per se implies no impairment in judgment, stability, reliability, or general social or vocational capabilities" (633). In subsequent years and decades, the World Health Organization and others similarly denounced the notion that homosexuality is a mental illness. Still, there are numerous countries in Africa and the Middle East that have not signed the United Nations 2011 declaration of the rights of gay and lesbian people and where homosexuality continues to be treated as a crime—often with serious and deadly punishments.

Contemporary Scientific Understandings of Homosexuality

According to the American Psychological Association (2008), "There is no consensus among scientists about the exact reasons that an individual develops a heterosexual, bisexual, gay, or lesbian orientation" (2). While sociologists and psychologists believe that nature and nurture both play a role in sexual development, a growing body of research has identified biological linkages to sexual orientation. While early physicians and psychiatrists *speculated* that sexual orientation is an inborn trait—reflecting

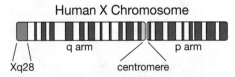

Human X Chromosome

Xq28   q arm   centromere   p arm

Is there a "gay brain"? Some research finds that the brains of lesbians resemble those of straight men while the brains of gay men resemble those of straight women.

genetics, hormones, and the intrauterine environment—modern science allows this hypothesis to be investigated.

Since the early 1990s, inquiry into "the gay brain" has been among the most visible forms of essentialist research on homosexuality. In his pioneering books *The Sexual Brain* and *Queer Science*, neuroscientist Simon LeVay (1994, 1997) documented systematic differences in the size of the hypothalamus in the brains of homosexual and heterosexual men. Although he *speculated* that such differences are likely produced by hormonal fluctuations during fetal development, LeVay cautioned that his studies did not prove a genetic *cause* of homosexuality; they simply identified morphological differences within a relatively small sample (N = 41) of deceased men's brains.

Studies on brain differences have continued to accumulate evidence, including a widely cited 2008 study by Ivanka Savic and Per Lindström of Sweden's Karolinska Institute. Using medical imaging to investigate the brains of 90 living humans, researchers concluded that the structure and composition (namely in the amygdala) of gay men's brains more closely resemble those of straight women, while the brains of lesbians more closely mirror those of straight men. Although their research was novel in identifying systematic differences in a part of the brain not linked to sexual behavior, Savic and Lindstrom distanced themselves from claims that they had "discovered" a genetic link to sexual orientation. These authors acknowledged that observed brain differences could be either a cause or a consequence of sexual orientation and sexual behaviors.

A 2009 study by Alicia Garcia-Falgueras and Dick Swaab, however, struck a more definitive tone. By analyzing the effects of hormones on intrauterine sexual differentiation and on brain development, these authors assert that a shift in hormones during pregnancy may result in the development of distinctly male genitalia with a more feminized brain structure (and vice versa). Accordingly, the authors conclude, "gender identity . . . and sexual orientation are programmed or organized into our brain structures when we are still in the womb. . . . There is no indication that social environment after birth has an effect on gender identity or sexual orientation" (p. 22). According to these authors, we *are* born this way.

Since the early 1990s, scholars have been exploring whether a "gay gene" might predispose some people to same-sex attractions. Instead of brain images, these studies use samples of DNA among family members—often twins—to identify whether there exists a shared genetic trait among those who identify as straight or gay. A string of studies co-authored by J. Michael Bailey and Richard Pillard (1991) concluded that such a link is likely. They found that among identical twins, if one was gay, the chance that the other was also gay exceeded 50 percent; among nonidentical twins, the likelihood was about 22 percent (this compares to only 11 percent among adopted brothers raised in the same home). Quoted in a *New York Times* article, J. Michael Bailey of Northwestern University asserted that this "is exactly the kind of pattern you would want to see if something genetic were going on."

In another study using DNA from men and their family members, Dean Hamer discovered a pattern of shared genetic markers among gay men along the maternal line. Since publishing his discovery in 1993, a number of other researchers have replicated the finding that a specific marker on one of the X chromosomes, known as Xq28, was more common among brothers who identified as gay and, to a lesser extent, among uncles on the maternal side. Because no one gene on its own produces *any* human trait or behavior, questions remain over how a particular genetic marker—or even set of markers—shapes human sexual behavior and desire.

Along with these efforts, researchers have branched out to examine how other factors—ranging from finger length (more specifically the ratio between the second and fourth fingers) to birth order—may be associated with sexual orientation. Many of these studies have found significant linkages, including some indicating that the more sons a woman gives birth to, the greater the likelihood that later sons will identify as gay. According to Ray Blanchard (2001), the father of such research, over time pregnant women develop antibodies in the presence of a male fetus, which then cross over the "blood/brain barrier" (BBB) and have a feminizing effect on the brain.

The Sociological Response to Research on the Biological Roots of Human Sexuality

Since the early 1990s, there has been a steady accumulation of research indicating a genetic linkage to sexual orientation. These studies increasingly suggest that we may be born this way and that being born this way is nonpathological. While these studies span diverse fields—from genetics to neuroscience to psychology—and have been subjected to scientific scrutiny, they are not perfect. These studies are limited, for example, by the fact that they use small sample sizes, rely on self-selected populations (rather than random samples), and have a difficult time sorting out causality (were biological differences present at birth, or did they emerge in response to environmental or behavioral factors?). Further, like much scientific research, these studies have either relied only on male subjects or have produced significant findings only among male subjects. Therefore, we know less about the possible genetic bases of lesbianism.

Despite these scientific insights, many remain skeptical of the notion that humans are born with a particular sexual orientation. For some with conservative religious beliefs, human sexuality and homosexuality, in particular, are *choices*—choices with moral implications. Conversion therapy works from the assumption that practicing homosexuals have been tempted into sinful behavior and that through diligence and prayer, they can make choices that are spiritually healthier. Some sociologists are also skeptical of essentialist claims. Indeed, essentialist claims have long been used to justify unequal treatment, whether in terms of gender, race, or sexual orientation. That said, these findings have real political implications. Evidence of a "gay brain" or "gay gene" has been celebrated by some, heralded as evidence that homosexuality is normal and should be treated like any other trait that people have no control over, such as skin color. Indeed, this logic has figured prominently into the civil rights discourse surrounding homosexuality, including efforts to legalize marriage among same-sex partners. Others worry that if fetuses are discovered to have a "gay gene," societies that stigmatize homosexuality might use this as a justification for abortion. These questions about the genetic basis of one's sexual desires are not merely academic; rather, they affect people's day-to-day life experiences, opportunities, and social standing.

NURTURE AND THE SOCIAL CONSTRUCTIONIST PERSPECTIVE

If sexual orientation is, as the essentialist perspective suggests, a reflection of underlying biological traits, why is it only in modern Western societies that we see a large number of gay people? Has the increased visibility of gay and lesbian people come about through certain genetic "mutations" that have begun occurring only during the last few hundred years and only in certain societies? This is likely not the case. The fact that homosexuality appears to be more prevalent today reflects a complex interaction of biology (nature) and the environment (nurture). In this case, "environment" does not mean the home environment. In fact, sociologists like Judith Stacey and Timothy Biblarz (2001) are quick to point out that there is virtually no scientific evidence to suggest that having gay parents or being raised in a gender-atypical environment leads to the expression of a gay or lesbian identity. The social constructionist perspective, instead, shows how cultural, historical, and macro-structural arrangements influence the environment in which sexuality is expressed and defined. By looking at cross-cultural and historical variations in sexual expression, we learn that similar kinds of behaviors have been given different definitions in different places and at different times.

THE STUDY ABROAD TRIP

Imagine, if you will, a particular sex act. Because it is a rather evocative (and provocative) example within contemporary American society, I suggest you imagine two men engaged in a sexual act. That said, other sex acts—including those between men and women—could also be used to make my point. What would we learn if we took a study abroad trip to explore the sexual behaviors of people living in other cultural contexts? While sex acts between men have occurred within other cultures and in different time periods, the social constructionist perspective shows that how this particular sex act is defined is determined by the overarching cultural and historical context. While some would clearly label the aforementioned act "homosexual sex," in other places and at other times, different labels and understandings would emerge. This insight is illustrated perhaps most powerfully by Gilbert Herdt's (1999) research on the "Sambia."

The first stop on our metaphorical study abroad trip takes us, once again, to Papua New Guinea—the culturally diverse nation in the South Pacific. In his anthropological study of the Sambia—a pseudonym—Gilbert Herdt documented a multi-stage rite of passage that involves fellatio between pre-adolescent boys and unmarried "bachelors." While this thought may inspire culture shock in many in the West, tribe members believe that men can only become properly masculinized by ingesting the semen of older males. After a period of ritualized fellatio—first as givers and then as receivers—it is believed that young men achieve a sufficient level of *jerungdu* (masculine strength and spirit). They are then expected to marry women and cease all sexual contact with men.

While a Western cultural lens would lead the reader to conclude that these men are, in fact, gay or are at least involved in erotic acts between men, members of the Sambia tribe would view this act differently. They see this as a highly specific rite of passage, not as a lifestyle choice per se. In fact, while same-sex contact is expected within the context of this ritual, men who engage in fellatio outside of the ritual or who express an exclusive preference for same-sex contact are scorned and considered insufficiently masculine. Moreover, this cultural ritual cannot be properly understood without examining Sambian gender roles. There, femininity is a degradable characteristic; contact with women is viewed as contaminating. As such, men can achieve status only through contact with other men; moreover, if a man were to engage in sex acts with other men *after* he had begun having intercourse with women, he would risk polluting another man. To do so would be deplorable.

The second stop on our study abroad trip takes us to Guadalajara, Mexico, a bustling city in the center of the country. In a city colonized by Spanish settlers in the 1500s, that cultural influence is still evident in both architecture and understandings of gender and sexuality. After a delicious meal of *pozole* soup and a concert by a mariachi band, our intellectual guide, Joseph Carrier, would explain to us how locals understand sexual relations among men. The same-sex act that most American's would label "homosexual" is viewed quite differently there; in fact, the two men engaged in the same act would be viewed differently from one another. In his book *De Los Otros*, Carrier (1995) described the role of the *activo* and *pasivo* sexual partners. The activo male takes the dominant position during sex; by being the "insertive" partner (what is sometimes called the "top" in the United States), he is viewed as dominant, simply doing what men do. As such, his *macho* identity is not called into question, nor is he labeled a homosexual (p.17). By contrast, the pasivo takes the submissive position during sex; as the "receiving" partner (sometimes called the "bottom" in the United States), he is viewed as feminine. With his masculinity called into question, he may be labeled stigmatized as "homosexual."

With two sets of terms for these roles, Mexican slang further clarifies the difference of these two sexual identities. While the activo is called *mayate*, *chichifo*, or *picador*, the pasivo is called *puto*, *joto*, or *maricon* (Carrier 1995:17). The terms that denote the activo have a masculine flavor—especially *picador*, which essentially means to pierce (like the heroic bullfighter). By contrast, the epithet *puto* has the connotation of coward, and *maricon* is a cruder version of the word "sissy." These linguistic differ-ences illustrate once again that cultural understandings of gender strongly influence cultural understandings of sexuality. In a society where masculinity is more highly valued than femininity, behaviors and identities that seem to threaten masculine privilege—like being the submissive sexual partner—are viewed more critically than those associated with *machismo*. This example illustrates further that a particular act involving genitalia has no inherent meaning; rather, its meaning is constructed within a broader social and cultural context.

In our final stop, we journey not to an exotic foreign land but to a unique cultural setting within the United States. The goal of this trip is to understand how masculinity and sexuality are expressed within the prison system. A report from Human Rights Watch estimates that 22 percent of male inmates have been coerced into sex while in prison. As in the Mexican context, men who engage in prison sex are viewed differently from one another: the dominant male receives little scrutiny and avoids the label "ho-mosexual," but the submissive male is labeled as homosexual, and given a variety of derogatory names. While prison sexuality may be hard for outsiders to understand, those who have studied the phenomenon generally see this "homosexual" activity as situational—a unique form of sexual expression that emerges within the prison context, but where the participants typically return to heterosexual behavior once released.

In order to understand these perspectives on same-sex contact, it is important to understand the hard realities of prison life, a place with its own culture and hierar-chies. Within that world, some men seek to prove their dominance through their sexu-ality; others are coerced into "riding with" their partners on the condition that they receive protection from more brutal forms of sexual and physical violence. *Protective pairing*, a term used by Stephen Donaldson (N.D.) in a blog-post for *Just Detention International*, reflects the fact that prisoners "have to constantly take orders from the authorities, which makes them feel like slaves of the state. As a compensation they like to find a way to be the boss with someone else and give orders themselves. Sex is a ve-hicle for a jocker (the dominant male) to express all these non-sexual needs." It is im-portant to note that even if this sexual interaction may serve a "function" within the confines of prison culture, many inmates are traumatized because of it; fortunately, organizations like Just Detention International and the California Coalition against Sexual Assault are committed to raising awareness of the issue and helping survivors.

EXPLORING INTERSECTIONALITY: RACE, SEXUAL ORIENTATION, AND BEING ON THE "DOWN LOW"

During the fall of 2012, the Gallup organization released some surprising poll results. According to their survey of 121,000 Americans, black and Hispanic men between the ages of 18 and 29 were about 50 percent more likely to identify as gay, bisexual, or trans-gender compared to white men. A similar, but less dramatic, pattern was found among men between 30 and 50. These results surprised many—academics, clergy, and ordinary citizens alike—due to the perception that homosexuality is considerably less accepted and, therefore, less common among minorities than among whites. Results from the General Social Survey, for example, show that about 72 percent of blacks and 52 percent of whites believe that homosexuality is "always wrong" (Glick and Golden 2010).

Researchers have been concerned for several decades that the stigma on homosexuality among black Americans is contributing to the problem of HIV/AIDS within that demographic (Lemelle and Battle 2004). Researchers and journalists alike attribute the relatively high rates of HIV/AIDS among black Americans to the "down-low" phenomenon; that is, men who have sex with both men and women but do not identify as gay or bisexual. By having closeted and covert sexual relations with other men, some black men have been accused of transmitting HIV to unsuspecting black female partners.

According to journalists like Benoit Denizet-Lewis and sociologists like Anthony Lemelle, being on the "down low" ("the DL") reflects a belief among black men that equates homosexuality with whiteness and effeminacy—neither of which they embrace. Because they see themselves as masculine and are expected to project a masculine demeanor, many black men reject a gay identity—even if they have sex with other men. The premium on masculinity is evident in William, a man profiled in Denizet-Lewis's 2003 *New York Times* piece, who reports using the America Online chat room DLThugs to look for "real guys" rather than "flaming queens who like to pretend they're thugs and on the DL." Although many men on the DL identify exclusively as dominant "tops," others describe themselves in their online profiles as "masculine bottom brothas." While Gallup's poll results may herald a new level of acceptance of homosexuality among minorities and, therefore, future declines in the rate of new HIV infections, by looking at the intersection of race and sexual orientation, we see once again that gender role expectations are intimately bound up in attitudes toward homosexuality.

TRAVELING BACK IN TIME

In our travels from Papua New Guinea to Mexico and back to the United States, we have encountered examples of how the same sexual act is labeled differently depending on the cultural context. As it turns out, the same lesson can be learned by traveling back in time. By jumping into our metaphorical time machine, we see that things we often assume have a clear meaning—like particular sex acts—have been understood very differently across time.

Although same-sex activities may have taken place throughout history, how these acts have been defined has varied tremendously. Within modern Western history, the rise of scientific authority has played a considerable role in shaping understandings of human sexuality. It is not implausible to talk about homosexuality, heterosexuality, and the idea that one has a "sexual orientation" as a scientific invention—as a conceptual *tool* that didn't exist previously. As discussed in our overview of German sexology, the notion that a person has a sexual orientation dates back only to the mid-1800s. It was not that same-sex activities did not exist previously; it was that these activities were labeled differently. Prior to that time, there were homosexual acts, but not homosexual people. According to historians like John Boswell, under the sway of religious authority these acts were considered sinful, but they did not define a particular kind of person. In fact, homosexual activities were generally grouped alongside other sinful sexual acts, such as adultery or masturbation. As noted by social philosophers like Michel Foucault, it was primarily through the rise of scientific authority—namely psychiatry and medical doctors—that these same-sex behaviors came to represent a particular kind of person. In the words of sexologist John De Cecco (1990), "homosexual" went from being an adjective that described a particular type of sex act (something you *do*) to being a noun that described a particular type of person (someone you *are*).

The fact that homosexual people were "invented" during the late nineteenth century did not simply reflect the rise of scientific authority. The emergence of a "homosexual identity" came about through other macro-level social processes, namely industrialization and urbanization. Within Western society, changing social conditions made it *possible* for gay and lesbian people to emerge. Prior to the Industrial Revolution of the 1800s, the family formed the lifeblood of society, both in terms of social organization and economic life. Quite simply, people could not exist outside of the traditional family structure. With industrialization, large numbers of people encountered the option of living and working outside of the family structure; now, they could get jobs in factories and live economically and socially independent lives. With the rise of factories and other new forms of technology, people moved from isolated rural areas into more densely populated urban areas. In doing so, face-to-face contact with familiar people declined and social interactions became more anonymous. It then became increasingly likely that people with same-sex attractions would discover that there were others like themselves; they may also have felt greater freedom to express these sentiments within a more anonymous urban environment. It was in this context that organizations and publications emerged to join together people with same-sex attractions.

By getting into our time machine and traveling back to New York City in the early 1900s, we learn an important lesson: while the underlying genetic predisposition toward homosexuality may have existed for many centuries, it took a particular set of social conditions—scientific knowledge, the industrial economy, and increased urbanization—for these behaviors to become an identity. Particular sexual acts and particular sexual identities cannot be understood outside of their historical and cultural context.

What could we learn by traveling to a much older point in Western history? By getting into our time machine and going to Ancient Greece (anywhere between the eighth and third centuries B.C.), we again learn that while certain human sexual behaviors have long existed, their meanings have shifted over time. As among the Sambia in more recent times, **pederasty** was a common form of sexual expression among

Ancient Greek pottery provides evidence of the elevated social status of men and the sexualized relations between them.

Ancient Greeks; pederasty refers to sexual relations between adult men and adolescent boys (ages 12–17). At that time, lifelong sexual partnering with women was the norm; indeed, heterosexual family relations were at the heart of Ancient Greek society—and virtually every Western society thereafter. Yet like the Sambia, the Ancient Greeks also participated in rites of passage where masculinity was cultivated through sexual relations between older and younger men. As in Mexican culture, moreover, the dominant role was associated with masculinity and higher social status, while the passive role was associated with femininity and lower social status.

In order to understand the meaning of this act, one must understand the culture of Ancient Greece more broadly. As Beert Verstraete and Vernon Provencal (2006) show in their book *Same-Sex Desire and Love in Greco-Roman Antiquity and in the Classical Tradition of the West*, art, philosophy, politics, and military life flourished at this time. At the forefront of society were philosophers and military leaders—men who had a deep appreciation for men's minds and bodies. Sculpture, pottery, and the original Olympic games (where men typically competed in the nude) were testaments to masculinity. Women, again, were generally considered unworthy—both physically and mentally—of erotic attachment. As in some of our other examples, sexual relations between Ancient Greek men took place within a specific social context. Likewise, it was expected that men would form lifelong partnerships with women; if they continued to engage in sexual relations with other men—especially as the passive partner—they would be subject to ridicule and stigma. Thus, while homosexual acts surely took place, it is unclear as to whether the participants can accurately be called homosexual men.

THE FIVE Ps OF HUMAN SEXUALITY

Through our travels across cultures and back in time, we have discovered a core socio-logical truth: while modern science has improved our understanding of the biological underpinnings of our sexual desires, our cultural understanding of these acts has only become more complicated. I encourage you, again, to imagine a particular sex act. While the example used throughout has involved two men, feel free to imagine two women making out or even a man and a woman engaged in intercourse. To say that human sexuality is "socially constructed" is to say that until you know more about the context in which a particular sex act takes place, you have no idea what that act *means*. Our cross-cultural and historical journeys reveal, quite simply, that no sex act has a fixed or inherent meaning. Almost any sex acts, depending on the context, could fall under any one of "the Five Ps of Human Sexuality."

From an historical and cross-cultural perspective, (1) *procreation* has been per-haps the most enduring function and meaning of human sexuality. In many times and places, this was the primary mode of sexual expression. Indeed, human society would not have survived without it. Individual sexual acts can also be viewed as (2) acts of *pleasure*; as driven by erotic desire. Although modern Western society seems almost obsessed with sexual pleasure, it may come as a surprise to know that sex as a form of recreation or as a way of connecting with another person is a relatively new invention. In fact, as recently as the Victorian era of the 1800s, people have been warned of the danger of sexual pleasures and were encouraged to use sex primarily as a tool for pro-creation. Today, most acts involving genitals fall into the pleasure category, as we have come to view sexuality as an erotic outlet and expression of our sexual orientation. The discovery of reliable modes of preventing pregnancy partially explains why most sex now takes place for the purpose of pleasure, whereas in the past its purpose was primarily procreative.

The examples used in this chapter also show that under other circumstances, gen-ital contact can be viewed as an (3) act of *power* (and/or protection). When men engage in sexual relations with other men in prison, we cannot automatically assume that they are gay or that they are motivated by feelings of pleasure. There, the rules are dif-ferent; the unique cultural norms of the prison construct human sexuality as an act of power, above all else. This is not so different from how sexuality has been constructed in Ancient Greece or modern Mexico; an expression of male dominance. Activists have also worked hard to define rape as an act of power, rather than an act of sexual desire. Sexual acts and genital contact may also (4) represent a *passage*, as in a rite of passage. In many societies, sexual acts have signaled a rite of passage into adulthood—especially within the context of marriage. In addition to a marriage certificate or li-cense, it was the consummation of the marriage that certified the married state. For the Sambia, sexual relations between younger and older men certified the passage into adulthood. Although some degree of eroticism was involved in these acts, their pri-mary meaning was not pleasure but a social passage into a properly masculine state.

Finally, sexual relations and genital contact may also fall under the category of (5) *profit*. Although difficult to determine whether prostitution is, in fact, the "oldest profession," it was codified in the Mesopotamian legal code as far back as the eighteenth century B.C. (Hammurabi's Code). Today, commercial sex workers include prostitutes, escorts, and adult film actors. While some are skeptical that a person can engage in sexual acts for pay and not be attracted to the persons with whom they partner, others emphasize the flexible nature of human sexuality and believe that it is completely plausible for a person to engage in sexual behaviors that are discordant with their sexual orientation—and not be defined by those acts. Within the adult film industry the term "gay for pay" refers to performers who identify as straight but have sex on film with partners of the same sex. While many label these performers as bisexual and leave it at that, others note that those performers are motivated to cross sexual lines due to the fact that male actors get paid more for having sex with men than for having sex with women; in an industry that glorifies female stars, this also gives male performers a chance to gain celebrity in a different film genre.

When sociologists note that social phenomena are socially constructed, they highlight the endless flexibility and creativity of human beings. With the power of symbolically constructing our worlds, humans take the same essential thing—in this case particular sex acts—and give it an endless array of meanings. It is important to understand, moreover, that humans do not construct these meanings out of thin air; rather, these meanings evolve out of the broader social context. Particular sexual acts and the identities of those who engage in them derive meaning from the broader social context, including the state of gender relations, economic conditions, and the role of authority in society (religious versus scientific). These examples clearly show that scientific insight into the essence of our "sexual orientation" *and* cross-cultural and historical knowledge are both necessary to properly understand human sexual behavior.

WHAT ABOUT THE SEXUALITY OF WOMEN?

By this point in the chapter, you may have asked yourself: What about the sexuality of women? Why have virtually all of the examples presented focused on men?! The answers to this question are sociologically insightful. With respect to the essentialist perspective on sexual orientation, it is simply the case that women have less frequently been subjects in scientific studies. To some extent, this is because men have been viewed as the "universal human," with the assumption that what happens in men's bodies must also happen in women's bodies. The male bias in medical research is evident not just in terms of inquiries into the biological basis of sexuality but also in studies of diabetes, heart disease, and most cancers. It is only recently that medical researchers have begun to understand that women's bodies are different from men's and worthy of investigation in their own right.

With respect to the social constructionist perspective on sexual orientation, our metaphorical travels abroad and back in time have focused on men for similar reasons: scholars seem less interested in the meaning of women's sexual partnering. We know little about what Sambian and Greek women were up to while their men were off engaging in their rites of passage, nor do we know much about how sexual relations among women are understood in Mexico or in U.S. prisons. One possible explanation for this lack of scholarship is that Western society puts a premium on men's activities—whether in terms of their biological makeup (as noted above), their role in history, or their sexual partnering. Similarly, as suggested in the previous chapter, because masculinity is so highly valued, deviations from its proper expression warrant greater concern from scholars and the public at large. While the MTV program *True Life* depicted a heterosexual man who partners with other men in adult films, there was no such segment devoted to a female performer. In fact, the concept of "gay for pay" has been applied almost exclusively to men; relatively few viewers seem concerned about the "real" sexual orientation of female actors who partner with other women. In fact, the success of this film genre is built partially on male viewers' assumption that such female performers are not *actually* lesbians and that under the right circumstances they are even game for hooking up with themselves!

The scholarly record is not completely devoid of accounts of physical relations among women. The Ancient Greek poet Sappho—whose verse focused on female objects of affection—and her island home of Lesbos are, after all, key symbols in *lesbian* culture. Although not as well documented as the activities of men, it is thought that Ancient Greek women also expressed intimate affections for other women (Page 1979). Since the Renaissance, female "homoerotic" relationships have been documented across Europe (Jennings 2007). Especially during the Victorian era, affectionate—bordering on romantic—relationships between women were common in England and the United States. According to historian Lillian Faderman (1981), these relationships flourished during the late 1800s when more women went away to college. Lifelong relations of this kind were called **Boston marriages**. While it is unclear whether these relationships included genital contact, they were characterized by handholding and romantic letter writing. In terms of passionate feelings, these friendships often exceeded those of heterosexual partnerships and were generally considered pure and ennobling—not suspicious or subject to stigma.

Today, the media and scholars alike seem interested in college-aged (presumably heterosexual) women who make out—often publicly—with other women. While heterosexual men often find them titillating, sociologist Laura Hamilton (2007) warns that these interludes may inadvertently trivialize lesbianism and lead to lower levels of social acceptance. Aside from the implications of their erotic play, a double standard is evident in the fact that these young women are rarely, if ever, judged to be actual lesbians. This is quite different from beliefs I have observed among some of my students, where any amount of same-sex contact among males makes them gay! Both casual and academic observations show that, compared to women, men are less accepting of homosexuality and are even less accepting of gay men than they are of lesbians. When women's sexual practices have received social and academic scrutiny, it is the number of partners she has had rather than the gender of her partners that has received approbation. A key takeaway, then, is that gender and sexuality cannot easily be separated from one another, as gender inevitably informs how we view particular sexual acts as well as the individuals who engage in them.

BEHIND CLOSED DOORS: THE SOCIAL STRUCTURING OF SEXUAL BEHAVIOR

When it comes to human sexuality, it is not only sexual orientation that can be examined sociologically. In fact, most of what we do sexually is profoundly social—not just because it involves other people, but because sexual activities are shaped by social norms and expectations. While sexual desires and behaviors are partially driven by essentialist forces (like hormones), whom we partner with, how we do it, and how we feel about it are socially constructed.

First, some basic facts. On second thought, when it comes to sex research, is there such a thing? Perhaps more than any other area of research, sex research suffers from **social desirability bias**; that is, the tendency for people, especially in survey research, to provide socially acceptable answers. Yet when it comes to sex research, it is hard to know what kind of answer would be socially desirable: Should a respondent claim early or later loss of virginity? Would a respondent look better by indicating numerous sexual partners or a few? The fact that people are likely to exaggerate in both directions means that social desirability bias may be washed out, producing relatively valid results. What is more important when it comes to sex research is to consider the source. While there are inherent problems with asking about things that take place behind closed doors (hopefully!), research by scholars associated with the Kinsey Institute or other reputable organizations is surely better than reports found in magazines like *Maxim* or *Cosmopolitan*.

One basic fact that almost everyone wants to know is whether today's teens are sexually out of control. Despite endless media portrayals to the contrary, most research indicates that this is hardly the case. The Alan Guttmacher Institute reports that the average age at first intercourse (penile-vaginal) is about 17 for males and 17.5 for females (lower for black but higher for Asian teens). To put this in context, the average age at first intercourse was about 18 during the 1950s. The Centers for Disease Control and Prevention (CDC) reports that about 42 percent of females between the ages of 15 and 19 have had sexual intercourse—a rate that has been declining since 1988, when 51 percent of this age group had had sex. Moreover, much teen sexual activity occurs within the context of relatively stable relationships. Finally, while some argue that oral sex among teens has exploded in popularity and become a "gateway" sexual activity, numbers do not confirm this. Among 15- to 19-year-olds, 43 percent of females and 35 percent of males have given oral sex, while 41 percent of females and 47 percent of males have been recipients. When it comes to sexual intercourse and teen pregnancies, high-quality data show a slow but steady trend toward lower levels of involvement.

Despite these patterns, rates of teen pregnancy in the United States are still among the highest in the developed world. American teens, for example, have a birth rate that is two times higher than peers in the United Kingdom and nearly 10 times higher than teens in the Netherlands. Throughout Europe, teen pregnancy is less common than it is in the United States, despite the fact that teen sexual activity is actually more common! What the research of sociologist Amy Schalet (2011) shows is that teens do not have sex in a social vacuum. That is, the broader social, economic, medical, and religious environment shapes whether and how teens will act on their "raging hormones." While focusing specifically on teens in the Netherlands, Schalet found that teen sexuality was generally normalized across Europe—viewed as a natural aspect of becoming an adult. Accordingly, comprehensive sex education and access to contraception are common. In the United States, by contrast, higher levels of religiosity and a focus on abstinence-only sex education means that frank conversations about sex are rare. More broadly, teen sexuality is considered "dangerous" in the United States. While many European societies have extensive social programs and resources to prevent teen pregnancy, sexually active teens are generally on their own in the United States. A lack of contraception and a lack of options when pregnancy occurs means that our social fears about teen pregnancy are often realized. This example shows further that the sex acts that human engage in, their meanings, and their consequences are strongly shaped by the social and cultural environment.

When it comes to sex, our behaviors are limited only by desire and imagination. And yet sociological research indicates that there are systematic patterns in terms of who engages in what activities. Take just one example: oral sex. Across the globe and throughout history, fellatio has in some cultures been considered an erotic art, while others have constructed it as a dirty and degrading activity. In the United States, the likelihood that a person has engaged in oral sex reflects underlying social traits, including age, education, and race. With respect to age, oral sex seems to be a fad or fashion that expanded after the 1960s, stimulated in part by the adult film classic, *Deep Throat* (1972). In the most comprehensive sexual study to date, the authors of *Sex in America* (Michael et al. 1994) found that among young adults born after 1970, a full 73 percent reported either giving or receiving oral sex; among adults born in the 1930s, only 48 percent reported any experience with oral sex—despite having about 30 more years in which to practice! Higher levels of education are also associated with oral sex. *Sex in America* reports that adults who attended college were nearly twice as likely to have given or received oral sex compared to adults who did not finish high school. This study (and others) found that race is also linked to participation in oral sex. While 51 percent of black adults have either given or received oral sex, this number is 81 percent among whites and 66 percent among Hispanics.

If most people are aware that oral sex exists, why are some less likely to try it? Sociologists believe that part of the answer lies in social networks. Higher education, in particular, expands a person's social network. Those who go onto college simply have more opportunity to learn about new stuff within their newly expanded network—whether that means the ideas of Karl Marx, Thai food, or what to do behind closed doors. The same is true with race/ethnicity: because most people partner with others of the same racial/ethnic group, if there are fewer people in your network who engage in oral sex, it is less likely you will be introduced to the behavior (and vice versa). Perhaps another reason that oral sex is less widely practiced by blacks is its historical association with the sexual abuse that took place between black female slaves and white slave masters in the plantation system (Faust 1985).

As it turns out, sexual response is also sociologically predictable—especially for women. Despite jokes about people's sex lives disappearing once they marry, research shows that married people enjoy their sex lives more than others. Married women, for example, report that they "usually" or "always" orgasm during sex at a rate of 75 percent; pity those single and cohabitating women, whose rate is only 62 percent (Michael et al. 1994:127). According to Waite and Gallagher (2001), married life is sexier than nonmarried life because partners have a chance to learn what makes the other "tick" sexually—and a long-term incentive for figuring out how to do so. Speaking of having an especially successful sex life, would you believe that religion also plays a role? Although it might seem that religiously liberal folks would have wildly fulfilling sex lives and religiously conservative folks less so, the opposite appears to be true. Whereas only 22 percent of women with no religion report "always" having an orgasm during sex, a full 32 percent of conservative Protestants (e.g., Baptists and Evangelicals) do so.

According to Robert T. Michael and his co-authors, "Perhaps conservative Protestant women firmly believe in the holiness of marriage and of sexuality as an expression of their love" (p. 127). What these examples show is that sexual experiences and appetites are not simply driven by essentialist forces like hormones or genital structure; instead, history and social context strongly influence how people pick from the menu of sexual options as well as how satisfied they are with their "meal."

EXPLORING ACTIVISM: QUEER YOUTH AND THE PROMISE THAT "IT GETS BETTER"

While adolescents and young adults are significantly more supportive of LGBTQ (Lesbian, Gay, Bisexual, Transgender, and Queer) rights compared to older generations, they still face incredible pressures in coming out and embracing their own sexual identities. Compared to their straight (or believed to be straight) peers, LGBTQ youth and adolescents experience higher rates of bullying, depression, and suicide, as well as greater struggles with drugs and alcohol and lower grades. Within middle and high schools across the nation, budding activists have sought to stem these negative experiences and promote a healthier environment for these young people under the national umbrella organization "Gay-Straight Alliance." According to the national organization's website, a Gay-Straight Alliance (GSA) is a student-run club in a high school or middle school that brings together LGBTQ and straight students to support each other, provide a safe place to socialize, and create a platform for activism to fight homophobia and transphobia." It is estimated that there are as many as 4,000 GSAs across the country, where chapters have specially trained leaders and sponsor events that include both days devoted to celebration and increased visibility, as well as programming dedicated to lobbying and political activism.

Despite the increased visibility of and support for LGBTQ youth within U.S. high schools, there has also been opposition to and backlashes against those wanting to

Pledging that "It Gets Better" is author and activist Dan Savage.

establish a GSA. In 2009 in Yulee, Florida, school officials repeatedly blocked students' request to establish a GSA. As a compromise, the school principal indicated that the club could form as long as they removed any reference to sexuality or sexual orientation from their name. Supporters of the club, however, responded that their organization has little to do with sex per se. According to one student organizer, Hannah Page, "We just want the club so that straight and gay kids can get together to talk about harassment and discrimination against gay kids in an open environment. The school is discriminating against us and that's exactly the kind of thing we want to talk about and prevent."

With backing from the American Civil Liberties Union (ACLU), these students took their school leaders to court—and won. After hearing the suit, the judge concluded that Hannah Page and Jacob Brock—her co-plaintiff—have the legal right (under the Federal Equal Access Act) to organize a GSA at their school. In his ruling, Judge Henry Lee Adams Jr. concluded that the school must:

- Allow the club to hold meetings on campus
- Allow the students to use the name Gay-Straight Alliance rather than one that does not use the word "gay"
- Allow the club to further its goals of advocating "for tolerance, respect and equality of gay, lesbian, bisexual, and transgender (LGBT) people" and curbing bullying and harassment against LGBT students
- Refrain from retaliating against students and faculty who participate in the GSA and the lawsuit

This struggle highlights the fact that LGBTQ youth still face hostility from peers and adults alike but that they have successfully lobbied for the right to express themselves.

Increasingly, adult activists have taken up the charge of supporting gay and lesbian youth. With the motto "It Gets Better," journalist and activist Dan Savage (along with his husband) kicked off a movement that has gained considerable strength worldwide. In 2010, after a series of suicides and incidents of bullying among LGBTQ youth that received national attention, the It Gets Better Project was created to show young LGBTQ people the levels of happiness, potential, and positivity their lives will reach—if they can just get through their teen years. Since then, the movement has gone viral. The organization's website features tens of thousands of videos that include personal testimonies of growth and survival; these videos have been viewed by millions. The movement, moreover, has gained the formal support of Barack and Michelle Obama, as well as MTV; the video project has been acknowledged with an Emmy Award. Today, It Gets Better operates as a full-fledged not-for-profit organization. In addition to using video and books to tell the stories of those who have survived bullying and depression, it also updates its audience with legal and social progress relevant to LGBTQ individuals and sells merchandise. In becoming both a mission and a brand, the hope now is that youth and young adults all across the country can tangibly benefit from the popular, viral activism kicked off by Dan Savage. The next frontier may be giving as much support to trans youth, many of whom experience bullying, depression, and suicidal thoughts.

WHAT DOES IT ALL MEAN? THE SOCIOLOGICAL TAKEAWAY ON SEXUAL ORIENTATION AND HUMAN SEXUALITY

When it comes to human sexuality, whether in terms of sexual orientation, sexual activity, or response, the sociological perspective provides insight into the degree to which we are "born this way." The research presented in this chapter reveals that there is a biological foundation to our sexual desires and identities. Especially when it comes to the question of whether we identify as gay, straight, or other, the latest scientific research suggests a degree of innateness to our sexual identities. For that reason, we may expect to see growing acceptance of gay and lesbian individuals, as well as legal condemnation and skepticism levied against organizations that claim to treat or "cure" homosexuality.

Yet, as with questions of gender identity, when it comes to sexual identity and desires, it is important to emphasize the complex interplay of nature and nurture. While biology may give us all certain sexual "predispositions," it is the human experience that shapes whether and how we act upon these predispositions, as well as what those acts mean. Hormones in men and women, as well as the shape of their genitals, do not vary much from culture to culture or across historical time. Yet how people act upon those biological forces and how they label them vary tremendously. Again, and finally, we take the example of oral sex. If nothing else, this chapter has shown the sociological significance of this particular act. Although this is, theoretically, a pleasurable act for many to engage in, it has also been embraced as a rite of passage (Sambian and Greek warriors) and as an act of social and sexual domination (prison, slavery). It is clearly the case that while some of our sexuality is biologically fixed, humans creatively define the meaning of their sexuality. Because social context matters, we need to know where, when, and how an act occurs in order to determine whether it is an instance of pleasure, profit, power, or something else.

A final sociological takeaway from this chapter is that there are social and political consequences associated with these definitions. For many decades in the United States (and abroad), not only has sex other than intercourse been defined as strange or immoral, it has also been defined as criminal. Over time, the very laws that govern what people do behind closed doors have changed and in so doing have opened the doors of acceptance for a broader array of sexual expression. Laws have been passed at the state and local levels, providing civil rights based on sexual orientation, along with the right for gays and lesbians to marry in 37 states and the District of Columbia. Yet groups *within* the LGBT community have sized each other up and questioned whether they want to embrace a broader "queer" identity, or whether they gain greater power and legitimacy by identifying the differences between them. Some gay and lesbian activists argue, for example, that they have concerns that are distinct from bisexual and transgender individuals and that they may make more progress by distancing themselves from those under the same umbrella. In the end, we learn that when it comes to questions about what determines a person's sexual orientation (and desires) and how many identities and possibilities there are, social and scientific understandings have changed over time and will, in all likelihood, continue to change in the future.

CHAPTER 3: REVIEW OF KEY POINTS

- Sexual behavior and sexual orientation are two different things; sexual orientation is longer, more enduring, and rooted in desires—or the lack thereof—rather than behaviors.
- Like sex, gender, and the other identities in this book, sexual orientation can be conceptualized as an identity that is discrete and categorical or one that is flexible and arrayed on a continuum.
- Researchers, activists, and individuals are giving increased attention to emerging concepts like asexuality and pansexuality.
- The *essentialist perspective* sees sexual orientation and sexual behavior as rooted in underlying biological phenomena.
- The *social constructionist perspective* sees sexual orientation and sexual behavior as historically and cross-culturally variable—largely created and reinforced by humans through socialization and the social structure.
- The notion of "sexual orientation" or sexual identity is a fairly recent "invention." It emerged in the 1800s, as religious explanations for social phenomena were replaced by scientific explanations.

- The social constructionist perspective shows that this same behavior has been viewed in distinct ways historically and cross-culturally. *The Five Ps* illustrate how the same behavior can be viewed differently depending on the social context.
- Historically and even in contemporary research and commentary, more attention has been paid to the sexual behavior of men than women. This tells us something about the power and privilege associated with masculinity.
- Human sexual behavior is *patterned* and structured by our social identities. Traits like age, race, education, and religion shape our propensities to have tried certain sexual activities, along with how "excited" we feel when we engage in certain activities.

CHAPTER 3: QUESTIONS FOR REVIEW

1. What is sexual orientation? How does it differ from sexual behavior?

2. "Sexual orientation" can be viewed as a categorical identity—where a person checks the box that best fits his or her identity—or as existing along a continuum. Explain these two approaches to sexual orientation and why they are both plausible.

3. The essentialist perspective sees sexual orientation (and human sexuality and sexual drives) as primarily rooted in biology. What evidence do they use to argue this case?

4. The social constructionist perspective sees sexual orientation (and human sexuality and sexual drives) as reflective of historically- and culturally-specific norms and social structures. What evidence do they use to argue this case?

5. What are some of the social consequences associated with looking at sexual orientation as biologically rooted—either positive or negative? Do you think there are negative consequences associated with looking at differences in gender behavior as a product of human social interaction?

6. The "Five Ps of Human Sexuality" illustrate the complexity that surrounds definitions of human sexuality. What are these five forms of expression? Do you find convincing the argument that genital contact can mean a lot of different things, depending on the context? Why or why not?

7. Sociologists find that the particular sexual behaviors and activities that a person chooses to participate in—and how they feel about it—are socially structured. How so? How does this information provide a critique against the notion that human sexuality is all hormonal or animal instinct?

KEY TERMS

asexuality

Boston marriages

concordance

discordance

essentialist

homosexual

Kinsey Scale

pansexuals

Paragraph 175

pederasty

queer

sexual inverts

sexual orientation

social constructionist

social desirability bias

REFERENCES

American Psychological Association. 2008. "Sexual Orientation and Homosexuality: Answers to Your Questions for a Better Understanding." Washington, D.C.: American Psychological Association. Retrieved April 17, 2015 (http://www.apa.org/topics/lgbt/orientation.pdf)

Bailey, J. Michael, and Richard C. Pillard. 1991. "A Genetic Study of Male Sexual Orientation." *Archives of General Psychiatry* 48(12): 1089–1096.

Blanchard, Ray. 2001. "Fraternal Birth Order and the Maternal Immune Hypothesis of Male Homosexuality." *Hormones and Behavior* 40(2): 105–114.

Bogaert, Anthony F. 2007. "Towards a Conceptual Understanding of Asexuality." *Review of General Psychology* 10:241–250.

Boswell, John. 1980. *Christianity, Social Tolerance, and Homosexuality.* Chicago: University of Chicago Press.

Carrier, Joseph. 1995. *De Los Otros: Intimacy and Homosexuality among Mexican Men.* New York: Columbia University Press.

Chandra, Anjani, William D. Mosher, Casey Copen, and Catlainn Sionean. 2011. "Sexual Behavior, Sexual Attraction, and Sexual Identity in the United States: Data from the 2006–2008 National Survey of Family Growth." Hyattsville, MD: National Center for Health Statistics.

Conger, John J. 1975. "Proceedings of the American Psychological Association, Incorporated, for the Year 1974: Minutes of the Annual Meeting of the Council of Representatives." *American Psychologist* 30(6): 620–651.

De Cecco, John. 1990. "Confusing the Actor with the Act." *Archives of Sexual Behavior* 19:409–412.

Denizet-Lewis, Benoit. 2003. "Double Lives on the Down Low." *New York Times*, August 3rd. Retrieved April 17, 2015 (http://www.nytimes.com/2003/08/03/magazine/double-lives-on-the-down-low.html)

Diamond, Lisa and Molly Butterworth. 2008. "Questioning Gender and Sexual Identity: Dynamic Links over Time." *Sex Roles* 59:365–376.

Donaldson, Stephen. N.D. "Hooking Up: Protective for Punks." Retrieved April 17, 2015 (http://www.justdetention.org/en/ps_hookingup.aspx)

Faderman, Lillian. 1981. *Surpassing the Love of Men: Romantic Friendship and Love between Women from the Renaissance to the Present.* New York: William Morrow & Company

Faust, Drew Gilpin. 1985. *James Henry Hammond and the Old South: A Design for Mastery.* Baton Rouge: Louisiana State University Press.

Garcia-Falgueras, Alicia and Dick F. Swaab. 2009. "Sexual Hormones and the Brain: An Essential Alliance for Sexual Identity and Sexual Orientation." *Pediatric Neuroendocrinology* 17: 22–35.

Glick, Sarah Nelson and Matthew R. Golden. 2010. "Persistence of Racial Differences in Attitudes towards Homosexuality in the United States." *Journal of Acquired Immune Deficiency Syndrome* 55:516–523.

Hamilton, Laura. 2007. "Trading on Heterosexuality: College Women's Gender Strategies and Homophobia." *Gender and Society* 21:145–172.

Herdt, Gilbert. 1999. *Sambia Sexual Culture: Essays from the Field.* Chicago: University of Chicago Press.

Human Rights Watch. 2001. *No Escape: Male Rape in U.S. Prisons.* New York: Human Rights Watch.

Jennings, Rebecca. 2007. *A Lesbian History of Britain: Love and Sex between Women Since 1500.* Westport, CT: Greenwood World Publishing

Klein. Fritz. 1978. *The Bisexual Option.* Philadelphia: Harrington Park Press.

LaMar, Lisa and Mary Kite. 1998. "Sex Differences in Attitudes toward Gay Men and Lesbians: A Multidimensional Perspective." *The Journal of Sex Research* 35:189–196.

Lemelle, Anthony J., Jr. and Juan Battle. 2004. "Black Masculinity Matters in Attitudes toward Gay Males." *Journal of Homosexuality* 47:39–51.

LeVay, Simon. 1994. *The Sexual Brain.* Cambridge, MA: MIT Press.

LeVay, Simon. 1997. *Queer Science: The Use and Abuse of Research Into Homosexuality.* Cambridge, MA: MIT Press.

Michael, Robert T., John H. Gagnon, Edward O. Laumann, and Gina Kolata. 1994. *Sex in America: A Definitive Survey.* Boston: Little, Brown.

New York Times. 1991. "Gay Men in Twin Study." *New York Times* December 17th. Retrieved April 17, 2015 (http://www.nytimes.com/1991/12/17/science/gay-men-in-twin-study.html)

Page, Denys. 1979. *Sappho and Alcaeus: An Introduction to the Study of Ancient Lesbian Poetry.* New York: Oxford University Press.

Prause, Nicole and Cynthia A. Graham. 2007. "Asexuality: Classification and Characterization." *Archives of Sexual Behavior* 36:341–356.

Savic, Ivanka, and Per Lindström. 2008. "PET and MRI Show Differences in Cerebral Asymmetry and Functional Connectivity Between Homo- and Heterosexual Subjects." *Proceedings of the National Academy of Sciences* 105(27): 9403–9408.

Schalet, Amy T. 2011. *Not Under My Roof: Parents, Teens, and the Culture of Sex.* Chicago: University of Chicago Press.

Stacey, Judith and Timothy J. Biblarz. 2001. "(How) Does the Sexual Orientation of Parents Matter?" *American Sociological Review* 66: 159–183.

Verstraete, Beert and Vernon Provencal. 2006. *Same-Sex Desire and Love in Greco-Roman Antiquity and in the Classical Tradition of the West.* New York: Routledge.

Waite, Linda and Maggie Gallagher. 2001. *The Case for Marriage: Why Married People Are Happier, Healthier, and Better Off Financially.* New York: Broadway Books.

Weinberg, Martin S., Collin J. Williams, and Douglas W. Pryor. 1995. *Dual Attraction: Understanding Bisexuality.* New York: Oxford University Press.

More Than Skin Deep?

Understanding Race and Ethnicity

When Barack Obama was elected during the fall of 2008, he was quickly labeled the United States' "first black president." Obama was elected with 95 percent of the black vote in 2008; when he was re-elected in 2012, he garnered 93 percent of this demographic. While blacks have supported Democratic candidates for decades (including Clinton, with 83 percent of this portion of the electorate in 1992 and 84 percent in 1996), Obama was embraced and celebrated as one of their own.

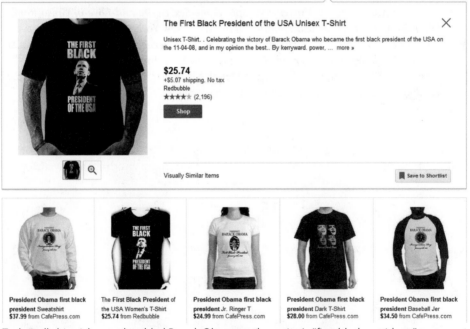

Technically biracial, many heralded Barack Obama as the nation's "first *black* president."

Although Barack Obama continues to be referred to as a "black president"—in outlets ranging from CNN to rap songs by Young Jeezy and Jay Z—questions exist about his race. On the one hand, there are those who wish to clarify that Obama is technically our nation's first "biracial" president—a man of black descent on his father's side, who was raised largely by his white mother and her parents. The biracial angle is endorsed by those who seek a more accurate and inclusive understanding of race in America, such as *Washington Post* columnist Clinton Yates (2012)—himself a black man. In commenting on Obama's race, he observed that "pride in not being solely one thing seems to be a high point, which is a good thing. Diversity within us, never mind among us, doesn't hurt." Conversations about Obama's race also include those who do not know what to make of his identity. With the name *Barack Hussein Obama*, some commentators have framed him not as a familiar type of black American but as an exotic man of Kenyan descent, possibly even a foreign-born Muslim. Finally, there are those who insist that at the end of the day Barack Obama is, despite his mixed-race parentage, a black man. In his online column, Casey Gane-McCalla (2008) provided a "Top 10 list" of reasons why Obama is black. While including some humorous items (Obama is black because he plays basketball), Gane-McCalla concludes that as long as the police see you and treat you as a black person, you are black. Obama himself has said that as long as "you look African-American in this society, you're treated as an African-American."

So what *is* the race of President Obama? If he is not actually black, why is he routinely labeled as such? The fact that President Obama's race has been the focus of such intense debate highlights just how contentious race continues to be in American society. Yet it also highlights the slipperiness of the very concept of race. As discussed above, the argument that Barack Obama is the nation's first black president rests on the following points: his genetic origins can be traced back to Africa; he *looks* black; and he *says* he's black. These various ways of defining blackness show that while race is partially a matter of genetics (at least in terms of phenotype), it is also a matter of history and self-identification. Race is, in short, both a descriptive and a political concept.

The goal of this chapter is to provide a sociological understanding of race and ethnicity. As in our chapters on sex, gender, and sexuality, the sociological assumption that guides this chapter is that while there is a biological basis to our race, this concept is, to a great extent, socially constructed. To begin our understanding of how and why race is socially constructed, we must first define our terms.

DEFINING RACE AND ETHNICITY: WHAT IS IT AND HOW MANY ARE THERE?

While the question of President Obama's race captures some of the challenges of racial classification, it is fair to say that racial classification is a prominent feature of everyday life. Earlier today, I filled out a survey online asking me to define my race. The survey game me five options: Asian, black, Hispanic, white, and other. Racial classification is also evident in the media. Black Entertainment Television (BET) has been around since 1980. Although there is officially no "White Entertainment Television," other ethnic groups (and foreign language speakers) also have specialized channels, including Univision, Telemundo, Al Jazeera English, and Filipino TV. Racial classification is also present in our everyday lives. According to research by Phyllis Katz and Jennifer Kofkin (1997), children as young as 4 years old are able to categorize others according to their race. In a study where they were asked to sort photographs of other children into piles, 68 percent of children spontaneously sorted them based on race, while only 16 percent grouped the photos based on gender. Such tendencies continue into adulthood, as we typically label the people with whom we come into contact in terms of sociologically relevant traits, like race and gender.

The task of racial classification begs two important questions: What determines a person's race and how many races are there? As stated above, President Obama is often categorized as black because he *looks* black. But what does it mean to "look black"—or Asian, or Hispanic, or white, for that matter? Systems of racial categorization typically focus on a person's **phenotype;** that is, their external observable traits, which are an expression of their genes, the environment, and interactions between the two. The first phenotypic trait that typically provides information about a person's race is their skin color. The darkest skin tones result in the label of "black"; brown skin with red or tan undertones generally gets the label Hispanic; brown skin with yellow undertones gets the label Asian; and white people are those with light skin, whose undertones may vary from pink to olive.

But what if skin color proves inconclusive? When a person's race is not immediately apparent in their skin tone, we typically look to another set of phenotypic traits, like hair or facial features. If we find a person with brown skin, but cannot tell their race (or ethnicity), we may look at the shape of their eyes, lips, or nose, or even hair texture for clues about their race. This set of traits usually comes together to help determine a person's race. But what about a person with dark skin and a short Afro who is also a native Spanish speaker? Does dark skin and an Afro make someone "black," or does the fact that someone is a native Spanish speaker make him or her Hispanic? Could I take a sample of their DNA in order to definitively determine their race?

To sort out these questions, it is necessary to define our terms. **Race can be defined as a socially constructed label used to categorize people based on real or perceived biological/physical characteristics.** The notion that race is a "socially constructed label" means that it is humans who invented and define this concept. It is humans who invented this term, decided how many races there are, and identified which traits are necessary to categorize people as one race or another. It also means that we as humans must learn which traits we are *supposed* to pay attention to when it comes to race. We have to learn, for example, that a person's skin color puts them into a certain category. We are trained, moreover, to pay attention to some differences and ignore others. For example, although a person with blond hair, light skin, and pink undertones looks very different from someone with dark hair and olive skin within the context of the contemporary United States, we have learned that both are "white." Our racial socialization, moreover, provides the "lesson" that a person's nose, eyes, lips, and hair texture are indicators of their race. Paying attention to these differences is not an automatic feature of being human. In fact, we could easily be re-socialized to pay attention to none of these features, to pay greater attention to distinctions among these features, or even to believe that earlobe or forehead size is the *true* indicator of who a person is.

While the terms "race" and "ethnicity" are often used interchangeably, they are different. **Ethnicity** refers to a socially defined category based on a common culture or, sometimes, nationality. As a group with a shared cultural background, people with the same ethnicity typically share language, religion, symbols and traditions, as well as history. Thus, while race deals with (perceived) *biological* differences, ethnicity deals with *cultural* differences. To further illustrate the differences between the two, it may help to note that one (race) of these you are (allegedly) born with, and the other (ethnicity) you learn through the experience of being born in a particular place and time. It may be useful to think about race as a concept similar to sex and ethnicity as a concept similar to gender.

Each of us has both a race and an ethnicity. In my case, I am white (race) and American (ethnicity). In identifying myself as "American," I note that I speak a particular version of the English language and have been socialized in a culture that endorses certain values, including individualism, equality, and progress. Being an American also includes the trivial—such as cheering for my country in the Olympic games—and the nontrivial—such as identifying on a personal and emotional level with major events of U.S. history, including the Vietnam War, the civil rights movement, and the 9/11 attacks. While I identify simply as "American," others may choose to identify as Italian American, African American, or Jewish American if their personal and family histories include the linguistic, culinary, or historic aspects of those culture.

The distinction between race and ethnicity returns us to a question asked earlier: What is the race of a person with dark skin and tightly curled, coarse hair who is also a native Spanish speaker? Depending on where you grew up, the answer to this question might be obvious. Yet if you are like me, having grown up in a relatively homogeneous environment, you might be as perplexed as I was the day I landed in New York's LaGuardia Airport and was greeted by young women with dark brown skin who were speaking Spanish. After some mental processing I figured out that these young women were probably New Yorkers from the Dominican Republic. While some readers may find my naiveté shocking, it helps make the following distinction: being Hispanic is not a race—it is currently defined as an ethnicity. "Hispanic" is an ethnicity because Hispanic people generally share a language (Spanish), a religion (historically Catholic, but less so in recent decades), and a history that involves coming from a country that was colonized by Spain. Being Hispanic is not technically a race because Hispanic people are of many different races. This is obvious if you know more than a handful of people from Cuba, Puerto Rico, or the Dominican Republic—where people may be racially categorized as white, black, or even Indian—like the indigenous Taíno of the Caribbean islands. It is, therefore, possible to be black *and* Hispanic. Also, a small segment of Hispanics is of Asian descent. In Peru, for example, waves of immigration dating back to the 1850s brought Chinese, Japanese, and Filipino people to work agricultural jobs. Although they retain some Asian customs, members of this unique ethnic group have also adopted aspects of the local Hispanic culture. These examples, again, help distinguish between race, which refers to external phenotypic traits, and ethnicity, which refers to adopted or socialized cultural traits.

If we now know that race refers to categorizations based on biological—and especially phenotypic—traits, we should now ask: How many races are there? Unfortunately, the answer to this question is complex. On the one hand, there is only one "human race." All humans belong to the group *Homo sapiens*; on the level of DNA, there is not enough biological variation among humans to separate us into subspecies. On the other hand, there are forms and official conventions like the U.S. Census that categorize humans into a finite set of races—usually six (white; black; Asian; Native Hawaiian, Pacific Islander, American Indian, and Alaska Native; other; and multiracial). Finally, as we will see later, humans across the globe and throughout history provide very different answers to the question of how many races there are. Therefore, it is entirely possible to answer the question of how many races there with one, six, or "however many we say there are" and still be correct. In order to understand why each of these answers might be considered correct, it is necessary to first explore scientific efforts to understand the concept of race and then move on to exploring the social constructionist approach.

MORE THAN SKIN DEEP? EXPLAINING RACIAL AND ETHNIC DIFFERENCES

Socially, there are many differences between racial and ethnic groups. Statistically, some groups earn more than others, are more likely to go to college, have more contact with the criminal justice system, and have different rates of marriage and divorce. Within the realm of stereotypes, some groups carry a reputation for being loud, musical, and athletic; others are seen as passionate, devoted to family, and hardworking; others still are thought to be a little uptight and ignorant of groups other than their own. When it comes to differences across racial and ethnic groups, we have to ask: Are these differences more than skin deep? In the following section, we explore two ways of thinking about race: the essentialist perspective sees race and racial differences as real reflections of underlying biology; the social constructionist perspective—the one typically favored by sociologists—sees these apparent differences as rooted in history, politics, and shifting social practices.

THE ESSENTIALIST PERSPECTIVE: SCIENTIFIC EFFORTS TO CATEGORIZE AND EXPLAIN RACIAL DIFFERENCES

Since the late 1600s, as European exploration of the globe expanded, so too did social and scientific efforts to understand the astounding forms of human variation encountered. For nearly 400 years, scientific efforts to understand the concept of race have focused on two core questions: How many races are there, and how and why do they differ from one another?

Although the French physician François Bernier may have been the first to use the term "race" in his 1684 publication *Nouvelle Division de la Terre par les Différents Espèces ou Races qui l'Habitent* ("New Division of Earth by the Different Species or Races Which Inhabit It), it is the Swedish scientist **Carl Linnaeus** who is generally credited with developing the first racial **taxonomy**—or system of classification—during the mid-1700s. Writing in the 10th edition of his classic, *Systemae Naturae,* Linnaeus identified four races, based largely on continental geographic origins and skin color variations: Americanus, Asiaticus, Africanus, and Europeaus. Embedded in this early taxonomy was the assumption that people from different geographical regions don't simply look different from one another, they also have different natures. While Linnaeus described *Homo sapiens Europeaus* as having a gentle character and inventive mind, the *Americanus* was described as stubborn and easily angered, and the *Africanus* as crafty, lazy, and careless. It seems that as soon as the concept of race became systematized, so did the tendency to think of race in a hierarchical manner, classifying one as better than the others.

Over the next 200 years, the revolution in scientific thinking inspired biologists and anthropologists alike to refine their understandings of this thing called "race." The advent of scientific thinking and new tools for measuring and making comparisons spawned the field of **anthropometry**—literally, the "measurement of man." By measuring human skulls (craniometry), Johann Friedrich Blumenbach first proposed in 1775 the notion that there are five races: Caucasoid (white), Mongoloid (Asian), Ethiopian (later Negroid), Malay (South Pacific), and American. While his racial taxonomy made a lasting impression within the field of anthropology, quickly forgotten among his peers was

Working from an essentialist perspective, Swedish scientist Carl Linneaus formalized one of the first racial taxonomies.

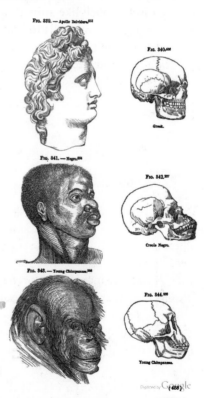

Many racial taxonomies saw people of African descent as a lower form of human life—a distinct race between white Europeans and primates.

his belief that physical differences among races did not necessarily correlate with physical or social deficiencies between them.

Among most race scientists of the 1800s, however, the general assumption was that the outward physical differences between the races were related to different and unequal inner virtues. This notion is called **physiognomy**. Beginning in the 1820s, for example, an American physician named Samuel Morton moved from measuring skulls to measuring the brains they contained. Using measurements from hundreds of skulls gathered from around the world, Morton (1939) concluded in his book *Crania Americana* that Europeans have the largest brain capacities, followed by Asians, Malay, American Indians, and lastly those of African descent. For Morton, a bigger brain is a superior brain; as such, he characterized the Caucasian race as "distinguished for the facility with which it attains the highest intellectual endowments . . . [who] have peopled the finest portions of the earth, and given birth to its fairest inhabitants," while Africans were described as "the lowest grade of humanity" (5).

The notion that nonwhite people are both exotic and backward became a social and scientific preoccupation from the 1850s through the early 1900s. While American and European citizens flocked to racial exhibitions that put people from Africa and Asia on display much like animals at a zoo, scientists treated these specimens as objects of inquiry. From skulls to brains, to limbs, to skin color, to hair texture, every physical feature of nonwhite people was scientifically poked and prodded, measured and examined, and often concluded to be deficient.

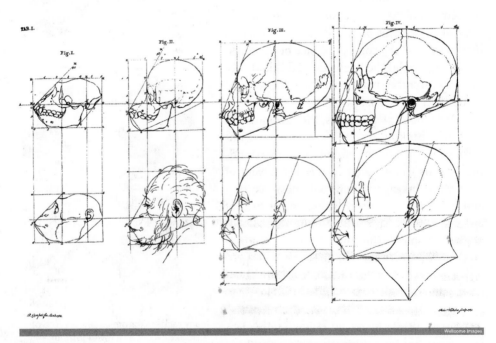

Scientists devoted considerable attention to documenting physical differences among "races" and used these differences to justify unequal treatment.

In many cases, these scientific inquiries were not merely scientific. Indeed, the findings of many race scientists were used to advance social and political goals. In the context of slavery, scientific evidence purporting to show that people of African descent have limited intelligence and a lazy character were used to justify their subjugation. Not only were black slaves thought to be feebleminded, but their bodies were seen as weak and prone to sickness; because little could be made of this allegedly inferior race, their best and highest use was to be put to work and, in the case of female slaves, to breed future workers. Outside of the slave system, physicians offered similar justifications for using people of African descent as subjects in medical experiments—most of which were done without the consent of the patients and some without providing basic technologies that were available at the time, including anesthesia. Again, we see the essentialist perspective has been used to justify racial inequality, just as it was used to exclude women from higher education.

The science of race reached its most troubling chapter in the study of **eugenics** during the early twentieth century. Literally meaning "well born," eugenics refers to scientific efforts to identify the best traits of humans and then engage in efforts to promote reproduction in those with the most desired traits and inhibit the reproduction of those with less desired traits. Fundamental to eugenics was the assumption that each racial group is genetically distinct from the others and passes its own unique set of physical, social, and psychological characteristics through its bloodline. In their studies, proponents of eugenics like the English anthropologist Sir Francis Galton and American psychologist H. H. Goddard argued that because intelligence is an inherited trait, and because certain races have demonstrably lower levels of intelligence, they should be considered unfit and discouraged from reproducing.

Throughout the early 1900s, the study of eugenics—which was mainstream scientific thinking at the time—influenced social policy in profound ways. Testimony from scientists was used, for example, to pass immigration laws limiting the influx of southern and eastern Europeans into the United States and marriage laws across the United States prohibiting **miscegenation**—interracial marriage—under the assumption that reproduction across racial lines would weaken and dilute the "superior" white race. Throughout Europe and the United States, these beliefs led to forced sterilizations and forced abortions where mothers were deemed genetically unfit (whether because of race, low levels of intelligence, physical disability, or perceived promiscuity). Yet it was in the Nazi **genocide**—the mass killing of an entire group of people—that eugenics was used for the most destructive purposes. Pseudoscientific claims fueled systematic efforts to destroy those races deemed unfit (Jews of the "Semitic" race" and Roma) and promote the (white) Aryan and Nordic races. It was only at this point, during the 1930s, that a significant backlash against eugenics emerged among American and European scientists, as they recognized the brutal ends to which their ideas could be put.

Today, while the scientific tools for studying race have improved dramatically, there remain lively debates on the question of race. One question that has generally been resolved is the question of how many races there are. Today, the dominant scientific belief is that there is just one race—*Homo sapiens*. There are no separate races, per se, because scientists have not been able to identify distinct groups with clearly defined genetic boundaries—where members of the population share significant traits with one another and have traits that distinguish them from others. In fact, using complicated scientific procedures, some biologists and geneticists argue that there is more genetic variation *within* the groups we call races than there is *between* them. Others point out that phenotypic traits—like skin color—vary in a continuous way, with no distinct boundary—genetic, geographic, social, or otherwise—marking the border between each race. Such traits—including eye shape and even certain racially patterned medical conditions like Tay-Sachs disease and sickle cell trait—are generally considered *environmental* adaptions among people living in particular geographic locations. In the case of skin color, lighter tones are thought to better facilitate the absorption of vitamin D and darker tones thought to defend better against ultraviolet exposure.

At the end of the twentieth century, geneticists like Luigi Luca Cavalli-Sforza and his co-authors (1994) declared that "The classification into races has proven to be a futile exercise" (19). A sample of **DNA**—the sequence of molecular material containing information about the human genetic code—cannot be used to determine a person's race. Similarly, there are no genetic markers that definitively indicate a person's racial identity. Scientists today are able to use **genetic analysis** (of DNA) and analysis of forensic remains not to determine a specimen's race, per se, but to identify its geographic origins. This process has been celebrated on television programs like TLC's *Who Do You Think You Are?* and PBS's *Finding Your Roots*. For just $195, a kit from Ancestry by DNA can be used to take a sample of DNA, submit it for analysis, and receive a report with information about one's "racial admixture." As illustrated by Table 4.1, such tests provide insight into the proportion of a person's DNA that can be connected to what the company calls "the four founding populations": European, indigenous American, sub-Saharan African, and East Asian. In fact, most people within the United States have DNA that exhibits a mixture of two or more of these geographic areas—despite the fact that relatively few of us look or identify as "multiracial." The takeaway point is that while our genes may provide insight into our geographic origins, our social identities and self-identification often trump (and sometimes contradict) this seemingly scientific evidence.

Table 4.1 **DNA Analysis**

Region	Percentage of Geographic Ancestry
East Asian	12
European	88
Indigenous American	0
Sub-Saharan African	0

Finally, another futile exercise from the standpoint of contemporary science is the effort to connect genetic markers to social or psychological differences between humans. While it may be tempting to believe that different "racial groups" have unique traits and talents, the scientific evidence does not support this. Those claims by early race scientists that some races are more intelligent than others, more hot-tempered, more rhythmic or musically gifted, or more physically resilient have not been confirmed by scientific analysis. Although measures of intelligence, like IQ, do show variations among racial and ethnic groups, the general consensus—led by psychologist Robert Sternberg and economist Thomas Sowell—is that these differences reflect social and environmental factors rather than underlying racial or genetic differences. Similarly, despite the significant success of "black people" in athletics, there is little to suggest that race-based genetics is the reason for this. While journalist John Entine (2000) argues in his book, *Taboo*, that the success of East African marathon runners may be attributable to "slow twitch" muscle fibers, other careful analysis suggests that the high elevations of parts of East Africa—an environmental factor—are a more likely explanation of their success.

The science of race, with a long and bumpy history, continues to evolve. What we know at this time is that while genetic traits vary across populations, from a biological perspective, there is just one race (*Homo sapiens*). Moreover, the concept of race has not just scientific purposes; it has also been used for social and political purposes—as with the eugenics movement. Finally, while there may be real social differences across groups that we call races—differences in terms of life expectancy, school success, and even athletic success—there is little to suggest that racial differences can be understood as substantially rooted in underlying genetic differences. For these very reasons, we now must turn to the social constructionist perspective to develop a broader sociological understanding of the concept of race.

NURTURE AND THE SOCIAL CONSTRUCTIONIST PERSPECTIVE

It has become common within sociology, anthropology, and other fields of study to declare that race is a "myth." Calling race a myth does two things: one, it calls into question the scientific evidence used in previous eras to argue for different and unequal racial groups; two, it highlights the notion that race is a social and political invention. Within sociology, we say that race is "socially constructed." Take, for example, President Obama. Although he has a fixed set of genetic and phenotypic traits, whether he is categorized as a "black man" depends on location and culture; what it might mean for him to be a black man, within a particular place or time, varies as well. In this section we explore the social construction of race. To do so, I show the tremendous cross-cultural and historical variations in how societies have dealt with questions such as: How many races are there; how does a person become classified as a member of a particular race; and what are the social meanings and consequences associated with being a member of a particular race? In doing so, we see this thing called race is not a biological inevitability but a human creation.

THE STUDY ABROAD TRIP

Pack your bags, and don't forget a swim suit—we're off on an adventure to see how two societies have constructed race in two very different ways. Our trip will take us to two locations that have much in common: beautiful beaches, a history of Colonial rule, diverse populations, and modern economies built on agriculture and mining. Yet their recent histories differ considerably in terms of how they count and categorize race, along with the social consequences associated with being categorized in one group versus another. Our journey will show that while South Africa has had a history of rigid racial categorization and harsh racial inequalities, Brazil has had a relatively fluid approach to race and a history that is less clearly marked by racial inequality.

Our first stop is South Africa, the African nation settled by the British, who later lost control of the nation in the Boer War with the Dutch during the early 1900s. While South Africa is known today as a nation with beautiful beaches, amazing wildlife, and high-quality vineyards, its recent past is most notably marked by its approach to race. While reaching its most profound expression under a system of segregation known as **apartheid** (literally, *being apart*), lasting from 1948 to 1994, South Africa's roots of racial inequality go back decades earlier, and today the nation is trying to heal its racial wounds. Under the system of apartheid, the country of South Africa officially recognized four races; White, Indian, Coloured, and Black. Although some of these categories include complex identities—for example, White could be broken down into English and Afrikaans (of Dutch descent), and Coloured included those of mixed-race

Under South Africa's rigid Apartheid system, legal segregation characterized many facets of life; citizens were also required to carry racial identification cards.

backgrounds and possibly some of Asian descent—the government officially recognized four races and then formally organized society around these groups.

While race today, especially in the United States, is to some extent a matter of self-identification (i.e., Barack Obama is black because he says he is), racial identity and racial categorization was a matter of governmental policy under apartheid. Under the **Population Registration Act of 1950**, each resident of South Africa received an official racial classification and was required to carry an identity card with this information. With respect to earning a particular racial designation, the Act defined a white person as "one who is in appearance obviously white—and not generally accepted as Coloured—or who is generally accepted as White—and is not obviously Non-White."

With this convoluted wording, it sometimes became necessary for an appointed board to determine whether a person should be considered White or Coloured. To do so, factors beyond skin color were taken into account, including socioeconomic status and employment. Here, being sufficiently advantaged in terms of economic status could tip the scale toward White. In other instances, the board was called upon to determine whether a person with ambiguous features should be defined as Black or Coloured. In these cases, a final determination was sometimes made using **the pencil test**. As described by Troy Duster in the book *The Making and Unmaking of Whiteness*, a person would be categorized as Coloured if, when asked to put a pencil in his or her hair and shake his or her head, the pencil then fell out; if the pencil remained in place, he or she would be classified as Black. Ultimately, the power to determine someone's race rested with official bureaucratic procedures.

Once an individual was given a particular identity and an identity card, it could be determined whether his or her behavior was in accordance with the laws of apartheid or whether his or her behaviors defied the law and called for punishment. And within the context of apartheid South Africa, almost no behavior went unregulated. As with Jim Crow–era policies in the United States, nearly all public facilities were segregated. "Whites Only" signs covered almost every facet of public space. Another similarity to racial inequality in the United States is that marriage and sexual relations between members of different racial groups were penalized under **anti-miscegenation laws**—one of which was the Immorality Act of 1950. Under the Group Areas Act, residential segregation took on an extreme form. While members of different racial groups once lived together side by side, beginning in 1950, each group was given its own space within which they were allowed to live and own businesses. It was through forcible relocation that black residents were eventually consolidated onto lands that were generally smaller compared to those allotted to whites, and often required them to travel longer commutes to work. Moreover, movement between areas was controlled using documentation similar to a passport.

Outside of the urban areas, members of the different black ethnic groups were forced into a system of *homelands*. While those designated Black made up nearly 70 percent of the overall population, they were consolidated onto a system of reservations—or **Bantustans**—that made up only 13 percent of the nation's land. Moreover, these lands were often substandard and agriculturally unproductive. Individual homelands functioned as a state-within-a-state. Black residents of Transkei or QwaQwa, for example, were citizens of those homelands, rather than citizens of South Africa. With their citizenship effectively revoked, entirely separate governmental structures emerged to serve and manage the black populations. While black workers were still needed to fuel the manufacturing and service sectors of South Africa proper, they were often treated like migrant guest workers, if not illegal immigrants.

Apartheid was not a system of "separate but equal." Under apartheid, nonwhites experienced higher rates of poverty and limited access to political representation, education, and health care. Civil rights abuses and imprisonment of activists were also common. Under this system, Coloureds and Indians experienced similar, but less severe, forms of oppression. Throughout the 1980s, however, both violent and diplomatic pressure mounted against the South African government, led by courageous domestic leaders like Nelson Mandela, global intervention and boycotts, and internationally acclaimed musical stars. Today, April 27 marks the day of independence formally granted in 1994. While significant social and political changes have taken place, South Africa remains a nation scarred by its lengthy history of racial inequality, where the health and well-being of nonwhites lags behind.

The case of South Africa shows the following: in some cases, race is divided into relatively few categories; moreover, assignment into those categories may be an official process. Finally, once assigned to a racial category, the consequences may be vast—with substantial privileges given to whites and many disadvantages to nonwhites. To see how race may be constructed very differently in other settings, we must now board an airplane bound for Rio de Janeiro, Brazil. To get our bearings, we stop off for a day at the beach, followed by a traditional Brazilian meal of *feijoada* (meat and bean stew) accompanied by a refreshing *caipirinha* cocktail. The next morning, our study of race begins.

Colonized by the Portuguese, but home to an indigenous population, Brazil has a racial history involving both the slave trade and extensive European migration. In fact, during the colonial period, Brazil received significantly more slaves than did the United States, and more European immigrants. Because of these patterns, Brazil has a population base that has some parallels with the United States. The history of race, though, is another story. Anthropologists and sociologists who have studied Brazil have been struck by the relative absence of sharply defined racial categories. Remarking in a classic 1964 article, anthropologist Marvin Harris wrote that "what is most distinctive about Brazilian race relations in comparison with other inter-racial systems [is the] plethora of racial terms and the abstract and referential ambiguity surrounding their application" (22). While the Brazilian census officially acknowledges five main racial groups (see Figure 4.1), the day-to-day realities of race are much more complicated. Surveys of communities, for example, have found that Brazilians readily identify 40 or so main racial terms, while colloquial speech may reveal more than a hundred ways of describing race.

To understand these complexities, it is important to understand the basis for racial classification in Brazil. As opposed to the official system of classification in South Africa, racial classification in Brazil is a complex, fluid, and contextual affair. As in

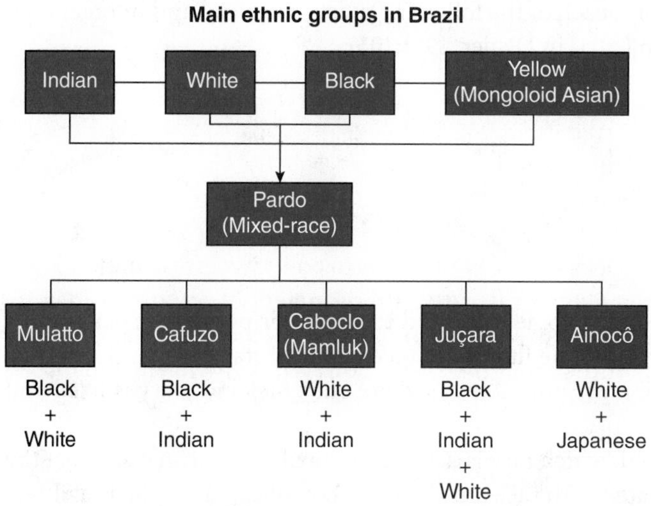

Main ethnic groups in Brazil

Figure 4.1 Main ethnic groups in Brazil. For official purposes, Brazil recognizes a specific number of racial categories; in everyday life, however, people identify many more racial distinctions.

South Africa and the United States, racial classification is based more on phenotype (appearance) than descent (family origins, bloodline). In Brazil, however, attention to the variations in phenotype is quite nuanced. While skin color, hair, and facial features are all part of racial categorization in the United States, Brazilians pay more attention to these subtleties and create additional categories to account for seeming contradictions between, for example, hair color (blond) and skin color (dark). Further, where most Americans would typically see "black" or "white" skin, the average Brazilian would be more aware of ruddy, olive, or even blue undertones in the skin—and consider these racial subtypes. The result is an extensive racial taxonomy that includes an array of terms that read like a menu of coffees or ice creams: *Acastanhada* (cashew-like tint; caramel colored); *Branca-avermelhada* (peach white); *Café-com-leite* (coffee with milk); *Cor-de-canela* (tint of cinnamon); *Jambo* (like a fruit the deep-red color of a blood orange); and *Saraúba* (like a white meringue).

To say that race is based more on phenotype than on descent means that two siblings with the same biological parents may have different racial identities. In fact, if they look sufficiently different from one another, every member of the same household—all related by blood—may end up with a unique racial classification. Yet in Brazil, the racial classification of any particular individual is also fluid, as context shapes how a person's race is identified. For example, if a person dyes their hair or develops a deep sun tan, their race may change. A person's race may also be viewed differently depending on whether they are one of the lightest or one of the darkest persons in a particular social situation. Within the Brazilian context, a person's race does not exist in a vacuum; rather, it emerges in conjunction with the racial identities of those around them. Further, the Brazilian phrase "money whitens" suggests that a person's race and class cannot be separated from one another. The tendency for wealthier and higher-status Brazilians with dark skin to be considered by others as members of a "lighter" racial group was described by Marvin Harris in the 1960s;

according to his observations, each of the following meets the social and interactional definition of a white person (cited in Degler, 1971:105):

White who is wealthy

White of average wealth

White who is poor

Wealthy mulatto

Mulatto of average wealth

Negro who is wealthy

These examples show that how people dress and their real or perceived social status affects perceptions of their race. The fluidity of race in Brazil stands in stark contrast to the system of classification in South Africa, where one's racial identity is fixed and official.

Given the complexity with which race is defined in Brazil, it is only natural that the social consequences associated with race are also quite complicated. While Brazil certainly has a history of racial inequality, including a history marked by the end of slavery in 1888, there are different opinions as to how severe this history has been. On the one hand, scholars have proclaimed Brazil to be a **racial democracy**—a place where various racial groups live and work side by side with few problems. As evidence, some point out that, unlike the United States and South Africa, Brazil never instituted laws against racial mixing (anti-miscegenation laws). In fact, racial mixing, or *mestizaje*, is a prominent part of Brazil's racial history. It is estimated that perhaps as many as one in five white Brazilians marries someone of a different color (Lima 2007); this contrasts with about 9 percent of recent such marriages in the United States. Throughout the 1900s, concerns about racial purity or formal practices of racial segregation were unheard of in Brazil. Indeed, throughout the twentieth century, Brazilian scholars, citizens, and politicians expressed a sense of pride in having distinctly "fraternal" (brotherly) interracial relations.

Other scholars have commented on the profound inequalities in Brazil. While the most prominent form of inequality is found across social classes, some have critiqued the notion that Brazil is a "racial democracy." Scholars like Florestan Fernandes and Edward Telles have pointed out that, just like the United States, the racial culture of Brazil varies across regions, so that while one region may appear to have relatively democratic race relations, other regions may be characterized by greater racial inequality—depending, for example, on who has settled in those areas and the degree of mixing that has taken place. A more dramatic point of view comes from American historian Carl Degler (1971), who argues that Brazil's racial mixing can be viewed as a sign of racism, rather than evidence against. In his view, the Brazilian government invited migration from Europe while internal populations embraced interracial marriages (mestizaje) as a way to dilute the black (former) slave population and, essentially, whiten it. It is, moreover, well documented that the standard of living in Brazil is higher among whites than it is among nonwhites. Brazilian census data, for example, show that whites earn nearly twice as much as nonwhites and are about three times more likely to finish or pursue a college degree.

Such disparities call into question the long-persistent national myth that Brazil is a racial democracy. It remains, though, that interracial mixing and a lack of legal segregation are part of the nation's history. In his groundbreaking book *Race in Another America*, the sociologist Edward Telles (2006) concludes that Brazil is marked by *both* relative equality of *interpersonal* relations and serious inequalities in the distribution of *institutionalized* wealth and power. The recognition that Brazil is not a racial democracy is evident in the fact that affirmative action policies—giving blacks an advantage in college admissions—have recently been implemented. Since the early 2000s in Brazil there has been, in the words of professor Ibram H. Rogers (2012), a "vibrant national mainstream discussion of racism, and new dynamic legislators and laws to undo its effects." What is fascinating about the affirmative action law is that implementation relies on a board of experts to view photographs and make determinations of applicants' racial identities. Thus, despite the fact that Brazil has long had a very fluid and contextual system of racial classification, these new procedures with the intention of reducing racial boundaries may have the unintended effect of both solidifying and formalizing the boundaries between groups.

The cases of South Africa and Brazil represent noticeably different approaches to the social construction of race. By taking a brief stopover in Europe, we can gather some final lessons on the topic. Throughout much of the continent, the notion of "race" has generally fallen out of favor. In part, this reflects the social uses to which this term was put during the Nazi Holocaust, where "race scientists" made claims about the alleged genetic inferiority of particular races and systematically exterminated them as such. Today, "The European Union rejects theories which attempt to determine the existence of separate human races" (Council Directive 2000/43/EC). By contrast, many European nations prefer the notion of ethnicity, both because of the baggage presented by the term "race" and because European history has been shaped by ethnic identities and struggles (e.g., Bosnians, Kosovar Albanians, and Serbians).

France provides another interesting approach to "race." An ethnically diverse country with immigrants from southern Europe and former African colonies, France is officially a **"race-blind" society**. What that means is that for the purposes of public policy, the French government neither collects census data on the racial characteristics of its residents nor implements policies that provide targeted benefits to specific racial groups. The race-blind policies are, to an extent, a reaction to Nazi race science and neo-Nazi groups that still seek to divide society based on racial grounds. Yet these policies also reflect the uniquely French concept of citizenship. An important part of French culture is to emphasize the collective French identity, focusing on citizenship, nationality, and language. From this perspective, being French comes first and should be emphasized above all other differences—whether based on language or race. To that end, France outlawed "hate speech," so that it is a crime to engage in racial defamation, provoke racial hatred, or organize a group that promotes racism. That said, racial and ethnic conflict is still an issue in France. Since 2005, there have been periodic riots throughout the country, many of which are seen as the result of economic frustrations felt by young immigrants from Africa. Soccer stadiums have erupted in ethnic taunts by the fans against players from African countries, while coaches for national development programs have admitted to setting quotas that limit players of African descent. Despite these events, writes political scientist Erick Bleich (2001), "France has proven less interested in and adept at punishing discrimination in jobs, housing, and in provision of goods and services" compared to other European countries and the United States. Thus, while France seems committed to addressing racism on the one hand, it has not escaped racial and ethnic inequality, on the other.

EXPLORING ACTIVISM:
THE CAMPAIGN AGAINST ETHNIC STUDIES

Does talking about race perpetuate racism and inequality? What about learning about racial and ethnic history in schools? Is it possible that courses devoted to multicultural topics or "ethnic studies" do more harm than good? From the perspective of some politicians, the answer is "Yes." In 2010, the Arizona legislators passed House Bill 2281 on the premise that "public school pupils should be taught to treat and value each other as individuals and not be taught to resent or hate other races or classes of people." In accordance with this principle, the state banned any course within the public school system that:

1. Promotes the overthrow of the federal or state government or the Constitution
2. Promotes resentment toward any race or class (e.g., racism and classism)
3. Advocates ethnic solidarity instead of being individuals
4. Is designed for a certain ethnicity

That said, the bill still allows for courses that include the discussion of controversial issues, including the "holocaust, any other instance of genocide," or the "historical oppression of a particular group of people based on ethnicity, race, or class."

One of the strongest supporters of the bill was Tom Horne, who served as Arizona's attorney general from 2011–2015, and the state's superintendent of public instruction from 2003–2011. Of primary importance was his wish to do away with Mexican American studies programs, arguing that the program teaches "destructive ethnic chauvinism" (excessive group pride) and works from the assumption that Mexican Americans are oppressed. Horne, however, believed that "people are individuals, not exemplars of racial groups." Within the context of a society that offers ample opportunity, he would rather students learn "what they can do, their ability to appreciate beauty, their character, and not what race into which they are born." The goal of his law, then, is to teach about ethnicity in relation to individual attributes rather than group conflict. In fact, other conservative groups—including the Ayn Rand Institute—agree that ethnic studies programs sometimes promote a new form of racism and encourage ethnic overidentification; a higher goal of educational institutions, they believe, should be to emphasize individual identities and achievement.

While HB 2281 stands as law, there exists ongoing opposition to the bill. Bloggers and some in the liberal news media have characterized it as "whitewashing the curriculum and writing Mexican Americans, Native Americans and other non-Anglo ethnic groups out of the curriculum" (alternet.com.) According to the *Chronicle of Higher Education*, the bill represents "a huge loss for dominant culture students who will also be schooled in ignorance and a sadly flattened understanding of our world." A student protest group, UNIDOS (United Non-Discriminatory Individuals Demanding Our Studies), has spoken out before legislators and school board members. According to their website, their primary goal is to "increase student interest in education and give us a chance to learn about not only our own culture, but others as well" (Biggers 2011). From their point of view, a broader historical understanding and the ability to see one's own group within it has a positive educational payoff.

While research is hard to come by, the question remains as to whether learning about ethnic identities and conflict enhances education or whether it further divides. Gordon Allport's **contact hypothesis** postulates that interpersonal contact is one of the best mechanisms for reducing racial and ethnic prejudice. Simply having contact with or understanding of other groups, according to this perspective, may be sufficient for altering stereotypes and generating greater appreciation for diversity. It remains, though, that what is taught in our schools is a matter for political debate and social activism. As pointed out by sociologist Amy Binder in her award-winning book *Contentious Curricula*, these debates are about much more than social and scientific "truths;" indeed, they capture tensions as activists fight over whose perspectives should be told, how, and with what consequences.

TRAVELING BACK IN TIME

While much can be learned about the social construction of race by traveling to places like South Africa and Brazil, it is also true that similar lessons can be learned by examining the notion of race within the United States. Here, we jump into our time machine to see how, even within the United States, the concept of race has been in a continual state of change. Once again, our lesson shows significant variability—variability that cannot be linked to emerging science—in terms of how many racial groups are acknowledged, how individuals are assigned to particular racial groups, and the consequences associated with being placed in one group versus another. Yet in order to take this historical journey, we must return to the question when the concept of "race" was initially invented within Western thought.

As mentioned earlier, sociologists generally think of race as an invention. While humans had been traveling the globe for centuries, encountering people who looked different from the ones back home, these differences were not always explained in "racial" or biological terms. Within Western society, during the Age of Exploration, phenotypic differences were typically interpreted through a religious lens. Coming from a society where the Bible and religious authorities explained most social and natural phenomena, the "discovery" of different-looking people in Asia, Africa, and the

New World was viewed through the biblical story of Ham—Noah's cursed son. As described in the book of Genesis, Ham betrayed his father and was then cast out of Israel; sent into Africa and cursed by God with the mark of black skin. During the eighteenth and nineteenth centuries, this biblical story was used as justification for why black Africans deserved to be exploited under slavery. In short, prior to the invention of race as a scientific concept, within Western cultures people with dark skin were constructed as a savage race of heathens, in contrast to the civilized and Christian people of Europe.

Even after emerging as a scientific concept, the notion of race has been reinvented periodically within the United States. Throughout its history, the U.S. Census has been an important source of information on how race has been constructed. As a window into official definitions of race, the Census indicates that the number of races identified within the United States has fluctuated dramatically over time. Since its first appearance in 1790, the U.S. Census has included questions about race. Initially, the main distinction was between "free white" persons and slaves. Throughout the 1800s, the Census introduced new questions, broadening its inquiry into whites, slaves, free "colored" people, and eventually mulattos—mixed race persons. It was in the 1870 Census that, for the first time, census takers were asked to classify whether residents were Chinese (a broad category including all Asians) or American Indian. Over the next 100 years, the "Chinese" category was broken down into more specific Asian nationalities. Today, the race question on the Census asks people of Asian descent to select their specific national background; the government then aggregates these responses into a broader "Asian" racial category. The term "race" was first used in the 1890 census.

The fact that race is more a social concept than a biological concept is seen in the various ways in which "black people" have been categorized by the Census. Returning to the case of President Obama, this means that his race is not actually dependent on his biological makeup; it is dependent on the particular historical period in which he might find himself. When the term race was first used in the 1890 census, the government officially recognized four different racial groups of African (black) descent: black, mulatto (half black), quadroon (one-quarter black), and octoroon (one-eighth black). In 1930, the U.S. Census fundamentally transformed the categorization of black people. Rather than identify distinctions within this group, as had been done previously, the U.S. Census adopted the rule of **hypodescent**: anyone with a single drop of black blood" would now be considered black—known as "the one-drop rule." The one-drop rule illustrates the notion that race is a social and political concept due to the fact that it came about at the same time that race science and the eugenics movement sought to draw firmer boundaries around the "pure" white race. Now, only people whose ancestry was 100 percent white could legitimately claim to be white; conversely, a person who is virtually all white but has *one* black four-times-great-grandparent would now be classified as *Negro*. Across the nation, people saw their race change with this new taxonomy (and laws such as Virginia's Racial Integrity Act of 1924). Within the context of a segregated society, this meant that many people's rights and privileges (like whether they can vote or where they can go to school) changed right along with it. While this change lasted for only one 10-year census cycle, it demonstrates that the concept of race serves the social and political interests of the powerful, as they draw boundaries around groups and allocate or deny privileges to them accordingly.

Similar fluctuations have also appeared in the U.S. Census with respect to Hispanics (or Latinos). Prior to 1940, Mexican was considered a separate race; after 1940, the category of Mexican was eliminated and Mexicans were then categorized as white. It was in 1980 that the United States first asked separate questions about Hispanic origins and race. To this day, the U.S. Census is structured in a way that allows individuals to identify, first, that they are Hispanic in terms of ethnicity and, second, that they

➔ **NOTE: Please answer BOTH Question 5 about Hispanic origin and Question 6 about race. For this census, Hispanic origins are not races.**

5. Is this person of Hispanic, Latino, or Spanish origin?

- ☐ **No,** not of Hispanic, Latino, or Spanish origin
- ☐ Yes, Mexican, Mexican Am., Chicano
- ☐ Yes, Puerto Rican
- ☐ Yes, Cuban
- ☐ Yes, another Hispanic, Latino, or Spanish origin — *Print origin, for example, Argentinean, Colombian, Dominican, Nicaraguan, Salvadoran, Spaniard, and so on.* ↘

[   ]

6. What is this person's race? *Mark* ☒ *one or more boxes.*

- ☐ White
- ☐ Black, African Am., or Negro
- ☐ American Indian or Alaska Native — *Print name of enrolled or principal tribe.* ↘

[   ]

☐ Asian Indian	☐ Japanese	☐ Native Hawaiian
☐ Chinese	☐ Korean	☐ Guamanian or Chamorro
☐ Filipino	☐ Vietnamese	☐ Samoan
☐ Other Asian — *Print race, for example, Hmong, Laotian, Thai, Pakistani, Cambodian, and so on.* ↘		☐ Other Pacific Islander — *Print race, for example, Fijian, Tongan, and so on.* ↘

[   ]

- ☐ Some other race — *Print race.* ↘

[   ]

Illustrating the socially constructed nature of race, U.S. Census classification has changed numerous times. Currently, "Hispanic" is not considered a race.

are white, black, or other in terms of race. Presently, however, the U.S. Census is considering re-categorizing "Hispanic" as a race. Nancy Lopez, director of the Institute for the Study of "Race" and Social Justice at the University of New Mexico, opposes the idea. She worries that lumping all Hispanics into one race would result in less detailed ethnic data, making it more difficult to monitor discrimination in housing, employment, political participation, education, and elsewhere. "If we collapse race and ethnicity as interchangeable concepts," she said, "we may miss the opportunity to examine whether there are unique experiences among co-ethnics that may occupy very different racial statuses" (Lopez 2013). Angelo Falcón, the president of the National Institute for Latino Policy and former census official, opposes the change on practical grounds. According to Falcón, focus groups on the matter found that "by combining the two questions, you get a better response rate. . . . It was clearer to people and more inclusive" (Ayala and Huet 2013) The classification of Hispanics, again, shows that there is nothing absolute or definitive about the concept of race; that understandings and classifications change when political pressures and practicalities come into play.

Outside of formal classifications of race, our time travels would also show considerable fluctuations in how Americans *informally* identify and enumerate the concept of race. While never as wide-ranging as the Brazilian taxonomy, informal notions of race in the United States have included far more categories than the formal systems of categorization. For example, at the turn of the twenty-first century, white Americans may have been further differentiated into Anglo-Saxon, Nordic, Semitic, Alpine, and Mediterranean "races." These distinctions were especially popular during the early twentieth century: as immigration from southern and eastern Europe swelled, politicians and other leaders became dissatisfied with such an inclusive definition of whiteness and responded by creating a hierarchy of whites. Informally, there are also colloquial distinctions among those defined as black in the United States. Although they do not constitute separate racial groups, variations in pigmentation among black people include *chocolate*, *café au lait*, *mocha*, *caramel*, *high yellow*, and *redbone* (the latter two referring to light-skinned blacks, like Beyoncé). With the onset of social media, people have even begun posting to sites like Twitter using the hashtag *#teamredbone* as a way of embracing their unique version of blackness. These distinctions, though, sometimes cause tensions, as there are perceptions that "light is right" and those with lighter skin experience more privilege in society. Also known as *colorism*, this phenomenon will be discussed in greater detail in Chapter 8.

The social construction of race is also evident in how race is assigned. Our historical journey through the United States would reveal that never has the United States been as rigid as South Africa when it comes to determining a person's race. With respect to formal procedures, prior to 1960, it was U.S. Census policy that census workers (enumerators) would determine the race of those they interviewed. Surely, by searching for visual clues and asking questions mainly about their country of origin, enumerators made mistakes in their data collection. In the 1960s, individuals were given, for the first time, the opportunity to *self-identify* their racial group. Therefore, were President Obama filling out Census forms in 1990, he would have the choice of

checking white or black. It was not until 2000, though, that the U.S. Census first offered people the right to self-identify as members of one or more racial groups. With
this new "multiracial option," Mr. Obama—and millions like him—would see their
race officially change within the context of official government statistics.

In a few rare, but fascinating, cases, various courts have offered legal rulings to determine an individual's race. First, in 1923, Baghat Singh Thind petitioned for U.S. citizenship. When his petition was denied, a legal battle ensured to determine whether
he—a native of India—could qualify as white under the law. In the United States today,
race or nationality cannot be used to deny someone citizenship; at that time, only
"whites" could become naturalized citizens. The definition of "white," however, was a
bit murky. Anthropological definitions focused on the *Caucasoid* race—referring to
groups with origins west of the Caucasus Mountains. Thind and his lawyers argued
that as someone of Aryan descent—a geographical area that includes northern India
and feeds into the Caucasus—he is, technically, white. The court, however, did not
concur. While Thind and his lawyers were technically correct, the judges ultimately
ruled that "white" has a popularly accepted social meaning, above and beyond its scientific meaning, and that those of Asian or Indo-European descent did not fit this popularly accepted notion.

The notion that you can be "black
by law" but not by self-identification
describes the ruling of a 1983 legal case.
With the plans of traveling to South
America for her honeymoon, Susie
Guillory Phipps sought a copy of her
birth certificate to apply for a passport.
After identifying as white for all of her
48 years, Phipps was shocked to learn
that her Louisiana birth certificate listed
her as "Colored." An ensuing investigation revealed that this racial designation
was not a mistake; rather, Phipps's great-
great-great-great-grandmother was an
enslaved black woman. Under law, anyone
having 1/32 "Negro blood" was classified
as black. The court battle began when
Phipps and her siblings sought to have
their race re-classified—and to do away
with Louisiana's method of racial classification. Ultimately, the family lost their
case. Although the state of Louisiana
eventually repealed their "one-drop"
rule, the decision was not retroactively
applied. Therefore, Phipps and her siblings

Bhagat Singh Thind sued the U.S., claiming he
qualified as White. He was denied, illustrating
the shifting and political nature of racial
classification.

remained black under the law—a reality that she rejected by describing her social reality: "I am White. I am all White. I was raised as a White child. I went to White schools. I married White twice."

One other fascinating aspect of race in the United States is the shifting boundaries that surround various racial groups. For example, the racial group we call "white" has gradually expanded its boundaries over time. Through the magic of time travel, many of us would be given different racial identities, depending on when and where we emerged from our time machine. Perhaps the example that best illustrates this is Americans of Irish descent. Despite the fact that they originate from islands separated by only about 12 miles at its closest point, during the 1700s and 1800s, English and Irish people in the United States were generally considered different "races." There were the civilized, Protestant "Anglos," on the one hand, and the more barbaric, Catholic Irish, on the other. In some states, birth certificates and marriage licenses listed those of Irish descent as "Colored." Although this labeling was not uniform across the United States, it is clear that through the late 1800s, Irish Americans were not viewed as white or as falling into the same category as Americans of English, German, or Scandinavian descent. In many cities, anti-Irish sentiment was common, with "Irish Need Not Apply" or "Protestant Only" signs appearing in help-wanted ads and apartment buildings. As immigrants to America, some of whom came through indentured servitude, the waves of Irish newcomers often started their lives in the United States close to the bottom of the hierarchy; there, they competed for jobs with black Americans, with whom they seemed to have more in common than their European brethren.

How is it, then, that the Americans of Irish descent "became white"? Sociologists Michael Omi and Howard Winant (1994) coined the term **racialization** to describe the process by which new racial meanings are applied to groups or social practices. The strength of this term is that it draws attention to the fact that it is humans, through the process of social construction, who define the meaning of race, the number of races, and the lines between racial groups. In the case of Irish Americans, they became white in part by actively distancing themselves from Chinese immigrants in California and

What is the race of Susie Guillory Phipps? There is no one answer. Racial classification depends on historical and cultural context.

black Americans elsewhere and in part by becoming middle class. As described in the work of historian Noel Ignatiev (2008), Irish immigrants banded together in neighborhoods and job sites, forming social and political organizations where they sought to exclude Chinese and black workers and ensure their own economic and political success. By the early 1900s, the economic upward mobility of Irish Americans, together with the fact that new waves of immigrants were arriving from southern and eastern Europe, meant that the Irish gradually moved closer to white Americans and were replaced with a new racial "other."

Throughout the first half of the twentieth century, various groups that had once been considered an exotic other—including those of Polish, Greek, Romanian, and Jewish descent—were absorbed into the category known as "white." In her book *How Jews Became White Folks and What That Says about Race in America*, Karen Brodkin (1998) identifies two general mechanisms in the racialization of these groups. First, as their representation swelled through immigration to America, these groups became increasingly visible and increasingly threatening and exotic to the existing racial order. Second, over several decades, these groups gradually moved into the economic mainstream. In doing so, like the Irish a decade or two earlier, they grew closer to the white or "WASP" (white Anglo-Saxon Protestant) establishment and further from the more marginal black and brown populations. It was the G.I. Bill (a package of benefits for veterans) following World War II that gave Jews increased access to higher education, suburban lifestyles, and small business ownership. Echoing the pattern of an earlier generation, black G.I.s were excluded from these benefits, in part due to residential and educational segregation.

By the time we emerged from our time capsule in the mid-1950s, we would encounter a society with a broad, inclusive definition of whiteness and a society in which the primary racial divide was that separating whites and blacks. By taking a historical look at race in the United States, and especially by looking at the experiences of Americans of Irish and Jewish descent, we learn that "white" is not a fixed category based on underlying genetic traits, that the boundaries around racial groups are in a state of flux, and that "money whitens"—even in the United States.

EXPLORING INTERSEXUALITY:
RACE, CLASS, AND BEING NATIVE

Across the United States, strict laws exist to determine who can be considered a legitimate member of a Native American tribe. While the specific guidelines vary from tribe to tribe, many use a **blood quantum** rule to establish tribal membership; blood quantum refers to the proportion of ancestry that is of direct tribal descent. Where the Yomba Shoshone tribe of Nevada requires ½ blood quantum—a fairly rigorous standard—other tribes, such as the Eastern Band of Cherokees of North Carolina, confer tribal membership to those with only 1/16 blood quantum (the equivalent of having one great-great-grandparent with tribal blood).

Like many Native American tribes, the Mdewakanton Sioux use a specific "blood quantum" to determine tribal membership. This membership can be quite valuable.

Officially dating back to the Indian Reorganization Act of 1934, the purpose of the blood quantum rule was to identify those who might qualify for any financial benefits that might accrue to tribal members through treaties with the U.S. federal government (from the sale of lands, for example). In recent decades, some of these regulations have become more hotly contested. The reason for the recent controversy surrounding these laws is that some Native American tribes are generating substantial revenues from casino gaming and other forms of economic development. In light of these new sources of income, some tribes have implemented new rules to make tribal membership more restrictive.

Although gambling is heavily restricted and regulated in the United States, treaty agreements have given many Native American tribes the right to establish casinos on their reservations. It is reported that revenues from "Indian gaming" may reach $27 billion annually; law requires that these revenues be fed back into the community through economic development programs. Yet because 65 percent of all gaming revenues are earned by just 12 percent of all casinos, the economic benefits from Indian gaming are not widely shared. Whereas some reservations have used revenues to create jobs and build new hospitals and schools, economic development programs remain, as the average poverty rate on Native American reservations across the United States remains at 28 percent—twice the national rate!

Yet in some tribes—usually those lucky enough to be located near an urban center—casino gaming has been incredibly successful. In such cases, casino revenues may be used both for economic development and direct payments to tribal members. In such tribes, "race" becomes a class issue: those who can document their tribal membership benefit tremendously, while those who cannot, lose out. The Mdewakanton Sioux, who operate the Mystic Lake Casino outside of Minneapolis-St. Paul, have kept their tribal membership small. The *New York Times* reported in 2012 that tribal members receive more than $1 million per year from casino revenues—making them, by far, the most well compensated of all Native tribes.

Within Native American tribes, the issue of tribal membership can cause economic inequalities, tensions, and claims about who is a "real Indian." That said, competition resulting from the rush to build new casinos, combined with loosening restrictions on Internet gaming, may put in peril the revenues of successful and less successful tribes alike.

WHAT DOES IT ALL MEAN? THE FUTURE OF RACE

At the heart of the social construction of race is the insight that the concept of race—how many there are, who's in which group—has changed over time. It is entirely reasonable, then, to assume that the future of race will be different from the present. One question regarding the future of race asks whether new groups will be incorporated into the "white" category in years to come. Sociologist Min Zhou (2004), in particular, asks whether Asian Americans are "becoming white." On the one hand, she argues that by climbing of the economic ladder, intermarrying with whites, and assimilating into majority-white schools and communities, they have followed a pattern similar to Irish and Jewish Americans before them. On the basis of these patterns, Asian Americans are often referred to as the **model minority**—a group that has defied many of the negative patterns commonly found among minority populations, and a model that should be emulated by others. At the same time, Zhou also points out that many Americans of Asian descent embrace their ethnic identities. Rather than wishing to **assimilate**—or blend, melting-pot style—into the dominant culture, their goal is to retain their cultural distinctness, as Vietnamese, Cambodian, Filipino, etc., while obtaining the same rights and legitimacy of those simply considered American. As they gain many markers of mainstream success, members of some of these groups also wish to point out that despite their "model minority" status, many Asian Americans still face discrimination, as well as the pressure to continually prove that they are loyal to the United States and as American as anyone else.

A second pattern that demands attention is that within the United States, the racial composition is expected to change significantly in the next several decades. If we were to take our time machine into the future, we would learn that by 2060, whites will no longer be the numerical majority. Based on projections calculated by the U.S. Census Bureau, the white (non-Hispanic) population is expected to decrease from about 63 percent to 34 percent, and the Hispanic population is expected to nearly double, going from about 17 percent to 31 percent. Overall, no group will constitute a simple majority (see Figure 4.2). These changing demographics reflect two underlying patterns: one, that white Americans have fewer babies than Hispanics (and others); and two, that immigration from Latin American and Asian countries continues, while immigration from European countries has largely leveled off.

What will these changing demographics mean for social, economic, and political life? If white Americans no longer represent a numerical majority of the

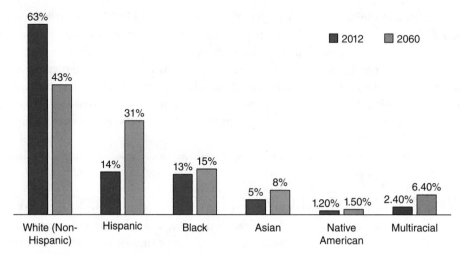

Figure 4.2 Race in the United States.
(Source: U.S. Census)

population, does that mean that they will no longer hold the majority of economic and political power? It is important to recall that even though white people were long the numerical minority in South Africa, they still held majority control over most social institutions. Currently in the United States, the two major political parties—Democrats and Republicans—are courting the expanding Hispanic population; their goal is to make sure their party remains true to its core message while also appealing to this growing demographic. Indeed, many commentators concluded that Barack Obama won the presidency in 2012 due to his ability to attract the vote of Hispanic Americans. Although Hispanic Americans remain significantly underrepresented in the U.S. Congress—where they constitute about 6 percent of elected officials but comprise 13 percent of the overall American population—it is clear that their influence is growing, along with the expanding Asian American population.

Finally, it is worth considering whether the boundaries dividing particular racial groups may be blurring. As mentioned earlier, the 2000 Census was the first to provide Americans the option of identifying with one or more race. This change came about from groups who wanted greater accuracy in describing their race. According to the 2010 census, nearly 3 percent of Americans identify as multiracial. Some expect this number to rise to 20 percent by 2050. For sociologists Jennifer Lee and Frank Bean (2003), the rising number of multiracial Americans represents "a profound loosening of rigid racial and ethnic boundaries" (p. 26), with people increasingly willing to see race as a complex, multifaceted identity. Although one part of this trend involves new waves of immigrants to the United States—immigrants not subjected to the baggage of the "one-drop rule"—it also reflects rising rates of intermarriage and the children of those unions. Since the early 1970s, the percentage of those who marry across racial and ethnic lines has increased more than 500 percent—from less than 1 percent of all marriages in 1970 to more than 5 percent of all marriages in recent years. The increase in interracial marriages across all groups, along with individuals' increased desire to claim a mixed-race background, has led some to claim that we are becoming a nation of "mutts"—a true melting pot with increasingly blurred lines.

For the time being, though, the projection of a nation of mutts may be premature. Perhaps the biggest reason is that rates of interracial marriage vary across groups. Data from the Pew Research Center indicate that while nearly 31 percent of all "new" marriages among Asians are across racial and ethnic lines, only 9 percent of whites and 15 percent of blacks married outside of their racial groups. Looking at all existing marriages, only about 3 percent of whites are in interracial marriages; among blacks this number is about 5.5 percent. These numbers are considerably smaller than the relatively high rates of interracial marriage among Asian Americans and Hispanics— where about 16 percent married outside their group (often with whites). From a sociological perspective, these numbers indicate a lessening of "social distance" and greater contact across groups; yet the boundaries between racial groups are not shifting evenly. Looking at these patterns, perhaps the future of race will involve little revision in who "counts" as black, with more mixing and blurring among those who identify as Asian, Hispanic, and white.

CHAPTER 4: REVIEW OF KEY POINTS

- *Race* refers to a category based on phenotypical or perceived biological traits, while *ethnicity* refers to a social and cultural category.
- Although the classification of Hispanic has changed over time, the U.S. Census currently labels Hispanic as an ethnicity rather than a race.
- The concept of race identity is a fairly recent "invention." It emerged in the 1800s, as religious explanations for social phenomena were replaced by scientific explanations.
- Swedish biologist Carl Linnaeus was the first to develop a racial taxonomy. He believed that racial groups were genetically distinct, had clear boundaries around them, and were characterized by different traits or "humors."
- Modern biology identifies only one race: *Homo sapiens*. Genetic research shows that there is no genetic variation across populations to subdivide them into racial groups.
- The *essentialist perspective* sees racial differences as being rooted in underlying biological differences. The essentialist perspective and *scientific racism* have been used to justify racial inequality.
- The *social constructionist perspective* sees race as historically and cross-culturally variable. Racial boundaries and differences between races are created and reinforced by humans through socialization and the social structure.
- Examples from South Africa, Brazil, France, earlier periods in the United States, and Native American tribes show profound differences in how many groups were identified, how firmly the boundaries were drawn between them, and the social consequences (privilege) associated with being in one group as opposed to another.
- The rise of cross-racial and cross-ethnic relationships and childbearing suggests a blurring of some racial and ethnic lines in the United States. This suggests a marked increase in the population of multiracial Americans.
- Because whites and blacks have the lowest level of interracial relationships, the "boundaries" around these racial groups are not expected to fade or change significantly in upcoming decades.

CHAPTER 4: QUESTIONS FOR REVIEW

1. What is race? What is ethnicity? Based on your reading of this chapter, how would you label your race and ethnicity? Remember, everyone has both a race and an ethnicity—so you should try to label both.

2. How does the essentialist perspective conceptualize race? More specifically, how does it approach the categorization of races and explain the apparent differences between racial groups?

3. In what sense do supporters of the social constructionist perspective see race as "a myth"? How do they use cross-cultural and historical evidence to argue their case?

4. Throughout history, how have biological or essentialist arguments about race been used to justify racial inequality? To what extent do you think that the belief that Africans and African Americans are superior athletes reflects the essentialist perspective? To what extent do you think such beliefs are harmful?

5. Based on the information presented in this chapter, along with your own critical thinking, what do you think the future of race is in the United States? To what extent do you see shifts among current racial and ethnic categorizations? Do you see the concepts of race and ethnicity having less importance in the future? Why or why not?

KEY TERMS

anthropometry

anti-miscegenation laws

apartheid

assimilate

Bantustans

blood quantum

Carl Linnaeus

contact hypothesis

DNA

eugenics

genetic analysis

genocide

hypodescent

miscegenation

model minority

pencil test

phenotype

physiognomy

Population Registration Act of 1950

race

"race-blind" society

racial democracy

racialization

taxonomy

REFERENCES

Ayala, Elaine and Ellen Huet. 2013. "Hispanic May Be a Race on 2020 Census." *SFGate*, February 4th. Retrieved April 17, 2015 (http://www.sfgate.com/nation/article/Hispanic-may-be-a-race-on-2020-census-4250866.php)

Biggers, Jeff. 2011. "UNIDOS Present Ten Point Resolution on Arizona Ethnic Studies Crisis: 'We Want an Educational System Where Many Cultures Fit.'" Alternet April 27. Retrieved April 17, 2015 (http://www.alternet.org/speakeasy/2011/04/27/unidos-present-ten-point-resolution-on-arizona-ethnic-studies-crisis-%25e2%2580%259cwe-want-an-educational-system-where-many-cultures-fit%25e2%2580%259d)

Bleich, Erik. 2001. "Race Policy in France." *The Brookings Institution* May 1. Retrieved April 17, 2015 (http://www.brookings.edu/research/articles/2001/05/france-bleich)

Brodkin, Karen. 1998. *How Jews Became White Folks and What That Says about Race in America*. New Brunswick, NJ: Rutgers University Press.

Cavalli-Sforza, Luigi Luca, Paolo Menozzi, Alberto Piazza. 1994. *The History and Geography of Human Genes*. Princeton, NJ: Princeton University Press.

Degler, Carl N. 1971. *Neither Black nor White: Slavery and Race Relations in Brazil and the United States*. Madison: University of Wisconsin Press.

Entine, Jon. 2000. *Taboo: Why Black Athletes Dominate Sports and Why We're Afraid to Talk About It*. New York: Public Affairs.

European Union. 2000. *Implementing the Principle of Equal Treatment Between Persons Irrespective of Racial or Ethnic Origin* 2000/43/EC

Gane-McCalla, Casey. 2008. "Top 10 Reasons Obama is Black." Retrieved April 17, 2015 (http://www.dailykos.com/story/2008/12/02/668481/-Top-10-Reasons-Obama-is-Black#)

Harris, Marvin D. 1964. "Racial identity in Brazil." *Luso-Brazilian Review* 1(2): 21–28.

Ignatiev, Noel. 2008. *How the Irish Became White*. London: Routledge.

Katz, Phyllis and Jennifer A. Kofkin. 1997. "Race, Gender, and Young Children." Chapter 3 in *Developmental Psychopathology: Perspectives on Adjustment, Risk, and Disorder*, edited by Suniya S. Luthar, Jacob A. Burack, Dante Cicchetti, and John R. Weisz. Cambridge, UK: Cambridge University Press.

Lee, Jennifer and Frank D. Bean. 2003. "Beyond Black and White: Remaking Race in America." *Contexts* 2:26–33.

Lima, Marcus Eugenio Oliveira. 2007. "Race Relations and Racism in Brazil" (a review essay). *Culture and Psychology* 13:461–473.

Lopez, Nancy. 2013. "Some Critical Thoughts on the Census Bureau's Proposals to Change the Race and Hispanic Questions." *La Prensa* January 11. Retrieved April 17, 2015 (http://laprensa-sandiego.org/editorial-and-commentary/commentary/some-critical-thoughts-on-the-census-bureaus-proposals-to-change-the-race-and-hispanic-questions/)

Morton, Samuel George. 1839. *Crania Americana*. Philadelphia, PA: J. Dobson.

Omi, Michael and Howard Winant. 1994. *Racial Formations in the United States: from the 1960s to the 1990s*. London: Routledge.

Rasmussen, Birgit Brander, Irene J. Nexica, Eric Klinenberg, and Matt Wray. 2001. *The Making and Unmaking of Whiteness*. Durham, NC: Duke University Press.

Rogers, Ibrahm H. 2012. "Brazil's Affirmative-Action Quotas—Progress?" *The Chronicle of Higher Education* November 12. Retrieved April 17, 2015 (http://chronicle.com/blogs/conversation/2012/11/05/brazils-affirmative-action-quotas-progress/)

Yates, Clinton. 2012. "Barack Obama: Let's Not Forget That He's America's First Bi-racial President." *Washington Post* November, 8. Retrieved on April 17, 2015 (http://www.washingtonpost.com/blogs/therootdc/post/barack-obama-lets-not-forget-that-hes-americas-first-bi-racial-president/2012/11/08/938765d4-29b1-11e2-b4e0-346287b7e56c_blog.html)

Zhou, Min. 2004. "Are Asian Americans Becoming 'White'?" *Contexts* 3:29–37.

Living the American Dream?
Understanding Social Class

I was five years old the first time I rode an airplane; it was the private airplane of the 1970s folk music legend, John Denver. Depending on your age and musical interests, you may not have heard of him, but he was a big deal. At the time I rode on his plane, I was also on welfare. The fact that these two facets of my childhood could coexist provides valuable insight into the concept of *social class*. With my parents' divorce in the mid-1970s, my dad moved to the exclusive resort town of Aspen, Colorado, a place where locals embraced, in the words of John Denver, a "Rocky Mountain High" life-style (if you know what I mean). There, my dad rubbed shoulders with wealthy people on ski vacations, celebrities, and other movers and shakers. As two guys who had spent some time living in Minnesota, John Denver and my dad struck up rapport; soon, my dad went to work for him, building custom furniture and helping with projects around the house. When I boarded John's private plane in the winter of 1976, and flew from Minnesota to Aspen, the flight was a personal favor from John to my dad. Meanwhile, my parents' divorce left my mom struggling. As she went back to college to pursue an associate's degree, she applied for welfare and began work as a grocery store cashier. Each day at school I got in the line marked "Free and Reduced Lunch"; at home I became accustomed to statements like, "We'll have to wait until my check comes on the first of the month . . ." or "Maybe we can go shopping when I get my tax return."

Nearly 40 years later, I am solidly middle class; it's been a long time since I've been on welfare *or* had a personal brush with celebrity fame. Yet some aspects of my dad's life continue to raise intriguing questions about social class. For example, as a skilled carpenter and construction supervisor in Aspen, he works on houses with market values well over $15 million. His clients include names and faces familiar in the media, entertainment, and corporate worlds. One of his most recent projects was a nearly $30 million house for someone who made a fortune selling products on a home shopping channel. While my dad makes a solid income, he also lives in what is technically sub-sidized housing. In a town like Aspen, Colorado, where the *median* home price is around $4 million, the city offers "employee housing" so that locals with ordinary jobs

What is social class? While exposed to elite cultural capital, I grew up with very modest financial capital.

can afford to live and work there. Employee housing typically includes modest townhomes in the price range $350,000 (with some newer and larger properties valued in excess of $1 million); because the local government subsidizes these housing options, there is a limit to how much they are allowed to appreciate in value (thus limiting profits for sellers). Meanwhile, my dad continues to rub shoulders with local artists and architects and has made plenty of friends among the wealthy clients he has built homes for and sold his works of art to.

The examples from my own life raise important questions about both what social class is and the kinds of social class inequalities that exist in the United States. The fact that I enjoyed the luxury of flying on a private plane while living close to poverty raises confusing questions about how social class is defined. When it comes to social class, what matters—income, wealth, education, social connections, or lifestyle? My dad's story, on the other hand, raises troubling questions about social class inequality in the United States: Why is it that some Americans are able to own homes—sometimes several of them—with values well into the millions, while others—including hardworking Americans—live in subsidized housing and struggle to make ends meet?

What makes the topic of social class unique compared to other identities discussed in this text is that sociologists disagree—sometimes vehemently—over how a person's social class is defined, how many social classes there are, and why socioeconomic inequality exists. Where sociologists agree, however, is that there is a tremendous amount of social class inequality in the United States—and that it seems to be increasing.

DEFINING SOCIAL CLASS: WHAT IS IT AND HOW MANY ARE THERE?

When it comes to *social class*, sociologists disagree about what it is and how many there are. The heated nature of this discussion makes sense when you consider that many sociologists see social class as the most important concept in their field. It is this concept that captivated sociologists when they developed the field 150 years ago, and it continues to be the most common topic of sociological research. For simplicity's sake, let's define **social class** as a group of people with shared life chances, economic opportunities, and lifestyle. While the concept of "economic opportunities" acknowledges that money matters, this broader definition hints at sociologists' belief that it is not the only thing that determines a person's social class.

One sociological model of social class often features the image of a pyramid, where each layer is composed of people with different levels of education, occupational skills, and, above all else, income. Included in the image of the pyramid are several assumptions. First is the notion that there are more people at the bottom of the class structure than at the top. Second is the notion that social classes are organized into strata (layers) that are organized hierarchically: each class is situated above, below, or between the others. While the exact number of strata is open to debate, Americans typically use terms like middle, upper-middle, and lower-middle to identity the classes within this system (see Figure 5.1). While this pyramid or layer cake–like model of social class reflects how many Americans think about social class—with lots of levels and slight variations among them—some sociologists think of social class in a very different way.

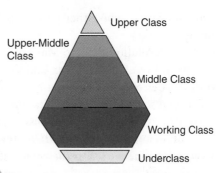

Figure 5.1 Conventional model of social class.
(Sources: Thompson & Hickey, Society in Focus, 2005; U.S. Census Bureau personal income & education of individuals 25+, 2005)

The oldest, simplest, and most controversial definition of social class was offered by German philosopher and aspiring revolutionary Karl Marx. Born in 1818, Marx came of age in an era of rapid social change. As he traveled throughout Europe, he observed the transformations of the **Industrial Revolution**. With industrialization and urbanization, workers and families went from having direct control over their work and economic output to working in factories where they had little control. As the factory system grew, Marx hypothesized, workers would become more and more exploited, while factory owners would become more and more powerful. His work brings to mind images like those of Victor Hugo's *Les Miserables*, Charles Dickens's *Oliver Twist* and *Bleak House*, which depicted poverty within Victorian England, and the photographs of factory workers in the United States, where women and children were routinely locked inside of factories and had few, if any, rights. In his best known work, *Das Kapital* (1867), Marx described factory owners as "vampires" who "suck" the life out of the workers.

Marx viewed the social class system as incredibly simple, composed of two and only two classes. According to Marx, a person's social class is determined by their relationship to the **means of production**—those things that are used to generate profit. In Marx's time, they were the factories; in today's *postindustrial economy* they are still the factories, but they are also the banks, and media, and technology companies that produce our culture and communications. Marx argued that there are only two possible relationships to the means of production: either you own them and control them *or* you work for the people who own them and control them. Marx referred to these two groups as the **bourgeoisie** (owners) and **proletariat** (workers), respectively. The simplicity of Marx's system derived from his belief that capitalism is an inherently exploitative system, where one group controls their own fate and another group is at their disposal.

In Marx's theory, those who control the means of production—the bourgeoisie—control every aspect of society. Those who control the economic foundations of society, Marx posited, eventually assume control of the political structure, along with the educational system and media. Accordingly, those who do not control the means of production—the proletariat—are at the mercy of the bourgeoisie in terms of political power, educational experiences, and the ideas and information transmitted through the media. For Marx, people share a social class when they comprise a group of people who either have autonomy and control over their lives (and others) or do not.

As a revolutionary, Karl Marx thought that one day this system of *haves* and *have nots* would break down. Marx said that the capitalist system "contains the seeds of its own self-destruction." Eventually, he theorized, the proletariat would become so miserable and so aware of its exploitation that they would no longer support the capitalist class. By developing a sense of **class consciousness**, they would realize that they have strength in numbers and would eventually rise up against the bourgeoisie and usher in a system that better serves their interests. Marx called this new system communism.

For Karl Marx, social class was a very simple thing: Do you control the means of production or do you not? For him, it all boiled down to exploitation.

Because Karl Marx formulated his ideas about 150 years ago, and because he formulated them amidst very different economic conditions, it is worth asking whether his ideas of the two-class system are still relevant. For Neo-Marxist scholars like Robert Perrucci and Earl Wysong (2008), the more things change, the more they stay the same. While the postindustrial economy is more complicated than the one observed by Marx—for example, many Americans are now stockholders in the companies they work for, making them both workers and owners—the basic premise remains: some have control over their economic fates while others are at the mercy of the system. In their book *The New Class Society*, Perrucci and Wysong argue that there are *still* just two social classes: the Privileged Class, which makes up 20 percent of American society, and the New Working Class, which makes up the remaining 80 percent. By taking into account people's incomes, wealth, academic credentials, and social connections (what they call *generative capital*), Perrucci and Wysong conclude that the class system is composed of those who have a considerable safety net, one that can sustain them in the event of almost any crisis, and those who lack any real safety, who are one crisis away from devastation. For these Neo-Marxists, there is no middle class: either you have control over your life or you do not.

Max Weber saw complexity in social class. In addition to economic standing and social power, he saw culture and lifestyle as part of social stratification.

Arriving on the scene some 40 years after Marx, Max Weber, a fellow German sociologist, also observed the social changes of the Industrial Revolution. Compared to Marx, he saw social inequality and social standing in more complex terms. First, rather than focus on one trait that determines a person's class (e.g., Marx's emphasis on one's relationship to the means of production), Weber identified *three* traits that determine a person's **socioeconomic status** (SES).

For Weber, a person's social standing is composed of a person's *class*, meaning their economic well-being; *status*, meaning the respect and prestige one possesses; and *power*, or the influence one has over others. Accordingly, SES is defined as more than an economic reality; it also takes into account culture and lifestyle. In this way, a person may occupy a complicated or contradictory social class position. A college professor, for example, may earn an average income, enjoy high status or respect by working in the educational field, and may also have some degree of power especially if she serves as a representative in the local labor union and negotiates work conditions with the university's president or board of trustees.

Max Weber's model of social class is also complicated in terms of how many social classes it identifies. Where Marx saw two and only two classes, Weber saw an indeterminate number of social classes. Because social class is comprised of three elements, and because an individual may be high on one element and relatively low on another, Weber was doubtful that people would unite into clearly defined social classes. While the notion of socioeconomic status partially resembles a continuum, people would naturally "jockey" for position and continually shift boundaries and identification. At times, they may identify with those sharing similar economic positions; at other times, identification may shift to those with whom they share status or lifestyle. Although both he and Marx saw capitalism as contributing to economic exploitation, Weber did not believe that people would develop a sense of class consciousness that would lead them to join together to fight for a more equitable class system.

During the second half of the twentieth century, the most innovative ideas about social class emerged from the mind of French sociologist Pierre Bourdieu. While Bourdieu agreed with Marx and Weber in that he too saw social classes as groups bound together by similar economic realities, he argued that cultural factors play an equally important role in delineating social classes and perpetuating inequality. Central to Bourdieu's model of social class is the concept of **cultural capital**. Cultural capital includes: (1) the cultural items that people consume (*objectified cultural capital*), like a wine cellar or collection of first-edition books; (2) the cultural knowledge that people possess (*embodied cultural capital*), like knowing how to pair wine with food or how to interact at a cocktail party; and (3) the affiliations and connections a person has (*institutionalized cultural capital*), like a degree from a prestigious school or *social capital* in the form of social and business ties.

In his book *Distinction*, Bourdieu (1984) developed a four-class model that combined economic and cultural capital:

1. Those with high economic capital and high cultural capital ("old money" families, CEOs, executives, doctors, and lawyers)
2. Those with high economic capital and low cultural capital ("new money families," entertainers, athletes, and the "Real Housewives" of anywhere)
3. Those with lower economic capital and higher cultural capital (many educators, artists, journalists, and other creative professionals)
4. Those with lower economic capital and lower cultural capital (a large portion of Americans, including custodians, truck drivers, nursing assistants)

The novel contributions of Bourdieu's theory are several. First is the idea that people's cultural knowledge and behaviors help define their class position: cultural capital binds some people together and can be used as a justification for excluding others (from a job, club, social circle, etc.). Second, cultural capital can be exchanged for economic capital (and vice versa). Individuals whose cultural capital (having gone to a prestigious college, knowing about Abstract Expressionist art) marks them as a member of the elite may be welcomed into that group and may be given financial opportunities because of it (jobs, contracts, art sales, etc.). Third, rather than a model with hierarchical layers, this model shows—like Weber's—that social class is quite complicated, with individuals having privilege in one domain but not in another.

Learning about Bourdieu's theory of cultural capital as an undergraduate was an epiphany for me. It helped me understand some of the contradictions in my own social class position growing up. While my family's economic capital was low enough to qualify us for welfare, my mother and father both possessed high cultural capital. Their interest in art, culture, exotic cuisines, and world religions marked them as sophisticated people—although neither possessed a four-year college degree; this opened up opportunities they may not have had otherwise (like riding on a celebrity's private plane). Subsequently, my ability to attend an Ivy League university and climb the social class ladder was surely facilitated by the cultural capital I acquired growing up.

While Karl Marx, Max Weber, Pierre Bourdieu, and others have developed theoretical models of social class, none of them backed their theories with extensive statistical evidence. In the next section we examine the nature of the class structure empirically by asking: From a statistical standpoint, how unequal are we in the United States? By exploring the *degree* of inequality in the United States using empirical evidence, we also gain new insight into the question of how many social classes there are.

WHEN IT COMES TO CLASS, HOW UNEQUAL IS THE UNITED STATES?

When it comes to social class, how unequal *is* the United States? Your initial reaction may be "very," "somewhat," or "not especially." Answering this question requires two additional questions: (1) What aspects of social class should we consider, and (2) to whom should we compare ourselves? Later in this chapter we will compare the level of inequality in the United States to that found in other countries and to our historical selves. While we could measure inequality using a number of indicators, the two most tangible are income and wealth.

Income refers to money, wages, or payments that people receive from occupations, government programs, or investments; it can then be categorized as *earned*, *unearned*, or *investment income* (e.g., "capital gains"). While it is possible to measure *individual income*, sociologists, economists, and the government typically focus on *household income*—an indicator that aggregates the income of all household members

Table 5.1 **Median Household Income by Race**

Racial/Ethnic Group	Median Income in Dollars
Asian Americans	$68,600
Whites	$57,000
Hispanics	$39,000
Blacks/African Americans	$33,300

U.S. Census Bureau 2013 "Income, Poverty, and Health Insurance Coverage in the United States: 2012"

above the age of 15 (related or not). Within the United States, the median household income is about $51,000 (all data are from the U.S. Census Bureau, unless otherwise stated). Half of all households earn more than this figure, and half earn less.

Median household incomes in the United States vary according to race, in part because members of some racial and ethnic groups have higher levels of education than others and because they are more likely to have multiple wage earners in the home. Table 5.1 indicates current median household incomes across racial groups. While Asian Americans have the highest household incomes at $68,600 and Hispanics the lowest incomes at $39,000, there is considerable variation within these groups. Data from the Pew Research Center show that the median household income among Indian Americans is $88,000, while that of Korean Americans is $50,000. Among Hispanics, the median household income among people of Colombian and Ecuadorian descent is $50,000, while that of Dominican Americans is $34,000.

To answer the question of how unequal are we, researchers measure the gap between the highest and lowest income earners (or wealth holders). They do so by dividing the population into **quintiles**—five segments, each of which represents 20 percent of the population. In terms of income, we can talk about the top quintile (richest 20 percent), the bottom quintile (the poorest 20 percent), and the three quintiles in between. Then, we can see how much income is earned by each quintile, or how income is distributed. Note that if we lived in a perfectly equal society, each quintile would earn 20 percent of all income.

To visualize this concept, imagine a group of five people sitting down to share a pizza. If we draw the parallel to income, we can see how much pizza each quintile would get. Figure 5.2 shows that the top quintile earns about 50 percent of all income! In the pizza parallel, this means that the richest of the five diners would have half of the pizza on their plate. The poorest quintile in the United States earns just 3.3 percent of all income. The poorest diner represents the same number of people as the richest diner, but his or her piece of the pie is much smaller. Expressed as a ratio, the richest quintile earns 15 times as much as the poorest quintile. If this were a dinner party featuring five diners and a single pizza, the richest diner would consume a meal that is 15 times greater, or has 15 times as many calories, as the poorest diner. Figure 5.2 shows the amount of income earned by each of the five quintiles.

Looking at this data, we can ask: How many social classes are there? Just because there are five quintiles does not automatically mean there are five classes. Remember: a class is defined as a group of people with shared life chances, economic opportunities, and lifestyles. How many different economic *realities* do you see represented in this chart? Two? Three? Five? Convincing arguments can be made for any of those answers.

While researchers commonly use the quintile to measure economic inequalities, it does not lend itself to an easy interpretation. Although this measure shows that the richest quintile earns 15 dollars for every dollar earned by the poorest, it does not show the actual incomes of those within each quintile. Figure 5.2 shows the income ranges earned within each quintile. It shows me, for example, that I grew up in the second lowest quintile but am currently in the second highest. It also provides different insight into the question of how many social classes there are. While the pie chart suggests that there is one very wealthy class (quintile) and four others with lower incomes, Table 5.2 shows that there is considerable variation *within* each quintile—especially the top one. It, for example, includes those earning $100,000 per year as well as those earning $25,000,000 and above.

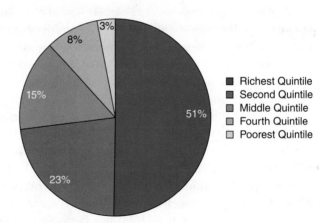

Figure 5.2: Income distribution
by quintile
(Source: U.S. Census Bureau 2013)

Table 5.2 Income Share and Income Ranges within Each Quintile

	Income Share Percentage	Income Ranges (dollars)
Top quintile (richest)	51.0	105,910 and above
Second quintile	23.0	65,501–105,909
Middle quintile	14.4	40,187–65,500
Fourth quintile	8.3	20,901–40,186
Bottom quintile (poorest)	3.2	20,900 and below

Source: U.S. Census Bureau 2013 and Historical Income Tables 2013.

In recent years, it has become increasingly common to talk about the top 1 percent, or the "superrich." During the fall of 2011, activists involved in the Occupy movement called attention to this group, claiming, "We are the 99%." They were, essentially, taking a Marxist approach by describing a society composed of two groups: the elite 1 percent who control the economic and political system and the remaining 99 percent who have little control. In terms of income, the cutoff point to get into the top 1 percent is $370,000 annually. This group, which comprises 1 percent of the population, earns about 20 percent of all income; in other words, about one of every five dollars is earned by the top 1 percent.

While there is considerable income inequality in the United States, these numbers pale in comparison to inequalities in **wealth**. Wealth refers to accumulated assets in the form of valued goods, such as savings, real estate, cars, art, jewelry, etc. To calculate a person's wealth (or net worth), you must add up their assets and then subtract their debts (credit cards, student loans, car loan, etc.). These calculations become tricky when it comes to things like cars and houses: if you owe more on your car than it's worth (what you could sell it for), it is not an asset; if you owe more on your home mortgage than you could sell it for, your home is not an asset. In these cases, car owners and homeowners are said to be "upside down" or "underwater" on their loans.

Returning to the concept of the quintile, Figure 5.3 depicts the distribution of wealth across the population. While the richest quintile *earns* 50 percent of all income, it *possesses* 84 percent of all wealth! This means that the remaining 16 percent of the wealth is distributed among 80 percent of the population. Returning to the pizza metaphor, one diner (the top quintile) gets more than four slices of the pizza, while the remaining four diners must share (less than) one slice. A more detailed look shows that the two bottom quintiles—or 40 percent of the population—possess less than 1 percent of all wealth. The second richest quintile, by contrast, possesses 11 percent, and the middle quintile possesses just 4 percent of all wealth. These data are made more concrete by looking at the median level of wealth per quintile, as reported by the Pew Economic Mobility Project (see Figure 5.3). Here, we see that the top quintile possesses wealth above $370,000 and the bottom quintile possesses wealth below $20,000.

Looking at these data, we return to the question: In terms of wealth, how many social classes—or distinct economic realities—are there? One could argue that there are three social classes: the top quintile that possesses the majority of all wealth; the two bottom quintiles that have basically no wealth (and, therefore, a very limited safety net); and the two middle quintiles that have modest shares of wealth (and a very modest safety net). While it may not sound as if $30,000 constitutes a weak safety net, that amount would cover the expenses of a middle-class family for about seven months; it would put only a small dent in a hospital bill in the event of a serious illness.

The conversation becomes more complicated when considering the superrich. The top 1 percent of the population holds 35 percent of all wealth and the top 10 percent of the population holds about 75 percent of all wealth (Kennickell 2009). These groups are in a class by themselves! Using another food analogy, imagine a birthday party

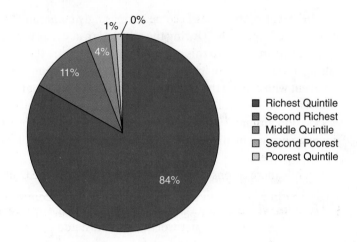

Figure 5.3 Wealth distribution by quintile Source: Norton and Ariely 2011)

Table 5.3 **Wealth Share and Wealth Ranges within Each Quintile**

	Wealth Share Percentage	Median Wealth (dollars)
Top quintile (richest)	84	367,100 and above
Second quintile	11	164,200–367,100
Middle quintile	4	73,100–164,200
Fourth quintile	1	20,300–73,100
Bottom quintile (poorest)	0	20,300 and below

Source: Norton, Michael I. and Dan Ariely. 2011.

where the birthday girl got 7.5 cupcakes all to herself and her 9 guests had to share the remaining 2.5 cupcakes. While imperfect, this analogy provides a visual tool for seeing how wealth is distributed in the United States.

Alas, cupcakes are not wealth. Cupcakes dry out and are only delicious for a limited period of time. Wealth, on the other hand, generally increases over time. The things that make up wealth—like homes and investments—tend to *appreciate* in value: because of increasing home values and the rate of return on investments, wealth tends to grow. Therefore, a person who has considerable wealth in 2015 is likely to have even greater wealth in 2025. (When housing or stock market bubbles occur, this does not happen.) This is why sociologists think that questions about social inequality should focus on wealth rather than income. Another reason sociologists emphasize wealth over income is that wealth brings power. Consider stock ownership. When stocks perform well, they clearly enhance a person's wealth; yet stock ownership also brings power when stockholders participate in corporate governance, as those with significant holdings vote on the composition of boards of directors, executive compensation packages, and other issues.

Table 5.4 **Distribution of Stock Ownership**

	1989	1995	1998	2004
Richest 1%	47%	51%	53%	39%
Richest 10%	84%	88%	92%	82%

Source: Mishel et al. 2007.

Table 5.4 represents the distribution of stock ownership in the United States. It shows that the richest 10 percent of the population controls about 80 percent of all stocks, while the richest 1 percent controls about 40 percent. This means that the remaining 20 percent of all stocks is divided among 90 percent of the population (Mishel, Bernstein, and Allegretto 2007). Although some middle-class individuals—including myself—are vested in the stock market through employee pensions and retirement plans, our stake in the system is miniscule compared to the wealthiest 10 percent. As you think through the question of how many social classes there are in the United States, you may wish to consider this piece of evidence.

EXPLORING INTERSECTIONALITY: THE COMPLICATED RELATIONSHIP BETWEEN SOCIAL CLASS, GENDER, AND SEXUAL ORIENTATION

During the 1990s, advertisers turned to gay men and lesbian women as a promising new source of revenue. Categorized as DINKs ("dual-income, no kids"), gay men and lesbians were viewed as an untapped market with plentiful disposable income. Accordingly, restaurants, hotels, cruise lines, and other entities began courting this demographic. Television programs like *Will and Grace* and *Queer Eye for the Straight Guy* similarly portrayed gay men as cosmopolitan urbanites with sophisticated tastes and money set aside for luxury goods and services.

Alongside this romantic and optimistic portrayal of affluence among gays and lesbians is the reality that within the United States, there are no federal workplace protections based on sexual orientation (20 states and municipalities have passed their own legislation, 13 of which include protections for transgender individuals under "gender expression" clauses). This means that gay men, lesbians, and anyone else who does not identify as heterosexual can experience discrimination at work—being paid less than equally qualified heterosexual peers, being fired without cause—and receive no legal protection. This begs the possibility that workplace discrimination may result in lower pay for nonheterosexuals. Considering these two contradictory possibilities, what do sociologists and economists know about how social class, income, and sexual orientation intersect?

A detailed look at the earnings of gay men and lesbians suggests that gay men earn less than straight men while lesbian women earn more than straight women

(Allegretto and Arthur 2001; Blandford 2003). If widespread discrimination against gays and lesbians existed, we would expect that the incomes of both groups would be below those of similarly qualified heterosexuals. Yet this is not what we see. What we do see is that gay men experience a wage "penalty" of $5,000 compared to straight men, while lesbian women experience a "premium" of about $3,000 (in 1992 dollars, when the data were collected).

So how can we explain these patterns? Rather than suggest that gay men in particular are victims of discrimination, scholars believe that the lower wages of gay men—who actually have higher levels of education than straight men—reflect the fact that they choose different occupations. Compared to straight men, they are more likely to work in female-dominated service-related professions, which typically earn lower wages (Antecol, Jong, and Steinberger 2008). Reflecting perhaps the fact that they do not experience pressure to care for children or be the primary breadwinner, they also log fewer work hours. The converse of these patterns appears among lesbian women (Black, Sanders, and Taylor 2007). They tend to be overrepresented in higher-paying male-dominated professions and work more hours than straight women. Because lesbian women are half as likely as straight women to have children at home (Jepsen 2007), they may be less likely to take time off to care for a child; consequently, they accumulate more seniority and higher earnings.

These findings illustrate how gender roles and sexuality intersect, especially in the context of a gendered workplace. (The notion of the gendered workplace will be explored in greater detail in Chapter 13.) While gay men may not have the affluence and disposable incomes that advertisers imagine, neither does it appear that widespread, systemic discrimination suppresses the wages of gays and lesbians. That said, workplace discrimination against gay men, lesbians, and transgender workers does occur. Researchers estimate that there are nearly 5 cases of discrimination based on sexual orientation for every 10,000 workers—a figure similar to the rate for women and just slightly less than the rate for discrimination based on race (Ramos, Sears, and Badgett 2008). But with the Employment Non-Discrimination Act (ENDA) stalled in the U.S. House of Representatives, those who do experience discrimination based on sexual orientation or gender expression currently lack a legal means of redress, especially at the federal level.

FINDING YOUR RUNG ON THE LADDER: EXPLAINING SOCIAL CLASS DIFFERENCES

When it comes to social class, there is no shortage of statistics to take into account. Yet what these statistics *mean* is a matter of interpretation. While the term "social class" should have a clear and precise meaning, this is not the case. Because there is no agreement on its definition, it is difficult to determine how many social classes there are. When looking at indicators like income and wealth, one could argue that there are two, three, or five social classes. Yet the fact that there is so much variation just at the top of the class structure leads to the conclusion that there are almost infinite variations of social class. The *degree* of inequality in the United States is also a matter of both fact and interpretation. While it is a fact that the United States is the most unequal Western industrialized country—a fact we explore in more detail later—it is less clear why this is the case or what should be done about it. We turn to these questions in the next section.

THE ESSENTIALIST PERSPECTIVE: BIOLOGICAL EFFORTS TO EXPLAIN SOCIAL CLASS DIFFERENCES

When it comes to sex, gender, and sexual orientation, sociologists understand that there is some biological basis to these social identities. But is there any evidence to suggest that underlying genetic differences can explain a person's social class position? Are there biological markers or other inborn traits that correlate to the class position a person ends up in or the traits of people within a particular social class? According to Richard Herrnstein and Charles Murray (1994), authors of *The Bell Curve: Intelligence and Class Structure in American Life*, there is such a correlation. For these authors, a person's intelligence—as measured by IQ or intelligence quotient—is an important predictor of their class position.

Prior to the modern era, a person's intelligence was of little importance to his or her social standing. The top social positions in China's ancient dynasties and Europe's monarchies were occupied through heredity: one did not rise through cunning or mental sophistication; one was born into his or her position. Premodern societies, moreover, lacked diversity in terms of how much intelligence and skill were needed to do particular jobs. Because most people toiled in lower-skilled jobs, intelligence or ingenuity were not especially useful and, therefore, largely irrelevant to a person's class position.

Through the technological revolutions of the twentieth century, and the greater differentiation of skilled positions, intelligence now has greater importance. High-skilled jobs now require higher intelligence. Accordingly, they also garner higher pay. Moreover, once in those high-skilled and high-pay positions, members of the "cognitive elite" pair off. Through marriage and childbearing, these highly intelligent and well-paid people reproduce, pass on their genetic advantage, and, thereby, produce the next generation of cognitive and economic elites. Over time, Herrnstein and Murray theorized, the upper classes would isolate and consolidate their privileges, leaving behind a less intelligent mass of society. Due to their genetic deficiencies, this group would be relegated to lower-class positions. Herrnstein and Murray's theory offers a micro-level, essentialist explanation for why *individuals* end up in particular class positions; yet their theory also provides a macro-level explanation for why social inequality has become so pervasive in contemporary societies.

So how has this theory been received? Over the last 200 years, studies linking intelligence to social class and race have had enduring appeal. The essentialist perspective, which links social experiences to underlying biological conditions, provides an easy explanation and justification for social inequality: it's rooted in our genetic makeup. The rich are rich because they are smart, and the poor are poor because they are less smart. Sociologists, however, are deeply skeptical of these explanations. So too are geneticists, who have not found a stable or reliable link between race, class, and intelligence.

Recent research on the link between genes and social class, in fact, highlights the importance of the environment in which a child grows up. While the genes of kids raised in middle- and upper-class families do predict their intelligence, as measured by IQ, the same is not true for kids raised in lower-income families (Turkheimer et al. 2003). A child raised by a lower-income family with strong genetic potential for a high IQ often faces adverse conditions at home, (e.g., lead poisoning, poor nutrition, less verbal stimulation); this adverse environment makes it difficult for a child's underlying intelligence to express itself. Other research shows that the risk of poverty and other poor life outcomes begins during fetal development. Fetal exposure to high levels of cortisol—a stress hormone that is higher among lower-income pregnant women—compromises brain development. During childhood and adolescence, the toxic stress of fetal development puts academic achievement at risk and is thought to be correlated with higher levels of aggression and propensity for criminal behavior (Knudsen et al. 2006).

This emerging scientific research is of utmost importance for critiquing the essentialist perspective on genes, intelligence, and social class. It is not that the poor are born less intelligent or genetically deficient but that their environments do not allow intelligence to express itself, thereby limiting socioeconomic opportunities.

HISTORY, POLICY, AND THE SOCIAL CONSTRUCTIONIST PERSPECTIVE

According to sociologist Claude S. Fischer and his co-authors, social class inequality "is not the natural and inevitable consequence of intelligence operating in a free market" (1996:7); rather, it is a social construction—a reflection of historical forces and policy decisions made by *humans*. If you want to know why my dad lives in subsidized housing while he travels each day to a multi-million dollar job site, you've got to adopt the social constructionist perspective.

A cursory glance across history and across the globe leads to the following conclusion: social inequality is inevitable. It is virtually impossible to find a society devoid of social class distinctions. But while social class inequality may be inevitable, the *degree* of inequality is not. A look across the globe and across historical epochs shows that societies vary tremendously in terms of *how* unequal they are. Figure 5.4 provides a snapshot of inequality in select countries, indicating the degree of income inequality between rich and poor. It is the social constructionist perspective—which takes historical changes, cultural values, and social policy into account—that best explains why social inequality exists.

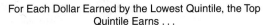

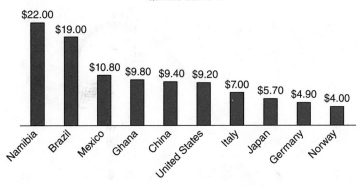

Figure 5.4 Snapshot of global income inequalities. (Source: World Bank 2014)

THE STUDY ABROAD TRIP

To what extent have societies approached economic equality? And why are some societies especially unequal? To answer these questions, we must pack our bags for an extensive study abroad trip. The first stop on our journey takes us to those societies with the highest degree of economic inequality. South America is home to the countries with the largest gap between rich and poor. Whether in the mountainous rain forests of Colombia and Venezuela with their coffee and banana plantations or the mineral-rich areas of Bolivia's high Andean plains, members of the highest income quintile typically earn $35–40 for every dollar earned by the members of the lowest quintile (recall that the ratio is $15:1 in the United States). In urban areas and the countryside, the poor typically live in small, simple homes where hot water is lacking and access to electricity may exist for only a few hours a day. Meanwhile, the wealthy live in gated communities and high-rise apartments, where their needs are tended to by drivers and maids. When I visited my sister who was studying abroad in La Paz, Bolivia, I felt a sense of both luxury and discomfort when we were served a multi-course lunch at 1:00 each day by her host family's *empleada domestica*, Felisa. In extreme cases, the wealthy are protected by bodyguards and security personnel due to real and perceived threats of violence from poorer members of society. Such scenes are echoed through the world, from Rio de Janeiro, Brazil, to New Delhi, India, to Nairobi, Kenya, and beyond.

So what explains whether a particular society has a staggering or a modest gap between rich and poor? Part of the answer has to do with a country's level of economic development, namely in terms of how industrialized they are.

Developed by the economist Simon Kuznets, the **Kuznets Curve** describes the relationship between a society's level of economic development and its level of inequality (see Figure 5.5). It shows that the most unequal type of society is an *agrarian* society—one that is organized primarily around agriculture (and, in some cases, mining

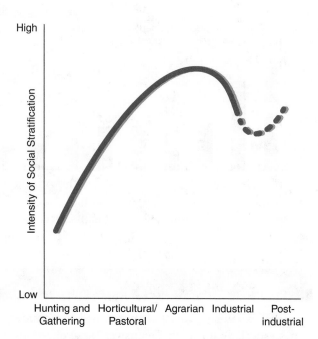

Figure 5.5 Kuznets Curve: economic development and social stratification. (Source: Kuznets 1955)

or mineral extraction). Such societies are highly unequal because the means of production—e.g., the rubber and banana plantations of Brazil (a rapidly industrializing society) and the diamond mines of South Africa—are owned by a small group. The mines and plantations, moreover, require a large labor force—one that is generally poorly educated and unskilled. Because the labor force lacks education, skill, and influence, owners are able to extract profit from the workers' labor and hold onto it for their benefit.

The fact that the countries of Europe and Asia have lower levels of economic inequality partially reflects the fact that they have modernized and reached the *industrial* stage of development. This is depicted in the Kuznets Curve where the line dips, indicating a reduction in inequality. Throughout the nineteenth century, the nations of Europe (and later Asia) developed new ways of generating power; these technologies then led to rapid economic change, a period known as the Industrial Revolution. As factories sprang up, new and more differentiated skills were needed by the labor force. These changes created the need for a more formally educated labor force. As the labor force became more educated, they became more literate, politically active, and empowered. This led to the formation of organizations like labor unions, which advocated on the workers' behalf. Over time, these general historical changes led to greater productivity and higher wages and more protections for workers, while spreading economic resources more evenly across the population.

Looking at the Kuznets Curve, it might seem like all nations will eventually industrialize and that when they do, inequality will decline. Unfortunately, that is not necessarily the case. To understand why some countries are more unequal than others, a second explanation is needed. According to **dependency theory** and **world systems**

theory, some nations remain poor and unequal due to exploitation by rich ones. According to Immanuel Wallerstein, raw materials and resources are extracted from poor nations—what he referred to as the **periphery**; once extracted, these resources are turned into usable goods within the **semi-periphery** (middle-income countries like Portugal, India, Mexico, and China); in the final step, the profits generated by selling these goods flow into rich, **core** nations (rich, developed nations that sell and profit from finished goods). Ultimately, poor countries—many of which are rich in natural resources—become *dependent* on rich ones—for loans and investment—which locks them in a state of underdevelopment and fuels their internal social class divisions.

To understand dependency theory, we must make a stop in Cochabamba, Bolivia. Located in a valley of the Andes Mountains at an elevation of 8,000 feet, Cochabamba is a city of more than 1,000,000 inhabitants. Originally settled by indigenous Quechua people, the city grew in size and wealth after the colonial Spanish began mining silver in nearby Potosi in the sixteenth century. Sometimes known as "The Garden City," things were not so peaceful when protests broke out in the year 2000. The cause of these protests was the fact that, due to an international economic agreement, the average Bolivian worker was spending about 25 percent of his or her monthly wages on water. In an effort to improve the country's water system, the Bolivian government approached the World Bank for a loan. The **World Bank** is an international financial institution that provides loans to developing countries for large-scale projects. The loan was needed to improve the system of dams and water transport so that more of the population could have safe and reliable access. One condition of the loan required the Bolivian government to *privatize* the water system. This natural resource was taken out of government control, which previously treated it as a not-for-profit natural resource, and transformed into a high-priced commodity. When the international consortium known as *Aguas del Tunari* took control of the system, they implemented rate hikes and even outlawed the collection of rain water from rooftops!

Changes to the water system were perceived as both a financial burden

In protesting privatization and rising fees for water access, Bolivian protestors proclaimed, "Water is for the people!"

and a human rights violation. Because of rate increases, workers withdrew their children from school (which require fees) and cut back on other essential services, like health care. Under the leadership of Oscar Olivera, four months of protests ensued, where The Coalition in Defense of Water and Life—composed of peasants, factory workers, and homeless street children—met with police officers wielding guns and tear gas. In April of 2000, after the killing of a teenage protestor was aired on television, the Bolivian government signed a peace agreement with Oscar Olivera and revoked its agreement with *Aguas del Tunari*. While nearly half of the population still lacks reliable access to water, control over the water system has been returned to the government.

The Cochabamba Water War reflects the economic dynamics that reverberate between rich and poor nations. Loans from organizations like the World Bank often perpetuate inequalities within poor countries: while the goal may be to build infrastructure and aid economic development, loan terms often "handcuff" these nations. Interest rates tend to be extremely high, making repayment difficult; as more money is spent repaying loans, less money is spent on education, medical facilities, and other needs. Accordingly, education remains out of reach for the poorest citizens—which perpetuates their poverty. Such loans may also require governments to shift production to single-crop economies. Loans to develop cotton production in the Central Asian republic of Uzbekistan, for example, required that land use be shifted from growing food to growing cotton. As a consequence, food now needs to be imported, rather than grown locally, which increases food costs. Expansion of the cotton crop also required substantial irrigation from the Aral Sea. Over time, the sea and its tributaries dried up (due in part to an outdated, inefficient irrigation system). This set off a chain reaction where declining sea levels led to the loss of fishing jobs and fish to eat; as the sea dried up, dust storms stirred up soils laced with pesticides, resulting in an epidemic of asthma and other illnesses. Moreover, according to Human Rights Watch, the government requires teachers and schoolchildren to participate in the harvest in order to meet quotas—an effort that surely takes away from their education.

Clearly, economic development efforts like these come with costs to the average citizen. Meanwhile, local elites and corrupt government officials benefit from these arrangements, given their stakes in the economic and political institutions at the heart of these multi-million dollar deals. These dynamics, then, not only keep such countries in a state of economic underdevelopment but also perpetuate the gap between rich and poor. At the same time, consumers in core nations like the United States benefit by having access to cheap products—whether cotton clothing, electronic goods, or food.

Our journey, then, leaves us with two important lessons: (1) it is within poor nations that we generally find the largest gap between rich and poor; and (2) this gap reflects the country's low level of economic development—a situation that partially reflects international economic arrangements that lock them into a state of underdevelopment. How then, can we explain why countries with the *same* level of economic development have different levels of inequality and social class structures? Considering Figure 5.6 and Table 5.5, why does the income gap between rich and poor vary so much *among* Western industrialized countries?

Western industrialized countries are those that have highly developed economies and advanced technological infrastructures. Found among the "advanced" nations of Europe, North America, and parts of Asia, they also tend to have capitalist economic systems and democratic political systems. Among these nations, some have a small gap between rich and poor, as seen in Denmark and Sweden, where the wealthiest quintile earns about $4 for every dollar earned by the poorest. At the other end of the spectrum is the United States—the most unequal of all Western industrialized countries. There, members of the richest quintile earn about $15 for every dollar earned by the poorest quintile. To explain why these nations, similar in economic development and democratic structure, are so different in terms of their degree of inequality, we must pack our bags and travel to Scandinavia and the Nordic countries.

Touching down in Oslo, Norway, a metropolitan area of more than a million, we are greeted by crisp air, pine-covered hills, and a deep blue fjord (inlet). Arriving in the winter, we would see sporty Norwegians traversing the city with cross-country skis; in summer we would see hordes of people relaxing in parks or enjoying coffee or beer in an outdoor café. A driving tour of the neighborhoods surrounding the fjord reveals a mix of historic and modern architecture. In the working-class East End we would see many apartment buildings and more single- and multi-family homes in the middle-class West End. Almost nowhere would we witness a homeless person, nor anything resembling the ghettos or housing projects of many American cities. Our journey would also lack the opportunity to gaze upon the lifestyle of Norway's rich and famous, because, unlike in most American cities, we would be hard-pressed to find an enclave of staggeringly large and well-manicured estates. It would be almost impossible to film a version of MTV's "Cribs" in Oslo. What we would see is a modern city filled with public transportation, modest Volvos, Toyotas, and Volkswagens, and a population that seems active and diverse (25 percent of the city's population is non-Norwegian, with Pakistanis and Somalis as the largest groups). Had we descended upon Stockholm, Sweden, Copenhagen, Denmark, or Reykjavik, Iceland, we would find a similar scene.

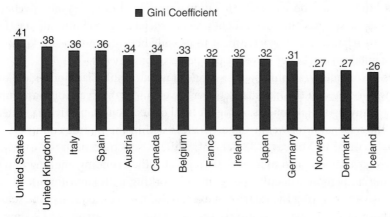

Figure 5.6 Income inequality in Western industrialized countries.
(Source: World Bank, World Development Indicators 2014)

One reason the gap between rich and poor is greater in the United States than in many European nations has to do with the complex interplay of social philosophy and social policy. Each nation has its own philosophy about the relationship between the people and the government, especially in terms of what role the government plays in maximizing the well-being of the people. Within Europe's Nordic countries, the underlying philosophy is that citizens should be guaranteed equality of condition. While equality of condition is a priority, the capitalist "free market" is seen as a threat to the individual's democratic standing. Consequently, these countries have developed a set of social policies that increase the scope of its **welfare state,** and mitigate the fluctuations of the capitalist market. The welfare state refers to the system of taxing and spending aimed at protecting and promoting the economic and social well-being of the people. Because the Nordic countries have a set of policies that extend a wide array of benefits (education, employment, health care, retirement pensions, etc.) *universally* across the population, they are a **social-democratic welfare state** (Esping-Andersen 1990). While some critics have called these systems "nanny states," based on the belief that these policies are overprotective and intrusive, defenders of the system believe they are "meant to cultivate cross class solidarity" and a collective spirit among the citizenry (Esping-Andersen 1990:25).

Danish-born sociologist Gøsta Esping-Andersen categorizes the United States as a **liberal welfare state,** based on the fact that it provides a smaller set of social policies to a smaller subset of the population. Australia, Canada, and Japan also fall into this category. In these countries, it is typically the poor who receive income assistance or help with housing, health care, and food; this help is usually temporary and minimal in scope. This contrasts with the Social Democratic system, where *everyone* receives benefits—like the $160 monthly child allowance to *all* Swedish parents. Within the United States and other liberal welfare states, however, there is a much stronger emphasis on the individual, rather than collective, good. Instead of *equality of outcomes*, as emphasized in the social democratic countries, conservative welfare states like the United States emphasize *equality of opportunity*. Americans generally embrace the idea that everyone has the same chances, but whether you succeed or fail is up to you. Within conservative welfare states there is skepticism over the government's role in social and economic affairs; therefore, there is less reliance on the government to provide benefits and greater faith that free market capitalism can better serve the people's economic needs.

These two underlying philosophies—one of which emphasizes individual over collective well-being and the free market over government intervention—are supported by accompanying social policies. A higher level of taxation, in particular, is needed to pay for the wide array of welfare state services within the Nordic countries. The top marginal tax rate in Norway is 48 percent, while it is 38 percent in the United States. Norway's government also more strictly regulates the economy, making home loans and credit cards more difficult to obtain and working with labor unions to ensure a living wage and limiting the salaries of executives. As a consequence, the social policies of these countries place a ceiling of sorts on how rich a person can become, as well as a floor beneath which few can fall. While the median household incomes between

Table 5.5 **Comparative Wealth Inequality**

Country	Percentage of Wealth Held by Richest 10% of Families
Switzerland	71
United States	70
Sweden	59
Great Britain	56
Canada	53
Norway	50
Italy	48
Australia	45
Germany	44
Spain	42
Japan	39

Source: Davis et al. 2006.

these two countries are not very different, the social class structure in the Nordic countries (and throughout most of Europe) is relatively compressed, while in the United States it is one of extremes. Our travels to Europe provide an important take-away: that modern nations differ in the degree to which they use social policies to reduce inequality and structure the social class system.

TRAVELING BACK IN TIME

Currently, the United States has the largest gap between rich and poor among Western industrialized countries. But has this always been the case? Has the United States always been a nation with unique opportunities to get rich alongside the tragedy of deep poverty? To some extent, yes, there have always been rich and poor in this nation. Yet the size of this gap is a relatively modern phenomenon—one where the United States set out on its own path in the early 1970s and has continued ever since. To understand how inequality and the class structure have changed over time in the United States, we must jump into our time machine.

While reasonable people argue about how much inequality is too much (or not enough) and what the ideal gap between rich and poor should be, it is a fact that the period of the greatest economic *equality* within the modern era was the 1950s and '60s. Our time machine, then, takes us to this era, an era that many romanticize as having strong values, strong families, and a strong economy (Coontz 1997). Whether our time machine dropped us in New York, Philadelphia, Cincinnati, Milwaukee,

Denver, or Seattle, we would encounter a scene of rapid suburbanization. In new housing developments across the nation, the Baby Boom brought infants, who grew into teens, who spent their weekends at drive-in movies and screamed along to the Beatles. Meanwhile, most families (especially white ones) were supported by a single wage earner—usually a father who spent his days working a white-collar job or in any one of the hundreds of factories that hummed along and rebuilt the United States and Europe after World War II. At the same time, racism and legal segregation made it difficult or impossible for nonwhites to share in the prosperity, and white poverty remained hidden in areas like the mountains of Appalachia. Still, many prospered. From the early 1950s through the early 1970s, men's incomes grew steadily and significantly, increasing from about $23,000 to $35,000 in inflation-adjusted dollars.

Since the early 1970s, things have changed. For one, men's wages and median household incomes have largely *stagnated* since the early 1970s. The income gains that the average American family experienced during the 1950s and '60s did not continue into the '70s, '80s, or beyond. In addition, the gap between rich and poor has expanded, with the share of income and wealth going to the "superrich" becoming larger and more concentrated. Besides the current era, only the Great Depression witnessed a larger gap between rich and poor.

Figure 5.7 uses the Gini coefficient to show how income inequality has changed within the United States over the last 100 years. The Gini coefficient, named after the Italian statistician and sociologist Corrado Gini, is a statistical measure of how income is spread across the population. Although a Gini coefficient of, say, .36 has no easy translation, it is easy to see that a higher Gini coefficient denotes a higher level of inequality (larger gap between rich and poor), and a smaller Gini denotes a smaller level. Accordingly, Figure 5.7 shows that the income gap between rich and poor has increased since the early 1970s. The amount of wealth concentrated in the hands of the superrich follows a similar pattern. Between 1945 and the early 1970s, the richest 1 percent of the population held between 20 and 25 percent of all wealth (see Table 5.6).

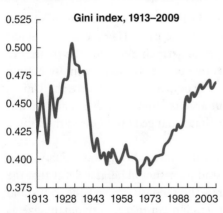

Figure 5.7 Changes in U.S. income inequality over time.
(Source: Atkinson 2010).

Since the early 1970s, however, the superrich have held a greater share—somewhere between 34 and 42 percent of all wealth.

While the U.S. economy has prospered over the last 40 years, especially in terms of the growth of GDP (gross domestic product), this growth has not benefited everyone equally. There is more money in the economy, but it's going to fewer people. While economic gains were shared more widely during the 1940s, '50s, and '60s, the gains have been increasingly concentrated in the hands of the wealthy since the 1970s. Data from the U.S Census Bureau show that 80 percent of the population—that is, all but

Table 5.6 **Wealth Share among the Superrich**

Year	Percentage of Wealth Held by Top 1%
1922	31.6
1929	36.3
1933	28.3
1939	30.6
1945	23.3
1949	20.8
1953	24.3
1958	23.8
1962	22.0
1965	23.4
1969	20.1
1972	20.7
1989	38.3
1995	38.5
1998	38.1
2004	34.3
2010	35.4

Source: Mishel et al. 2009; Wolff 2010.

the top quintile—has a smaller share of the income "pie" now compared to the late 1960s. Imagine, for example, five people sitting down to a pizza meal in the late 1960s. Even at that time, the size of each diner's portion would have been unequal. If the same group sat down to the same meal in 2010, however, four of the five diners would find the size of their portion had decreased by an average of 8 percent. Meanwhile, the richest diner—the one who represents the wealthiest quintile—would enjoy a meal that had increased by more than 11 percent.

Returning to the question of how many social classes there are, these patterns can be used to argue that there are just two classes: the rich, who have increased their fortunes over time, and the remaining 80 percent, who have seen their fortunes decline. These patterns have only become more pronounced since the "Great Recession" that began in 2007. According to University of California economist Emmanuel Saez (2013), the *average* increase of family income during the years of recovery was 1.7 percent. This average, however, conceals considerable variation: the incomes of the top 1 percent grew by 11.2 percent while those of the other 99 percent declined by 0.4 percent. The top 1 percent, then, captured 121 percent of the income gains in the first two years of the recovery. As the stock market bounced back, the wealthy were best positioned to take advantage of the improving economy.

Still, the gains to the wealthy are not simply an artifact of the recent recession and moderate economic recovery. As suggested above, we are in the midst of a decades-long trend in which the wealthy have captured a significantly higher portion of the economic gains. A report from the Center on Budget and Policy Priorities shows that since 1979, the top 1 percent of the population has seen its after-tax income increase by about 281 percent; those in the middle quintile (the middle class, essentially), by contrast, have seen their incomes increase by about 25 percent during this time frame (see Figure 5.8). Over the last three decades, the income gains of the superrich have been about 11 times greater than the average American household.

Why were the 1950s and '60s a period of relatively greater equality, and why has economic inequality in the United States since increased? Is it the case, as Herrnstein and Murray suggest in *The Bell Curve*, that intelligent people are mating with intelligent people and, therefore, producing a class that is better positioned to maximize their economic well-being? Is there any evidence that the majority of Americans have become considerably lazier than they were in the past, while a smaller segment of the population has become more innovative and hardworking? Rather than look at the failings or successes of individual people, sociologists see growing economic inequality as a reflection of long-term economic transformations coupled with social and economic policy choices.

The United States has entered the **postindustrial stage** of economic development. This means that the economy has shifted from manufacturing (clothing, electronics, cars, etc.) to service industries (banking, information processing, entertainment, hospitality). Looking again at the Kuznets Curve, inequality begins to increase when societies enter the postindustrial stage. In the move toward a service-based economy, semi-skilled manufacturing jobs are replaced by lower-skilled, mechanized jobs. Whereas the skilled and semi-skilled manufacturing jobs of the 1950s, '60s, and early '70s paid relatively high wages and were relatively secure, they have been replaced by jobs that require less skill, command less pay, and are less secure. Meanwhile, new jobs have been created at the high end of the economy. These jobs are more specialized, higher paying, and generally require a four-year college degree (or more). There are, in

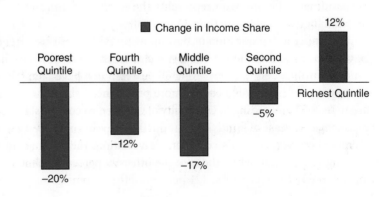

Figure 5.8 Income gains and losses by quintile, 1967–2013. (Source: U.S. Census Bureau 2014)

addition, new jobs that have been created in the service sector: more Americans are eating out, buying more and cheaper clothing, and beautifying themselves like never before (note the explosion of nail salons in your town or city). A large portion of "middle-class jobs" have been lost through these transformations, replaced by jobs at both the lower and higher ends (in terms of skill and pay) of the occupational spectrum—thereby contributing to a larger gap between the top and bottom.

The expansion of inequality also involves economic and policy choices. The economic prosperity of the postwar decades, for example, required extensive support from the federal government. The expansion of the middle class during the 1950s was achieved partially through benefits extended to returning soldiers through the **G.I. Bill** (officially called the Servicemen's Readjustment Act). Beginning in 1944, the G.I. Bill provided low-cost mortgages, low-interest loans to start a business, and considerable financial aid to attend college or vocational school. Through this effort, more than 8 million veterans received some form of postsecondary education (Bound and Turner 2002). In *Over Here: How the G.I. Bill Transformed the American Dream*, journalist Edward Humes (2006:1) wrote that the "G.I. Bill made homeowners, college graduates, professionals, rocket scientists, and a booming middle class out of a Depression-era generation." In a sense, the stable middle class that emerged in that era was a government creation.

The gap between rich and poor was also moderated by the fiscal policies of the 1950s and '60s. The top marginal tax rate ranged from 91 percent under Dwight Eisenhower in the 1950s to 70 percent under Richard Nixon in the late 1960s. Moreover, **estate taxes**—taxes paid on inheritance—were nearly 50 percent higher during this era: 77 percent compared to 55 percent today. Consequently, the government used to collect more tax from the wealthy, leaving them with lower after-tax income and less wealth to pass on. The federally mandated minimum wage was also more generous during these decades. With steady increases during the '50s and '60s, the minimum wage reached its highest level in 1968 when it was equivalent to $10.64 (today, by contrast, it is $7.25). While the booming economy of the '50s and '60s required hard work and ingenuity on the part of individuals, the government was intimately involved in economic affairs. Through its policies, it limited the incomes and wealth of the upper class, provided a living wage for the lower classes, and subsidized the growth of the middle class. It is these kinds of policies that currently create a relatively small economic gap in many European countries.

Since the early 1970s, wage and tax policies have changed. While the federal minimum wage rose slowly but steadily up until 1980, there have been only modest increases in the years since. Although only 5 percent of workers hold minimum-wage jobs, it is difficult for these workers to earn a **living wage**—one that provides enough income to meet basic housing, food, and clothing needs. Rather than $7.25, a worker would need to be paid $11–13 to make a "living wage." With respect to tax policies, the 1980s ushered in a period of **Reaganomics**: a supply-side approach built on the notion that tax cuts for the wealthy would have a "trickle-down" effect and stimulate the economy, creating jobs for the middle and lower classes. Decreased spending on social welfare programs was also part of Reaganomics. Assistance to poor and lower-income

Americans declined during this period, as "the American safety net became less effective at reducing poverty" (Mishel and Bernstein 1993:12). While the policies ushered in by Ronald Reagan were associated with economic growth and increases in GDP as well as lower unemployment rates, the jury is out on whether these economic policies led to greater prosperity for Americans *as a whole*—though most analysts doubt it.

Finally, the growing economic gap can be explained in part by declining **labor union** membership. A labor union is a group that binds workers together and provides the opportunity to negotiate wages and workplace conditions through a process called collective bargaining. Union membership was highest during the 1950s, when approximately 35 percent of workers were members; today, only about 12 percent of workers are members (often teachers and public sector workers). Critics see unions as inefficient, prone to corruption, and damaging to business. Over time, the government and employers have developed greater opposition towards unions—breaking strikes, locking out workers, and firing workers for organizing (Norwood 2002; Smith 2003). The economist Joseph Stiglitz (2013:38), however, argues that "Strong unions have helped to reduce inequality, whereas weaker unions have made it easier for CEOs ... to increase it." Fellow economist David Card (2001) estimates that perhaps as much as 20 percent of the growth in income inequality among male workers can be attributed to declining labor union strength.

A time machine journey through the last 100 years confirms the following: while economic inequalities have been an inevitable feature of American life, with periods of greater or lesser intensity, the gap between rich and poor has increased since the 1970s. As Figure 5.9 shows, even though the economy has grown steadily since the mid-1990s, it is the top 1 percent that has disproportionately benefited from those gains. While our time machine does not allow us to travel into the future, it does offer a hazy glimpse into the decades ahead. Based on projections published by Euromonitor International, it is expected that within the United States and other developed countries, the economic slowdown, unemployment, budget cuts, and an aging population that puts pressure on public expenditures will contribute to even greater income disparities in the future.

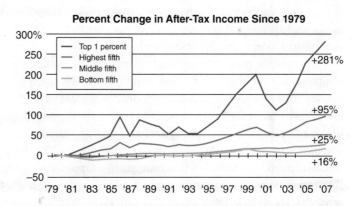

Percent Change in After-Tax Income Since 1979

Figure 5.9 Income gains of the superrich. (Source: Stone et al. 2015)

EXPLORING ACTIVISM:
THE OCCUPY MOVEMENT

While the trends toward greater economic inequality have been underway for four decades, most Americans seem either ignorant of these trends, indifferent toward them, or unsure of how to fight against them. In fact, research suggests that Americans have a fairly weak sense of class consciousness—that is, they do not identify strongly with a social class, nor do they see it as an important source of group identity—and are relatively tolerant of social inequality. During the fall of 2011, in the wake of the financial crisis—sometimes called "The Great Recession"a group emerged to protest growing social and economic inequality. The **Occupy movement** sprang up first in New York City, with its headquarters in Zuccotti Park near Wall Street—a choice that strategically and symbolically allowed protesters to draw attention to the recent bank bailouts. The movement soon spread to as many as 95 cities in the United States and dozens of countries around the world.

The goal of the Occupy movement was to create more equitable economic arrangements as well as more democratic and participatory political processes. Under the rallying cry "We are the 99%," they hoped to gather strength by drawing attention to the growing economic power of the richest 1 percent and the common ground shared by the vast majority of the population. In public parks across the nation, protesters staged "general assemblies," where proposals and decisions were made through democratic

Occupy Wall Street protestors brought increased attention to socioeconomic inequality in the United States. Hoping to build solidarity and awareness, they declared: "We are the 99%."

participation and consensus building. While semi-formal *teach-ins* offered the opportunity to learn about issues ranging from tax and trade policies to media ownership to food insecurity and environmental justice, informal *stacking* gave participants the opportunity to ask questions or share information and opinions. The movement also harnessed the power of social media to spread awareness and gather support.

Throughout, the Occupy movement was criticized for its lack of formal structure and the lack of clearly specified goals. Movement leaders, however, defended the practices, emphasizing the goal of a democratic, local, and grassroots movement—even if it meant a lack of formal proposals or structures. Some conservative politicians and media commentators characterized the Occupy movement as an act of "class warfare"—a Marxist-inspired effort to divide the population into two opposing groups and wage war against the successful and the capitalism system that creates them. Meanwhile, President Obama offered lukewarm support to the movement, and Comedy Central stars Jon Stewart and Stephen Colbert provided comedic political commentary that raised the awareness of many young adults.

By the winter of 2012, the formal movement had died down, and protestors were removed from New York's Zuccotti Park. Due to its lack of formal agenda, it is difficult to assess the movement's success. Sometimes portrayed as a ragtag group of disaffected hippies, the Occupy movement failed to establish lasting coalitions with labor union activists or leaders of other progressive social causes. Perhaps the most significant short-term achievement of the movement is that it did inspire a national conversation about economic inequality and a slight change in consciousness. A national survey of college students has shown, for example, that since the economic collapse, students express greater support for higher taxes on the wealthy (Eagan et al. 2013). To date, however, no major changes have occurred with respect to tax policies, corporate governance, or campaign finance reform that would significantly alter the degree of economic inequality in the United States.

RISING ECONOMIC INEQUALITY: SO WHAT?

For many of us, all of these facts and their explanations can get lost in a pool of abstractions. It can be hard to connect these statistics and seemingly technical explanations to one's own life. If the United States remains the world's largest economy (as measured by GDP), why does it matter that inequality is growing? Further, isn't some degree of inequality good for society?

Indeed, some sociologists and economics argue that some amount of inequality is good for society. According to Kingsley Davis and Wilbur Moore's (1945) **functionalist perspective**, social inequality is necessary in order to provide incentives for people to perform society's most difficult and important jobs. Without the proper economic rewards, the **Davis-Moore thesis** asserts, there would be no motivation for people to take on difficult and important jobs, like being a doctor, or risky jobs that provide innovation and help society move forward. One reason that communist countries failed is that in the interest of economic equality, they did not provide the proper incentives for people to take on jobs that would help society innovate. Unfortunately, when Davis and Moore created this theory during the 1940s, they did not state *how much* inequality was necessary to ensure progress. They did not, moreover, consider that excessive inequality would spell dysfunction for society.

Is it possible that the level of inequality in the United States—where the richest quintile earns $15 for every dollar earned by the poorest quintile—is dysfunctional? The large and growing gap between rich and poor comes with costs. Moreover, we all pay these costs. Poverty is associated with poor health, including higher levels of diabetes, heart disease, hypertension, and cancer. Poor women are significantly more likely to give birth prematurely and have low-birthweight babies. The March of Dimes (2002) estimates that the lifetime costs of a baby born prematurely are about $500,000, with annual costs of $26 billion for all premature babies (Behrman and Stith Butler 2007). Because many poor women lack health insurance, these costs filter through the system, as "hospitals and insurance companies pass their costs on in various ways, ultimately resulting in higher insurance premiums paid by everyone" (Rank 2004:112).

Many children born into poverty also struggle in school. Currently, about 22 percent of all children in the United States live in poverty. Their academic and cognitive difficulties reflect the higher likelihood of being born premature or of low birthweight, as well as exposure to lead paint (a neurotoxin), stressors at home, and hunger and malnutrition. Millions of children go to school every day unable to absorb the material presented to them. Over time, this means a loss of creativity and productivity. They are not, however, the only ones who pay the costs of their poverty. The economy as a whole suffers when millions of people do not have the tools to contribute to the labor force. According to a report by Harry Holzer and colleagues (2007), the annual costs associated with childhood poverty—in terms of health care, education, and crime—may be as high as $500 billion annually. Clearly, significant economic costs are associated with poverty—costs born by society as a whole—as when poor Americans are too sick, too poorly educated, or too enticed by crime to contribute to society.

In his book *One Nation, Underprivileged: Why American Poverty Affects Us All*, Mark Rank (2004) argues that Americans pay a high cost for social inequality in terms of our core civic values, namely liberty, justice, and democracy. Poverty, Rank writes, severely constrains people's choices, power, and ability to act as they please; their destitution imposes significant limitations on their daily realities. The democratic system, moreover, is compromised as poor people lack access to leaders and the power to lobby or influence leaders in meaningful ways. The poor do not constitute a special interest group with which most politicians want to align; therefore, their interests often go unaddressed.

While many Americans acknowledge the fact of social inequality as well as the costs associated with social inequality, there is strong disagreement about what—if anything—should be done about it. Further, because social class is such a complicated and contradictory identity—some days even I am not sure what social class I belong to—many Americans have a hard time identifying which, if any, group they fit into and how they might advocate for change. Finally, while inequality may be an inevitable fact of life, the degree of inequality is not. Indeed, social inequality is a reflection of macro-level social and political choices. The question, then, is whether we will continue making choices that widen social inequality or whether the choice will be made to reverse this course.

CHAPTER 5: REVIEW OF KEY POINTS

- Although class can be defined as a group of people with shared life chances, economic opportunities, and lifestyle, sociologists disagree intensely on how to define these concepts and, especially, which of these components is most important.
- Karl Marx defined social class in simple terms, focusing on autonomy, social control, and exploitation; Max Weber and Pierre Bourdieu placed greater emphasis on culture and the subjective aspects of social class.
- When it comes to income, the richest quintile earns about 50 percent of all income. Wealth is distributed much more unequally, with the richest quintile holding 84 percent of all income and the bottom two quintiles possessing negligible portions.
- When focusing on economic inequality, more emphasis should be placed on wealth since it comprises a person's safety net and because it tends to appreciate in value over time.
- Some theorists have applied the *essentialist perspective* to explaining social class differences, arguing that intelligence is innate (genetic) and closely linked to the social class a person occupies.
- The *social constructionist perspective* shows us that over the course of history, the degree and significance of socioeconomic inequality has varied widely; it also shows that social policies can either mitigate or exacerbate the degree of inequality in a society.
- *Dependency* argues that poor countries remain poor because they are locked into exploitative relationships with richer countries; they often have rich natural resources and corrupt leaders that make them ripe for exploitation.
- Scandinavian countries and other European countries have lower levels of economic inequality because they have strong *welfare state* policies that limit economic inequalities and promote social well-being.
- Due to various large-scale structural changes (macro; "The Game"), the United States has become increasingly unequal since the early 1970s.
- Even though many Americans are living comfortable middle- and upper-middle-class lives, we should all care about inequality because we all pay the price—in terms of taxes for programs that address poverty and in terms of having a legitimate democratic society.

CHAPTER 5: QUESTIONS FOR REVIEW

1. Karl Marx and Max Weber developed two of the earliest sociological theories about social class. What are the key points of similarity and difference in their theories, especially in terms of what determines a person's social class, how many classes there are (how social class is structured), and the social consequences of class inequality?
2. In the late twentieth century, Pierre Bourdieu made an important contribution to theories of social class inequality. What is cultural capital, and how does it add to understandings of social class inequality?
3. Looking at statistical information about economic inequality in the United States, how much inequality currently exists in this country?
4. Thinking about both the theories of social class and the data on economic inequality in the United States, where do you think you stand in terms of social class? How would you label

your social class? How do your economic resources and cultural capital affect your choice of a label?

5. On what basis do Herrnstein and Murray argue that social class differences are genetically based?

6. According to the information in this chapter, why are some societies much richer and more equal than others? What dynamics account for the inequalities in the "developing world" compared to industrialized countries? What dynamics account for differences across industrialized countries?

7. What factors account for the fact that economic inequality in the United States has been growing since the late 1960s?

8. Why should anyone be concerned about a society's level of inequality? To what extent are you concerned about the level of inequality in the United States—whether for personal reasons or for broader social reasons?

KEY TERMS

bourgeoisie

class consciousness

core

cultural capital

Davis-Moore thesis

dependency theory

estate taxes

functionalist perspective

G.I. Bill

income

Industrial Revolution

Kuznets Curve

labor union

liberal welfare state

living wage

means of production

Occupy movement

periphery

postindustrial stage

proletariat

quintile

Reaganomics

semi-periphery

social class

social-democratic welfare state

socioeconomic status

wealth

welfare state

World Bank

world systems theory

REFERENCES

Allegretto, Sylvia A. and Michelle M. Arthur. 2001. "An Empirical Analysis of Homosexual/Heterosexual Male Earnings Differentials: Unmarried and Unequal?" *Industrial and Labor Relations Review* 54(3):631–646.

Antecol, Heather, Anneke Jong, and Michael Steinberger. 2008. "The Sexual Orientation Wage Gap: The Role of Occupational Sorting and Human Capital." *Industrial and Labor Relations Review* 61(4):518–543.

Atkinson, Anthony B. 2010. "Income Inequality in Historical and Comparative Perspective." Paper presented at the opening conference of the GINI Project, March 19, London, U.K.

Behrman, Richard E. and Adrienne Stith Butler. 2007. "Preterm Birth: Causes, Consequences, and Prevention. Institute of Medicine Committee on Understanding Premature Birth and Assuring Healthy Outcomes." Washington, D.C: National Academies Press.

Black, Dan A., Seth G. Sanders, and Lowell J. Taylor. 2007. "The Economics of Lesbian and Gay Families." *Journal of Economic Perspectives* 21(2):53–70.

Blandford, John M. 2003. "The Nexus of Sexual Orientation and Gender in the Determination of Earnings." *Industrial and Labor Relations Review* 56(4):622–642.

Bound, John and Sarah Turner. 2002. "Going to War and Going to College: Did World War II and the GI Bill Increase Educational Attainment for Returning Veterans?" *Journal of Labor Economics* 20(4):784–815.

Bourdieu, Pierre. 1984. *Distinction: A Social Critique of the Judgement of Taste*. Cambridge, MA: Harvard University Press.

Card, David. 2001. "The Effect of Unions on Wage Inequality in the U.S. Labor Market." *Industrial and Labor Relations Review* 54: 296–315.

Coontz, Stephanie. 1997. *The Way We Really Are: Coming to Terms With America's Changing Families*. New York: Basic Books.

Davis, James, Susanna Sundstrom, Anthony Shorrocks, and Edward Wolff. 2006. "World Distribution of Household Wealth." Helsinki, Finland: United Nations University World Institute for Development Economics Research. Retrieved April 20, 2015 (http://www.wider.unu.edu/publications/working-papers/discussion-papers/2008/en_GB/dp2008-03/)

Davis, Kingsley and Wilbert E. Moore. 1945. "Some Principles of Stratification." *American Sociological Review* 10(2):242–249.

Eagan, Kevin, Jennifer B. Lozano, Sylvia Hurtado, and Matthew H. Case 2013. *The American Freshman: National Norms 2013*. Los Angeles: Cooperative Institutional Research Program at the Higher Education Research Institute at UCLA. Retrieved September 3, 2014 (http://www.heri.ucla.edu/monographs/TheAmericanFreshman2013.pdf).

Fischer, Claude S., Michael Hout, Martin Sanchez Jankowski, Samuel R. Lucas, Ann Swidler, Kim Voss, and Lawrence Bobo. 1996. *Inequality by Design: Cracking the Bell Curve Myth*. Princeton, NJ: Princeton University Press,

Gøsta, Esping-Andersen. 1990. *The Three Worlds of Welfare Capitalism*. Cambridge, U.K.: Polity.

Herrnstein, Richard J. and Charles Murray. 1994. *The Bell Curve: Intelligence and Class Structure in American Life*. New York: Simon and Schuster.

Holzer, Harry, Diane Whitmore Schanzenbach, Greg Duncan, and Jens Ludwig. 2007. "The Economic Costs of Poverty in the United States: Subsequent Effects of Children Growing Up Poor." Washington, DC: Institute for Research on Poverty.

Humes, Edward. 2006. *Over Here: How the G.I. Bill Transformed the American Dream*. Boston: Houghton Mifflin Harcourt.

Jepsen, Lisa Kay. 2007. "Comparing the Earnings of Cohabiting Lesbians, Cohabiting Heterosexual Women, and Married Women: Evidence from the 2000 Census." *Industrial Relations: A Journal of Economy and Society* 46(4):699–727.

Kennickell, Arthur B. 2009. *Ponds and Streams: Wealth and Income in the US, 1989 to 2007*. Washington, D.C.: Divisions of Research & Statistics and Monetary Affairs, Federal Reserve Board.

Knudsen, Eric I., James J. Heckman, Judy L. Cameron, and Jack Shonkoff. 2006. "Economic, Neurobiological, and Behavioral Perspectives on Building America's Future Workforce." *Proceedings of the National Academy of the Sciences* 103(27):10155–10162.

Kuznets, Simon. 1955. Economic Growth and Income Inequality. *American Economic Review* 45 (March):1–28.

Mishel, Lawrence and Jared Bernstein. 1993. *The State of Working America, 1992–1993*. Armonk, NY: M.E. Sharpe/Economic Policy Institute.

Mishel, Lawrence, Jared Bernstein, and Sylvia Allegretto. 2007. *The State of Working America*. Ithaca, NY: ILR Press.

Mishel, Lawrence, Jared Bernstein, and Heidi Shierholz. 2009. *The State of Working America: 2008/2009*. Ithaca, NY: Economic Policy Institute, Cornell University Press.

Norton, Michael I. and Dan Ariely. 2011. "Building a Better America—One Wealth Quintile at a Time." *Perspectives on Psychological Science* 6(1) 9–12.

Norwood, Stephen H. 2002. *Strikebreaking and Intimidation: Mercenaries and Masculinity in Twentieth Century America*. Chapel Hill: University of North Carolina Press.

Perrucci, Robert and Earl Wysong. 2008. *The New Class Society: Goodbye American Dream?* Lanham, MD: Rowman and Littlefield.

Pew Research Center. 2010. "Marrying Out: One-in-Seven New U.S. Marriages Is Interracial or Interethnic." Washington, DC.

Ramos, Christopher, Brad Sears, and M. V. Lee Badgett. 2008. "Evidence of Employment Discrimination on the Basis of Sexual Orientation and Gender Identity: Complaints Filed with State Enforcement Agencies 1999–2007." Los Angeles: The Williams Institute at the UCLA School of Law. Retrieved September 8, 2014 (http://williamsinstitute.law.ucla.edu/wp-content/uploads/Badgett-Sears-Ramos-Emply-Discrim-1999-2007-Nov-08.pdf).

Rank, Mark. 2004. *One Nation, Underprivileged: Why American Poverty Affects Us All*. New York: Oxford University Press.

Saez, Emmanuel. 2013. "Striking it Richer: The Evolution of Top Incomes in the United States (updated with 2012 preliminary estimates)." Berkeley: University of California, Department of Economics.

Smith, Robert Michael. 2003. *From Blackjacks to Briefcases: A History of Commercialized Strikebreaking and Unionbusting in the United States*. Athens, OH: Ohio University Press.

Stiglitz, Joseph. 2013. *The Price of Inequality: How Today's Divided Society Endangers Our Future*. New York: W.W. Norton.

Stone, Chad, Danilo Trisi, Arloc Sherman, and Brandon DeBot. 2015. "A Guide to Statistics on Historical Trends in Income Inequality." Washington, D.C.: Center on Budget and Policy Priorities. Retrieved April 20, 2015 (http://www.cbpp.org/files/11-28-11pov.pdf)

Thompson, William and Joseph Hickey. 2005. *Society in Focus*. Boston, MA: Pearson.

Turkheimer, Eric, Andreana Haley, Mary Waldron, Brian D'Onofrio, and Irving I. Gottesman. 2003. "Socioeconomic Status Modifies Heritability of IQ in Young Children." *Psychological Science* 14(6):623–628.

United States Census Bureau. 2014. "Historical Income Tables: Income Inequality. Share of Aggregate Income Received by Each Fifth and Top 5 Percent of Households" Washington, D.C. Retrieved on April 18, 2015. (http://www.census.gov/hhes/www/income/data/historical/inequality/).

U.S. Bureau of the Census. 2013. "Income, Poverty, and Health Insurance Coverage in the United States: 2012." Washington, DC. Retrieved April 18, 2015 (http://www.census.gov/prod/2013pubs/p60-245.pdf).

Wolff, Edward N. 2010. "Recent Trends in Household Wealth in the United States: Rising Debt and the Middle-Class Squeeze—an Update to 2007." Annandale-on-Hudson, NY: Levy Economics Institute of Bard College.

World Bank. 2014. "World Development Indicators: 2014." Washington, D.C. Retrieved April 20, 2015 (http://data.worldbank.org/sites/default/files/wdi-2014-book.pdf)

Deficit or Difference?
Understanding Disabilities

In the summer of 2009, I became a member of the largest minority group in the United States. I did not miraculously change my race; nor did I come out of the closet and join the increasingly diverse group of Americans who identify as "queer" (a term sometimes used for people whose gender and/or sexuality do not follow normative conventions). Instead, after months of medical tests, I was diagnosed with a chronic health condition—one that relatively few people *die from*, but rather *die with*, often after years of debilitating health and well-being. With this diagnosis, I became a person with a disability. To confirm my status, I registered with the office of ADA compliance on campus (which ensures employees' protections under the Americans with Disabilities Act) and then cruised over to the Department of Motor Vehicles to pick up my "handicapped-parking" hangtag.

When the attendant looked at me with disbelief, and then questioned the legitimacy of my request for a handicapped-parking hangtag, I had two profound realizations about the nature of disability. First, I immediately felt the sting of stigma that often accompanies having a disability. In many cases, people with disabilities are the object of scrutiny and suspicion, with frequent questions about the legitimacy of their condition and why they can and cannot perform certain tasks. Second, I realized how large and unwieldy the disabilities umbrella is. While my doctors had classified me as having a physical disability and authorized me certain legal protections (under the ADA), it felt strange that I technically was a member of a group that also includes my 26-year-old cousin, a young man with severe autism, who has never spoken and cannot care for his own basic needs. What did we have in common, I wondered, and how useful is it to include under the umbrella of disabled persons those with such different types of disability?

This chapter explores the newest "frontier" in sociological studies of inequality and diversity: people with disabilities. First, we begin with basic definitions and background: Who is included in this large umbrella, and what is the difference between *having a disability* (me) and *being disabled* (my cousin)? Second, we explore the different ways of framing or understanding people with disabilities. From one perspective, people with disabilities—whether intellectual, physical, or mental—are people with deficiencies, whose lives can be improved with intervention from experts. From another perspective, having a disability is a social construction. Accordingly, whether and how having a disability equates with having a deficit is a matter of social and structural conditions, rather than an inherent reflection of the individual or group. Further, the social constructionist perspective often frames people with disabilities as a minority group—that is, a group that differs in some sense from the norm, experiences that difference in fundamental ways on a daily basis, and generally has less power and opportunity than people who are part of the majority. Finally, we take a closer look at controversial topics within disability studies, such as how technologies have both costs and benefits for people with a disability.

MATTERS OF DEFINITION: COUNTING AND CLARIFYING *PEOPLE WITH DISABILITIES* AND *THE DISABLED*

As noted above, one of the biggest challenges in understanding the topic of disabilities is the wide net that is cast over this group and the diverse conditions and levels of severity it encompasses. Drawing on data from the U.S. Census, the Centers for Disease Control and Prevention estimates that about 57 million Americans are living with some type of disability; of that group, about 38 million have a severe disability. Expressed in other terms, nearly 19 percent of Americans has some type of disability. Not surprisingly, the likelihood of having a disability increases with age. Whereas only 8.4 percent of people under the age of 15 have some type of disability, this number rises to 19.7 percent among 45- to 54-year-olds and 70 percent of those above the age of 80. It is estimated that 19 percent of all Americans have some type of disability, which qualifies it as the largest minority group in the United States.

The wide-ranging estimates of those who have a disability, and the category of "severe disability," point to the importance of establishing some definitions. **Disability** is an umbrella term that refers to an impairment that is physical, cognitive, mental, sensory, emotional, developmental, or some combination of these. *Impairment* generally refers to a problem with the structure of functioning of some physical, mental, or sensory feature. Many definitions of disability, including those used by the **Americans with Disabilities Act** (a topic that will be addressed later in the chapter), emphasize that disability occurs when a person experiences a condition that substantially limits at least one "major life activity." This phrase itself is a matter of some debate. While undefined by the ADA, it is generally assumed to include walking, hearing, seeing, performing manual tasks, learning, and working. The ability to drive is *not* considered a major life activity; sexual function occupies a murky area: while being able to perform with vigor and stamina is not considered a major life function, being able to reproduce might be.

The notion of disability, then, covers a wide array of physical, mental, and cognitive conditions. The definition also includes conditions that range from mild to severe. A person with a severe disability may not be able to care for oneself, communicate, learn, or work. Compare someone with these impairments to someone with a mild form of multiple sclerosis, who has few symptoms on a day-to-day basis. A flare-up or exacerbation may bring on temporary impairments in mobility, vision, or other core functions, but one's daily life is generally free of impairment. The considerable variation that occurs within the category of people with disabilities also suggests that many people have *non*visible disabilities. People with Crohn's disease, arthritis, dyslexia, and many other conditions may experience very real challenges to their daily functions, but these challenges may go unnoticed or even be minimized by those around them due to the largely invisible nature of their disability.

One trait that makes people with disabilities a unique group is that, unlike race or ethnicity, it is a category that most people are not born into but rather join later in life. What I mean is that most disabilities are not congenital, but rather acquired. Disabilities like Down syndrome, cystic fibrosis, missing limbs, and severe autism are present at birth. Yet the majority of those who have a disability—perhaps as many as 85 percent—acquire it later in life. This may be due to a car accident requiring a limb amputation or an accident causing a traumatic brain injury (TBI). Acquired disabilities also include conditions that have some combination of genetic and environmental causes often appearing in advanced adulthood, such as Parkinson's disease, Alzheimer's disease, and multiple sclerosis.

The concept of disability becomes even stickier when it comes to official governmental recognition. On the one hand, the ADA provides a broad definition with few qualifying terms. The core characteristic, as noted above, is that a person experiences substantial limitations in one or more major life activity. In contrast to this wide umbrella, the notion of *being disabled* by official government standards is quite narrow. The Social Security Administration determines who is disabled and, therefore, qualifies for financial support from the government. Their definitions focus more specifically on the ability to work. A person may be considered disabled if extensive medical documentation indicates they are unable to perform significant gainful activity—generally defined as unable to work to one's full capacity or within his or her established occupational field. Although just one example, this shows that debates over the definition of disability are important because they determine who may deserve certain benefits and which categories of people may be protected by legislation that prohibits discrimination.

THEORIZING DISABILITY: COMPARING THE MEDICAL AND SOCIAL MODELS

Across many societies, the history of people with disabilities is not a pretty one. In addition to the fact that people with disabilities differ from the norm and lack social power, they can also be considered a minority group due to a long history of discrimination. This discrimination has included everything from banishment and isolation to forced sterilization to death. It has only been in recent decades that perspectives and treatment of people with disabilities have shifted. In part, this shift represents the transition from a *medical model* for thinking about disabilities to a *social model*.

THE ESSENTIALIST PERSPECTIVE: USING A MEDICAL MODEL TO UNDERSTAND DISABILITIES

Recently enrolled in one of my classes was a woman who requested that PowerPoint slides, handouts, and other documents for the course be printed on yellow paper. This student can read, does not sit near the front of the class, and does not require large-print materials. She is registered with our campus's Disability Resource Center, where they work with her to transfer the assigned reading materials to yellow paper. Last year, I worked with a remarkable deaf student. Enrolled in my Qualitative Research Methods class, she conducted a marvelous project on deaf culture and perspectives on *cochlear implants* (devices that improve the sensory abilities of people who are hard of hearing). In the classroom, she lip-read, voiced, used her own cochlear implant, and had an assistant, assigned by the Disability Resource Center, who provided real-time captioning (and immediate transcription of course content). While both of these students received accommodations from our campus's Disability Resource Center, I ask the provocative question: Are they disabled?

Looked at from the perspective of the medical model, the answer clearly is yes. The **medical model of disability** parallels the essentialist perspective discussed throughout this text. It assumes, first, that there is a real physical, mental, or emotional deviation present in the disabled person's body. Second, it assumes that the condition is rooted in the individual's body—rather than caused by the social environment. Third, it assumes that this condition is, in fact, a problem. The medical model, in short, sees disability as a *personal tragedy* (Oliver 1990)—where each of those words neatly captures a key part of the perspective. In the above examples, the medical model would simply label the first student as having a visual impairment and the second student as having a hearing impairment. In the realm of disabilities, these notions are often subtly embedded in our language. For example, one website sells a special keyboard with black letters printed on bright yellow keys—perfect perhaps for the student I mentioned. It describes its products as "designed for individuals who *suffer* from visual impairments" (emphasis added). The notion of impairment suggests that the condition in question is not just a statistical deviation from the norm, but a characteristic that makes the person lesser and in need of fixing.

Finally, perhaps most central to the name of this approach, the medical model proposes a variety of therapies—physical and mental—and accommodations aimed at repairing the disabled person. It situates the problem in the individual and the cure or treatment in the hands of trained medical professionals. According to this perspective, a person who has a hearing impairment may be helped through the surgical implantation of a cochlear implant, a device that stimulates auditory nerves to improve hearing. In addition to regular monitoring by audiologists, he or she may receive the assistance of an occupational therapist to help successfully navigate home and work environments. Because the range of disabilities is so large, there is almost no limit to the types of surgical, pharmaceutical, and therapeutic interventions a disabled person may receive.

So far, this approach doesn't sound so bad. In fact, it sounds like a holistic way of ensuring that the person in question may function according to their highest capabilities within society. Yet the history of this approach is one that concentrated power in the hands of medical professionals and severely mistreated people with disabilities, given the tendency at the core of this approach to pathologize people with disabilities (to pathologize means to define a condition not simply as a statistical deviation from normal, but as a disease or sickness). As a social identity, this pathology becomes a basis for stigma. Sociologists like Erving Goffman have defined stigma as a trait that marks a person as deviant and undesirable, with consequences ranging from judgment, to exclusion, to discrimination, to death (Link and Phelan 2001).

TRAVELING BACK IN TIME

Indeed, the arc of Western history—from the Ancient Greeks to today—shows that death and exclusion were common responses to disability throughout history. Over time, however, social understandings of disability shifted from religiously based explanations to biological or scientific explanations. Like many of the topics discussed in this book—from explanations of racial differences to human sexuality—scientific explanations began to replace religious or theological explanations during the 1700s. In the 1800s, for example, deafness was a concern primarily because without language, deaf people were "beyond the reach of the gospel" (Baynton 1996). In other cases, people with disabilities were thought to have been punished by God for their sins. As scientific thinking began to replace religious thinking as the primary source of authority, disabilities began to be seen as problematic because they brought medical afflictions or compromised the individual's capacity for reason. This shift meant that people who were once considered the responsibility of the local church parish, which relegated them to almshouses and workhouses, became the responsibility of the government and the medical establishment.

Across Europe and the United States, the 1700s marked the beginning of an era in which people with disabilities were increasingly institutionalized. This means they were formally housed in asylums and largely isolated from the wider society—a process philosopher Michel Foucault called "the Great Confinement." Soon, in England and the United States, once-charitable attitudes toward those with disabilities began to harden. Whereas workhouses once had a human design, facilities built in the 1800s were designed as miserable places to live; they were made so unappealing that those with the capacity to work would seek occupation rather than a "free ride" within the institution. As a consequence, these institutions led to increased isolation for those with physical disabilities and the mentally ill.

Filth, crowding, and inattention were part of the truly deplorable conditions in which people with disabilities were kept for many decades.

Inside the asylum, medical professionals known as "alienists" believed that within the peaceful confines, patients could be restored by "moral treatment." Instead of punishment or restraint, these early psychiatrists approached their patients with kindness, fresh air, and light work. Within decades, this optimism died away, giving birth to a system that housed severe and chronic cases, which many professionals regarded as incurable, if not hopeless. Meanwhile, some special schools for people with epilepsy, blindness, and deafness did flourish under innovative leadership.

While many today may believe that people with disabilities can be responsibly helped by medical professionals, French philosopher Michel Foucault was critical of the degree to which the medical establishment claimed power within this domain. Foucault argued that patients were increasingly subjected to the "**medical gaze**" in clinics and asylums. He used this term to describe the medical profession's dehumanizing separation of the patient as a body (in need of repair) from the patient as a person. Moreover, he was critical of the fact that by carving out a domain of power and expertise, doctors transformed patients into possible targets of professional manipulation. He saw the birth of modern medicine, alongside the emergence of those facilities serving people with disabilities, as more focused on gaining power and authority, and the ability of the medical profession to define reality, than about caring for the patient.

The power of the medical profession to define the reality of those with disabilities is seen most insidiously in the eugenics movement of the late 1800s and mid-1900s. Rather than rehabilitate or attempt to cure people with disabilities, the eugenics movement sought to eliminate them altogether. As discussed in Chapter 4, eugenics means *well born*. It refers to a social philosophy—most closely associated with Sir Francis Galton—and medical practices that promoted reproduction among those with socially desirable traits and eliminating reproduction among those with less desirable traits—racial and ethnic minorities—as well as those with physical and mental disabilities. Scientists and medical doctors played prominent roles in this movement, lending their expertise to the genetic theories that motivated the movement, the surgical efforts that accompanied it, and the social policies that enforced it.

Throughout the 1900s, at least 27 states in the United States joined a number of European countries in passing compulsory sterilization laws. Under these laws, both men and women with disabilities were sterilized against their will, rendering them infertile; women who were already pregnant were sometimes forced to have an abortion. Eugenics thinking was so prevalent that in 1927, the U.S. Supreme Court ruled that forced sterilizations did not violate a person's Constitutional rights. In **Buck v. Bell**, Supreme Court Justice Oliver Wendell Holmes Jr. ruled that compulsory sterilization of the intellectually disabled "for the protection and health of the state" did not violate the 14th Amendment's Due Process clause. Instead, eliminating the "feebleminded" "defectives" from the gene pool was viewed as in the best interest of the public welfare. Indeed, Holmes wrote in his decisions that it was reasonable for individuals to make this "sacrifice" so that people with disabilities did not "sap the strength" of the nation. While this Supreme Court ruling has never formally been reversed, by the early 1960s forced sterilization was no longer practiced. In 2011, the state of North Carolina became the first to discuss providing compensation to those who were forcibly sterilized after being declared mentally unfit.

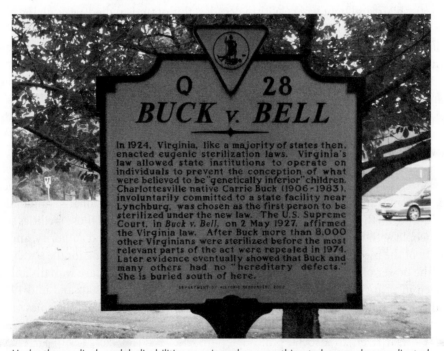

Under the medical model, disabilities are viewed as something to be cured or eradicated.

While many of these examples may seem like a dark chapter from an earlier time, some observers fear that eugenics is alive and well. They argue that the use of **genetic testing** is a modern example of how science and the medical model are being used to rid the population of unwanted traits (Kitcher 1997). In this case, genetic testing is used as an umbrella term to refer to a variety of tests given to a woman and her fetus during pregnancy; a more specific term is prenatal testing. While some genetic testing is less invasive and simply extracts a sample of DNA from one's hair, saliva, or other tissues, other forms are more invasive and potentially dangerous, such as amniocentesis, during which a sample is drawn by inserting a needle through the abdomen into the amniotic fluid surrounding the uterus. These tests can detect hundreds of traits, including sex, lactose intolerance, extra digits (fingers), short limbs or bowed legs, poor vision, dwarfism, deafness, fragile X syndrome (which can cause an intellectual disability or what was previously called mental retardation), and Down syndrome.

So how might you respond if you learned that you or your partner was pregnant with a fetus showing the possibility of being born with Down syndrome? While genetic and prenatal testing can be used to detect particular conditions and help parents prepare for the birth of a disabled child, it can also lead to the choice to abort the developing fetus. This is sometimes called selective abortion, referring not to a general desire to become unpregnant but to the desire not to give birth to a fetus with specific traits. In some cases, this may be because a parent already has three boys and would prefer not to give birth to another boy; in other cases, people may feel ill-equipped to parent a child with a disability or may fear that the child's quality of life would be severely compromised. Although estimates are hard to come by, one study finds that within the United States, 67 percent of pregnancies with a definitive diagnosis of Down syndrome are terminated (Natoli et al. 2012).

The topic of genetic and prenatal testing raises a number of ethical questions and in so doing points to the dark side of the medical perspective on disabilities. First, many of the tests result in false-positives (Bianchi et al. 2014; Malone et al. 2005). These tests are imperfect and sometimes provide incorrect results. Yet because they have the authority of scientific or medical knowledge, they sometimes lead potential parents to falsely believe their developing fetus is at risk for a disability and a decision to terminate the pregnancy. The tests are also limited in that they cannot detect the degree of disability—from mild to severe. Further, some of the more invasive tests actually cause a fetus to abort in 1–2 percent of all cases. Many in the disability rights movement worry that the reduction of genetic and neurodiversity through selective abortions may result in less financial support for groups that promote research, support, and awareness for various disabilities. Yet another concern is that with fewer people being born with various disabilities, stigma and intolerance may increase for those who are born with a disability (Parens and Asch 2003). Genetic counselors are employed by many hospitals and clinics to help parents work though these difficult questions, providing patients with information about the risks of testing, the consequences of having a child with particular conditions, and resources for supporting that child. Ultimately, these scientific innovations raise troubling questions about who deserves to be born and what kinds of lives are worth living (Hubbard 2006).

It would be unfair and inaccurate to suggest that medical practitioners in general carry within them a perspective that sees those with disabilities as fundamentally pathological. A tremendous number of physicians have made it their life work to improve through research and treatments the lives of those with disabilities. The point made herein is that one prevailing belief is that those with disabilities are deviant from the norm and that medical professionals hold the tools for helping them overcome their limitations. In a number of noteworthy instances, this same perspective has been used to bolster the legitimacy and power of science and medicine, with deleterious consequences for people with disabilities. It is, therefore, necessary to turn our attention toward another lens through which the topic of disabilities can be viewed.

THE SOCIAL CONSTRUCTIONIST PERSPECTIVE: USING A SOCIAL MODEL TO UNDERSTAND DISABILITIES

The assertion that a person who is deaf does not actually have a disability is quite provocative. Ordinarily, it would seem obvious that a person who cannot hear is impaired and, therefore, has a disability. The **social model of disability**, however, challenges this interpretation. The social model of disability acknowledges that some people have physical, mental, and cognitive functioning that places them outside the statistical norm. Yet advocates of this perspective do not automatically conclude that the atypical individual is impaired. Rather, they contend it is the social context that disables people, through the imposition of social, structural, and environmental barriers (Oliver 2009; Shakespeare 2006). From this perspective, deafness is a problem because the wider social environment is built around the assumption that everyone can hear. Yet deaf people *can* communicate. Accordingly, they are not inherently disabled; rather, it is the social environment that disables them. With assumptions like these, the social model seeks to *destigmatize* people with disabilities and raise difficult questions about how society is itself organized. Rather than attempt to "fix" the disabled person, as the medical model would, the social model approaches disability as a civil rights issue. It "places the moral responsibility on society to remove the burdens which have been imposed, and to enable disabled people to participate" (Shakespeare 2006:199).

There are parallels between the social model of disability and the social constructionist perspective described throughout this book, just as there are parallels between the medical model and the essentialist perspective. The social model parallels the social constructionist perspective in the sense that what counts as a disability and who counts as being disabled have fluctuated across time and across cultures. The same mental, physical, or cognitive manifestations that may be considered a disability in one context may be constructed very differently elsewhere. This suggests that while there may be some common patterns in terms of what is seen as disabling, there are few things that are universally defined as a disability.

Take, for example, people we would today label as having a mental health problem or emotional disability, something along the lines of schizophrenia or bipolar disorder. In his classic book *Madness and Civilization* (originally published in 1964),

Michel Foucault shows how conceptions of "madness" changed over time in western Europe. During the Renaissance, for example, people with mental or emotional "deviations" were thought to possess unique and valuable forms of humor, wisdom, and insight. They sometimes appeared in royal courts as "natural fools," where their performances pointed out truths or ironies about the human condition that only they could see. Only during the Age of Reason of the late 1600s, with the increased emphasis on rationality and systematic thought, did "madness" come to be viewed as both a personal flaw and a threat to the social order.

Looking at various constructions of physical disability, it has already been stated that such conditions have been considered a moral or religious curse. Elsewhere, the blind prophet—such as Tiresias of Greek mythology—represents an image of how disabilities have been positively, yet mysteriously, construed. Without language, deaf people during the 1800s were thought to possess unique wisdom and freedom from corrupt thoughts (Baynton 1996). Indeed, ever since the 1600s, social attitudes toward people with disabilities have been, in a word, ambivalent. Alongside confinement and stigma, the popularity of "freak shows"—where people with disabilities sometimes performed astounding feats—attests to our curiosity about human difference. Many of the traveling shows of the 1700s and 1800s included acts that performed fantastical or heroic tasks. The German performer Matthias Buchinger, for example, was born without arms or legs but publicly performed music and astounding magic tricks. Yet as medical understandings of disability emerged, these entertainments fell out of favor and, somewhat ironically, brought greater stigma to those with disabilities.

ARGUING AGAINST DISABILITY: TWO ILLUSTRATIONS

Maybe a couple of examples will better illustrate the social model of disability. Being deaf or hard of hearing represents perhaps the best developed illustration of this perspective. When it comes to deafness, many argue against medical conceptions and reject the notion that it is, in fact, a disability. It is important to note that being *hard of hearing* is an umbrella term—one characterized by variations in hearing loss. Many definitions assume full hearing as the default condition and measure deafness as the degree of impairment from this standard. Accordingly, medical definitions emphasize both the timing and causes of hearing loss, as well as the degree of hearing loss, ranging from mild (up to 40 decibels of hearing loss) to severe (greater than 91 decibels of hearing loss) to totally deaf.

In arguing against deafness as a disability, the central point is that deaf people are not *unable* to communicate. Deafness is not a deficiency; rather, it is merely a difference. Instead of communicating aurally, deaf people communicate using other means, the most common of which is sign language. The notion that being deaf is a disability has been called **audism**. If refers, more specifically, to the belief that being able to hear is superior to not being able to hear, and that life without hearing is futile and miserable. It frames, for example, being able to enjoy music as a fundamental joy of the human experience, without considering the possibility that deaf people may have unique sensory or linguistic abilities. The famed neurologist Oliver Sacks (1989)

A controversial technology, some see cochlear implants as a tool to help deaf people function in the world; others see them as an assault on Deaf Culture.

challenged this assumption in his book *Seeing Voices*, where he describes sign language as a beautiful visual language capable of great poetry and as linguistically rich and expressive as any spoken language. It is not a partial substitute for spoken language but a complete language unto itself.

Because deaf people do have obvious language capabilities, theorists and advocates like Harlan Lane (2006) prefer to see them as members of a linguistic minority group—in the same sense that Spanish speakers are a linguistic minority in the United States and French speakers a linguistic minority in Canada. Others have expanded this notion to argue that deaf individuals can function as an autonomous minority or ethnic group, a group that has been labeled **"Deaf Culture."** When written with a "Big-D," identifying as Deaf represents a fundamental identity and comprehensive way of life (Padden and Humphries 2005). This is distinct from deafness with a "small-d," which refers to an *auditory condition* characterized by deafness or hearing loss. Those who claim membership within Deaf Culture are typically those who were born without hearing or experienced hearing loss early in childhood. Accordingly, they likely grew up with American Sign Language (ASL) as their first language and experienced other unique, immersive experiences (such as attending schools and camps for deaf students). According to Harlan Lane (1999), the Deaf Culture resembles other minority groups in the sense that members have a sense of collective identity; values and behavioral norms (e.g., a more collectivist culture with emphasis on finding common ground rather than individualist); distinct language; kinship ties within the group (through birth or marriage); and a history characterized by folk tales, significant figures, events, and places.

Because members of Deaf Culture tend to reject the notion that they are disabled, there have been passionate reactions to the use of cochlear implants. As mentioned above, **cochlear implants** are surgically implanted devices that stimulate auditory nerves to improve hearing. While some see cochlear implants as a miracle device that allows people with hearing loss to participate more fully in social, educational, and work environments, Deaf Culture activists have historically opposed them. The fundamental basis for their opposition is that they do not view deafness as an impairment that needs to be fixed. They reject the medical model because it places power and authority in the hands of doctors and other experts while undermining the distinctiveness and functionality of Deaf Culture. Many activists worry, moreover, that the widespread use of cochlear implants will fracture and fragment Deaf Culture, that rather than a cohesive group with a strong cultural identity, it will transform into a loose group of those who move back and forth between oral and manual language (sign), between hearing and deaf communities. Further, some activists worry that children who receive the implants will experience alienation from both hearing and deaf communities. While they may have skills to communicate with both, neither oral nor manual language will be their native language, so they may lack full acceptance in either group. From the standpoint of identity and inclusion, as well as recognition of the legitimacy of their culture, some members of Deaf Culture are wary of this technology.

Moving to a second case study, there is also controversy around whether autism should be considered a disability. On my campus and perhaps on yours, autistic students are treated as having a disability, with many receiving services through the Disability Resource Center. **Autism** is conventionally defined as a range of complex brain disorders, characterized by a variety of social impairments, communication difficulties, along with restricted and repetitive behaviors, and sensory sensitivities. The autism spectrum includes *autism disorder* on one end, *Asperger's syndrome* in the middle, and *pervasive developmental disorder–not otherwise specified* on the other end (revisions frequently occur in what is included in the spectrum and where it is placed). Note that these conventional medical definitions emphasize impairments and disorders rather than differences. Indeed, the medical community has been active in terms of identifying the causes of autism, how to diagnose it, and how to treat it—typically using medical and behavioral interventions.

The social perspective, in conjunction with members of the autism rights movement, sees the condition as a difference rather than a disability. Instead of curing autism, their goal is to recognize and appreciate the unique abilities that people with autism may have while reducing barriers in the social and educational environment that exacerbate their functioning. Activists within this community seek greater recognition of the neurodiversity that exists within the population; that is, they emphasize the wide range of social and cognitive traits that exist among humans and, therefore, see autism as a nonpathological *variation*, rather than a disease. This wide-ranging difference includes those with dyslexia, dyspraxia, dyscalculia, attention deficit disorder, Tourette's syndrome, and more. It also includes *neurotypicals*—a term coined within the autism rights movement to refer to those who are not on the autism spectrum.

Perhaps the most visible contingent within the autism rights movement consists of people with Asperger's and their advocates. Asperger's is a form of autism characterized by high levels of verbal and cognitive functioning; indeed, many people with Asperger's attend college and perform at a high level. Its most noteworthy characteristic tends to be difficulty in social interaction, especially in terms of reading nonverbal cues, expressing empathy, and picking up on subtleties of humor. Some people with Asperger's may also display a fascination with maps, schedules, molecular structures, or other figures that display complex visual patterns. Indeed, this speaks to the finding that people with Asperger's have unique skills in auditory, visual, or other sensory perception. Psychologist Simon Baron-Cohen noted that "In the social world, there is no great benefit to a precise eye for detail, but in the worlds of maths, computing, cataloging, music, linguistics, engineering, and science, such an eye for detail can lead to success rather than failure" (2002:189).

One of the most well-known people with autism is animal rights activist Temple Grandin. While she has described herself as feeling like "an anthropologist on Mars"

Scholar and activist Temple Grandin has raised awareness of the unique abilities many people with autism have.

among neurotypical people, Grandin has an especially keen understanding of animals. This has made her a sought-after consultant by the livestock industry, where she has lent her expertise to help build systems that treat animals with empathy. Grandin's life, and the research of Baron-Cohen, among others, had led many to emphasize the unique skills of people with autism and Asperger's rather than their deficits—and ultimately argue against the medical model of disability.

As with those who are deaf, there is debate and discord among people with autism and their allies. Some argue that while it may be appropriate to argue against the disability model for people with Asperger's and high-functioning autistic people, this happy, empowered image may not apply across the spectrum. This group acknowledges that some autistic people have amazing gifts and the ability to live independently; they also believe that the wider society can work to reduce the stigma it places on autistic people and become more accepting of behavioral tics and other repetitive behaviors. Yet they emphasize that many people with autism have very real needs, including medication and behavioral therapy. They worry, moreover, that the success of the autism rights movement and an unrealistic positive emphasis on *neurodiversity* may jeopardize funding for research into autism and, therefore, make life more difficult for people with autism.

EXPLORING INTERSECTIONALITY: GENDER AND THE EXPERIENCE OF DISABILITY

While differences in terms of race, class, and gender have been virtually invisible in this chapter so far, it is impossible to speak of *people with disabilities* as if they were a homogeneous group. As with virtually all social experiences, the experience of disability is bound up with sex, race, social class, sexuality, age, and other factors. Indeed, writers across fields have increasingly brought an intersectional approach to their work, with especially fruitful work focusing on feminist approaches to disability. The work of these scholars is varied, but one central theme is the assumption that women with disabilities (and minorities with disabilities, and queer people with disabilities) face a "double whammy"—such that the disadvantage of being disabled and a woman are multiplicative, rather than additive.

Alongside these voices have emerged some critiques and counterpoints. What if men, these voices ask, *also* experience unique and powerful forms of disenfranchisement when disabled? Indeed, notions of masculinity are often centered on a powerful and able male body; masculine identity, in many cases, is virtually synonymous with strength—both emotional and physical. So what happens when a man can no longer express his masculinity in socially expected ways? What if he is no longer able to play sports, do physical tasks around the house, or feels compelled to internalize his stress or pain? Although women certainly face inequality in society, the rigidity of the male gender role can be disempowering for men.

In their analysis of British men who sustained spinal cord injuries while playing competitive rugby, Brett Smith and Andrew Sparkes (2004) uncovered several unique masculine discourses of their experiences. Many men described their bodies as machines that had broken down, while also using metaphors of war and battle. A man named Eamonn, for example, said: "One thing rugby taught me was that you have to *fight* if you are going to get anywhere in life. And, y'know, I've taken this view into how I see disability and myself now. 'Cos I will walk again and make a *comeback*. I will *fight* to make a *comeback*."

While the "supercrip" image can be empowering, it can also reinforce masculine stereotypes that emphasize toughness, competition, and physicality.

(p. 602). The words *fight*, *battle*, and *comeback* resonated throughout their interviews. Other research has found that sport and exercise can be helpful for men with serious mental illness (Carless and Douglas 2008a), with patients and the social workers who counsel them describing their activity and achievements as truly transformative:

"What's different about him is that he, more or less, he started doing the football and, more or less, most of the changes have been of his own volition. He's chosen to do those things rather than me saying, 'Come on, I'll pick you up in the car, I'll take you there, I'll sort it all out for you,' but he's actually run with the ball himself. That would be the most dramatic thing I think, that he's started to take control of his own life" (Carless and Douglas 2008b:146).

Although people with disabilities are sometimes pitied, they are in other cases seen as courageous heroes. This is sometimes called the **"supercrip" stereotype**, which involve tales of determination and remarkable feats. In the realm of disability and masculinity, this image is evident in the intensely competitive wheelchair athlete (Berger 2008; Silva and Howe 2012). The documentary *Murderball* profiles the physically intense world of wheelchair rugby, whose players are typically quadriplegic. As the film's promotional poster shows, its central images are hypermasculine men who are physically gifted and intensely competitive to their core. The book *Wheelchair Warrior*, which tells the story of Melvin Juette—a black male who took up wheelchair basketball after being paralyzed in a gang-related shooting—highlights similar themes: an uplifting story where a man is able to "overcome" his disability through intense physical and emotional dedication.

Scholarly studies and popular depictions show that while their bodies and minds may be stressed or weakened, men can regain a masculine sense of power and independence by maintaining an approach of activity, achievement, and aggression through athletic involvement. Yet while managing to smash damaging stereotypes about disabilities, they also confirm stereotypes of masculinity that emphasize toughness, competition, and physicality. These men's achievements, moreover, may have negative spillover for those who are not able to overcome their limitations or prove their abilities, potentially contributing to the notion that disability is something that people can overcome, but only if they try hard enough.

DISABILITY AS A CIVIL RIGHTS ISSUE

Another aspect that draws a parallel between the experiences of other minority groups in the United States and people with a disability is that both have participated in social movements to draw attention to their struggles for civil rights. Drawing strength from the movements for gender, racial, and sexual equality that rose during the 1960s, the **disability rights movement** emerged in conjunction, seeking justice, inclusion, and equal rights for people with disabilities. It also emphasizes the notion that having a disability is not just a condition but an *identity*—one that has been oppressed but should be embraced. Initially, the strongest voices in the movement were those of advocates for and people with physical disabilities. Their concerns pointed quite convincingly at the array of physical barriers present in society; barriers in schools, workplaces, and public settings that made it difficult or impossible for people with disabilities to participate. At its core, the movement sought to call attention to the injustices caused by *ableism.*

Ableism refers to both individual prejudices against people with disabilities and the social conditions that pose barriers and create inequality for them. In addition to overt discrimination against people with disabilities, ableism includes the subtle yet pervasive assumption that all members of society have the same capabilities—in terms of mobility, sight, vision, and more. With respect to the latter, think about the room in which you are now situated. When it was built, assumptions were made about what kind of lighting is suitable, how people will move about the space, and so forth. Many of the classrooms in which I teach are stadium-style; this, for example, assumes that people are capable of navigating the stairs and selecting the seat they prefer. The default lighting in these classrooms—and most public spaces—is bright and fluorescent; while this lighting is bright and effective for most, it can cause problems for those with certain visual and neurological conditions. The disability rights movement, then, sought to draw attention to seemingly subtle barriers such as these, so that more people can more fully participate in society.

Like the social movements aimed at racial and gender justice, the disability rights movement similarly has noteworthy leaders, significant events, and resulting legislation. A key turning point in the movement was the 1977 sit-in at government office buildings across the U.S., protesting lack of action on legislation that would provide protection to people with disabilities. Led by activist Frank Bowe, nearly 300 people

Leaders of the disability rights movement used many of the same tactics—like sit-ins—introduced by leaders of the civil rights movement.

staged a protest in Washington, D.C., with hundreds more lending support in other U.S. cities. In San Francisco, for example, a smaller number of 120 protestors occupied a city office building for 25 days—making it the longest occupation of a federal office building in U.S. history. Ultimately, these protests led to the signing of Section 504 by Health and Human Services Secretary Joseph Califano, stating: "No otherwise qualified handicapped individual in the United States, shall, solely by reason of his handicap, be excluded from the participation in, be denied the benefits of, or be subjected to discrimination under any program or activity receiving federal financial assistance."

The occupation of federal office buildings is noteworthy for several reasons. First, it resulted in the first passage of legislation requiring equal rights for people with disabilities. Moreover, like other powerful social movements, it involved coalitions—in this case, partnership with organizations seeking justice for racial and social class issues, as well as a broad coalition of people with different disabilities. While the movement was previously fragmented into separate interest groups for those with polio, hearing loss, visual impairments, cerebral palsy, and the like, this event unified them into a powerful group with shared concerns.

As many organizations have staged marches on Washington, the disability rights movement reached a second turning point in 1990 as they descended on Washington, D.C., to further gather support for their cause. In particular, activists wished to hasten the passage of the Americans with Disabilities Act (ADA)—a piece of legislation introduced by Iowa Senator Tom Harkin, which seemed to be delayed. Culminating in the "Capitol Crawl," members of the movement proved just how far they had come. With 1,000 protestors participating in the event, the march climaxed when approximately 60 activists abandoned their wheelchairs and walkers to climb—or crawl—the steps of the Capitol. This dramatic act illustrated their determination to highlight both their disability and their ability and to challenge misconceptions held by the general public. This demonstration is credited with hastening the signing of the Americans with Disabilities Act.

In the "Capital Crawl," disability activists drew increased attention to both their disabilities and their determination.

Mirroring the content of other civil rights legislation, the Americans with Disabilities Act (ADA) was signed into law on July 26, 1990, by President

With activists at his side, President George H. W. Bush signs the Americans with Disabilities Act (1990) into law.

George H. W. Bush. The law prohibits discrimination against people with disabilities and focuses especially on employment, public entities (public transportation and government buildings), public accommodations (movie theaters, malls, airports), the workplace, and telecommunications services. It does so in part by providing explicit regulation of building codes to make buildings accessible and by providing reasonable accommodations in employment and other settings. The law defines "disability" as a "physical or mental impairment that substantially limits a major life activity." In 2009, the law was amended to define "major life activities" as caring for oneself, performing manual tasks, seeing, hearing, eating, sleeping, walking, standing, lifting, bending, speaking, breathing, learning, reading, concentrating, thinking, communicating, and working. Because it calls for changing the social and physical environment in which we live, the ADA reflects the social perspective on disease as it seeks to empower people with disabilities and acknowledges the barriers posed by the social world.

Reading the legislation for the ADA can be a thankless exercise in legalese and technical definitions, but shifting your attention to concrete scenarios can help illustrate how the act may improve a person's life. Think about the room in which your class meets or a movie theater. In order to comply with the ADA, public accommodations must be *accessible*—that is, able to be used by people with a variety of disabilities. As a result of the ADA, numerous seemingly minute design features ensure that public spaces can be used effectively by people with various disabilities. Start with the doorway: Title III of the ADA legislates the width of doorways, ensuring that

Structures with demonstrated historical significance, like the Castillo San Marcos in St. Augustine, Florida, are exempt from ADA regulations.

wheelchair users can easily enter and exit. Flooring too may be a product of ADA regulations: whether carpeted, concrete, or tiled, it must be amenable to navigation by wheelchair, walker, and cane—not too smooth and not too rough. While shag carpet may have hipster cred, its high pile is certainly not ADA compliant. The lighting should be adjustable, and exit signs must be illuminated and written in font sizes visible to most. Elsewhere on campus, restrooms and elevators must be big enough for wheelchairs to rotate on their axes; walkways must be at an angle that is not too steep and will not cause uncontrolled acceleration. Meanwhile, all major signage must have several features that maximize its readability, playing up font size, reducing surface glare, and providing contrast between foreground and background (see Figure 6.1).

Although the ADA passed with wide, bipartisan support, there was some opposition to it. Some business groups and religious organizations

Figure 6.1 Sign identifying ADA features. Many seemingly ordinary building features, like this restroom sign, are actually engineered to provide accessibility to people with disabilities.

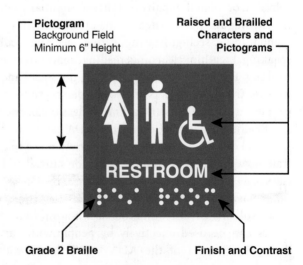

Pictogram
Background Field
Minimum 6" Height

Raised and Brailled
Characters and
Pictograms

RESTROOM

Grade 2 Braille

Finish and Contrast

opposed the legislation, for example, on the basis that it would be too cumbersome and too costly to implement. They worried, in particular, that churches, businesses, and other entities would have to spend money on costly modifications to bring their services and facilities up to code. As a compromise, the legislation stipulates that while all new buildings must comply, older buildings are subject to "the balancing test"— where the costs and ease of bringing the building up to code are balanced *against* ability of the business owners to bear those costs. Other groups exempt from the regulations on public accommodations include private clubs, religious organizations, and noteworthy historic sites. Many historic sites may be granted a waiver if "following the usual standards [of modification] would threaten or destroy the historic significance." The website of one of my favorite local historic sites, a Spanish fort in St. Augustine, Florida, reads: "The Castillo de San Marcos was built for ancient warfare, not for public touring. Unfortunately, the need to preserve the historical and architectural integrity of the fortress limits access to some areas."

DISABILITY RIGHTS AT WORK

The Americans with Disabilities Act also protects people from discrimination at work. I found this out when I was diagnosed with my disability, as I quickly registered myself with my campus's office of ADA compliance. One way the ADA provides protection is by ensuring that workers do not face discrimination in hiring or promotions and that they are provided "**reasonable accommodations**" so they can do their job. A key feature of this part of the law (Title I) is that protections are given only if the person in question is otherwise qualified to execute the duties of the position. The law defines a reasonable accommodation as "any change in the work environment or in the way things are customarily done that enables an individual with a disability to enjoy equal employment opportunities" while *not* causing undue hardship on the employer (in terms of cost or lost productivity). In my case, I am still expected to adhere to my contractual duties of teaching three classes per term, maintaining regular office hours, and keeping up with research. I receive accommodations, though, by being assigned a classroom close to my office for mobility reasons and not teaching long classes at night when I might experience fatigue. For others, this may mean having work equipment modified, so that telephones, computer screens, lighting, office furniture, printed materials, and training manuals are usable for that employee. Outside of an office setting, a grocery store cashier with lupus (an autoimmune disease) may be provided with a stool at work. He can still execute all of the duties of his job, but having a stool provides reasonable relief from pain and fatigue. This allows the individual to remain gainfully employed while costing the employer next to nothing.

One significant achievement of the disability rights movement, and the ADA, has been the notion of universal design. **Universal design** refers to the broad spectrum of ideas that are meant to generate products, buildings, and environments that are accessible to everyone. At its core is the notion that good design can produce good living for all. Rather than thinking about places and products for disabled individuals and non-disabled individuals, universal design aims at creating quality of life for everyone.

Take a simple, almost trivial, example: bathrooms "for" disabled people. These spaces are typically bigger and more comfortable than the tiny stalls "for" nondisabled people. The notion of universal design suggests that those bathroom stalls should not be saved or set aside for people with disabilities; rather, we should all use those bathrooms and put pressure on those who build such facilities to make them functional and aesthetically pleasing for *all*. Doing so would simultaneously reduce the stigma on those for whom those facilities are "set aside," by putting all users on an equal plane.

You know that dip at the corner of sidewalk curb that gradually brings it down to street level? That's called a "curb cut"—the innovation that made universal design famous. Created and promoted by Selwyn Goldsmith—an architect with polio—this urban design feature made navigation more accessible to those using wheelchairs, walkers, and really anyone who doesn't enjoy the sudden drop-off at the end of the sidewalk. In addition to some of the design features listed above, universal design includes buses that "kneel" or have on-ramps, flat panel light switches, door handles in the shape of levers to push rather than knobs to twist, listening devices at museums, and even electric toothbrushes. The beauty of universal design is that it has the potential to erode, if not erase, the distinction between people with disabilities and everyone else, as it highlights the notion that good design is good for everyone. Moreover, it helps illustrate the social perspective on disability, showing how the environment itself can disable the person.

DISABILITY RIGHTS IN EDUCATION

Until fairly recently, most children with disabilities were either educated in specialized schools or not educated at all. Following the model of civil rights movements that sought greater inclusion and educational resources for minority children, activists began seeking a more equal and appropriate education for children with disabilities during the 1970s. Central to this movement were parents of children with disabilities and organizations advocating on their behalf. The **Individuals with Disabilities Education Act**, or IDEA, was initially passed in 1975 as the Education for All Handicapped Children Act. The law applies to those with educational, emotional, and physical disabilities. Its goal is to provide a free and appropriate education to all children with disabilities, one that will prepare them for further education, employment, or independent living.

When I was in elementary school in the 1970s, students in "special education" were relegated to their own classroom. At the time, this was considered the best way to meet these students' educational and emotional needs. Yet it also isolated them and created ideal conditions for stigmatizing them. Today, the law requires children with disabilities to be educated in the "least restrictive environment." This principle, also called *inclusion* and *mainstreaming*, typically means placing them in classrooms with nondisabled peers for the majority of the school day and exposing them to a general education curriculum. Ideally, no more than 2 hours per day should be spent in a separate *resource* classroom. In conjunction, a team of education specialists along with the parents devise an individualized educational program (IEP) for the student, which spells out an educational plan uniquely tailored to that student's strengths, weaknesses, needs, and goals. Together, these principles are meant to achieve two objectives: reducing the stigma those with disabilities often experience, while allowing each individual an appropriate opportunity to learn.

Legislation like IDEA has surely improved the lives of those with disabilities. In addition to higher graduation rates and better cognitive skills, research suggests that the inclusive environment provided by IDEA is linked to improvements in self-esteem and social skills (Koegel et al. 2005; National Research Center on Disabilities 2007; Whitaker 2004; Wolfberg and Schuler 1999). Yet sociological insights indicate lingering issues of inequality and problems associated with the social construction of disability. One such issue is the disproportionate representation in special education programs of students who are minorities and come from lower-income households. Estimates from the U.S. Department of Education, for example, suggest that African American students are twice as likely to be identified as learning disabled or having an emotional disturbance compared to other students. The question becomes whether their higher representation is a reflection of real underlying issues and their special needs or culturally biased testing materials, a clash of cultures, or the tendency to see disruptive behaviors as indicators of disability when presented by students with these traits.

As students who are more likely to have grown up in the urban core, and who may have exposure to environmental toxins and other traumas, it is possible that lower-income and minority students may, indeed, face unique educational and behavioral challenges. Yet others are concerned that lower-income and minority students are mistakenly placed in special education programs. One concern is that the educational professionals who make referrals to special education programs may lack *cultural competence*; that is, they may lack adequate knowledge of cultural differences in norms and behaviors. Within an educational setting, a first-grade child who does not respond to a teacher's questions during story time may be labeled slow, whereas this child may come from a cultural group with different storytelling traditions and simply may be unaccustomed to what the teacher defines as normal behavior. Other research shows that educators define the same types of social behaviors differently depending on the race of the student. Something as seemingly minor as a middle-school student walking with "swagger" was interpreted differently by educators depending on whether the student was white or black. The same physical style was more likely to be seen as aggressive and threatening when displayed by a black student; moreover, that student was more likely to be judged as needing special education services (Neal et al. 2003). More generally, research shows that white teachers consistently rate the behaviors of black students as more problematic and more indicative of ADHD (attention deficit hyperactivity disorder), when compared to their ratings for white students and the ratings given by black teachers (Pigott and Cowen 2000; Zimmerman et al. 1995).

The implications and insights from these studies are sociologically important. First, on a practical level, being placed in special education without cause can have deleterious social and academic consequences. In addition to bringing even greater stigma to a child who may be struggling, misdiagnosing that student's struggles may also mean that student goes without needed resources. Second, on a theoretical level, these insights further demonstrate how social inequalities are perpetuated by seemingly minor acts—actions and reactions based on socially constructed notions of proper and problematic behavior.

EXPLORING ACTIVISM: MAKING HIGHER EDUCATION ACCESSIBLE TO NEW POPULATIONS

The law mandates that schools educate children with disabilities through age 18 or 21, but what happens when those children age out of high school? To what extent is it feasible or appropriate for students with disabilities to pursue a college education? My home institution, the University of North Florida (UNF), in Jacksonville, has several innovative programs that promote higher education for students with disabilities. Like many campuses across the country, UNF has a Disability Resource Center (DRC) that provides accommodations for students with documented disabilities. In addition to extended test times for students with dyslexia or ADD, the Center also provides an array of interpreting services for deaf and hard-of-hearing students, as well as text modification for blind and low-vision students. Currently, the DRC serves more than 800 students on a campus of nearly 16,000. An essential part of the DRC's mission is the expectation that faculty do not "dumb-down" the curriculum for students with disabilities. Rather, the Center ensures "reasonable accommodations" that allow students to demonstrate their knowledge within a framework appropriate to their situation.

Another thing that makes UNF unique is its efforts to educate students who face additional barriers in higher education. Concerned that adults with autism are too often unemployed or unable to reach their potential, three graduate students founded Project THRIVE to help students build situational social skills and independent living skills and to assist with career development. Begun in 2011 with 6 students, THRIVE—which stands for Transition to Health, Resources, Independence, Viable careers, and Education—has grown to serve 40 students. Comparative programs across the country cost students and their families thousands of dollars a semester. With a unique cost-neutral design, THRIVE serves it students' needs by harnessing the mentoring skills of graduate students in Special Education and Mental Health Counseling and advanced undergraduates in select majors. Although the program is too young to evaluate in terms of its graduation record, students like Ian Cleary attest to the value it has added to their college experience: "I joined THRIVE when I was 19 and am still figuring out how to deal with college and my newfound independence as an adult with Asperger's syndrome. The THRIVE program helped me develop agency and confidence and gave me a safe space to talk about things I was struggling with socially, practically, and emotionally. Most importantly, my skills of self-analysis and problem-solving have greatly improved and I've become much more independent than I was two years ago."

Finally, UNF also runs an innovative program for non–degree-seeking students. Built on the assumption that students with intellectual disabilities—including Down syndrome and those with low IQs—can benefit from being exposed to the college environment, the On Campus Transitions program brings students to campus for an educational experience that involves academic and social programming. Instead of seeking a degree, the 25 or so students in the program attend classes, make friends, live away from home, work or volunteer, and engage in recreation, all with the goal of easing the transition to adulthood. The program operates in conjunction with professional guidance from The ARC—a national advocacy group for people with intellectual disabilities—and staff from AmeriCorps, a national service organization. Each week, nearly 200 degree-seeking students volunteer to act as social, academic, or recreational mentors to these students. Upon graduation, the professional staff works hard to place students in residential and occupational positions that maximize their independence.

Begun by activists and advocates, these programs began with the goal of generating greater educational access for people with a range of disabilities and providing them with more options and accommodations to reach their full potential. Yet through their visibility on campus and in the wider community, these programs provide a form of activism by normalizing the experiences of people with disability in society, providing images and examples of ability, and—ideally—reducing the stigma that sometimes comes with having an intellectual disability.

NEW DIRECTIONS FOR THE SOCIOLOGY OF DISABILITIES

Disabilities studies is a relatively new field. Emerging in the 1980s, one of its initial tasks was to examine the socially constructed nature of disability, investigating historical and cross-cultural variations in what is considered a disability and how people with disabilities are treated. In addition, it has framed the issue of disability within an *oppression* model, focusing on the way in which those with disabilities constitute a minority group and face systematic discrimination within society. As in many sociological fields, scholars have also added an intersectional perspective to their studies. They know, for example, that the experience of being black and deaf is unique, just as there are important differences in the experience of having a physical disability, whether the person in question is male or female.

Despite the relative youth of disabilities studies, the field is already keenly focused on the future. One central question scholars are now grappling with, as hinted at throughout this chapter, is the role of technology in the lives of people with disabilities. When it comes to technology, one fundamental sociological insight is that such advancements can both solve problems and create new ones. In decades past, the notion that hearing could be restored through a device like a cochlear implant may have been heralded as a miracle. Today, the device remains controversial and raises questions about the nature of deafness and the degree to which it is a condition that should be cured. Prenatal testing has the capacity to detect hundreds of conditions and to inform parents of any special needs their child may be born with. Yet many

In the future, more and more humans may use technologies like the "eyeborg" to enhance their natural abilities. Such technologies blur the lines between ability and disability and raise questions about whether and how humans should be "fixed."

parents, when informed that their child *may* be born with Down syndrome or an extra finger, choose to abort that fetus. This technology, then, raises questions about medical ethics, and the especially troubling question of which lives are worth living. Some technologies even blur the line between humans and their mechanical counterparts, such as pacemakers, insulin pumps, prosthetic limbs, and other devices to assist in seeing and hearing. In a TED talk, color-blind artist Neil Harbisson discussed his use of a device that transforms colors into audible frequencies. This device has been called an *eyeborg*—a play on the word cyborg, which means an organism with organic (human) and mechanical parts, designed to enhance natural abilities. Rather than simply providing him with a capacity he previously lacked, Harbisson sees himself as *becoming one* with his eyeborg. According to Harbisson, this blurring of man and machine occurred when he started to dream in color. "The software and my brain had united," he said, "because in my dreams, it was my brain creating electronic sounds."

Because technological knowledge and tools will continue to advance, questions about their role in the lives of people with disabilities are likely to become even more relevant. While the medical perspective on disability may celebrate these advancements and see them as tools to improve the lives of those with impairments, it is likely that the social model of disability will continue to take a very different approach. Concerns are likely to remain fixed on the notion that it is the social environment that disables people, and the environment that needs altering, rather than the person. Beyond focusing on individuals, the social perspective on disability will continue to ask questions about how a "fix" for one person may spell greater burdens for others (perhaps those who cannot or do not opt to get "fixed"). If more and more people use technologies to address their disabilities, will this mean greater stigma against and less support for those with disabilities?

If Disabilities Studies is to become a core focus within sociology, the question of definitions may need to be resolved. Right now, the field is both energized and limited by its expansive definitions. In terms of who counts as being disabled and what a disability is, there remain fine distinctions between having a disability and being disabled—where the former is an umbrella term and the latter is a medico-legal designation. Similarly, the field brings together those with mild and those with severe disabilities. Historically, the movement has gained power by uniting these categories and by conceptually bonding physical, intellectual, and emotional disabilities. The field will continue to grow as it clarifies the common ground upon which these categories stand, as well as the distinctions among them.

CHAPTER 6: REVIEW OF KEY POINTS

- The term "disability" is a broad umbrella; it describes people with mild to severe limitations in major life activities due to physical, cognitive, and emotional conditions.
- Having a disability and being disabled are two different things; the latter is a medico-legal term that typically applies to those who are no longer able to earn a living or function independently.
- The medical model assumes that disabilities are rooted in people's bodies and that medical knowledge, authority, and techniques can be used to lessen disability. The medical model often results in stigma being placed on those with disabilities.
- The social model of disability assumes that disabilities are socially constructed and that some aspects of the social context or environment *disable* people. This model further assumes that functionality can be restored by fixing the environment rather using medical techniques to fix the person.
- Being deaf or hard of hearing and having autism are two specific conditions that illustrate the socially constructed nature of disability; these two conditions also help illustrate the notion that "people with disabilities" may simply have a different range of abilities. They are different, rather than inherently deficient.
- The disability rights movement emerged after the civil rights movement for racial justice. It, too, aimed to reduce prejudice and discrimination against people with disabilities and remove barriers for their full participation in society.
- The disability rights movement resulted in legislation that protects the rights and opportunities for disabled people in employment, education, and public accommodations. Passed in 1991, The Americans with Disabilities Act is the central piece of legislation in this movement.

CHAPTER 6: QUESTIONS FOR REVIEW

1. In what sense do people with a disability constitute the largest minority group in the United States? From your point of view, does it make sense to think of those with a disability as members of a minority group? Why or why not?
2. What is the medical model of disability? In what cases does it make sense for you to think of having a disability through the lens of the medical model? In what cases does it not make sense?

3. What is the social model of disability? Considering the examples given in this chapter, what are the advantages of thinking about disability through the social model? What are the limitations?

4. How has the disability rights movement paralleled other social movements, especially those focusing on civil right?

5. Some people believe that legislation designed to protect the civil rights of people with disabilities is too extensive and potentially expensive. To what extent do you have concerns with existing laws designed to protect the civil rights of those with disabilities, whether in school, at work, or in public accommodations?

6. Imagine that you are an employer. To what extent do you believe you have the right to know whether applicants for a position in your business have a disability?

KEY TERMS

ableism

Americans with Disabilities Act

audism

Autism

Buck v. Bell

cochlear implants

Deaf Culture

disability

disability rights movement

Individuals with Disabilities
   Education Act

medical gaze

medical model of disability

"reasonable accommodations"

social model of disability

"supercrip" stereotype

universal design

REFERENCES

Baron-Cohen, Simon. 2002. "Is Asperger Syndrome Necessarily Viewed as a Disability?" *Focus on Autism and Other Developmental Disabilities* 17(3):186–191.

Baynton, Douglas. 1996. *Forbidden Signs: American Culture and the Campaign against Sign Language.* Chicago: University of Chicago Press.

Berger, Ronald J. 2008. "Disability and the Dedicated Wheelchair Athlete: Beyond the 'Supercrip' Critique." *Journal of Contemporary Ethnography* 37(6):647–678.

Bianchi, Diana W. R. Lamar Parker, Jeffrey Wentworth, Rajeevi Madankumar, Craig Saffer, Anita F. Das, Joseph A. Craig, Darya I. Chudova, Patricia L. Devers, Keith W. Jones, Kelly Oliver, Richard P. Rava, and Amy J. Sehnert. 2014. "DNA Sequencing versus Standard Prenatal Aneuploidy Screening." *The New England Journal of Medicine* 370:799–808.

Carless, David and Kitrina Douglas. 2008a. "Narrative, Identity and Mental Health: How Men with Serious Mental Illness Re-story Their Lives Through Sport and Exercise." *Psychology of Sport and Exercise* 9(5):576–594.

Carless, David and Kitrina Douglas. 2008b. "The Role of Sport and Exercise in Recovery from Serious Mental Illness: Two Case Studies." *International Journal of Men's Health* 7(2):137–156.

Foucault, Michel. 1988. *Madness and Civilization: A History of Insanity in the Age of Reason.* New York: Vintage Books.

Hubbard, Ruth. 2006. "Abortion and Disability: Who Should and Who Should Not Inhabit the World?" Pp. 93–104 in *The Disability Studies Reader,* 2nd ed., edited by Lennard J. Davis. New York: Routledge.

Juette, Melvin and Ronald. J. Berger. 2008. *Wheelchair Warriors: Gangs, Disability, and Basketball.* Philadelphia: Temple University Press.

Kitcher, Philip. 1997. *The Lives to Come: The Genetic Revolution and Human Possibilities.* New York: Free Press.

Lane, Harlan. 1999. *The Mask of Benevolence: Disabling the Deaf Community.* San Diego, CA: DawnSignPress.

Lane, Harlan. 2006. "Construction of Deafness." Pp. 79–92 in *The Disability Studies Reader,* 2nd ed., edited by Lennard J. Davis. New York: Routledge.

Link, Bruce G. and Jo C. Phelan. 2001. "Conceptualizing Stigma." *Annual Review of Sociology* 27:363–385.

Koegel, Robert L., Grace A. Werner, Laurie A. Vismara, and Lynn Kern Koegel. 2005. "The Effectiveness of Contextually Supported Play Date Interactions between Children with Autism and Typically Developing Peers." *Research and Practice for Persons with Severe Disabilities* 30(2):93–102.

Malone, Fergal D., Jacob A. Canick, Robert H. Ball, David A. Nyberg, Christine H. Comstock, Radek Bukowski, Richard L. Berkowitz, Susan J. Gross, Lorraine Dugoff, Sabrina D. Craigo, Ilan E. Timor-Tritsch, Stephen R. Carr, Honor M. Wolfe, Kimberly Dukes, Diana W. Bianchi, Alicja R. Rudnicka, Allan K. Hackshaw, Geralyn Lambert-Messerlian, Nicholas J. Wald, and Mary E. D'Alton. 2005. "First-Trimester or Second-Trimester Screening, or Both, for Down's Syndrome." *The New England Journal of Medicine* 353:2001–2011.

National Research Center on Disabilities. 2007. "Twenty-Five Years of Progress in Educating Children with Disabilities through IDEA." Washington, DC. Retrieved March 10, 2014 (http://www.nrcld.org/resources/osep/historyidea.html).

Natoli, Jaime L., Deborah L. Ackerman, Suzanne McDermott, and Janice G. Edwards. 2012. "Prenatal Diagnosis of Down Syndrome: A Systematic Review of Termination Rates (1995–2011). *Prenatal Diagnosis* 32(2):142–153.

Neal, LaVonne I., Audrey Davis McCray, Gwendolyn Webb-Johnson, and Scott T. Bridgest. 2003. "The Effects of African American Movement Styles on Teachers' Perceptions and Reactions." *The Journal of Special Education* 37(1):49–57.

Oliver, Michael. 1990. *The Politics of Disablement: A Sociological Approach.* Hampshire, UK: Palgrave Macmillan.

Oliver, Michael. 2009. *Understanding Disability: From Theory to Practice.* Hampshire, UK: Palgrave Macmillan.

Padden, Carol A. and Tom L. Humphries. 2005. *Inside Deaf Culture.* Cambridge, MA: Harvard University Press.

Parens, Erik and Adrienne Asch. 2003. "Disability Rights Critique of Prenatal Genetic Testing: Reflections and Recommendations." *Mental Retardation and Developmental Disabilities Research Reviews* 9(1):40–47.

Pigott, Rowan L. and Emory L. Cowen. 2000. "Teacher Race, Child Race, Racial Congruence, and Teacher Ratings of Children's School Adjustment." *Journal of School Psychology* 38(2): 177–195.

Sacks, Oliver. 1989. *Seeing Voices.* New York: Vintage Books.

Shakespeare, Tom. 2006. "The Social Model of Disability." Pp. 197–204 in *The Disability Studies Reader*, 2nd ed., edited by Lennard J. Davis. New York: Routledge.

Silva, Carla Philomena and P. David Howe. 2012. "The (In)validity of Supercrip Representation of Paralympian Athletes." *Journal of Sport and Social Issues* 36(2):174–194

Smith, Brett and Andrew C. Sparkes. 2004. "Men, Sport, and Spinal Cord Injury: An Analysis of Metaphors and Narrative Types." *Disability & Society* 19(6):613–626.

Whitaker, Philip. 2004. "Fostering Communication and Shared Play between Mainstream Peers and Children with Autism: Approaches, Outcomes and Experiences." *British Journal of Special Education* 31(4):215–222.

Wolfberg, Pamela J. and Adriana L. Schuler. 1999. "Fostering Peer Interaction, Imaginative Play and Spontaneous Language in Children with Autism." *Child Language and Teaching Therapy* 15(1):41–52.

Zimmerman, Rick S., Elizabeth L. Khoury, William A. Vega, Andres G. Gil, and George J. Warheit. 1995. "Teacher and Parent Perceptions of Behavior Problems among a Sample of African American, Hispanic, and Non-Hispanic White Students." *American Journal of Community Psychology* 23(2):181–197.

Socialization: The Process by Which We Become Who We Are

When talking about gender differences in the educational system, I often hear from my students: "Maybe teachers treat female students more delicately because they know girls are more sensitive and don't want to be embarrassed." Embedded in this statement is a powerful sociological puzzle: Do our social interactions reflect who we inherently are, or are we who we are because of the nature of our social interactions? Do we treat girls a particular way because they are inherently more sensitive and easily embarrassed, or do girls become sensitive and easily embarrassed over time *because* of how they are treated? In Unit 2 we focus on the concept of *socialization*—the lifelong process by which we learn our society's culture while also developing our individual personalities and social identities. While sociologists acknowledge that biology and our unique human capacities establish the foundation of who we are, they strongly believe that when it comes to identities like sex/gender, race, and social class, much of who we are is learned.

Over the next three chapters, we explore how our sex/gender, race, and social class identities are the product of socialization. From the moment we are born, our identities are being molded; this molding begins with *primary socialization* in our families of origin and continues throughout secondary socialization in school, among peers, and through the media. What is important about the concept of socialization is that it demonstrates, as illustrated in Unit 1 of this text, that biology is not destiny. Instead, human beings are remarkably malleable creatures, influenced considerably by social interaction and the broader cultural messages they receive. Second, because humans are so malleable, we learn that social change and transformation can occur by altering patterns of socialization and interaction. If, for example, we believe that gender, race, and social class socialization is too restrictive or contributes unduly to social inequality, we can look for ways to transform how we interact. Finally, a key point of this section is to emphasize that what seems completely normal, natural, and unremarkable in the realm of human social identities is actually the reflection of multitudinous minute interactions. It is the contribution of sociology to bring greater attention to the seemingly small, but ultimately consequential, ways in which humans create their social worlds.

Enlisting in Gender Boot Camp: How We Become Gendered Beings

Imagine a child reared without human interaction. Whether locked in a basement or raised by animals in the wild, what would that child be like? Would the child exhibit any of the traits we associate with normal little boys or girls? Every so often, such a child is discovered. Children who are raised without human contact are sometimes called **feral children**. In the fall of 1970, child protective services in suburban Los Angeles discovered "Genie," one of the most infamous cases of a child raised in isolation. While she was 12 years old at the time of discovery, Genie appeared much younger. Fragile and skittish, she had the habit of spitting, clawing, and cowering in the presence of animals. After lengthy investigation, authorities concluded that Genie spent most of her life confined to one room, where she passed her days tied to a potty chair and her nights confined to a crib. Evidence suggested that she was beaten for vocalizing by both her father and her brother and was fed a poor diet of primarily nonsolid foods. Her toys consisted of plastic food containers and spools of thread (Rymer 1993). She could not speak, and it was assumed that she had experienced very limited verbal interaction growing up (Curtiss 1977).

The story of Genie raises many questions about human development. One question has to do with gender: When it comes to our gender identities, how much of who we are is a product of nature (biology), and how much is a product of nurture (or social environment)? Imagine, for example, if Genie had been let loose at a Toys "R" Us soon after her discovery. Would she naturally gravitate to the "girls' section," drawn to the little dolls she never had, wanting to give them love and affection? Imagine, alternately, that she were introduced to other children on a playground. Would she automatically identify the other little girls and be drawn to them as playmates? If she were taken on a shopping spree, would she revel in the many varieties of pink clothing adorned with butterflies, hearts, and flowers?

In this chapter we explore the processes by which we become gendered beings. While sociologists acknowledge that biology plays a role in shaping our identities, personalities, interests, and talents, they focus more intently on the ways in which

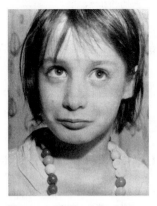

The case of "Genie" raises many questions about human development, including the role of socialization in the formation of gender identities.

social structural and social interactional forces mold our gender identities. From the day we are born—and sometimes even before—our gender identities are constructed through our parents or guardians; later, it is at school and among peers that we are shaped into gendered beings and we shape others into gendered beings. Finally, during childhood and beyond, gender identities are molded in the symbolic realm, where books, the media, games, and more convey to us messages about what it means to be an ideal or culturally appropriate male and female. Throughout, human beings take in these messages, sometimes accept and internalize them, and at other times reject them or incorporate the messages in new and creative ways. Ultimately, we become gendered beings partially because of our underlying biology, but also because of the subtle, ongoing force of human social interaction.

GENDER BOOT CAMP: SOCIALIZATION AND THE PROCESS OF LEARNING GENDER

As discussed in Chapter 2, underlying biological forces—including hormones and brain structures—contribute to gender role differences. Sociologists, however, show that socialization both magnifies these underlying gender differences and creates new ones. **Socialization** refers to the lifelong process by which we learn our society's culture (norms, values, expectations) while also developing our individual personalities and social identities (race, class, gender, etc.). With respect to gender, the concept of socialization illustrates the fact that humans are born with a sex, but we must *learn* what it means to be male or female; we must acquire a culturally specific gender role. Sociologists Candace West and Don Zimmerman (1987) described this as "doing gender." By coining this term they hoped to show that gender is not something we *have* or *are* but something *we* do: it is a role we play. Most of this learning takes place through the face-to-face interactions that are the foundation of socialization. Because Genie lacked this social interaction, it is possible to say that she lacked a well-defined gender role.

While perhaps extreme, the metaphor of **gender boot camp** illustrates the process by which we become gendered beings. To compare gender socialization to military boot camp is to highlight several parallels between two processes that at first seem quite different. Although children in the United States are generally nurtured and treated as precious beings, military recruits are disciplined and generally spared any emotional indulgence. Yet both gender socialization and military boot camp share the same goal: to transform the individual into a functioning member of a larger group. While parents and other adults may not have this goal at the forefront of their minds (they would probably describe their efforts in terms of love and protection), it surely is implicit in all they do and say.

Gender boot camp and military boot camp also use many of the same methods. First, new recruits are initiated into the group by an elder who has greater experience with the culture; the sense of expertise and hierarchy embedded in the process helps new recruits accept their training. Further, the authority figure generally wants what's best for the young person, given his or her understanding of how the world/military works, and adjusts his or her behavior accordingly. Second, the authority figure—whether parents or a drill sergeant—has at his or her disposal a system of rewards and punishments ("Good boy" versus "Drop and give me 20"). Because new recruits identify with their superiors and generally seek their approval, these rewards and punishments successfully produce desired behaviors. Finally, both forms of boot camp involve ongoing, repetitive training routines. While military personnel participate in drills using verbal commands and physical routines, parents (and guardians) spend many hours each day verbally and physically interacting with their own little recruits. Over time this repetition instills a sense of cause and effect in the infant or child, so that child knows—in conjunction with rewards and punishments—which behaviors garner which results.

With respect to the development of a gender identity, children have a sense of their own gender around the age of two, in the sense that they can label themselves as a "little boy" or a "little girl." Soon thereafter they are able to identify other little boys and girls and begin modeling the behaviors of gender-similar adults. Occasionally, children do not identify with the gender they have been assigned, which can make boot camp especially painful for that child. For most children, though, it is through these ongoing processes that we effectively *become* the boys and girls, men and women, we are thought to be in the first place.

LEARNING GENDER DURING PRIMARY SOCIALIZATION: THE ROLE OF PARENTS AND GUARDIANS

When you were a teenager, your parents or guardians probably worried that your peers, the Internet, or other forms of media were having an undue and maybe even dangerous influence on you. They need not have worried: in the grand scheme of things, parents and guardians have the most significant and enduring impact on the people we become. The socialization we receive from our parents and guardians is called **primary socialization**. It is a powerful force in human development for two main reasons: one, we are largely blank slates when our parents and guardians begin interacting with us; therefore, they have the first crack at molding us. Two, as creatures who need *attachment* in order to thrive, we feel compelled to behave in ways that are consistent with parents' and guardians' wishes. Further, because we hope to elicit positive rewards (attention, a hug, a smile, etc.) from our parents, we learn to act in ways that earn these rewards. This is called **reinforcement**. When it comes to primary socialization, the routines that start in infancy and carry through childhood are strongly gendered. Because they are also repetitive, these routines and interactions mold us into gendered teens and adults.

From the moment children are born, parents interact with them verbally. These repetitive and gendered interactions are a part of gender boot camp. Observational studies show that parents—both moms and dads—use more varied and more frequent emotion words when talking to their female children (Adams et al. 1995; Fivush et al. 2000). When talking about sad or happy events, parents are less likely to discuss emotional nuances with male children. For example, parents may talk to boys about feeling angry, while conversations with girls may refer to feeling hurt, sad, and disappointed (Brody 2001; Fivush 1989). By the age of 6, research shows, little girls have a wider vocabulary of emotion words than little boys. As time goes on, both girls (Denham, Zoller, and Couchoud 1994) and women (Hall and Matsumoto 2004) are more adept at interpreting the emotional states of others compared to boys and men; they may also experience their emotions more intensely (Brody 2001). During early years mothers also spend more time verbally interacting with female children compared to male children; their conversations, moreover, focus disproportionately on questions and conversational give-and-take (even if infants and toddlers can't act as true conversational partners). Little boys, by contrast, receive more directives and factual statements (Clearfield and Nelson 2006).

If parents speak less about emotions to little boys, what do they talk about? Research shows that adults may use more words focusing on shapes, numbers, actions, and scientific concepts when speaking with boy children (Weitzman, Birns, and Friend 1985). One observational study focused on mothers interacting with their elementary-school–aged children in a laboratory setting. While playing with a set of magnets, mothers incorporated more scientific terms and concepts when interacting with their sons than with their daughters (Tenenbaum et al. 2005). It is in part through these ongoing verbal interactions that little girls and little boys develop the emotional and conversational capacities that are part of their gender roles.

Experimental research shows that we often see what we want to see in terms of gender. Even when looking at infants of objectively similar size, parents describe newborn girls as finer featured and more delicate than newborn boys, whom they describe as strong and sturdy (Karraker et al. 1995). A classic study by Condry and Condry (1976) shows that assumptions about a child's gender influence how adults interpret that child's emotions. In this study, infants were observed playing with a jack-in-the-box. When the jack-in-the-box sprang open, infants typically began crying. When told that the child was a boy (sometimes a girl dressed as a boy), adults interpreted crying as a sign of anger; when told that the child was a girl (sometimes a boy dressed as a girl), the same emotional expression was described as fear. Studies with adults show similar results: when people believe they are looking at photos of men, they describe emotional displays as anger; the same emotional displays are interpreted as sadness among women (Johnson, McKay, and Pollick 2011; Plant et al. 2000).

While much of parents' verbal interaction with children seems unintentional, parents sometimes act like drill instructors, intentionally instilling what they consider gender-appropriate behaviors. When fathers call their sons "sissies" or berate them for playing with "girls' toys" they send explicit verbal messages about what it means to be a boy. According to sociologist Emily Kane, fathers are more intense drill sergeants than mothers—especially with their male children—and are more likely to admonish behaviors they see as threatening to their sons' budding masculinity and heterosexuality. Through these verbal interactions, Michael Kimmel (2008) concludes, boys learn that "independence, aggression, and suppression are rewarded" (p. 141). When little girls are told to cross their legs or act "like a good little girl," they also receive explicit messages about gender expectations, perhaps that their bodies are shameful. Given the frequency and consistency of these messages, it is likely that they mold a child's gender behavior and identity—especially to the extent that children alter their behaviors to receive positive reinforcement from parents and other adults.

Like military boot camp, gender boot camp also involves physical training. Although gender boot camp does not involve rigorous physical drills, it parallels military boot camp in the sense that new recruits develop their identities through repetitive physical interactions under the guidance of authority figures. Take, for example, studies focusing on physical interactions between mothers and infants. A classic study by Carol Malatesta and her co-authors (1989) used videotaped observations of mothers playing with their children. The authors found that mothers used more frequent and longer eye contact with female infants compared to male infants. This behavior, which psychologists call **gazing**, is significant because eye contact is associated with feelings of trust; it is thought to contribute to healthy parent–child attachments. During childhood, male children exhibit more discomfort and anxiety when adults hold their gaze. Over time, these physical interactions may translate into the development of men who exhibit lower levels of trust and intimacy.

Research also shows that parents hold newborn males longer than female infants and keep them in close physical proximity. Around six months, however, these patterns reverse. Fathers, in particular, maintain greater physical proximity to female children (Bronstein 1988; Snow, Jacklin, and Maccoby 1983). In an observational study of more than a thousand families visiting the zoo, Alyson Burns and her co-authors (1989) found that fathers were more likely to carry female children, while male children were more likely to walk on their own or ride in strollers. In their physical interactions with infants, fathers initiate rougher styles of play with little boys, tossing them in the air, play wrestling, or simulating clapping, boxing, or bicycle riding (Carson, Burk, and Parke 1993; Lindsey and Mize 2001; MacDonald and Parke 1986). Girls, by contrast, receive more verbal play

Gazing and physical contact are some of the ways in which even the smallest of infants develop gender identities and behaviors.

and are given more guidance when completing physical tasks. Through these interactions, especially if they are repetitive, boys are more likely to hone their fine and gross motor skills (Renzetti and Curran 1999) while also cultivating a sense of autonomy and independence. The physical part of gender boot camp for girls, by contrast, may result in a greater sense of dependence and desire for physical closeness. Another component of military boot camp involves the new recruit donning a uniform that denotes his or her status. As in the military, the clothes we wear *mark us* and *make us*. To say that clothes mark us means that our clothes declare to others who we are. In the military, the bars, stars, and insignia that decorate a service member's uniform convey rich information about rank, status, specialties, etc. In gender boot camp, we are marked by clothes that color-code us. When little boys are dressed in blue and little girls dressed in pink, they declare their gender to the world at large.

To say that clothes *make us* means that our clothes mold us into specific kinds of people. The clothes of a high-ranking military official, for example, suggest that he or she should be treated with deference and respect. Over time, the manner in which people interact with him or her transforms that individual into a person with a confident demeanor and impressive bearing. The color-coding of little boys and girls conveys their gender to the outside world; subsequently, people treat the infant or child in a manner they deem suitable to that gender. Our clothes also make us by enabling or constraining physical activity; clothes can control the way we hold our bodies and what they allow us to do. In part because of their gendered uniforms, little girls become the sweet, delicate things they are assumed to be, while little boys become the rugged, adventurous creatures they were thought to be all along.

A quick trip to a children's clothing store reveals a world of gendered uniforms. The first distinction among these clothes, from infancy on up, is their color. Boys' clothes, for the most part, feature intense primary colors, most frequently blue. Girls' clothes feature soft pastel tones, with pink being especially popular. The color-coding of children contributes to the belief that there are two *opposite* sexes. There is very little "gray area" when it comes to children's clothes; instead, there are clear-cut differences. These differences exist in part to communicate to strangers who the child is and how to interact with it. If any confusion remains, parents can adorn the bald heads of their baby girls with lacy headbands. Rather than hold hair back from her eyes, the headband tells the world that she is a girl and should be spoken to softly and described as sweet and delicate, rather than strong and sturdy.

Children's clothes also differ in the symbols and images that adorn them. Girls' clothes are decorated with butterflies, hearts, rainbows, and flowers, often with ribbons or lace appliques. Boys' clothes feature animals—especially strong and vicious ones—vehicles (fire trucks, tanks, motorcycles), and sports equipment. If these images don't say enough about the child wearing them, many clothes also feature sayings or mottos. While a pink T-shirt proclaims "Daddy's Little Sweetie," a blue one featuring construction equipment says "Daddy's Little Helper." A gray and red T-shirt from the boys' department declares that the two-year-old wearing it is "Born to Rock;" a similar style featuring a guitar says "Make Some Noise." Over in the girls' section, a red

T-shirt with Minnie Mouse says, "He Loves Me, He Loves Me Not," while a pink T-shirt says "J'adore des Fleurs" ("I Love Flowers").

Admittedly, many of these clothes are cute. Personally, I struggle to buy gifts for a baby shower when the parents don't yet know the sex of the baby. The gender-neutral world of yellow and green just isn't as appealing. Yet these clothes, whether purchased from the Gap, Target, Wal-Mart, or Gymboree, reflect cultural assumptions about what little girls and boys are like. With respect to these decorations, the theme that emerges is that boys are adventurers and doers; they are active and creative, whether building or destroying with earthmovers or rocking out on a guitar. These symbols convey the assumption that girls are soft, delicate creatures; rather than active creators, they are emotional, passive, and even decorative. Even as toddlers, girls are concerned with whether boys like them and whether they will find their Prince Charming.

Rather than mere symbols that mark us, these clothes make us. Because children wear clothes every day, and because those clothes are clearly gendered, over time what we wear contributes to gender role differences. In part this occurs because children's clothes differ in the fabric they are made from. Boys' clothing is durable. Their pants and overalls are typically made of denim, corduroy, or canvas; even their T-shirts are made of beefier cotton than the sheer cotton typical of girls' clothing. These clothes demand to be played in; they are clothes that can easily be washed to rid them of mud

Adventure, building, and problem-solving are some of the themes emphasized in boys' clothing.

Nature, beautification, and even foreign culture ("Bonjour") are some of the themes emphasized in girls' clothing.

and grass stains. Little girls' clothes are thin and delicate; while there are more knit pants and simple T-shirts for girls today compared to years gone by, with all of the lace and ribbon adornments, it's not as easy to throw them into the washing machine. Girls, then, may be told not to get their clothes dirty and may be cautioned against stomping in puddles, climbing trees, or building a fort in the backyard.

According to sociologist Karin Martin (1998), the clothes little girls wear teach them to be aware of and potentially uncomfortable with their bodies. In her observation of preschool children, pre-school teachers often pulled little girls' skirts down or twisted their tights back into place. As women grow older, they often check to see if underpants or a bra strap are showing; the skinny jeans that are popular in recent years serve as a constant reminder of women's bodily contours. Meanwhile, adults remind little girls to keep their knees together and pull their dresses down to make sure they are properly covered. Because these interactions are repetitive, Martin argues, they remind women to take up less space with their bodies, to sit in closed positions with arms and legs crossed, and generally use smaller and more restricted movements. Men and boys, by contrast, wear clothing that sets their bodies free.

Whether men and women take up space or try to be as small as possible is not without consequences. Amy Cuddy (2011), a social psychologist and professor at the Harvard Business School, shows that standing in a "power pose"—tall, hands on hips, taking up plenty of space—can affect a person's hormone levels, making them behave more confidently and take more risks. These physical gestures, she theorizes, can lead to success in stressful situations, like job interviews. In a laboratory study, she found that when subjects were instructed to stand in the power pose for two minutes, they were evaluated as more confident and worthy of being hired than those who did not practice the power pose for two minutes prior to a mock job interview. If men more so than women are socialized to take up these "power poses," it is likely that their bodies will both convey and create more success.

Toys are also an important part of gender boot camp. They allow children to engage in imaginative play that also provides the chance to engage in developmentally necessary role-playing games. For developmental psychologists, children use play as a way to model and therefore learn gender-appropriate behaviors. A trip through almost any toy store reveals an array of gender lessons. In brick and mortar stores and on its website, Toys "R" Us declares the world of play to be divided into two distinct camps. Color-coded signs hang from the rafters (or large buttons on the website) to signal shoppers to "gender-appropriate sections." The organization of the store provides very little gender-neutral territory. Once inside, additional themes emerge when investigating the contents of these gendered aisles.

Walking into the boys' section, one is immediately struck by the color scheme: black, blue, red, and green dominate. The toys, moreover, allow plentiful opportunities for little boys to explore, compete, build, and destroy. There are (increasingly muscle-bound) action figures, Nerf guns, science sets, Legos, Lincoln Logs, as well as dump trucks, fire engines, and race cars. When exploring outdoor play options, little dudes can mimic daddy, making burgers on the grill, riding his (tricycle) Harley Davidson, whacking some weeds, and mowing the lawn. How fun! These toys are certainly fun and—perhaps—innocent, yet they play an important role in gender socialization. Through their play, boys learn and practice two sets of themes: the first is to build, create, and explore; the second is to compete. Many games, even role-playing games with action figures, involve domination, destruction, and the eventual production of winners and losers.

The girls' section, meanwhile, is characterized by full-scale *pinkification*! Everywhere you look there are variations of pink and purple. Many toys involve baby dolls, Barbies, Disney Princesses, tea sets, miniature kitchens, and even pinkified vacuum cleaners! Day in and day out, these toys allow little girls to model mommy (vacuuming is fun!) and practice a more passive, communal form of play. Rather than winners and losers, games focus on role-playing that involves sharing, bonding, and occasional scolding (as when playing school or house). In her book *Cinderella Ate My Daughter: Dispatches from the Front Lines of the New Girlie-Girl Culture*, Peggy Orenstein points out that girls' toys inculcate the practice of **body management**. Girls' toys, while fun, also foster a preoccupation with appearance: whether playing dress-up, dabbling in makeup kits, or indulging her creativity with a jewelry-making kit, the end goal of girls' "play" seems to be improving her appearance. Even a seemingly intellectual game like Scrabble is not immune from the pinkification and the emphasis on body

Care to play? By "pinkifying" their products, companies may find new markets for their goods.

management. The pink "Designer Edition" features tiles spelling "fun" and "fashion" on the front of the box.

Girls' toys also teach a profound lesson of consumerism, as girls learn to shop through play. While the American Girl brand can be credited with promoting diversity, knowledge of history, and the recognition that there are a lot of unique ways to be a cool little girl (dolls that are snowboarders and scientists), this and many other girls' toy brands promote an insatiable appetite to consume. American Girl dolls offer an endless opportunity to accessorize (there is even an orthodontic-themed accessory kit with "headgear"); moreover, they allow mother, daughter, and the doll herself to wear the same outfit. If that isn't enough, the girls can conclude their shopping trips with a delicious lunch at one of the epic American Girl stores—true palaces of consumerism. Thus, while American Girl can be credited with promoting more inclusive and achievement-oriented values than Barbie, what the two brands have in common is the fact that they train girls to want through product lines that change season after season and offer endless ways to extend one's relationship to the brand.

A closer look at the areas of the store that seem to sell gender-neutral toys reinforces another theme of gender socialization: while girls can tread into boys' territory, the opposite is not true. Over in the sporting equipment aisles, there are tennis rackets and t-ball sets for little girls. How do you know they are gender specific? The color-coding, of course, along with the photographs on the packages (featuring only little girls, if the product is pink; both boys and girls if the product is blue). There are glitzy pink soccer balls, basketball hoops, tents, and sleeping bags. Little girls *can* do physical adventurous things, especially if they are properly color-coded. Nowhere to be found, though, were there any toughened-up versions of tea sets or feather boas or any dude-ified leotards or ice skating costumes.

The argument here is not that a lack of eye contact, wearing jeans, or playing with an action figure *causes* little boys to become detached, competitive creatures. Rather, the goal is to identify (1) the repetitive nature of gender boot camp and (2) the themes that cross-cut how parents interact with and dress their children and what toys they provide. All together, these patterns illustrate the bundle of traits associated with masculinity and femininity in our society and how these traits get coded in us. Without gender boot camp, Genie scarcely had the opportunity to become a little girl. Indeed, a look at gender boot camp shows just how much work—whether in terms of verbal and physical "drills" or the donning of a new uniform—goes into making little girls and little boys. Through these processes, parents encourage little boys to be active and develop greater independence and emotional self-control (Leaper 2002), while the socialization of little girls encourages passivity and finely honed skills for human connection.

It goes without saying that not all children (or parents) conform to these patterns. Increasingly, transgender or "gender-nonconforming" children confound the gender binary. These children reject the gender identity given to them at birth and their given name and embrace the toys, clothing, hairstyles, and identity of the other gender. In a *New York Magazine* article by Jesse Green (2012), psychotherapist Jean Malpas is quoted as saying that children who reject their assigned gender (sometimes called **gender dysphoria**) are not mentally ill. In "the vast majority of cases it [gender dysphoria] is not caused by psychopathology. . . . Nor is it generally caused by a particular family pattern, any more than gayness is caused by the old stereotype of controlling mother and passive father. It is just an essential part of who you are. Not that there aren't any coexisting psychosocial issues. But the problems generally come from outside." To deal with the social stigma and logistical challenges transpeople may face, new resources are emerging. Parents and schools, for example, are working together to identify which bathrooms children should use, to determine how teachers should address them ("he," "she," or "they"), and to support their mental health. Nationally, the organization Trans Youth Family Allies advocates for transchildren in schools; there are also local support groups and even Camp Aranu'tiq for "transgender and gender-variant kids" aged 6 through 16. While no child conforms completely to the social expectations associated with masculinity and femininity, transchildren illustrate most clearly the fact that flexibility and nonconformity is part of gender expression from very early on.

Camp Aranu'tiq offers a traditional summer camp experience—and safe space—to transgender and gender-variant kids.

EXPLORING INTERSECTIONALITY:
RACE, CLASS, AND SEXUALITY WITHIN GENDER BOOT CAMP

If much of what has been described in this chapter so far sounds a bit stereotypical, this may be because much of the research on gender and parenting has focused on white, middle-class, heterosexual, two-parent families. In recent decades, however, there has been an expansion of research on gender and parenting into diverse family types. This research shows that race and sexuality, in particular, intersect in the production of gendered beings.

When it comes to race and parenting, research reveals that black parents engage in less stereotypical behaviors than white parents. Black parents, for example, tend to stress independence (Hale-Benson 1986) and academic achievement for both male and female children (Hill and Sprague 1999). Indeed, some evidence suggests that black parents are especially supportive of daughters excelling in science classes and careers (Hanson 2007). Moreover, black sons are taught to take on supervisory duties for younger children (Hill 2001). Social class is, however, an important intersecting variable. Compared to upper-income families, lower-income black parents express less support for gender flexibility and stronger expressions of homophobia (Hill 2002). On the macro-level, the emphasis on achievement and independence for black girls may reflect the historically higher percentages of female-headed households and maternal employment among black Americans and the push for black boys to take on domestic duties may reflect the higher rates of mother-headed households within that demographic.

Patterns of gender socialization within Latino families also have their unique traits. Research using in-depth interviews and surveys indicates that Latinos emphasize gender differences in their parenting, in part by imposing stricter rules on female children (Raffaelli and Ontai 2004). Latina adolescents, for example, typically begin dating later than their male peers; they are also more likely to date within their race and to date someone older (Raffaelli 2005). The cultural emphasis on machismo—an expectation in Latin American cultures that men be strong, chivalrous, and dominant (Ramirez 1999)—may help explain these patterns. Some studies also suggest a stronger gender division in parenting roles among Latino families, where fathers take greater responsibility for raising sons and mothers for raising daughters. This same-sex identification has measurable consequences, as girls' academic achievement is linked to encouragement from mothers, and boys' from fathers (Alfaro, Umaña-Taylor, and Bamáca 2006). Patterns of gender socialization vary, though, depending on how long families have been in the United States and whether they speak English. This suggests that acculturation within the United States may lessen these gender distinctions over time.

Finally, emerging research suggests that parents' sexual orientation also influences gender socialization. Studies show, for example, that gay and lesbian parents raise their children with greater gender flexibility compared to heterosexual parents (Biblarz and Savci 2010; Stacey and Biblarz 2001) and express greater openness to gender-atypical clothing choices, activities and interests, and occupational aspirations. With respect to their sexual socialization, children raised by gay and lesbian parents are no more likely to claim a gay or lesbian identity themselves compared to those raised by heterosexual parents; they express, however, more support for sexual experimentation. As adults, men raised by nonheterosexual parents report having fewer sexual partners than their counterparts raised by heterosexual parents, while women raised by non-heterosexual parents report more partners (Tasker and Golombok 1997). These results show that men vary in terms of how rigidly they transmit gender expectations. These studies, moreover, emphasize a key sociological point: while it is possible to identify patterned behaviors within society as a whole, these patterns often intersect with race/ethnicity, social class, and sexual orientation.

LEARNING RACE DURING SECONDARY SOCIALIZATION: EXPERIENCES AT SCHOOL

After children are initially molded by parents and guardians, they are ready for secondary socialization. **Secondary socialization** takes place outside of the home—usually in schools, among peers, in religious settings, or through the media. It is how we learn about diversity, social differences, and how to operate in small groups and society at large. Although many lessons are learned through secondary socialization, one set of lessons focuses on gender role expectations. In their classic work spanning several decades, Myra Sadker and David Sadker (1995; Sadker and Zittleman 2009) show that the educational system both reflects and creates gender differences, often to the detriment of female students.

Extending the metaphor of gender boot camp, once in school children receive their official training manuals. These "training manuals" are the books and lessons that comprise the formal curriculum. The elementary and middle-school curriculum is characterized by lessons that focus on and celebrate the accomplishments of men and boys. That the history and science curriculum focuses on men's accomplishments may not be surprising, given that historically women had fewer official roles in politics, science, culture, or the arts. Within these texts, Sadker and Sadker found, men grossly outnumbered women; one middle-school history text, for example mentioned only 11 females. Yet male characters also outnumbered female characters in fiction and language arts texts—at a ratio of nearly two to one (McCabe et al. 2011; Sadker and Sadker 1995). In addition to being more numerous, male characters were more likely to be central characters—the ones facing challenges and solving problems. Females, by contrast, typically play supporting roles. In storybooks with primary female characters, beauty is a common theme, with female characters both rewarded and punished for their looks (Baker-Sperry and Grauerholz 2003). While these patterns have changed over time, especially with female characters taking on more leadership roles, there has not been a similar shift of male characters into domestic or supporting roles (Gooden and Gooden 2001).

If children only read a couple of books during their school year, these gender differences may not be a problem. Yet most children are exposed to these lessons, day in and day out, for 12 years. What is learned through these lessons? Scholars refer to the underrepresentation of female characters in literature and the media as **symbolic annihilation** (Tuchman, Daniels, and Benet 1978). When one group is underrepresented in the media, their members are made invisible; the underlying message is that they are uninteresting and unimportant. It is difficult to measure the long-term consequences of these patterns. On the most trivial level, it may explain why my boyfriend refuses to watch "chick flicks" with me and insists that females don't make good comedians. On a more serious level, this repeated imagery may contribute narrow ideas of each gender's skills and capacities, and how little boys and little girls envision their futures.

At school, children meet a new drill instructor: their classroom teacher. He or she plays a critical role in gender socialization. The daily routine involves lining students up in two separate lines, dividing them by gender for the purposes of competition, and generally organizing classrooms in ways that continually reinforce the notion of gender differences (Thorne 1993). With respect to the content of their interactions, Sadker and Sadker found in videotaped observations of 100 classrooms that boys get more attention from teachers than do girls. First, boys are called on more frequently during class discussion and are less likely to be reprimanded for talking out of turn. With respect to the kind of feedback teachers gave to students, Sadker and Sadker found that boys were more likely to be "praised, corrected, helped and criticized" (p. 55). While girls received superficial feedback such as "Okay," "Good," or "Not quite," boys were given more opportunities to engage in critical thinking and make connections ("Tell me more about why you think that," or "How does that point connect to yesterday's lesson?"). Sadker and Sadker also found that teachers waited longer for male students to answer questions during class discussion before moving onto another student. They called this the **bombing rate.** When teachers "lob" questions out to their students, they move on more quickly when a female student does not quickly come up with an answer. Girls do receive some positive feedback in the classroom, though. Indeed, they are often complimented for their appearance or the neatness of their work. Boys, though, are more often complimented on the quality of their thoughts (Sadker and Sadker 1995).

Why do teachers do this? Do they quickly move on from female students because they don't want to embarrass them if they don't know the answer? Do they push male students harder during class discussion because they need to be corralled and engaged? While these are plausible explanations, it is difficult to observe teachers' motivations. It is easier to speculate about the consequences of these interactions. Sadker and Sadker conclude that over time these daily repetitive interactions—most of which escape teachers' and students' attention—contribute to a lack of confidence in female students. While male students are given practice in defending their point of view or rethinking an incorrect answer—becoming the "prime actors" in their classrooms (Sadker and Zittleman 2009:9)—female students are praised for giving correct answers but are not encouraged to be risky or nuanced in their thought processes.

If these patterns typify the daily interactions of elementary, middle, and high school, do they have long-term consequences for students' academic achievement? Given that females are more common on college campuses than males, it is difficult to argue that our educational system is "failing at fairness," as Sadker and Sadker suggest. In fact, some scholars now argue that the school system disadvantages young boys. They point to the higher levels of behavioral and learning problems among boys; they conclude that the rigid, tightly organized structure of schooling is poorly suited to young boys' brain development, energy level, and learning style (Gurian 2006; Kindlon and Thompson 2000; Sax 2009).

The question of how these differences affect students over the long term is complicated. While female high school graduates have higher GPAs than their male peers, they have lower SAT scores. Yet the notion of average differences can be deceiving. The fact that more female students take the SAT may explain this pattern: when more

According to existing research, the teacher will most likely call on a boy.

students take the test, there is a greater variation in their abilities and a likelihood of lower scores. Data also show greater variation in the scores of male students (a higher "standard deviation"), with more males scoring at the lower and higher ends; the scores of females, by contrast, cluster more in the middle.

Even if female students perform well academically, these patterns may partially explain why females are underrepresented in STEM fields (science, technology, engineering, and math). In mathematics textbooks, girls constitute only 12 percent of the "characters" used in word problems (Sadker and Zittleman 2009). In lab science classes, teachers may *tell* male students how to conduct an experiment but *do* the experiment for female students (Sandler, Silverberg, and Hall 1996). Research has shown that male students tend to overestimate their academic abilities while females tend to underestimate theirs (Cole et al. 1999); these tendencies, moreover, increase as children spend more years in school. Thus, while female students are not failing per se, school socialization molds them into strong and steady, but more tentative, students; males, meanwhile, are molded into active and visible students who perform at both the highest and lowest levels.

GENDER AND THE INFLUENCE OF PEERS

A second part of secondary socialization is peer socialization. This is where children and adolescents can create their own autonomous worlds, with unique norms and values, separate from the adult world (Corsaro 2010). As children interact with one another, they reinforce gender differences and gender role expectations. From very early ages, children contribute to the distinction between little boys and little girls, drawing firm boundaries between them. More in schools than in their neighborhoods, sociologist Barrie Thorne (1993) observed, children segregate themselves based on sex—in classrooms or during lunch or recess. Moreover, they police the boundary that separates them, warning of "cooties" when one group crosses over into enemy lines. Thorne calls this a **contamination ritual**—and observes that boys are less welcoming of "invaders" than girls. In the popular culture, this is illustrated by the He-Man Woman Haters Club featured in the old *Our Gang* television show and in the more recent *Little Rascals* movie.

Not only are boys more aggressive than girls in protecting their territory, they also have more territory to protect. In classrooms and on playgrounds, boys claim more space: sprawling out or crawling around during story time and building forts in the classroom (Martin 1998) or colonizing vast spaces during recess. In her ethnographic study of a number of diverse California elementary schools, Barrie Thorne concluded that boys take up about 10 times the playground space that girls take up (1993:44). School is a place where boys continue to cultivate a sense of comfort and adventure, playing in larger groups, while girls continue taking up less space, interacting in smaller more intimate social groups and staying in closer proximity to authority figures (Thorne and Luria 1986).

Peer socialization is also where notions of popularity and gender expectations collide. Even today, an adolescent's position within the peer group is strongly shaped by their conformity to traditional gender role expectations: while boys gain status for being athletic, funny, and daring in their behaviors (Kimmel 2008; Pascoe 2007), girls generally climb the social ladder based on appearance and performance in appearance-based activities, like cheerleading (Adler, Kless, and Adler 1992; Bettie 2003; Eder 1995). As sociologist Donna Eder points out, these standards can be problematic for girls. Whereas boys historically have had athletic teams and other avenues to prove their masculinity, girls face other restrictions, as there are only so many positions on the cheerleading squad. While girls now have more options in extracurricular involvements than in decades past, the structural lack of avenues for girls to gain approval and status may cause competition, nastiness, and "mean girl" behavior.

Gendered dynamics of popularity create another difficulty for adolescent females. While young men's popularity is rooted in athletics and personal achievement, girls are rewarded more based on appearance—something over which they have less control. Unless young girls win the genetic lottery or have the advantage of social class resources, they may have a harder time navigating peer groups. From elementary school (Eder 1995) on up to college (Armstrong and Hamilton 2013), young girls face pressures to groom themselves in socially approved ways (thin, tan, straightened and highlighted hair, properly outfitted and accessorized) and are rewarded by peers, teachers, and parents for doing so. This, however, requires money and know-how; it may be especially hard for lower-income females to find their place at school (Bettie 2003). Using one's social skills to attain popularity also requires incredible work: young girls must maintain the reputation of being nice, but not too nice. Someone who has too many friends and is too accessible to her peers is, by definition, no longer popular, given that popularity and exclusivity are nearly synonymous within adolescent peer cultures (Eder 1985; Merten 1997). Adolescence is a tough time for females: their self-esteem drops first with the move into middle school and second after high school graduation (Robins et al. 2002). While boys' self-esteem also drops during these periods, the drop is greater for girls (Robins and Trzesniewski 2005)—in large part due to increased dissatisfaction with their appearance and bodies (Paxton, Eisenberg, and Neumark-Sztainer 2006).

Boys face their own pressures. As discussed in Chapter 2, the male gender role involves a narrower set of behaviors than the female gender role. Adolescent boys, moreover, are intense drill sergeants in their own right, verbally and physically encouraging their peers to adhere to this role. Through their peer interactions, sociologist Michael Kimmel (2008) shows, adolescent males internalize **the guy code**: the collection of attitudes, values, and traits that together comprise what it means to be a man. At its core, it is the expectation to be tough, unemotional, and never show weakness. In locker rooms, classrooms, and beyond, boys chastise each other for being "babies," "sissies," and worse. Kimmel is concerned that over time, boys turn inward and dull their own emotions; dampening their empathy and ability to connect. In more extreme cases, the guy code may contribute to violent behaviors and tolerance of sexual harassment, misogyny, and homophobia.

In adolescent peer culture, it can be difficult to see where informal sanctioning and social pressures leave off and bullying begins. Sociologist C. J. Pascoe (2007) explores this line in her book, *Dude, You're a Fag: Masculinity and Sexuality in High School*. Gender policing among high school boys, Pascoe found, relied on the **fag discourse**—a term they applied when their peers violated the guy code: showing emotion, dancing well or performing in school productions, caring about one's appearance, or being physically uncoordinated. Especially for white high school students, this term was an insult and a hot potato: one could distance oneself from accusations of being a "fag" by tossing the term onto another student. Yet being called a "fag," for Pascoe, is not truly an insult to one's sexuality; the boys she observed in a California high school were aware of and generally comfortable with gay students. Instead, she concludes, it is a tool that adolescent boys skillfully utilize to enforce socially approved notions of masculinity.

Not all high school environments are as traditional as the ones discussed above. Some schools have their own unique gender, race, and social class dynamics, so that differences and deviations from the norm do exist. Similarly, not all adolescents participate in traditional peer cultures. Some teens participate in subcultural groups that place them outside of the mainstream. A **subculture** is a group that establishes its own cultural values, behavioral norms, fashion sense, and lingo. Among adolescents, this may include metalheads, Goths, punks, gamers, drama kids, or "band geeks." For some teens, these alternate spaces provide greater freedom of expression and their own "rules" when it comes to gender. Pascoe observed that tomboyish "basketball girls" were well liked, despite their deviation from mainstream gender role expectations and ambiguous sexual identities. Not *all* girls need to be cheerleaders to fit in at school. Further, although they were relatively low on the school's social hierarchy, boys in drama club experienced it as a space that was free from "the fag discourse."

Online gaming also offers the opportunity for new gender dynamics to emerge. Within the virtual world and especially in MMORPGS ("massively multiplayer online role-playing games)," players can "become" any sex and, in doing so, create complicated ways for real and virtual gender expressions to intersect (Beavis and Charles 2007). Yet in many ways, the virtual world mirrors the physical world in terms of gender interactions: "gender swapping" is less common among adolescent male players than among adult males (Griffiths et al. 2004); female gaming is still highly sexualized (Taylor et al. 2009); and female players report segregation and discrimination in online spaces (Delamere and Shaw 2008). Sociologist Ross Haenfler (2010), though, has coined the term **nerd masculinity** to describe the ways in which men may both reject and reinforce traditional expressions of masculinity. While some young men may criticize "jocks" and "frat boys" for their alleged tendency toward dominance and aggression, they still talk trash within the context of online gaming ("I owned you!") and treat women—at least in the abstract—as sexual objects (Kendall 2002). Within adolescent peer cultures, nerd masculinity may be evident in online gaming, the drama club, Goths (Wilkins 2008), and even the recent emergence of the Brony phenomenon (male fans of *My Little Pony: Friendship Is Magic*).

For adolescents who don't fit in—in many cases because of their gender or sexual expression—bullying is a fact of life. **Bullying** is defined as the use of force to intimidate others. With firm data hard to come by, the American Psychological Association estimates that 40–80 percent of adolescents experience some form of bullying at some point in their school careers; other studies offer lower estimates (Cook et al. 2010). Targets are often bullied based on their religion, race, sexual orientation, disability status, weight, or social class. It is unclear, though, whether bullies are motivated by power and aggression or by their own feelings of shame and anxiety. Sociologists see bullying—which escalates during adolescence (Espelage, Bosworth, and Simon 2001)—as an effort to gain popularity (Corsaro and Eder 1990). In terms of gender, most researchers believe that boys are more likely than girls to bully. In terms of tactics, males are more likely to engage in physical aggression—often motivated by homophobia or anti-gay sentiment—whereas females are more likely to engage in social aggression, including gossip and social isolation, often targeted at other females based on appearance.

SECONDARY SOCIALIZATION—LEARNING GENDER THROUGH THE SYMBOLIC WORLD AND THE MEDIA

During infancy and throughout our lives, we are also socialized through the symbolic world of the media. For the majority of human history, all communication was face to face. With the advent of mass communication, we are now molded by distant forces—forces that convey information and entertain and also mold our identities in subtle and not-so-subtle ways. Today, children and adults spend a considerable amount of time in front of a screen—whether a television, cell phone, or computer. According to a Kaiser Family Foundation study, infants on up to adults watch about 5 hours of television a day and spend nearly 7.5 hours a day in front of a screen. Given its ubiquity, what do we learn about gender from the media?

One thing we learn is that much of the media is gender segregated. While toddlers and young boys and girls are exposed to similar movies, television programs, and books, segregation takes over during the tween years. From there on out, there is Spike TV and several versions of ESPN for male viewers, and TLC and Lifetime ("Television for Women") for female viewers. While women get "chick flicks," male viewers are targeted with action movies (*Fast and Furious*) and "gross-out" films like *The Hangover*. An enduring theme, though, is that while female media consumers can trespass onto male turf, the reverse is rarely true. It sometimes seems that even a minute of exposure to *"Pretty Little Liars," Grey's Anatomy*, *The Notebook*, or *Love, Actually* might "contaminate" a male viewer with a small dose of dreaded femininity!

A second lesson from the mass media is that unlike the real world, where men and women exist in roughly equal numbers, men outnumber women on the big and small screens. As in children's storybooks, women experience *symbolic annihilation* in television and movies. Researchers from the Annenberg School of Communication and Journalism at the University of Southern California find that only 11 percent of family-oriented films and 22 percent of prime-time programs have "gender-balanced casts." On prime-time television, women comprise only about 37 percent of all characters. They are, moreover, generally portrayed in stereotypical roles. For example, male characters are more likely to work than female characters, while female characters are more consumed with romantic relationships. In family-oriented films, females represent only about 30 percent of characters. Again, portrayals are fairly stereotypical: women are three times more likely than men to be *sexualized*—appearing either nude or in sexy attire or conforming to social standards of physical beauty. Females, moreover, often fall into three main character types: mothers, hypersexualized vixens, or damsels in distress. Discrepancies between the real world and the media also appear to be increasing over time. With respect to weight and body type, women in adult magazines and beauty contests are getting smaller while those in the real world have been growing in size (Spitzer, Henderson, and Zivian 1999).

Even behind the scenes, men outnumber women. Martha Lauzen of San Diego State University found that during the 2010–11 prime-time television season, women accounted for 25 percent of all creators, producers, directors, writers, editors, and directors of photography. In her study of the top 250 grossing films of 2010, she found that women comprised 16 percent of these same roles. Even popular television programs that promote sexually empowered, career-oriented women like *Sex and the City* are often created and written by men. Because the creative forces behind the scenes lack diversity in terms of gender, it may be hard to create complicated, nuanced female characters. While powerful women like Shonda Rhimes (*Grey's Anatomy* and *Scandal*), Tina Fey (*30 Rock* and *"The Unbreakable Kimmy Schmidt"*), Amy Poehler (*Parks and Recreation*), Lena Dunham (*Girls*), and Mindy Kaling (*The Mindy Project*) have taken control of their own media projects, researchers find that little has changed over the last several decades with either the number of women involved in mass media or how they are presented.

THEORIES OF THE MEDIA'S IMPACT

Researchers have developed a variety of theories on how the media affects users. **Behaviorist theories**, which have their grounding in psychology, speculate that the media acts as a stimulus that directly influences behavior. For example, when children view violent or aggressive cartoons, they will behave in violent or aggressive ways; alternately, media advertising will stimulate wants and desires in those who view the images. Alfred Bandura's classic **Bobo doll experiments** represent this school of thought (Bandura, Ross, and Ross 1963). In one experiment, one group of children (aged 2–6) was shown a video depicting violent behavior toward a Bobo doll and another group was not. Next, researchers placed the children in a playroom with a Bobo doll to see if exposure to violent imagery would cause them to behave more violently. The children who had been exposed to the aggressive behavior demonstrated nearly twice as much aggressive behavior than the control group (those who did not view the aggressive behavior). Moreover, boys exhibited more aggression than girls. While some have concluded that this research shows that the media can influence violent behavior, it is limited in the sense that it provides only a one-time snapshot: it cannot tell us much about the behaviors of those who are exposed to a steady diet of particular media images.

Cultivation theory, by contrast, looks at how the media affects viewers *over time*. This theory, which emerged from communications studies, posits that heavy exposure to the mass media *cultivates* in viewers a distinct worldview and set of behaviors.

When exposed to violent stimuli, children typically behave more violently—at least in the short term.

Media scholar George Gerbner (1998), for example, found that when it comes to violent media, *heavy viewers* are much more fearful of the world around them compared to *light viewers*; this is what he termed the **mean-world syndrome**. When it comes to gender socialization, researchers find that television viewing "makes an independent contribution to adolescents' sex-role attitudes over time" (Morgan 1987), so that heavy viewers have more rigid beliefs about male and female roles (Signoreilli and Lears 1992). "Independent contribution" means that other factors have been controlled for statistically, so that television viewing *itself* seems to cause stereotypical gender beliefs. Similar findings have been confirmed for Latino youth (Rivadeneyra and Ward 2005). It is unclear, though, whether television viewing affects actual gendered *behaviors* among children and adolescents.

Some researchers, though, provide evidence that media exposure contributes to the *sexualization* of youth and adolescents (Ward 2003). Psychologists L. Monique Ward and Rocio Rivadeneyra (1999) found that greater exposure to sexual content on television is associated with higher rates of sexual activity, as well as greater endorsement of casual sex. For Kristen Firminger (2006), the media also contributes to female adolescents' investment in romance. Advice columns, for example, suggest that success in attracting the "right" boy and finding love depends on girls' self-regulation and good choices. Moreover, girls are told that it is both their duty and within their power to rein in boys' bad behavior. The enduring theme in teen magazines is that successful romantic relationships are girls' responsibility; with appropriate levels of self-esteem and the proper beauty and hygiene products, they can train and control their male partners.

The ideas of media activist Jackson Katz also correspond to this theoretical perspective. It is not only women who are negatively affected by the media, he argues. The constant barrage of violent and aggressive imagery—especially in media targeting men and young boys—also contributes to personal and social problems. In the documentary film *Tough Guise* (Jhally 1999) Katz links issues like bullying, school shootings, gay bashing, and sexual assault to the way masculinity is portrayed in the media. Although he does not argue that the media *causes* these behaviors, he draws a connection between media constructions of masculinity and how masculinity is lived and experienced by men and boys. In an interview with the *American Men's Studies Association* (Maurino 2013:3) Katz commented: "Boys are taught and thus learn at an early age that being a man means being powerful and in control; violence is an instrumental means of gaining or maintaining that power and control." This message is conveyed by everything from daring television shows like *Jackass* and *"Ridiculousness,"* to professional wrestling and mixed martial arts programming, to mundane commercials. Even children's television shows are filled with instances of "happy violence" (Gerbner 1998)—acts of violence portrayed either with humor or swiftly and without consequence.

The media's impact, then, is not simply a "monkey see, monkey do" dynamic. Given its pervasiveness, the media contributes to a cultural environment in which aggression is normalized and naturalized. Boys will be boys, after all. While this may occasionally erupt into spectacular instances of violence—like the school shooting at Sandy Hook Elementary School or the party rape perpetrated by male athletes in Steubenville, Ohio—the more ordinary result of these cultural images may be men who feel inadequate and alienated from themselves and the people around them.

Finally, **constructivist theories** take a different approach to media's role in socialization. These theories, which emerged from the minds of sociologists, assume that viewers and consumers are creative; they don't simply absorb the media as it is fed to them. With respect to gender, children, and the media, sociologist William Corsaro argues that children "creatively appropriate information from the adult world [and use it] to produce their own unique peer cultures" (1992:160). In this regard, media consumption is a fundamentally social event, as media consumers interact with others to construct their own understandings of a particular media event (violent video game, cartoon, etc.). Children may role-play, for example, taking scenarios they observed in the media and infusing them with values and characters from their own real and imagined worlds. Corsaro calls this process **interpretive reproduction**.

In her study of middle schools girls, Laura Fingerson (1999) found that girls use their own family experiences to critically evaluate dynamics and plots in television programs about family life. In talking to their peers about these programs, girls try to make sense of the morals and values promoted, given their own life experiences. They develop understandings of these shows by talking with others, showing that the media's impact is mediated through social processes. In a similar observational study, Meenakshi Durham (1999) found that adolescent females do absorb messages about beauty and relationships from magazines like *Seventeen* and *YM*; girls who are minorities or from lower-income families, however, may be more apt to reject these images and question the relevance to their own lives. While some worry that viewers may be harmed by unrealistic media images, scholars find that viewers have understood the differences between what is presented in the media and their actual lives.

With the growth of the Internet and other new technology, cultural consumers have new ways of interacting with their favorite media. **Fandom** allows consumers to form or join subcultures with other fans; these subcultures allow participants to interact with other fans and create art, videos, fan fiction, or other artifacts. Some of the media phenomena that have given rise to expressions of fandom are *Star Trek*, *Dr. Who*, *Naruto*, and even Jane Austen. In a sense, fandom allows participants to transform themselves from consumers of the culture to creators of the culture. In recent years, one of the most surprising instances of fandom emerged in the **Brony phenomenon**, a group composed largely of male fans of *My Little Pony: Friendship Is Magic*. This animated series—originally targeted at young girls—has attracted older viewers who have unabashedly embraced the positive values promoted by the show, while challenging preconceived gender roles. In a *Wired* magazine article profiling the phenomenon, one viewer was quoted saying that he learned more about "friendships and social interactions" from one season of the show than he had learned his entire adult life. Whether it is the lessons of such shows that make them unique or the opportunities to participate in fandom, these examples show that media consumers do not simply and passively absorb what the media offers.

EXPLORING ACTIVISM: "NOT BUYING IT" WHEN IT COMES TO GENDER AND CONSUMER CULTURE

While commentators like Jackson Katz and sociologists like Michael Kimmel are deeply worried that the media promote aggression and misogyny to young men, social activists are more vocal and organized when it comes to concerns about the impact of the media on girls and young women. Although large-scale national movements are yet to emerge, voices are bubbling up that encourage girls and women to reject both sexualizing media messages and the consumerism that often accompanies these messages. Shown on college campuses throughout the nation, the documentary film Miss Representation offers a call to action, arguing that media images that infantilize and sexualize women are partially to blame for women's underrepresentation in corporate and political settings. According to the film's website, director Jennifer Siebel Newsom's film "challenges the media's limited and often disparaging portrayals of women and girls, which make it difficult for women to achieve leadership positions and for the average woman to feel powerful herself."

Harnessing the power of social media, the film has spun off the "Not Buying It" app and Twitter hashtag (#notbuyingit). According to the app's website, "users will be able to upload sexist or inspiring media they see, scroll through images posted by others, and immediately let brands on Twitter know how they feel!" The site's users have called out Carl's Jr. (fast food), Radio Shack, Beats by Dre (headphones), Abercrombie & Fitch, and American Apparel for what users see as degrading imagery. According to the site's press, their actions have encouraged retailers like Hallmark Cards and Amazon to remove sexist products.

Even if it is difficult to show that sexualized media images cause either violence against women or the lack of representation of women in politics or corporate leadership, the patterned nature of these media representations do convey powerful messages about women's place in society. Although some may dismiss these images as mere entertainment, others have taken up the charge as either activists or professionals. Organizations like the Women's Media Center and the Geena Davis Institute on Gender in Media offer internships and careers to men and women who are interested in research and education on this topic. The Geena Davis Institute has spearheaded a program called "See Jane," whose mission is "to engage the entertainment industry and recognize the need for gender balance and varied portrayals of females and male characters into movies, TV, and other media aimed at children 11 and under." Moving beyond the voices of social media users, these organizations "work cooperatively and collaboratively with entertainment creators to encourage them to be leaders in creating positive change."

BIOLOGY, SOCIOLOGY, AND THE LIMITS OF GENDER SOCIALIZATION

During the early twentieth century, psychologist John B. Watson (1930: 82) was quoted as saying: "Give me a dozen healthy infants, well-formed, and my own specified world to bring them up in and I'll guarantee to take any one at random and train him to become any type of specialist I might select—doctor, lawyer, artist, merchant-chief and, yes, even beggar-man and thief, regardless of his talents, penchants, tendencies, abilities, vocations, and race of his ancestors."

Are human beings that malleable? With enough skill and enough exposure to gender boot camp, could John Watson turn a boy into a girl? As it turns out, biology seems to impose real limits on gender socialization. The case of David Reimer illustrates this. Born a healthy male in 1968, as an infant Reimer suffered a "botched circumcision" that seriously damaged his penis. His parents brought him to famed doctor John Money at Johns Hopkins University in the hopes that through surgical intervention and proper gender role socialization, the parents could raise David as a girl. Given the name Brenda, David's parents worked with him and his twin brother under the guidance of Dr. Money to promote healthy gender development. Yet as he moved into his teen years, David was unable to embrace his female identity, and became severely depressed. At age 14, he reverted to a male gender identity and began surgical procedures to rebuild his penis. His life ended tragically, however. While he did marry a woman and help raise her children from a previous relationship, depression plagued him. Two years after his twin brother died from a drug overdose, David Reimer took his own life. Despite his gender socialization and medical intervention, David could not be transformed into Brenda.

The stories of Genie and David Reimer contribute important insights to our understanding of gender. From David, we learn that biology may provide a foundation upon which our gender identities are built. From Genie we learn that social interaction is essential for molding our gender identities; without it, no one would become a "properly" gendered boy or girl (woman or man). In this sense, I use the term "properly" to indicate that gender expectations are often rigid and accompanied by rewards and punishments. The story of Genie and the research presented in this chapter also show that becoming a gendered being requires lots of work—from parents, teachers, peers, and the media. In conjunction with the lessons from Chapter 2 on sex and gender, we should remind ourselves that the interactions that make up gender boot camp are cross-culturally and historically variable. As the historical and structural context in which gender role expectations change, so too does the gender training passed on by parents, teachers, peers, and the media. In turn, when parents and children push back against these gender expectations or revise them in novel ways, they play a part in transforming the structure of gender within society.

CHAPTER 7: REVIEW OF KEY POINTS

- Although some gender distinctions may be rooted in biology, sociologists focus on the role of socialization in shaping gender roles and gender identities.
- Gender boot camp is the metaphor used to illustrate how gender is learned during primary socialization. Gender identities are learned and reinforced through physical interaction, verbal interaction, uniforms, and "equipment."
- While most children are at least initially raised within a binary system that categorizes them as "boys" or "girls," transgender or gender-nonconforming children do exist. For these children, being socialized into strict binary gender roles may be difficult; with greater awareness and new resources, these children can be raised with healthy identities.
- Gender intersects with race and ethnicity, so that gender distinctions between males and females tend to be firmer among Latinos and less firm among black Americans.
- In secondary socialization, children learn gender lessons outside of their families. At school, for example, boys are often given more space for physical and intellectual exploration; girls, meanwhile, learn to give correct answers, color inside the lines, and take fewer risks.
- Different theories exist to explain how the media may affect viewers, in this case in terms of shaping their gender identities and expectations. While behaviorist theories see a more linear impact of media representations on viewers, constructivist theories see viewers as creatively reinterpreting and giving meaning to the messages they receive from the media.
- Two broad themes running through gender socialization in the United States are that boys are raised to be adventurous, competitive risk takers, while females are raised to be cautious, collaborative, and correct. These patterns reflect broader social structural arrangements and are always subject to variations and evolution.
- When it comes to the sexualization of young girls and their socialization into consumer society, some groups are raising awareness and encouraging consumers to make more conscious choices.
- This chapter shows that gender role identities are not a foregone conclusion or rooted in biology; rather, many threads within society are woven together to almost seamlessly produce the men and women we already believe that we are.

CHAPTER 7: QUESTIONS FOR REVIEW

1. How does gender boot camp parallel military boot camp? How does gender socialization and the process of becoming a boy or a girl resemble military socialization and the process by which civilians become soldiers?
2. During primary socialization, what are some key differences in the ways that parents (and other adults) interact with boys and girls? To what extent do you believe that these interactions are instrumental in the process by which males and females take on gender roles?
3. During secondary socialization in school, what are some key differences in the socialization of male and female students? How do students themselves socialize each other to take on "proper" gender roles?
4. Perhaps you are skeptical of the notion that these seemingly minute social interactions are responsible for the social differences that characterize men and women. Can you think of ways to test the hypotheses that gender differences are rooted in biology rather than socialization?
5. When it comes to theories of the media's impact on viewers, how do psychologically based theories differ from sociologically based theories? Of the three theories mentioned, which do you think best describes the media's impact on consumers?

6. One of the themes of gender socialization is that males receive the message that the range of acceptable gender expression is quite narrow, and that males—in both childhood and adulthood—are more likely to "police" gender expression. Why do you think this is true? What are some of the reasons, in other words, that girls experience more flexibility than boys when it comes to acceptable forms of gender expression?

KEY TERMS

behaviorist theories

Bobo doll experiments

body management

bombing rate

Brony phenomenon

bullying

constructivist theories

contamination ritual

cultivation theory

fag discourse

fandom

feral children

gazing

gender boot camp

gender dysphoria

guy code

interpretive reproduction

mean-world syndrome

nerd masculinity

primary socialization

reinforcement

secondary socialization

socialization

subculture

symbolic annihilation

REFERENCES

Adams, Susan, Janet Kuebli, Patricia A. Boyle, and Robyn Fivush. 1995. "Gender Differences in Parent-Child Conversations about Past Emotions: A Longitudinal Investigation." *Sex Roles* 33(5–6):309–323.

Adler, Patricia A., Steven J. Kless, and Peter Adler. 1992. "Socialization to Gender Roles: Popularity among Elementary School Boys and Girls." *Sociology of Education* 65(3):169–187.

Alfaro, Edna C., Adriana J. Umaña-Taylor, and Mayra Y. Bámaca. 2006. "The Influence of Academic Support on Latino Adolescents' Academic Motivation." *Family Relations* 55(3):279–291.

Armstrong, Elizabeth A. and Laura T. Hamilton. 2013. *Paying for the Party: How College Maintains Inequality*. Cambridge, MA: Harvard University Press.

Baker-Sperry, Lori and Liz Grauerholz. 2003. "The Pervasiveness and Persistence of the Feminine Beauty Ideal in Children's Fairy Tales." *Gender and Society* 17(5):711–726.

Bandura, Albert, Dorothy Ross, and Sheila Ross. 1963. "Imitation of Film-Mediated Aggressive Models." *Journal of Abnormal and Social Psychology* 66(1):3–11.

Beavis, Catherine and Claire Charles. 2007. "Would the 'Real' Girl Gamer Please Stand Up? Gender, LAN Cafes, and the Reformulation of the 'Girl" Gamer." *Gender and Education* 19(6):691–705.

Bettie, Julie. 2003. *Women without Class: Girls, Race, and Identity*. Berkeley, CA: University of California Press.

Biblarz, Timothy J. and Evren Savci. 2010. "Lesbian, Gay, Bisexual, and Transgender Families." *Journal of Marriage and Family* 72:480–497.

Brody, Leslie. 2001. *Gender, Emotion, and the Family.* Cambridge, MA: Harvard University Press.

Bronstein, Phyllis. 1988. "Father-Child Interaction." Pp. 107–124 in *Fatherhood Today: Men's Changing Role in the Family*, edited by Phyllis Bronstein and Carolyn Pape Cowan. New York: John Wiley.

Burns, Alyson L., G. Mitchell, and Stephanie Obradovich. 1989. "Of Sex Roles and Strollers: Female and Male Attention to Toddlers at the Zoo." *Sex Roles* 20:309–315.

Carson, James, Virginia Burk, and Ross D. Parke. 1993. "Parent-Child Physical Play: Determinants and Consequences." Pp. 197–219 in *Parent-Child Play: Descriptions and Implications*, edited by Kevin B. MacDonald. Albany, NY: SUNY Press.

Clearfield, Melissa W. and Naree M. Nelson. 2006. "Sex Differences in Mothers' Speech and Play Behavior with 6-, 9-, and 14-month-old Infants." *Sex Roles* 54:127–137.

Cole, David A., Joan A. Martin, Lachlan A. Peeke, A. D. Seroczynski, and Jonathan Fier. 1999. "Children's Over- and Underestimation of Academic Competence; A Longitudinal Study of Gender Differences, Depression, and Anxiety." *Child Development* 70:459–473.

Condry, John and Sandra Condry. 1976. "Sex Differences: A Study of the Eye of the Beholder." *Child Development* 47:812–819.

Cook, Clayton R., Kirk R. Williams, Nancy G. Guerra, Tia E. Kim, and Shelly Sadek. 2010. "Predictors of Bullying and Victimization in Childhood and Adolescence: A Meta-analytic Investigation." *Social Psychological Quarterly* 25:65–83.

Corsaro, William. 1992. "Interpretive Reproduction in Children's Peer Cultures." *Social Psychology Quarterly* 55:160–177.

Corsaro, William. 2010. *Sociology of Childhood.* Thousand Oaks, CA: Sage Publications.

Corsaro, William A. and Donna Eder. 1990. "Children's Peer Cultures." *Annual Review of Sociology* 16:197–220.

Cuddy Amy J.C. 2011. "Dear Negotiation Coach: Striking a Powerful Pose." *Negotiation* 14:8.

Curtiss, Susan. 1977. *Genie: A Psycholinguistic Study of a Modern Day Wild Child.* New York: Academic Press.

Delamere, Fern M. and Susan M. Shaw. 2008. "'They See It as a Guy's Game': The Politics of Gender in Digital Games." *Leisure* 32:279–302.

Denham, Suzanne A., Daniel Zoller, and Elizabeth A. Couchoud. 1994. "Socialization of Preschoolers' Emotional Understanding." *Developmental Psychology* 30:928–938.

Durham, Meenakshi Gigi. 1999. "Girls, Media, and the Negotiation of Sexuality: A Study of Race, Class, and Gender in Adolescent Peer Groups." *Mass Media and Journalism Communication Quarterly* 76:193–216.

Eder, Donna. 1985. "The Cycle of Popularity: Interpersonal Relations among Female Adolescents." *Sociology of Education* 58:154–165.

Eder, Donna, with Catherine Collins Evans and Stephen Parker. 1995. *School Talk: Gender and Adolescent Culture.* New Brunswick, NJ: Rutgers University Press.

Espelage, Dorothy L., Kris Bosworth, and Thomas S. Simon. 2001. "Short-term Stability and Change of Bullying in Middle School Students: An Examination of Demographic, Psychosocial, and Environmental Correlates." *Violence and Victims* 16(4):411–426.

Fingerson, Laura. 1999. "Active Viewing: Girls' Interpretations of Family Television Programs." *Journal of Contemporary Ethnography* 28:389–418.

Firminger, Kristen. 2006. "Is He Boyfriend Material? Representation of Males in Teenage Girls' Magazines." *Men and Masculinities* 8(3):298–308.

Fivush, Robyn. 1989. "Exploring Sex Differences in the Emotional Content of Mother-Child Conversations about the Past." *Sex Roles* 20:675–691.

Fivush, Robyn, Melissa A. Brotman, Janine P. Bruckner, and Sherryl H. Goodman. 2000. "Gender Differences in Parent-Child Emotion Narratives." *Sex Roles* 42:233–253.

Gerbner, George. 1998. "Cultivation Analysis: An Overview." *Mass Communication and Society* 1:175–194.

Gooden, Angela M. and Mark A. Gooden. 2001. "Gender Representation in Notable Children's Picture Books: 1995–1999." *Sex Roles* 45:89–101.

Green, Jesse. 2012. "S/He." *New York Magazine.* Retrieved August 24, 2013 (http://nymag.com/news/features/transgender-children-2012-6/index1.html).

Griffiths, M. D., Mark N. O. Davies, and Darren Chappell. 2004. "Online Computer Gaming: A Comparison of Adolescent and Adult Gamers." *Journal of Adolescence* 27:87–96.

Gurian, Michael. 2006. *The Wonder of Boys.* New York City: Tarcher.

Haenfler, Ross. 2010. *Goths, Gamers, and Grrrls: Deviance and Youth Subcultures.* New York: Oxford University Press.

Hale-Benson, Janice. 1986. *Black Children: Their Roots, Culture, and Learning Styles.* Annapolis, MD: Johns Hopkins University Press.

Hall, Judith A. and David Matsumoto. 2004. "Gender Differences in Judgments of Multiple Emotions from Facial Expressions." *Emotion* 4: 201–206.

Hanson, Sandra L. 2007. "Success in Science among Young African American Women: The Role of Minority Families." *The Journal of Family Issues* 28:3–33.

Hill, Shirley A. 2001. "Class, Race, and Gender Dimensions of Child Rearing in African American Families." *Journal of Black Studies* 31:494–508.

Hill, Shirley A. 2002. "Teaching and Doing Gender in African American Families." *Sex Roles* 47:493–507.

Hill, Shirley A. and Joey Sprague. 1999. "Parenting in Black and White Families: The Interaction of Gender with Race and Class." *Gender and Society* 13:480–502.

Jhally, Sut. 1999. "Tough Guise: Violence, Media, and the Crisis in Masculinity." Northampton, MA: Media Education Foundation.

Johnson, Kerri L., Lawrie S. McKay, and Frank E. Pollick. 2011. "He Throws Like a Girl (But Only When He's Sad): Emotion Affects Sex-Decoding of Biological Motion Displays." *Cognition* 119(2):265–280.

Kane, Emily W. 2012. *The Gender Trap: Parents and the Pitfalls of Raising Boys and Girls.* New York: New York University Press.

Karraker, Katherine Hildebrandt, Dena Ann Vogel, and Margaret Ann Lake. 1995. "Parents' Gender-Stereotyped Perceptions of Newborns: The Eye of the Beholder Revisited." *Sex Roles* 33:687–701.

Kendall, Lori. 2002. *Hanging Out in the Virtual Pub: Masculinities and Relationships Online.* Berkeley: University of California Press.

Kimmel, Michael. 2008. *Guyland: The Perilous World Where Boys Become Men.* New York City: Harper Collins.

Kindlon, Dan and Michael Thompson. 2000. *Raising Cain: Protecting the Emotional Life of Boys.* New York: Random House.

Leaper, Campbell. 2002. "Parenting Girls and Boys." Chapter 7 in *The Handbook of Parenting*, Vol. 1, edited by Marc H. Bornstein. Mahwah, NJ: Lawrence Erlbaum Associates.

Lindsey, Eric W. and Jacquelyn Mize. 2001. "Contextual Differences in Parent-Child Play: Implications for Children's Gender Role Development." *Sex Roles* 44:155–176.

MacDonald, Kevin and Ross D. Parke. 1986. "Parent-Child Physical Play: The Effects of Sex and Age of Children and Parents." *Sex Roles* 15:367–378.

Malatesta, Carol Z., Clayton Culver, Johanna Rich Tesman, and Beth Shepard. 1989. "The Development of Emotion Expression in the First Two Years of Life." Monographs of the Society for Research in Child Development 54: i-136.

Martin, Karin A. 1998. "Becoming a Gendered Body: Practices of Preschools." *American Sociological Review* 63:494–511.

McCabe, Janice, Emily Fairchild, Liz Grauerholz, Bernice Pescosolido, and Daniel Tope. 2011 "Gender in Twentieth-Century Children's Books: Patterns of Disparity in Titles and Central Characters." *Gender & Society* 25(2):197–226.

Maurino, James P., ed. 2013. "An Interview with Jackson Katz, Ph.D., on the Gendered Nature of Gun Violence." *AMSA Newsletter* 3(1):3–8.

Merten, Don E. 1997. "The Meaning of Meanness: Popularity, Competition, and Conflict among Junior High School Girls." *Sociology of Education* 70:175–191.

Morgan, Michael. 1987. 'Television, Sex-Role Attitudes, and Sex-Role Behaviors." *Journal of Early Adolescence* 7:269–282.

Pascoe, C.J. 2007. *Dude, You're a Fag: Masculinity and Sexuality in High School.* Berkeley: University of California Press.

Paxton, Susan J., Marla E. Eisenberg and Dianne Neumark-Sztainer. 2006. "Prospective Predictors of Body Dissatisfaction in Adolescent Girls and Boys: A Five-Year Longitudinal Study." *Developmental Psychology* 42:888–899.

Plant, E. Ashby, Janet Shibley Hyde, Dacher Keltner, and Patricia C. Devine. 2000. "The Gender Stereotyping of Emotions." *Psychology of Women Quarterly* 24:81–92.

Raffaelli, Marcela. 2005. "Adolescent Dating Experiences Described by Latino College Students." *Journal of Adolescence* 28:559–572.

Raffaelli, Marcela and Lenna L. Ontai. 2004. "Gender Socialization in Latino/a Families: Results from Two Retrospective Studies." *Sex Roles* 50:287–299.

Ramirez, Rafael. 1999. *What It Means to be a Man: Reflections on Puerto Rican Masculinity.* New Brunswick, NJ: Rutgers University Press.

Renzetti, Claire M. and Daniel J. Curran. 1999. *Women, Men, and Society*, 4th ed. Boston: Allyn and Bacon.

Rivadeneyra, Rocio and L. Monique Ward. 2005. "From Ally McBeal to Sábado Gigante: Contributions of Television Viewing to the Gender Role Attitudes of Latino Adolescents." *Journal of Adolescent Research* 20:453–475.

Robins, Richard W. and Kali H. Trzesniewski. 2005. "Self-Esteem Development across the Lifespan." *Current Directions in Psychological Science* 14:158–162.

Robins, Richard W., Kali H. Trzesniewski, Jessica L. Tracy, Samuel D. Gosling, and Jeff Potter. 2002. "Global Self-Esteem across the Life Span." *Psychology and Aging* 17:423–434.

Rymer, Russ. 1993. *Genie: A Scientific Tragedy.* New York: Harper Perennial.

Sadker, Myra and David Sadker. 1995. *Failing at Fairness: How Our Schools Cheat Girls.* New York: Scribner.

Sadker, David and Karen Zittleman. 2009. *Still Failing at Fairness: How Gender Bias Cheats Girls and Boys in School and What We Can Do About It*. New York: Scribner.

Sandler, Bernice R., Lisa A. Silverberg and Roberta M. Hall. 1996. *The Chilly Classroom Climate: A Guide to Improve the Education of Women*. Washington, DC: National Association for Women in Education.

Sax, Leonard. 2009. *Boys Adrift. The Five Factors Driving the Growing Epidemic of Unmotivated Boys and Underachieving Young Men*. New York City: Basic Books.

Signoreilli, Nancy and Margaret Lears. 1992. "Children, Television, and Conceptions about Chores: Attitudes and Behaviors." *Sex Roles* 27:157–170.

Snow, Margaret Ellis, Carol Nagy Jacklin, and Eleanor E. Maccoby. 1983. "Sex-of-Child Differences in Father-Child Interaction at One Year of Age." Child Development 54:227–232.

Spitzer, Brenda L., Katherine A. Henderson, and Marilyn Zivian. 1999. "Gender Differences in Population versus Media Body Sizes: A Comparison over Four Decades." *Sex Roles* 40:545–565.

Stacey, Judith and Timothy J. Biblarz. 2001. "(How) Does the Sexual Orientation of Parents Matter?" *American Sociological Review* 66: 159–183.

Tasker, Fiona L. and Susan Golombok. 1997. *Growing Up in a Lesbian Family*. New York: Guilford.

Taylor, Nicholas, Jen Jensen, and Suzanne de Castell. 2009. "Cheerleaders/Booth Babes/*Halo* Hoes: Pro-gaming, Gender and Jobs for the Boys." *Digital Creativity* 20:239–252.

Tenenbaum, Harriet R., Catherine E. Snow, Kevin A. Roach, and Brenda Kurland. 2005. "Talking and Reading Science: Longitudinal Data on Sex Differences in Mother-Children Conversations in Low-Income Families." *Journal of Applied Developmental Psychology* 26(1):1–19.

Thorne, Barrie. 1993. *Gender Play: Boys and Girls in Schools*. New Brunswick, NJ: Rutgers University Press.

Thorne, Barrie and Zella Luria. 1986. "Sexuality and Gender in Children's Daily Worlds." *Social Problems* 33:176–190.

Tuchman, Gaye, Arlene Kaplan Daniels, and James Benet. 1978. *Hearth and Home: Images of Women in the Mass Media*. New York: Oxford University Press.

Ward, L. Monique. 2003. "Understanding the Role of Entertainment Media in the Sexual Socialization of American Youth: A Review of Empirical Research." *Developmental Review* 23: 347–388.

Ward, L. Monique and Rocio Rivadeneyra. 1999. "Contributions of Entertainment Television to Adolescents' Sexual Attitudes and Expectations: The Role of Viewing Amount versus Viewer Involvement." *Journal of Sex Research* 36: 237–249.

Watson, John B. 1930. *Behaviorism* (Revised edition). Chicago: University of Chicago Press.

Weitzman, Nancy, Beverley Birns, and Ronald Friend. 1985. "Traditional and Non-traditional Mothers' Communication with their Daughters and Sons." *Child Development* 56:894–898.

West, Candace and Don H. Zimmerman. 1987. "Doing Gender." *Gender and Society* 1(2):125–151.

Wilkins, Amy. 2008. *Wannabes, Goths, and Christians: The Boundaries of Sex, Style, and Status*. Chicago: University of Chicago Press.

Chapter 8

"We Make Each Other Racial": How We Become Racialized Beings

In 1972, the National Association of Black Social Workers (NABSW) issued their "Position Statement on Trans-Racial Adoption." In this document, leaders of this professional organization spoke against the "placement of black children in white homes for any reason." With respect to foster care and adoption, it was and is the position of this organization that black children should be raised in black families. According to the organization's leaders, that is where black children "belong physically, psychologically and culturally," and it is only there they can "receive the total sense of themselves and develop a sound projection of their future." With the goal of strengthening black families, the NABSW emphasized the importance of socialization and stressed that an authentic connection to one's cultural heritage is an essential part of strong families and healthy personal development. When black children are placed with white families, efforts to learn how to "handle black children's hair" and familiarize the child with "black culture . . . puts normal family activities in the form of special family projects to accommodate the odd member of the family" (NABSW 1972: 3) Considering the racial history of the United States and continued racism and inequality, the NABSW argued that a black child cannot become properly black outside of a black home.

While the position of the NABSW remains controversial—in part because of the many black children within the foster care system who may eventually qualify for adoption—it raises an important sociological question about how racial and ethnic identities are *learned*. One lesson learned in Chapter 3 is that the amount of genetic variation in the human population is scant, not enough to divide the population into subspecies called races. Yet we also learned that race and ethnicity are powerful social constructs—constructs molded by historical forces and embedded in social arrangements. Given the minimal genetic differences that exist among the groups we call races, we can conclude that some of the social differences that exist among groups are a product of social learning. While we learn these differences within a society that is already characterized by deep inequalities, the lesson of this chapter is that through socialization, we *become* racialized beings. This means that even though we are born with phenotypic differences that are used to categorize us as "white," "black," "Asian," and "Latino" (in addition to other groups), what it means to be a member of these groups and the way in which we embody these identities is partially a product of socialization—a process that involves primary socialization at home and secondary socialization within the school system and the media.

SOCIALIZATION AND THE PROCESS OF LEARNING RACE

As with gender, children are born into a world that is already structured around race. When parents socialize their children, they do so within a social context in which race matters and where people of different races and ethnicities occupy different (and often unequal) positions. These positions are different and unequal in that racial and ethnic groups in the United States differ in terms of family structure, income, and the neighborhoods in which they live. While the families within any one racial or ethnic group are incredibly diverse, aggregate differences at the group level make members of some groups more likely than others to experience economic stability, relationships with two parents or other guardians, and a neighborhood that is safe and filled with good schools. These characteristics lay the foundation upon which socialization takes place.

With respect to family structure, children from different racial and ethnic groups experience differences from the day they are born. Data from the Centers for Disease Control and Prevention (CDC) indicate that about 40 percent of all children are born to unmarried women. For children born to black mothers this number is nearly 73 percent. At 17 percent, Asian American children are least likely to be born out of wedlock. As Table 8.1 shows, other racial and ethnic groups fall between these poles. Another indicator of family structure is the percentage of children living in "married couple families." Data reported by the National Center for Education Statistics show that 82 percent of Asian American children live with two married parents; among black children this figure is only 37 percent. Children from other racial and ethnic groups fall in between. Although these data do not indicate whether a child's unmarried parents are cohabiting or in a stable relationship, they provide some insight into the family structures experienced by children of different racial and ethnic groups.

How do these patterns in family structure shape the childhood socialization of children from different racial and ethnic groups? On average, not having two adults in the home has negative consequences for economic well-being. The fact that black households are less likely to have two adults present partially explains why their median *family* incomes are about $35,500, compared to the national median of about $57,200. Accordingly, being raised in a single-parent family is strongly associated with experiencing economic instability and childhood poverty. As Table 8.1 shows, rates of childhood poverty vary significantly across racial and ethnic groups. According to the

Table 8.1 Family Demographics by Race and Ethnicity

Group	Births to Unwed Mothers	Children Living in Two-Parent Families	Median Income (Families with 1 or More Children)	Child Poverty Rate
Black/African American (non-Hispanic)	72.5%	37%	$35,500	39%
Native American	64%	51%	—	34%
Hispanic	53%	63%	37,400	34%
White (non-Hispanic)	29%	73%	61,900	12.5%
Asian American	17%	82%	76,400	13.5%

National Center for Children in Poverty, children raised in single-parent households are more than twice as likely (70 percent) to live in low-income families as those with married parents (32 percent).

In terms of childhood experiences, sociologist Sara McLanahan (2011) shows that when families lack financial resources, they move more frequently. Even though their parents may love and care for them, residential instability disrupts a child's educational experiences, as frequent moves are associated with lower levels of academic achievement and lower rates of high school graduation and college enrollment. Frequent moves also make it difficult for parents and children to accumulate social capital. **Social capital** refers to the social connections that exist among people and within communities. People can use social capital to access information (how to find a good tutor, where to enroll a child in guitar lessons) and support (help babysitting, sharing a cup of sugar, commiserating); social capital also helps to reinforce social norms and maintain order within a community (keeping an eye on kids, keeping kids in line). The fact that children of different racial and ethnic backgrounds tend to live in different family structures, which are associated with different economic realities, suggests that their access to social capital differs early on.

The fact that black children are less likely than others to live in married, two-parent families does not automatically mean that they experience less social support. Sociologists and anthropologists have shown that kinship networks can be remarkably strong within black communities. **Kinship** usually refers to relationships built through reproduction or marriage. Kinship can also include **fictive kin**. These are relationships with people who are *like* family, in the sense that these ties involve regularized interaction, the giving and receiving of support (reciprocity), and social control (efforts to reinforce social norms). Colloquially, some black people may refer to someone as "Auntie" or "cousin," even though they are not related by blood or marriage. Because of their nurturing and supervisory roles, sociologist Patricia Hill Collins (1991) refers to older female fictive kin as "other mothers."

The sentiment that fictive kin are like family members may reach back to slavery, where the plantation system made it difficult for slaves to maintain legal family ties;

accordingly, they developed family systems of their own. As Carol Stack wrote in her 1974 ethnographic classic *All Our Kin*, fictive kin networks can help families survive in challenging times. Her study of a poor black community showed residents caring for one another, looking out for and disciplining each other's children, and developing collaborative strategies to cover the costs of food and rent. The picture that emerges from her work is a community that is poor in financial terms but rich and adaptive in terms of social support.

Another variation across racial and ethnic groups is the likelihood of being raised in a multigenerational family. Multigenerational families include two or more generations of adults living under the same roof, usually including at least one grandparent. For white Americans—especially those who have been in the United States for several generations—multigenerational families are rare. Yet the number of multigenerational families in the United States is growing, mainly due to higher levels of Asian and Latin American immigration. According to the Pew Research Center, Hispanics (22 percent), blacks (23 percent) and Asians (25 percent) are all significantly more likely than whites (13 percent) to live in a multigenerational family household.

While the need to pool economic resources is one reason multigenerational families have increased, this family structure is also embraced for social and cultural reasons. For immigrants living in a new country, multigenerational families are essential for maintaining and passing on shared rituals, holidays, and other special events. According to the website for the organization Generations United, "some individuals believe it is healthier to live in age-integrated communities where young can benefit from the wisdom of elders and older adults feel connected to the future." Research has shown, moreover, that teens living with a single mother and grandparent may have better developmental outcomes (lower rates of drinking and sexual activity, higher levels of academic performance) than those in two-parent families (Deliere and Kalil 2002).

Within multigenerational immigrant families, parents and grandparents may also benefit from younger generations. Children of immigrants raised in the United States, for example, may act as brokers, advocates, and even surrogate parents in their families, helping older non–English-speaking relatives navigate interactions in banks, schools, doctors' offices, and other settings (Katz 2010; Valenzuela 1999). According to Orellana, Dorner, and Pulido (2003), this brings children into the front and center of their families, where they take on essential legal and economic roles. While relatively few children report feeling burdened or embarrassed by these roles (Tse 1995), these interactions can put them in compromising positions—especially if their family members are not in the United States legally. In these situations, children may hide their own or family members' medical and educational problems, fearing that if they come forward, they may compromise their parents' or grandparents' residency in the United States (Gonzalez 2009; Passel and Cohn 2009).

These differences in family structure establish the context in which children from different racial and ethnic groups are socialized. While aggregate differences exist in terms of financial resources and family structure, a cross-cutting theme is that parents and communities across racial and ethnic boundaries work to provide children with meaningful support and social ties.

LEARNING RACE DURING PRIMARY SOCIALIZATION: THE ROLE OF PARENTS AND GUARDIANS

If race and racial identities are learned, when and how are these lessons imparted? Further, how does the process and content of socialization differ across racial lines? With respect to the timing of racial socialization, psychologists and sociologists speculate that infants develop a sense of racial differences after they have developed a sense of gender differences. Some believe that learning just two categories—male and female—is developmentally easier than learning the complex variations that come with race and ethnicity. Psychologist Phyllis Katz spent much of her career studying racial awareness and racial preferences among infants and young children. In a laboratory study, Katz and her collaborator Jennifer Kofkin (1997) found that infants as young as six months old stare longer at the faces of people with skin color that is different from their parents than at faces with similar complexions. When Katz and Kofkin studied the same group as three-year-olds, they found that more than half the children were able to label themselves in terms of race, suggesting the formation of racial identities around this time. As five- and six-year-olds, study participants were given a stack of photographs and told to separate them into piles. While 16 percent of the children divided the cards up in terms of gender, 68 percent sorted them in terms of race.

Yet being aware of race is different from applying meanings to these differences or expressing racial preferences. As primary socialization unfolds, children begin to receive messages about race, which shape how they think about their own and others' race. So what kinds of messages do children receive? One difference in racial socialization is the degree to which parents talk to their children about race. Using a nationally representative sample of 17,000 kindergartners and their families, Brown et al. (2007) found that nonwhite parents are three times more likely to talk to their children about race as white parents. In a study using quantitative data, Lesane-Brown and co-authors (2010) reported that 60 percent of white parents *never* or *almost never* talked to their children about racial or cultural heritage; the numbers were 15 percent for Native American parents and 30 percent for black parents.

The silence of white parents on questions of race and ethnicity may come from two different places. One, their silence may simply reflect the fact that as members of the majority, they are less aware of how race affects their everyday lives. The privilege of being part of the majority may mean that race is a less salient aspect of their identity. For many white Americans, identifying with a particular race or ethnicity feels optional, given that the uniqueness of their racial or ethnic group is not often highlighted (Waters 1996). Yet another reason for their silence may be a combination of feeling awkward and the hope that by not talking about race, children will develop a "color-blind" outlook. While she hoped to conduct a study examining what happens when white parents do talk to their children about race, Birgitte Vittrup encountered a barrier: many white parents refused to participate in the study or were unable to have meaningful conversations with their children on the topic (Bronson and Merryman 2009). When white parents did discuss race with their children, they made generic statements like "Everyone is equal" and "We are all the same on the inside." What their conversations lacked was historical context or factual attention to the ways that race has shaped this nation's history.

Meanwhile, conversations about race and ethnicity seem to be a key feature of growing up in minority families. Sociologist Shirley Hill notes that "Because race has been the central defining factor in the African American experience, one of the greatest challenges facing parents has always been to counter pervasive, destructive stereotypes and myths about Black people" (2001:498). In fact, even as young children, minority youth may express a preference for white playmates and a sense of shame in their own racial identity. When Katz and Kofkin followed up their research participants as five-year-olds, they found that 82 percent of white children but only 32 percent of black children preferred playmates of their *own race*. That is, both white and black children expressed a preference for white playmates.

Psychologists Mamie and Kenneth Clark most famously documented this preference in their "doll study." In a series of studies conducted in the 1940s, this husband-and-wife team explored children's feelings about race. In a laboratory setting, a white-skinned doll with blond hair and a brown-skinned doll with black hair were set in front of children. Children were then asked which doll they wanted to play with, which was the nice doll, which was the bad doll, and which doll looked like them. Using hundreds of respondents, a majority of children—both black and white—expressed a preference for playing with the white doll; they were also more likely to associate positive traits with the white doll and negative traits with the black one. These results were persuasively used in the 1954 *Brown vs. Board of Education* U.S. Supreme Court case—which ultimately outlawed school segregation—to argue that segregation and inequality exacerbate feelings of inferiority among black children.

In their classic "doll study," Mamie and Kenneth Clark found that black children preferred to play with white dolls and associated them with more positive traits.

In terms of what minority parents talk to children about in conversations about race, researchers have uncovered three themes. Parents impart lessons that focus on *egalitarianism*, *group pride*, and *preparation for adversity* (Hill 2001; Hughes and Chen 1997; Scottham and Smalls 2009). According to Shirley Hill, minority parents must "teach their children to expect and cope with racism and racial exclusion while not allowing it to become a rationale for failure or despair" (2001:498). Black children raised in the 1950s may have been warned not to "show your color."

According to award-winning playwright August Wilson, this phrase means "Don't act out" or "Don't be yourself"—especially in public settings inhabited by whites. Elders were essentially telling him, "Go down there and try to act . . . like you see white folks acting." Looking back on this warning, Wilson reflected: "If you say showing your color is bad, you're saying 'Don't go down there and act like a [n-word]; don't go down there and act black.'" For *Chicago Tribune* journalist Clarence Page, this admonition encouraged black children to be colorless; to avoid drawing attention to themselves and try to blend in. For black children growing up in the 1950s, parents may have intended this as a way to protect their children, given that lynchings and other dangers were an ongoing threat.

When 17-year-old Trayvon Martin was shot in an Orlando suburb during the winter of 2012, the media highlighted another conversation that some black parents have with their children, commonly referred to as **"The Talk."** The need for "The Talk" was reinforced repeatedly in 2014, with the high-profile police-involved deaths of Michael Brown in Ferguson, Missouri, Tamir Rice in Cleveland, Ohio, and Eric Garner in Staten Island, New York.

While adolescents across the United States may get a talk from their parents about sex, drugs, and alcohol, "The Talk" seems to be a unique feature of adolescent socialization among black Americans, especially young men. As described by *New York Times* blogger KJ Dell-Antonia, "The Talk" prepares adolescents for how to deal with police officers and other authorities. In "The Talk," young black men are advised to stand up straight, keep hands visible at all times, and "don't let your anger get the best of you." If interrogated by the police, cooperate and be polite. The assumption underlying this conversation is that police officers are not always helpful allies; it reflects the fact that for members of some minority groups, police intrusions may be a regular occurrence. Quoted in the *New York Post*, Reverend Conrad Tiller of Brooklyn commented: "It's really a painful paradox when you know you haven't done anything wrong. . . . Even though you may be in the right, life and death may hang in the balance. You can't win in that situation." You must, New York state senator Eric Adams said, not just behave respectfully but bend over backward to avoid a confrontation. Presumably, "The Talk" is not exclusive to black Americans. It is likely that parents of Latino youth speak to their children about the same issues, especially if they live in an area where police have been cracking down on undocumented or illegal immigrants. The significance of "The Talk" is that some minority youth are raised from an early age to expect tensions with authorities and are given advice about how to respond.

It is worth asking: Why does it matter whether and how parents talk to their children about race? According to Rebecca Bigler (Bronson and Merryman 2009), when white children learn more about the details of discrimination—rather than stories simply praising the accomplishments of heroes like Jackie Robinson and Martin Luther King Jr.—they develop more positive attitudes toward minority groups. Allison Briscoe-Smith (2010) found that children whose parents talked to them about race were better able to identify racism when they saw it and were more likely to have positive views about ethnic minorities. Research by Anna Beth Doyle and Frances Aboud

(1995) reinforces the notion that talking about race can improve children's attitudes toward minority groups.

For black children, there is a delicate balance when it comes to *how* parents talk to children about race. On the one hand, African American children whose parents do not talk to them about race feel less prepared to handle discrimination and less control over their environment; those who were socialized to be *aware* of racial barriers had better academic performance (Bowman and Howard 1985). Further, April Harris-Britt and her co-authors found that children who heard more stories emphasizing racial or ethnic pride had higher levels of self-esteem and school involvement (2007). On the flip side, children who more frequently heard stories about discrimination were more likely to blame their failures on others (Bronson and Merryman 2009). It appears, then, that there is a "sweet spot," in terms of how and how much parents should talk to children about racial issues.

So other than family structure or lessons about racial discrimination, how does culture influence childhood socialization? Culture is more than the foods we eat or holidays we celebrate. When it comes to the culture of parenting, differences do emerge across racial and ethnic groups. One primary divide seems to be the emphasis on individualism and child-centered socialization among white American families and the emphasis on collectivism and **familism** among Asian and Hispanic American families. Children raised with a sense of familism are raised with a sense of interconnectedness and an emphasis on placing the family's needs above one's own. Within Asian cultures, this is sometimes referred to as **filial piety**. It is a cultural approach in which children are expected to take on chores to help the entire family, attend family events, and, as they grow up, live close to the family and continue to offer tangible support (a home, rides to medical appointments) to elders (Kiang and Fuligni 2009). Among immigrant families in the United States, familism is considered essential for preserving the culture across generations (Zayas and Solari 1994).

Within Hispanic communities, children are also socialized to give respect (*dar respeto*). **Respeto** refers to a cultural emphasis on obedience to authority, deference to elders, and proper decorum in public settings (Calzada, Fernandez, and Cortes 2010). Children are expected to behave deferentially and respect boundaries with adults. Illustrating this principle, one mother in the study by Calzada, Fernandez, and Cortes was quoted thusly: "So I would say to him [her son], 'Who invited you into this discussion?' That looks bad. That reflects poorly on you. It is bad manners to get involved in adult conversations" (2010:82). While some mothers in this study suggested that instilling a sense of *respeto* is a natural part of everyday interactions, others spoke of using "harsh methods" to do so. "There are times," one mother said, "when one has to smack [a child], especially now that children are so head-strong" (2010:82). Indeed, the Dominican and Puerto Rican mothers in this study suggested that spanking is a necessary tool for proper childrearing. While it would seem that respect and decorum are universally appreciated traits for children to learn, it appears that white American families place less emphasis on these traits while putting greater emphasis on self-direction, dialogue, and critical thinking.

This leads to the question of whether mothers like the one quoted above are typical of Hispanic mothers and, more generally, whether disciplinary techniques vary across racial and ethnic families. Are some children socialized with spanking and physical and verbal discipline as a common feature of childhood? To the extent that researchers have uncovered racial differences in disciplinary styles, efforts have been made to determine whether these differences are due to race itself or the fact that minority groups tend to have lower levels of education and income. Using data from thousands of children and efforts to statistically control for a variety of factors (including income), researchers find that black parents are likely to use physical discipline and verbal punishment (shouting, negative comments) more frequently than white or Hispanic parents (Berlin et al. 2009; Gershoff et al. 2012). Yet social class also matters: middle- and upper-income black parents are less likely to endorse physical discipline than their lower-income counterparts (Horn, Cheng, and Joseph 2004).

Among some African Americans physical punishment is a hot-button issue. Some African Americans defend physical punishment as a legitimate parenting tool, so that questioning the use of corporal punishment can provoke a defensive reaction. "It's culturally embedded in America that spanking is a legitimate and good way to discipline children," said Dr. Alvin Poussaint of Harvard Medical School in a CNN blog post. "But the fact is, nearly all studies, except for a few, say it is not a good way of disciplining and can actually produce damage." Longitudinal studies—ones that follow the same individuals over a period of time—have also found that harsh disciplinary techniques can produce negative outcomes. Youngsters who were spanked frequently exhibited more aggressive behaviors over time (Gershoff et al. 2012), and also scored lower on scales of cognitive development (Berlin et al. 2009).

While "harsh" in other ways, Amy Chua caused a stir in 2011 with her book *Battle Hymn of the Tiger Mother*. In this book she describes the parenting practices of the typical Chinese family—what she calls tiger mothering. This parenting style emphasizes academic drills and long sessions practicing violin or piano, along with a lack of play dates or emotional indulgence. Some readers were taken aback by her suggestion that providing positive feedback to children could be damaging and cringed at the notion that good results can be achieved by withholding praise or calling children shameful names. Chua attributes these parenting styles to most Asian and immigrants groups and also claims these techniques produce strong, successful children. Recent research, however, challenges Chua's claims. First, Su Yeong Kim and her co-authors (2012) found that relatively few Asian American parents can be considered true "tiger parents." Instead, most used a supportive parenting style, emphasizing warmth and reasoning with minimal punishment. Second, researchers found that supportive parenting—rather than authoritarian methods—produced the best results in children, as measured by high GPA and lack of depressive symptoms.

One commonality among nonwhite racial and ethnic minorities is that during childhood they typically receive messages about *both* how the "outside" world views their race or color *and* how their race or color is viewed within their own community. These lessons often reflect on colorism. **Colorism** is a form of prejudice or discrimination, often occurring within minority communities, where people are treated differently based on skin color. Colorism has its roots in the systems of slavery, where the sexual exploitation of Black female slaves by White male slave owners resulted in mixed-race offspring (Hunter 2007; Keith and Herring 1991). Although they were still slaves, these offspring were often assigned less strenuous tasks inside the home. Over time, slaves with a white background and lighter skin gained more advantages. After slavery, the lightest of these individuals sometimes passed as white in society at large. In Africa, Asia, and Latin America, similar dynamics emerged in association with colonization by European powers (Hernandez 2006; Hunter 2007; Lynn 2008; Mukhtar 2007).

Scholars have increasingly turned their attention to "colorism," or discrimination based on pigment (skin tone) *among* people of color.

As a reflection of this history, nonwhite children with darker skin may be told from early on that they are not as pretty or favored as their light-skinned peers. Statements like "You're pretty for a dark girl," or "He's dark, but smart" may be common (Thompson and Keith 2003). In their research on socialization within black families, JeffriAnne Wilder and Colleen Cain (2011) found that relatives sometimes instilled within younger generations a sense of internal bias and judgment. They quote one dark-skinned respondent, Tessa, reflecting: "I remember my young cousins growing up who were lighter skinned and had the good hair, . . . they were just expected to be smart, to say smart things, to kind of carry on the family name. . . . I was never expected to be smart" (2011:591). Filipina students have told me stories of being chastised by older relatives for spending too much time in the sun and being encouraged to use skin-bleaching creams. Family members, then, sometimes perpetuate internalized racism—meaning ways that people of color embrace the racial standards and preferences of society at large, including the preference for light skin and straight hair.

Over time, research shows, these messages penetrate a person's sense of identity and well-being. Using a nationally representative sample of black Americans, Thompson and Keith (2001) found that light skin is associated with higher levels of self-esteem for women and self-efficacy for men (feeling competent to complete tasks and reach goals). Research on immigrant Latinas also shows that those with darker skin have lower self-esteem and feelings of attractiveness and a stronger desire for lighter skin (Telzer and Vazquez Garcia 2009). While the negative impacts on identity appear to be stronger for females than males, researchers also find that black women with darker skin who come from wealthier families are less negatively impacted by colorism than those from poor families (Thompson and Keith 2001)—suggesting that social class can be a buffer for these negative feelings. Finally, Wilder and Cain show that some families serve as a "fairly positive socializing agent, [where] women learned to challenge and oppose colorist ideology" (2011:594) and adopt a sense of racial pride. One of their respondents, Callea, recalled that her father "always told us, (my sister and I) that we're beautiful, natural hair is African silk, and you are beautiful the way you are. I guess that is because he knew how society is . . ." (2011:595).

Beyond one's own family, research has repeatedly shown that colorism is associated with long-term consequences in terms of health, education, and income. People of color with light skin, across black, Latin American, and Asian American populations tend to reach higher levels of education and earn higher incomes—even when other relevant traits (like their social class origins) are statistically controlled (Allen, Telles, and Hunter 2000; Hughes and Hertel 1990; Hunter 2002, 2007; Villareal 2010).

If light skin has positive connotations among people of color, does that mean that biracial people—especially those with one white parent—have positive social experiences? In earlier eras, individuals with mixed-race heritage were defined as mulatto, quadroon, or octoroon; later, individuals with just "one drop" of black blood were defined as black. Today, about 2 percent of Americans claim a "multiracial" identity; their numbers are expected to grow over the next decades. The identities and experiences of mixed-race individuals are variable. Some research shows that multiracial or biracial individuals have difficulty achieving a coherent identity or identification with a larger social group (Bowles 1993), and that biracial teens and adolescents experience rejection from peers on both sides of their racial or ethnic identity (Herring 1992). Yet with respect to social and emotional well-being, research shows that multiracial individuals are happiest and most well adjusted when they are able to identify with all of their racial and ethnic identities (Shih and Sanchez 2009).

Using in-depth interviews, sociologists provide insight into how bi- and multiracial individuals *do* race. In their interviews with biracial college students, Rockquemore and Brunsma (2008) found that the most common approach for multiracial students was to embrace an identity that is *neither* white *nor* black—where biracial constitutes its own identity. While these individuals may be defined as black by outsiders, at home they blend their black and white families and elements of their black and white culture. A smaller percentage of students in their study embraced a singular, "black-only" identity. A third group of students described a racial identity that shifts depending on context. These students tend to "culture switch": draw on experiences and slang that help them feel at home in settings with people of color, while also maintaining contact with white family members and using different cultural references and interactional styles with them. Sociologists show that being biracial is not fixed identity; rather, biracial individuals actively construct their racial and ethnic identities, highlighting some traits and downplaying others as they seek to present a particular racial self (Khanna and Johnson 2010).

Although biracial children with one white parent and one black parent are most common, children are being raised and socialized by parents with many other racial and ethnic combinations. Among individuals with white-Asian or white-Hispanic parentage, a key factor affecting their identity is the degree to which the individual *looks* nonwhite: those who look less white are less likely to identify with their white heritage (Herman 2004; Khanna 2004). Social psychologists note that *reflected appraisals*—the messages we receive from others about who we are—play a strong role in shaping our self-identification. Among biracial youth who appear white, there is a tendency for peers to see them as "whitewashed" and refer to them using slang terms or racial slurs. Research also shows that biracial individuals who attend diverse schools are also more likely to emphasize their Asian or Hispanic heritage (Eschbach and Gomez 1998); an individual's familiarity with one's Asian culture affects the degree to which they identify with that culture (Khanna 2004).

When it comes to how we learn our race during primary socialization, it is almost impossible to draw generalizations, in part because there are tremendous differences within each racial and ethnic group. We must differentiate between low- and high-income families within each group and note that groups like "Asian Americans" and "Latinos" contain people from disparate lands and cultures. When it comes to immigrant families, there are significant differences in identity and cultural practices between newcomers and those of the second and third generations.

Cross-cutting these patterns and variations, though, is the conclusion that white families instill in their children a greater sense of individualism compared to nonwhite families. Meanwhile, many nonwhite children learn that the collective good and the group's reputation within society as a whole are shared responsibilities. Second, for whites, talk about race and the active cultivation of a particular racial identity are rare, while the topic of race is more common among nonwhite children. The silence of many white parents suggests that race is a less salient, if not largely invisible, issue for those in the majority.

EXPLORING INTERSECTIONALITY: THE UNIQUE TENSIONS OF BEING BLACK AND MIDDLE CLASS

Although black American families earn less, on average, than the average American family, the black middle class has grown in recent decades. Black children from middle-class and affluent families face unique challenges—unique compared to both lower-income black and middle-class white families. Looking at the typical middle-class black family, one thing that stands out is that they tend to live in neighborhoods that are poorer and more economically diverse than those of middle-class white families (Pattillo 2005). Their neighborhoods, moreover, have higher crime rates and more vacant buildings and other signs of social disorder. With fewer educated adults in these neighborhoods, children there grow up with less access to social capital that might help them excel in school or get involved in extracurricular activities.

According to sociologists who have researched black middle-class neighborhoods, the people living there often balance two cultural orientations: street and decent (Anderson 2000; Pattillo-McCoy 2000). At one extreme, the pull of the street refers to the ever-present existence of gangs, along with criminal and near-criminal elements. Young boys and young girls may feel the allure of the street, as they aspire to high-priced consumer goods and autonomy from their parents. At the other pole is the decent—where young girls and boys remain involved in and identify with legitimate activities involving school, athletics, and church. In her ethnography of the Groveland neighborhood on Chicago's South Side, Mary Pattillo-McCoy (2000) described the delicate balance between "privilege and peril" among local families. She described teens like Neisha and Tyson, who were as likely to fall into downward mobility by being pulled into teen pregnancy and drug dealing as they were to become upwardly mobile by attending selective high schools and staying on the straight and narrow through college. As long as they live in mixed-class neighborhoods like Groveland, black middle-class teens must "culture switch," moving back and forth between demonstrating their **street** credibility and moving forward with **decent** educational and career goals.

In her book Blue Chip Black: Race, Class, and Status in the New Black Middle Class, Karyn Lacy (2007) examines the experiences of upper middle-class black families living in majority-white suburbs. While these families have moved into wealthier and safer neighborhoods, they still face challenges in raising their children. Lacy describes these black parents as socializing their children using "strategic assimilation." On the one hand, parents teach their children to behave in ways that convey their social class and reduce the risk of discrimination (not "showing their color"). For example, parents may emphasize speaking "Standard" American English and avoiding

Exclusive clubs, organizations, and even vacation spots are maintained by "the black elite." Here, members of Jack and Jill participate in a *cotillion*.

African American slang while in public. On the other hand, privileged parents also want their children to develop a positive racial identity, so they encourage their children to participate in activities with other black children and families, like attending majority-black churches. In these ways, parents try to make sure their children can fit in with both the privileged whites, with whom they share a social class identity, and blacks, with whom they share a racial identity.

One step higher on the socioeconomic ladder is the "black elite." Children raised in the black elite, unlike their middle-class counterparts, are typically raised in neighborhoods where they are the minority. Surrounded by affluent whites, their parents work hard to make sure that their children have access to the best schools and activities possible. Yet because they spend most of their days in majority-white environments, parents also work hard to make sure their children are able to connect to their black peers. In his book Our Kind of People: Inside America's Black Upper Class (1999), Lawrence Otis Graham describes the invitation-only organization "Jack and Jill," where children of the black elite meet for community service, etiquette lessons, social networking, and maybe an eventual marriage proposal. He quotes in his book a father named James, who said, "Even if you send your children to the best private schools and colleges, it doesn't mean they will get to meet black role models who inspire them and make them feel they can succeed in a white world. That's what Jack and Jill can do" (1999:23).

According to Graham, the children of the black elite (of which he considers himself a member) move through life attending particular colleges (Howard University, Spellman College, Morehouse College), joining Greek organizations ("The Divine 9"), and being invited into select clubs (the Boulé and so-called "Blue Vein Societies"). While they spend most of their days surrounded by white people, they strategically maintain contact with other black people. Graham also describes the black elite as a group with complex emotional pulls: On the one hand, he and other successful blacks feel immense pride in their accomplishments, with occasional feelings of superiority; on the other hand, there is an ever-present desire to give back and use one's success to bring greater opportunities to other blacks (1999:18). Over the years, these issues have been portrayed in the mainstream media, including shows like A Different World, The Cosby Show, The Fresh-Prince of Bel Air, and the most recent program, Black-ish. Whether addressed by scholars, journalists, or television producers, these conversations speak to the complex history of race in the United States, where racial identities are powerful and often transcend social class identities in terms of salience.

LEARNING RACE DURING SECONDARY SOCIALIZATION: EXPERIENCES AT SCHOOL

During secondary socialization, children—and later adults—have the opportunity to learn about the world beyond their own homes and families of origin. It is a chance to learn about other groups and other ways of doing things. When it comes to race, however, the segregated nature of our social world means that secondary socialization may offer relatively few opportunities—especially for whites—to learn about race beyond lessons that may have been imparted at home. Still, the sociological perspective illustrates that we become racialized beings through social interaction. It is through social interaction that the phenotypic variations among us take on meaning. In the words of one of the high school students in Laurie Olsen's ethnographic book, *Made in America*, "We make each other racial."

Race and the influence of peers

Because social identities are molded through social interactions, we learn about race and acquire our racial and ethnic identities in school. These identities are molded through interactions with peers and teachers, and through the formal curriculum. But in terms of learning about our own and others' racial and ethnic identities, the segregated nature of American schooling must first be acknowledged. Because most Americans live in segregated neighborhoods, most children attend schools where their own group is the majority (see Table 8.2). Gary Orfield and his co-authors (2012) report that the average white student attends a school where 75 percent of his or her classmates are also white. Conversely, about 75 percent of black and Hispanic students attend schools where minority students are a numerical majority; in fact, about 40 percent of black and Latino students attend schools in which 90 percent of their peers are also minorities. These percentages are much higher than one would expect given the racial composition of the nation's public schools. Only Asian American students attend truly diverse schools. For example, about 42 percent of Asian Americans attend "multiracial schools," while only 15 percent of whites do so; for blacks and Hispanics, this is about 26 percent. Otherwise, all groups except Asian Americans attend schools in which their own group is the majority. These data also reveal that the segregation of black and Hispanic students has increased over the last decade.

Scholars are concerned about racial segregation in schools for several reasons. When schools are intensely segregated along racial and ethnic lines, those same

Table 8.2 **School Segregation/Racial Composition**

	Percentage Attending Multiracial School	Percentage Attending High-Poverty Schools	Percentage Attending Intensely Segregated School
African-American (black)	26	64	38
Asian American	42	39	—
Latino	27	64	43
Native American	20	—	—
White	15	37	—

Source: Orfield, Kucsera, and Siegel-Hawley 2012.

schools are more likely to experience concentrated poverty. Schools characterized by concentrated poverty, as I explain in Chapter 12, tend to have less school funding. A 2012 report from Gary Orfield's Civil Rights Project notes that concentrated poverty and racial/ethnic segregation in schools are associated with factors that limit educational opportunities and outcomes. In addition to lower-quality teachers and inadequate facilities, there is mounting evidence "that desegregated schools are linked to important benefits for all children, including prejudice reduction, heightened civic engagement, more complex thinking and better learning outcomes in general" (2).

While the schools that children attend are themselves segregated, students within those settings tend to segregate themselves further. In her ethnographic study of a preschool, Debra Van Ausdale observed one to three racial "episodes" each day, many of them involving exclusion. During play time she observed a girl named Elizabeth trying to join a play group. "Rita shakes her head vigorously, saying, 'No, only people who can speak Spanish can come in.' Elizabeth frowns and says, 'I can come in.' Rita counters, 'Can you speak Spanish?' Elizabeth shakes her head no, and Rita repeats, 'Well, then you aren't allowed in'" (Van Ausdale and Feagin 1996:781). Other children were observed using racial epithets and citing skin color as a reason why another child could not take the classroom rabbit home for the weekend.

In her ethnographic study of a racially mixed preschool, Caryn Park (2011) found that instances of social exclusion disproportionately involved white females excluding children of color. According to the author, exclusion and rejection "took subtle forms, such as two White girls refusing to look at or touch the show-and-tell object of a student of color when it was being passed around for admiration or making up play situations in which a student of color was the 'bad guy' who would come to hurt them" (p. 407). In her study of a racially mixed summer camp, Valerie Ann Moore (2003) observed white pre-adolescents ignoring and excluding their black peers; in a predominately black day camp, Moore observed the reverse behavior, with white campers occasionally stigmatized and excluded. Such sociological studies show that, from very young ages, children have sophisticated understandings of race and ethnicity and they often use race as a basis for excluding their peers.

As students move through the educational system, their friendships are characterized by racial homophily. **Homophily** means that things that are similar are drawn to one another; racial homophily describes the fact that most friendships among children are with same-race peers. Using a nationally representative data set with 90,000 schoolchildren, Kara Joyner and Grace Kao (2000) found that 10 percent of white, 20 percent of black, and 40 percent of Asian and Hispanic students have at least one friend of another race. Yet when taking into account the racial populations of their schools and the statistical chance of making cross-racial friends, white males were actually 1.4 times more likely than their nonwhite peers to have a cross-race friendship, and white females were 1.6 times more likely to do so. Yet researchers have found that cross-racial friendships tend to be less stable than same-race friendships (Rude and Herda 2010) and that they also tend to be less intense in terms of the kinds of activities and interactions they involve (Kao and Joyner 2004).

While the lack of diverse friendships may reflect a preference for familiarity and/or racial prejudice, sociological studies show that context matters for our friendship patterns. If the typical white student attends a school where other whites make up more than 70 percent of the population, it is not surprising that most of her friends will be white. Using a nationally representative data set, James Moody (2001) found that racial homophily is greatest in schools with "moderately high" levels of diversity. In diverse schools where two or three main groups are balanced in size, tension and competition tends to emerge, thereby deterring cross-race friendships. By contrast, cross-racial friendships are somewhat more likely in schools that have either minimal or very high levels of diversity. Moody notes that schools can promote racial mixing by minimizing racial segregation within schools, ensuring, for example, that both classrooms and extracurricular activities are places where students from different racial and ethnic groups have contact with one another.

By why should schools "promote" cross-racial friendships? As it turns out, there are a number of positive outcomes associated with cross-racial friendships. Consistent with the contact hypothesis, familiarity with people from different backgrounds can increase positive feelings toward those groups. For minority students, cross-race friendships may have academic benefits. At least among college students, black students who have white roommates have higher GPAs than those with same-race roommates. Shook and Fazio (2008), the study's authors, speculate that African American students may adjust better to college when they have a roommate who can help them navigate the cultural norms and expectations of a predominantly White university.

Not every school in the United States is a segregated school. There are, indeed, schools—often urban magnet schools—where students from diverse racial and ethnic backgrounds attend classes and socialize with one another. Yet national data sources suggest that the most common aspect of racial socialization in schools is that students have relatively few opportunities to learn about race and ethnicity through face-to-face interaction.

Learning Race at School through the Curriculum

Does the formal curriculum offer more opportunity to learn about other races and ethnicities? When it comes to race and ethnicity in the formal curriculum, underrepresentation, sanitization and silence, and segregation are typical. In fictional stories and literature, for example, nonwhite characters are underrepresented—appearing rarely as central characters and more often as supporting characters. In their detailed historical analysis, Bernice Pescosolido, Elizabeth Grauerholz, and Melissa Milkie (1997) found that the number of black children in children's books has gradually increased over the decades, but that during periods of racial conflict (like the civil rights movement), their representation actually decreased. In books where black characters do appear, stories tend to focus on historical events or racial issues, only rarely in ordinary stories focusing on friendships or family.

Within the academic curriculum, racial and ethnic issues may be silenced or sanitized. This means teachers are able to ignore some historical events and that the curriculum makes difficult and unflattering issues more acceptable to an audience that has come to expect positive accounts of U.S. history. While many high school textbooks mention the Trail of Tears, they typically understate the scope and significance of this event, which forcibly removed Native Americans from their homes and relocated them—on foot and often without proper clothes or footwear—to reservations on Western lands. Absent from these retellings are the words "genocide" and "death march," which scholars like Howard Zinn (*A People's History of the United States*) and James Loewen (*Lies My Teacher Told Me*) believe more accurately describe President Andrew Jackson's 1830 Indian Removal Act. An inaccurate understanding of history does little to understand the ongoing racial and ethnic struggles; it also runs the risk of unjustly celebrating the historical accomplishments of European Americans.

Finally, with respect to segregation in the formal curriculum, schools often observe the historical significance of minority groups in themed months, like "Black History Month" and "National Hispanic Heritage Month." During these months, schools may feature plays, speakers, projects, and lessons designed to teach students about the accomplishments and struggles of minority groups. When Black History Month was first introduced in 1926 by historian Carter G. Woodson (then, "Negro History Week"), its goal was to give blacks a sense of pride in their accomplishments and to educate whites on the historical contributions of African Americans.

The notion that specific months should be set aside to address racial and ethnic issues rubs many people the wrong way. Some see it as giving minorities special treatment and, therefore, ask "What about white history month?" Others think these events actually undermine the importance of minorities in history, science, etc. In an on-line blog post, columnist Earl Ofari Hutchinson (N.D.) wrote that when Black History Month ends, "it's back to business as usual. . . . Black achievements vanish from the screen, the concert halls, and the speeches of politicians." By treating blacks, Hispanics, and Asians as tokens, these academic rituals reinforce racial differences. "When the experience of blacks is accepted as central to the American story," Hutchinson argues, "Black history will be what it always should have been— American history."

Some educators and activists have proposed that schools—especially ones with diverse student bodies—implement multicultural curricula. Multicultural curricula use a set of strategies and materials to provide students with knowledge about the histories, cultures, and contributions of diverse groups. As opposed to confining this knowledge to a particular month, multicultural curricula integrate race into lessons about science, history, and literature throughout the year. Advocates believe that the educational achievement of minority students will improve when they feel more connected to the lessons taught in school—when the curriculum incorporates these students' lived experiences by tackling issues like hunger, poverty, violence, and the experience of being an immigrant or refugee. Advocates believe these lessons will be valuable to white students as well, in that learning about other social groups will reduce prejudice and promote civic engagement (Banks 2008; Nieto 2004).

Beyond the formal curriculum, schools socialize students through the **hidden curriculum**, which includes the subtle, informal lessons taught in schools, through which students learn socially desirable values, beliefs, and behaviors. The daily recitation of the Pledge of Allegiance, for example, operates as a way of learning patriotism; the star-studded ranking of students that hangs on the classroom wall conveys the importance of competition and hard work. The hidden curriculum is also part of the method by which people from diverse cultures are incorporated into a more unified, homogeneous culture. This is called cultural assimilation. It is within the school system that the children of immigrants learn English and are taught the history and traditions of the United States. Some observers are critical, however, of this process. They argue that assimilation often involves a cultural clash, resulting in a loss or de-valuing of culture among immigrant and minority groups.

Perhaps the best example of this cultural clash was the widespread building of boarding schools for Native American students in the late 1800s. The explicit goal of these schools was to "Americanize" Native Americans. Sometimes taken from parents against their will, children were away from their families, their language, and their religious traditions. In a move that sounds like racial boot camp, boarding school students were also given new haircuts, Western-style clothing, and European-American names. In 1928, the Meriam Report noted widespread disease, poor nutrition, and unsanitary conditions at these schools. Enrollment in Indian boarding schools peaked in the 1970s; it has declined ever since. The 1970s also brought recognition by the federal government that Native American culture should be protected and preserved, as shown by the American Indian Religious Freedom Act (1978) and the Native American Graves Protection and Repatriation Act (1990).

Today, a culture clash occurs between the socialization of some Latino children and the cultural values and expectations promoted within the U.S. educational system. In her study of Mexican families in the United States, Guadalupe Valdes (1996) found that immigrant parents value education and see it as essential for getting a job. They are skeptical, however, of people with "too much education"—whom they see as inept and having abandoned their family responsibilities. In a culture where family comes first (*familism*), parents may pull children out of school to spend time with a sick or dying grandparent. School personnel then question the parents' commitment to education. Parents, meanwhile, mistrust the schools' message that education is an important vehicle for social mobility and economic success. With the emphasis on *respeto* among Mexican immigrants, kids who go off to college are sometimes viewed as abandoning their families; moving away from family to get a better-paying job may be viewed a moral failure. Other scholars have criticized the U.S. educational system for dismissing the definition of education held within many Latino communities—one that emphasizes moral training and personal connections above competition and individual achievement (Suárez-Orozco, Suárez-Orozco, and Todorova 2010; Valenzuela 1999).

While many immigrants and minorities succeed within this system, some scholars note that the socialization of Latino children may cause teachers to question these families' commitment to education and to label them as deviant or problematic. By meting out discipline or disappointment, students may conclude that teachers do not care about their culture or their life experiences. Over time, this cultural clash may undermine Latino students' interest in school and slowly set in motion a process that ends in their dropping out of school.

Another cultural clash occurs between the verbal styles used at school and the language socialization experienced within different racial and social class groups. Language socialization involves the subtle interactions through which we learn language, including both grammatical conventions and social norms of how to use language. Here, the conflict is not over what is taught or the goals of the educational system; it is over pedagogy, or teaching methods. For 10 years, anthropologist Shirley Brice Heath (1983) observed how parents talk to children and how children learn to speak in three distinct North Carolina communities. Among white middle-class families, parents treat children as legitimate conversational partners, actively engaging them in conversation. In the very structured ritual of the bedtime story, adults read to children while breaking the story down into discrete parts, asking toddlers and children, "What color is the bunny's nose?" or "What is the puppy doing there?" While this may sound like a perfectly normal and healthy routine, Heath observed lower-income black children learning language differently. In these homes, children were passive listeners to adult conversations. For them, learning language was more about listening to adults tell stories and figuring out the connections and context on their own—rather than being asked detail-oriented questions.

While both forms of language socialization are useful within their own contexts, the clash occurs because most classrooms operate according to cultural styles that mirror middle-class homes. During story time, when the teacher asks her kindergartners "How many baby ducks are in the pond?" or "What shape is the birthday present?" some students may be more familiar than others with this type of questioning. Although the answer to these questions may seem self-evident, black children have not been socialized to pick out obvious, descriptive elements of stories; instead, they learn to focus on motivations, feelings, and the musical sounds of words. Teachers, though, may label kids academically deficient or problematic when they are unable or unwilling to participate in such seemingly simple dialogue.

As black children move through the school system, these culture clashes continue. According to some scholars, the lower level of academic achievement among black and Latino students partially reflects the fact that the school system deems their cultural style, language use, and behaviors as disruptive and delinquent. In her book *Keepin' It Real: School Success beyond Black and White*, Prudence Carter (2005) spent a year observing the day-to-day experiences of a group of lower-income black and Latino students. While some of these students were exceptionally clever and creative in using black vernacular language (slang or Ebonics) and had a deep interest in the poetry of Nikki Giovanni and Amiri Baraka, their skills and interests were not recognized within the school system. Without an interest in canonical poets like William Butler Yeats, Elizabeth Barrett Browning, or T. S. Eliot, and by not adopting a conventional use of the English language, these students were dismissed as defiant or deficient. Over time, these students began to believe that the educational system privileges and prioritizes the styles, tastes, and understandings of white middle-class students. According to Carter, black and Latino children struggle in school because the school system rejects their unique cultural skills and knowledge and delivers the message that they simply don't belong.

Because children spend a significant portion of their lives in schools, it stands to reason that much of what they learn about themselves and others occurs within that context. A common theme when it comes to racial and ethnic socialization is that white students typically experience a "cultural match" within the school system. First, they attend schools in which their racial group is the majority. Second, the interactional styles and teaching methods used by teachers typically mirror their own primary socialization. When teachers expect that students will look them in the eye or that they will eagerly respond to seemingly self-evident questions during story time, they use a cultural style that may not be familiar to all students. Finally, within the formal curriculum, the experiences of racial and ethnic minority groups are segregated into separate units, while the historical accomplishments of European Americans are treated simply as "history." Throughout this process, whiteness becomes invisible and white students are unknowingly socialized to see themselves and their experiences as the norm. Meanwhile, students of color—especially those who are black and Latino—may be viewed as deviating from the norm and potentially problematic.

EXPLORING ACTIVISM: IMPROVING THE EDUCATION OF NATIVE AMERICAN STUDENTS

Across the nation, Native Americans have the lowest educational outcomes of any racial or ethnic group. Fifty-one percent of Native American students receive their high school diplomas; the rates are 80 percent for white and Asian students, 68 percent for Latino students, and 62 percent for black students. Although college enrollment rates for Native Americans have doubled since the 1970s, only 13 percent of Native American adults have completed a bachelor's degree or higher. This compares to 50 percent among Asian Americans, 29 percent among whites, 18 percent among blacks, and 13 percent among Hispanics. For many activists, the key to improving the educational outcomes of Native Americans is to provide a culturally relevant education—one that addresses the unique cultural needs of Native Americans and highlights their cultural accomplishments.

One group aimed at this goal is the National Indian Education Association (NIEA), whose mission is to advance "comprehensive educational opportunities for American Indians, Alaska Natives, and Native Hawaiians throughout the United States." They do so by promoting a culturally relevant education that allows Native students to preserve tribal languages and traditions and to expand the educational opportunities of Native students. Their work focuses on the 10 percent of Native students who attend schools in tribal areas controlled by the Bureau of Indian Education as well as the 90 percent who do not. Working with legislative aides in the nation's capital, organizers from the NIEA seek to strengthen tribal control of education and invest in cultural and language revitalization. The organization's website notes that Native students perform better academically when they have a strong foundation in their language and culture and when there is greater tribal control of education.

Another strategy of education activists is to expand opportunities at tribal colleges and universities (TCUs). With roots dating back to the 1970s, tribal colleges are controlled by tribal authorities—whose goal is to build the skills of native students using culturally relevant pedagogy and curricula. Currently, there are 34 fully accredited tribal col-

Native American tribal colleges equip students with job skills and a culturally relevant curriculum, with the explicit goal of preparing them to "give back" and improve tribal life.

leges across 15 states (and one Canadian province), serving about 17,000 students. With programs ranging from vocational education to master's degrees, these colleges focus on issues relevant to Indian communities, such as sustainable agriculture, water quality, wildlife conservation, and diabetes prevention.

To better understand this mission, it is important to bear in mind the often brutal history of Native Americans in the United States As discussed in this chapter, Native American people have experienced mass killings at the hands white settlers and armies, as well as the systematic erasure of their culture and history. Treaties and other economic policies continue to hinder the economic standing of Native tribes. This is part of the context in which Native Americans today struggle in terms of health, education, and economic well-being. The assumption is that these problems can be mitigated by socializing young Native Americans with a positive racial identity. Although comprehensive research remains scant, small studies suggest that programs using indigenous cultures and language result in improved academic performance (Lipka 2002; McCarty 2003).

SECONDARY SOCIALIZATION—LEARNING RACE THROUGH THE SYMBOLIC WORLD AND THE MEDIA

Beyond our face-to-face interactions, secondary socialization occurs through exposure to the media. As discussed in the previous chapter, both children and adults spend a considerable amount of time interacting with the "symbolic world" that is transmitted through television, movies, video games, and the like. These media sources constitute a symbolic world in the sense that they provide representations and constructions of what our world is like. Although we expect viewers to understand that the media represents a sort of fantasy world, these representations nonetheless convey socializing messages about race and ethnicity.

When comparing the symbolic world to the "real world," there is a disjuncture between these two worlds. As with representations of women, minorities are underrepresented in the media. In children's programming, 85 percent of television shows have main characters who are white (Greenberg and Mastro 2008); this compares to 70 percent of the population as a whole. Racial representations in top-grossing G-rated films are similar (Kelly and Smith 2006). According to Greenberg and Mastro, public television stations like PBS "provide a richer racial and ethnic environment with attention specifically paid to issues of diversity, both in terms of character composition and dialogue" (2008:80). For example, White people comprise about 55 percent of the characters in children's programming on PBS and black characters comprise 32 percent. This means, however, that Asians and Latinos are still underrepresented.

On prime-time television, the only group represented in proportion to its population in the United States is black Americans; by contrast, white characters are overrepresented and Asian and Latinos are underrepresented (Behm-Morawitz and Ortiz 2012). Despite the transformation of television programming to include television networks aimed at black audiences (BET and, to a lesser extent, the CW), there are few television programs that feature majority-black casts—especially outside the comedy genre. More common in recent decades is programming that features a "potpourri" approach to casting. Seen in shows as diverse as *Lost*, *The Office*, *Glee*, and *Grey's Anatomy*, this approach features "one-of-each" casting of characters across racial and ethnic groups, and even sexual orientation and ability status. While programs with multiethnic casts have been on the rise in recent decades, there have been few dramatic programs with minority leads or casts.

Media commentators are critical of the fact that there is one place where minorities—namely blacks and Latinos—are well represented: crime stories. In crime stories, minority characters are more than twice as common as whites; they are also more likely to be depicted as menacing, shown in disheveled mug shots, handcuffs, or prison uniforms (Dixon and Linz 2002). The rate at which minorities are shown as perpetrators of crime on television is not proportional to the rate at which they commit crimes out in the "real world." In this regard, media viewers are socialized to see minorities as more criminal and threatening than they actually are, while being spared images of criminal, menacing whites (with the exception of the occasional white-collar criminal).

The fact that minorities are overrepresented in crime stories relates to a broader theme regarding media representations of race and ethnicity: the narrow and stereotypical nature of these representations. Although there are noteworthy exceptions (e.g., Kerry Washington in *Scandal*, Idris Elba in *Luther*), black and Latino characters are overrepresented in comedic roles and underrepresented in dramatic roles.

In recent decades there has been a trend toward more authoritative and hardworking black male characters (in crime dramas, for example). Another stereotypical media portrayal is the fact that nightly news and newsmagazine programs "portray the poor as substantially more Black than is really the case" (Gilens 1996:515). This leads to distorted beliefs about both what black people are like and who is poor in America, given that whites are clearly the majority of those living in poverty.

When it comes to stereotypical portrayals of black women in the media, sociologist Patricia Hill Collins (1991) has coined a specific term. She calls these controlling images. According to Collins, media images of black women have historically fallen into these categories:

The Mammy: The wise and loving black woman; faithful and obedient, she is often portrayed taking care of white children. Represented historically by Mammy in *Gone with the Wind*, Florida in *Maude* and *Good Times*, and more recently by the domestic workers in *The Help*

The Matriarch: The strong, if not domineering, black woman; often a single mother or grandmother whose work takes her away from her family; may share traits with the "angry black woman" stereotype. Madea from the Tyler Perry movies is one example, and Cookie from "Empire" provides a modern take on the theme.

The Welfare Mother: The lazy, freeloading black woman; manipulates the welfare system and also tries to trap men into being their "Baby Daddy." Appears most frequently on shows hosted by Geraldo, Maury Povich ("You are not the father"), and Judges Mathis, Judy, et al.

The Jezebel: The highly sexualized black woman; she sometimes uses her sexuality to manipulate men; related to the "Gold Digger." Some female rappers and R&B artists like Nicki Minaj and Lil' Kim adopt this persona to demonstrate their sexual power.

According to Collins, "controlling images are designed to make racism, sexism, poverty, and other forms of social injustice appear to be natural, normal, and inevitable parts of everyday life" (1991:69). The repetition of these images can hide or normalize inequality by making it appear that the individual in question has voluntarily and maybe even happily taken on the oppressed position. "The Mammy," for example, is a beloved media character, romanticized for her close relationship with the white children or women for whom she works. Yet like all "controlling images," this portrayal conceals the downsides of her position, ignoring her low wages, lack of autonomy, and the structural conditions that make this one of few jobs available.

The concept of "controlling images" can be applied to other groups. For example, media representation of Native Americans that portrays them as strong and stoic warriors conceals the systematic abuse and genocide they faced. Whether these stereotypical images condemn or celebrate the people in question, they have the common characteristic of minimizing or erasing historical realities and social injustice.

Finally, because Asians appear so infrequently in the mainstream media, it is difficult to generalize about their representation. Some tentative generalizations can be made (Behm-Morawitz and Ortiz 2012): Asian men are portrayed *either* as devious villains or de-sexualized white-collar professionals; Asian women may appear as exotic

"GONE WITH THE WIND." ● David O. Selznick Technicolor Production released by Metro-Goldwyn-Mayer

The "Mammy figure," such as the image from *Gone with the Wind*, has been described as an image that controls and oppresses black women.

and sexually dangerous. Danger and violence are also themes for those of Middle Eastern descent, who are also rarely depicted on television outside of roles focusing on terrorist threats. One recent exception is the Bravo reality television program *The Shahs of Sunset*, which profiled a group of wealthy Persian friends (mainly Iranian) and portrayed them as gossipy and materialistic. Finally, with even less frequent representation, Native Americans typically appear in either historical or spiritual roles.

How does this stream of stereotypes reflect macro-level forces in the entertainment industry? In recent decades, more television stations have emerged to meet the needs of diverse audiences. Some have hoped that networks like BET, Telemundo, and Univision would provide more nuanced representations of race and ethnicity. Unfortunately, this has not happened. While Telemundo and Univision offer legitimate news and sports programming, some of their signature shows are stereotype-laden *telenovelas* and variety shows (*Sabado Gigante*). After debuting as a full-time network in 1983, BET offered an array of news and public affairs programming, with personalities like Ed Gordon and Tavis Smiley. Over time, many of these programs have been replaced by a heavier rotation of videos, movie reruns, and reality programs like *Sunday Best*, *Hell Date*, and *Baldwin Hills*.

With respect to BET, some attribute this shift to the change in ownership after the founders Sheila and Robert L. Johnson sold the network to media giant Viacom (Telemundo is owned by NBC Universal; Univision is an independent company).

Indeed, all media representations must be interpreted in light of the fact that the media is a business and that there are relatively few companies competing with this sector. More generally, the limited range of representations reflects the underrepresentation of people of color as writers, directors, and producers. It is difficult to create complicated characters representing diverse backgrounds. According to Thad Mumford, television writer and producer, "Many writers who create black characters don't have the remotest idea of how such people would really act. They create stereotypes because their own perceptions are based on stereotypical images that they've seen or read." It is hard to imagine that these images will change without prior changes to the creative forces behind these images.

When it comes to media representations of race and ethnicity, the most important question is: So what? Among children, high levels of media consumption are associated with higher rates of prejudice and stereotypical beliefs (Zuckerman, Singer, and Singer 1980). Among adults, heavier media consumers are more likely to call for harsher penalties for criminals and support politicians who are "tough on crime" (Valentino 1999). They also tend to be more fearful of crime and more likely to perceive themselves as possible victims of crimes. Media analyst George Gerbner calls this the mean world syndrome—a worldview ostensibly influenced by the racialized and inaccurate portrayals of crime in the media. These attitudes are problematic given that media portrayals of crime and violence do not mirror real-world patterns. Finally, in terms of consequences, some research suggests that minorities who consume media with higher levels of stereotypical depictions (sports and music for black viewers, soap operas for Latinos) have lower levels of self-esteem and self-confidence (Ward 2004).

While researchers typically focus on the negative impact of media depictions of race and ethnicity, there are some positive outcomes. Some suggest that with the rise of multiethnic casts, viewers can learn to model positive and productive examples of cross-racial interaction (Ortiz and Harwood 2007). In studies focusing on short-term effects, those exposed to more frequent examples of successful African Americans in the media had less stereotypical views and were more sympathetic to issues of discrimination compared to others (Greenberg and Mastro 2008).

LEARNING RACE, INHERITING DIFFERENCE, AND NAVIGATING INEQUALITY

To say that whiteness or blackness or being Asian or Hispanic is learned is to say that our racial identities, while marked by biologically rooted phenotypic traits, are also a product of socialization. Yet this socialization does not take place in a vacuum. It takes place within a society that is deeply marked by racial tensions and tragedies and structured by racial inequality. This is the context in which the National Association of Black Social Workers made its recommendation against transracial adoptions. Their position reflected the history of racial oppression and the belief that the continued tendency for whiteness to be treated as the norm in schools and the media means that the best place for a black child is in a home with black adults. The Indian Child Welfare Act of 1978 makes a similar case for the socialization and adoption of Indian children.

Although research does not show that black children raised by white parents differ from those raised by black parents in terms of psychological outcomes or racial self-concept (Lee 2003), it does show that socialization differs along racial and ethnic lines. Racial and ethnic differences in parenting practices, experiences in school, and representations in the media all contribute to the development of our own racial and ethnic identities and our broader understandings of race and ethnicity. Different, though, does not necessarily mean deficient. Thus, sociologists argue that some differences in socialization contribute simply to different cultural styles and personalities, but that one is not better than the other. Other differences, though, such as those that play out in the school system—where some students' culture gets them defined as deviant or dim—are part of the process by which racial and ethnic inequalities are reproduced across generations.

CHAPTER 8: REVIEW OF KEY POINTS

- The structure of families and the socialization of children within families vary by race and ethnicity in the United States. This is part of the process by which we acquire our racial and ethnic identities.

- Categorization of people by race is a learned task. Research suggests that children begin to learn racial schema and categorize people by race around the age of 5.

- Within families, White parents are relatively silent when it comes to talking about race with their children; children raised by black parents, however, are often talked to about race. They often learn lessons about adversity, discrimination, and how to represent their race in public.

- In the United States, children of Asian descent often learn lessons of *filial piety*, while children of Hispanic descent are raised with the notion of *respeto*. Both of these lessons formalize the notion that elders should be respected.

- Children of the *same* racial or ethnic background may also receive differing messages about their race. *Colorism* cross-cuts racial and ethnic lines and communicates to many a cultural preference for lighter skin. This sometimes constitutes a form of prejudice and discrimination within racial and ethnic groups.

- Looking at secondary socialization, we find that many of us learn lessons about race within the context of racially segregated schools. Within racially mixed environments, children begin to separate themselves as early as preschool.

- When looking at the school curriculum, lessons about the accomplishments of minorities are few; lessons about race and ethnic conflict are also few, and when they are told they tend to tell a "sanitized" version of events.

- Messages about race and racial socialization through the media take place through programming and content in which whites are statistically overrepresented and minorities are statistically underrepresented.

- Characters and portrayals of race and ethnicity within the media have historically presented rather stereotypical images (e.g., whites are victims of crimes while blacks and Hispanics commit crimes). These patterns appear to be changing.

CHAPTER 8: QUESTIONS FOR REVIEW

1. In terms of family structure, how do the experiences of children from different racial and ethnic groups compare? Moreover, how do these structural differences influence the experiences of children from different racial and ethnic groups?

2. During primary socialization, what are some key differences in the ways in which parents from different racial and ethnic groups raise their children? What kinds of messages do children from different racial and ethnic groups receive about their identities and where they fit into society?

3. How do the notions of colorism and the experience of being biracial (or multiracial) add nuance to our understanding of identity among racial and ethnic minorities?

4. During secondary socialization in school, what are some key differences in the experiences of children from different racial and ethnic groups? What differences have been documented among peer groups and friendships? What differences exist in the formal curriculum?

5. According to this chapter, what are some of the differences in the media representation and portrayals of people from different racial and ethnic groups? What are some of the social consequences of these representations?

6. One of the themes of gender socialization is that whites are raised in a context where they are rarely prompted to think about race, while members of racial and ethnic minorities receive more explicit messages about their group's identity. To what extent does this theme resonate with your own social experiences? To the extent that it does resonate with you, what do you think the consequences of this pattern are?

KEY TERMS

colorism	kinship
decent	respeto
familism	social capital
fictive kin	strategic assimilation
filial piety	street
hidden curriculum	"The Talk"
homophily	

REFERENCES

Allen, Walter, Edward E. Telles, and Margaret Hunter. 2000. "Skin Color, Income and Education: A Comparison of African Americans and Mexican Americans." *National Journal of Sociology* 12:129–180.

Anderson, Elijah. 2000. *Code of the Street: Decency, Violence, and the Moral Life of the Inner City*. New York: W.W. Norton and Co.

Banks, James A. 2008. *An Introduction to Multicultural Education*, 4th ed. Upper Saddle River, NJ: Pearson.

Behm-Morawitz, Elizabeth and Michelle Ortiz. 2012. "Race, Ethnicity, and the Media." Pp. 252–266 in *The Oxford Handbook of Media Psychology*, edited by Karen E. Dill. New York: Oxford University Press.

Berlin, Lisa J., Jean M. Ispa, Mark A. Fine, Patrick S. Malone, Jeanne Brooks-Dunn, Christie Brady-Smith, Catherine Ayoub, and Yu Bai. 2009. "Correlates and Consequences of Spanking and Verbal Punishment for Low-Income White, African American, and Mexican American Toddlers." *Child Development* 80(5):1403–1420.

Bowles, Dorcas D. 1993. "Bi-racial Identity: Children Born to African-American and White Couples." *Clinical Social Work Journal* 21(4):417–428.

Bowman, Phillip J. and Cleopatra Howard. 1985. "Race-Related Socialization, Motivation, and Academic Achievement: A Study of Black Youths in Three-Generation Families." *Journal of the American Academy of Child Psychiatry* 24(2):134–141.

Briscoe-Smith, Allison. 2010. "How to Talk with Kids about Race." Pp. 58–63 in *Are We Born Racist? New Insights from Neuroscience and Positive Psychology*, edited by Jeremy A. Smith, Jason Marsh, and Rodolfo Mendoza-Denton. Boston: Beacon Press.

Bronson, Po and Ashley Merryman. 2009. *Nurture Shock: New Thinking about Children*. New York: Twelve.

Brown, Tony N., Emily E. Tanner-Smith, Chase L. Lesane-Brown, and Michael E. Ezell. 2007. "Child, Parent, and Situational Correlates of Familial Ethnic/Race Socialization." *The Journal of Marriage and Family* 69(1):4–25.

Calzada, Esther J., Yenny Fernandez, and Dharma E. Cortes. 2010. "Incorporating the Cultural Value of *Respeto* into a Framework of Latino Parenting." *Cultural Diversity and Ethnic Minority Psychology* 16(1):77–86.

Carter, Prudence. 2005. *Keepin' It Real: School Success beyond Black and White*. New York: Oxford University Press.

Civil Rights Project. 2012. "*E Pluribus…* Separation Deepening Double Segregation for More Students: Executive Summary." University of California, Los Angeles: Civil Rights Project. Retrieved April 20, 2015 (http://civilrightsproject.ucla.edu/research/k-12-education/integration-and-diversity/mlk-national/e-pluribus...separation-deepening-double-segregation-for-more-students/orfield_ePluribus_executive_2012.pdf).

Collins, Patricia Hill. 1991. *Black Feminist Thought: Knowledge, Consciousness, and the Politics of Empowerment*. New York: Routledge.

Deliere, Thomas and Ariel Kalil. 2002. "Good Things Come in Threes: Single-Parent Multigenerational Family Structure and Adolescent Adjustment." *Demography* 39(2):393–413.

Dixon, Travis L. and Daniel Linz. 2002. "Television News, Prejudicial Pretrial Publicity, and the Depiction of Race." *Journal of Broadcasting & Electronic Media* 46(1):112–136.

Doyle, Anna Beth and Frances E. Aboud. 1995. "Longitudinal Study of White Children's Racial Prejudice as a Social-Cognitive Development." *Merrill-Palmer Quarterly* 41(2):209–228.

Eschbach, Karl and Christina Gomez. 1998. "Choosing Hispanic Identity: Ethnic Identity Switching among Respondents in High School and Beyond." *Social Science Quarterly* 79(1):74–90.

Gershoff Elizabeth T., Jennifer E. Lansford, Holly R. Sexton, Pamela Davis-Kean, and Arnold J. Sameroff. 2012. "Longitudinal Links between Spanking and Children's Externalizing Behaviors in a National Sample of White, Black, Hispanic, and Asian American Families." *Child Development* 83(3):838–843.

Gilens, Martin. 1996. "Race and Poverty in America: Public Misperceptions and the American News Media." *Public Opinion Quarterly* 60(6):515–541.

Gonzalez, David. 2009. "A Family Divided by Two Worlds, Legal and Illegal." *New York Times*, April 26, pp. A1, 20–21.

Graham, Lawrence Otis. 1999. *Our Kind of People: Inside America's Black Upper Class*. New York: Harper Collins.

Greenberg, Bradley S. and Dana E. Mastro. 2008. "Children, Race, Ethnicity, and Media." Pp. 74–97 in *The Handbook of Children, Media, and Development*, edited by Sandra L. Calvert and Barbara J. Wilson. Hoboken, NJ: Wiley-Blackwell.

Harris-Britt, April, Cecelia R. Valrie, Beth Kurtz-Costes, and Stephanie J. Rowley. 2007. "Perceived Racial Discrimination and Self-Esteem in African American Youth: Racial Socialization as a Protective Factor." *Journal of Research on Adolescence* 17(4):669–682.

Heath, Shirley Brice. 1983. *Ways with Words: Language, Life and Work in Communities and Classrooms*. Cambridge, UK: Cambridge University Press.

Herman, Melissa R. 2004. "Forced to Choose: Some Determinants of Racial Identification Among Multiracial Adolescents." *Child Development* 75(3):730–748.

Hernandez, Tanya K. 2006. "Bringing Clarity to Race Relations in Brazil." *Diverse: Issues in Higher Education* 23(18):85.

Herring, Roger D. 1992. "Biracial Children: An Increasing Concern for Elementary and Middle School Counselors." *Elementary School Guidance & Counseling* 27:123–130.

Hill, Shirley A. 2001. "Class, Race, and Gender Dimensions of Child Rearing in African-American Families." *Journal of Black Studies* 31(4):494–508.

Horn, Ivor B., Tina L. Cheng, and Jill Joseph. 2004. "Discipline in the African American Community: The Impact of Socioeconomic Status on Beliefs and Practices." *Pediatrics* 113(5): 1236–1241.

Hughes, Diane and Lisa Chen. 1997. "When and What Parents Tell Children about Race: An Examination of Race-Related Socialization among African-American Families." *Applied Developmental Science* 1(4):200–214.

Hughes, Michael and Bradley R. Hertel. 1990. "The Significance of Color Remains: A Study of Life Chances, Mate Selection, and Ethnic Consciousness among Black Americans." *Social Forces* 68(4):1105–1120.

Hunter, Margaret. 2002. "'If You're Light You're Alright': Light Skin Color as Social Capital for Women of Color." *Gender and Society* 16(2):175–193.

Hunter, Margaret. 2007. "The Persistent Problem of Colorism: Skin Tone, Status, and Inequality." *Sociological Compass* 1:237–254.

Hutchinson, Earl Ofari. N.D. "Black History is American History." Retrieved April 20, 2015 (http://www.afrocentricnews.com/html/ofari_blkhistory.html)

Joyner, Kara and Grace Kao. 2000. "School Racial Composition and Adolescent Racial Homophily." *Social Science Quarterly* 81(3):810–825.

Kao, Grace and Kara Joyner. 2004. "Do Race and Ethnicity Matter among Friends? Activities among Interracial, Interethnic, and Intraethnic Adolescent Friends." *The Sociological Quarterly* 45:557–573.

Katz, Phyllis A. and Jennifer A. Kofkin. 1997. "Race, Gender, and Young Children." Pp. 51–74 in *Developmental Psychopathology: Perspectives on Adjustment, Risk, and Disorder*, edited by Suniya S. Luthar, Jacob A. Burack, Dante Cicchetti and John R. Weisz. New York: Cambridge University Press.

Katz, Vikki S. 2010. "How Children of Immigrants Use Media to Connect Their Families to the Community: The Case of Latinos in Los Angeles." *Journal of Children and Media* 4(3):298–315.

Keith, Verna and Cedric Herring. 1991. "Skin Tone and Stratification in the Black Community." *American Journal of Sociology* 97(3):760–778.

Kelly, Joe and Stacy Smith. 2006. "G Movies Give Boys a D: Portraying Males as Dominant, Disconnected, and Dangerous." See Jane Program at Dads and Daughters (SeeJane.org).

Khanna, Nikki. 2004. "The Role of Reflected Appraisals in Racial Identity: The Case of Multi-racial Asians." *Social Psychology Quarterly* 67(2):115–131.

Khanna, Nikki and Cathryn Johnson. 2010. "Passing as Black: Racial Identity Work among Biracial Americans." *Social Psychology Quarterly* 73(4):380–397.

Kiang, Lisa and Andrew Fuligni. 2009. "Ethnic Identity and Family Processes in Adolescents with Latin American, Asian, and European Backgrounds." *Journal of Youth and Adolescence* 38 (2):228–241.

Kim, Su Yeong, Yijie Wang, Diana Orozco-Lapray, Yishan Shen, and Mohammed Murtuza. 2012. "Does 'Tiger Parenting' Exist? Parenting Profiles of Chinese Americans and Adolescent Developmental Outcomes." *Asian-American Journal of Psychology* 4(1):7–18.

Lacy, Karyn. 2007. *Blue-Chip Black: Race, Class, and Status in the New Black Middle Class.* Berkeley: University of California Press.

Lee, Richard B. 2003. "The Transracial Adoption Paradox: History, Research, and Counseling Implications of Cultural Socialization." *Counseling Psychology* 31(6):711–744.

Lesane-Brown, Chase, Tony N. Brown, Emily E. Tanner-Smith, and Marino A. Bruce. 2010. "Negotiating Boundaries and Bonds: Frequency of Young Children's Socialization to their Ethnic/Racial Heritage." *Journal of Cross-Cultural Psychology* 41(3):457–464.

Lipka, Jerry. 2002. *Schooling for Self-Determination: Research on the Effects of Including Native Language and Culture in the Schools. ERIC Digest.* Charleston, WV: ERIC Clearinghouse on Rural Education and Small Schools (ERIC ED459989).

Loewen, James W. 2007. *Lies My Teacher Told Me: Everything Your American History Textbook Got Wrong.* New York: Touchstone.

Lynn, Richard. 2008. "Pigmentocracy: Racial Hierarchies in the Caribbean and Latin America." *The Occidental Quarterly* 8:25–44.

McCarty, Teresa L. 2003. "Revitalising Indigenous Languages in Homogenising Times." *Comparative Education* 39(2):147–163.

McLanahan, Sara. 2011. "Family Instability and Complexity After a Nonmarital Birth." Pp. 108–133 in *Social Class and Changing Families in an Unequal America*, edited by Marcia Carlson and Paula England. Palo Alto, CA: Stanford University Press.

Moody, James. 2001. "Race, School Integration, and Friendship Segregation in America." *American Journal of Sociology* 107(3):697–716.

Moore, Valerie Ann. 2003. "Kids' Approaches to Whiteness in Racially Distinct Summer Day Camps." *The Sociological Quarterly* 44(3):505–522.

Mukhtar, Al-Baqir al-Afif. 2007. "The Crisis of Identity in Northern Sudan: The Dilemma of a Black People with a White Culture." Pp. 213–224 in *Race and Identity in the Nile*, edited by Carolyn Fluehr-Lobban and Kharyssa Rhodes. Trenton, NJ: Red Sea Press.

National Association of Black Social Workers. 1972. "Position Statement on Transracial Adoption." Retrieved April 20, 2015 (http://nabsw.org/?page=PositionStatements)

Nieto, Sonia. 2004. *Affirming Diversity: The Sociopolitical Context of Multicultural Education*, 4th ed. Boston: Allyn and Bacon.

Orellana, Marjorie Faulstich, Lisa Dorner, and Lucila Pulido. 2003. "Accessing Assets: Immigrant Youth's Work as Family Translators or 'Para-phrasers.'" *Social Problems* 50(4):505–524.

Orfield, Gary, John Kucsera, and Genevieve Siegel-Hawley. 2012. "E Pluribus . . . Separation." The Civil Rights Project, Proyecto Derechos Civiles. University of California Los Angeles. Retrieved September 4, 2013 (http://civilrightsproject.ucla.edu/research/k-12-education/

integration-and-diversity/mlk-national/e-pluribus...separation-deepening-double-segregation-for-more-students).

Ortiz, Michelle and Jake Harwood. 2007. "A Social Cognitive Theory Approach to the Effects of Mediated Intergroup Contact on Intergroup Attitudes." *Journal of Broadcasting and Electronic Media* 51(4):615–631.

Park, Caryn C. 2011. "Young Children Making Sense of Racial and Ethnic Differences: A Sociocultural Approach." *American Educational Research Journal* 48(2):387–420.

Passel, Jeffrey and D'Vera Cohn. 2009. *A Portrait of Unauthorized Immigrants in the United States.* Washington, DC: Pew Hispanic Center.

Pattillo, Mary. 2005. "Black Middle Class Neighborhoods." *Annual Review of Sociology* 31: 305–329.

Pattillo-McCoy, Mary. 2000. *Black Picket Fences, Second Edition: Privilege and Peril among the Black Middle Class.* Chicago: University of Chicago Press.

Pescosolido, Bernice A., Elizabeth Grauerholz, and Melissa A. Milkie. 1997. "Culture and Conflict: The Portrayal of Blacks in U.S. Children's Picture Books through the Mid- and Late-Twentieth Century." *American Sociological Review* 62:443–464.

Rockquemore, Kerry A. and David L. Brunsma. 2008. *Beyond Black: Biracial Identity in America,* 2nd ed. Lanham, MD: Rowman & Littlefield.

Rude, Jesse and Daniel Herda. 2010. "Best Friends Forever? Race and the Stability of Adolescent Friendships." *Social Forces* 89(2):585–607.

Scottham, Krista Maywalt and Ciara P. Smalls. 2009. "Unpacking Racial Socialization: Considering Female African-American Primary Care-Givers' Racial Identity." *Journal of Marriage and Family* 71(4):807–818.

Shih, Margaret and Diana T. Sanchez. 2009. "When Race Becomes Even More Complex: Toward Understanding the Landscape of Multiracial Identity and Experiences." *Journal of Social Issues* 65(1):1–11.

Shook, Natalie J. and Russell H. Fazio. 2008. "Roommate Relationships: A Comparison of Interracial and Same-Race Living Situations." *Group Processes and Intergroup Relations* 11(4):425–437.

Stack, Carol. 1974. *All Our Kin: Strategies for a Survival in a Black Community.* New York: Harper & Row.

Suárez-Orozco, Carola, Marcelo M. Suárez-Orozco, and Irina Todorova. 2010. *Learning a New Land: Immigrant Students in American Society.* Cambridge, MA: Harvard University Press.

Telzer, Eva H. and Heidie A. Vazquez Garcia. 2009. "Skin Color and Self-Perceptions of Immigrant and U.S.-Born Latinas: The Moderating Role of Racial Socialization and Ethnic Identity." *Hispanic Journal of Behavioral Sciences* 31(3):357–374.

Thompson, Maxine S. and Verna M. Keith. 2003. "Copper Brown and Blue Black: Colorism and Self-Evaluation." Pp. 45–64 in *Skin Deep: How Race and Complexion Matter in the "Color-Blind" Era,* edited by Cedric Herring, Verna M. Keith, and Hayward Derrick Horton. Chicago and Urbana: Institute for Research on Race and Public Policy, University of Illinois at Chicago, and University of Illinois Press.

Thompson, Maxine S. and Verna M. Keith. 2001. "The Blacker the Berry: Gender, Skin Tone, Self-Esteem, and Self-Efficacy." *Gender and Society* 15(3):336–357.

Tse, Lucy. 1995. "Language Brokering among Latino Adolescents: Prevalence, Attitudes, and School Performance." *Hispanic Journal of Behavioral Sciences* 17(2):180–193.

Valdes, Guadalupe. 1996. *Con Respeto: Bridging the Distances between Culturally Diverse Families and Schools: An Ethnographic Portrait.* New York: Teachers College, Columbia University.

Valenzuela, Abel, Jr. 1999. "Gender Roles and Settlement Activities among Children and Their Immigrant Families." *American Behavioral Scientist* 42(4):720–742.

Valentino, Nicolas A. 1999. "Crime News and the Priming of Racial Attitudes during Evaluations of the President." *Public Opinion Quarterly* 63(3):293–320.

Van Ausdale, Debra and Joe R. Feagin. 1996. "Using Racial and Ethnic Concepts: The Critical Case of Very Young Children." *American Sociological Review* 61(5):779–793.

Villareal, Andres. 2010. "Stratification by Skin Color in Contemporary Mexico." *American Sociological Review* 75(2):652–678.

Ward, L. Monique. 2004. "Wading Through the Stereotypes: Positive and Negative Associations between Media Use and Black Adolescents' Conceptions of Self." *Developmental Psychology* 40(2):284–294.

Waters, Mary C. 1996. "Optional Ethnicities: For Whites Only?" Pp. 444–454 in *Origins and Destinies: Immigration, Race and Ethnicity in America*, edited by Sylvia Pedraza and Ruben Rumbaut. Belmont, CA: Wadsworth Press.

Wilder, JeffriAnne and Colleen Cain. 2011. "Teaching and Learning Color Consciousness in Black Families: Exploring Family Processes and Women's Experiences with Colorism." *Journal of Family Issues* 32:577–604.

Zayas, Luis H. and Solari, Fabiana. 1994. "Early Childhood Socialization in Hispanic Families: Context, Culture, and Practice Implications." *Professional Psychology: Research and Practice* 25(3):200–206.

Zinn, Howard. 2005. *A People's History of the United States, 1492–Present*. New York: Harper Perennial Modern Classics.

Zuckerman, Diana M., Dorothy G. Singer, and Jerome L. Singer. 1980. "Children's Television Viewing, Racial and Sex-Role Attitudes." *Journal of Applied Social Psychology* 10(4):281–294.

Calling Class to Order:
How We Become Classed Beings

"So, how did it go?" my sister asked over the phone.

"I'm not sure. It was kind of weird."

"What do you mean?"

"Well, his mom didn't ask me any questions about myself."

After dating for about a month, I met my new boyfriend's mother and family for the first time. Having recently moved to Jacksonville for a job as a professor, I was a little anxious about meeting Kurt's family—working-class people who had built a respectable family business—for the first time. When my sister called to ask about it, I struggled to articulate why the encounter felt a bit off. The only way I could express why our meeting felt strained was that his mother hadn't engaged me in conversation or asked me "questions about myself."

What does it mean that a social encounter might feel awkward—perhaps because someone doesn't engage you in the way you're used to? In this case, my reaction to meeting Kurt's mother could be interpreted as that of a narcissist: Was I frustrated because I am self-centered and have a need to talk about myself? Or maybe the awkwardness was simply a reflection of different personality types. Some people are more reserved, after all, while others are more outgoing. Yet a savvy sociologist might offer a different interpretation: perhaps the awkwardness of this interaction reflects a clash of social class cultures. Although asking people questions about themselves may be common among the middle-class, working-class people may view the same behavior as obnoxious or intrusive.

When people click and interactions go smoothly—or when they don't—there is a tendency to attribute that to compatible personalities. Yet sociologists believe that social class socialization plays an important role in shaping what we think of as personality and, by extension, the degree to which we feel comfortable in certain situations. Moreover, sociologists believe that there are real consequences associated with whether we feel comfortable in certain interactions. Think, for a moment, of all of the interactions where it's important that people "click": a first date, meeting your new girlfriend's parents, a college interview, a job interview, fraternity or sorority recruitment, viewing a new apartment. These interactions are gateways to gaining access to valuable opportunities in education, employment, and our personal lives. For sociologists, one reason social class inequalities persist across generations is that some interactions feel right, while others feel slightly off. Over time, the fact that some people naturally seem to get along partially explains why some people gain access to desired social opportunities while others do not. Social class socialization lies at the heart of this matter.

This chapter explores what it means to become a social classed being. It focuses on the social interactions and social meanings that characterize the socialization of people who occupy different social class locations. Throughout the life course, this socialization molds us into people who occupy social positions marked not just by different levels of wealth and income but also cultures and identities.

SOCIALIZATION AND THE PROCESS OF LEARNING SOCIAL CLASS

What does it mean to *become* a classed being? In what sense is social class an identity that is socialized, as opposed to a position determined by the amount of money you earn? Sociologists commonly agree that a person's social class is partially defined by their income and wealth (and, sometimes, education). In this sense, it is a position or social location we occupy—as in one metaphor, a rung on a ladder. Yet many sociologists also agree that people who occupy different class locations have different cultural styles and different ways of being. In this sense, social class is something that you are or *do* in all of your interactions. Moreover, they argue, we learn these cultural styles as children and carry them with us as we grow and move through schools, jobs, and society at large. As we develop, these cultural styles open and close doors along the way. This is one reason social class inequalities tend to persist across generations.

LEARNING SOCIAL CLASS DURING PRIMARY SOCIALIZATION: THE ROLE OF PARENTS AND GUARDIANS

Naturally, children raised in different social class locations have different material realities. That is, some may have fancy cribs and strollers, nannies, delightful wardrobes, and books as well as the latest educational devices. Others may share a bed with siblings or parents, wear hand-me-down clothes or even just a diaper on hot days, and have few toys or stimulating games. Beyond these obvious material differences, sociologists have documented cultural differences in how parents from different social classes interact, or socialize, with their children.

From the day children are born, some parenting practices differ along social class lines. For example, the U.S. Surgeon General reports that education—an indicator of social class—is strongly correlated with breastfeeding. Among women who are high school graduates, 66 percent nurse their child; among college graduates, this number is 88 percent. The American Academy of Pediatrics recommends exclusive breastfeeding for the first six months of life and continued breastfeeding for the first year of life and beyond, if desired by mother and child.

Given this recommendation, why do parents from different social classes have different rates of breastfeeding? According to the classic theories of psychologist Urie Bronfenbrenner (1958), this reflects the tendency of middle-class parents to follow and comply with the parenting advice of so-called experts. Compared to less educated parents they are more likely to read parenting manuals, internalize the messages, and treat their children like a project or a puzzle to be solved. Sociologists focus on the social context of breastfeeding. As more women have entered the labor force, lower-income and less educated mothers return to work more quickly than mothers with higher incomes and education. Mothers with higher levels of education are more likely to receive paid time off (or afford unpaid time off), have flexible jobs that allow mothers to work from home, or have access to a *lactation room* at work (where they can nurse or use a breast pump). In this sense, the *opportunity* to breastfeed is a social class issue.

Why does it matter whether parents breastfeed? Accumulating research has documented diverse advantages for infants, mothers, families, and society, including benefits to health, cognitive development, and psychological well-being (American Academy of Pediatrics 2012). A study from the United Kingdom even found that children who were breastfed moved higher up in social class than their nonbreastfed counterparts (Sacker et al. 2013). In this longitudinal study of about 34,000 children, breastfeeding increased the odds of moving into a higher social class position by 24 percent and reduced the chance of downward movement by about 20 percent—all else equal. The authors of the study were not certain of the mechanisms driving this relationship: Was it the boost to health, the benefits associated with parent–child bonding, or some other factor?

Social class, indeed, is a powerful force in how parents parent and where children later end up in the social class structure. Beyond breastfeeding—an event that kicks off the parenting process—how do parenting styles differ along social class lines, and how does social class socialization impact our experiences through the life course?

A major assumption of sociologists is that children from different social classes are socialized differently. From day one they experience different social interactions and, therefore, adopt different ways of acting, thinking, and being. Melvin Kohn, a social psychologist, was among the first to explore class differences in socialization. While he did not directly observe family interactions, his research uncovered social class differences in **parental values**. Using a survey of 400 families, Kohn (1959) found that both working- and middle-class parents value traits like honesty and dependability. Where differences in parents emerged, though, was in the emphasis on *conformity* (obedience) among working-class parents and the emphasis on *self-direction* (motivation, personal responsibility) among middle-class parents.

Imagine you are standing in the checkout line at Target, Wal-Mart, or your local grocery store. In the lanes on each side of you, a child is grabbing at the tempting items and pleading with a parent to buy the fruit snacks, animal crackers, or what have you. To your left, the working-class parent tersely says, "No." When the five-year-old asks why not, her parent replies, "Because I said so," and then grabs the child's hand and says, "Keep your hands to yourself." To your right, the middle-class parent gives a different reply: "You've already had a snack, but we can buy it, and you can have it tomorrow." As the child's eyes widen with excitement, the parent adds, "I just want you to pick the one you think is healthiest."

Kohn's goal was to explain these different interactions. The fact that one child was given permission to select a snack is not simply about the fact that his parents can better afford the treat. The nature of this interaction, according to Kohn (1963), reflects the fact that "Members of different social classes, by virtue of enjoying (or suffering) different conditions of life, come to see the world differently—to develop different conceptions of social reality, different aspirations and hopes and fears, different conceptions of the desirable" (p. 471). What he means is that the daily experiences of a factory worker cultivate in them certain traits: obedience, promptness, and teamwork. Advertising executives, who occupy middle-class positions, have different daily realities: their livelihoods depend on creativity, thinking outside of the box, and self-direction. Parents employ childrearing techniques that reflect these day-to-day experiences: a working-class parent may expect her child to stop touching snacks and asking to buy them in the checkout line, while a middle-class parent may ask the child to use self-control and critical thinking when selecting a snack. Kohn's contribution is that he drew a connection between the macro- and micro-levels, showing that people from different social classes occupy different positions in the class structure (macro) and that over time these differences contribute to what manifest as personality differences (micro).

During the 1970s, French sociologist Pierre Bourdieu began to explore the link between social class and cultural practices and in so doing developed a theory about how social inequalities get perpetuated. For Bourdieu, *cultural capital* and the *habitus* operate as two mechanisms by which children end up in the same social class as their parents. As discussed in Chapter 5, **cultural capital** is comprised of three components:

1. *Objectified cultural capital*: Concrete items that a person owns or consumes, like fine wines, the latest technological gadgets, trendy athletic shoes, or status jewelry.
2. *Institutionalized cultural capital*: The affiliations and connections a person has, like a degree from a prestigious school or *social capital* in the form of friendships, club memberships, and business ties.
3. *Embodied cultural capital*, or **habitus:** The cultural knowledge that a person has; their values and dispositions, as well as how they stand, talk, eat, and interact. This includes knowing how to pair wine with food, but also preferences for how to engage people in conversation the first time you meet them.

So how do these terms relate to social class socialization? According to Bourdieu, a person's cultural capital and habitus are linked to their social class and transmitted *through* socialization. Like Kohn, Bourdieu theorized that people who inhabit different social class positions experience different *material conditions*, especially at work: while middle-class people experience freedom, creativity, and autonomy, working-class people experience rules, constraints, and external supervision. Echoing Kohn, Bourdieu asserted that parents mirror the material conditions they face at work in many of their cultural styles and preferences, including their childrearing practices. Accordingly, middle-class parents typically interact with their children in ways that foster creativity and autonomy, while working-class parents interact with their children in ways that foster obedience. Meanwhile, both pass onto their children social connections (institutionalized cultural capital) that reflect their social class positions, as well as material objects (objectified cultural capital) that mark their social class.

Looking into the day-to-day experiences inside middle- and working-class homes, Bourdieu's theories can be applied to what happens at mealtimes. Do families gather together formally around a table; what do they eat and does the meal require use of cutlery; what do they talk about during dinner and how do they talk about it; is there music or a television playing in the background? Although Bourdieu (1984) did not directly observe family mealtimes, his work in *Distinction: A Social Critique of the Judgment of Taste* might suggest that middle-class families eat formally around a dinner table, perhaps experimenting with different "ethnic foods;" that mealtime is fairly orderly with an effort among parents to talk about their day at work and to engage children in conversations about current events or things going on at school. The scene in working-class homes might be different: more informal, with more familiar and fewer "exotic" foods, less conversation, and more attention paid to the television show in the background.

For Bourdieu, these seemingly inconsequential differences become consequential once children enter the school system. With his co-author Jean-Claude Passeron, Bourdieu (1977 [1990]) argued that schools do not operate according to class-neutral norms; rather, the norms and expectations of the educational system are those of the privileged classes. This means that teachers define "good students" as those who speak quickly and directly, engage confidently with authority figures, and bring certain cultural knowledge to class. If a teacher is delivering a lesson about Renaissance art, and a student has traveled to Paris and seen the *Mona Lisa* first-hand, that student's contribution to the discussion may mark him or her as intelligent. Students who are street-smart, have common sense, or knowledge of small engine repair (as opposed to French culture) may zone out during this seemingly abstract lesson and have their cultural capital dismissed. The problem is that the school system never explicitly defines these subtle codes of conduct. According to Bourdieu:

> By doing away with giving explicitly to everyone what it implicitly demands of everyone, the education system demands of everyone alike that they have what it does not give. This consists mainly of linguistic and cultural competence and that relationship of familiarity with culture which can only be produced by family upbringing when it transmits the dominant culture. (1977:494)

According to Bourdieu and Passeron, children from privileged families succeed not because they are naturally more gifted than their less privileged peers but because their cultural capital is better matched with the expectations of the school system. Over time, students from less privileged families may reject school or opt out, as they come to feel that their knowledge is not respected within the school system and the school system has not explicitly conveyed their expectations.

Other scholars have taken a close look at language socialization as a mechanism through which social class inequalities get perpetuated. As discussed in earlier chapters, **language socialization** refers to the subtle interactional techniques by which we learn how to use language. The field of **sociolinguistics** assumes that language is a tool for communication but that this tool is not socially or culturally neutral. There are cultural norms and expectations associated with how language is used, so that some language practices are defined as correct while others are defined as incorrect and deficient. Usually, it is the language styles used by privileged groups (in terms of social class and race) that are defined as correct, while the language of less privileged groups is deemed deficient.

In his classic book *Class, Codes, and Control*, British sociologist Basil Bernstein (1971) argued that social class differences in language both reflect and reproduce social class inequalities. Generally speaking, Bernstein said, members of the working and less privileged classes use a **restricted speech code**. This way of speaking packs a lot of meaning into few words. Effective when spoken among intimate groups with shared understandings, it is speech code that is simple and direct but less clear to outsiders. By contrast, members of the middle and privileged classes more frequently use an **elaborated speech code**. This is an explicit and detailed way of speaking, where context is made clear and outsiders can easily understand the meaning. Perhaps an example is needed to bring these concepts to life.

Imagine a first-grade teacher holding up a picture to her class and asking students to tell a story about the image. The picture shows an empty fishbowl, water spilled on the counter, and a cat with a guilty look on its face. According to Bernstein, a predictable response from a working-class child would be, "He ate it." In this restricted speech code, neither "he" nor "it" is named. A predictable response from a middle-class child would be "The cat ate the goldfish." Using an elaborated speech code, the listener can understand the story without seeing the picture; the other statement is less clear. As children move through the school system and academic tasks become more complex, the restricted speech code becomes less effective for discussions with teachers and written work.

The issue for Bernstein is not that one speech code is better than the other. Both have their appropriate uses. The issue for Bernstein is that schools and middle-class jobs operate according to elaborated speech codes: you have to clearly explain what you mean to people so that ideas are thoroughly explained, leaving no ambiguities. Consequently, those who have been socialized to use elaborated speech codes are more likely to be defined as clear and intelligent, while those socialized to use the restricted speech code risk being labeled lazy or less intelligent.

Table 9.1 **Social Class, Parenting, and Language Use**

Socioeconomic Status	Words Spoken Per Hour	Vocabulary Size at Age 3	Ratio of Encouragements to Discouragements
Poor (low-SES)	616	525	6:1
Working-class (medium-SES)	1251	750	2:1
Professional (high-SES)	2153	1100	1:2

Source: Hart and Risley 1995.

Another landmark study focusing on social class and language was published by Betty Hart and Todd Risley (1995). Their research is noteworthy for its detailed observations: the authors followed 42 families for nearly two and a half years; each month, they made detailed recordings of how the families interacted with one another for a one-hour period. After amassing 30,000 pages of data, Hart and Risley discovered both quantitative and qualitative differences in how families talk (see Table 9.1). *Quantitatively*, more affluent families are more talkative families: more words were uttered in "professional" homes (middle- and upper middle-class doctors, lawyers, executives, teachers, accountants, for example) than in working-class (custodians, cashiers) and poor homes. In conversations focusing on mundane subjects like eating, bathing, and toilet training, the children of professionals heard 2,153 words an hour and the children of poor parents heard about 616 words. The authors extrapolate that by the time they are four years old, children of professional parents have heard 48 million words, while children of poor families have heard 13 million words.

According to Hart and Risley, this difference is significant because the number of words a child hears influences his or her vocabulary size. At age three, children from poor families had a vocabulary size of 525 words; for working-class children, the number was 750, and for affluent families the number was 1,100. Even at age three, these language patterns matter: the larger the vocabulary, the higher the IQ scores. A practical takeaway of this research is that encouraging parents to talk more to their children may increase their academic aptitude and school success.

Hart and Risley also uncovered *qualitative* differences in how parents talk to children. Using a detailed system of coding and categorization, the authors found that professional parents use more *encouragements and affirmations* than *discouragements and prohibitions*; among lower-income families, discouragements were more common. In professional families, children hear about six encouraging statements for every discouragement. Day in and day out they are told "Good job on your test," "I appreciate the way you helped your brother with his homework," and "I was really proud of how you handled the loss at your basketball game." Working-class or poor children, by contrast, are more likely to hear statements like "Don't touch that," "Leave your sister alone," or "You wanna try out for the team? Who do you think you are, LeBron James?" By age four, a child from a professional family has heard 750,000 instances of praise and 120,000 admonitions, while a child from a working-class family has heard about 120,000 instances of praise and 250,000 admonitions.

Another social class difference was parents' use of *questions* versus *prohibitions* (or directives). In poor and working-class families, questions were less common than prohibitions; children were more likely to hear statements like "Put this in your room" or "Turn that thing down" than "What would you like for dinner?" or "What did you think of the presidential debate?" In addition, poor and working-class parents were less likely to respond to children's efforts to engage them in conversation and had shorter conversations with less turn-taking and elaboration.

Because of these kinds of interactions, by the time four-year-olds enter pre-school they are, according to Jessi Streib (2011), already skilled "class actors." Although their behaviors are unintentional, they actively perform and reproduce class through their linguistic styles. Streib's ethnographic examination of a preschool found that upper middle-class children speak, interrupt, ask for help, and argue more often than working-class children. The linguistic style of upper middle-class children silences working-class students, giving them less influence in the class-room and fewer opportunities to develop their own language skills. By using their words to argue for why they should be able to play with toys and take a turn in class-room conversation, four-year-olds from privileged families learn how to gain power within the preschool world. Jessica McCrory Calarco (2011) demonstrates that these help-seeking behaviors also exist in later elementary classrooms, wherein verbally skilled, attention-seeking students from more advantaged backgrounds demand more attention from teachers and, consequently, "create their own advantages and contribute to inequalities in the classroom" and beyond (p. 862).

As the years roll on, language socialization molds us into people with distinct personalities and cultural styles. It is partially language socialization that shapes afflu-ent kids into secure, confident teens and young adults—people who are accustomed to positive feedback and being asked to voice their opinions. Less affluent kids are shaped into more tentative beings, ones who have thick skins and are less accustomed to ex-tended conversations and requests to give or defend their opinions.

Influenced by Pierre Bourdieu, Annette Lareau (2003) developed in her book *Un-equal Childhoods* one of the most comprehensive models of class socialization to date. After lengthy observation, Lareau coined the term **concerted cultivation** to describe the parenting style of middle-class families and the **logic of natural growth** to de-scribe the parenting style of working-class families. These parenting styles differ in three main ways. First, in terms of the *organization of daily life*, middle-class children participate in numerous formal, age-graded extracurricular activities—such as piano, gymnastics, and soccer. While adults plan these activities, daily life is focused on chil-dren's enjoyment and development. Children in working-class families have looser schedules; participating in few, if any, organized activities, their daily lives focus on hanging out with siblings, cousins, or peers in the neighborhood. In general, their needs are secondary to the parents' needs.

Second, Lareau also observed social class differences in *language use*. As she accompanied families to birthday parties, doctors' appointments, and sports practices, Lareau saw middle-class parents actively cultivate in their children a sophisticated use of language. Parents were keen to educate their children on the meaning of words and engage in wordplay. Their conversations were also characterized by reasoning and negotiation, with parents asking children to defend opinions and talk through choices. Language use in working-class homes was different: Lareau observed less talk, fewer questions and negotiations, and less effort by parents to engage children as conversational partners.

Finally, parents modeled different ways *of interacting with institutional authorities*. When riding to a doctor's appointment, for example, middle-class Ms. Williams encouraged her son Alex to think up a few questions to ask the doctor, so that he could practice interacting with experts. When another middle-class parent, Mrs. Marshall, perceived her daughter's gymnastic coach as being too hard on her, she confronted the coach and asked her to soften her approach and give her daughter more individualized attention. By contrast, when Katie Driver was struggling in school, her working-class mother did not intervene in her teachers' decisions, nor did she request special testing. Instead, she supported the teachers' efforts to help her daughter but trusted their authority rather than trying to guide their actions.

What are the consequences of these parenting styles? As a result of the logic of natural growth, working-class children develop an **emerging sense of constraint**. They are socialized to defer to the authority of teachers, doctors, and coaches—and later bosses and landlords. Without extensive participation in extracurricular activities, they have less experience interacting with strangers, traveling, and being out of their comfort zone. The concerted cultivation of middle-class kids, on the other hand, contributes to an **emerging sense of entitlement**. Through their daily interactions, they learn to use their voices and critical thinking skills, to feel comfortable in new situations and with strangers, and to make sure when interacting with authorities that their needs are met.

While Lareau was quick to note that neither parenting style was better than the other, she argued that children raised using concerted cultivation are better equipped to step into middle-class jobs and social circles, while those raised with the logic of natural growth feel less comfortable in those settings and, perhaps, less likely to succeed. In this way, her work illustrates the link between social class socialization and the reproduction of social class inequality—in the same way that other studies on language socialization and the inculcation of cultural capital show that the socialization of middle-class children produces a cultural match with major social institutions and the socialization of working-class children sometimes produces a clash.

WHAT CAN SOCIAL MOBILITY TELL US ABOUT SOCIAL CLASS?

Much sociological research indicates that children born into a particular social class will end up in the same social class later in life. But surely some people change social classes in their lifetime? Indeed they do—it is a phenomenon called **social mobility**. From a *quantitative*—or statistical—perspective, social mobility was a common feature of life in the United States during the twentieth century. Throughout the twentieth century, researchers report, nearly two-thirds of all Americans changed social classes—with the majority moving up the class ladder. Most of this social mobility, though, was *structural* in nature: due to structural expansion of middle-class jobs during the twentieth century, more and more people were able to change social classes. As agriculture and unskilled manufacturing declined, the job market saw an increase in white-collar jobs, skilled service jobs, and jobs in information technology. These structural changes made social mobility almost inevitable. Since the 1980s, mobility in the United States has slowed considerably: maybe one in 10 children born in the lowest class will rise to the highest.

Yet sociological research on the experience of mobility sheds interesting light on the concept of social class. *Qualitative* researchers find that social mobility is difficult—not because it requires hard work and diligence, but because once people move up the class ladder, they may find that they lack the "right" cultural capital. Upwardly mobile individuals mention feeling like frauds and impostors, lacking the clothing and conversational styles that would help them blend in and feel at ease among their middle-class peers. Reflecting on her move from a working-class background into a stable, upper middle-class adulthood, psychologist and writing instructor Barbara Jensen wrote: "I wandered into a whole new world where few rules of my first world . . . apply" (2012:10). Putting a more pointed spin on the same idea, Professor Donna Langston wrote: "Coming from a working-class background guarantees that you will feel uncomfortable in middle- and upper-middle-class settings" (1993:67). For her, "Keeping up a different set of 'manners' and pretentious small talk [was] an exhausting experience" (p. 67). Despite her academic achievements, Langston felt she didn't have the cultural tools to blend in with her middle-class peers. Over time, she chose to attend less frequently dinners in fancy restaurants and other networking opportunities—choices that may have limited her professional success.

In his research on working-class students pursuing law degrees at an Ivy League university, Robert Granfield (1991) observed little by little students shedding the markers of their working-class upbringing and acquiring the markers of their new middle-class identities. Yet buying a new Brooks Brothers suit was the easy part; they struggled with the advice from their advisors to downplay their own personal stories of upward mobility and shift their aspirations from jobs in public interest law to more lucrative legal specialties. In my own research, I found some working-class students feel outclassed by their peers on campus and intimidated by the ease that their more affluent peers seemed to have participating in class discussions and making friends.

Upward mobility typically brings important benefits: higher salaries, more independence at work, less stress, and more job stability. Yet there can also be costs. In Alfred Lubrano's *Limbo: Blue-Collar Roots, White-Collar Dreams*, a memoir of his own social mobility, a woman named Rebecca is quoted as saying: "The strange thing about getting an education and piercing a class level higher than your parents' is you gain a better lifestyle, money, and status, but you lose your family" (2005:70). You lose your family, she and other upwardly mobile people note, because by changing social classes you take on a set of cultural codes that may cause separation and alienation from one's working-class origins. Together, sociological accounts of social mobility provide two important takeaway points: (1) social mobility was an important part of many Americans' economic reality during the twentieth century, in large part due to economic transformations; (2) social class is more than an economic state—it is also a cultural state.

Other research, including my own, shows that upwardly mobile people can be quite successful, in part because they have the cultural know-how of two distinct class locations. One woman I spoke to worked as a lawyer for a labor union, where she moved back and forth in her daily work tasks, conversing alternately with blue-collar workers—like her own father—and corporate managers. About this experience she proudly claimed:

> I can hang out with a bunch of factory workers who made bombs for the Pentagon and sort of shoot the shit and talk about their kids, etc., etc., and then walk directly from there into a room full of lawyers where, you want to talk big words to me, I can talk big words. I know how to put the posture on. I know how to dress; I know what quiche is. But seriously, I'm not lost if you want to talk to me about quiche or sushi. I've had good red wine and all that stuff. (Stuber, 2005:158)

This research shows that as people move up the class ladder in terms of income and occupation, they may struggle to acquire the cultural capital that accompanies the new position—even if some of them do eventually make peace with and utilize the cultural capital of their class origins.

LEARNING SOCIAL CLASS DURING SECONDARY SOCIALIZATION: EXPERIENCES AT SCHOOL

Beyond the family, social class identities and differences are also cultivated in school settings. In part, this is due to social interactions among peers. At a young age, children are aware of social class differences; as they move through the school system, both inside and outside of the classroom, they create and reinforce social class distinctions through their friendships. Yet socialization and social interaction never take place in a vacuum. What makes the sociological perspective unique is the attention paid to the structure of schooling and the context in which socialization takes place. For sociologists, the educational system is not a class-neutral setting; as stated earlier, sociologists believe that the educational system presents advantages to students from privileged backgrounds and disadvantages to those from less privileged backgrounds.

School organization and academic culture

Among the first to systematically describe the class structure of the educational system were Samuel Bowles and Herbert Gintis (1976). In their classic book *Schooling in Capitalist America*, these economists argued that rather than function as a place where hardworking students can move up the class ladder, the educational system is set up to

The "hidden curriculum" of the schools helps transmit values like obedience and patriotism

keep people within their social class positions. It does so due to the fact that the "structure of the educational experience is admirably suited to nurturing attitudes and behaviors consonant with participation in the labor force" (p. 9). The authors do not mean that at school students learn human capital and job skills; rather, through the **hidden curriculum** students acquire a personality type centered on punctuality, conformity, and respect for authority. In doing so, the authors argued, the educational system actually dulls students' curiosity and essentially turns out compliant workers who will not rock the boat and will accept their subordinate positions within the class structure.

One way in which students become compliant and accepting of social inequality is through the formal curriculum, which molds social class worldviews and ideologies. An **ideology** is a set of beliefs and values that explain and justify social inequality. The dominant ideology of the United States has as its centerpiece the notion that the individual, rather than the government, is responsible for shaping his or her opportunities and well-being. It also includes a belief in **meritocracy**—the notion that we live in a society where people earn their positions through competition and hard work (i.e., their own *merits*). These beliefs generally lead us to condemn the poor and celebrate the wealthy.

Within the school system, the dominant ideology is transmitted through the formal curriculum. In most school textbooks, the economic and social contributions of workers and labor unions tend to be omitted, obscured, or downplayed; meanwhile the negative consequences of capitalist enterprise (monopolies, price-fixing, low wages, and poor working conditions) are ignored or given superficial treatment (Chafel 1997). Textbooks typically celebrate the accomplishments of industrialists, "robber barons," high-tech pioneers, and the capitalist system while ignoring instances of U.S. governmental forces attacking workers or breaking up union organizing; the dysfunctions of capitalism, like the underlying causes of housing bubbles and stock market crashes, are also given cursory treatment (Loewen 2007; Zinn 2005). In her classic work, Jean Anyon concluded that textbooks "imply that we should regard the poor as responsible for their own poverty: poverty is a consequence of the failure of individuals, rather than the failure of society to distribute economic resources universally. This ideology encourages education and other actions that attempt to change the individual, while leaving the unequal economic structures intact" (1979:383). The school system, in other words, socializes students to blame lower-income people for their problems and ignore the macro-level or structural factors that contribute to the success of some and failure of others.

By casting a microscopic eye on what happens in school classrooms, Anyon (1981) extended the argument that the structure of schooling reproduces social class inequalities. In her influential research, Anyon explored the curriculum and instruction at a set of elementary schools, each serving a different social class population. She found that schools serving working-class students teach students to follow orders, to be punctual, and to respect authority. While they used many of the same textbooks as the middle- and upper middle-class students, teachers used them in a different way: emphasizing memorization and facts above analysis and interpretation, for example. By the time these students reached 5th grade, they were disengaged and disruptive, with few expressing confidence in their ability to attend college. When asked about their behaviors, students told Anyon they were bored "[b]ecause he [the teacher] don't teach us nothin'" and checked out because "[t]hey give us too many punishments."

Schools serving economically privileged children, by contrast, teach students to be independent and creative, to work at their own pace, and to use critical thinking. Whereas one teacher of working-class students said her goal was to "keep them [students] busy," a teacher serving the children of professional parents said: "My goal is to have the children learn from experience. I want them to think for themselves." Students in these schools were more likely to see themselves as creators of knowledge, while their less privileged peers were socialized to see knowledge as coming from books and authority figures. The textbooks of privileged students, moreover, emphasized "competing worldviews" and multiple interpretations of cultural and historic events; textbooks at schools serving lower-income students provided a more narrow and sanitized version of history. They especially lacked lessons on social class struggles or the contributions of working-class people to building this nation. And while the education of privileged students gives them cultural capital and critical thinking skills, Anyon worried that it also contributes to a sense of **narcissism**, or excessive individualism—what Annette Lareau called entitlement.

As students move from elementary school into middle and high school, similar dynamics play out in a process known as tracking. In academic **tracking**, students are grouped into courses based on academic ability. While supporters believe students learn better when they are placed into classes tailored to their abilities, some worry that social class (and race) is partially the basis by which students are assigned to tracks, with higher-class students placed in higher tracks and lower-class students in lower tracks. In her classic book *Keeping Track: How Schools Structure Inequality*, Jeannie Oakes (1985) described the curriculum and pedagogy of high-track classes as transmitting "high status knowledge"; knowledge that emphasizes critical thinking, creativity and self-direction. Meanwhile, lower tracks transmit "low status knowledge"—knowledge that emphasizes conformity, memorization, practical skills, and punctuality. Teachers in low-track classrooms also spent less time on instruction and more time on procedures and "bookkeeping"; teachers also exhibit warmer interactions with high-track students while ignoring or isolating low-track students (Clark-Ibáñez 2005).

For Oakes, one of the most detrimental aspects of tracking is that it labels and stigmatizes students. Over time, through interactions with teachers and peers, students take on the labels of their groups and perform accordingly: those who are labeled bright and motivated *become* bright and motivated, and those who are labeled slow or unmotivated *become* slow and unmotivated. Track placements, in a sense, become **self-fulfilling prophecies**. This is also how tracking contributes to the reproduction of social inequalities.

Despite the labeling of students as bright and cooperative, on the one hand, and slow and defiant, on the other, some students resist these labels and develop an **oppositional culture**—one that rejects the importance of schooling and good behavior and imposes in its place a culture of toughness and rebellion. After years of having their culture denigrated—being told that their language is wrong, their behaviors inappropriate, and that working-class people did little to build their nation's history—students may rebel. Paul Willis (1977) described the British working-class high-school aged **Lads** in his classic *Learning to Labour* as primarily concerned with "having a laff." After coming to feel that the school system would never recognize the value of their working-class culture, these high school students found that the only way to gain respect among their peers was to adopt an oppositional culture based on drinking, smoking, cursing, and crude sexist attitudes. Willis sees the "bad behavior" of these students in a new way: rather than seeing them as unintelligent, deviant ingrates or victims of a middle-class school system, he sees them as working-class students who deal with rejection from school by developing their own cultural standards of respect. Willis emphasizes these students' **agency**: their ability to act creatively and forge their own positions in society. The irony, though, is that by rejecting an educational system that seems to privilege middle-class culture, these working-class youth end up holding working-class jobs, thereby reproducing the social class structure they were rebelling against in the first place.

A final example of how social class socialization reproduces inequality is seen in the education of elites at select boarding schools. For those who have attended ordinary urban and suburban high schools, many boarding schools look like a mixture of an elite country club and a classic English college. At the nation's elite boarding schools, where the annual cost of attendance runs about $45,000, the education is truly top-notch. With highly selective admissions and class sizes of about 15, students take literature courses with titles like "Road Trip!" and "Rebels and Nonconformists" and social science courses with titles like "War and Peace in Modern Times," "Capitalism and Its Critics," and "Why Are Poor Nations Poor?" What does it mean that the typical public school curriculum rarely raises complicated questions about capitalism and the class structure, but at elite boarding schools privileged students dive right in?

Beyond the formal curriculum, experiences outside the boarding school classroom also play a role in socialization. Community service is typically required, as is participation in at least one competitive athletic team; extracurricular options are diverse and well funded. Phillips-Exeter Academy in New Hampshire offers 90 student clubs, including a capella singing groups (like The Warblers on the TV show *Glee*), the ski and snowboard club, the filmmaking club, and the "Culinary Society of Exeter"—commonly known as the cooking club. Many of these high schools also offer study-abroad programs. According to the website of Connecticut's Choate Rosemary Hall,

Elite boarding schools transmit the cultural capital of the upper classes, emphasizing athletics, volunteerism, foreign travel, and an appreciation for "high culture."

"Rather than offering students the typical sightseeing experience," these programs "extend the rare invitation to adopt the daily routines and cultural habits of another country for an extended period of time." The website also declares that "the sooner adolescents learn to overcome the personal challenges inherent in moving outside the familiar and encountering new cultural practices and ways of thinking, the better their chances of acquiring resourcefulness, flexibility, and versatility, that thriving in today's world demands."

What these schools do best is *prepare students for power* (Cookson and Persell 1985) and teach them to *embody privilege* (Khan 2011). They do so by inculcating students with the cultural capital of the elites. Students learn classical art and literature, sophisticated ways of engaging in critical issues, physical discipline and self-presentation (dress codes typically require shirt and tie for boys), and a sense of worldliness and opportunity. The chance to build social capital is also unparalleled, as these schools have illustrious alumni and students who come from families that are leaders in business, education, medicine, entertainment, and the arts. "For students seeking to be the best," Cookson and Persell write, this exposure provides "a sense of importance and empowerment" (1985:83). With increasingly international student bodies, attendees also learn how to interact in a diverse world. One final advantage of attending an elite boarding school is their ability to "charter and barter" in college admissions (Cookson and Persell 1985). Many of these schools maintain tight relationships with admissions counselors at top universities, so that their students have an advantage in the college application process—even when their SAT scores and GPAs are lower than an applicant from an unknown urban high school (Stevens 2007). All told, these schools offer already-privileged students an advantage in maintaining their privilege.

Peer interactions and class identification

Many sociologists believe that in order to understand social inequality, it is important to understand real people's experiences and worldviews. In terms of social class socialization, this means that people develop a sense of their own and others' social class identities through social interaction. Just as researchers have found that children are aware of racial differences and build racial boundaries at an early age, researchers have discovered similar dynamics in terms of social class. At the age of six children can categorize based on social class, typically using material goods and possessions as markers (Leahy 1983). In her study using **photo elicitation**—a research technique where respondents are shown photos and asked questions about what they see— Patricia Ramsey (1991) found that while preschoolers did not spontaneously mention social class when describing the photos, they were adept at classifying rich and poor people when asked. In another study using photo elicitation, Susan Weinger (2000) found that middle-class children did not identify or empathize with the lower classes and sometimes blamed them for their poverty; lower-income children, by contrast, expressed feelings of empathy, warmth, and even pity for other lower-income people. Middle-class children, moreover, described lower-income people as "dirty," "lazy" and "mean," as well as prone to anger and destructive behaviors like "busting windows." While most middle-class children expressed a desire to play with other middle-class children, describing them as "normal" and someone they could "relate to," lower-income children preferred lower-income playmates, explaining:

> "I really don't want a rich friend that thinks he's better than me. When we're friends we know that we're friends because we like each other, and not that we just want each other for money and stuff."

> "This kid (poor) would probably treat me nice and this kid (middle-class) would probably treat me badly because she's rich and she wants a lot of friends who are rich." (Weinger 2000:143)

Indeed, numerous studies have identified feelings of shame and exclusion among lower-income children. Exclusion was felt, for example, by poor children who could not participate in field trips requiring a parental contribution. Not only did they feel excluded from a fun activity, they also worried about being "outed" and looked down upon (Ridge 2002; Wikeley et al. 2007). In schools where children wear uniforms, "dress-down days" that "rewarded" children with the opportunity to wear their own clothes caused anxiety for children who worried about being teased or laughed at for their lack of fashionable clothing (Taylor and Fraser 2003). Anxieties about not having the right toys or clothes (Pugh 2009), as well as painful memories of being laughed at for having the wrong clothes, seem characteristic of some lower-income children. According to Sandi Nenga (2003), these experiences contribute to a *structure of feeling* where shame is a central emotion through which lower-income and working-class people experience the world.

As children move into middle and high school, social class identities are honed further, with exclusion continuing to characterize their socialization. In her qualitative study of working- and middle-class adolescents, Ellen Brantlinger (1993) found that lower-income youth were more aware of their higher-income peers and more sensitive to class dynamics at school. They could, for example, name wealthy students' social groups (Jocks, Preppies, Snobs, Popular Kids), individual members, and their shifting friendships. They also saw themselves as alienated from their teachers and characterized their affluent peers as teachers' pets. Despite their insights into and criticism of the class system, they tended to internalize messages transmitted by school and society, blaming themselves for their school failures and socioeconomic situation. Upper-income youth, by contrast, seemed unaware of their lower-income peers, identifying only a few names for their social groups (Stoners, Rednecks, Headbangers). Their discourses, moreover, reflected a meritocratic view of social and school hierarchies, where middle-class students viewed their class privilege and school success through the lens of entitlement and self-congratulation.

While most high schools in the United States are strongly segregated along racial and ethnic lines, social class segregation is less apparent. When students attend schools with diverse social class groups, they tend to self-segregate into their own camps and tribes. While the groups' names may differ across schools, an **oppositional social structure** develops in schools whereby wealthier kids and less wealthy kids define themselves in relation to one another (Eckert 1989). Over time, these "two categories progressively separate their worlds, developing opposing territories, appearances, demeanors, and activities" (p. 49). Wealthier kids tend to be highly involved in school activities and committed to the official goals of the school; less wealthy kids—like the Lads described by Paul Willis—develop their own internal system of values and often look to establish credibility in the adult world rather than the high school world. As wealthier students ingratiate themselves with school authorities, they are able to use their extracurricular involvement as an excuse to skip class and goof off. Less wealthy kids have no such alibi and lack the verbal skills to talk themselves out of tricky situations. By the time they graduate, this class-based polarization of student cultures means that students from the same high school may feel as if they attended entirely different schools.

Once in college, these dynamics may continue. Although lower-income students are less likely to attend college than their more affluent peers, they are present on campuses across the country. In my book *Inside the College Gates: How Class and Culture Matter in Higher Education* (Stuber 2011), I found that working-class students were more aware of class dynamics on campus and more sensitive to class differences than their more affluent peers. For one working-class male, the move to a large university with a larger population of wealthy students honed his class awareness:

> I can just *see* it so much clearer now. I can just constantly see it in everyday life, whereas before, I wouldn't really notice it. But now, I notice it just like driving through a certain neighborhood. Now I'm like, "Oh, this is a real rich neighborhood or this is a real poor neighborhood." Or going into classrooms and being able to see it. Or going into school and just interacting with students here. I can definitely tell, "Oh, you're from a rich neighborhood; you definitely have two parents," or this or that (p. 142).

One working-class female at a selective liberal arts college described feeling alienated on campus and pressured to present a serious, refined persona: "I like to be goofy and just be really silly and I just don't feel like I can do that here, 'cause people constantly look down on other people. I feel like this is a very high class, elite college and I feel I'm under a microscope and I can't ever have that funny, goofy side of me come out" (p. 149).

Upper middle-class students were less aware of social class on campus and generally dismissed its importance. One affluent student rejected the notion that social class mattered at her liberal arts college: "If you're involved enough and work hard enough to immerse yourself in the campus and try hard to have every experience you can, then it really doesn't matter. It shouldn't shape who you are and what you want to do." Affluent students were, however, aware of and concerned with social class differences among their affluent peers. Many of them minimized their own privilege with comparisons to students who were better-off, like the one who declared: "I only own seven items from Juicy Couture (a popular brand of clothing at the time) as opposed to these two girls down the hallway, who have like a hundred." This student claimed she did not want to be perceived as a snob, and wanted to "prove" to the middle-class students in her dorm that she was "on their level." Yet elsewhere in our conversations, she noted: "I can get my mom to do whatever I want her to do, but it's at a lower level, I feel, than some people" (Stuber 2011:125). This young woman echoed the sentiment of many affluent students: despite their advantages, they see themselves as disadvantaged in some ways.

Social class socialization in college extends to students' participation in extracurricular activities. Research shows that lower-income and **first-generation college students** (those with neither parent having attained a college degree) are less likely to be involved in campus activities, including clubs and organizations, Greek life, and study-abroad programs, compared to their more affluent peers. In my research I found that upper middle-class students were excited about meeting new people, traveling abroad, and acquiring new cultural experiences outside the classroom. They took for granted that this was a key part of the college experience. Working-class students, by contrast, saw those activities as a distraction and irrelevant to what they saw as the true purpose of college. As long as they got good grades and a degree, they felt confident that they would be able to prove their worth to employers.

This and other research shows that the **experiential core** of college life—the space comprised of extracurricular activities and social life—is a site for the formation of social class identities (Stevens, Armstrong, and Arum 2008). Because of their different approaches to college, upper middle-class students spent their time on campus acquiring valuable social and cultural capital while working-class students maintained relationships to people from home and focused on acquiring *human capital*, or a college degree.

These patterns echo the socialization described by Annette Lareau, where privileged kids grow up participating in formal activities and cultivating outgoing, inquisitive selves, while less privileged students have more limited experiences and maintain connections with family and familiars. In terms of social reproduction, it is true that working-class college graduates have positioned themselves for upward mobility; yet their paths are likely to be more modest than their upper middle-class peers, who have attained in college not only a valuable credential but the kinds of social and cultural capital that can help them navigate the social and occupational worlds of the privileged class.

EXPLORING ACTIVISM: DISRUPTING CLASS ON COLLEGE CAMPUSES

If upwardly mobile students from working-class and first-generation backgrounds struggle in college, why don't we see more efforts on campus to address their needs and feelings of dislocation? Why are there not more clubs and organizations or "resource centers" devoted to their needs, as there are for students who are veterans, LGBTQ/sexual minorities, or black, Hispanic, or Asian? Indeed, since the early 1970s, college activism around social class has been relatively silent.

That said, there have been some recent efforts to raise class consciousness on college campuses. According to its website, "Class Action" is a network of 100+ college-based organizations devoted to providing "a dynamic framework [for] analysis, as well as a safe space, for people of all backgrounds to identify and address issues of class and classism." At the elite women's college, the Smith Association for Class Activists was formed to raise awareness of class diversity and provide resources to students facing class-based struggles. Quoted in the campus newspaper, student leader Melissa Mac-Donald said that when talking about social class, "Ideas don't come across well and it gets personal. It's a continual process to renegotiate." As in many student groups, their work includes movie screenings, workshops, and panel discussions. The organization also connects current students to alumnae from low-income homes to create networking opportunities and address the unique needs of lower-income students who lack professional connections or may feel out of place in interviews.

On many campuses, these groups have struggled to maintain activity and visibility. To date, they have not become as institutionally recognized as groups devoted to religious, sexual, or racial/ethnic minorities. Why not? Is it that these groups do not resonate with student needs or administrators' priorities? We know that social class identities lack salience for many Americans. Accordingly, social class issues may be hard to articulate or identify. Moreover, in a society characterized by an ideology based on hard work, individualism, and self-reliance, groups wanting to raise class consciousness may run up against the dominant ideology. It is also possible that lower-income students are reticent to "come out" of the class closet and proclaim their economic disadvantage. Despite my own class-based struggles in college, I was mainly concerned with fitting in with my more affluent peers; joining a "class action" group would have seriously compromised my efforts to pass. In my own research, a student named Patty Ellis echoed this sentiment, scoffing at the idea of wearing a T-shirt with the name of her scholarship organization on it "because of the whole income thing." For her, there is a stigma associated with participating in an income-based scholarship organization. Because social class is not as immediately visible as race and ethnicity, students have the option of remaining invisible.

The example of the Occupy movement notwithstanding, the United States is not in a moment of strong class consciousness. Until that time comes, organizations that seek to raise class awareness or alter class arrangements may remain marginalized. And college students like Patty Ellis may continue to struggle in silence.

EXPLORING INTERSECTIONALITY: SOCIAL CLASS AND THE EDUCATION OF ELITE WOMEN

Wealthy students in the United States are socialized to approach education in particular ways, and while in school their socialization reinforces their privilege. Yet gender also enters the equation, whereby the experiences of privileged females and privileged males differ from one another. From middle-school onward, female students cultivate a sense of competitiveness and intelligence, coupled with heightened expectations of beauty, style, and sexual expression.

To understand how gender and social class intersect in school socialization, it is necessary to listen to middle, high school, and college students talk about the ways female bodies are indelibly *marked* by social class. In reflecting on the degree to which they fit in, how they make friends, and how they feel when excluded by peers, markers of social status appear as a constant preoccupation (Armstrong and Hamilton 2013; Bettie 2003; Chase 2008; Proweller 1998; Stuber, Klugman, and Daniel 2011). There seems to be a well-known catalog of items that young women "must have" if they want to fit in. Although specific items shift over time, in recent years these have included furry Ugg boots and rugged Hunter rain boots, Vera Bradley and Lilly Pulitzer tote bags, Tiffany jewelry, Michael Kors watches, and cozy but chic North Face fleece jackets. Although some young women reject these mainstream signifiers and develop alternative aesthetics, for many trying to navigate their peer groups, these status symbols present a no-win situation: while many female students consider these items essential for gaining acceptance to desired friendship groups or the "right sorority," they are chastised for being superficial and overly materialistic if they do have these items (Stuber, Klugman, and Daniel 2011). Whereas college students characterize guys as chill and laid back, unconcerned about social status, both male and female students made mildly pejorative comments about female students, like this one from Suzanne Sorensen: "I don't think it [social status] really matters to guys. But like to girls, you see them together with all the same stuff on—Kate Spade, Ralph Lauren, Tiffany necklaces, Gucci. Guys could care less . . . they're like, if you don't have a lot of money, big deal, come party, you know. But for girls, most of 'em are daddy's little rich girls" (p. 438).

In addition to negotiating the peer group, once in college, privileged women must find a major, develop extracurricular interests, and manage romantic and/or sexual relationships. For women who wish to preserve their privilege, these competing demands can be tricky. Although college represents an ideal time to find a long-term romantic partner, possibly even a spouse, Laura T. Hamilton and Elizabeth A. Armstrong (2009) found that many affluent women see serious relationships as a threat to their career goals. While working-class women had more modest career goals and were focused on maintaining serious, monogamous relationships, affluent women engaged in casual hookups to avoid being distracted from their social life and campus activities. While negotiating the hookup culture, they also faced the challenge of avoiding being labeled a "slut."

By looking at the intersection of gender and social class, we see that it's not just lower-income people who feel pressured to fit in or who are squeezed by class socialization. For many affluent young women, a Duke University report attests, there exists a cultural expectation of **"effortless perfection"**: an "expectation that one would be smart, accomplished, fit, beautiful, and popular, and that all this would happen without visible effort." Perfect without effort? That's a tall order, one that may result in eating disorders, cutting, depression, or simply running one's self ragged. The Women's Initiative, who produced the report at Duke University, concluded that these cultural expectations contribute to a "climate . . . that too often stifles the kind of vigorous exploration of selfhood and development" that is assumed to be what college is about.

Admittedly, the men and women who graduate from elite universities often have excellent social and economic outcomes. Yet this research finds that such social and economic benefits do not always come without costs. For affluent college women, there may be unique pressures to present a gendered and classed self, one built on "effortless perfection."

SECONDARY SOCIALIZATION—LEARNING SOCIAL CLASS THROUGH THE SYMBOLIC WORLD AND THE MEDIA

While sociologists believe that social class is perhaps the strongest force shaping our lives—influencing our educational attainment, income, marital stability, and health and well-being—social class identities are not particularly **salient** for most Americans: they don't rank highly in our conscious thoughts of who we are. Moreover, decades of research shows that Americans are not terribly critical of social class inequality. For the most part, our ideologies tell us that social class inequality is inevitable and that people's fortune or misfortune is their own doing. Yet how do we come to hold these beliefs? How are we socialized to either ignore or tolerate the vast social inequalities among us? Scholars have a word to describe the process by which inequalities come to be viewed as normal and natural: it is called **legitimation**.

To some extent, social inequality is legitimated through the formal curriculum and stories that herald rags-to-riches success, the evils of communism, and the moral and financial victories of capitalism. Yet legitimation also occurs within the mass media: in everything from news coverage to broadcasts of *The Simpsons*. For sociologists and other scholars, a steady media diet can similarly shape our perspectives on social inequality, the economic system, and the class structure. Yet to understand *what* we see, hear, and read in the media, we must first understand *who* owns the media. The fact that about five companies in the United States (and 12 companies globally) control almost all of the media (radio, films, magazines, newspapers, television) we receive is called **media concentration** (see Figure 9.1) While media concentration may be an efficient business model, critics warn that it limits the diversity of opinions we are exposed to; more pointedly, the fact that a few powerful companies dominate the market means that the interests of a minority elite pervade the public airwaves. If media companies are major contributors to political organizations and have a stake in political candidates, they are likely to promote stories and viewpoints that do not alienate them from political favor. In reports on congressional negotiations on tax policy, for example, conservative media outlets may label efforts to raise corporate or income taxes as "class warfare"—implying that less successful individuals are wrongly clamoring to claim the benefits of the more successful. They may also characterize protestors like those in the Occupy Wall Street movement or at G8 economic summits as disgruntled, out-of-touch radicals.

A second concern of media critics is that media concentration by large, for-profit companies results in a system that is commercially driven and loyal to advertisers and

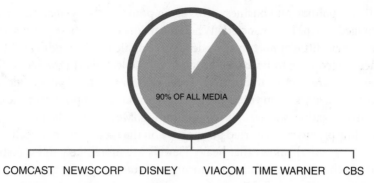

Figure 9.1 Media concentration. Some argue that "media concentration"—where a few parent companies own almost all media outlets—leads to transmission of fewer viewpoints and a "pro-business" message.

government, rather than to the public interest. Consequently, certain media outlets may be reluctant to report that Disney—one of the large media conglomerates—has been accused of unfair child labor practices in the foreign factories that produce their toys. Moreover, when discussing a new movie on morning news programs like *The Today Show* and *Good Morning America*, commentators may be likely to give positive reviews because their television network is owned by the same company that produced the film. When radio stations, television stations, film studios, and other media outlets are owned by the same company, this is called **vertical integration**. This ownership structure, where economic interests are interlinked, tends to be monopolistic and promote consumer-oriented, pro-business messages.

It cannot be said that the media ignores issues of economic inequality. In addition to nightly newscasts on unemployment or the housing collapse of 2009, there are periodic specials by commentators like Oprah Winfrey, Diane Sawyer, and Anderson Cooper that focus on urban and rural poverty, along with the misdeeds and questionable practices of corporate entities. Yet when these issues are presented, the framing tends to be sanitized. An *Oprah* segment on poverty in Detroit and a *20/20* special on poverty in Appalachia both provided compassionate portraits of people experiencing poverty but did not question the macro-level forces that contribute to high levels of poverty in these regions. Instead of focusing on the boom and bust of the auto and coal industries, respectively, media portrayals show hopeful individuals who are convinced that through their own hard work they can transcend the structural conditions that have impoverished their areas. By focusing on the virtues of hard work, many media outlets legitimate the dominant ideology and downplay the complicated macro-level forces at work.

Media socialization plays out more subtly in dramatic programming and sitcoms. Paralleling the earlier discussions of gender and race in the media, lower-income and working-class people are also *underrepresented* in prime-time programming. Working-class people are statistically less common on television than they are in "real life;" instead, glamorous, successful professionals dominant the airwaves, with jobs in law, medicine, politics, and business. This again points to the *symbolic annihilation* of disadvantaged groups in our society. When the media deems these groups uninteresting, viewers have little opportunity to develop realistic understandings of their lived experiences. According to Barbara Ehrenreich, "The less 'we' know about 'them,' the more likely 'we' are to cling to our stereotypes—or forget 'them' altogether" (1995:42). This has consequences when voters form their opinions about political candidates and issues such as taxation, wages, and school funding. Meanwhile, the media's emphasis on the wealthy provides a distorted perspective on the socioeconomic reality in which we live. Some research shows that heavy viewers are more likely to overestimate the affluence of others, perceive a large and unsatisfying economic gap between themselves and others (Yang and Oliver 2010), and develop feelings of envy and desire for material goods (O'Guinn et al. 1989).

The depiction of characters—in both scripted programs and reality shows—also provides insight into how the media molds our social class worldviews. Working-class men are commonly portrayed as buffoons, "dumb, immature, irresponsible, or lacking in common sense" (Butsch 1995:404). Think momentarily about Homer Simpson, Kevin James of *King of Queens*, Burt Chance of *Raising Hope*, and the biggest buffoon of all—Archie Bunker from the 1970s classic *All in the Family*. Meanwhile, middle-class fathers are often portrayed as wise and hardworking. Classic examples include *Leave it to Beaver*'s Ward Cleaver, Mike, the patriarch of the *Brady Bunch*, Bill Cosby, and more current examples like *7th Heaven*'s Eric Camden (the fathers from *Malcolm in the Middle* and *Modern Family* notwithstanding).

In the last decade, reality television has provided plenty of confusing messages when it comes to social class. During the mid-2000s, a crop of shows devoted to the lifestyles of the rich and famous popped up. MTVs *Cribs* took viewers into the tricked-out mansions of celebrities, while *My Super Sweet 16* gave viewers a look at the extravagant

Media images of the working class praise their authenticity and down-to-earth nature, while also depicting them as crude or ignorant buffoons (left). Archie from *All in the Family* and Honey Boo Boo both fit this archetype (right).

birthday parties of wealthy teens. Paris Hilton and Nicole Richie gained fame as they got a taste of *The Simple Life*, and *Rich Girls* depicted the ups and downs of two wealthy teens completing high school and getting ready for college—with stints vacationing in the Hamptons and visits to rehab in between. Bravo television, meanwhile, packed its nightly lineup with wealthy housewives, Manhattan prep school students, millionaire bachelors, and sellers of "million dollar listings." Currently, E! broadcasts a superficial, fast-edit profile of wealthy young people, cleverly titled *#RichKids*. Through the gossip, infighting, and bad behavior, coupled with images of opulence and success, viewers may be confused as to whether they should envy and aspire to the lifestyles of the elite or feel morally superior to them and thankful for their own comparatively simple lives.

A more recent phenomenon has been the explosion of reality television shows devoted to the poor and working classes. Many of these shows focus on quirky men with unique hobbies and occupations—*Duck Dynasty*, *Hillbilly Handfishin'*, *Moonshiners*, *Gator Boys*, and *Billy the Exterminator*. While relatively few of these shows focus on women, *Extreme Couponing* highlights the thrift of some working-class women, and *Here Comes Honey Boo Boo* captures the scents and sounds of a fun-loving, down-to-earth Georgia family. These shows, in contrast to the ones featuring the wealthy, often highlight these folks' authenticity, humor, creativity, and family values. While they are still framed as exotic creatures, these working-class people are portrayed with some degree of respect.

What all of these shows have in common—whether focusing on the foibles of the rich or the authenticity of the not-so-rich—is their entertainment value. In their playful portrayals of both affluence and the lack thereof, these shows distract viewers from serious social issues and give them a questionable lens for considering the real inequalities in the world around them.

SOCIAL CLASS IDENTITIES AND THE REPRODUCTION OF CLASS INEQUALITY

As we move into our adult years, we continue to develop an understanding of our own and others' social class identities. Especially for members of the lower and working classes, researchers find there are "hidden injuries" (Sennett and Cobb 1972) or minor indignities suffered in their daily lives. Their levels of stress are higher, and their lack of autonomy (or self-direction) at work digs in and erodes their health and well-being. They may find dignity in what they do, however, and develop pride in their authenticity and work ethic (Kefalas 2003; Lamont 2002). Professional men have a pride of their own, but as Michèle Lamont finds, it's based more on their financial and professional accomplishments than their character (1992). Meanwhile, upper middle-class women—many of whom have careers of their own—are devoted to cultivating the next generation of privileged children and making sure they have access to the best educational opportunities (Brantlinger 2003; Lareau 2003).

Although social class identities are not especially salient in the United States, social class is both deeply felt and continually enacted. We feel social class in those moments when we experience either shame or accomplishment; we also feel it in those moments when we are either included or excluded from valued opportunities, like jobs, friendships, and club memberships. It can explain why upon meeting my boyfriend's family for the first time, I felt awkward and out of place. We are, moreover, always *doing* social class, whether in terms of how we hold our bodies, how we order food at a restaurant, or how we act when meeting new people.

These different ways of doing and feeling social class are important for one major reason: our most powerful social institutions operate according to the norms and culture of the middle and upper classes. Therefore, following the insights of scholars like Pierre Bourdieu and Annette Lareau, those whose culture matches the cultural norms of the school and workplace will likely succeed in those settings, while those who have the skills to compete but lack the cultural and social capital may wonder why they got left out. It is in these ways that social class socialization and social interactions play a critical role in the reproduction of social class inequality.

CHAPTER 9: REVIEW OF KEY POINTS

- Children raised in different social classes are typically socialized differently. These differences in socialization both reflect existing social class differences and, in many instances, reproduce social class differences in adulthood.
- Middle-class parents tend to emphasize creativity and self-direction in raising their children, while working-class parents tend to emphasize obedience. As explained by Pierre Bourdieu, these differences reflect the values and material conditions that middle- and working-class parents face at work.
- Social class differences also exist in language socialization. Working-class children are spoken to less, overall, and hear more directives and discouragements. Middle-class children, by contrast, are spoken to more and are also more likely to hear questions and encouragements.
- For Annette Lareau, children in poor and working-class families are socialized in a way that produces a sense of constraint, while children in middle-class families are socialized in a way that produces a sense of entitlement. Like the other patterns mentioned, this pattern helps privileged children succeed at school and work, while holding less privileged children back.
- Studies of social mobility (moving from one social class to another) show class mobility was quite common throughout the twentieth century but has become less common over time. These studies also show that when people move up in terms of social class, they often struggle culturally to fit in.
- Some sociologists believe the educational system also reproduces social inequality and existing class divisions. They argue that the formal curriculum and the hidden curriculum socialize less privileged students to remain compliant and content with their inferior positions, while socializing already privileged students to become privileged adults.
- Even young children have an awareness of social class differences. Some children carry an awareness of class differences with them through their time at school, feeling shame and exclusion or superiority and comfort as they size themselves up in relation to peers and teachers.
- The mainstream media also socializes us in terms of our class identities and awareness. One common pattern is that the media does not call serious attention to social class inequalities or

social problems. Reality programming may feature the lives of both the poor (authentic and fun) and the rich (superficial and annoying)—yet these portrayals are for entertainment value and rarely help viewers think about social class in serious ways.

CHAPTER 9: QUESTIONS FOR REVIEW

1. During primary socialization, what are some differences in the ways that parents from different social class backgrounds raise their children? How and why do these differences matter, especially when it comes to children's experiences at school?

2. During secondary socialization in school, what are some key differences in the socialization of children from different social class backgrounds? What do kids learn about social class through the formal curriculum? Through social interactions and other policies and procedures that structure the school environment?

3. For many Americans, social class is not an especially salient identity. Yet the research presented in this chapter shows that social class is understood and enacted at fairly early ages. How, according to research presented in this chapter, do children and adolescents understand social class differences?

4. What "lessons" can be learned about social class through the mainstream media? Generally speaking, what messages are transmitted about social class through the mainstream media, especially television?

5. Thinking about the ideas presented in this chapter, does it make sense to think about a person's social class position as more than simply the amount of money they have access to? According to the research presented in this chapter, how do the cultural differences among social classes impact the kind of people we become as adults?

6. Imagine that you had been born into a different social class. Over the course of your childhood and adolescence, how do you think that this would have influenced the person you are today?

KEY TERMS

agency	logic of natural growth
concerted cultivation	media concentration
cultural capital	meritocracy
effortless perfection	narcissism
elaborated speech code	oppositional culture
emerging sense of constraint	oppositional social structure
emerging sense of entitlement	parental values
experiential core	photo elicitation
first-generation college students	restricted speech code
habitus	salient
hidden curriculum	self-fulfilling prophecies
ideology	social mobility
Lads	sociolinguistics
language socialization	tracking
legitimation	vertical integration

REFERENCES

American Academy of Pediatrics, Section on Breastfeeding. 2012. "Breastfeeding and the Use of Human Milk" [Policy Statement]. *Pediatrics* 129: e827–e841.

Anyon, Jean. 1979. "Ideology and United States History Textbooks." *Harvard Educational Review* 49(3):361–386.

Anyon, Jean. 1981. "Social Class and School Knowledge." *Curriculum Inquiry* 11(1):3–42.

Armstrong, Elizabeth A. and Laura T. Hamilton. 2013. *Paying for the Party: How College Maintains Inequality.* Cambridge, MA: Harvard University Press.

Bernstein, Basil. 1971. *Class, Codes, and Control: Theoretical Studies towards a Sociology of Language*, Vol. 1. London: Routledge and Kegan Paul.

Bettie, Julie. 2003. *Women without Class: Girls, Race, and Identity.* Berkeley: University of California Press.

Bourdieu, Pierre. 1977. "Cultural Reproduction and Social Reproduction." Pp. 487–510 in *Power and Ideology in Education*, edited by Jerome Karabel and A. H. Halsey. Oxford, UK: Oxford University Press.

Bourdieu, Pierre. 1984. *Distinction: A Social Critique of the Judgment of Taste.* Cambridge, MA: Harvard University Press.

Bourdieu, Pierre and Jean-Claude Passeron. 1977 [1990]. *Reproduction in Education, Society, and Culture.* Translated by Richard Nice. Newbury Park, CA: Sage.

Bowles, Samuel and Herbert Gintis. 1976. *Schooling in Capitalist America: Educational Reform and the Contradictions of Economic Life.* New York: Basic Books.

Brantlinger, Ellen. 1993. *The Politics of Social Class in Secondary School: Views of Affluent and Impoverished Youth.* New York: Teachers College Press, Columbia University.

Brantlinger, Ellen. 2003. *Dividing Classes: How the Middle Class Negotiates and Rationalizes School Advantage.* New York: RoutlegeFalmer.

Bronfenbrenner, Urie. 1958. "Socialization and Social Class through Time and Space." Pp. 400–425 in *Readings in Social Psychology*, 3rd ed., edited by Eleanor E. Maccoby, Theodore M. Newcomb, and Eugene L. Hartley. New York: Holt, Rinehart & Winston.

Butsch, Richard. 1995. "Ralph, Fred, Archie, and Homer: Why Television Keeps Recreating the White Male Working-Class Buffoon." Pp. 403–412 in *Gender, Race, and Class in Media*, edited by Gail Dines and Jean M. Humez. Thousand Oaks, CA: Sage Publications.

Chafel, Judith A. 1997. "Children's Views of Social Inequality: A Review of Research and Implications for Teaching." *Educational Forum* 61(1):46–57.

Chase, Sarah A. 2008. *Perfectly Prep: Gender Extremes at a New England Prep School.* New York: Oxford University Press.

Clark-Ibáñez, Marisol. 2005. "Making Meaning of Ability Grouping in Two Urban Schools." *International Review of Modern Sociology* 31:57–79.

Cookson, Peter W., Jr. and Caroline Hodges Persell. 1985. *Preparing for Power: America's Elite Boarding Schools.* New York: Basic Books.

Eckert, Penelope. 1989. *Jocks and Burnouts: Social Categories and Identity in the High School.* New York: Teachers College Press, Columbia University.

Ehrenreich, Barbara. 1995. "The Silenced Majority: Why the Average Working Person Has Disappeared from American Media and Culture." Pp. 40–42 in *Gender, Race, and Class in Media*, edited by Gail Dines and Jean M. Humez. Thousand Oaks, CA: Sage Publications.

Granfield, Robert. 1991. "Faking It by Making It: Working-Class Students in an Elite Academic Environment." *Journal of Contemporary Ethnography* 20(3):331–351.

Hamilton, Laura and Elizabeth A. Armstrong. 2009. "Gendered Sexuality in Young Adulthood: Double Binds and Flawed Options." *Gender & Society* 23(5):589–616.

Hart, Betty and Todd R. Risley. 1995. *Meaningful Differences in the Everyday Experience of Young American Children*. Baltimore, MD: Paul H. Brookes Publishing Co.

Jensen, Barbara. 2012. *Reading Classes: On Culture and Classism in America*. Ithaca, NY: Cornell University Press.

Kefalas, Maria. 2003. *Working-Class Heroes: Protecting Home, Community, and Nation in a Chicago Neighborhood*. Berkeley: University of California Press.

Khan, Shamus. 2011. *Privilege: The Making of an Adolescent Elite at St. Paul's School*. Princeton, NJ: Princeton University Press.

Kohn, Melvin L. 1959. "Social Class and Parental Values." *American Journal of Sociology* 64(4):337–351.

Kohn, Melvin. 1963. "Social Class and Parent-Child Relationships: An Interpretation." *American Journal of Sociology* 68(4):471–480.

Lamont, Michèle. 1992. *Money, Morals, and Manners*. Chicago: University of Chicago Press.

Lamont, Michèle. 2002. *The Dignity of Working Men: Morality and the Boundaries of Race, Class, and Immigration*. Cambridge, MA: Harvard University Press.

Langston, Donna. 1993. "Who Am I Now?: The Politics of Identity." Pp. 60–72 in *Working-Class Women in the Academy: Laborers in the Knowledge Factory*, edited by Michelle M. Tokarczyk and Elizabeth A. Fay. Amherst: University of Massachusetts Press.

Lareau, Annette. 2003. *Unequal Childhoods: Class, Race, and Family Life*. Berkeley: University of California Press.

Leahy, Robert L. 1983. *The Child's Construction of Social Inequality*. New York: Academic Press.

Loewen, James W. 2007. *Lies My Teacher Told Me*. New York: Touchstone.

Lubrano, Alfred. 2005. *Limbo: Blue-Collar Roots, White-Collar Dreams*. Hoboken, NJ: Wiley Press.

McCrory Calarco, Jessica. 2011. "'I Need Help!' Social Class and Children's Help-Seeking in Elementary School." *American Sociological Review* 76(6):862–882.

Nenga, Sandi Kawecka. 2003. "Social Class and Structures of Feeling in Women's Childhood Memories of Clothing, Food and Leisure." *Journal of Contemporary Ethnography* 32:167–199.

Oakes Jeannie. 1985. *Keeping Track: How Schools Structure Inequality*. New Haven, CT: Yale University Press.

O'Guinn, Thomas C., Ronald J. Faber, Nadine J. J. Curias, and Kay Schmitt. 1989. "The Cultivation of Consumer Norms." *Advances in Consumer Research* 16:779–785.

Proweller, Amira. 1998. *Constructing Female Identities: Meaning Making in an Upper Middle Class Youth Culture*. Albany, NY: SUNY Press.

Pugh, Allison. 2009. *Longing and Belonging: Parents, Children, and Consumer Culture*. Berkeley: University of California Press.

Ramsey, Patricia G. 1991. "Young Children's Awareness and Understanding of Social Class Differences." *The Journal of Genetic Psychology: Research and Theory on Human Development* 152:71–82.

Ridge, Tess. 2002. *Childhood Poverty and Social Exclusion: From a Child's Perspective*. Bristol, UK: Policy Press.

Sacker, Amanda, Yvonne Kelly, Maria Iacovou, Mariko Cable, and Mel Bartley. 2013. "Breast Feeding and Intergenerational Social Mobility: What Are the Mechanisms?" *Archives of Disease in Childhood* 98(9):666–667.

Sennett, Richard and Jonathan Cobb. 1972. *The Hidden Injuries of Class*. New York: Vintage.

Stevens, Mitchell. 2007. *Creating a Class: College Admissions and the Education of Elites*. Cambridge, MA: Harvard University Press.

Stevens, Mitchell L., Elizabeth A. Armstrong, and Richard Arum. 2008. "Sieve, Incubator, Temple, Hub: Empirical and Theoretical Advances in the Sociology of Higher Education." *Annual Review of Sociology* 34:127–151.

Streib, Jessi. 2011. "Class Reproduction by Four Year Olds." *Qualitative Sociology* 34:337–352.

Stuber, Jenny M. 2005. "Asset and Liability?: The Importance of Context in the Occupational Experiences of Upwardly Mobile White Adults." *Sociological Forum* 20:139–166.

Stuber, Jenny M. 2011. *Inside the College Gates: How Class and Culture Matter in Higher Education*. Lanham, MD: Lexington Press.

Stuber, Jenny M., Joshua Klugman, and Caitlin Daniel. 2011. "Gender, Social Class, and Exclusion: Collegiate Peer Cultures and Social Reproduction." *Sociological Perspectives* 54: 431–451.

Taylor, Janet and Alex Fraser. 2003. *Eleven Plus: Life Chances and Family Income*. Melbourne, Australia: Brotherhood of St Laurence.

Weinger, Susan. 2000. "Economic Status: Middle Class and Poor Children's Views." *Children and Society* 14(2):135–146.

Wikeley, Felicity, Kate Bullock, Yolande Muschamp, and Tess Ridge. 2007. "Educational Relationships Outside School: Why Access Is Important." [Discussion Paper] York, UK: Joseph Rowntree Foundation.

Willis, Paul. 1977. *Learning to Labour: How Working Class Kids Get Working Class Jobs*. New York: Columbia University Press.

Yang, Hyeseung and Mary Beth Oliver. 2010. "Exploring the Effects of Television Viewing on Perceived Life Quality: A Combined Perspective of Material Value and Upward Social Comparison." *Mass Communication and Society* 13(2):118–138.

Zinn, Howard. 2005. *A People's History of the United States: 1492–Present*. New York: Harper Perennial Modern Classics.

Of Prejudice and Privilege: A Sociologist's Toolkit

"I'm not a racist, but. . . ." I have heard this phrase many times. You probably have, too. In my experience, this phrase is often followed by statements like "I would never date someone who isn't Hispanic," or "I don't get why there's a Black History Month, but no White History Month." Statements such as these sometimes raise suspicion among ordinary observers, sociologists, and other scholars who study race. Perhaps the fact that a person prefaces his or her statement in this way does, indeed, indicate underlying racial judgment or antipathy. But does that make them racist?

Terms like racist and racism are often used quite casually in our society. Many people deflect from themselves the label of "racist," as discussed above, and sometimes apply the label to others as a way to call their moral judgment into question. The two chapters that comprise this unit explore sociological approaches to prejudice, discrimination, and racism. The main goal of these two chapters is to answer this question: To what extent is racial inequality and racism alive and well in today's society? This question will be answered with a diverse array of evidence, including public opinion polls, scales and measures developed by researchers, audit studies, and legal cases. The goal of presenting this information is to provide insight into the tools that sociologists and other social scientists use to investigate their research question and draw empirically based conclusions about a variety of social issues.

A second goal in asking about race and racism in contemporary society is to further illustrate two key components of the sociological perspective. In the first chapter of this unit, racial inequality and racism are approached as social phenomena that occur at the micro-level: among individuals, in their consciousness and through their face-to-face interactions. From this perspective, racial inequality reflects the thoughts and actions of bigoted individuals. Logically, it also includes the assumption that racial inequality can be alleviated by changing the thoughts and actions of bigoted individuals. The second chapter in this unit, however, considers the possibility that racial inequality can persist, even if there are no bigoted racists to perpetuate it. It shifts our attention to the macro-level and explores the ways in which racial inequalities are perpetuated by policies and procedures that are embedded in our social intuitions and subtly woven through the ideologies and worldviews that govern our everyday experiences. Together, the chapters in this unit highlight the fact that any social phenomenon can best be understood by bringing together an understanding of dynamics at the micro-level—referred to in this text as "the player"—with those at the macro-level referred to as "the game."

Bigots, Cheats, and Unsportsmanlike Players

Understanding Inequality at the Micro-Level

A few summers ago, when a new colleague was hired at my university, I decided to extend my hospitality and offered to help her find a new place to live. After booking a set of appointments with an apartment broker and looking at a number of promising units in a neighborhood called Avondale, we were wrapping up the day at our final listing. Almost immediately upon being greeted by the apartment owner—a white male who appeared to be in his late 50s—he declared, "I can tell already you're not the type of person I'm looking for." Still standing in the front room of the apartment, we were immediately taken aback. What did he mean that my new colleague wasn't the "type of person" he was looking for?

To add intrigue to this story, it is necessary to know that the neighborhood in which we were apartment hunting is primarily inhabited by middle- and upper middle-class whites, and the new professor at my university was black. On the day that we went apartment hunting, she and I were dressed almost identically: casual summer dresses, jewelry, lightly embellished sandals. Both in our 30s at the time, she and I are also similar in build and had the same short bob haircut. The main difference between us is our skin color. Therefore, when the landlord interjected that she wasn't the type of person he was looking for, I had to ask myself: Is it because she's black? In any event, the apartment wasn't to her liking, and my new colleague found a lovely apartment in another neighborhood.

Approximately six months later, I wanted to downsize and was driving around the same neighborhood looking for a new apartment. When I spotted a promising location, I pulled over and called the number listed on the "For Rent" sign. When I asked about viewing the apartment the owner said, "Just come on over and get the keys; you can check it out on your own." I was surprised that he did not insist on being present during the tour and was comfortable handing the keys over to a stranger. The man on the phone added, "I can usually get an impression of someone right off the bat." He then gave me the address where I could pick the keys up, just a couple of blocks away. Imagine my surprise when I approached an all-too-familiar building, only to be greeted by the same man who had turned a cold shoulder to my colleague and me months earlier.

Although this may be a personal anecdote, these two interactions illustrate the process by which many people find a place to live. The route to finding a home usually begins with either a phone call or a face-to-face meeting with a stranger. So what did it mean that the man who immediately proclaimed my colleague wasn't the type of person he was looking for virtually rolled out the red carpet for me after a brief telephone conversation? What was it about her appearance and my voice that produced these two very different outcomes? Interactions like this happen every day—sometimes involving housing searches, other times involving job searches. In these exchanges, doors close and doors open, sometimes begging the question whether the outcome has been influenced by race—or gender, or sexuality, or religion.

The question that guides this chapter is: Are racial inequality and racism alive and well in today's society? In instances like the ones above, we may never know if the interaction was shaped by race or any other social identity. We may have a hunch but no hard evidence. In order to answer this question, we need to go above and beyond our personal experiences and look at the **empirical evidence**—evidence that is systematically collected and measured. The discussion of whether racism is alive and well centers on the *concepts* and *methods* used by social scientists. These concepts and methods highlight two unique perspectives: the micro- and macro-levels. The **micro-level** perspective focuses on the individual level. It assumes that social phenomena emerge from face-to-face interactions between individuals. In this book I use the metaphor of "the player" to illustrate the micro-level perspective. The macro-level perspective, in contrast, focuses on the structural level. It assumes that social phenomena emerge from and are structured by social policies, social institutions, and other patterns that transcend the individual. I use the metaphor of "the game" to illustrate the macro-level perspective.

While this chapter focuses primarily on understanding inequality at the micro-level, these are not isolated perspectives; indeed, the player (micro-) and the game (macro-) are intimately linked and mutually constituted. The next chapter explores the dynamics of social inequality at the macro-level. Although most of the examples used in this chapter focus on racial inequality, the same *perspective* and *methods* can be used to understand inequalities in terms of sex and gender, sexual orientation, disability, age, and other statuses. Occasionally, examples from these identities are highlighted to broaden the discussion.

RESEARCHING AND UNDERSTANDING INEQUALITY AT THE MICRO-LEVEL

In the last 150 years, the United States has come a long way in terms of social equality. Slavery was outlawed in the 1860s; in the 1950s, the U.S. Supreme Court case *Brown v. Board of Education* outlawed segregation; in the 1960s, civil rights legislation enacted protections for racial and ethnic minorities in housing, education, employment, and voting. Since the early 1900s, women have gained the right to vote, hold property in their own names, and initiate legal proceedings like divorce; they now represent nearly 60 percent of all college students and nearly half of all workers in the U.S. labor force. Legislative and judicial changes have extended *some* protections to gays and lesbians: while they now have the right to marry in 37 states, there is no federal law protecting people from discrimination based on sexual preference (or gender expression). Because of such changes, many people believe prejudice and discrimination are a thing of the past. Others, however, continue to see and experience injustices and closed doors on a daily basis. In my story about apartment hunting, for example, do *you* think the landlord closed the door to my colleague but opened it to me because of race? Adjudicating between these two perspectives on contemporary racial inequalities requires an understanding of sociological concepts and research techniques.

Public opinion polls are one method used by social scientists to understand the degree to which social inequality is alive and well. High-quality public opinion polls can gauge how Americans think about particular issues by using a **representative sample**—one that presents Americans as a whole in terms of gender, age, race and ethnicity, income and/or education, and geography. The Gallup organization and the General Social Survey routinely ask Americans questions about racial inequality, affirmative action, interracial marriage, homosexuality, and other social and political issues (e.g., gun control, immigration). Their findings indicate that how you interpret my apartment hunting experiences may depend on your own race. When asked whether racism against blacks is a problem in the United States, the Gallup organization found that respondents' opinions differ along racial lines. As indicated in Figure 10.1, whites are less likely to think that anti-black racism is a problem compared to blacks and Hispanics. Although the tendency to attribute social experiences to discrimination has declined among black Americans, a 2013 Gallup poll shows that 52 percent of blacks are still dissatisfied with "how blacks are treated in U.S. society." This number, though, has also declined from a high of 68 percent in 2007.

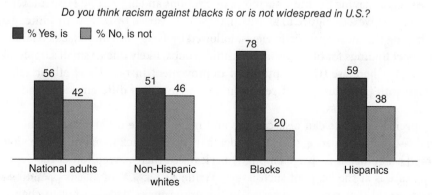

Figure 10.1 Gallup findings on racial attitudes.
(Source: USA Today/Gallup poll, June 5–July 6, 2008)

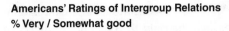

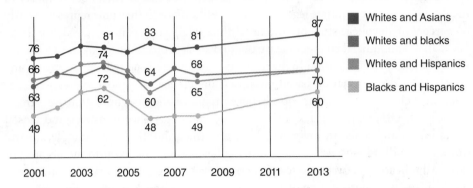

Americans' Ratings of Intergroup Relations
% Very / Somewhat good

Perceptions of Relations Between Groups, by Race and Ethnicity
% Very / Somewhat good

	Non-Hispanic whites	Blacks	Hispanics
	%	%	%
Whites and Asians	89	84	82
Whites and blacks	72	66	64
Whites and Hispanics	72	63	71
Blacks and Hispanics	56	76	64

Figure 10.2 Gallup findings on intergroup relations.
(Source: Gallup)

When considering how Americans feel about contemporary race relations, public opinion polls document detailed patterns. Americans as a whole have positive assessments of intergroup relations—although some groups are perceived as having better relations than others. Gallup data collected in 2013 suggest that Americans view whites and Asians as having the most harmonious relations and blacks and Hispanics having the least positive (see Figure 10.2). Again, these data varied by race, with whites generally having the most optimistic views, followed by Hispanics and blacks (Gallup did not report findings for other racial or ethnic groups, likely due to small sample sizes). Two themes here are (1) perceptions of improvement in racial and ethnic relations coupled with (2) enduring differences in how members of different racial and ethnic groups perceive the issue.

Specific incidents can also capture and magnify race differences on hot-button social issues. During 2014, several incidents involving black men and police violence showed a significant cleavage among Americans in their perception of the degree to which race is at the heart of such issues. While 64 percent of blacks polled by Pew Research said that race was a factor in the grand jury's decision not to charge the police officer in the Ferguson, Missouri, shooting of Michael Brown, only 16 percent of whites offered the same response. Virtually identical results were obtained by a Pew poll asking the same question about the strangling death of Eric Garner in Staten Island, New York.

PREJUDICE: THE ATTITUDINAL FOUNDATION OF RACIAL INEQUALITY

Understanding racism, sexism, and other forms of social inequality begins with a focus on the individual, or what academics sometimes call the micro-level. Focusing first on the micro-level allows insight into the real-life people and interactions that form the basis of our society. Social inequalities do not emerge out of thin air; rather, real people with real beliefs and behaviors give rise to social inequality. When looked at from the micro-level, prejudice forms the foundation of social inequality. **Prejudice** refers to negative attitudes toward an entire category of people. The idea that some groups are cheap or lazy or bad tippers or sexually perverted are prejudicial beliefs. Unlike stereotypes, which can be positive or negative, prejudices are usually negative judgments. As with stereotypes, many people form prejudices on the basis of incomplete or partial information. Their beliefs are learned and stem from negative portrayals in the media or stories passed down through the generations; they may also emerge from personal experiences, such as when a person attributes an interaction to someone's race, ethnicity, gender, or sexual orientation. Finally, prejudice is considered an *attitudinal* or *affective* indicator of racial inequality (or sexism, homophobia, etc.). In other words, it is a sentiment rather than an action or behavior.

Researchers have a number of tools for measuring prejudice. One of the first was the **Bogardus Social Distance Scale**, developed by Emory Bogardus way back in 1925. This scale was built on the assumption that the more prejudiced someone is, the more social distance that person wants to put between him- or herself and members of particular groups (racial, ethnic, religious, etc.). As illustrated in Figure 10.3, someone who would entirely exclude members of a particular group—say Irish or Koreans— from that's person's country is defined as more prejudiced than one who would allow

How would you feel about having members of the following groups:	Irish	Korean
As a relative by marriage	☐	☐
In my club as a personal friend	☐	☐
On my street as a neighbor	☐	☐
Working alongside me in my job	☐	☐
As citizens in my country	☐	☐
As visitors to my country	☐	☐
I'd exclude them from my country	☐	☐

Figure 10.3 Social Distance Scale example.
(Source: Bogardus 1933)

(a) Social Distance Scale

I would accept a[n] [minority category] as a...

1	2	3	4	5	6
family member by marriage.	close friend.	neighbor.	co-worker.	speaking acquaintance.	visitor to my country.	I would bar from my country.

(Less social distance / greater acceptance)   (Greater social distance / less acceptance)

(b)	1925	1946	1956	1966	1977	2001
Mean Score for All Categories:	2.14	2.14	2.08	1.92	1.93	1.44
Range of Averages:	2.85	2.57	1.75	1.55	1.38	0.87

(c) Mean Social Distance Score by Category, 2001

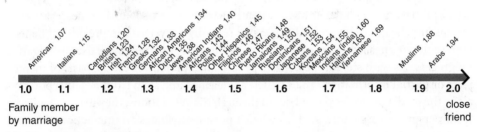

1.0	1.1	1.2	1.3	1.4	1.5	1.6	1.7	1.8	1.9	2.0

Family member by marriage

close friend

Figure 10.4 Social Distance Scale results.
(Source: Parrillo and Donoghue 2005)

him or her to enter the country, but only as a visitor. A person who would allow an Irish or Korean person to marry into his or her own family is considered the least prejudiced, as that relationship represents a minimum level of social distance.

Research using the Bogardus Social Distance Scale reveals some interesting results (see Figure 10.4). Over time, there has been a reduction in the mean social distance score; this suggests a steady erosion in feelings of prejudice since the early 1900s (Parrillo and Donoghue 2005; Weaver 2008). Second, the most recent research shows that Americans have the highest levels of prejudice toward Arabs and Muslims: with a score of 1.94, the average American would feel comfortable having an Arab or Muslim person in their social club or neighborhood but stop short of welcoming that person into their own family. Some caution is needed in interpreting these results, however, since this study was conducted soon after the 9/11 attacks. Finally, research on prejudice also indicates that females are generally more tolerant and less prejudiced than males. This is consistent with research showing that women generally have more liberal social views than men.

Corroborating the finding of declining levels of prejudice are data on interracial marriages. Public opinion polls show that Americans' attitudes toward interracial marriages have changed considerably over time. When asked in 1958 whether they approved or disapproved of marriage between blacks and whites, only 4 percent of respondents answered that they approved. With consistent but gradual increases over time, Gallup data report that as of 2011, 86 percent of the population approved of interracial marriages. Again, though, the race of the respondents matters, with approval rates of 96 percent among blacks and 84 percent among whites (data was not provided for other races). These attitudes, moreover, are supported by changing behaviors: since the early 1970s, there has been a fivefold increase in the rate of interracial marriages, with Hispanics and Latinos having the highest incidence.

Think about Bogardus Social Distance Scale: What if people lie, or provide only the most politically correct responses? What if they hold beliefs they are not consciously aware of and cannot articulate? To overcome potential limitations of self-reported data, psychologists at Harvard University developed the Implicit Association Test. The **Implicit Association Test** (IAT) is designed to measure people's implicit or underlying beliefs; it is especially geared toward minimizing **social desirability bias**—the tendency of respondents to provide responses they believe will meet with social or cultural approval. Since 1998, researchers have designed tests to tap into underlying racial attitudes, as well as prejudices, in the realm of religion, gender, age, and body type (*fat-ism*). Rather than asking people directly about their attitudes or beliefs about certain groups, the test asks respondents to make split-second associations between images and words flashing on a computer screen. First, respondents see a series of black faces and white faces and are asked to hit keys labeling them. Then, they are shown a series of positive and negative words—like "glorious" and "wonderful" and "nasty" and "bad"—and are asked to categorize them. After additional exercises, where these words and images are eventually brought together, the respondent receives results indicating he or she has, perhaps, a "slight preference for European Americans" (whites), or a "strong preference for African Americans."

If you take the IAT online—which you should—it may be hard to believe that this rapid-fire activity accurately taps into underlying associations or prejudices. Some critics argue that the test may actually measure cultural knowledge or the cognitive ability to rapidly switch between words and images. Despite these criticisms, it endures as one tool for measuring prejudice.

Working from the assumption that snap judgments can reveal underlying prejudice, some researchers have investigated what this means for racial bias in professional athletics. Are basketball referees prejudiced? Do white referees make

Do you have any unconscious biases? The Implicit Association Test is designed to measure a person's implicit (underlying) attitudes toward various social groups.

more foul calls against black players and do black referees make a disproportionate number of calls against white players? In a paper examining this question, Joseph Price and Justin Wolfers found that "more personal fouls are awarded against players when they are officiated by an opposite-race officiating crew than when they are officiated by an own-race refereeing crew" in NBA (National Basketball Association) games (2010:1859). When done carefully, this kind of research can provide powerful insights. The researchers, however, need to know a lot about basketball and must control for numerous factors in their analyses. These authors, for example, statistically accounted for the fact that centers tend to draw more fouls—and are disproportionately white; that veteran players and All-Stars tend to draw foul calls at different rates than rookies and nonstars; and that some players are substituted into games specifically to commit fouls. After taking these and other factors into account, the authors concluded that racial biases in officiating are large enough to "affect the outcome of an appreciable number of games" (p. 1859). Not surprisingly, the NBA disputes these claims, as I am sure would many sports fans. This careful research, however, suggests that snap racial judgments—rather than conscious racial bias—may influence outcomes in surprising social settings.

Although contact with individuals and groups from different backgrounds has been shown to erode our prejudices, there is something about the nature of prejudice that makes it relatively resistant to change. One psychological mechanism that keeps our prejudices in place is confirmation bias (discussed in Chapter 1). **Confirmation bias** is the tendency for people to pay attention to or retain information that supports (*confirms*) their existing beliefs (and ignore information that contradicts). Say, for example, a server takes a new job at The Burger Factory, a casual dining spot. On her first day of training, she observes a fellow server approach the hostess stand and say, "Please, please don't seat any more black people in my section. I need to make rent this week and they are the worst tippers." I use this example because students often bring it up in my own class discussions. This comment sticks in the new server's mind, and over time she begins to hold this same impression. Due to confirmation bias the server notices every instance where she receives a "bad tip" from a black table but fails to notice when they provide good or average tips. Moreover, when she receives a bad tip from a white party, she does not attribute it to race. Prejudices, then, stay firmly rooted in our brains because they form a simplified mental schema that is resistant to new or complicated information.

While confirmation bias provides one explanation for why prejudices remain in place, it cannot explain how or why people come to hold prejudicial beliefs in the first place. One psychological theory is that some people come to hold prejudicial beliefs because of their personality types. As a result of particularly harsh childhood discipline, for example, some people develop an **authoritarian personality** type; feelings of prejudice, then, are part of a broader personality type characterized by a rigid set of beliefs, conventional values, and intolerance for those who deviate from the norm. **Scapegoating theory** takes this idea one step further, speculating that people develop prejudicial beliefs as a way of explaining or alleviating their own failures. Blaming

Humorously depicted on *The Office*, diversity seminars are designed to increase cross-cultural familiarity and reduce prejudices at the micro-level.

immigrants for coming into the country illegally, using social services they're not entitled to, and taking all of the jobs may be the prejudicial reaction of someone who feels like a victim or a failure. A similar perspective is used by sociologists, who see prejudice as a social phenomenon that allows one group to maintain a position of superiority over another. This is called **exploitation theory**: prejudices are created and exploited as a justification for limiting access or opportunities to groups who don't deserve them. Rather than a belief that stems from an individual's mind, to explain his or her situation, this perspective sees prejudice as a structural mechanism that allows one group to dominate or exploit another group (whites over nonwhites, Christians over Muslims, etc.).

Because it is generally accepted that these belief systems form the foundation of more harmful behaviors, changing people's attitudes is commonly used as a way to reduce prejudice This perspective reflects the **contact hypothesis**: the notion that intergroup contact, or greater familiarity with diverse individuals, helps erode prejudicial beliefs. Well-intentioned efforts on college campuses, in workplaces, churches, and other settings encourage people to talk about prejudice and learn about diverse groups in a safe setting. This is called **diversity training**. Michael Scott, the lead character on the television sitcom *The Office*, is the humorous "poster child" for this type of effort. In the iconic "Diversity Day" episode, Michael Scott tries to bring greater racial tolerance to the workplace—after having been accused of racial insensitivity—by having his colleagues guess the name of the ethnic group written on the card fixed to their foreheads by asking their colleagues questions about that group, in the style of "20 questions." Despite the intended humor, the episode echoes the assumption that if we can simply realize the ridiculousness of our prejudices, while also increasing our familiarity with diverse people, we will go a long way toward reducing social inequality. While this approach has merit, it does little to address the macro-level, or structural, sources of social inequality.

TURNING ATTITUDES INTO ACTION: DISCRIMINATION

While prejudice forms the foundation of inequalities generated at the micro-level, it becomes insidious and damaging when these attitudes are translated into action. On an everyday level, stereotypes may manifest as microaggressions. **Microaggressions** are those small everyday interactions—many of them not even conscious or intentional—which convey derogatory or negative messages to members of a marginalized group. With respect to gender, this may be as seemingly minor as assuming that a woman with a stethoscope is a nurse rather than a doctor, or referring to a female leader as "bossy" rather than "assertive." Similarly, a blind person may feel annoyed and aggrieved by a person who tries to be helpful by speaking to them in a louder voice (when it is their sight that is impaired, not their hearing); an Asian American, born and raised in the United States, may not appreciate the praise when complimented for speaking "good English." Although such comments are not illegal, they can aggregate over time and convey the message that some groups occupy a privileged position, while others are marginalized and suspect. Microaggressions, then, provide a window into how deeply embedded beliefs about superiority and inferiority and normality and deviance manifest in everyday interactions.

Taking these beliefs to a more concrete level, **discrimination** refers to the unfair treatment of people in various categories, whereby some people are given opportunities and others are denied them *because of* their race (or gender, sexual orientation, age, disability, etc.). Discrimination is not mere bigotry or maltreatment. In a legal sense, discrimination occurs when otherwise qualified persons are excluded from opportunities that are socially desirable and consequential, such as pursuing an education, living where you want, getting a job, or even paying a fair price for a car. For the moment, discrimination can be viewed as a micro-level source of social inequality, namely in that it emerges from individual, face-to-face interactions. As I show later, individual actions can aggregate and take on a patterned quality; when they do, they become a macro-level phenomenon.

Detecting discrimination through audit studies

Researchers have a number of tools for documenting discrimination. Consider Table 10.1, drawn from a study by Ian Ayres and Peter Siegelman (1995). Looking at the markup paid when buying a car, could one conclude that black men and women are victims of discrimination?

Table 10.1 shows that black men and women pay a higher markup than whites when purchasing a new car. While some might use this data to conclude that discrimination is alive and well, this table poses more questions than answers. For example, maybe black and white buyers purchase different cars, with different profit margins, so that dealers are able to give a better discount to some buyers than others. Maybe white buyers have just learned to negotiate more effectively. What about the possibility that black buyers rely on dealer financing, which creates an incentive for sellers to mark up the price? If any of these conditions were true, we would be unable to conclude that racial discrimination is at the heart of these numbers, as the real explanation for the different prices paid would lie elsewhere.

Because it is difficult to know with certainty that race is the reason for different outcomes, scientists have developed specialized research methods. One tool is the **audit study**—a technique considered far more reliable that individual perceptions

Table 10.1 **Discrimination in Car Buying (Ayres and Siegelman 1995)**

Purchasers	Initial Offer	Final Offer	Average Markup
White males	$1,019	$564	5.18%
White females	$1,127	$656	6.04%
Black males	$1,954	$1,665	14.61%
Black females	$1,337	$975	7.2%

when considering the prevalence of discrimination. Ayres and Siegelman (1995) used this technique in their study of discrimination in the car-buying market. Audit studies use a quasi-experimental design to test the researchers' hypothesis. Take this hypothesis: black people experience more discrimination when buying a car than white people. Researchers then assemble a pool of test subjects, known as *testers* or *auditors*, and make sure that they resemble one another on virtually every relevant criterion other than race. They do this to control for other possible explanations for their findings. Ayres and Siegelman controlled for all of the factors mentioned above in their study and also made sure that testers dressed the same when they set out for the dealership. If black auditors end up paying a higher price than white auditors, the researchers can conclude that race is the likely reason, rather than some other factor. In addition to being able to control for a wide array of factors, audit studies get their strength from the fact that they use hundreds if not thousands of repeated observations. Ayres and Siegelman, for example, based their findings on more than 300 observations (negotiations). Also called *field experiments* (because they take place out in the field, rather than in a laboratory), audit studies are used by sociologists, psychologists, and economists; they can be applied to racial discrimination, as well as discrimination based on gender, age, and other characteristics.

As part of an undergraduate course in sociology at the University of Pennsylvania, Douglas Massey and Garvey Lundy (2001) used their students as testers to see whether some races face more discrimination than others when it comes to renting an apartment. Because a phone call is a common first step when apartment hunting, the authors had their testers call 79 separate agents to inquire about advertised units (large managed complexes and independent owners). Yet rather than simply test whether racial discrimination exists, the authors wanted to find out if social class matters as well. Accordingly, some students called using "Black English Vernacular" and others used "Black Accented English." The authors hypothesized that "when an African-American speaks Standard English with a black pronunciation of certain words (BAE), listeners infer that the speaker is black but of middle-class origins, whereas the combination of nonstandard grammar with a black accent (BEV) signals lower-class origins" (p. 456). Unfortunately, the authors were only able to test middle-class white English because the students enrolled in this class spoke with no accents or dialects associated with the lower classes. After making a total of 474 calls, the authors found evidence of racial—and class—discrimination (see Figure 10.5): white callers were most likely to be told an apartment was available (68 percent), followed by middle-class black callers (60 percent), and finally lower-income black callers (41 percent).

To ensure the rigor of their research, the authors controlled for a number of factors. For example, testers were trained with a specific script, giving them relatively uniform identities and instructions about the kind of apartment they were seeking. The testers all had a maximum budget of $800, held similar jobs (billing at a hospital), with similar incomes ($25,000–$30,000) and were 25, single, and without children. Although there is no way of knowing whether the person answering the phone could tell the race of the tester, it is clear that some accents were more successful than others

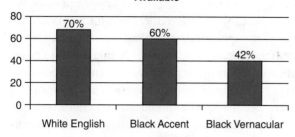

Figure 10.5 Discrimination in Apartment Rentals (Source: Massey and Lundy 2001)

when requesting information about an apartment. By making sure that the primary way these renters differed was the racial inflection of their voices, these authors concluded that race and class discrimination do exist in rental housing—and that it can be triggered simply by the sound of one's voice.

So what about employment—does race influence the likelihood of a qualified person getting a job? A team of sociologists explored this question with an **in-person audit study**—one where testers physically interacted with potential employers (Pager, Western, and Bonikowski 2009). To isolate the effect of race in employment, the authors selected testers who were clean-cut and well-spoken and matched in terms of age, height, and physical attractiveness, as well as "verbal skills [and] interactional styles (level of eye contact, demeanor, and verbosity)" (p. 781). If they were not already matched on other relevant characteristics, the research team made sure the applicants' résumés did not differ in educational attainment (and type of high school attended), work history, and other traits that might disqualify them. To ensure this level of rigor, the authors interviewed more than 300 applicants and selected the 10 who best fit their criteria.

After training applicants, having them dress in similar attire, and sending them out to apply for 340 entry-level jobs (restaurants, retail sales, warehouse workers, telemarketers, customer service, delivery drivers) in New York City, the authors found that 31 percent of white applicants, 25 percent of Latino (English-speaking, no accent), but only 15 percent of black applicants received a callback after submitting applications. According to the authors, "these results indicate that, relative to equally qualified blacks, employers significantly prefer white and Latino job applicants." The consequence is that "a black applicant has to search twice as long as an equally qualified white applicant before receiving a callback or job offer from an employer" (Pager et al. 2009:785).

Yet even when minority applicants were called back, the authors found, they experienced another subtle form of discrimination. In **race-coded job channeling**, minority candidates were given the opportunity to interview for a lesser position than the one to which they initially applied. When Joe, a black tester, told the hiring manager of a Japanese restaurant that he was there to apply for the waiter position, she told him no such positions were available and that the job advertisement contained a mistake. "She said all she had available was a busboy position," Joe recounted to the authors; he went ahead and applied for the busboy position. Later that day, Kevin, his white test partner, was hired on the spot for the server position (Pager et al. 2009:790). In fact, in another instance of race-coded job channeling, white applicants were occasionally *upgraded* in terms of job opportunities; given interviews for line cooks instead of prep cooks, for example, or office supervisor rather than receptionist.

In her earlier work, Devah Pager (2003) was curious about whether having a criminal record would make white applicants less appealing to potential employers. Using pairs of white and black testers, matched again in terms of physical appearance and interactional style, as well as relevant occupational and educational characteristics, Pager examined whether identifying potential applicants as having allegedly committed drug-related felonies might alter patterns of racial discrimination in hiring. Based on 350 cases, with testers being paired and sent to employers advertising entry-level jobs in the city of Milwaukee, Pager uncovered some surprising results (see Figure 10.6).

The fact that white applicants with a criminal record were more likely to receive a call back than black applicants without a criminal record speaks loudly of the racial attitudes of the employers in this study. Moreover, these racial attitudes suggest serious implications for the perpetuating of racial inequality. As Pager writes: "In our frenzy of locking people up, our 'crime control' policies may in fact exacerbate the very conditions that lead to crime in the first place," leaving black men with a criminal record "with few viable alternatives" to get their lives back on track (Pager, 2003:961).

What's in a name? Have you ever wondered whether your name or the names you give your children (if you have any) may affect life chances, like the ability to get a job or live in a desired location? Two economists—Marianne Bertrand and Sendhil Mullainathan (2004)—explored this question, looking specifically at white- and black-"sounding names." To so do, they used a **correspondence-based audit study**—one using only résumés sent by mail, thereby reducing the human element of "tester effects." To conduct their study, the authors first needed to define what they meant by black- and white-"sounding names." They did so by examining birth certificates from children born in Massachusetts from 1974 through 1979, looking for names that were frequent for one race but rare for the other. After assembling a list of racially distinct

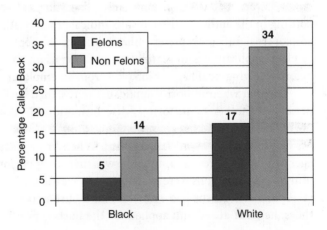

Figure 10.6 Discrimination in Employment.
(Source: Pager 2003)

names, the authors gave the list to a set of residents in the city of Chicago and asked them to assess whether each name belongs to a white or black person. If the respondent thought that a name could be either, that name was disqualified. Next, the authors created a bank of corresponding résumés. Résumés were matched but not made identical in terms of home address, schools attended, academic performance, job experience (server at Chili's versus server at Applebee's, for example), and other factors, including volunteer experience and foreign-language skill. The authors then sent 5,000 well-matched resumes to 1,300 separate employers.

The selected names and callback rates are shown in Figure 10.7. Results show that résumés with white-sounding names were 50 percent more likely than those with black-sounding names to receive callbacks from employers (about 10 percent versus 6.5 percent). On a practical level, this means that in order to get a callback, black applicants need to send out 15 résumés for every 10 résumés sent out by a white applicant. In a tight job market, these data suggest, black applicants have to work harder than similarly qualified white applicants to find employment.

So what are the practical implications of research like this? What are real-life people supposed to do with this information? Parents cannot choose the race of their baby, but they can choose their child's name. Do these results suggest that minority parents can and should protect their children from discrimination by giving them a "white-sounding" name? What do you think potential parents should do with this information?

When considering the usefulness of audit studies, it is worth asking why audit studies focus mainly on whites and blacks—and occasionally Hispanics—with relatively little consideration to other racial groups. Unfortunately, audit studies do not yet represent the racial and ethnic diversity that exists in the United States. One reason is

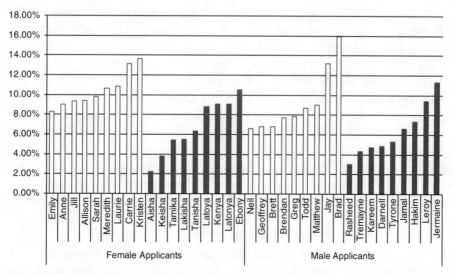

Figure 10.7 Percent receiving a callback.
(Source: Bertrand and Mullainathan 2004)

statistical: to achieve robust results, each test scenario needs to be run many, many times. In the United States, where Asian and Arab Americans comprise a small portion of the population (4 percent and 1 percent, respectively), it is difficult to obtain appropriate testers to participate in the study, and it may also be implausible that an employer or apartment rental agent would suddenly be deluged with Asian and Arab applicants. Another reason that Hispanics and Asians have not been studied as extensively as black applicants is that black applicants are more likely to be legal residents of the United States and native English speakers. If an audit study uncovered that Hispanic or Asian applicants in San Diego were less likely to get a callback from a job interview than white applicants, it would be difficult to disentangle whether racism or questions about their language or legal status were at the root. Finally, the categories "Asian" and "Hispanic" represent diverse cultural groups. In some areas of the country—like the West Coast—Chinese Americans are well established; although they faced plenty of discrimination in the past, it is likely that they face less discrimination today than new immigrants from Laos or Vietnam. Similar dynamics may play out in South Florida, where Cubans are well established and historically have held middle-class positions, while Dominicans, Mexicans, and Central Americans bring different cultural, educational, and legal backgrounds to the labor market. In the future perhaps researchers will find ways to disentangle these many complicated factors so that they can better illuminate issues of racial and ethnic discrimination in the United States.

Thinking about questions of discrimination in contemporary society, audit studies show persistent racial inequalities in housing, employment, and the consumer marketplace. Audit studies, however, are not perfect. For one, they typically capture dynamics taking place within a particular city or region. It is difficult to know whether the car-buying market of Chicago or the housing market of Philadelphia or the job markets of New York or Milwaukee are typical. Would substantially different results emerge had these studies taken place in Birmingham, Alabama, Missoula, Montana, or Tempe, Arizona? Another limitation of audit studies is that researchers cannot control every possible factor. In particular, they cannot control for who answers the phone at the apartment complex, who receives the résumé at the worksite, or which sales agent first approaches the customer on the car lot. There are, then, unknown interactions between the race and gender of the tester and whomever they encounter in the field. These unknown factors may bias results. That said, audit studies probably *underestimate* the actual incidence of discrimination. The real world is not a controlled experiment; in the real world, car buyers and job applicants do not dress the same, talk the same, or come in with the same employment experiences or credit histories. The factors that are controlled for in the experimental context are likely to give an advantage to whites in the real world, thereby increasing racial disparities in these settings.

Exploring Internationally: Prejudice and Discrimination Abroad

Racial inequality and racism are such fundamental features of American history that many students raised in the United States may wonder whether these problems are unique to their society or whether other societies deal with similar issues. While most of Europe lacks the history of slavery and immigration that is central to the racial and ethnic diversity of the United States, increasingly many European countries struggle with how to incorporate diverse others. Today, the percentage of foreign-born people living in European countries ranges from less than 5 percent to more than 15 percent (13 percent of those living in the United States are foreign born). Germany has historically had a large population of Turkish immigrants, many of whom initially arrived in the 1960s through a guest-worker program; in recent decades they have received refugees fleeing ethnic conflict in Bosnia. Nordic countries like Sweden and Norway have also allowed refugee resettlements from Iraq and Bosnia. France and Spain have recently received immigrants—both legal and undocumented—from a variety of African countries. Throughout Europe, the quasi-nomadic Roma people—also known by the pejorative term "Gypsies"—have experienced long-standing stigma. A 2012 "Eurobarometer" report from the European Commission found that 56 percent of Europeans believe that discrimination based on ethnicity is widespread and that 75 percent agree that the Roma people, in particular, experience discrimination. Yet perceptions of discrimination vary across the Continent: they are highest in France and Sweden (about 75 percent) and lowest in former Soviet republics like Latvia and Lithuania (about 20 percent).

Throughout Europe, racial and ethnic inequalities resemble those in the United States, with minority groups having less education, lower wages, and less political representation. Self-segregation into ethnic enclaves and exclusion by natives are common. Although these groups occupy a lower position in the social hierarchy than native-born people, their differences are defined as primarily cultural in nature (attributable to ethnic or racial differences), rather than *racial*, per se. Immigrant groups are sometimes seen as cultural outsiders, threatening to tradition, and unwilling or unable to assimilate. During periods of economic recession, immigrants are also seen as taking jobs and threatening the economic well-being of the native born. Within this context, riots have periodically erupted in France, with African immigrants—many of whom are Muslim—feeling excluded from French society. Tensions have also emerged in Nordic countries, most notably in the mass shooting at a Norwegian summer camp, where the shooter Anders Behring Breivik explained his actions as an effort to gain attention for his socially conservative, anti-Muslim views. Elsewhere in Europe, nationalist political parties, including Neo-Nazi parties, have gained strength, promising tighter restrictions on immigration and a return to more "traditional" policies, including fewer freedoms for gays and lesbians. In France, Jean-Marie Le Pen of the National Front party won a stunning symbolic victory, coming in second in the 2002 presidential election. Declaring himself a defender of French traditions, his comments about Jews and Muslims have, nevertheless, caused him to be convicted of the crime of "inciting racial hatred."

A common theme in diverse societies is the existence of tension and inequality along racial or ethnic lines. Even seemingly homogeneous societies have their tensions. In Japan, immigrant groups from Korea (the Zainichi) who have been in Japan for generations experience stigma and lower social outcomes than native Japanese.

There are few truly **pluralistic societies** across the globe—those where diverse groups experience relatively equal rights, political representation, and economic and social outcomes. Instead, diverse societies struggle with the issue of **assimilation**: the notion that newcomers should adopt and adhere to the traditions of the long-standing majority. Unfortunately, this belief system often results in exclusion and marginalization for newcomers, many of whom want to hang onto their own cultural traditions *while* learning the language and culture of the majority. The United States, then, is not unique in terms of contemporary struggles with racial and ethnic discrimination—even if its history of racial inequality is more checkered and deeply entrenched.

Detecting and Dealing with Discrimination through the Legal System

When a business posts a sign declaring "We reserve the right to refuse anyone service," does that mean that business can deny someone service based on race or religion? If my landlord wished not to rent to a black tenant, does he have that right? What if he chose not to allow gays or lesbians to rent in his buildings? This section answers these questions by focusing on how claims of discrimination are adjudicated within the legal system.

Court rulings and legal statutes provide a window into enduring forms of racism, sexism, and other forms of inequality. Because of legislation emerging from the civil rights movement of the 1960s, many forms of discrimination are illegal in the United States. Based on centuries of documented and systematic discrimination, the **Civil Rights Act of 1964** created a set of protected classes of persons, giving them legal protection in specific settings. This landmark federal law, signed by President Lyndon Baines Johnson, outlawed discrimination against racial, ethnic, national, and religious minorities and women, namely in voting, education, the workplace, and public accommodations (restaurants, hotels, theaters, malls, etc.). It is, therefore, illegal to refuse to hire someone or deny housing to them based on their race, ethnicity, religion, or gender if they are otherwise qualified. One group not included in this federal civil rights legislation is gays, lesbians, transgender people, or anyone who would be considered a sexual minority.

Because sexual orientation and gender identity are not included in federal civil rights legislation, there is no federal protection for sexual minorities. Therefore, in many states it is not illegal to deny employment, housing, or service to members of this group. A school district in Florida, for example, can fire a teacher for being gay, just as an apartment owner in Idaho can evict a renter if he or she is transgender. Individual states, cities, and municipal districts, however, have passed their own civil rights statutes. Although these numbers change from time to time, there are presently 29 states that provide no legal protection in housing based on sexual orientation or gender identity, along with 19 states that provide no such protections in employment.

While the rights of same-sex couples to marry legally have been increasing over the years—gays and lesbians can now marry in 37 states—it is remarkable that the sexual activities of gay men and lesbians were criminalized in many states up until 2003. While being gay was not itself a crime, *sodomy* (sex acts not involving both penis and vagina) was. In 2003, however, the U.S. Supreme Court overturned these laws in the case ***Lawrence v. Texas***. In this case, the Court declared that adults have the right to privacy when it comes to consensual sexual activities, as protected by the due process clause of the Fourteenth Amendment. While this court ruling loosened the sexual restrictions on anyone participating in oral or anal sex—regardless of sexual orientation—it was especially considered a victory for gays and lesbians, the original targets of these anti-sodomy laws. Writing for the majority, Justice Anthony Kennedy said: "The petitioners [Lawrence and Garner] are entitled to respect for their private lives. The State cannot demean their existence or control their destiny by making their private sexual conduct a crime."

Finally, in some of the most heinous crimes of racism or homophobia, perpetrators can receive enhanced penalties if convicted of a hate crime. A **hate crime** (also called a *bias crime*) is one where the perpetrator is motivated not by mere malice but where the perpetrator targets a victim because of their membership (real or perceived) in a particular social group. The crime itself usually involves harassment, injury, assault, or murder. Because research suggests that victims of these crimes experience higher levels of post-traumatic stress and because the perpetrators are motivated by hatred, criminal justice and civil rights authorities believe they warrant harsher penalties. To determine whether a crime is a hate crime, investigators must explore the identities and backgrounds of the perpetrators as well as comments made during the commission of the crime or evidence left behind. Kidnapping and branding a victim with a swastika or writing "white power" and "KKK" on a body after an assault would be considered adequate evidence. In such instances, if the perpetrators were found guilty, they would receive harsher sentences than they would for "simple" kidnapping or assault.

In 2009 the U.S. federal government passed the **Matthew Shepard and James Byrd Jr. Hate Crimes Prevention Act**. Named after two high-profile hate-crime victims, this is the first federal law to provide enhanced prosecution for crimes motivated by race, ethnicity, national origin, religion, sexual orientation, gender identity (including transgender persons), and disability. Matthew Shepard was a gay college student who was tortured and murdered in Laramie, Wyoming, in 1998, the same year that James Byrd, a black man, was dragged along a dirt road from the back of a truck and eventually decapitated by white supremacists near Jasper, Texas. Neither case was prosecuted as a hate crime, since no such legislation existed in those states at the time. FBI statistics from 2011 indicate that 21 percent of hate crimes were motivated by sexual orientation, while 47 percent were motivated by race.

Returning to the issue of discrimination, imagine you and a co-worker were both interviewed for a promotion; although you thought her job performance was subpar, she received the promotion. If you suspected that you were denied a promotion due to your gender, age, or race, what should you do? The **Equal Opportunity Employment Commission** (EEOC) is a federal agency charged with enforcing civil rights laws and investigating claims of workplace discrimination. Each year, the Commission receives nearly 100,000 complaints—about one-third based on claims of gender discrimination and another third alleging discrimination based on race or ethnicity. Based on its investigations, the Commission ultimately dismisses more than 60 percent of initial complaints. The fact that so many cases are found to be without merit suggests two possibilities: one, many people are sensitive to the perception of discrimination; and/or two, proving discrimination is difficult. Of the complaints found to have merit, the vast majority is settled out of court; only a small proportion goes to trial. Between 2000 and 2012, the number of suits resulting in court trial ranged from 122 to 388 annually. Most settlements, whether in or out of court, usually result in monetary compensation and restoration of employment if the finding is in favor of the complainant.

When it is found that individual complaints form a larger pattern of discrimination, these cases may become a class-action lawsuit. In a **class-action lawsuit**, a group of people bring a case to trial on the basis that they represent a broader *class* of people who have experienced a similar fate. Rather than an individual bigot who doesn't want to hire minorities or women, the aggregation of cases indicates a systematic pattern of discrimination within an organization. It is in this way that individual experiences of discrimination at the micro-level aggregate into a broader pattern of experiences that comprise the macro-level.

If all of this sounds like technical terminology or a set of abstract claims by disgruntled employees elsewhere, rest assured that there have been some high-profile cases dealing with discrimination that relate to many college students' lives. In 2005, retailer Abercrombie & Fitch reached an out-of-court settlement amounting to $40 million in a class-action lawsuit alleging a systematic practice of failing to hire women and minorities, of placing them in low-visibility positions, and firing them without cause. The lead plaintiff in *Gonzalez v. Abercrombie & Fitch*, Eduardo Gonzalez—then a student at Stanford University—said that the manager encouraged him to apply for a job in the stockroom. "It was like they're pushing me to the only nonvisible jobs, they don't want me to be seen in public," Mr. Gonzalez said. "And it was weird: all the store's posters were white, blond-haired, blue-eyed." As it turns out, Mr. Gonzalez was not alone in his experience; ultimately, 10,000 individuals signed onto the class-action suit.

But doesn't a business have the right to hire whom it wants in order to promote its brand? Abercrombie & Fitch thought so. In their defense, they maintained that they had the right to hire in accordance with the "A&F Look," which they described as "classic American." In practice, this meant that their stores and advertisements were populated primarily by white, athletic, blond, blue-eyed individuals. Yet their legal shortcoming was that the term "classic American" means different things to different people. Quoted in a *New York Times* profile on the case (Greenhouse 2003), a plaintiff named Juan Carlos Gomez-Montejano took issue with Abercrombie's narrow definition: "It disgusted me because my family name has been on this continent for centuries, and they have the audacity to say I'm not American enough." In the end, the arbitrators sided with Gomez-Montejano. In his comments, the EEOC's general counsel, Eric Dreiband, stated: "The retail industry and other industries need to know that businesses cannot discriminate against individuals under the auspice of a marketing strategy or a particular 'look.' Race and sex discrimination in employment are unlawful, and the EEOC will continue to aggressively pursue employers who choose to

Failing to demonstrate its "all-American" brand identity, Abercrombie & Fitch settled a lawsuit alleging discrimination against racial and ethnic minorities.

Arguing that a defined image is embedded in their brand, Hooters has successfully defended their right to hire only slim and busty women as servers.

engage in such practices" (USA Today 2004). In the consent decree, plaintiffs were awarded settlements ranging from a few hundred to a few thousand dollars, and A&F was ordered to institute a range of policies and programs to promote diversity among its workforce and to prevent future instances of discrimination.

In more recent years, A&F has continued to find itself in legal hot water, with two cases alleging religious discrimination for refusing to hire Muslim applicants who wore headscarves. In a 2010 suit, the plaintiff said: "This was the first job I ever applied for, and I was excited about the idea of working for Abercrombie & Fitch. I was into fashion, and wore skinny jeans and imported scarves that matched my outfits. The interview crushed me because I never imagined anyone in the Bay Area would reject me because of my head scarf" (EEOC 2010). In 2011 it settled a case initiated by Samantha Elauf, who alleged that Abercrombie refused to make an exception to its dress code to accommodate her religious practices, though it had previously allowed a Jewish employee to wear a yarmulke. The company, moreover, could not prove that allowing an employee to wear a headscarf would damage its bottom line or compromise "the look." Elauf was awarded a $20,000 settlement.

But what about Hooters—you know, the chicken-wing restaurant with the signature orange short-shorts and owl-embellished tank tops? If Abercrombie can't hire a staff with a particular look, why can Hooters hire only female waitresses with a particular look? In fact, every so often an isolated male plaintiff initiates a complaint against Hooters on these grounds. Each time such a case has emerged, judges have ruled on behalf of Hooters, identifying the BFOQ exception to rules on workplace discrimination. **BFOQ** stands for *bona fide occupational qualification*—a legal concept that applies in cases where the essence of the business operation and its unique brand would be compromised if it did *not* engage in discrimination. Because Hooters clearly proclaims its brand identity with its name and logo, it is on solid ground in hiring female waitresses with a certain look. As a result of these cases, the restaurant has agreed to set aside gender-neutral kitchen and bar positions for male employees. This same legal principle explains why Japanese steakhouses and sushi bars seem to hire mainly Asian employees and why organizations like the Rockettes dance troupe can establish weight or even age restrictions. In some well-defined cases, organizations can go beyond traditional qualifications and hire employees based on race, ethnicity, or gender, engaging in what would otherwise be considered discrimination.

Have you ever received exceptionally poor service at a restaurant? Have you ever wondered whether it was *because* of your race, age, or other social identity? Although the civil rights legislation of the 1960s outlawed discrimination in public accommodations, some high-profile cases indicate that these behaviors did not end in the 1960s. In 1994, Denny's restaurant chain paid $54 million to settle a lawsuit alleging racial discrimination. The suit, which involved 4,300 claimants at 1,500 restaurants, described a pattern where black diners were refused service, made to wait longer for tables, or charged more than other customers. At one location in South Carolina, black diners were asked to pay in advance for their food, yet white diners were not asked to do the same. The fact that this was a class-action lawsuit shows that these were not isolated instances of poor service; rather, the suit's assertion that Dennys violated black cus-tomers' civil rights by treating them rudely and giving preferential treatment to whites is shown by the widespread nature of these complaints, which suggests a systemic cul-ture embedded within the corporation.

Incidentally, not every claim of discrimination is shown to have merit. Waffle House, another iconic breakfast chain, was accused of racial discrimination, with claimants asserting that servers deliberately served unsanitary food to minority cus-tomers, that servers directed racial epithets at blacks, and that servers became verbally abusive when asked to wait on blacks. When juries found a lack of evidence in these cases, the plaintiffs were ordered to pay Waffle House's legal costs. Still, in recent years many high-profile companies, including FedEx, Walgreens, Pepsi, and the Albertson's grocery chain, have been found guilty of *systemic* racial discrimination—usually re-fusing to hire or promote minority employees, but occasionally tolerating a climate of racial harassment.

The fact that nearly all of the cases discussed so far focus on minorities begs the question: Is there evidence that white people can be victims of discrimination? When discrimination occurs against members of a dominant group (men, whites) in favor of members of a minority or historically disadvantaged group, this is sometimes called **reverse discrimination.** This term is frequently applied to instances when whites (or men) are denied opportunities in education or employment due to affirmative action policies that favor minorities and women. According to a 2008 Gallup poll question, 55 percent of whites believe there is widespread racism against whites in the United States. Academic studies suggest that white people increasingly see themselves as vic-tims of discrimination—with some suggestion that whites see discrimination against whites as a *bigger* problem than discrimination against blacks (Norton and Sommers 2011). While these perceptions are important, they are not currently backed by evi-dence. Complaints from whites to the Equal Employment Opportunity Commission are exceedingly rare. Even more rarely are these complaints found to be backed by evidence (Reskin 1998).

That said, there have been some high-profile cases in which whites were found to be victims of racial discrimination. In the 2009 U.S. Supreme Court case **Ricci v. DeStefano**, the justices found that white firefighters in New Haven, Connecticut, were wrongly denied promotions. These firefighters sued the fire department after it threw out the results of the written test upon which promotions are based. Because no black firefighters and only one Hispanic firefighter scored high enough to receive a promo-tion, the fire department threw out the test—fearing that the test might have been ra-cially biased—and denied promotions to high-scoring whites. Upon hearing the facts of the case, the Court found that the white firefighters' civil rights had been violated and restored their promotions.

In 2012, a white man named Doug Carl was awarded a $1.3 million settlement against his employer, Fulton County, Georgia. He charged the county with racial dis-crimination when he was passed over for a promotion to human services director in favor of a black candidate. The jury agreed and sided in his favor. Because the case has

Although statistically rare, the U.S. Supreme Court found in *Ricci v. DiStefano* that white firefighters had been victims of racial discrimination.

been appealed, Mr. Carl has not yet received a payment. Despite these cases, and despite the perception of many whites that they are now subject to racial discrimination, the legal facts do not bear this out. Even with the controversial issue of affirmative action in higher education—a topic covered in more detail in Chapter 12—researchers estimate that if affirmative action were repealed, the chances that a white applicant would gain admission would increase only to 26 percent from 25 percent (Bowen and Bok 2000). The fact that there has not yet been a settlement finding discrimination against whites as a class suggests that despite these individual instances, whites do not face systemic discrimination at the macro-level.

EXPLORING ACTIVISM: GROUPS THAT DEFEND CIVIL RIGHTS AND CIVIL LIBERTIES

While individuals can and do fight prejudice and discrimination on their own, many who feel they have been victims of discrimination are backed by national civil rights organizations. Alive and well in the United States are a range of groups actively engaged in social and legal campaigns to reduce prejudice and provide legal assistance in cases of discrimination. One of the oldest of such organizations is the **American Civil Liberties Union** (ACLU). Founded in 1920, the ACLU describes itself as "our nation's guardian of liberty, working daily in courts, legislatures and communities to defend and preserve the individual rights and liberties that the Constitution and laws of the United States guarantee" (aclu.org). In addition to working on privacy issues for all Americans (illegal wiretapping and unnecessary surveillance, freedom of speech, consumer privacy, etc.), the organization's national and state chapters provide legal and legislative action on issues related to religious freedom, sexual orientation, women's issues, and racial justice. It has provided legal assistance in groundbreaking legal cases including *Gideon v. Wainwright* (which extended legal assistance to the poor in 1963), *Miranda v. Arizona* (which required police to notify suspects of their legal rights in 1966), and *Loving v. Virginia* (which outlawed bans against interracial marriage in 1969).

Two other groups have missions devoted to anti-racism and the dismantling of white supremacy. Founded in 1971, the **Southern Poverty Law Center** (SPLC) maintains the agenda of the civil rights movement and is "dedicated to fighting hate and bigotry, and to seeking justice for the most vulnerable members of society" (splc.org). While a recent case involved defending the right of parents of an intersex infant to refuse sex-reassignment surgery, it has a history of fighting jails and prisons that use cruel and unusual punishment (like the prisoner who was handcuffed to a hitching post and left virtually without water in the Alabama sun for seven hours) and prosecuting hate groups like the Ku Klux Klan (KKK). The **Anti-Defamation League** (ADL) was founded in 1913 "to stop the defamation of the Jewish people and to secure justice and fair treatment to all" (adl.org). Today, it fights anti-Semitism and other forms of bigotry, especially targeting "white power" groups that carry on Adolf Hitler's message and tactics. In addition to developing educational programs and outreach, the ADL investigates Internet activity and reports to government and law enforcement officials on the activities of hate groups and domestic (and international) terrorists.

Both founded in 1968, the **National Council of La Raza** (La Raza) and the **Mexican American Legal Defense Fund** (MALDEF) are devoted to the civil rights of Latinos. Broadly speaking, these groups focus on "social change through advocacy, communications, community education, and litigation in the areas of education, employment, immigrant rights, and political access" (maldef.org). Working inside Latino communities, providing education and outreach to improve health and economic outcomes, these groups also work outside Latino communities, focusing on civil rights issues through legislation and legal defense. Sometimes called the "law firm of the Latino community," MALDEF won an important legal victory in the U.S. Supreme Court case *Plyler v. Doe* (1982), where the Court struck down a Texas law allowing districts to charge tuition to children of undocumented immigrant parents. Today, voting rights and immigration issues are on the forefront of these two groups' agendas.

Finally, **Lambda Legal** was founded in 1973 to fight for the civil rights of gays, lesbians, and transgender individuals; in recent years it has been especially active in the fight for marriage equality. Historically, Lambda Legal has fought against bullying in schools and for the rights of students to form Gay-Straight Alliances; for the employment rights of people with HIV/AIDS; and the right to privacy and sexual freedom in the landmark 2003 U.S. Supreme Court case *Lawrence v. Texas* (mentioned above). As a legal defense organization, it goes beyond filing *amicus curiae briefs* (friend of the court); it provides active support for nationally significant legal cases that would increase the rights of gays, lesbians, and transgender persons and typically has 65 dockets, or cases, open at any given time (lambdalegal.org).

Civil rights organizations like these are not without their critics. Many see them as radical groups fighting for a liberal agenda and against traditional values. That said, the ACLU has fought for the civil rights of racial and ethnic minorities, just as it has fought for the free-speech rights of those considered bigots who exacerbate racial problems, including the KKK. Moreover, many of these organizations receive funding from mainstream groups, including the Ford Foundation, the Bill and Melinda Gates Foundation, Citigroup, and Wal-Mart.

Other critics see these civil rights groups as quick to "play the race card" and inclined to overlook instances where the civil rights of whites may be violated. Standing in opposition to what it sees as the government's tendency to elevate minority group interests above the interests of individuals is the **Center for Individual Rights** (CIR). Established in 1988, the CIR is a "nonprofit public interest law firm dedicated to the defense of individual liberties against the increasingly aggressive and unchecked authority of federal and state governments . . . [seeking] to enforce constitutional limits on state and federal power" (cir-usa.org). Its most visible cases have been those dealing with affirmative action, policies that provide racial preferences for minorities. In 2003 the organization represented a white woman named Jennifer Gratz in the U.S. Supreme Court case *Gratz v. Bollinger.* After being rejected from the University of Michigan, Gratz and the CIR argued that her civil rights had been violated by the university's admissions system, a system that awarded extra points to applicants who were from racial and ethnic minorities (scholarship athletes, low-income students, and children of alumni also got extra points in this system). As a white individual, the CIR argued, Gratz was subjected to an unfair standard. The Court agreed and declared this point system unconstitutional (although it did not declare affirmative action itself unconstitutional). The CIR continues to back cases promoting free speech and protecting the civil liberties of people it sees as disadvantaged or ignored by mainstream perspectives on discrimination and civil rights litigation.

COLOR-BLIND RACISM AND THE TRANSFORMATION OF RACIAL IDEOLOGIES

This chapter asks whether racism and racial inequality are alive and well in contemporary society. Racial attitudes have come a long way since black slaves counted as 3/5 of a person and Asian immigrants were barred from entering the United States; since nonwhites were considered biologically deficient; and since legal segregation characterized the lives of many Americans. Since the election of Barack Obama as president, some commentators have declared that we live in a "postracial America." The notion that we live in **a postracial America** reflects the belief that prejudice and discrimination are a thing of the past. The very fact that Obama was elected (not once, but twice), the logic goes, is proof that race is no longer an issue in this society. Other claims that we live in a postracial society point toward increases in interracial marriage and interracial childbearing and the general sentiment that racial diversity in the United States is so vast and so complicated that traditional racial boundaries and sentiments no longer apply.

Most sociologists reject the claim that we live in a "postracial society." Instead, they argue that the nature of our racial beliefs has simply changed and that many Americans now espouse what they call **color-blind racism.** Color-blind racism is different from the overtly prejudicial or racist beliefs and practices that existed in the past. It is a more covert form of racism: rather than argue that blacks or Hispanics cannot achieve the same social status as whites because they are genetically, socially, intellectually, or physically inferior, a color-blind racist would argue that racial and ethnic minorities have unequal outcomes due to *nonracial* dynamics. According to Eduardo Bonilla-Silva, a major theorist on this topic, color-blind racists claim that minorities themselves are "responsible for whatever 'race problem' we have in this country [the United States]" (2010:1). Residential segregation exists not because of formal housing segregation or the informal exclusion of whites, but because people simply prefer to live with others who are like them (in terms of culture or socioeconomic status); minorities have poorer educational and occupational outcomes not because they are inherently inferior, but because of the choices they make or their cultural preferences (they don't value education or work hard enough). Color-blind racism, according to Bonilla-Silva, is racism lite (2010:3). Rather than oppose interracial marriage on explicitly racial grounds, a color-blind racist will argue that the children born of such unions should not be subjected to confusion and stigma due to their parents' choices (Bonilla-Silva and Forman 2000).

For Eduardo Bonilla-Silva, surveys showing an improvement in Americans' racial views and a reduction of prejudice are fundamentally flawed. Because the questions used in such surveys were created in a different historical context, they cannot capture the changing and subtle nature of contemporary racial animus. According to critics, these new racial ideologies are problematic because they conceal the underlying patterns by which neighborhoods have become segregated in the first place or the reasons why some minorities may become disengaged from school. At the individual level, color-blind racism is especially insidious because it allows people the opportunity to deny that they are racist while obscuring the degree to which inequality is generated by macro-level phenomena: vestiges of conscious and deliberate actions on the part of city councils, zoning boards, real estate developers, school boards, and other such organizations.

THE LIMITS OF THE MICRO-LEVEL PERSPECTIVE

From the sociological perspective, the social world is made up of processes that occur at the micro- and macro-levels. Racial inequality is one aspect of the social world: members of different groups have different and unequal outcomes when it comes to education, employment, political participation, renting a house, purchasing a car, and even life expectancy. This chapter shows that starting from the bottom up, social inequalities partially reflect dynamics at the micro-level: individuals who have prejudicial beliefs and/or engage in discriminatory behaviors. Further, the research presented in this chapter shows that while racial prejudice has declined over time, racial animus has also transformed. Finally, both audit studies and legal cases show that discrimination in housing and employment are persistent social problems.

The micro-level perspective leads to the conclusion that racial inequalities can be reduced by changing individuals' beliefs and practices. It leads to the conclusion that we simply need to train our "players" to be more "sportsmanlike": not to talk smack about the other team, so to speak, or cheat to gain an unfair advantage. On a practical level, diversity training is often used in educational and corporate settings as a way to reduce prejudice and discrimination. Within the college setting, courses on cultural diversity, educational programs within residence halls, and clubs and organizations tailored to various identity groups work from this notion. By changing the mindsets of individuals, the logic goes, progress can be made.

While nothing in society changes without changing the individuals who make up society, the next chapter highlights the limits of the micro-level perspective. By shifting our attention to the macro-level, we see that the game itself is fundamentally flawed, with rules that privilege some and disadvantage others from the outset.

CHAPTER 10: REVIEW OF KEY POINTS

- This chapter focuses on explaining racism and racial inequality at the micro-level. This perspective examines the role of the individual, their beliefs, and social interactions in perpetuating racial inequality.
- Public opinion polls provide one window into racial inequality, focusing on people's beliefs. Such polls indicate that minorities are more likely than whites to believe that racism is still a problem in society and are less likely to characterize race relations in a positive way.
- Prejudice is an attitudinal form of racial animus; social scientists have measured it using self-reports (like the Bogardus scale) and by tapping into underlying beliefs (like the Implicit Association Test).
- Some theories suggest that fostering *contact* with people from different groups is one way to reduce prejudice at the micro-level. Workshops or seminars focused on diversity, where people interact and learn about differences in a nonthreatening, noncompetitive environment, is one such example.
- Where prejudice is about beliefs, discrimination is about action; specifically about actions that deny qualified people access to education, jobs, housing, and so forth.
- Audit studies are an experimental tool used by researchers to assess discrimination. These studies routinely find evidence of discrimination in housing, hiring, and other domains.
- Another source of information on lingering inequalities is the legal system. Legal cases—whether settled in or out of court—and the Equal Employment Opportunity Commission (EEOC) illustrate instances and patterns of discrimination.
- While legislation has been passed since the civil rights era to protect people from discrimination on the basis of gender, race, national origin, and religion, there is no federal legislation that protects people from discrimination based on sexual orientation or gender expression (for transpeople, for example).
- Although some court cases have identified instances of discrimination against whites, most claims brought to the EEOC by whites alleging racial discrimination have been found not to have merit.
- To the extent that the beliefs and actions of individuals contribute to racism and racial inequality, the solution for fixing racial inequality would also be found among individuals. Logically, this means changing their beliefs, firing or retraining employees and others who engage in acts of discrimination, and other efforts that target specific individuals.

CHAPTER 10: QUESTIONS FOR REVIEW

1. Public opinion polls are one tool to understand people's thoughts on current issues. How do public opinion polls work? What do they reveal about contemporary views on race?

2. What is prejudice? What are some tools developed by social scientists to measure prejudice?

3. How does discrimination compare to prejudice? From your perspective, is prejudice as harmful as discrimination? Why or why not?

4. Audit studies are one tool to measure discrimination. What are audit studies? What are their advantages and what are their disadvantages?

5. Looking at legal cases dealing with discrimination, what do we learn about what discrimination means in a legal sense? What characteristics does it involve, and who can and who cannot be discriminated against?

6. Do you believe that employers and landlords should be able to select whomever they want for employment or housing, regardless of race? That is, what do you see as the pros and cons of allowing individuals to maintain their own racial preferences when it comes to selecting candidates for employment and housing?

7. As you reflect on your own life experiences, where do you see evidence of prejudice and discrimination? Which groups seem to be the recipients of this prejudice and discrimination, and with what consequences?

KEY TERMS

American Civil Liberties Union
Anti-Defamation League
assimilation
audit study
authoritarian personality
BFOQ
Bogardus Social Distance Scale
Center for Individual Rights
Civil Rights Act of 1964
class-action lawsuit
color-blind racism
confirmation bias
contact hypothesis
correspondence-based audit study
discrimination
diversity training
empirical evidence
Equal Opportunity Employment Commission
exploitation theory

hate crime
Implicit Association Test
in-person audit study
Lambda Legal
Matthew Shepard and James Byrd Jr. Hate Crimes Prevention Act
Mexican American Legal Defense Fund
microaggressions
micro-level
National Council of La Raza
pluralistic societies
postracial America
prejudice
race-coded job channeling
representative sample
reverse discrimination
scapegoating theory
social desirability bias
Southern Poverty Law Center

REFERENCES

Ayres, Ian and Peter Siegelman. 1995. "Race and Gender Discrimination in Bargaining for a New Car." *American Economic Review* 85(3):304–321.

Bertrand, Marianne and Sendhil Mullainathan. 2004. "Are Emily and Greg More Employable Than Lakisha and Jamal? A Field Experiment on Labor Market Discrimination." *American Economic Review* 94(4):991–1013.

Bogardus, Emory Stephen. 1933. "A Social Distance Scale." *Sociology & Social Research* 17:265–271.

Bonilla-Silva, Eduardo. 2010. *Racism without Racists: Color-Blind Racism and the Persistence of Racial Inequality in America*, 3rd ed. Lanham, MD: Rowman & Littlefield.

Bonilla-Silva, Eduardo and Tyrone A. Forman. 2000. "'I'm Not a Racist, But . . .': Mapping College Students' Racial Ideology in the USA." *Discourse and Society* 11(1):50–85.

Bowen, William G. and Derek Bok. 2000. *The Shape of the River: Long-Term Consequences of Considering Race in College and University Admissions*. Princeton, NJ: Princeton University Press.

Equal Employment Opportunity Commission. 2010. "Abercrombie & Fitch Sued For Religious Discrimination" (Press Release). Washington, D.C.: *U.S. Equal Employment Opportunity Commission*.

Greenhouse, Steven. 2003. "Clothing Chain Accused of Discrimination." *New York Times* June, 27. Retrieved April 21, 2015 (http://www.nytimes.com/2003/06/17/national/17STOR.html)

Massey, Douglas and Garvey Lundy. 2001. "Use of Black English and Racial Discrimination in Urban Housing Markets: New Methods and Findings." *Urban Affairs Review* 36(4):452–469.

Norton, Michael I. and Samuel R. Sommers. 2011. "Whites See Racism as a Zero-Sum Game That They Are Now Losing." *Perspectives on Psychological Science* 6(3):215–218.

Pager, Devah. 2003. "The Mark of a Criminal Record." *American Journal of Sociology* 108(5): 937–975.

Pager, Devah, Bruce Western, and Bart Bonikowski. 2009. "Discrimination in a Low-Wage Labor Market: A Field Experiment." *American Sociological Review* 74(5):777–799.

Parrillo, Vincent N. and Christopher Donoghue. 2005. "Updating the Bogardus Social Distance Studies: A New National Study." *The Social Science Journal* 42(2):257–271.

Price, Joseph and Justin Wolfers. 2010. "Racial Discrimination among NBA Referees." *The Quarterly Journal of Economics* 125(4):1859–1887.

Reskin, Barbara. 1998. *The Realities of Affirmative Action in Employment*. Washington, DC: The American Sociological Association.

USA Today. 2004. "Abercrombie & Fitch to Pay $40 Million to Settle Bias Case." *USA Today* November, 16. Retrieved April 21, 2015 (http://usatoday30.usatoday.com/money/industries/retail/2004-11-16-anf-bias_x.htm)

Weaver, Charles N. 2008. "Social Distance as a Measure of Prejudice among Ethnic Groups in the United States." *Journal of Applied Social Psychology* 38(3):779–795.

Don't Hate the Player, Hate the Game

Understanding Inequality at the Macro-Level

Imagine a country where convicted drug dealers are able to turn the tables and take on the criminal justice system. Imagine, moreover, that convicted drug dealers can take on the highest court in the land, challenge the basis of their conviction, and win. Where is such a thing possible? Indeed, it is in the United States. In 2007, Derrick Kimbrough, a convicted drug dealer, took on the U.S. Supreme Court. He was not there to argue his innocence; no, he acknowledged his drug offenses. Rather, Kimbrough appeared in court to argue that the penalties he received as a convicted drug dealer were unfair; that they deprived him of his constitutional rights. In hearing the details of his case, the Court's majority agreed. It ruled that U.S. drug penalties not only violated Kimbrough's rights, but that they systematically violated the rights of a particular class of drug offenders. (Specific details of this case will be discussed later in this chapter.) By showing that an entire class of people—namely racial and ethnic minorities—had been denied equal protection under the law in federal drug prosecutions, in this particular case, the U.S. Supreme Court made an important and provocative statement: Don't hate the player, hate the game. That is, they called attention to systematic inequities that exist in our society and the ways in which inequalities are produced and perpetuated at the macro-level.

The goal of this chapter is to illustrate how social inequalities are produced and perpetuated at the macro-level. From a sociological perspective, racism, sexism, and classism are macro-level phenomena in that they form an overarching system of inequality. They form a system in the sense that they are embedded in many of society's core social institutions, including the economy, the educational system, the criminal justice system, and health care. Macro-level sources of social inequality are especially pernicious because there are no bigots or cheating "players" who are directly responsible for generating this inequality. You can't simply fire or retrain these "bad apples."

Instead, social inequality emerges simply from how things work and the disparate impact institutions and their policies have on racial or ethnic minorities, women, lower-income people, and others. The tricky thing about these systems of disadvantage and privilege is they exist independently of the individual social actors (or "players") that either benefit from or are harmed by their operation. That means that to alleviate these inequalities, it is not enough to hold diversity seminars or retraining workshops all across the land; rather, changes can only be made by fundamentally transforming these deeply institutionalized policies—by going all the way to the U.S. Supreme Court, for example, and demanding new penalties for drug offenders.

This chapter focuses on the "rules" of "the game" that systematically produce and perpetuate social inequality. Two of the specific macro-level "rules" that constitute the focus of this chapter are institutional discrimination and group privilege. While the majority of the examples used in this chapter focus on how these two macro-level phenomena relate to racial inequality, the same concepts apply to understanding sexism, classism, and homophobia.

RIGGING THE GAME THROUGH INSTITUTIONAL DISCRIMINATION

One of the most difficult questions in all of sociology has to do with differentiating between the micro- and macro-levels. At the micro- or individual level, inequality derives from specific face-to-face interactions that privilege some and disadvantage others (when seeking a job, an apartment, or a new car). At the macro- or societal level, inequality derives from institutional policies and procedures. The line between the two isn't always clear—there had to be, after all, specific people with specific motives who created these policies and procedures in the first place. For our purposes, micro-level interactions transform into macro-level phenomena when individual acts take on a repetitive, patterned quality and eventually become institutionalized or embedded within the social structure or social institutions. This is called **institutional discrimination.**

To illustrate this concept more fully, imagine that my new colleague (from Chapter 10) faced repeated rejection from landlords all over town, especially in so-called desirable neighborhoods inhabited by whites, so that her only housing option was to live in a lower-income black neighborhood. Imagine, moreover, that she wasn't the only person this was happening to; rather than an isolated incident, people with her racial identity faced similar discrimination at the hands of people with a different racial identity. Another example draws upon the class-action lawsuits discussed in the previous chapter. Imagine, then, that it wasn't simply Abercrombie & Fitch that preferred to hire sales associates who have a particular "all-American look;" imagine that all across the land, racial and ethnic minorities faced almost impossible odds of landing a job in a retail setting. While both of these examples are extreme, they help illustrate the concept of institutional discrimination.

Institutional discrimination can take numerous forms. **Institutional racism**, for example, refers to macro-level policies and procedures that have a disparate racial impact. *Disparate impact* means that they have a systematic negative impact on one group or groups and a systematic positive impact on another group or groups. Institutional sexism refers not to the individual acts of people who engage in sexual harassment or crude jokes in the workplace, but those policies and procedures that systematically disadvantage women and advantage men. That topic, and how it applies to the gender gap in pay, is the subject of Chapter 13. While it is possible that some policies systematically advantage women and disadvantage men, this seems to be extremely rare historically and in the current era. Finally, it is possible to refer to institutional homophobia and institutional classism as policies and procedures that have disparate impacts on the basis of sexual orientation and social class standing, respectively.

INSTITUTIONAL RACISM IN HOUSING

Why are there such extreme disparities in *wealth* between whites and minorities? Looking at median net worth, the typical white family has $22 for every $1 of the median black family ($110,729 vs. $4,995). The gap is also large between whites and Hispanics, where the ratio is $15 to $1 ($110,729 vs. $7,424). Although the answer is surely multifaceted, much of the racial disparity in wealth has to do with institutionalized differences in home ownership and the ability to build equity. While it may be tempting to conclude that these racial differences reflect little more than individual desires to purchase and invest in a home, a historical perspective shows that these current disparities reflect institutionally rooted policies and procedures that have contributed to one group's ability to accumulate wealth—wealth that can be passed down and creates intergenerational financial stability—and another group's difficulties in accumulating wealth. Because today's racial disparities in wealth are generations in the making, we need to get back into that time machine.

INSTITUTIONAL RACISM AND INDIVIDUAL FAMILY WEALTH

In the not-so-distant past, segregation in housing was common throughout the United States. Up until 1948, **restrictive covenants** were used by housing developers and owners to prevent categories of people from moving into particular neighborhoods. Property deeds, for example, included clauses restricting blacks, Jews, and in some cases even working-class whites and Catholics from purchasing these homes (Fogelson 2005; Miyares 2004). During the post–World War II housing boom, this meant that many black

Through the mid-1960s, segregation in housing was legal. Signs like these publicly expressed local preferences and prohibitions.

5. The lot, nor any part thereof, shall not be sold to any persons either of whole or part blood, of the Mongolian, Malay or Ethiopian races, nor shall the same nor any part thereof be rented to persons of such races.

"Restrictive covenants" spelled out which groups—"races," ethnic groups, and religions—were excluded from ownership or habitation. In the language of its time, this covenant prohibited occupation by blacks (Ethiopian) and Asians (Malay and Mongolians).

Banks refused to offer mortgages for properties in "redlined" neighborhoods. This made it difficult for blacks to accumulate home equity, a form of wealth.

families (and others) were systematically closed out of the rapidly expanding suburbs—where home values were increasing and generating equity for owners.

If black homebuyers were systematically excluded from the suburbs and majority-white housing developments, what was to prevent them from purchasing homes in black neighborhoods and generating equity that way? Here, another systematic policy made it difficult for minority homeowners to generate wealth. A policy known as **redlining** meant that many banks refused to give mortgages to buyers who wished to purchase homes in "redlined" areas. In 1934, the Federal Home Loan Bank Board conducted a national appraisal of neighborhoods in 239 U.S. cities. Because the U.S. federal government had recently gotten into the business of guaranteeing home loans through the Federal Housing Administration, the goal of the appraisal system was to protect the investments of the federal government. It did so by drawing "residential security maps" based on the assumption that neighborhoods differ in the degree to which they are a secure investment for the banks. The board concluded that homes in neighborhoods with large numbers of minorities were unlikely to increase in value; therefore, those areas were "redlined" and denied investment through home loans.

The policy of redlining illustrates several issues pertinent to institutional discrimination. One, the policy discriminated against an entire class of people, regardless of their qualifications. Thus, even if individual homebuyers had excellent credit, good incomes, and a history of maintaining their properties, they would be denied a mortgage if they wanted to purchase a home in a majority-black community. Two, as a policy, it is impossible to point to the bigot who is behind these denials; instead, this policy creates a nearly invisible source of discrimination. Three, there is a large social institution behind this policy. In this case, the institution was the U.S. federal government. It cannot be overstressed that many federal and state policies had a disparate racial impact. In this case, the U.S. government, by both offering home loans and creating the conditions that determined who got them, subsidized the growing wealth of many white American families and denied the same opportunities to many minority families. Yet not only did individual families struggle to acquire home equity, these policies also undervalued entire minority communities.

Another tricky aspect of institutional discrimination is that while these policies may not be racist in their intent, they are surely racist in their impact. The G.I. Bill, originally known as the Servicemen's Readjustment Act of 1944, further illustrates this point. When I reflect on my (white) grandfathers' accomplishments after serving in World War II, I have a lot to be proud of. They returned after their service, bought the suburban homes in which they would live the rest of their lives, had children and sent them to college, and established respectable careers in sales. Both of them built up equity and were able to pass some of that on to their children after they died. A look at the historical context, however, shows that they did not do this entirely on their own. As war veterans who served honorably, they used the G.I. Bill to establish this foundation.

As discussed in Chapter 5, the G.I. Bill extended benefits to veterans who served in World War II. The goal was to thank veterans for their war efforts and rebuild the nation after years of sacrifice. One benefit the G.I. Bill provided was access to low-downpayment, low-interest home loans; another was the opportunity to enroll in higher education. This government policy contributed not just to the formation of a strong middle class but especially to a strong *white* middle class. Although all veterans who had served at least 90 days and were honorably discharged received these benefits, not all veterans were able to use these benefits. Because of the racialized housing policies described earlier, minority veterans were largely unable to convert the G.I. Bill into a new home purchase with access for their children to good schools and the possibility of accumulating wealth. Because of legal segregation in education, veterans in many states were also unable to pursue a college degree. At the time, 17 southern states had legally segregated systems of higher education—meaning that black G.I.s were entirely shut out of most institutions in those states. Despite the presence of some schools that served black and Hispanic populations, these colleges and universities offered only a small range of degree programs and were especially unlikely to offer minority students the ability to pursue degrees in law, medicine, business, and other professions. The G.I. Bill, then, exacerbated inequalities as minority G.I.s were systematically denied opportunities while white veterans benefited from them. These disparities persist today and are evident in the intergenerational transmission of wealth and access to higher education along racial and ethnic lines. They may even play a role in shaping the kinds of resources that you and your family have access to.

INSTITUTIONAL RACISM AND NEIGHBORHOOD DEGRADATION

Institutional racism not only hindered individual minorities and their families in taking advantage of the opportunities to accumulate wealth; macro-level policies and procedures have also systematically contributed to the degradation of minority neighborhoods. The years following World War II were a boom not just for home ownership and college enrollment—they were also a boom for the expansion of cities, suburbs, and the highway system that connected these places and the growing businesses (e.g., auto manufacturing, industrial business parks) that surrounded them. In this hopeful time, the federal government provided money and established projects under the guise of urban renewal. **Urban renewal** refers to the planned demolition of structures and the relocation of businesses and people with the goal of improving a community's infrastructure and business opportunities.

One prong of urban renewal in the 1950s was the attempted conversion of "slum" neighborhoods into areas with newer and more affordable low-income housing. Under the Housing Acts of 1949 and 1954, the federal government bought up considerable land and buildings in urban areas and sold them to private developers with federally subsidized mortgages. This was a win for private business interests but a loss for local community members whose own businesses were lost in the process and residents who may have been evicted from their homes and then crowded into high-rise apartment complexes. Others were left scrambling to find housing: in Chicago, it is estimated that 425,000 housing units were razed under urban renewal programs while only 125,000 units were constructed (Bauman, Biles, and Szylvian 2000). Especially in larger cities, communities were left with housing "projects" that carried real and imagined social problems, including substandard housing conditions and an influx of prostitution and drug dealing.

The way that race more clearly enters this picture is seen in the class-action lawsuit *Dorothy Gautreaux v. Chicago Housing Authority*. In 1966, activist Dorothy Gautreaux sued the Chicago Housing Authority (CHA), alleging that its system of public housing subjected recipients to racial discrimination. With the backing of the American Civil Liberties Union (ACLU) (see Chapter 10), Gautreaux argued that public housing was substandard *and* built solely in areas with high concentrations of poor minorities. The case—which made it to the U.S. Supreme Court in 1976—demonstrated that the CHA violated the civil rights act. In representing the plaintiff, lawyer Alexander Polikoff successfully demonstrated that the CHA's policies were motivated by racial animus and an explicit desire to keep black people out of "white neighborhoods." Further research found this housing policy to be problematic because the deliberate concentration of minorities in impoverished areas further contributed to their poverty and deprived them

"Urban renewal" attempted to create new and better housing options for lower-income people, but instead it tended to concentrate poor people in large urban housing projects.

In many areas, local residents opposed the clearing away of older buildings and their way of life.

of legitimate opportunities to improve their condition—thereby perpetuating racial disparities.

Eventually this case led to a fundamental alteration in the way that low-income people are assigned to public housing. In a study known as the **Gautreaux Project**, sociologists Leonard Rubinowitz and James Rosenbaum (2000) demonstrated that poor urban residents who were randomly assigned to private housing units (urban or suburban) had better outcomes in terms of finding employment, leaving welfare, and moving their children through school than those who were randomly assigned to large-scale public housing complexes in areas with concentrated poverty. This research led to a policy of **scattered-site** housing placements, where people living in subsidized housing (e.g., Section 8) are not concentrated within low-income areas but spread *throughout* middle-class communities. The logic behind this policy is that it provides low-income people—many of whom are minorities—with better access to employment and good schools, as well as the opportunity to build a more diverse array of social capital.

A second prong of urban renewal was the transformation of American cities and suburbs through the Federal-Aid Highway Act of 1956. The goal of this act was to more efficiently connect people who were increasingly moving out to the suburbs with the still-vibrant urban centers where they worked. Doing this required the building of an interstate highway system on a national scale. Decisions about where to build highways, however, often corresponded with race and often hinged on the logic of building them in areas with the lowest property values and where citizens would be least likely to stage a successful fight against eminent domain. **Eminent domain** refers to the power, usually of the government, to forcibly acquire private property and use it for the public good. Because of this rationale, the U.S. highway system was disproportionately built in poor and minority neighborhoods.

The consequences of these federal policies were often devastating for the inner cities through which these new highways were built. Neighborhoods were effectively carved up by highways: residents became cut off from the parks and businesses that were physically close by but were now separated by highway overpasses and drainage ditches. Vibrant commercial districts were now isolated from potential customers as highways efficiently carried commuters high above them, back to the suburbs. Ultimately, these processes contributed to declining property values and, therefore, the tax dollars collected in these areas. Neighborhoods took on a patchwork feel and were no longer coherent and vibrant spaces. Over time, as prominent sociologist William Julius Wilson (1987, 1996) explored in his classic books *The Truly Disadvantaged* and *When Work Disappears*, employers moved to the suburbs, lured by cheaper land values and easier parking and transportation routes. While many white residents had the resources to move to the suburbs, to seek jobs and increasing home values, most blacks and Hispanics were left behind in fraying and decaying neighborhoods.

As neighborhoods were carved up by highways and became economically vulnerable, some also became environmentally vulnerable. Across the nation, minorities are more likely to live in close proximity to environmental hazards than whites are. In

The toxic donut surrounding Altgeld Gardens turned the American Dream of home ownership into a nightmare for many black residents.

urban areas blacks and Latinos live in greater proximity to chemical manufacturing plants, toxic landfills, and waste incinerators; nuclear waste sites may be built close to Native American reservations. A research initiative spearheaded by the United Church of Christ—in partnership with academic researchers—found that race is "the most potent variable in predicting where commercial hazardous waste facilities were located in the U.S, more powerful than household income, the value of homes and the estimated amount of hazardous waste generated" (Bullard et al. 2007:x). Their analyses, which span a period of more than 20 years, led to the popularization of the term **environmental racism**, referring to the disproportionate negative impact of environmental hazards on people of color. For residents of these communities, exposure to environmental hazards has been linked to increased risks of asthma and other respiratory illnesses, cancers, and brain tumors and higher rates of miscarriage.

When black veterans returned to the city of Chicago after World War II, many of them found homes in a new housing community called Altgeld Gardens, which was built over an abandoned industrial site. As white residents moved to the suburbs after the war, urban land values in this area dropped, and in came a number of industrial and manufacturing businesses to take the white residents' places. Despite black people's hopes of living in a middle-class community and fulfilling the American Dream, Altgeld Gardens came to be known as a "toxic donut." At the center of this donut is a community that is nearly all black with the majority living in poverty; forming the ring of the "donut" are 50 toxic waste dumps along with "contaminated lagoons, steel slag beds, a huge chemical waste incinerator, buried metal drums, and piles of loose trash . . . metal-plating shops, a paint company, and a sewage treatment plant" (OECD 1999).

Farther south is a region on the banks of the Mississippi River known as Cancer Alley. Spanning an 85-mile corridor between Baton Rouge and New Orleans,

The fact that many toxic waste sites are located near areas inhabited by poor people and minorities has been called "environmental racism."

Louisiana, this area, dotted with chemical manufacturing and industrial plants, has gained notoriety due to its high concentrations of cancer diagnoses. While it is clear that higher concentrations of poor and minority people live in close proximity to such environmental hazards, it is harder to prove that these hazards are directly responsible for higher rates of illness in these areas. There may be clusters of rare cancers that spring up in these areas, but conducting epidemiological research that pinpoints the cause is difficult due both to the small numbers of people affected (small, from a statistical standpoint) and the number of external factors that must be taken into account.

Adopting a macro-level perspective can help explain why neighborhoods inhabited by poor residents appear to be such unpleasant places to live. Next time you're driving on a highway that bypasses these areas (or if you live in one of these areas), you may see them in a different light. There is not merely a high correlation between minority neighborhoods and environmental hazards. The U.S. General Accountability Office (GAO)—the nonpartisan research wing of the U.S. Congress, which researches how the government spends taxpayer dollars—concluded in a landmark report that race and low incomes are the *cause* of this relationship. Many companies deliberately place their plants in these areas because they assume that community members lack the organizational skills and political power to resist or oppose their efforts. Compared to white and wealthier residents, they may also be less able to move from these areas and less likely to seek financial compensation from any damages they may suffer.

INSTITUTIONAL RACISM IN THE CRIMINAL JUSTICE AND POLITICAL SYSTEMS

The criminal justice and political systems are major social institutions in which institutional racism also plays out. Here, routine policies and procedures—from policing strategies to the allocation of punishments to what happens after leaving the criminal justice system—have a racially disparate impact, disadvantaging some groups and advantaging others. In many cases, the policies and procedures set in motion by the criminal justice system carry over into the political system and beyond. It is not, then, simply the fact that racial and ethnic minorities experience disadvantages in policing and criminal penalties; it is also that these disparities reverberate into other social domains and make it difficult—though not impossible—for racial and ethnic minorities to get an education, earn a living, and participate in the political system.

From the outset, strategies of policing and surveillance have a racially disparate effect. With limited resources, police departments are challenged by how best to deter criminal activity and catch criminals when crimes do occur. Police officers cannot be everywhere at all times; they must allocate resources to the neighborhoods and locations where crimes are most likely to occur. Many scholars and legal authorities, however, believe that these pressures may result in racial profiling. **Racial profiling** refers to police activity that uses race or ethnicity as a basis for where, when, and how to intervene in possible criminal activity. Racial profiling appears to be justified when you consider the fact that minorities are overrepresented among those arrested, sentenced, and incarcerated. According to Bureau of Justice statistics, blacks constitute about 13.6 percent of the total U.S. population, but they account for 39.4 percent of those incarcerated. Hispanics are also overrepresented in the criminal justice system: while they constitute 16.3 percent of the U.S. population, they make up 20.6 percent of those in jails and prisons. Yet when it comes to statistics like these, there is more than meets the eye.

Despite the apparent justification for racial profiling, it is a controversial way to address drug dealing, illegal immigrants, and terrorist activity. In fact, declared illegal in many jurisdictions—especially when used as the only motivation for stopping and searching suspects. Still, some police departments use race and/or ethnicity in decisions about where to patrol and whom to pull over in traffic stops or interrogate on the street. In terms of institutional racism, this means that formal policies shape the likelihood that some groups will get caught up in the criminal justice system as others escape its surveillance and grasp.

One well-publicized example of racial profiling is **driving while black** (DWB)—the idea that drivers may be pulled over and ticketed because of their race. Despite colloquially being called "driving while black," such racial profiling affects many racial and ethnic minorities. Research shows that some police departments explicitly train their officers to use this strategy—arguing that it helps them catch criminals. Not simply intended to stop or punish speeders, pulling over drivers based on race has been justified as a way to catch drug traffickers. Prior to coming under fire in 1999 for racially motivated policing, the New Jersey superintendent of police, Carl Williams, defended his department's tactics, saying "it's most likely a minority group that's

Playing off the infraction of "driving while intoxicated," "driving while black" (DWB) is a vernacular term for suspected racial profiling on the part of law enforcement officials.

involved with that (the local drug trade)" (McFadden 1999). This comment, and the subsequent discovery of police training procedures consistent with racial profiling, led to investigations into "driving while black" in a number of states.

So are police justified in racially targeting drivers based on race? Are members of some races statistically more likely to speed or drive recklessly than others? Are, in fact, drivers of some races more likely to carry drugs in their cars? In a landmark study, John Lamberth (1998) demonstrated the irrationality of racial profiling. By systematically researching drivers and arrest records in several states, Lamberth concluded that black drivers were no more likely than other drivers to speed but were nearly five times more likely to be stopped. Once stopped, they were 16.5 times more likely to be arrested. Using videotaped data from 313 traffic stops, other researchers found that traffic stops of black drivers were more *extensive* in terms of duration and the likelihood of being asked about weapons and drugs. In addition, when black drivers were stopped by white officers, the officers "displayed more indifference . . . were less approachable, were more dismissive of driver comments, showed a more pronounced appearance of superiority, gave less respect, and did less listening" (Dixon et al. 2008:541).

Because law enforcement officers sometimes find drugs when they search minorities (or find radical Muslims when they stop people of Arab descent), racial profiling becomes a self-fulfilling prophecy: inevitably, you find what you seek. Yet when looking at data from drivers who were searched after being stopped, Lamberth found that blacks were no more likely than whites to have contraband—illegal drugs—in their cars. Given the disproportionate focus on minority drivers, the ACLU alleges that "white drivers receive far less police attention, many of the drug dealers and possessors among them go unapprehended, and the perception that whites commit fewer drug offenses than minorities is perpetuated" (Harris 1999). Data suggest, moreover, that within the general population, whites, blacks, and Hispanics have similar rates of illegal drug use (Asians have the lowest rates and Native Americans the highest).

Statistical analyses by Lamberth and others have been used to conclude there is no benefit to racial profiling. While profiling based on psychological traits or behavior is legal, targeting people based on race—especially in the absence of other evidence—seems both inefficient and unconstitutional. It constitutes a fundamental violation of rights because the Fourth Amendment of the U.S. Constitution protects against police stops and seizures without probable cause. Analysis of crime data suggests that simply being a minority is not "probable cause."

The issue of racial profiling continues to draw attention. In 2013, a New York judge concluded that a procedure known as "stop-and-frisk" violates the constitutional rights of minorities. **Stop-and-frisk** is the name for a crime-reduction strategy where law enforcement officers have the right to stop and physically search—not just question—individuals on the street. The procedure gained popularity in New York City in the 1990s, and many credit it with helping reduce crime rates. While the policy requires *probable cause* (reasonable suspicion of having committed a crime or intending to do so) when detaining people on the street, critics suspected that officers were racially profiling suspects and only later coming up with justifications for their stops.

Data involving 4.4 million stops, gathered over an 8-year period, confirmed these suspicions: only 1 out of every 10 stops detected a criminal offense—meaning that 90 percent of those frisked were innocent. Critics were even more concerned about the racial breakdown of the data. While blacks and Hispanics make up about 50 percent of those living in New York City, they comprised 83 percent of those subjected to stop-and-frisk. If these stops were successful in identifying criminals, this targeting might be justified. Among blacks and Latinos stopped on the street, however, there was a lower chance of criminal activity among minorities compared to whites. The payoff for this procedure in terms of catching criminals is suspect, *and* its civil rights implications are troubling. Judge Shira Scheindlin, who decided the case, said: "The City's highest officials have turned a blind eye to the evidence that officers are conducting stops in a racially discriminatory manner. In their zeal to defend a policy that they believe to be effective, they have willfully ignored overwhelming proof that the policy of singling out 'the right people' is racially discriminatory and therefore violates the United States Constitution" (Goldstein 2013)—namely its equal protection clause (Fourteenth Amendment) and the right to be free of unlawful searches (Fourth Amendment).

Policing tactics such as these constitute a form of institutional racism because they create a sweeping policy with racially disparate effects. In this case, they affect the likelihood that a person will become caught up in the criminal justice system. Once a person is stopped, searched, or arrested, race continues to play a role in terms of punishments. This leads us back to the case of Derrick Kimbrough, convicted drug dealer.

So on what basis did Derrick Kimbrough take his drug case all the way to the U.S. Supreme Court? And why did the majority of the justices conclude that the drug penalties applied in his case constituted a violation of a whole class of people's constitutional rights? First, it is essential to establish that Kimbrough was a convicted drug offender: in 2004 he pled guilty to four drug charges, including conspiracy to distribute crack and powder cocaine; possession with intent to distribute more than 50 grams of crack cocaine; possession with intent to distribute powder cocaine; and possession of an illegal firearm. In the sentencing phase of his trial, Kimbrough received 180 months in jail. It was discovered, though, that if he had possessed the same quantity of cocaine, but *only* in powder form (rather than crack or rock), his sentence would have been 97–106 months. Ultimately, Kimbrough and his lawyer took their case to the Supreme Court, alleging—and proving—that sentencing guidelines that treated crack and powder cocaine differently were unjustified and, essentially, deprived those convicted of crack-related drug crimes of their constitutional rights.

Prior to the 2007 Supreme Court case **Kimbrough v. United States**, federal drug sentencing guidelines penalized those who trafficked in crack cocaine much more harshly than those who trafficked in powder cocaine. Five-year minimum sentences were mandated for those found guilty of possessing five grams of crack cocaine; an offender would need to possess 500 grams of powder cocaine to receive the same sentence. Various arguments were used to justify these disparate sentences. Some said that crack was more addictive than powder cocaine; that it was more damaging to developing fetuses; that it had a more devastating impact on the urban areas in which it was used and distributed. None of these arguments, however, held up in court.

Indeed, the Court ruled that these sentencing disparities were unjustified and, agreeing with an earlier Court ruling, concluded that it "fosters a lack of confidence in the criminal justice system because of a perception that it promotes an unwarranted divergence based on race" (Supreme Court of the United States 2007:2). This "unwarranted divergence based on race" was supported with data from U.S. Sentencing Commission indicating that blacks accounted for 27 percent of powder cocaine offenders but 81 percent of crack offenders. Whites, by contrast, were more likely to be convicted for powder cocaine offenses. That crack tends to be a "drug of the streets" while powder tends to be a "drug of the suites" (hotels, businesses) meant that black offenders were receiving disproportionately large sentences and whites were getting off with relatively light sentences. Because it could not be proven that sentencing disparities were justified by the drugs' effects, it appears that these guidelines systematically disadvantaged some and advantaged others. As a result, judges are now able to use more discretion when sentencing drug offenders, and those convicted pre-Kimbrough are able to appeal their convictions.

Across the criminal justice system, minorities appear to receive harsher sentences than whites for similar crimes (Reiman and Leighton 2012). This becomes a life-and-death issue in the case of capital punishment. While these data are especially hard to analyze, given the many complicated factors for each crime that need to be controlled, some patterns seem agreed upon. The landmark **Baldus Study** (Baldus, Woodworth, and Pulaski 1990), for example, used a sophisticated statistical design to conclude that the *race of the victim* is a major factor in deciding whether to apply the death penalty: blacks who victimize whites are significantly more likely to receive the death penalty than whites who victimize blacks—even when controlling for relevant factors. Subsequent studies across a number of states have confirmed this finding (e.g, Radelet and Pierce 2011).

These patterns suggest some form of widespread, institutional discrimination. While some scholars see these patterns as simply reflecting racist prosecutors and juries (Huff, Rattner, and Sagarin 1996), the reality is more complicated and more deeply rooted in macro-level patterns. For example, black defendants are more likely than whites to rely on the system of **indigent defense**—the federally mandated system that provides legal representation to those who cannot afford a lawyer. According to Bureau of Justice Statistics, 69 percent of white state prison inmates rely on this system, while 77 percent of black and 73 percent of Hispanics do so. This system has been criticized for being underfunded, so that public defenders have large caseloads, limited time to meet with clients, and few resources to conduct investigations. In short, those who use this service seem to be receiving substandard legal services, which may put them at risk for harsh sentences or even wrongful conviction (Bureau of Justice 2013).

The **jury selection** process may also systematically result in harsher penalties for minorities. The first step in selecting a jury is drawing from a list of registered voters or those holding state IDs. Because minorities are less likely than whites to register to vote or hold a state ID, they are less likely to be summoned for jury duty. Second, some argue that the jury screening process also contains racial biases (Alexander 2010). Although racial bias is prohibited in the selection of jurors, critics argue that some reasons given for dismissing a potential juror have racially coded undertones (Somers and Norton 2008). The Equal Justice Initiative, a not-for-profit research and advocacy group, found that potential black jurors were excluded for reasons including posture and style of walking ("shucked and jived"; 2010:18); marital status; involvement in an interracial relationship; having attended a historically black college or living in a black neighborhood; and claims of low intelligence and lack of sophistication—even for people who are college graduates and professionals. The fact that 80 percent of potential black jurors have been excluded in some southern counties means that many minority defendants are not judged by a jury of their peers. Critics and activists have a hard time, however, identifying intentional racial discrimination in these selection processes.

RACE, CRIME, AND THE LOSS OF CIVIL RIGHTS

Because of how convicted felons are treated after their release, reverberations of these policies continue long after the sentence has been served. One area where reverberations are felt is the political system, where felon disenfranchisement policies have a racially disproportionate effect. **Felon disenfranchisement** refers to the practice of prohibiting convicted felons from voting. All but two states suspend a felon's right to vote while incarcerated; some states suspend this right permanently or restore the right only after a lengthy process. Because minorities are disproportionately represented among convicted felons, they are disproportionately affected by these laws. In 2013 the Sentencing Project reported that 7.7 percent of black adults have lost the right to vote, compared to 1.8 percent of the nonblack population. In Florida, Virginia, and Kentucky, these numbers are above 20 percent. The logic behind felon disenfranchisement is that because convicted criminals have violated the social contract (social trust), they must give up some of their rights. The U.S. Supreme Court has declared felon disenfranchisement laws constitutional.

The implications of these policies are both obvious and immediate, and more subtle and long term. Clearly, the fact that large percentages of blacks in a number of states lack the right to vote means their voice is systematically lost in elections. In tight competitions, this can affect the outcome of elections. Some statistical analyses suggest that Al Gore would have won the highly contested 2000 presidential election (by winning the state of Florida) had it not been for these laws (Uggen and Manza 2002). With respect to the more subtle, long-term consequences of felon disenfranchisement, scholars argue that these laws affect the voting behavior of nonfelons as well. Melanie Bowers and Robert Preuhs (2009) found that felon disenfranchisement can bubble over, causing a sense of cynicism in the political system and reducing voter turnout in black communities. Children raised in this community may not be socialized to see political participation as effective, hence carrying the effects of disenfranchisement into the future. Interestingly, felon disenfranchisement does not have the same broad effect in white communities. The impact of this policy are also self-reinforcing: lower levels of political participation by minorities means that they exert less influence on this and other policies that might improve their well-being.

Even when they have the right to vote, some find that minorities are deprived of voting rights. Critics argue that voter ID laws constitute another form of institutional racism. **Voter ID laws** are state-level provisions that require voters to present an official form of identification when going to the polls. Supporters of these laws believe they are necessary to prevent or reduce voter fraud. Critics argue that evidence of voter fraud is scant and that these laws deliberately disenfranchise elderly, poor, and minority voters. Because official state IDs cost money (the ID itself, along with the fee for acquiring an official birth certificate), critics argue, they are a modern incarnation of a **poll tax**—a now-illegal fee that was used in many southern states to discourage blacks from voting (Mississippi's law was the last to fall in 1966). Although requiring voters to possess an ID to vote is a race-neutral policy, it may hit minorities harder, given that they are more likely to be poor and lack mobility. Indeed, while 11 percent of adult Americans lack an official government ID, these numbers are 25 percent among blacks, 18 percent among senior citizens, and 15 among low-income Americans (Brennan Center 2006).

Across the United States, voter ID laws are legal and growing in popularity. A 2012 poll from the Pew Research Center showed that a full 77 percent of Americas support these laws—with considerably greater support among Republicans (95 percent) than Democrats (61 percent). So far, the evidence is inconclusive as to whether voter ID laws reduce voter turnout or disproportionately affect minority voters. There is concern, though, that this is one of several policies that could impose barriers that systematically make it more difficult for some voters to participate in the political process. Apathy and skepticism already characterize the political views of some minorities. A 2012 Pew poll, for example, found that 60 percent of whites and Hispanics were confident that votes in their area are counted accurately, while only 44 percent of black respondents expressed this confidence.

Finally, beyond the political process, prisoners may find it hard to assimilate back into society. Despite doing their time and paying their debt to society, once released back into society, some ex-offenders continue to be stripped of their civil rights. Referred to as the **collateral consequences of criminal conviction**, this includes the loss or restriction of professional licenses (for engineer, accountants, hair stylists, athletic trainers), ineligibility for welfare benefits and student loans, loss of voting rights, and ineligibility for jury duty. Because of these laws, someone convicted of selling marijuana as a young adult may not be able to get a loan to go to college or technical school and would be prohibited from becoming licensed to practice law or social work. While these laws operate in a race-neutral way (they apply to all convicts), the historical record suggests that they were initially implemented in order to strip blacks of their civil rights (Chin 2002). Moreover, because minorities represent a higher proportion of those with criminal sentences, they are more likely to experience barriers to rehabilitating themselves and rejoining civil society. Rather than a restoration of their civil rights, some legal scholars have called this "civil death" (Chin 2012). These policies are especially problematic given the finding that while blacks are not more likely to commit drug crimes than members of other races, they are more likely to be arrested, prosecuted, convicted, and sentenced (Chin 2002:256).

When people are genuinely guilty of criminal activity, there is little need for sympathy or concerns about bias. Yet crime and punishment do not take place in a vacuum. Researchers have identified racial disparities in the criminal justice system, disparities that begin with surveillance and then carry over into prosecution and sentencing, and finally into release back into society. The examples given illustrate a pattern of institutional discrimination: they illustrate policies with widespread application that require no racist instigator and have racially disparate effects. In her book *The New Jim Crow*, legal scholar Michelle Alexander (2010) argues that our treatment of felons has effectively replaced earlier forms of discrimination in housing, employment, and politics; she argues that institutional racism is now practiced primarily through the criminal justice system. Finally, it is worth noting that while these examples apply most acutely and vividly to racial discrimination, many of them also have a disparate impact on lower-income Americans, thereby illustrating institutional classism.

EXPLORING ACTIVISM:
ACHIEVING JUSTICE THROUGH THE INNOCENCE PROJECT

If a person is guilty of a particularly heinous crime, regardless of race, he or she may receive the death penalty. Since the 1990s, however, more concern has been expressed about wrongful convictions. Wrongful convictions are those where innocent people are convicted and, occasionally, put to death. Although its mission is not specifically racial in nature, The Innocence Project was founded to achieve justice in the case of wrongful convictions. In the process they have highlighted some of the policies within the criminal justice system that produce racial disparities.

There is no more serious punishment than the death penalty. The Innocence Project was founded in 1992 with the goal of identifying and exonerating those wrongly convicted—especially those sentenced to death. Headed by lawyer Barry Scheck, its work has resulted in more than 300 exonerations (reversals of those previously convicted); other organizations have also worked on this cause, achieving more than 900 exonerations.

The work of The Innocence Project and other such organizations amounts to racial activism in the sense that minorities are disproportionately represented among the wrongly convicted. Race (and social class) enters the picture in this way: original prosecutions, perhaps because of the limited resources of the indigent defense system, are often unable to use DNA evidence effectively. The Innocence Project, then, works to identify appropriate DNA evidence and have the case retried. In other cases, false or coerced confessions have been thrown out—another symptom of an underfunded indigent defense system—and eyewitness testimony has also been called into question. Eyewitness identification may also be a racial issue; according to The Innocence Project, studies have shown that people are less able to recognize faces of a different race than their own.

While the typical person exonerated through this activist work has served 13 years, many cases involve those having served 20 or more years in jail. With greater attention and more resources devoted to these cases, lawyers are able not simply to exonerate the wrongly convicted but to win civil rights cases and monetary settlements on their behalf. Although an extreme case, in 2010 Barry Gibbs was awarded nearly $10 million in a civil rights settlement after serving 19 years in a New York jail. According to The Innocence Project, 65 percent of those wrongly convicted have

INNOCENCE PROJECT

Because minorities are more likely to be "wrongly convicted" than white defendants, organizations like The Innocence Project are a form of racial justice.

received financial compensation (usually based on the number of years served). What is more difficult to remedy, however, is one's criminal record. In many cases, the original conviction stays on his or her record permanently.

RIGGING THE GAME THROUGH GROUP PRIVILEGE

"Dr. Stuber," a student wrote to me in a private communication, "I have a problem. I requested a random roommate for fall and I just found out she's black. I looked her up on Facebook and I know it sounds like I am discriminating [against] her, but I know it would not work out. What should I do? Request a roommate change? But if I do request a roommate change, what do I tell her the reason why I do not want to live with her? HELP!"

While legal forms of discrimination are largely a thing of the past, and subtle forms of racial bias have been getting more attention in recent years, some macro-level sources of inequality remain virtually invisible. What is it that allowed my student (1) to freely express her feelings of racial antipathy and (2) assume that I—her white professor—would be an appropriate, if not sympathetic, person to whom she could express her feelings? Perhaps she was even beginning to question her own feelings on race and looked to me as a trusted person with whom she could begin processing this issue. Yet for scholars of race, gender, and sexual orientation, this student's posing of this question reflects a sense of group privilege—in her case, white privilege. **Group privilege** is different from overt forms of prejudice and discrimination. It refers to subtle cultural beliefs and, inevitably, social interactions that contribute to a *broader environment* where members of some groups experience social advantages and others do not. Group privilege is a macro-level form of racial inequality in the sense that it pervades our culture and has a disparate impact on members of various social groups but does not require explicit "work" on the part of individuals to keep it going.

WHITE PRIVILEGE

In her groundbreaking 1988 essay, scholar and activist Peggy McIntosh wrote: "As a white person, I realized I had been taught about racism as something which puts others at a disadvantage, but had been taught not to see one of its corollary aspects, white privilege which puts me at an advantage" (2007: 98). With this simple and logical observation, McIntosh made an important point: the flip side of disadvantage is advantage. There cannot be one without the other. When one group is being scoped out by the police, another group systematically escapes observation. In this essay McIntosh coined the term **white privilege**, defined as the automatic and unearned educational, social, and economic privileges that white people receive on account of their race.

The notion that one group—whether whites, men, or heterosexuals—*automatically* receives education, social, and economic privileges rubs many the wrong way. In the

United States, we have a strong sense of individualism and an emphasis on personal achievement. I, for one, did not *automatically* receive my Ph.D.—I worked for it. It's not like I, as a white person, receive discounts, freebies, and upgrades everywhere I go on account of my race. When thinking about the notion of group privilege, it is important to distinguish between earned and unearned advantages. Some of the advantages I experience have been earned: I worked hard for an education; this resulted in a stable and well-paying job and affords me good health insurance and the opportunity to live in a pretty and safe neighborhood. Unearned advantages, by contrast, are things that make a white person's (or man's) life educationally, economically, and socially easier—but he or she did not have to work to receive them.

To take the abstract and make it concrete, consider how race may affect your own educational experiences. If you are a white student, it is likely that for most of your life, you have been taught by another white person. Moreover, in many of your courses, you were probably taught a curriculum focusing on the achievements and experiences of white people. Finally, when other groups are discussed, they are often portrayed in an unfortunate or unfavorable light (historical struggles, lower life expectancies, higher poverty rates, etc.). If you are a nonwhite student, you have most likely been taught by a person of another race, with a focus on the achievements and experiences of other racial and ethnic groups, where your group has been portrayed as disadvantaged or different from the norm.

What is the impact of these educational experiences, year after year? Does a white student experience a sense of comfort in the classroom that eases the educational experience? Does this comfort give students the permission to freely express their thoughts—especially those reflecting doubts about racial inequality or even feelings of racial animosity—and assume that their instructors will understand their point of view? What about nonwhite students? Do they censor themselves in class, worried about how their instructor or classmates may respond to their comments? Do they experience discomfort when discussing some topics, making it more difficult for them to learn?

In her essay on white privilege, Peggy McIntosh (2007) identified numerous subtle settings and experiences where racial dynamics quietly confer either advantage or disadvantage. The same dynamics I describe within educational settings may also exist when going out to shop, dine, visit the doctor, apply for a job or new apartment, and watch, read, or listen to the news. In thinking about her daily life, McIntosh identified these forms of white privilege (99–100):

- I am generally able to attend decent schools, where people like myself are in charge, and where my cultural experiences are reflected in the curriculum.
- When I am told about our nation's history or the history of "the world," I can expect to see people of my race well represented.
- I can turn on the television or open the newspaper and see people of my race widely and positively represented.
- I generally pass unnoticed in stores, restaurants, and other public places.
- I am never asked to speak for all the people of my racial group.

- I can criticize our government and not be viewed as a bitter or a cultural outsider.
- I can swear, talk crudely, or dress in dirty or secondhand clothes without having people attribute these choices to the bad morals or poverty of my race.
- I can easily buy picture books, greeting cards, dolls, and toys featuring people of my race.
- When I buy Band-Aids, bandages, or blemish cover, I know that the "flesh" tone will more or less match my skin.
- When I do well or succeed, I am not called a credit to my race.

These examples help expand our understanding of group privilege. The one I relate to most is the assertion that I can criticize our government without being viewed as a bitter outsider. Indeed, teaching sociology is all about pointing out inequalities and injustices in our society. As a white professor, I believe my students listen to what I have to say with greater acceptance than if I were saying the same things as a minority or immigrant. White privilege for me is being considered credible and (relatively) unbiased, whereas if my racial or ethnic identity were different, I might be viewed as having a chip on my shoulder.

Where does group privilege come from in the first place? According to sociologist Michael Kimmel: "To be white, or straight, or male, or middle class is to be simultaneously ubiquitous and invisible. You're everywhere you look, you're the standard against which everyone else is measured" (2014:3). Group privilege, then, comes from being

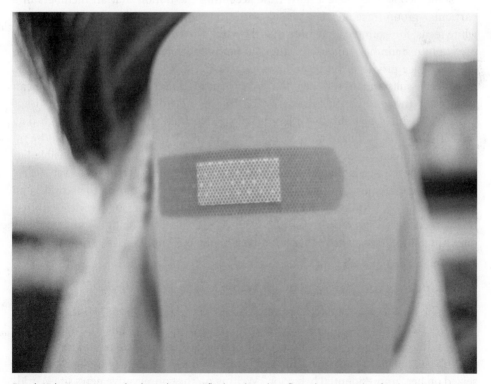

Band-Aids, crayons, and nylons that are "flesh-colored" reflect the principle of "white privilege." Whose "flesh" is considered the reference point?

part of the majority. While "the majority" often refers to the largest social group, it can also refer to the group with the most social power (political representation, business ownership). For example, white privilege certainly exists in South Africa, even though whites are not the numerical majority. White privilege, then, is the privilege that comes from being a member of the group whose culture is considered the norm in society. On a superficial level, it is the basis some use to conclude that there are "normal names" (Michael, Aaron, Kristin, and Allison) and "weird names" (Eboni, Shanquille, D'Andre, and Dajon)—without considering how normal names became the standard.

Although there are many ways of conceptualizing group privilege, one way that makes sense to me is that is the privilege of being invisible. I do not mean invisible in the sense that you are ignored when you go into a store, or no one notices you raising your hand in class. I mean that your existence as a *white* person is rarely acknowledged; in class discussions, your classmates rarely think, "Oooh . . . I wonder what the white person is going to say about this," or as a job applicant you rarely wonder if your race is the reason why you didn't receive a callback. While some people may refer to their "Filipino friend," their "gay colleague," or the "female sports anchor at ESPN," group privilege means that these qualifiers are rarely used to specify who you are, what you have achieved, or why you may say the things you do. Your whiteness or maleness is considered an invisible and irrelevant part of who you are.

Some people may have a hard time accepting the notion that all members of a particular group (race, gender, sexual orientation, or religion) have privilege. Some white teens, for example, may note that they are also followed in stores or given poor service in restaurants. It is useful, then, to point out that all white people have *some degree* of race privilege, yet some have more than others. White teens, for example, may receive substandard service if the server believes that they are poor tippers. It can be assured, though, that these teens will grow up and this disadvantage may disappear. Poor whites certainly have less privilege than affluent whites—although data indicate that they still have more freedom to live where they want and attend decent schools compared to poor minorities. White people with facial piercings, visible tattoos, and shaved heads may also wonder where their white privilege is. Yet if they remove their piercings and grow their hair out, they may discover the world is an easier place to be. Ultimately, age, socioeconomic status, and personal style are things that can change; one's racial or ethnic identity endures. Still, being white is not any one thing: it intersects with other identities, giving one more or less privilege, based on those other identities.

GENDER PRIVILEGE AND HETERONORMATIVITY

When she ran for the Democratic presidential nomination in 2008, Hillary Clinton was criticized for tearing up on the campaign trail. When asked how she managed the stress of the campaign trail, she emotionally replied, "I couldn't do it [run for office] if I didn't passionately think it was the right thing to do." Members of the press quickly seized on her "unpresidential behavior." Writing on the conservative news site World-NetDaily, journalist Chelsea Schilling asked: "Is this emotional behavior acceptable for a potential leader? And is crying a tactic she plans to use as president in negotiations with foreign tyrants?" She concluded her column by asserting: "If Senator Clinton wants to play with the big boys and be respected by foreign leaders, she had better drop the crying act."

The sentiment expressed by Schilling reflects **male privilege**. Like white privilege, it is the nearly invisible set of standards we use to evaluate social behaviors. In this example, it is the notion that crying and the overt expression of emotion are bad and that to be a good leader, one must adopt a rational and emotionally neutral demeanor. From this perspective, overly emotional leaders are more vulnerable and command less respect. Yet from the perspective of male privilege, emotional expressions are condemned simply *because* they are associated with women.

Notice that when we discuss the gender gap in pay, men's wages are considered the standard (Kimmel 2014). In stating that women earn 78 cents for every dollar earned by a man, his wage becomes the standard. Stated this way, discrimination *against* women is made visible. Rarely do we express the statistic in an alternate way: men earn $1.28 for every $1 earned by a woman. To do so would highlight men's *privilege*. Other linguistic subtleties also demonstrate male privilege. It would be strange if I walked into class and said, "Okay, girls, let's settle in and get started." Yet we rarely question the logic surrounding the fact that I regularly walk into a classroom that is 60 percent female and say, "Okay, guys, let's get started." The term "guys" has become our standard, even when it is factually incorrect. In many languages, the word "they" takes on a masculine form once one man is included in the group. If I wanted to say in Spanish "My students are very intelligent," I would say, "Ellos estan muy inteligentes." This would be the case even if the group in question contained just one male and 99 (or more) females.

Beyond examples of how male privilege is expressed in language, there are examples of how male privilege is related to more powerful forms of inequality. Some suggest, for example, that male behavioral norms—rather than universal standards of excellence—are used to judge job applicants and candidates for promotion in many occupational fields. Others argue that the structure of many professions—the 9-to-5, full-time–only model—is built on a male standard and, consequently, privileges male workers. I return to these examples in Chapter 13, where gender inequalities in pay and the workplace are examined in greater detail.

It should be mentioned that some dispute the concept of male privilege. In his book *The Myth of Male Power*, Warren Farrell (1993) argues that men are in many ways disadvantaged. From pressures to be the primary breadwinner and fight our nation's wars, to having higher rates than women of suicide, alcoholism, and criminal victimization, Farrell identifies many ways that men lack privilege. Farrell suggests, though, that it is partially male privilege and the expectation that men adhere to a dominant, aggressive version of masculinity that produces these negative results.

Finally, another form of group privilege is heterosexual privilege. Also called **heteronormativity**, it is the tendency to assume heterosexuality is the norm and to structure society in a way that reflects this assumption. Heteronormativity manifests in my classrooms when I make statements assuming that everyone is heterosexual and has the ability and desire to participate in heterosexual institutions like marriage. When discussing gender differences in communication, I may make a seemingly innocuous statement like, "When you fight with your boyfriend or girlfriend, you may get frustrated because...." This statement reflects the assumption that your boyfriend or girlfriend is of the *opposite* sex. Offhand comments like, "When you get married..." contain a similar assumption. While research on LGBTQ persons may be sprinkled throughout the semester, the basic assumption of many Sociology of the Family courses is that getting married is both possible and the ultimate goal. Beyond these subtle linguistic examples, heteronormativity is reflected in the belief that stable, monogamous relationships are the most desirable (they are the norm), alongside the sexual appetites and preferences of heterosexual people. Relationship styles (nonmonogamous) and sexual behaviors ("promiscuous") that deviate from this norm are considered problematic (Rubin 1984). These statements both stigmatize and exclude those who fall outside of the heterosexual norm.

It is not only social judgments that reflect heteronormativity. Many social institutions are also structured around this assumption. Family law, for example, operates in a heteronormative way, allowing legal marriage primarily to heterosexual couples and restricting—in some cases—the adoption options of nonheterosexual people. The assignment of roommates to college dorms also reflects this assumption: males and female students should be separated in order to protect people's privacy, promote their personal comfort, and keep sexual shenanigans to a minimum. As more students who are neither heterosexual nor traditionally gendered enroll in college, new questions arise as to how to make roommate placements (see Chapter 3). Prior to entering college, students may have attended a high school where only male–female couples were allowed at prom and homecoming. Finally, the health care system also assumes a heterosexual, traditionally gendered patient. When doctors take sexual histories of their patients, they usually restrict their focus to heterosexual relations in questions about number of partners, use of contraception, exposure to risks, etc. This perspective can limit doctors' ability to identify and treat patients in an appropriate way, possibly missing symptoms or underestimating risks.

EXPLORING INTERSECTIONALITY: VARIATIONS AND DEGREES OF PRIVILEGE

Although all whites have some degree of race privilege, and all men have some degree of gender privilege, and Christians within the United States have some degree of religious privilege, specific individuals will experience different degrees of privilege depending on their other social identities. Looking at this issue from an intersectional lens, there is no uniform condition called white or male privilege; rather, all forms of privilege exist across several axes, including race, gender, sexual orientation, religion, (dis)ability status, and more. A white man may experience both race and gender privilege, but if he is gay and has a physical disability, he may lack privilege in those domains.

In drawing attention to the phenomenon of "black male privilege," author and activist Jewel Woods says that for many, this term is an oxymoron: "three words that simply do not go together" (2014:29). Yet he argues that "the African-American community will never be able to overcome the serious issues we face if we as black men do not confront our role in promoting and sustaining male supremacist attitudes and actions" (p. 29). While black men may daily suffer the injuries of being on the flipside of white privilege, Woods believes that black men simultaneously experience advantages and privileges—some of which come at the expense of black women. In his "Black Male Privileges Checklist" he identifies the following examples (30–34):

- When I learn about the civil rights movements and leadership in the NAACP and the Black Power movements, most of the leaders I read about are black men.
- I do not have to worry about the tone of my skin or the straightness of my hair, nor am I expected to conform to a standard image of beauty the way black women are.
- I have the privilege of coming from a tradition of humor based largely on insulting and disrespecting women ("Your momma's so fat . . .").
- I have the privilege of believing that the failure of the black family is due in part to black women who are not allowing black men to "be men."
- In college I will have the opportunity to date outside my race at a higher rate than black women will.

In developing these ideas, Woods says he has received the greatest criticism and skepticism from other black men. The long-term and justified focus on racial domination has, he said, curtailed black men's ability to develop a "more expansive understanding of privilege and power" (p. 36). Accordingly, despite their position of racial disadvantage, they have been unable to see what they share in common with women, gays and lesbians, or other disadvantaged groups.

In their research on disabled, gay, and working-class men, Bethany Coston and Michael Kimmel are interested in how "marginalized" men "navigate and access their privilege within the confines of a particular social role that limits, devalues, and often stigmatizes them" (2012:99). Men who are marginalized in some way, they argue, respond in some cases by asserting and emphasizing their masculinity. Men who use wheelchairs, for example, may feel stigmatized in not living up to the strong, able-bodied ideal that hegemonic masculinity emphasizes. In addition to remaining stoic and avoiding emotional expressions, such men may also join athletic leagues (wheelchair basketball, tennis, racing, etc.) that reassert their masculinity. Some gay men, by contrast, may respond to stereotypes that portray them as effeminate by exaggerating their feminine traits. They may resist the expectations of hegemonic masculinity by performing in drag or speaking in an exaggeratedly feminine way.

These examples show that group privilege operates in complicated ways. There are some who are well aware of their lack of privilege but may be less aware of the ways they experience privilege at the expense of others. There are those, moreover, who have privileges that may daily be chipped away at and are reminded of the ways in which they are not universally advantaged.

BECOMING AN ALLY: PRIVILEGED RESPONSES TO GROUP PRIVILEGE

The notion of group privilege and how it contributes to social inequality can be difficult to absorb. Does it really exist? If so, how did it get to be that way and who allows it to continue? As one of the leading scholars of privilege, Michael Kimmel, argues: "Privilege needs to be made visible" (2014:3). We all need to see, he writes, that we are "stakeholders in understanding structural inequality." Racism and inequality affects everyone, in some way. What's more, we should recognize that all white people benefit from racial inequality, even if they themselves are not overtly racist. While some may find this concept too abstract and others may find it offensive, it highlights the fact that group privilege is a macro-level manifestation of social inequality. Because white privilege persists without the overt or conscious actions of a particular individual, and because the beliefs and interactions that result have racially disparate impacts, it is the case people today experience racial inequality even if they have never owned slaves, participated in legal segregation, or discriminated against anyone.

On a practical level, what is a person supposed to do with this information? According to Peggy McIntosh (1988), learning about privilege makes us "newly accountable." Individuals who recognize they have privilege based on race, gender, or sexual orientation must now do two things: (1) acknowledge their (unearned) benefits and (2) ask what they can do to end it. This is a tricky question—I can't give up being white; I didn't ask to be born this way, nor can I just renounce my color. Becoming accountable to your privilege—and *virtually everyone* has some form of privilege—means making yourself uncomfortable; opening your mouth when it would be more comfortable to remain silent; asking the store manager why you weren't asked to show your ID to pay with a check, but the person of color behind you was; tactfully pointing out comments on social media that seem racist or homophobic. Going from everyday experiences to bigger commitments, we can choose to put ourselves in situations that require us to give up, for whatever length of time, a degree of privilege: move into a multiracial neighborhood; attend a multiracial church; go to a meeting with a friend who is a member of an LGBTQ group on campus; choose to join a study group that takes you out of your comfort zone.

For those looking to make a bigger impact, one can become an ally. To be an **ally**—across racial lines, sexual orientation, religion, and so forth—one must stop thinking of "us" and "them." An ally to LGBTQ people does not join "their" fight or become a part of "their" cause; allies see themselves as having a stake in the cause, willing to give up the privilege of remaining silent or invisible. Being an ally may lead to becoming an activist. Activism has the goal of making a public declaration and a commitment, typically, to transforming social policies and institutions. As discussed throughout this book, there are many movements waiting to be joined or formed. So, even though group privilege is a macro-level phenomenon, permeating the air like an invisible ether, it can be dismantled by a series of micro-level responses.

RACISM WITHOUT RACISTS? THE PERSISTENCE OF RACIAL INEQUALITY

Can there be racism without racists? Can racial inequality persist, even if no one in society holds prejudicial beliefs or engages in individual acts of discrimination? This chapter provides an answer to those questions: yes. Racism and racial inequality can persist independently of the individuals who perpetuate it. Racism may still exist, even if there are no specific racist individuals. That's a deep thought. But the reason for this is that inequality—racism, sexism, and so forth—is generated at both the micro- and macro-levels. In addition to the players who put inequality into action, the rules of the game themselves perpetuate inequality.

The examples described in this section reflect a set of social dynamics at the macro-level; some of these dynamics reflect deeply embedded laws and social policies, while others are a reflection of what happens in a diverse society when a powerful majority group sets the norm. All of these examples illustrate dynamics at the macro-level that have produced and now perpetuate racial inequality. That said, there has been a steady pattern over time of dismantling the macro-level sources of inequality. By addressing dynamics at the macro-level—by changing laws and policies and through judicial actions—the racially disparate treatment experienced by millions of Americans has been reduced.

The focus on institutional racism reminds us that the patterns of inequality we see today—patterns involving racial disparities in income, wealth, educational attainment, and health and well-being—did not come out of nowhere. And they do not only reflect the actions or decisions of specific individuals. These patterns, which are likely to have shaped the life experience of you and your relatives, are historically rooted in policies that have systematically affected millions of people over several generations. While it is difficult to say whether the federal government enacted these policies—like the G.I. Bill or penalties for crack and powder cocaine—*in order* to disadvantage minorities and advantage whites, this has been their effect. The housing policies described in this chapter, for example, illustrate where there are racial disparities with respect to the accumulation of wealth, the ability to pass wealth intergenerationally, and the possibility of having home equity that can be used to take out educational loans.

In addition to the examples given here—which focus on housing policies, the criminal justice system, and the political process—institutional racism can also be found in the educational system, namely in terms of how schools are funded (local property taxes) and the criteria used in college admissions (legacy admissions, emphasis on the SAT). These examples are considered in the next chapter, which explores inequalities in the educational system. What unites all of these examples is the systematic nature of their application, as well as their nearly invisible reach, which means that groups within society experience advantages or disadvantages that often seem normal, natural, inevitable, and without malicious intent. Such is the pernicious nature of social inequality.

CHAPTER 11: REVIEW OF KEY POINTS

- This chapter focuses on explaining racism and racial inequality at the macro-level. This perspective examines the role of social structures, policies, and widespread cultural beliefs in perpetuating racial inequality.

- Institutional discrimination is one example of how inequalities are perpetuated at the macro-level. Intuitional racism refers to how racial inequalities are perpetuated by policies and structural arrangements, like housing policies. Even though racially discriminatory housing policies were outlawed in the 1960s, their effects on family wealth and tax revenues for local schools can still be seen today.

- Some sociologists argue that the placement of highways and toxic waste sites reflects explicitly racist beliefs. Regardless of whether such decisions are intentional, the consequences of these decisions have disproportionate negative impact on people of color and lower-income people. This is an example of institutional discrimination.

- Examples of institutional racism can also be seen in the criminal justice system—both in terms of day-to-day policing tactics (like stop-and-frisk) and the kinds of penalties that are attached to particular crimes.

- There are long-term consequences associated with racially disparate penalties in the criminal justice system. The collateral consequences of criminal conviction show that negative consequences follow offenders for many years and that these negative consequences ultimately contribute to racial disparities in income, educational attainment, and political involvement.

- Group privilege, seen more specifically in white privilege, male privilege, and heteronormativity, are macro-level sources of inequality. They are a macro-level force because the beliefs that maintain white privilege, male privilege, and heteronormativity are broad cultural belief systems, with consequences for large segments of the population.

- White privilege is a tricky concept: it suggests that I, as a white person, benefit from racism even if I myself do not hold prejudices or engage in discrimination. Male privilege and heteronormativity operate similarly.

- To the extent that structural arrangements and policies perpetuate racism and racial inequality, the solution for fixing racial inequality would also be found at the level of structural and social policy. Logically, this means changing arrangements at the macro-level, such as housing policies, policies that govern how schools are funded, policies that determine penalties for particular crimes, and admissions policies that determine what factors count in college admissions.

CHAPTER 11: QUESTIONS FOR REVIEW

1. What are the key differences between discrimination, as discussed in Chapter 10, and institutional discrimination, as presented in this chapter?

2. Thinking about the micro- and macro-level forms of discrimination, which do you see as the most pernicious? Similarly, at which level do you think the most progress can be made in terms of alleviating inequalities in race (or gender, sexual orientation, etc.)?

3. Both of my parents grew up in middle-class suburban households in the 1950s. According to the policies described in this chapter, what racial dynamics contributed to the growing wealth and stability of my white grandparents (and did not benefit racial and ethnic minorities)?

4. Currently, the criminal justice system is the site for growing racial inequalities. What are some of the policies that account for this? What are some of the long-term consequences of these racially disparate policies?

5. In this chapter, white privilege is conceptualized as a macro-level dynamic shaping racial inequality (and gender inequality, when thought of as male privilege). In what sense is white privilege a macro-level phenomenon as opposed to a micro-level phenomenon?

6. In what ways do you see (or not see) white privilege operating in the world around you—whether at your place of employment, on campus, or among your family and friends? Considering the class for which this text assigned, to what extent do you think your experience in the class would be different if your instructor had a different race? Do you see racial privilege operating in your classroom? What about gender privilege or heteronormativity?

KEY TERMS

Baldus Study

collateral consequences of criminal
  conviction

driving while black

eminent domain

environmental racism

felon disenfranchisement

Gautreaux Project

group privilege

heteronormativity

indigent defense

institutional discrimination

institutional racism

jury selection

male privilege

poll tax

racial profiling

redlining

restrictive covenants

scattered-site housing

stop-and-frisk

urban renewal

voter ID laws

white privilege

REFERENCES

Alexander, Michelle. 2010. *The New Jim Crow: Mass Incarceration in the Age of Colorblindness.* New York: The New Press.

Baldus, David C., George G. Woodworth, and Charles A. Pulaski. 1990. *Equal Justice and the Death Penalty: A Legal and Empirical Analysis.* Boston: Northeastern University Press.

Bauman, John F., Roger Biles, and Kristin M. Szylvian, eds. 2000. *From Tenements to the Taylor Homes: In Search of an Urban Housing Policy in Twentieth-Century America.* University Park: Pennsylvania State University Press.

Bowers, Melanie and Robert R. Preuhs. 2009. "Collateral Consequences of a Collateral Penalty: The Negative Effect of Felon Disenfranchisement Laws on the Political Participation of Nonfelons." *Social Science Quarterly* 90(3):722–743.

Brennan Center for Justice, NYU School of Law. 2006. "Citizens without Proof: A Survey of Americans' Possession of Documentary Proof of Citizenship and Photo Identification." Retrieved September 10, 2013 (http://www.brennancenter.org/sites/default/files/legacy/d/download_file_39242.pdf).

Bullard, Robert D., Paul Mohai, Robin Saha, and Beverley Wright. 2007. "Toxic Wastes at Twenty: 1987–2007. United Church of Christ. Retrieved August 28, 2013 (http://www.ejrc.cau.edu/TWART-light.pdf).

Bureau of Justice. 2013. "Indigent Defense Systems." Retrieved September 14, 2013 (http://www.bjs.gov/index.cfm?ty=tp&tid=28).

Chin, Gabriel J. 2002. "Race, the War on Drugs, and the Collateral Consequences of Criminal Conviction." *The Journal of Gender, Race, and Justice* 6:253–278.

Chin, Gabriel J. 2012. "The New Civil Death: Rethinking Punishment in the Era of Mass Conviction." *University of Pennsylvania Law Review* 160:1789–1833.

Coston, Bethany M. and Michael Kimmel. 2012. "Seeing Privilege Where It Isn't: Marginalized Masculinities and the Intersectionality of Privilege." *Journal of Social Issues* 68(1):97–111.

Dixon, Travis L, Terry L. Schell, Howard Giles, and Kristin L. Drogos. 2008. "The Influence of Race in Police-Civilian Interactions: A Content Analysis of Videotaped Interactions Taken During Cincinnati Police Traffic Stops." *Journal of Communication* 58(3):530–549.

Equal Justice Initiative. 2010. "Illegal Racial Discrimination in Jury Selection: A Continuing Legacy." Retrieved September 14, 2013 (http://www.eji.org/files/EJI%20Race%20and%20Jury%20Report.pdf).

Farrell, Warren. 1993. *The Myth of Male Power: Why Men Are the Disposable Sex*. New York: Simon & Schuster.

Fogelson, Robert M. 2005. *Bourgeois Nightmares: Suburbia 1870–1930*. New Haven, CT: Yale University Press.

Goldstein, Joseph. 2013. "Judge Rejects New York's Stop-and-Frisk Policy." *New York Times*, August 12. Retrieved April 22, 2015 (http://www.nytimes.com/2013/08/13/nyregion/stop-and-frisk-practice-violated-rights-judge-rules.html)

Harris, David A. 1999. "Driving While Black: Racial Profiling on our Nation's Highways." American Civil Liberties Union. Retrieved September 7, 2013 (https://www.aclu.org/racial-justice/driving-while-black-racial-profiling-our-nations-highways).

Huff, Ronald, Arye Rattner, and Edward Sagarin. 1996. *Convicted but Innocent: Wrongful Conviction and Public Policy*. Thousand Oaks, CA: Sage.

Kimmel, Michael S. 2014. "Introduction: Toward a Sociology of the Superordinate." Pp. 1–12 in *Privilege, A Reader*, 3rd ed., edited by Michael S. Kimmel and Abby L. Ferber. Boulder, CO: Westview Press.

Lamberth, John. 1998. "Driving While Black: A Statistician Proves That Prejudice Still Rules the Road." *Washington Post*, August 16, C01

McFadden, Robert D. 1999. "Whitman Dismisses State Police Chief for Race Remarks." *New York Times*, March 1. Retrieved April 22, 2015 (http://www.nytimes.com/1999/03/01/nyregion/whitman-dismisses-state-police-chief-for-race-remarks.html)

McIntosh, Peggy. 2007. "White Privilege: Unpacking the Invisible Knapsack." Pp. 98–102 in *Race, Class, & Gender: An Anthology*, edited by Margaret L. Anderson and Patricia Hill Collins. Belmont, CA: Wadsworth.

"White Privilege: Unpacking the Invisible Knapsack." *Race, Class, and Gender in the United States: An Integrated Study* 4:165–169.

Miyares, Ines M. 2004. "From Exclusionary Covenant to Ethnic Hyperdiversity in Jackson Heights, Queens." *Geographical Review* 94(4):462–483.

Organization for Economic Co-operation and Development (OECD). 1999. "OECD Seminar: Social and Environmental Interface Proceedings." Retrieved August 27, 2013 (http://www.oecd.org/environment/country-reviews/33848718.pdf).

Radelet, Michael L. and Glenn L. Pierce. 2011. "Race and Death Sentencing in North Carolina, 1980–2007." *North Carolina Law Review* 89(6): 2119–2159.

Reiman, Jeffery and Paul Leighton. 2012. *The Rich Get Richer and the Poor Get Prison*, 10th ed. Upper Saddle River, NJ: Pearson.

Rubin, Gayle. 1984. "Thinking Sex: Notes for a Radical Theory of the Politics of Sexuality." Pp. 267–319 in *Pleasure and Danger: Exploring Female Sexuality*, edited by Carole S. Vance. Boston: Routledge & Kegan Paul.

Rubinowitz, Leonard S. and James E. Rosenbaum. 2000. *Crossing the Class and Color Lines: From Public Housing to White Suburbia*. Chicago: University of Chicago Press.

Somers, Samuel R. and Michael I. Norton. 2008. "Race and Jury Selection Psychological Perspectives on the Peremptory Challenge Debate." *American Psychologist* 63(6):527–539.

Supreme Court of the United States. 2007. Syllabus for *Kimbrough v. United States* 552 US 85. Retrieved August 28, 2013 (http://www.scotusblog.com/wp-content/uploads/2007/12/06-6330.pdf).

The Sentencing Project. 2013. "Felony Disenfranchisement Laws in the United States." Retrieved September 9, 2013 (http://sentencingproject.org/doc/publications/fd_bs_fdlawsinus_Jun2013.pdf).

Uggen, Christopher and Jeff Manza. 2002. "Democratic Contraction? Political Consequences of Felon Disenfranchisement in the United States." *American Sociological Review* 67(6):777–803.

Wilson, William Julius. 1987. *The Truly Disadvantaged: The Inner City, the Underclass, and Public Policy*. Chicago: University of Chicago Press.

Wilson, William Julius. 1996. *When Work Disappears: The World of New Urban Poor*. New York: Vintage Books.

Woods, Jewel. 2014. "The Black Male Privilege Checklist." Pp. 28–38 in *Privilege, A Reader*, 3rd ed., edited by Michael S. Kimmel and Abby L. Ferber. Boulder, CO: Westview Press.

Unequal Outcomes: The Interplay of Micro- and Macro-Levels

People raised in the United States tend to be a tirelessly optimistic bunch. Many of us believe wholeheartedly in the "American Dream." According to a poll conducted by the *New York Times*, the vast majority of Americans believe that it is possible to start out poor and end up rich. These beliefs have held up, even in times of economic struggle, when fewer and fewer Americans are able to achieve such social mobility. Outside of the economic realm, the boundless optimism was evident during the 2014 FIFA World Cup, when American soccer fans chanted "I believe that we will win." This belief in faith and determination in the face of struggle was noteworthy, given the relatively poor performance of U.S.A. soccer on the world stage and the comment by the team's German coach that "You have to be realistic. Every year we are getting stronger. For us now talking about winning a World Cup, it is just not realistic."

Whether in reference to a sports team or the economic fortunes of the individual, Americans are an optimistic bunch. Their optimism, moreover, tends to reflect a deep and abiding emphasis on the individual. It is conventionally American, for example, to believe that—as noted in the first chapter of this book—"Anyone can make it if they try." Sociologically, "making it" translates to meaningful variables like completing a college degree, earning a fair and decent wage, and living a long and healthy life. This cultural mindset, which I've observed for 15 years among my students, typically holds that the only thing holding a person back from achieving their educational or occupational goals, or from living a long and healthy life, is him- or herself.

For those who hold such faith in the individual, sociology can be a tough sell. It's not that sociologists discount the importance of "free will" or dismiss the role of the individual in shaping his or her life chances; it is that sociologists believe that the emphasis on the individual provides only a partial understanding of why things are the way they are. This unit continues the emphasis on "the player" and "the game." Here, we explore some of the most significant forms of social inequality in the contemporary United States. Each chapter in this unit takes a basic social outcome—namely how much education a person receives, how much he or she gets paid, and how long one lives—and explores it from the sociological perspective. That means examining the degree to which these inequalities are shaped by individual life circumstances (e.g., the player) *as well as* the social factors that play out at the structural level (e.g., the game). Rather than provide a pessimistic account of why it is often difficult for individuals to achieve their goals, this chapter shows the complicated dynamics that characterize our social world and indicates that social inequalities can best be addressed by both micro-level factors at the individual level and macro-level factors within society at large.

Graduating with Honors?

Understanding Inequalities in Education

During the spring of my sister's senior year of high school, I accompanied her to a taping of the *Oprah Winfrey Show*. When I say that I accompanied her, I don't mean that we had finally secured tickets to sit in the audience of this immensely popular talk show. I accompanied her because she was selected to be a featured guest of Ms. Winfrey. In a program devoted to people who had "beat the odds"—those who had overcome significant obstacles to achieve remarkable educational success—my sister Caitlin was invited to tell her story. Her story was that we lost our mother when she was 11 years old; in the years following, her father (my stepfather) struggled with financial, as well as physical and mental health, issues so that she often lacked the stability she needed. Despite these challenges, she embarked on several service trips abroad, graduated near the top of her high school class, and was accepted at numerous prestigious colleges. After her appearance on the Oprah show, she went on to graduate from a prestigious college, spent two years doing research in South America through a highly selective Fulbright scholarship, and enrolled in a Ph.D. program at Harvard University.

My sister Caitlin's story raises an important question: Why do some people achieve greater educational success than others? To some extent, her story illustrates the notion of the American Dream—the belief that in the United States, individuals have the opportunity to overcome their circumstances and not be held back in their quest to achieve great things. Yet the fact that the theme of the Oprah Winfrey episode was individuals who "beat the odds" highlights just how unlikely it is that people will, in fact, defy the circumstances of their birth. People "beat the odds" when they defy the statistical pattern showing that those who grow up in disadvantaged circumstances have a difficult time achieving educational success, while those who grow up in advantaged circumstances are more likely to do so. The fact that they "beat the odds" means that the odds are stacked against them.

The question of why some people achieve greater educational success than others is significant because the educational system and people's experiences within it are linked to their economic and social well-being as adults. Higher levels of education are related to higher incomes, as well as greater marital stability, greater access to health care, higher levels of political participation, and other factors that improve people's lives. Yet in the United States, there are serious educational inequalities. These inequalities—involving race and social class—include how much education a person receives, the quality of their education, and the kinds of experiences they have in school.

This chapter begins with a description of educational inequalities in the United States in terms of college entrance, college selectivity, and college completion. The next task is to explain why these inequalities exist. Our explanation begins with the assumption that "the player" plays a significant role in shaping his or her success. The ability of the player to play the game reflects previous educational success, access to funding, and knowledge of how to play the game. Still, every player plays a game that has pre-existing rules and structure. Therefore, we expand our explanation of educational inequalities to the nature of the game—dynamics taking place at the macro-level. As it turns out, the nature of the "game" is such that the structure of education and educational policies reward some players more than others. Ultimately, these explanations reflect the core insight of sociology: that individual efforts and circumstances matter a great deal, but that any social phenomenon—like educational inequality—can best be understood by also paying attention to the context in which individual efforts and circumstances play out.

WHEN IT COMES TO EDUCATION, HOW UNEQUAL IS THE UNITED STATES?

Within the United States, how much and what kind of education a person receives is often a function of their social class and racial background. While schools play an important role in social mobility, the educational system can also thwart the American Dream and perpetuate inequality. We begin by exploring statistically the scope of educational inequalities. In terms of higher education, these inequalities include *whether* you go; *where* you go; and *whether* you complete your degree.

THE EDUCATIONAL PAYOFF

Currently in the United States, about 32 percent of adults have earned at least a Bachelor's degree.[1] Those who have earned a bachelor's degree have very different incomes compared to those who have not. As shown in Figure 12.1, the median weekly income of a person with a bachelor's degree is about $1,050, compared to about $638 for a person

---

[1] Unless otherwise noted, all data in this section come from the U.S. Census Bureau or the Bureau of Labor Statistics.

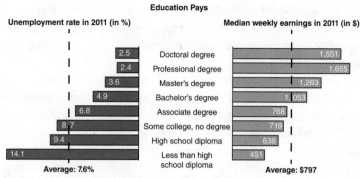

Figure 12.1 Education and weekly earnings.

(*Source:* Bureau of Labor Statistics, Current Population Survey)

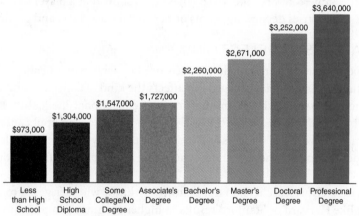

Figure 12.2 Median lifetime earnings by educational attainment, 2009.

(*Source:* Carnevale, Rose, and Cheah 2011)

with only a high school degree. On an annual basis, this means that adults with a bachelor's degree (or higher) earn twice as much as those with only a high school degree. There are, of course, variations within these numbers. While both hold a college degree, a petroleum engineer's median annual earnings are about $135,000, while a social worker's are only $42,000. Over time, these differences add up. Figure 12.2 shows that the average person with a bachelor's degree will earn nearly $2.3 million during their lifetime, while the average high school graduate will earn an average of $1.3 million. Over time, that extra million dollars translates not simply into more vacations or meals out, but also the ability to live in a safe neighborhood and plan for retirement.

INEQUALITIES IN ENROLLMENT

While it is clear that the "payoff" associated with higher education is substantial, there are big inequalities in terms of who achieves this goal. When researchers talk about educational inequality, one indicator they use is **educational attainment**—the number of years or highest degree a person achieves. When it comes to attaining a bachelor's degree, there are significant inequalities in college enrollments. Among high school graduates from the wealthiest families (top quintile), 80 percent enter college following high school. That number is 55 percent among high school graduates from the poorest families (bottom quintile).

Inequalities in college enrollment are also evident when it comes to race and, to a lesser extent, gender. The College Board, for example, reports that 70 percent of white high school graduates go on to some form of higher education; for black and Hispanic high school graduates, these numbers are 56 and 62 percent, respectively. Asian American students, by contrast, enroll at the highest rates. When it comes to gender inequalities in college enrollment, females have been the majority of all college students since the 1980s; today, they represent nearly 60 percent of all college students. In terms of college enrollment, approximately 72 percent of females go on to college after high school, while 66 percent of males do so. These data show that a player's chance of getting in the game varies depending on his or her social class, race, and gender.

INEQUALITIES IN SELECTIVITY

Educational inequalities are not simply measured by who goes to college in the first place. A student's social class background affects the kind of college or university they attend. Therefore, **selectivity** is another form of educational inequality. A selective school is, by definition, one that admits a smaller percentage of applicants. Selective schools tend to have fewer students and cost more than a typical public college or university. Does that mean, though, those schools are better or that their graduates earn more money?

Unfortunately, researchers do not definitively know whether going to a selective university like Harvard or Stanford results in higher earnings compared to going to a less selective school like California State at Fullerton or Mankato State University in Minnesota. Economic researchers Stacy Dale and Alan Krueger (2011) found that once you control for other things that might affect how much a person earns—like family background, SAT scores, and college GPA—attending one of the 150 schools rated as "highly selective" may not make much of a difference. Yet Paul Kingston and John Smart (1990) found that graduates from truly top-tier schools (e.g., Ivy League) have higher earnings than those who graduate from merely "good" schools (e.g., University of Illinois, Drake University). Where most researchers agree is that students from lower-income backgrounds, as well as African Americans and Latinos, earn more when they graduate from a highly selective school, controlling for other factors (Dale and Krueger 2011; Loury and Garman 1995). For students from less advantaged backgrounds, going to a selective school may play an important role in achieving the American Dream.

Beyond how much a person earns, there are other benefits associated with going to a selective college or university. For one, students who enroll in selective schools are more likely to finish their college degrees (Carnevale and Rose 2004). They are also more likely to rub shoulders with people from affluent backgrounds, thereby increasing their "social" and "cultural capital" (Stuber 2011). About 74 percent of students attending highly selective schools come from families with the highest incomes (Sacks 2007)—meaning that the typical student is wealthy and is surrounded by other wealthy students. Finally, students at selective schools are more likely to marry (and remain married to) another graduate of a selective school—which further contributes to higher lifetime earnings (Arum, Roksa, and Budig 2008). In these ways, going to a selective school perpetuates social inequality.

Despite the apparent benefits of going to a selective college, not everyone can get in or pay for such a school; others don't even aspire to attend. For many, starting off at a two-year college appears to be a good option. These schools are especially attractive to students who want a specific job skill or want to complete their "general education" requirements at a less expensive institution. Over the last 50 years, two-year colleges have expanded the educational opportunities for minorities and lower-income people. In fact, The National Center for Education Statistics reports that minorities represent only 21 percent of students enrolled at 4-year schools, but 31 percent of those at two-year schools.

While two-year colleges fit some students' needs, some researchers argue that they actually contribute to educational inequalities. In their classic book, *The Diverted Dream*, Steven Brint and Jerome Karabel (1989) show that community colleges have had a poor record moving students into four-year schools. Although some students at two-year colleges do not aspire to a bachelor's degree, many do. Unfortunately, many community colleges do a poor job helping students attain their goal. Perhaps one reason is that many of the classes students take at two-year schools are remedial in nature or do not offer transferrable college credits. Thus, while students may be enrolled in college, their courses are not helping them move through the college curriculum. In some cases, then, less selective schools attract students from more disadvantaged backgrounds and make it difficult for them to overcome that disadvantage.

INEQUALITIES IN COMPLETION

Not everyone who enrolls in college completes their degree. Researchers refer to this as **attrition**—a technical term for "dropping out." While some students leave college because they can no longer afford it or they cannot handle the academics, others—especially those from lower-income and minority backgrounds—leave because they have a hard time adjusting to campus climate. This partially explains why students from lower-income and minority backgrounds may have a harder time completing a degree once they enroll.

In terms of college completion, the U.S. Census Bureau reports that as of 2010, about 52 percent of Asian Americans have attained at least a bachelor's degree, followed by 30 percent of whites, 20 percent of African Americans, and 14 percent of Hispanics (see Figure 12.3). Among African Americans and Hispanics, women are more likely than men to have completed a college degree. Despite these lingering inequalities, since the 1970s the total enrollments of minorities have been growing, as have their completion rates. In fact, since 1980, the percentage of African American and Latino adults with a bachelor's degree has doubled.

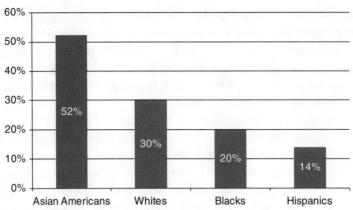

Figure 12.3 Bachelor's degree attainment by race/ethnicity.
(*Source:* Ewert and Kominski 2014)

Although Asian Americans are still more than twice as likely as African Americans to have completed a college degree, the most enduring inequality in education falls along economic lines. Students who grow up in the wealthiest families (top quartile) are about eight times more likely to finish a bachelor's degree than those who grow up in the poorest families (bottom quartile). What is truly astounding is that this figure has not changed in the last 40 years (Sacks 2007). Although the total number of colleges and universities in the United States, along with the overall number of students enrolled in higher education, has expanded dramatically over the last 40 years, the social class gap in college completion has not budged during that time frame. There is something about both the players and the game that continues to result in significant social class inequalities within the educational system.

EDUCATIONAL INEQUALITY AND THE ROLE OF "THE PLAYER"

From the sociological perspective, social phenomena can best be understood by combining the micro- and macro-levels. To understand why some groups end up with more education than others, we need to look at the role of "the player" (micro-level) and the nature of "the game" (macro-level). The player brings a lot to the table. Some players, for example, have an abundance of talent, drive, and motivation, as well as money and access to resources that enhance their ability to play the game. Other players are at a disadvantage—whether because of their lack of talent or motivation or the fact that they do not have access to money or resources that might help boost their performance. In terms of educational success, three of the most important factors shaping a player's ability to play the game are money, skills or talent, and know-how.

ACCESS TO MONEY: THE COST OF GETTING IN THE GAME

Players need an awful lot of money to enter the game of higher education. The National Center for Public Policy and Higher Education reports that one year of college currently costs more than $26,000. The costs of tuition plus room and board run an average of $39,000 at private institutions and $20,000 at public institutions. Students whose families lack financial resources or wish to save on the cost of higher education can live at home and attend a two-year college. This reduces annual costs to about $7,900. At the other end of the spectrum are expensive, highly selective colleges and universities. At nationally ranked liberal arts colleges and universities, annual costs typically run around $55,000 (tuition plus room and board). The fact that the average college costs more than half of what a lower-income family earns in an entire year helps explain why students from such families are less likely to graduate from college and why they are more likely to enroll in less selective two-year schools.

The costs of higher education are such that players need more money than ever to get in the game. Over the last 30 years, the cost of going to college has increased 440 percent; since the early 1980s, the cost of going to college has increased more than four times. The costs of health care have gone up by 250 percent during the same time frame, while the median family income has increased only 147 percent. In short, the cost of higher education has increased much more rapidly than most families' ability to pay for it.

Although college costs have skyrocketed, financial aid is available based on both merit (grades, accomplishments) and financial need. Whereas the average annual cost of attendance is about $20,000 at a public four-year school, the average financial aid package is around $8,000. Through a combination of grants, loans, and scholarships, the typical student's out-of-pocket costs are reduced to about $12,000. Even so, the average college student graduates with a considerable debt. Mark Kantrowitz (2011), who operates the website finaid.org, reports that the average debt for a graduate of the class of 2011 is about $27,000. When you factor in loans taken out by parents or guardians, this amount increases to $34,000.

On the surface, the fact that financial aid decreases the costs of attendance comes as a relief to families struggling to pay for college. Yet some financial aid policies may actually contribute to educational inequalities. How can it be that something that is intended to reduce college costs actually contributes to social class or racial inequalities? The answer lies in how financial aid policies have changed over the last 40 years. In fact, if you receive financial aid, these changes probably affect you in some way. I encourage you to find yourself in this discussion and consider whether you have been helped or hurt by these changes.

Financial aid comprises some combination of grants, loans, scholarships, and work study. Over the last 40 years, loans have replaced grants as the primary source of federal student aid (Price 2004). This means that college students must repay a greater share of their financial aid. Students during the 1970s or '80s, by contrast, received a larger share in grant-based aid—a type of financial aid that does not need to be paid back!

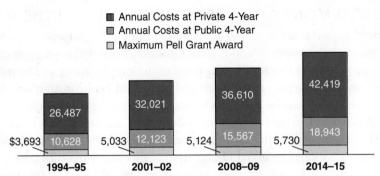

Figure 12.4: Declining public support for higher education: Pell Grant as a proportion of college costs (inflation adjusted).
(*Source:* "Trends in College Pricing, 2014," The College Board)

One federal grant program that has shrunk over the last several decades is the Pell Grant, named after Senator Claiborne Pell and formerly known as the Basic Education Opportunity Grant. Since the mid-1960s, the Pell Grant has been the largest source of aid to students from lower-income backgrounds. Unfortunately, with the rising costs of higher education, it now pays a smaller portion of a student's costs (see Figure 12.4). During the 1970s, the Pell Grant covered about 75 percent of a student's college costs; today, it covers only about one-third. While there are more loan options available today than in the past, members of minority groups are especially hesitant to take out loans. These changes, then, have placed barriers in the way of some aspiring college students.

At the same time, some changes in financial aid policies have increased the fortunes of upper-income students—especially those with demonstrated talents. While need-based aid has decreased, especially at public institutions, more financial aid dollars have been devoted to merit aid, or aid given for academic accomplishments and other talents. Although this shift in policy is designed to reward talented students, it has the effect of increasing the social class gap in education because middle- and upper-middle class students are more likely to have high school records that qualify them for merit aid (Schmidt 2007). As a consequence, there is relatively less aid for lower-income students.

Yet the story surrounding the increase in merit aid is more complicated still. Imagine how these policies may affect students in your state, students who wish to attend the "flagship" school, such as Rutgers, The State University of New Jersey, Indiana University, or the University of Florida. In order for these institutions to raise their prestige and move up the rankings of colleges and universities, they must attract students with high SAT scores. In the last several decades, many state schools have begun looking for students outside of their borders—students who can increase the academic prestige of the institution and also pay higher out-of-state tuition prices. Yet in order to entice these students to enroll and reduce the sting of out-of-state tuition, many public state schools have begun using merit aid and scholarships as the lure.

While it is in the university's best interest to admit the strongest students, doing so contributes to social class inequality: as these schools seek out academically talented students from outside their state's borders, in-state students with more modest academic records are turned away. This would not necessarily be a problem, except for the fact that these students and their families pay taxes to the state in question; consequently, they end up subsidizing the merit aid to out-of-state students, while they are increasingly shut out and end up enrolling at less selective schools.

When it comes to financial aid, do "players" who are black or Hispanic or Native American have an advantage over those who are white? With prominent advertisements from the United Negro College Fund and other groups that give scholarship money to students from particular racial and ethnic groups, it is tempting to conclude that minorities have a leg up when it comes to paying for college. Yet a review of the evidence indicates that this is not the case. According to financial aid guru Mark Kantrowitz (2011), white students represent 62 percent of all college students but receive 76 percent of all merit-based scholarships. Ultimately white students are 40 percent more likely than nonwhite students to receive private scholarships. When it comes to the player's ability to pay, Kantrowitz concludes that white students "receive more than their fair share" (p. 1) of scholarship money.

Over the last several decades, some of our nation's most elite universities have made incredible strides in providing financial assistance to lower-income students. Because they have large endowments, schools like Harvard, Stanford, and the University of North Carolina are able to admit talented lower-income students and help them graduate without any debt. This is no small accomplishment, given that a bachelor's degree from one of these schools has a sticker price of $220,000 or more. In fact, this is precisely how my sister Caitlin was able to attend a highly selective college. Yet gaining admissions to one of these schools is no small accomplishment. While elite schools may have made strides in increasing financial access, lower-income students often lack the academic preparation to get in the game.

SKILLS AND TALENT: ACADEMIC BARRIERS TO GETTING IN THE GAME

In order to succeed in the game of higher education, the player needs a variety of skills and talent. Whereas a basketball player needs to be adept at shooting, ball handling, footwork, and defensive play, success in the educational game requires intelligence, creativity, curiosity, and discipline. And while basketball players are recruited after recruiters review tape, make in-person visits, and assess where they might fit into a lineup, recruitment into the collegiate game typically occurs after a relatively brief review of an applicant's credentials. As it turns out, in the recruitment of college students and the specific "skills" assessed, some benefit more than others.

Imagine recruiting players for a basketball team by looking for players who have the highest field goal (shooting) percentage. Although making baskets is an extremely important skill—maybe even the most important one—it is not the only skill that makes an excellent basketball player. Moreover, if you're trying to put together a team, you'll want players with a variety of skills. If you end up selecting players based only on their field goal percentage, you're likely to end up with a lopsided team.

What does this analogy have to do with the game of higher education? Many colleges and universities have admissions policies that emphasize one trait above others, and, it turns out, this particular trait is highly correlated with social class. Since the early 1980s, the Scholastic Aptitude Test (SAT) has become increasingly important in the college admissions game. On the list of things that colleges and universities take into account, the SAT has risen to the top, while class rank has declined in importance. For colleges and universities that receive many applicants, admissions decisions may be based on SAT scores and GPA alone. At small, selective colleges and universities, or in the case of "borderline" applicants, other skills and talents are taken into account, including extracurricular involvement, service work, personal essays, and letters of recommendation.

The fact that SAT scores are strongly correlated with social class means that wealthier students score higher on the test (see Figure 12.5). According to data from the College Board—the organization that operates the SAT—there is about a 200-point gap between the SAT scores of low-income high school students and those of high-income students. The average combined score for an upper-income student is about 1140, while the average score for a low-income student is about 940 (out of 1600 on the Math and Critical Reading portions). Perhaps even more appalling is the fact that the social class gap in SAT scores has widened over the last several decades! In the context of a game where the SAT score is perhaps the most important recruitment tool, this has significant consequences for a student's college options.

What is it about social class that provides such an advantage on the SAT? Perhaps wealthier kids are just naturally or genetically smarter. That explanation, however, has

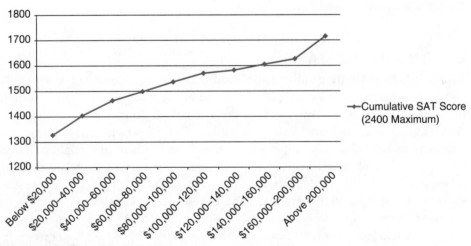

Figure 12.5 SAT and family income.
(*Source:* "Total Group Profile Report, 2013," The College Board)

been evaluated and rejected numerous times (Bowen, Kurzweil, and Tobin 2005; Fischer et al. 1996). Another possibility is that the test itself has a class bias built in. There is, in fact, some support for this explanation. Some researchers have found that certain questions in the critical reading (verbal) portion of the test contain words or cultural expressions that are not learned in school but tend to circulate among affluent whites (Santelices and Wilson 2010). The College Board is sensitive to charges that their test is biased toward different groups. Over the years, they have made changes to make it a more valid indicator of intelligence. Questions about analogies have been phased out, partially for this reason. Yet consider one question that has been used to illustrate a possible class bias (Pringle 2003):

Runner: Marathon

A) envoy: embassy
B) martyr: massacre
C) oarsman: regatta
D) referee: tournament
E) horse: stable

This question includes some terms that any high school student should be expected to know (e.g., martyr and massacre) but other terms that are culturally specific (oarsman and regatta). The class bias is certainly not intentional. It simply reflects the types of conversations and cultural references that are more likely to be found among affluent families. The correct answer to this question is C; while there are likely to be few academic lessons where these terms come up, they may be familiar to students of the upper classes, where knowledge of water sports like yachting and crew are more commonplace.

Another explanation for why kids from wealthier families tend to score higher on the SAT is that practice makes perfect—and students from higher-income families have more opportunities to practice. One opportunity they take advantage of is taking the test multiple times; perhaps by becoming more familiar with the test, they perform better. At $50 a pop, this is no small investment. In addition, schools in wealthier districts are also more likely to offer extensive test-prep as part of the regular curriculum. Beyond the school walls, the test-prep industry has become big business; according to *Time* magazine it is a $4 billion per year industry! Test preparation includes private tutors who may charge as much as $200 per hour, as well as expensive ($500–$1,400) test-prep courses from nationally known companies. If you think about SAT test-prep through the analogy of basketball, some players simply have access to the best personal coaches and trainers out there.

When it comes to understanding the racial gap in standardized testing, a very provocative explanation has been given by the social psychologist Claude Steele. Is it possible, he asks, that black students just "get tight" and fail to perform under pressure? In fact, Claude Steele's experimental research suggests that black students in particular have the skills but sometimes "choke" due to "stereotype threat." In an *Atlantic* magazine article Claude Steele defined **stereotype threat** as "the threat of

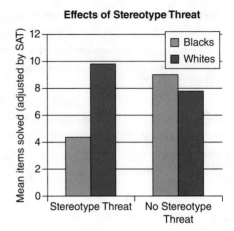

Figure 12.6 Effects of stereotype threat.
(*Source:* Adapted from Aronson, Steele, Salinas, and Lustina 1998)

being viewed through the lens of a negative stereotype, or the fear of doing something that would inadvertently confirm a stereotype." In other words, the fear of confirming a negative stereotype about unintelligent black students causes black students to perform below expectations. As shown in Figure 12.6, Claude Steele and his collaborators devised a number of clever experiments and found that when black students (and others) were prompted to think about their race or ethnicity before taking an exam, they did worse than when they were not primed to think about their race or ethnicity. This suggests that certain aspects of the test-taking scenario itself—such as asking test takers to fill in their race or ethnicity—contributes to the test score gap.

The growing emphasis on the SAT is partially responsible for race and social class inequalities in college attendance. Perhaps this matter would not be so controversial if it could be demonstrated that the SAT is a true indicator of intelligence and collegiate success. Unfortunately, it has only modest success in predicting collegiate success, whether in terms of GPA or graduation rates. For minority students, in particular, SAT scores have very little to do with how well they perform in college (Bowen and Bok 1998). The heavy reliance on SAT scores means that many colleges and universities end up with a narrowly skilled and less diverse student body. Indeed, studies of colleges and universities that have gone "SAT-optional" show that focusing on high school GPA in the admissions process results in an incoming class that is demonstrably more diverse and no less academically talented (Soares 2011).

EXPLORING INTERSECTIONALITY: RACE, GENDER, AND ACADEMIC PERFORMANCE

While persistent inequalities exist in the college completion rates of white and black students, the story becomes more complicated when taking an intersectional approach. While racial gaps in education certainly exist, there is also a large gender gap *among* black Americans (and, to a lesser extent, Latinos). At the grade school level, black boys and black girls perform similarly on standardized tests. Yet in high school, gender differences emerge. While black males and black females have similar scores on the SAT, a smaller percentage of black males take the test. A Manhattan Institute report based on data from 11 large urban school districts reveals that 59 percent of black females finish high school, compared to 48 percent of black males. From this group, fewer males go on to college; among those who do go, fewer males complete their degrees. All of this contributes to a pattern whereby black females generally have higher levels of educational attainment than black males.

Why do black males and females have such different educational outcomes? While the explanation is multifaceted, sociologist Prudence Carter (2006) argues that it partially boils down to the construction of gender roles. Numerous scholars—including Elijah Anderson (2000, 2013) and Patricia Hill Collins (2004)—have commented on the fact that the black male gender role is one that emphasizes hardness and being "streetwise." This includes adopting a cool, indifferent pose; using non-Standard English, Ebonics, or slang; and finding a way to make economic ends meet ("grind") outside of socially approved settings. As it turns out, these traits are largely at odds with prevailing definitions of academic success. In school, earnestness and engagement, as well as the use of "proper English," are seen as markers of success. Because of the tension between these two sets of expectations, Prudence Carter argues, school success has come to be defined as a girl thing, while success on the street has come to be defined as a guy thing. Therefore, when black males succeed in school, they run the risk of being labeled gay or effeminate. According to some scholars, then, black men must choose between academic success and masculinity.

While the roots of these gender inequalities are still being explored, the consequences are better understood. According to Nancy Lopez (2002) these educational experiences produce "hopeful girls" and "troubled boys." Still, these hopeful and academically successful black women face a "marriage squeeze"—a situation where they confront a shortage of potential marriage partners. The squeeze is partially due to the fact that black men are more likely to be involved in the criminal justice system and have lower levels of educational attainment than black women. Black women confront a dilemma: to enter into a relationship with a man who may not meet the traditional definition of a good provider, to enter into an interracial relationship; or to go it alone. The demographic and educational mismatch among black women and black men currently appears to be resulting in lower rates of marriage and higher rates of births to unmarried women (a trend that has roots broader than the educational mismatch). The consequences of the marriage squeeze—and the unique ways in which gender and race intersect within the educational realm—are expected to reverberate throughout future generations, given that nearly 70 percent of black children are born to unmarried mothers. These dynamics will likely have consequences for gender roles and economic well-being among black Americans for generations to come.

ACCESS TO KNOW-HOW: THE ROLE OF CULTURAL CAPITAL IN GETTING IN THE GAME

Finally, in order to play the game and perform well, players must know the rules of the game. As with sports, both skills and knowledge of the game itself are necessary for success. Knowledge of the game includes information about where to sign up, what kind of prior preparation is needed, and which league best suits a player's talents. In the complicated game of higher education, successful players—aka students—need a kind of know-how called **cultural capital**. French sociologist Pierre Bourdieu argued that students from higher social classes have more cultural capital—more knowledge of how the educational system works and appropriate cultural skills—and that this explains why they have better educational success.

Going way back to elementary school, Bourdieu said, teachers develop more positive feelings toward students who exhibit certain forms of cultural capital. Students, for example, who sit quietly during story time and answer the teachers' questions get noticed. Teachers also like students who can shake their hands, look them in the eye, and engage in conversation, almost like little adults. Teachers may get excited about students who can connect history lessons to their own family vacations or trips to museums. These subtle cultural traits capture positive attention from teachers and are interpreted as signs of intelligence.

As students move through high school, different forms of cultural capital affect how they play the game. Some players have an innate feel for the game. Students who come from wealthier backgrounds or who have college-educated parents may have an intuitive feel for things like which high school courses are necessary for college admissions; which standardized tests are required, where they are offered, and when they should be taken; admissions deadlines; financial aid opportunities; and more. Although it is the job of the school to provide students with this information, some students have the advantage of having these lessons reinforced at home. In my own research (Stuber 2011), I found that middle- and upper middle-class students often apply to the same colleges their parents and grandparents attended, so the routines and traditions associated with these educational experiences are passed down almost like their genetic material.

Educational aspirations, such as the desire to attend college, are one form of educational know-how. While researchers know that lower-income and minority students often have high educational aspirations, they don't always achieve their aspirations. Sociologist Roslyn Mickelson (1990) called this the **Attitude-Achievement Paradox**. Why, she and others have asked, do black and Latino students have positive educational attitudes but lower academic achievement? While minority students enjoy school, value school, and believe that education pays off (Downey, Ainsworth, and Qian 2009), these values do not translate into high levels of achievement. Scholars explain this paradox by noting that there is a difference between having *abstract* educational values and being able to convert those attitudes into *concrete* behaviors that produce educational achievement. The takeaway is that success in school requires a kind of know-how that translates values into behaviors that contribute to educational achievement.

When it comes to going to college, the lack of concrete know-how may be a hindrance. Lower-income and minority students may not know, for example, the differences between technical colleges, liberal arts colleges, and universities. For students who lack educationally specific cultural capital, simply going to "college" is the ultimate goal, without understanding that there are substantial variations between schools—variations that have implications for retention, employment, and earnings. Consequently, students sometimes end up in schools that are a poor fit for them—in terms of the campus culture or course offerings—and then leave.

When it comes to how students choose a college, researchers find that high-achieving students from lower-income families apply to schools that are "beneath" them in admissions standards; according to their academic credentials, these students are **undermatched** at the colleges in which they eventually enroll (Roderick, Coca, and Nagoka 2011). By contrast, lower-achieving students from wealthy families are more likely to apply to "reach" schools—ones that are above their qualifications in terms of admissions standards (Gerald and Haycock 2006). For students from wealthy families, a robust sense of entitlement (in the words of Annette Lareau) and feelings of financial security may encourage them to reach for the stars—even if those stars are academically beyond their reach. Lower-income students, by contrast, tend to overestimate how much it costs to go to college (Grodsky and Jones 2007), thereby limiting the schools to which they apply. Because of the college-going climate in their high schools, these students may also lack educationally-specific cultural capital, making them unaware of the fact that many highly selective schools have a "no-loan" financial aid policy, so that they could graduate debt free!

It's not just money that opens doors for some and closes them for others. Another aspect of cultural capital that guides the college choice process is the attitude toward going away to college. For many students from affluent backgrounds, "going away" is a mark of success and a rite of passage. Many lower-income and minority students, by contrast, prefer to attend college close to home (Kurlaender 2006). In so doing, they are able to maintain ties with home and engage in reciprocal relationships with family members, depending on each other for assistance. This choice, though, may have the unintended effect of derailing the child's education—given that students who attend two-year colleges and live at home are more likely to drop out. This is how cultural preferences and college-specific know-how contribute to social class and racial inequalities in education.

Focusing on the completion of a college degree as the key indicator of educational inequality, as I've done here, is a bit simplistic. Yet it is a significant culmination of educational experiences that have come before and the most significant educational divide in terms of income and other benefits (autonomy, safety, health, etc.). It is also simplistic to focus on the SAT as the key indicator of skill and talent among college applicants. Yet because of its significance in the game of college admissions, I focus on it, while also acknowledging that there are schools that evaluate applicants according to a diverse set of indicators. These schools, moreover, are more likely to admit students who are racially and economically diverse—as well as academically talented. Still, the field of higher education is characterized by "players" who vary in terms of their financial ability to play the game, the skills and talent they bring to the game, and their attitudes toward and understanding of the rules of the game. For these reasons, players from different racial and social class groups end up having different and unequal levels of educational success. Now, we must also examine how the game itself produces winners and losers.

EDUCATIONAL INEQUALITY AND THE RULES OF "THE GAME"

While educational success depends on what the player brings to the game, from a sociological perspective the rules of the game favor some players more than others. The game of higher education favors players from economically and racially advantaged backgrounds. In this section, I focus on how "the game" is funded, how it is structured, and how players are "recruited." These features allow some players to develop and demonstrate their talents while other players' talents remain underdeveloped and undiscovered.

OLD EQUIPMENT AND RUN-DOWN FACILITIES: INEQUALITIES IN SCHOOL FUNDING AND RESOURCES

As any student who has participated in competitive events during high school knows, schools differ considerably in their facilities and resources. A trip to an away football game may reveal an impressive stadium with nice bleachers and beautiful green fields, while one's home team may not even have its own field. As a member of my high school's "Quiz Bowl" team (super cool, I know), I discovered that our suburban competitors attended schools with newer facilities and coaches with more resources. Why are schools in the United States so diverse in terms of their facilities and resources, and how does this affect players' ability to compete?

Within the United States, schools are largely operated at the state and local levels. This means that what is taught in schools, how teachers are hired, fired, and evaluated, along with how schools are funded, is determined by the individual states and school districts. The people who wrote the rules of the game felt that what works in Massachusetts may not work in Georgia; therefore, each state should control how its children are educated. This approach is different from what happens in Europe, where schools are run at the national level. Not only are all French schools funded equally, but if it's 11:00 a.m. on November 12, third-graders across the nation are learning the same lesson. In the United States, by contrast, only a small percentage of a school's budget comes from federal sources; the rest comes from taxes collected at the state and local levels. This means that some states spend a lot of money on schools while others do not; it also means that within a given state, there may be considerable funding differences across school districts.

The U.S. Census Bureau indicates that Alaska, New Jersey, and New York spend the most per pupil—somewhere in the area of $17,000 per year (school budgets are typically reported at the "per pupil" level to control for the fact that some states and some schools have more students than others). At the other end of the spectrum, the states with the lowest per pupil funding—around $7,400 annually—are Arizona, Utah, and Idaho. To some extent, these differences reflect the fact that the cost of living varies from one state to another: $8,000 goes a lot further in Idaho than it does in New York, so it may not necessarily be the case that young Idahoans attend inferior schools or receive an inferior education.

There are also significant inequalities within states. This reflects the fact that nearly half of a school's budget comes from local property taxes. A 45-minute drive across your city or state immediately makes clear why this is significant. Imagine beginning your drive in a new suburban area—an area dotted with malls, movie theaters, business parks, and new homes valued at more than $250,000. A drive toward either the inner city or out to the rural areas will reveal different landscapes. In these areas, homes have lower property values; in the urban core, many properties are tax exempt, so that organizations like churches, hospitals, libraries, and schools don't pay property taxes. With a wealthier tax base in the suburbs and a crumbling tax base in many inner cities and rural areas, we see why some schools have larger budgets than others. In an urban area like Chicago, per pupil expenditures at the high school level are about $13,000 per year, while across the border in the neighboring suburban district (like Evanston, Niles, or New Trier), they are about $22,000! During a child's educational career, this may translate into more than a $100,000 difference in spending on education!

Funding differences then result in resource differences. As indicated in Figure 12.7, schools that serve low-income students are less likely than those serving higher-income students to have a working science lab or independent spaces devoted to art, music, or athletics. Low-income schools are also more likely to be overcrowded and to use portable buildings as classrooms.

It is situations like this that inspired the work of education activist Jonathan Kozol. In his classic book, *Savage Inequalities* (1991), Kozol traveled throughout the United States to document the dramatic differences in American schools. In the inner cities and rural areas, he found public schools with crumbling walls and infrastructure; sewage problems and asthma-triggering mold; out-of-date books and inoperable science labs. Out in the suburbs he found schools with beautiful common areas and lovely

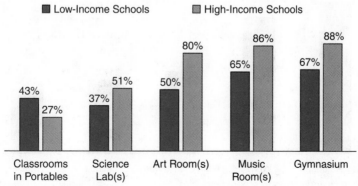

Figure 12.7 Social class and school resources.
(*Source:* Chaney and Lewis 2007)

landscaping; state-of-the art science equipment; and an extensive array of courses. He argued that these differences create not only different *opportunities* to learn but different *desires* to learn. Kozol quoted a young girl from East St. Louis, a district characterized by profound disadvantage, who asked: "Are we citizens of East St. Louis or of America?" (p. 30). Her question reflects the injustice and resignation she felt in attending schools in such deplorable conditions. By contrast, a student from the affluent suburb of Rye, New York, was quoted saying, "I don't see how that would benefit me" (p. 128), when asked whether she felt that her family should pay higher taxes in order to improve schools in poorer districts. This privileged student seems to reject the notion that the rules of the game are unfair and displays a sense of individualism and entitlement with respect to her own educational experiences. If we are to generalize from Kozol's examples, it seems that attending schools with unequal resources affects how students see themselves and their place in the world. Feelings of constraint and entitlement—terms coined by Annette Lareau and discussed in Chapter 9—are created and maintained not just by parents at home but also within the school environment.

So do these differences in school funding and resources ultimately matter? Do the rules of the game—rules that dictate that some students go to well-funded schools and others go to poorly funded schools—mean that some students get a better education than others? The answer seems like a no-brainer when considering the fact that school funding can be spent on a number of things that are likely to improve students' learning. Resources can be invested, for example, in computers and other technologies, well-stocked libraries, and advanced courses. The answer seems similarly apparent when you recognize that class sizes in the low 20s and others have class sizes in the upper 30s; and some schools have a student to counselor ratio of 1:24 and others have a ratio of 1:500. With respect to the impact on student achievement, A Schott Foundation (2009) report indicates that white and Asian American students are about twice as likely to attend schools that have good resources *and* high-performing students compared to Native American, black, and Latino Students (see Figure 12.8).

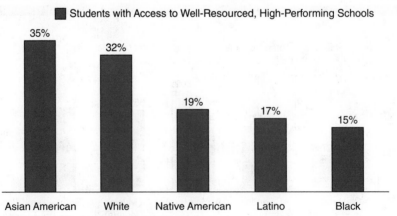

Figure 12.8 Race and access to school resources.
(*Source:* Schott Foundation, 2009)

It is not clear, though, that schools with higher per pupil expenditures *automatically* produce students with higher educational achievement or aspirations. One reason is that schools spend their money on different things. Imagine an older elementary school in a rural town: built in the 1930s, the building has high maintenance costs, not to mention higher heating bills due to old, inefficient construction. In addition, students need to be bused in from across the county. Because the county has had a spike in teen pregnancy, more money is needed so that social workers and counselors can help pregnant students stay in school. For these schools, the portion of the budget spent on teachers' salaries, books, and instructional equipment may be less than in a suburban high school two hours away.

Where money clearly matters, though, is in terms of teacher quality and class size. Schools with larger budgets can pay higher salaries; higher salaries, then, attract better teachers. Further, these teachers tend to stay in their jobs longer and develop even greater effectiveness. Imagine you live in Illinois and recently graduated with a degree in teaching. The starting salary at a top-paying district in the state is above $50,000; the lowest-paying districts, by contrast, offer only $26,000. Although some bright and dedicated teachers choose to work in schools that pay less and provide more challenges, many are not so altruistic. Moreover, districts with lower budgets, lower salaries, and lower-performing students have higher rates of teacher turnover. In terms of school funding, the rules of the game make it difficult for some schools to provide a consistently high quality of education to the lower-income and minority students they serve. Even if the players are bright and motivated, their development may be hindered by those who "coach" them on a day-to-day basis.

School funding and school resources also seem to matter in terms of class size. Perhaps the study that best makes this point is one conducted in the state of Tennessee in the 1980s and '90s. Because it was a true experimental design, researchers were able to explore what happens when some students are placed in smaller classrooms (approximately 15 students) and others are placed in classrooms with the "standard" number of students (approximately 23 students). After nearly 10 years of investigation, researchers found that students who were placed in smaller classes had higher scores on standardized tests in English and math, compared to those in larger classes. What is even more remarkable is that these educational benefits remained—even after students returned to standard-sized classes (Mosteller 1995).

The Tennessee class size study echoes another important finding: school resources seem to matter more for some students than others. While some students learn well in schools with modest resources, larger classes, and less qualified teachers, other students—namely minorities—do much better when they have access to high-quality educational resources. Starting with James Coleman's classic report in the 1960s, researchers have found that "it is for the most disadvantaged children that improvements in school quality will make the most difference in achievement" (Coleman, quoted in Arum, Beattie, and Ford 2010:132). One reason that resources matter more for minority students is that the school environment can make up for things that they don't have access to at home. Researchers find, for example, that kids who come from lower-income and minority backgrounds have fewer books at home and spend less time reading with parents or guardians. Schools with strong resources can help fill in these gaps.

Researchers have also discovered that black and Latino students have higher educational achievement and higher aspirations when they attend schools with higher percentages of white students. What is it about going to school with white students that provides this boost? Researchers believe that schools with more white students transmit a wider range of opportunities to students and have teachers who hold higher expectations, so that students develop higher aspirations over time. These higher expectations flow through both formal (teachers and counselors) and informal (friendship networks) channels within the school (Schofield 2001). Studies also show that cross-racial friendships boost the educational aspirations of both minorities and whites (Hallinan and Williams 1990) and later contribute to higher levels of racial comfort (at work, school, etc.) and a stronger desire to work across racial lines in political and community organizations (Kurlaender and Yun 2007).

Despite these findings, schools and school districts across the United States remain deeply segregated. In fact, most students attend schools where their own race is the majority. Asian Americans are an exception, as they are most likely to attend integrated schools. By contrast, 43 percent of Latino and 38 percent of black students attend a school that is nearly all black or Latino. When attending schools where less than 10 percent of their peers are white, these students can be said to attend "apartheid" or hypersegregated schools (Orfield, Kucsera, and Siegel-Hawley 2012). Using our metaphor of "the game," the fact that so many minority students attend segregated schools means that they are generally playing in an entirely different league than their white counterparts. This is another macro-level factor that affects students' experiences and their ability to succeed.

SUMMER BREAK OR SUMMER LEAGUE?: INEQUALITIES IN THE STRUCTURE OF THE SCHOOL CALENDAR

Competitive athletics have intensified since I was in high school. Back in the 1980s and '90s, student athletes typically played one or two sports a year and took the summer off. Since then, it seems like competitive middle- and high-school athletes have begun to specialize and to play all year round. Time off between seasons means taking a break from developing talents; at the beginning of the new season, players would spend too much time simply getting back in shape. Therefore, the structure of competitive athletics changed in order to ensure the highest level of performance among the players. As it turns out, the same thing happens in the academic realm.

When the American educational system was developed back around the 1830s, the structure of the school year was dictated by the fact that most Americans lived rural, agricultural lives. Therefore, an extended summer break was essential because the labor of school-aged children was needed for the harvest. Although only a small percentage of Americans work in agriculture, an extended summer break remains a key feature of the older educational system. From the perspective of educational inequalities, this seemingly harmless aspect of "the game" puts some students at risk, making it difficult for them to retain their talents.

"**Summer setback**" or "**summer reading loss**" refers to the pattern whereby over the summer, many low-income and minority students lose the academic gains that they make during the school year. Researchers know that at the beginning of the school year, a test score gap exists between low-income and upper-income students, as well as between white and minority students. During the course of the school year, low-income and minority students catch up and narrow that gap so that the test score gap is much smaller at the end of the school year than at the beginning. Over the summer, these students experience significant "reading loss." Researchers estimate that over the summer, students from disadvantaged backgrounds lose about a month and a half's worth of what they learned in school. By the time students reach the fifth grade less advantaged students have lost nearly a year and a half's worth of learning— much of it due to an academic calendar that includes an extended summer break (Allington and McGill-Franzen 2003; Cooper, Borman, and Fairchild 2010). Because lower-income and minority homes have less access to age-appropriate reading materials, and because reading is a skill that takes practice, many students suffer over the summer. Students from higher-income families, by contrast, continue to make academic gains and pull further ahead over the summer months, as their parents are more likely enroll their children in educational and cultural camps or take them on trips that expand their cultural capital.

This research shows that the educational system has the great capacity to equalize the educational achievements of students across social class and racial lines. Yet due to the way that the game is structured—by giving students time off during the summer— much of this capacity is lost. The rules of the game could be revised in order to promote greater educational equity across social class and racial lines. Although it might be wildly unpopular, extending the school year would go a long way toward reducing these gaps in learning. As long as the structure of schooling includes an extended summer break, where many parents and families continue their gains over the summer and others have a difficult time doing so, the rules of the game will continue to help some and hurt others.

TAKING THE GAME TO THE NEXT LEVEL: INEQUALITIES IN COLLEGE ADMISSIONS

The rules of the game, when it comes to the college admissions process, also favor some and disadvantage others. These dynamics are especially evident at the most selective schools, the ones that receive lots of applications, reject lots of students, and rank at the top of lists like those published by *U.S. News and World Report*. In the words of education scholar Peter Sacks, access to the "best" colleges and universities is "determined by an elaborate, self-perpetuating arrangement of social and economic privilege that systematically grants advantages to affluent, well-educated families while systematically shutting the gates of opportunity to those without such advantages" (2007:130).

SIGNING A LETTER OF INTENT: EARLY ADMISSIONS

One of these "elaborate" arrangements is the "early admissions" process. Imagine, for a moment, that you are an exceptionally talented high school student—meaning that your SAT scores place you above the 85th percentile nationally, you have a high GPA, an array of advanced courses, and a deep résumé of extracurricular activities. Next, imagine you have your heart set on going to one of the nation's top colleges—and that you just discovered an option that could substantially increase your chances of getting in. This option is the "early admissions" process, where students typically apply during November of their senior year and then generally agree to enroll automatically if accepted. Research indicates that 41 percent of early decision applicants are accepted at Princeton University, while the acceptance rate of regular decision applicants is only 8 percent. At Harvard, 21 percent of "early" applicants are accepted, while only 5 percent of regular applicants are. This advantage is equivalent to a boost of nearly 200 points on the SAT (Avery, Fairbanks, and Zeckhauser 2003). If early decision applicants are substantially more likely to be accepted than those who apply in the regular pool, how could this be a bad thing?

The answer is that while the early admissions game provides applicants with a unique advantage, not every student can reasonably take advantage of it. The downside of this process is that if you are admitted, you are expected to enroll. From the standpoint of the college or university, the early decision process makes sense because they can solidify their incoming class and grab those students who are most committed to their institution. The catch, though, is that applicants are expected to enroll without having information about their financial aid package. This is akin to requiring a customer to purchase a product without revealing its price. For affluent families, this may not be a deterrent; families who depend on financial aid and would like to weigh various financial aid packages against one another may not be able to use the early admissions game to their advantage.

CARRYING ON A FAMILY TRADITION: THE ADVANTAGE OF BEING A "LEGACY"

In the world of athletics, you sometimes see prowess and success across generations. In football, the Manning family is legendary, beginning with Archie and ending with Peyton and Eli, both of whom have won Super Bowl rings. In baseball there are both the Cal Ripkens and Ken Griffeys, senior and junior. The same thing is seen within education: families who, across generations, send their children to the same colleges and universities. While good genes and socialization within the family are surely part of these processes, the rules of the college admissions game give family ties unique consideration.

Many colleges and universities give special consideration to applicants who have **legacy status**. That is, applicants are given a boost if they have a family member who has previously graduated from that college or university. Legacy students are attractive to colleges and universities for a number of reasons. One is that they like the idea of attracting students who are familiar with the culture and traditions of their school and who are apt to extend those traditions into future generations. Another is the hope that legacies will become major donors to these colleges and universities. Many administrators believe that their university's fundraising efforts—which allow them to provide financial aid to other students—depend upon giving preferential treatment to those with family ties.

The scope of the legacy advantage is significant. If a given applicant has a 50 percent chance of being admitted to a particular college or university, having legacy status increases their chances to 70 percent. Looked at another way, while only 11 percent of Harvard's nonlegacy applicants are admitted, 40 percent of its legacy applicants are (Bowen et al. 2005). At other colleges and universities, the acceptance rate of legacy candidates is about twice that of regular applicants. Legacy applicants—who already are likely to have a number of advantages given their parents' educational successes—have an additional advantage in the college admissions "game." The rules of the game give them a special advantage, even when they have lesser demonstrated skills (i.e., lower SAT scores) as a "player."

PAY TO PLAY? MONEY AND COLLEGE ADMISSIONS

Can admissions to a top college or university simply be bought? What if credentials mattered little and the ability to pay tuition or donate to the university were counted in the college admissions process? There are some circumstances where this is precisely the case. Some top colleges and universities use "provost's discretion" and "development admits" as tools for admitting students whose credentials may not give them a chance in the regular admissions process. Daniel Golden's reporting for *The Wall Street Journal* suggests that in recent years Duke University has actively courted and admitted as many as 125 students annually whose families were uniquely positioned to make substantial donations to the university's endowment.

In recent years this type of practice seems to have expanded. Although top colleges like Harvard and Brown proudly tout their "need-blind admissions" process (where students are admitted without any consideration of their ability to pay), other colleges and universities have begun seeking out full-pay students or practicing "need-sensitive admissions." Full-pay students are attractive to colleges and universities because they add revenue and do not drain financial aid resources. Some colleges argue that they need full-pay students *in order* to admit students from lower-income backgrounds. Schools that practice "need-sensitive admissions" typically take ability to pay into account when considering "borderline" students. Essentially, the ability to pay full tuition—which runs around $45,000 at many of these schools—is one factor that makes a student "qualified" for admissions. Students who are more academically qualified but less affluent may be turned away. These examples of college admissions policies show that the rules of the game don't treat all players the same.

REWRITING THE RULES OF THE GAME: EFFORTS TO IMPROVE THE PLAYERS' PERFORMANCE

While it is widely recognized that the U.S. educational system is not performing up to expectations, people have different ideas about where the problems lie. While some observers place blame on individual players, others criticize the game itself. Education reformers typically adhere to the optimistic belief that by reforming the game, individual players will be able to perform at their best. Here we look at some efforts to rewrite the rules of the game.

Give the players more choice: Charter schools and school vouchers

Some education experts believe that educational failure and school inequalities exist because the system allows it. The key to improving the educational system, some argue, is to give students more options and force schools to compete. **Charter schools** are one reform effort that reflects this belief. A charter school is a public school that is allowed to operate with more flexibility than the typical public school—flexibility in terms of what is taught, how success is measured, who is hired, and how to fire ineffective teachers. This reform is supported by those who think that the public school system's failures stem from the fact that it is overburdened by regulations and lacks innovation.

Vouchers reform efforts reflect similar beliefs about public education. Like charter schools, **school vouchers** give students and their family more choice. In this case, students receive "vouchers" they can either apply to private school tuition or use to transfer out of their neighborhood school to a higher-performing public school. The assumption behind this reform is that the public school system lacks competition: schools are funded by public tax dollars, regardless of their results. Because of this steady stream of funding, schools have historically faced little pressure to reform. By allowing students and their families to "vote with their feet," vouchers force failing schools to become more effective—or risk losing their students and their funding.

Many people like charter schools and vouchers because they give parents and students more options and force schools to be more accountable. The logic is that more competition will produce better results. To date, however, the success of these programs has been mixed. A report from Stanford University found that 17 percent of charter schools showed academic gains but 46 percent performed no better than public schools—and 37 percent performed significantly worse (Center for Research on Education Outcomes 2009). When it comes to research on school vouchers, small studies on individual programs and school districts have found improvements in test scores and college entrance rates (Hoxby 2007; Chingos and Peterson 2012). Other studies, though, show no real gains for students or schools with voucher systems (Ladd 2002; Witte 2000). Moreover, critics point out that Cleveland, Milwaukee, and Washington, D.C. have had voucher systems for many years and, for just as many years, have been plagued by underachievement. To date, it is unclear whether changing these rules will produce more competitive players.

Lowering the goalpost? Affirmative action policies

Colleges and universities are also seeking to rewrite the rules of the game. One of the most sustained efforts to increase racial diversity within higher education is **affirmative action**. Initiated by Presidents John F. Kennedy and Lyndon Baines Johnson during the mid-1960s, affirmative action refers to a set of policies designed to bring greater diversity to educational settings and some workplaces. As practiced, affirmative action generally uses race or gender as a "tie-breaking" qualification. When two applicants are roughly similar in terms of SAT, GPA, and extracurricular involvement, the edge is given to the applicant who brings greater diversity.

Yet there is plenty of debate over this controversial policy. For critics of affirmative action, the practice is both unfair and foolish: unfair because another accomplished student may be excluded (and their rights violated) and foolish because some believe it results in recruiting students who are less qualified and bring less to the institution. Yet the constitutionality of affirmative action has been affirmed by the U.S. Supreme Court based on the notion that diverse schools and workplaces are good for everyone. While well-qualified individuals may be rejected in this process, the policy is permissible, the court has argued, because affirmative action serves the public's interest. That is, college students learn more when their campuses have a critical mass of diverse students; because class discussions are livelier and incorporate more diverse points of view, more learning takes place (Chang, Astin, and Kim 2004). Many employers also support affirmative action. Leaders from Fortune 500 companies to the U.S. military believe that their organizations function better when they include persons from diverse backgrounds. Sociologist Cedric Herring (2009) found that companies with higher levels of diversity earn higher profits and have greater market share. Diversity at work seems to bring a wider perspective, more outside-the-box thinking, and a wider array of social network connections.

Research on the consequences of affirmative action has reached mixed conclusions. William Bowen and Derek Bok (1998) have found that our nation's most selective colleges and universities are more diverse places because of affirmative action. Yet if affirmative action were one day found to be unconstitutional, there would be little impact at most colleges and universities, given that most do not practice affirmative action. There would, however, be a significant decline in the Latino and black populations at many elite institutions. Bowen and Bok also found that college students admitted through affirmative action are not less qualified: as they move through college, their GPAs, graduation rates, and likelihood of going to graduate school are no different from students who did not benefit from affirmative action. Further, they found that affirmative action seems to have almost no impact on the chances of admissions of white applicants and is not a form of "reverse racism." In fact, Bowen and Bok estimated that if affirmative action were eliminated, white applicants would see their admissions rates at these competitive colleges and universities go from 25 percent to 26 percent. The group that would benefit most from eliminating affirmation action is Asian Americans, given that they typically do not qualify for affirmative action and are less likely to have legacy preferences (Espenshade and Radford 2009).

Because affirmative action is so controversial and seems to violate the premium we place on individual merit, it is a hotly contested issue. While it has resulted in more racially diverse schools and workplaces, many see it as patently unfair. It is likely that the U.S. Supreme Court will continue to weigh in on this issue. In the meantime, many propose that affirmative action be instituted on the basis of economic, rather than racial, disadvantage. There are, moreover, those who argue that if the SAT were eliminated as the main criterion for college admissions, there would be no need for affirmative action. In this spirit many colleges and universities have rewritten the rules downplaying the SAT—some even moving to an SAT-optional format.

EXPLORING ACTIVISM: EDUCATIONAL OPPORTUNITY AND "THE DREAMERS"

Much is made of the opportunities offered by the American public school system. But what happens to those students who make it through the public school system as undocumented students? Within the United States, children who are in the country illegally are allowed to enroll in many public schools without providing proof of citizenship or residency. When these students graduate, however, they face a new set of rules; consequently, they confront barriers in enrolling in higher education—as unauthorized state residents they are not eligible for in-state or federal financial aid. Brought to the United States in many cases as young children, undocumented citizens who graduate from high school have an unusually hard time pursuing a college degree.

A movement has emerged in the United States to change this situation. Known as "Dreamers," members of this movement "strive to achieve equal access to higher education for all people, regardless of immigration status." The website for United We Dream states: "We aim to address the inequities and obstacles faced by immigrant youth and to develop a sustainable, grassroots movement, led by undocumented immigrant youth and their allies." While this movement gathered force under President Obama and his plans for immigration reform, its origins are found in a bipartisan proposal dating back to 2001, known as the DREAM Act (Development, Relief, and Education for Alien Minors). The goal of this proposal—which has been repeatedly introduced into Congress but never passed—is to provide a path to citizenship for undocumented youth. The pathway to citizenship, however, is conditional: only youth who were brought to the United States illegally as children, graduated from a U.S. high school, and have "good moral character" would be eligible for citizenship. In addition, they would have to complete at least a two-year college degree or serve in the military. Because individuals would still be responsible for their college costs, Dreamers have worked to pass bills that would help finance their education. These bills include legislation that would allow Dreamers to pay in-state tuition rates and in three states (Texas, New Mexico, and California), and gain access to state-supported—but not federal—financial aid.

Within organizations like United We Dream and their affiliates, Dreamers are trained as youth activists. They learn how to lobby politicians, spread their message,

Brought to the United States as children, these undocumented immigrants and their supporters are seeking access to higher education and the American Dream.

and mobilize others—often classmates and other youth—to fight for their cause. Their activism includes working with a diverse set of groups—including supporters of same-sex marriage (also known as "marriage equality")—to show the commonalities in their goals. While President Obama passed legislation known as Deferred Action for Childhood Arrivals (DACA) in order to slow the deportation of these students, a more permanent decision about their residency status and access to higher education remains on hold. While supporters argue that opening access to higher education will stimulate the economy by helping undocumented people develop relevant job skills, others oppose the Act because they believe it rewards illegal immigration and acts as a magnet for further waves of illegal immigration. This example shows that even those who are vulnerable are willing to become activists to help themselves and others like them.

THE FUTURE OF EDUCATIONAL INEQUALITY: DECLINING, VARYING, AND PERSISTENT DIVIDES

Since the end of the civil rights era in the 1960s, education has changed considerably. Opportunities for diverse groups have increased. Women, in particular, have experienced remarkable progress. While women faced quotas and other barriers to entry into higher education through the early 1970s, today they represent a majority of students at both the undergraduate and graduate levels. While high school females lag behind their male peers on SAT scores, they tend to have higher GPAs and take more advanced courses. Beginning in elementary school, male students are more likely to be labeled as learning disabled and to receive behavioral interventions. In high school they are more likely to be enrolled in remedial courses and less likely to go to college. For these reasons, sociologist Steven Brint (2006) has called gender the "declining divide" within education.

Race, by contrast, represents a "varying divide." One example of this variation is that Asian Americans have excelled educationally. Although there are complexities within this group—for example, Vietnamese Americans have lower achievement levels on average than Indian Americans—Asian Americans have the highest standardized test scores and college completion rates of all racial/ethnic groups. While Latinos and African Americans still lag behind, progress has been made over the last 50 years. It was not that long ago, after all, that educational segregation was the norm. The fact that many college campuses are diverse places is a significant accomplishment. This accomplishment has been achieved, in part, by narrowing the test score gap. From the 1970s through the early 1990s, the "black-white test score gap" decreased by 40 percent. These years also saw a significant increase in the percentage of black people with a college degree. Since then, however, progress has halted. There remains a stubborn gap in the educational achievements of white and Asian Americans, on the one hand, and African Americans and Latinos, on the other.

Perhaps the most persistent educational divide is the social class divide. As shown in this chapter, significant social gaps remain, especially when it comes to completing a college degree. Some students, though, do "beat the odds." My sister Caitlin is one of them. Her experiences as a lower-income, first-generation college student were statistically different from other kids who grew up in similar circumstances. There is no doubt that she was a skilled player, excelling academically and making friends with kids whose parents *were* college educated and who shared their cultural know-how when it came to navigating the educational system. Yet it was partially due to luck and good fortune that she lived in a high school district that offered a well-respected International Baccalaureate program and that she was able to enroll with relative ease. There she met kids whose parents had higher levels of education, which provided her access to valuable forms of social and cultural capital. Of course, it was up to her to take advantage of that opportunity and perform at her best. The rules of the game worked for her; they rarely work as well for the majority of students from less advantaged backgrounds.

So what is it about social class, in particular, that produces these persistent variations? Plenty of work remains for sociologists and other researchers to understand the enduring nature of this gap—and to make recommendations on how to close the gap. It is the premise of this chapter, though, that these recommendations should focus on both the player and the game. Focusing on the player, efforts must be made to enhance the skills and attributes of students from lower-income and underrepresented minority backgrounds. As it is, their academic skills, their financial situations, and their lack of education-related cultural capital make it difficult for them to compete successfully in this intensely competitive game. If players were better trained and better equipped, they might perform at a higher level. That said, the rules of the game must also be re-written, given that the current rules do not treat all players equally. In fact, the rules—those that govern the way that schools are funded, the schedule of the school year, and the college admissions process—systematically favor some players over others. It is the opinion of this sociologist that changing the rules of the game will create a situation where the players have the skills and motivation to perform at their best.

CHAPTER 12: REVIEW OF KEY POINTS

- This chapter explains educational inequalities by focusing on dynamics at the micro- and macro-levels. The fact that some people receive more and better education than others reflects both circumstances of individual "players" and the structure of "the game" (policies that govern education).

- Social class inequalities in education have been more persistent than racial or gender inequalities in education. These inequalities exist in whether one goes to college, where one goes, and whether one completes a degree once enrolled.

- Despite the expansion of the educational system, with more colleges existing now than ever before, there has been little change in the social class gap in college completion.

- Increasing college costs are one micro-level factor that contributes to the social class gap in education. College is more expensive than ever before, *and* financial aid policies at the macro-level mean that lower-income students have less access to an affordable college education.

- At the micro-level, scores on the SAT also correlate to a student's family income; at the macro-level, policies that emphasize the SAT in college admissions exacerbate the social class gap in education.

- Cultural capital also plays a role in educational inequality. While minorities and members of the lower classes may aspire to educational success, they may not have the concrete tools, knowledge, or cultural capital that allows them to achieve their goals.

- At the macro-level, the structure of school funding results in social class disparities in educational access. The reliance on the local tax base for school funding means that students who live in different types of neighborhoods will typically attend schools with vastly different resources.

- Some sociologists have pointed at the structure of the school calendar, which typically features a long summer break, as another macro-level factor that disadvantages already-disadvantaged students.

- When it comes to access to higher education, numerous college admissions policies systematically advantage students from already-advantaged backgrounds. This is especially the case when it comes to highly selective colleges and universities.

- Educational reformers support charter schools and school voucher programs as ways to improve the educational access and achievement of less advantaged students. These programs have shown some success but do not yet demonstrate clear advantages over traditional public schools.

- In order to ameliorate social class inequalities in education, changes can be implemented at both the micro- and macro-levels. The former would involve changing individual players and providing them with greater access to learning, financial aid, and so forth. The latter would involve changing the educational system so that students from all social class backgrounds receive similar benefits and treatment.

CHAPTER 12: QUESTIONS FOR REVIEW

1. Statistically speaking, what kinds of gaps or inequalities exist in higher education enrollment, selectivity, and completion?

2. Looking at the consequences of college attendance, what kinds of economic benefits come from completing a college degree? What kinds of benefits come with attending a highly selective college or university?

3. One important micro-level factor that contributes to educational inequalities is the player's ability to pay. How has the cost of college changed over time, and what changes have occurred in student financial aid? How do these changes contribute to class inequalities in college completion?

4. Another micro-level factor that contributes to educational inequality is test performance. What social class and racial biases sometimes influence how students perform on standardized tests? What kinds of changes may minimize these social class and racial gaps?

5. How do cultural factors and knowledge and attitudes toward higher education result in educational inequalities?

6. On the macro-level, larger structural factors, like policies and procedures, set the foundation for educational inequalities. How are public schools funded? How/why do the accompanying differences in resources matter? Further, can you imagine a different way of funding public schools?

7. In terms of how "the game" is structured, the school year typically runs from August until June. How does this macro-level facet affect race and class inequalities in school performance? What do you think would happen if the structure of the school year were altered to address these inequalities?

8. Looking at the college admissions system, what policies and procedures tend to provide advantages to students from higher social class backgrounds? From your point of view, do these policies make sense? Why or why not?

9. Currently, efforts exist to close some of the gaps in public education. What are some of these efforts, and what results have they shown?

KEY TERMS

affirmative action

Attitude-Achievement Paradox

attrition

charter schools

cultural capital

educational attainment

legacy status

school vouchers

selectivity

stereotype threat

summer setback

undermatched

REFERENCES

Allington, Richard L. and Anne McGill-Franzen. 2003. "The Impact of Summer Reading Setback on the Reading Achievement Gap." *Phi Delta Kappan* 85(1):68–75.

Anderson, Elijah. 2000. *Code of the Street: Decency, Violence, and the Moral Life of the Inner City.* New York: W.W. Norton & Company.

Anderson, Elijah. 2013. *Streetwise: Race, Class, and Change in an Urban Community.* Chicago: University of Chicago Press.

Aronson, Joshua, Claude M. Steele, Moises Salinas, and Michael J. Lustina. 1998. "The Effects of Stereotype Threat on the Sandardized Test Performance of College Students." Pp. 400–412 in *Readings about the Social Animal*, 8th ed., edited by Elliot Aronson. New York: Freeman.

Arum, Richard, Irenee R. Beattie, and Karly Ford, eds. 2010. *The Structure of Schooling: Readings in the Sociology of Education*. Thousand Oaks, CA: Pine Forge Press, Sage.

Arum, Richard, Josipa Roksa, and Michelle Budig. 2008. "The Romance of College Attendance: Higher Educational Stratification and Mate Selection." *Research in Social Stratification and Mobility* 26(2):107–121.

Avery, Christopher, Andrew Fairbanks, and Richard Zeckhauser. 2003. *The Early Admissions Game: Joining the Elite*. Cambridge, MA: Harvard University Press.

Bowen, William G. and Derek Bok. 1998. *The Shape of the River: Long-Term Consequences of Considering Race in College and University Admissions*. Princeton, NJ: Princeton University Press.

Bowen, William G., Martin A. Kurzweil, and Eugene M. Tobin. 2005. *Equity and Excellence in American Higher Education*. Charlottesville: University of Virginia Press.

Brint, Steven. 2006. *Schools and Societies*. Palo Alto, CA: Stanford University Press.

Brint, Steven and Jerome Karabel. 1989. *The Diverted Dream: Community Colleges and the Promise of Educational Opportunity in America, 1900–1985*. New York: Oxford University Press.

Bureau of Labor Statistics. 2014. "Earnings and Unemployment Rates by Educational Attainment." Washington, D.C.: Current Population Survey. Retrieved April 22, 2015 (http://www.bls.gov/emp/ep_chart_001.htm)

Carnevale, Anthony P. and Stephen J. Rose. 2004. "Socioeconomic Status, Race/Ethnicity, and Selective College Admissions." Pp. 101–156 in *America's Untapped Resource: Low-Income Students in Higher Education*, edited by Richard D. Kahlenberg. New York: The Century Foundation Press.

Carnevale, Anthony P., Stephen J. Rose, and Ban Cheah. 2011. "The College Payoff: Education, Occupations, and Lifetime Earnings." Washington, D.C.: The Georgetown University Center on Education and the Workforce.

Carter, Prudence L. 2006. "Intersecting Identities: 'Acting White,' Gender, and Academic Achievement." Pp. 111–132 in *Beyond Acting White: Reframing the Debate on Black Student Achievement*, edited by Erin McNamara Horvat and Carla O'Connor. Lanham, MD: Rowman and Littlefield.

Center for Research on Education and Outcomes. 2009. "Multiple Choice: Chapter School Performance in 16 States." Palo Alto, CA: Center for Research on Education Outcomes at Stanford University. Retrieved September 29, 2014 (http://credo.stanford.edu/reports/MULTIPLE_CHOICE_CREDO.pdf).

Chaney, Bradford and Laurie Lewis. 2007. "Public School Principals Report on their School Facilities, 2005." Washington, DC: National Center for Education Statistics.

Chingos, Matthew M., and Paul E. Peterson. 2012. "The Effects of School Vouchers on College Enrollment: Experimental Evidence from New York City." Washington, DC: The Brookings Institution.

College Board. 2014. "2013 College-Bound Seniors: Total Group Profile Report." Washington, D.C.: The College Board. Retrieved April 22, 2015 (http://media.collegeboard.com/digitalServices/pdf/research/2013/TotalGroup-2013.pdf)

College Board. 2014. "Trends in College Pricing: 2014." Washington, D.C.: The College Board. Retrieved April 22, 2015 (http://trends.collegeboard.org/)

Collins, Patricia Hill. 2004. *Black Sexual Politics: African Americans, Gender, and the New Racism.* New York: Routledge, 2004.

Cooper, Harris, Geoffrey Borman, and Ron Fairchild. 2010. "School Calendars and Academic Achievement." Pp. 342–355 in *Handbook of Research on Schools, Schooling, and Human Development*, edited by Judith L. Eecles and Jacquelynne S. Meece. New York: Routledge.

Chang, Mitchell J., Alexander W. Astin, and Dongbin Kim. 2004. "Cross-Racial Interaction among Undergraduates: Some Consequences, Causes, and Patterns." *Research in Higher Education* 45(5):529–553.

Dale, Stacy and Alan B. Krueger. 2011. "Estimating the Return to College Selectivity over the Career Using Administrative Earnings Data." National Bureau of Economic Research (NBER) Working Paper No. 17159.

Downey, Douglas B., James W. Ainsworth, and Zhenchao Qian. 2009. "Rethinking the Attitude-Achievement Paradox among Blacks." *Sociology of Education* 82:1–19.

Espenshade, Thomas J. and Alexandria Walton Radford. 2009. *No Longer Separate, Not Yet Equal: Race and Class in Elite College Admission and Campus Life.* Princeton, NJ: Princeton University Press.

Ewert, Stephanie and Robert Kominski. 2014. "Measuring Alternative Educational Credentials: 2012." Washington, D.C.: U.S. Bureau of the Census. Retrieved April 22, 2015 (http://www.census.gov/hhes/socdemo/education/data/files/p70-138.pdf

Fischer, Claude, Michael Hout, Martín Sánchez Jankowski, Samuel R. Lucas, Ann Swidler, and Kim Voss. 1996. *Inequality by Design: Cracking the Bell-Curve Myth.* Princeton, NJ: Princeton University Press.

Gerald, Danette and Kati Haycock. 2006. "Engines of Inequality: Diminishing Equity in the Nation's Premier Public Universities." Washington, DC: The Education Trust.Grodsky, Eric and Melanie T. Jones. 2007. "Real and Imagined Barriers to College Entry: Perceptions of Cost." *Social Science Research* 36(2):745–766.

Hallinan, Maureen T., and Richard A. Williams. 1990. "Students' Characteristics and the Peer-Influence Process." *Sociology of Education* 63(2):122–132.

Herring, Cedric. 2009. "Does Diversity Pay?: Race, Gender, and the Business Case for Diversity." *American Sociological Review* 74(2):208–224.

Hoxby, Caroline M., ed. 2007. *The Economics of School Choice.* Chicago: University of Chicago Press.

Kantrowitz, Mark. 2011. "Student Aid Policy Analysis: The Distribution of Grants and Scholarships by Race." Retrieved September 16, 2012 (http://www.finaid.org/scholarships/201109 02racescholarships.pdf.).

Kingston, Paul William and John C. Smart. 1990. "The Economic Pay-Off of Prestigious Colleges." Pp. 147–174 in *The High Status Track: Studies of Elite Schools and Stratification*, edited by Paul William Kingston and Lionel S. Lewis. Albany: State University of New York Press.

Kozol, Jonathan. 1991. *Savage Inequalities: Children in America's Schools.* New York: Harper Perennial.

Kurlaender, Michal. 2006. "Choosing Community College: Factors Affecting Latino College Choice." *New Directions for Community Colleges* 133:7–16.

Kurlaender, Michal and John T. Yun. 2007. "Measuring School Racial Composition and Student Outcomes in a Multiracial Society." *American Journal of Education* 113(2):213–242.

Ladd, Helen. 2002. "School Vouchers: A Critical Perspective." *Journal of Economic Perspectives* 16(4):3–24.

Lopez, Nancy. 2002. *Hopeful Girls Troubled Boys: Race and Gender Disparity in Urban Education*. New York: Routledge.

Loury, Linda Datcher and David Garman. 1995. "College Selectivity and Earnings." *Journal of Labor Economics* 13(2):289–308.

Mickelson, Roslyn Arlin. 1990. "The Attitude-Achievement Paradox among Black Adolescents." *Sociology of Education* 63(1):44–61.

Mosteller, Frederick. 1995. "The Tennessee Study of Class Size in the Early School Grades." *The Future of Children* 5(2):113–127.

Orfield, Gary, John Kucsera, and Genevieve Siegel-Hawley. 2012. "E Pluribus . . . Separation." The Civil Rights Project, Proyecto Derechos Civiles. University of California Los Angeles. Retrieved September 4, 2013 (http://civilrightsproject.ucla.edu/research/k-12-education/integration-and-diversity/mlk-national/e-pluribus...separation-deepening-double-segregation-for-more-students).

Price, Derek V. 2004. *Borrowing Inequality: Race, Class, and Student Loans*. Boulder, CO: Lynne Rienner Publishers.

Pringle, Paul. 2003. "College Board Scores With Critics of SAT Analogies." *Los Angeles Times*, July 27. Retrieved April 22, 2015 (http://articles.latimes.com/2003/jul/27/local/me-sat27)

Roderick, Melissa, Vanessa Coca, and Jenny Nagaoka. 2011. "Potholes on the Road to College: High School Effects in Shaping Urban Students' Participation in College Application, Four-Year College Enrollment, and College Match." *Sociology of Education* 84(3):178–211.

Sacks, Peter. 2007. *Tearing Down the Gates: Confronting the Class Divide in American Education*. Berkeley: University of California Press.

Santelices, Maria Veronica and Mark Wilson. 2010. "Unfair Treatment? The Case of Freedle, the SAT, and the Standardization Approach to Differential Item Functioning." *Harvard Educational Review* 80(1):106–134.

Schmidt, Peter. 2007. *Color and Money: How Rich White Kids Are Winning the War over Affirmative Action*. New York: Palgrave-MacMillan.

Schofield, Janet Ward. 2001. "Maximizing the Benefits of Student Diversity: Lessons from School Desegregation Research." Pp. 99–109 in *Diversity Challenged: Evidence on the Impact of Affirmative Action,* edited by Gary Orfield (with Michal Kurlaender). Cambridge, MA: Harvard Education Publishing Group.

Schott Foundation. 2009. "Lost Opportunity: A 50 State Report on the Opportunity to Learn in America." Cambridge, MA: The Schott Foundation for Public Education. Retrieved September 29, 2014 (http://www.otlstatereport.org/50_state_report_national_summary.pdf).

Soares, Joseph A., ed. 2011. *SAT Wars: The Case for Test-Optional College Admissions*. New York: Teachers College Press.

Stuber, Jenny. 2011. *Inside the College Gates: How Class and Culture Matter in Higher Education*. Lanham, MD: Lexington Books.

Witte, John F. 2000. *The Market Approach to Education: An Analysis of America's First Voucher Program*. Princeton, NJ: Princeton University Press.

Lean In or Opt Out?

Understanding Gender Inequalities at Work

I n 2012, journalist Hanna Rosin published a book provocatively titled *The End of Men: And the Rise of Women*. In it she argues that men are at an increasing disadvantage in the emerging postindustrial economy. As manufacturing jobs have disappeared, she says, it is men whose wages have declined and who have borne the brunt of the layoffs. The fact that fewer male high school graduates go off to college than females, coupled with the fact that they are less likely to major in fields that are expanding— and *feminized* (health care, social services)—means that men are poorly positioned to compete in the new economy. In an interview with National Public Radio, Rosin suggested that the "million-dollar question" for economists and sociologists is why women have heard the call of the changing economy—being more flexible in their job choices and following economic development—while men haven't. What Rosin sees as an era of increasing female financial power has profound consequences for the families and heterosexual relations, at the micro-level, and the organization of work at the macro-level.

Just one year later, Facebook executive Sheryl Sandberg published a book urging women to be more flexible and more aggressive in the workplace. In *Lean In: Women, Work, and the Will to Lead*, Sandberg combines academic studies with personal anecdotes to argue that women unintentionally make choices that hold them back at work. Despite Hanna Rosin's observation that women are on the rise and men on the decline, Sandberg pointed out that women hold just 14 percent of top corporate jobs and 17 percent of the seats on corporate boards of directors.

While Sandberg acknowledges the societal forces that shape these gender inequalities—even in subtle things like calling girls and women "bossy" and boys and men "assertive"—she ultimately urges women to *lean in* by not selling themselves short before even stepping foot in the game (i.e., curtailing their ambitions) and becoming more comfortable with touting their achievements—as long as they do it with a smile.

So which is it? Do women still face intractable barriers in the workplace, needing to be urged to "lean in" so that they can rise up, take on leadership positions, and finally close the gender gap in pay? Or is the modern reality one where, as Hanna Rosin suggests, "women are the new men"? This chapter explores gendered experiences in the workplace, focusing specifically on the gender gap in pay. The central question explored in this chapter is: Why do men continue to outearn women? Like all sociological explorations of inequality, this question is best answered by taking a look at dynamics taking place at the micro- and macro-levels. Accordingly, our exploration begins first with the role of "the player": the choices that individual women and men make that contribute to unequal earnings. Yet because sociologists know that no one lives in a bubble, we also explore how the choices of men and women are shaped by "the rules of the game"—in this case, the way that work is structured and how that impinges on men's and women's work experiences and wages. Although we explore the macro- and micro-levels separately, this chapter also shows that the structure of society at the macro-level influences people's micro-level behaviors *and* that decisions at the micro-level ultimately aggregate to form the macro-level architecture of our society.

THE GENDER GAP IN PAY—HOW UNEQUAL ARE WE?

When I was in graduate school, one of the student organizations on campus sponsored a "Feminist Bake Sale." Maybe you've seen one of these events on your campus. Spread across the table was an assortment of goodies—peanut butter cookies with Hershey kisses on top, neat square Rice Crispy treats, messy seven-layer bars, and more. What made this a "feminist" bake sale was that students were selling each item to women for 75 cents and to men for a dollar. The goal was to raise awareness of the gender gap in pay, charging men and women in proportion to their average earnings in society (at that time). While the University of Maine declared one of these bake sales on its campus illegal—alleging that it violated the state's civil rights laws—the gender gap in pay itself has not been declared illegal. First we explore some facts related to the gender gap in pay.

The **gender gap in pay**, as suggested above, is typically expressed as a ratio of how much the average woman earns for every dollar earned by the average man. As it turns out, there are a number of ways to measure this figure. When comparing *all working men* to *all working women*, women earn about 68 cents for every dollar earned by a man. Yet because women are less likely than men to work full-time, year-round, a different comparison is needed. Looking only at full-time, year-round workers (**FTYR**), Bureau of Labor Statistics data indicate that the gender gap in pay is about 81 cents to the dollar. At the Feminist Bake Sale I could buy a cupcake for 81 cents, while a male colleague would have to fork over a dollar. While women like me may get a deal at the bake sale, the broader social reality is one of disadvantage. On an annual basis, this

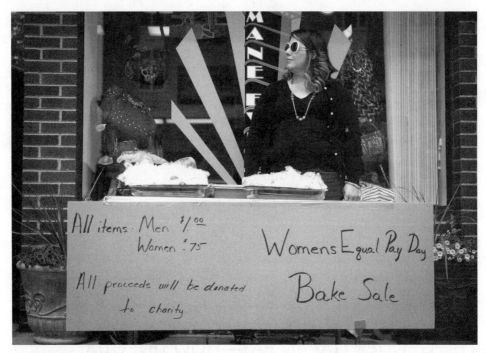

"Feminist bake sales"—where women pay less than men for the same baked goods—have been held on college campuses to draw attention to the gender gap in pay.

disparity translates into median earnings for a woman employed full-time of about $35,000, and $43,500 for a full-time employed man.

As Figure 13.1 shows, the pay gap among full-time workers has been closing over time. During the 1960s, the average women earned about 60 cents for every dollar earned by the average man. Given these steady increases in women's wages over the last 50 years, can we anticipate that the gap will continue to narrow as time goes on? That question is examined toward the end of this chapter.

Looking at this issue from an intersectional angle, Figure 13.2 shows that the gender gap in pay varies along racial lines. It is among the higher earning racial and ethnic groups—Asians and whites—that the gender gap in pay is also highest. For example, white women earn about 81 cents for every dollar earned by a white man. Among lower-paid disadvantaged minorities, namely blacks and Hispanics, the gender gap in pay is lowest. To illustrate, black women earn about 90 cents for every dollar earned by a black man. Why might this be the case? To plant the seed for a discussion later in the chapter, it reflects the fact that disadvantaged minority women may be financially less able to take time off of work when they have children, thereby minimizing the "experience gap" between themselves and men in their same racial/ethnic group.

Although it is useful to know *on average* how much women earn compared to men, this statistic conceals as much as it reveals. For example, it does not take into account hours worked or years of experience; performance or productivity; level of

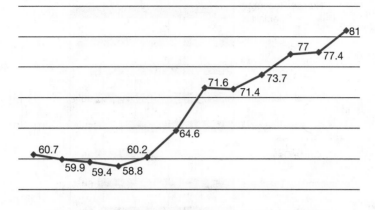

Women's Pay as a Percentage of Men's (Full Time, Year Round Workers)

Figure 13.1 Gender gap in pay over time.
(*Source:* U.S. Census Bureau 2014)

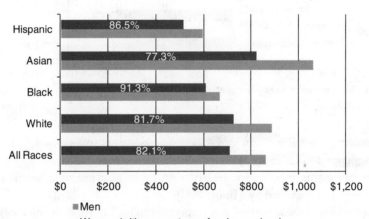

■ Men
■ Women (with percentage of male earnings)

Figure 13.2 Gender gap in pay by race/ethnicity.
(*Source:* Bureau of Labor Statistics/U.S. Census Bureau 2014)

education; *or* the *type* of work women and men do. Therefore, more refined comparisons are needed. Figure 13.3 illustrates the scope of the **gender pay gap across occupational sectors.** Again using data from the Bureau of Labor Statistics, men outearn women in all but 4 of the 108 occupational categories measured. Women outearn men by a few cents (on the dollar) in a number of lower-paying fields, including bakers, teacher assistants, and restaurant/bar "helpers" (earning about $1.05 cents for every $1 earned by a man). It is in some of the best paying fields that the largest gaps exist. For

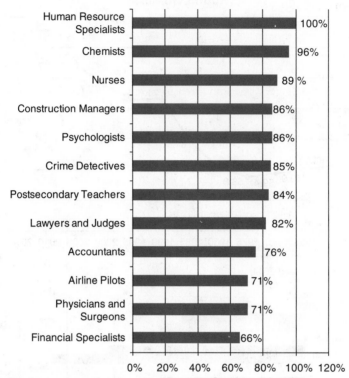

Figure 13.3 Gender gap in pay by occupational sector. (*Source:* Goldin 2014)

example, in the financial services jobs, women earn 66 cents for every dollar earned by a male counterpart (Goldin 2014). Surprisingly, there are some "brawny" fields where the gender pay gap is smaller. In construction trades, for example, women earn 86 cents for every dollar earned by a man.

When looking at these figures, it is important to look beyond the ratio of what the average woman earns for every dollar earned by the average man. On a weekly basis, the typical woman earns $706 while the typical man earns $860. This may or may not sound like a major difference to you. On an annual basis, though, this translates into an average income of about $35,000 for women and $43,500 for men—a difference of $8,500. Looking at lifetime earnings, a man with a college degree earns an average of $2.1 million, while a woman with the same level of education earns $1.4 million. Among those with a high school degree, men earn an average of $1.05 million by the age of retirement, while women earn an average of $.7 million ($700,000). While these numbers are substantial on their own, considering the fact that many jobs offer retirement plans based on a percentage of the workers' income, it becomes clear that disparities in wages also lead to disparities in retirement savings. The fact that retirement contributions are based on wages means that men who are fortunate enough to have these accounts accumulate tens—if not hundreds—of thousands of dollars more than female workers. In short, the gender gap in pay is real, substantial, and persistent through retirement.

THE GENDERED PLAYER—MICRO-LEVEL EXPLANATIONS FOR THE PAY GAP

The metaphor of the player draws our attention to the circumstances and choices made by individuals. When it comes to the pay gap, this means focusing on the gendered choices of men and women, as well as the possibility that some players are "poor sports" who cheat or otherwise give advantages to their own "team." The notion that some players may cheat refers, of course, to the possibility of discrimination at the micro-level. For decades, the assumption has been that individual players—usually men—use their power and position to create bastions of male privilege in the workplace, overtly discriminating against female applicants and employees. Statistical analyses, however, suggest that the rigging of the game by poor sports and cheats is relatively rare. In fact, researchers conclude that less than 7 percent of the gender gap in pay—about 1.4 cents out of the 20 cent difference—can be accounted for by overt discrimination.

A much more significant explanation for the pay gap reflects decisions men and women make—whether to go to college, what to major in, what type of job to pursue, and how to balance work and family obligations. The totality of these factors is referred to as **human capital**—differences among workers in terms of educational background, occupation, years of experience, hours worked, etc. Researchers conclude that a substantial portion of the gender gap in pay reflects differences in human capital: men and women are different kinds of workers, with different work histories and employment characteristics (Blau 2012; Blau and Khan 2008).

GENDER SEGREGATION IN THE WORKPLACE

Looking at gender differences in human capital, it is essential to point out that the labor force as a whole is segregated along gender lines. Think for a moment about the major you have chosen or the job you hope to have one day. Is this job considered a "man's" or a "woman's" job? Traditionally, men have been more heavily employed in white- and blue-collar jobs, while women have been concentrated in pink-collar jobs. Using the metaphor of the player, this means that men and women wear different "uniforms" and play in different occupational "leagues." Because men and women do different kinds of work, and because this work has been ascribed different economic and social value, men and women end up with unequal earnings.

Gender segregation in occupations starts early. Perhaps echoing and mimicking the toys they are given as youngsters, elementary and middle school children display a preference for "gender-typical" household chores (Etaugh and Liss 1992). Beyond chore type, young girls do more household chores than their male counterparts (Crouter et al. 2001; Raley and Bianchi 2006). According to Frank Stafford, an economist at the University of Michigan, the average girl does about seven hours of chores each week and the average boy about five (for similar findings, see Juster, Ono, and Stafford 2004). What is the average boy typically doing in his down time? He is not sleeping or doing homework, the study suggests, but playing and watching TV. This is called the **leisure gap**—showing that each week young boys experience about 2 hours more "free time" than young girls. Finally, even in our earliest years, gender distinctions in chores equate to differences in pay. Frank Stafford's study, which relied on a sample of 3,000 children living in the United States, found that despite these difference in work contributions, boys are more likely than girls to receive allowances—and larger allowances, at that.

Researchers have extensive ways of documenting the occupational choices of male and female workers once they enter the paid labor force as adults. Grouping workers into broad occupational categories, the Bureau of Labor Statistics reports that women comprise only 3–4 percent of workers in "Construction and Extraction Occupations" and "Installation, Maintenance and Repair Occupations." Men, by contrast, are underrepresented in "Office and Administrative Support Occupations," where they represent only 25 percent of all workers. The two sectors that come closest to **gender parity**—where men and women are represented relatively equally—are "Sales" and "Professional and Related Occupations" (a catch-all category that includes engineers, researchers, teachers, writers, and designers). These data are presented in Table 13.1.

Gender segregation in the workplace is so pronounced that some occupations can be called "hypersegregated." Table 13.2 documents some of these occupations, indicating for example that in the United States about 98 percent of preschool and kindergarten teachers are women and 97 percent of firefighters are men. To a great or lesser degree, most men and women go to work each day in settings where their own gender is the majority.

Looking at patterns of gender in the workplace, it appears that women and men choose to play for gender-segregated occupational "teams." Reflecting patterns of gender socialization in childhood, young men and women draw conclusions about what they are good at and what they are interested in; these beliefs then guide their

Table 13.1 Gender Segregation by Occupational Sector

Occupational Sector	Percent Male	Percent Female
Installation, Maintenance, and Repair Occupations	97	3
Construction and Extraction Operations	96	4
Transportation and Materials Moving Occupations	78	22
Farming, Fishing, and Forestry Occupations	74	26
Professional and Business Services	59	41
Sales and Related Occupations	38	62
Management, Business, and Financial Operations	47	53
Community/Social Service Occupations	34	64
Education and Health Services	25	75

Source: Bureau of Labor Statistics, 2014.

Table 13.2 Gender "Hypersegregation" in Occupations

Occupation	Percent Male	Percent Female
Auto Mechanics	99	1
Firefighters	97	3
Airline Pilots	96	4
Mechanical Engineers	95	5
Construction Management	94	6
Preschool and Kindergarten Teachers	2	98
Secretaries and Administrative Assistants	5	95
Nurses (RNs)	11	89
Librarians	13	87
Legal Assistants	14	86

Source: Bureau of Labor Statistics, 2014.

occupational choices (Correll 2001). In their book *Occupational Ghettos*, Maria Charles and David Grusky (2004) show that occupational segregation reflects notions of "gender essentialism"—deeply rooted cultural beliefs that women are (biologically) suited to jobs that require nurturing and human service (teaching, nursing), while men are (biologically) suited to jobs that require physical strength and abstract analysis (construction, engineering).

Although men and women may segregate themselves into sex-typed work, why are "female jobs" paid less than "male jobs"? It is tempting to conclude that men's jobs are paid more because they require more skill or are more difficult—either physically or mentally. Yet the notion that traditionally male jobs are paid a **danger wage premium**—higher pay due to difficult or dangerous conditions—has generally been rejected by researchers (Dorman and Hagstrom 1998; Herman 1999). Instead, it appears that jobs held by women are paid less not because of the inherent characteristics of the job but because they are held by women (Bielby and Baron 1987). The wage gap, then, may reflect a general social devaluation of women.

If this idea sounds a bit extreme to you, consider a few illustrations, starting with dentistry. It is reasonable to assume that the work dentists do is relatively similar across developed countries. Yet in the United States, dentistry is a more prestigious and high-paying job, while in many European countries it is merely average. What accounts for the difference? It could be, in part, because dentistry tends to be a female occupation in many European countries and (historically) a male occupation in the United States (Kimmel 2009).

Second, consider what happens when the gender composition of a particular occupation shifts. Researchers have documented that occupations increase in pay and prestige as men move into those fields, while occupations decrease in pay and prestige as women move in. Take the job of the computer operator. Back in the 1940s, women were the first computer operators; over time, more men became attracted to the job. As men entered this growing occupation, the job was redefined as an intellectually demanding task rather than a routine clerical task. While the job duties themselves changed little, computer programming was socially reconstructed as suitable for men and, consequently, commanded higher pay. Historical case studies show that as women have moved into pharmaceutical occupations, veterinary medicine, book publishing, banking, psychology, and clerical work, those formerly male-dominated positions have lost prestige and pay (Cohn 1985; Reskin and Roos 1990; Strober and Arnold 1987). These patterns again suggest that part of the reason that women are paid less is that the work they do is *constructed* as less difficult and less important.

ACADEMIC MAJORS AND PROFESSIONAL SPECIALIZATION

Although women now represent the majority of college students and new graduates, their wages continue to lag behind their male counterparts. As Figure 13.4 shows, men earn more than women at every level of education. One reason for this, as suggested above, is that men and women segregate themselves into different occupations; among college students, this means segregating themselves into different majors.

Consider your own major and the classes you are taking this term. While courses at the lower level—general education courses, especially—tend to be gender-integrated, once students move into their majors, many find themselves in classrooms where their own gender is the majority. Once again, based on years of socialization and assessments of what he or she might be good at and what they enjoy, individual players choose to play for gender-segregated teams. Gender patterns are especially evident in STEM fields (science, technology, engineering, and math). Not only are these fields growing and high paying, they are also heavily populated by males. As shown in Table 13.3, males make up 82 percent of those majoring in Engineering and Construction Trades and 83 percent of those in Computer and Information Sciences. Female students, by contrast, make up 85 percent of those majoring in Health Professions and 80 percent of those majoring in Education. It is worth noting that the broad field of social science is fairly balanced in terms of gender, yet men outnumber women in the subfield of economics while women outnumber men in the subfield of sociology.

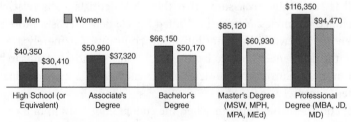

Full-time, Year-Round Workers

Figure 13.4 Gender, education, and the pay gap.
(*Source:* NCES 2012)

Table 13.3 Bachelor's Degrees Granted by Gender and Field of Study

Field of Study/Major	Percent Male	Percent Female
Health Professions	15	85
Education	20	80
English, Foreign Language, and Literatures	31	69
Communications	37	63
Business	51	49
Social Science and History	51	49
Mathematics and Statistics	57	43
Computer and Information Sciences	82	18
Engineering and Construction Trades	83	17

Source: NCES 2012.

While some may suspect that women are less likely to enter STEM fields due to lower abilities in math and science, this appears *not* to be the case. Even when female students have high math scores on the SAT, they are less likely than their male peers to major in fields like economics, math, or engineering (Turner and Bowen 1999). As with occupational choices more broadly, socialization plays a powerful role in shaping students' choice of major. Many college students appear to choose majors based on expectations of the future: male students may focus more on pay and the expectation of being a breadwinner, while female students may focus more on majors and jobs that help them balance work and family (Turner and Bowen 1999; Zafar 2009).

Finally, even when women and men major in the same fields, obtain the same graduate degrees, and enter the same occupations, gender differences in pay still exist. Today, women make up about half of those graduating with advanced degrees in law (JD), business (MBA), and medicine (MD). With each of those fields, women tend to specialize in subfields that provide more job flexibility but are lower paying. In law, for example, men are more likely to opt into the intense and highly paid field of patent law; women, by contrast, are more likely to opt into family law. Within medicine, women are more likely to become general practitioners or family doctors, while men select specialties like anesthesiology, transplantation, or cardiology. Again, we see how macro-level forces of gender socialization impact individual-level choices: the desire to balance work and family remains at the forefront of women's decisions, even when they earn advanced degrees.

SIGNING A "LETTER OF INTENT": GENDER AND WAGE NEGOTIATIONS

Once offered a job, the gender gap in pay is also shaped by differences among "players" in their negotiation strategies. At the micro-level, men are more likely to negotiate their salaries, and when they do negotiate, they negotiate harder. These findings are documented by economist Linda Babcock and her co-author Sara Laschever (2003) in their book, *Women Don't Ask: Gender and the Negotiation Divide*. They report that men initiate wage negotiations about four times as often as women. Moreover, while women described negotiations as a painful process, not unlike going to the dentist, men saw them as a lively competition. Finally, when they do negotiate, women typically ask for 30 percent less than men.

Perhaps these different appetites for negotiation reflect deep-seated messages of gender socialization. As discussed in Chapter 7, much of male gender socialization revolves around toys and social interactions that emphasize competition and one-upmanship. In her work on gendered patterns of communication, linguist Deborah Tannen (1996) argues that men tend to communicate using **report-talk**—a style of conversation that is built on establishing dominance and status. Female gender socialization revolves around toys and social interactions that emphasize consensus and common ground. According to Tannen, women tend to use **rapport-talk**, a style of communication aimed at harmony and the collective well-being, and avoids rocking the boat.

The significance of these patterns is found both outside and inside the workplace. Scholars use the term the **tyranny of nice** to describe one overarching message of gender socialization: that women should be nice and polite, deferential and cooperative, above all else (Martin 2003). This message may shape a woman's approach to wage negotiations, as well as how she approaches buying a car and working through interpersonal tensions. Yet research shows that by simply shifting the framing of this issue, women may become more comfortable talking about pay. Experimental research shows that women are less comfortable with the notion of *negotiating*, with its adversarial connotation, but more comfortable *asking* for a raise (Small et al. 2007). Women are more comfortable *asking* for a raise, since it is seen as a linguistic gesture of politeness and deference used when attempting to get something from another, which is consistent with low-power social roles that women have typically occupied at work (Brown and Levinson 1987).

Returning to the economic significance of the gender gap in pay, Babcock and Laschever note that what may start out as a relatively minimal salary difference between men and women in their first jobs tends to accumulate over time, since raises and retirement contributions are often distributed as a percentage of one's initial salary. By the age of retirement, an individual who does not negotiate their starting salary stands to lose more than $500,000 by age 60. These authors also report that women who consistently negotiate salary increases across their careers earn at least $1 million more than women who don't.

Although it may be tempting to recommend that women simply reframe the act of negotiating as a polite request in conversation, researchers have discovered that asking for a raise may itself bring penalties. Using an experimental research design, Hannah Riley Bowles and colleagues (2007) found that women who negotiated their salaries received negative evaluations: both male and female evaluators were less likely to want to hire them or work with them on a team (compared to men who negotiated).

Connecting this research to *the tyranny of nice*, women who negotiated were perceived as demanding and difficult to work with—two characteristics that can sink a woman's professional aspirations. It is possible that women's disinclination to negotiate is actually a rational strategy, given the social and economic costs that sometimes come with their decision to negotiate.

TRYING TO PLAY FOR TWO TEAMS: BALANCING WORK AND FAMILY

Can men and women "have it all"? Is it possible in this day and age for players to balance playing for two teams—the "home team" and the "work team"? Among the individual-level factors contributing to the gender pay gap, the real and perceived decision to have a family has a measurable and disparate impact on the work experiences of women and men. One of the biggest reasons women earn less than men, even in the same job, is that they are more likely to take time off of work and/or reduce their work hours when they have children. Among heterosexual couples, a very real calculation takes place: Who is best suited to provide for the child's needs (breastfeeding, for example), and whose earnings will take less of a hit by taking time off? Because the average woman earns less than the average man, in heterosexual relationships this often leads to the decision for the mother to stay home, to cut back at work, to pick the child up from school when sick, and so forth.

It is estimated that 60 percent of women with children under 2 work outside the home; this is referred to as their **labor force participation rate**. This means that 40 percent of women with young children have exited the labor force—at least for a period of time. The decision to take a break from work or move to part-time employment takes place within a macro-level context where women earn less than men. In the short term, it makes sense for women who earn less than their male partners to take time off. Over time, these individual-level decisions result in substantial differences in human capital in terms of skill and seniority, as workers with less human capital are worth less in the labor market. It is estimated that among married women, the birth of each child results in a 7 percent decrease in wage (Budig and England 2001). In short, the decision for female players to expand their "home team" is expensive.

The tendency for women with children to exit the labor force or cut back at work has been called the **mommy track**. In a *New York Times Magazine* article on the subject, journalist Lisa Belkin (2013) profiled a group of women who "opted out" of the labor force, despite their prestigious degrees and high-profile jobs. According to Belkin, these women were actively making choices—choices they did not seem to regret—to reject the world of work and redefine the meaning of success. "'I don't want to be on the fast track leading to a partnership at a prestigious law firm,'" Katherine Brokaw told Belkin. "Some people define that as success. I don't." These women touted the joys of motherhood and admitted that they simply didn't want to "work that hard." Some women used the language of *essentialism* and suggested that as women, they had been born with less desire to compete and more desire to nurture. In asking "Why don't women run the world?" Belkin concludes: "Maybe it's because they don't want to."

The decision to opt out of the labor force does not take place in a vacuum. When men and women make decisions about how to balance work and family, they do so within a macro-level context. It may not be the case that women find motherhood uniquely gratifying or that they feel the biological pull to nurture. Across the globe, women in many societies don't *opt out*—suggesting that something *social* is also at work. It may be the case that the social organization of work in the United States is unfriendly to family life and that the social construction of gender, which emphasizes men's need to compete and women's desire to nurture, provides women the opportunity to gracefully exit the labor force.

THE GENDERED GAME—MACRO-LEVEL EXPLANATIONS FOR THE PAY GAP

The benefit of the sociological perspective is that it emphasizes social dynamics at the micro- and macro-levels. Although the efforts and decisions of the player are important for shaping social outcomes—like the gender gap in pay—these efforts and decisions do not take place in a vacuum. Decisions about what kind of career to select are molded by broad, cultural messages about gender roles; decisions about whether to hire a particular candidate are also influenced by cultural beliefs about gender; and individual decisions about whether and how to balance work and family are shaped by the social organization of employment and the presence or absence of "family-friendly" policies. Here we discuss the gendered aspects of the game and how they perpetuate unequal gender experiences at work.

CHEATS AND UNSPORTSMANLIKE CONDUCT?: THE ROLE OF OVERT DISCRIMINATION

Although games have rules, "cheating" and bending the rules are also part of many games. When it comes to gendered experiences in the workplace, what is the role of cheating and unsportsmanlike conduct (i.e., discrimination)? In terms of **gender discrimination**, researchers believe that overt and intentionally sexist attitudes and behaviors exert a statistically small, though socially significant, impact on workplace inequalities.

One facet of gender discrimination in the workplace involves the belief that men make better workers than women; this belief then affects the selection and promotion of men over women. High-profile legal cases sometimes bring public awareness to this phenomenon. In 1997, for example, the Publix grocery chain was accused of systematically denying women opportunities to advance. One female employee was told by a male supervisor that women simply are not capable of supervisory roles; another was told she could not be promoted because she was not the head of her household. An investigation found that promotions were typically awarded in an informal manner; rather than advertising job openings and have interested parties apply, management filled vacancies using personal connections and the "old boys' network." In what was the largest class-action gender discrimination case at its time, Publix agreed to pay $81.5 million to those affected by its systematic gender bias.

Similar allegations have been leveled against Wal-Mart, yet for technical reasons, that class-action case—involving more than 1.5 million women—has not moved forward. Both cases illustrate the **glass ceiling** women sometimes face at work: an invisible yet unbreakable barrier that impedes advancement to higher positions.

A second form of discrimination some women face at work is sexual harassment. **Sexual harassment** takes several forms: pressuring workers to trade sex for favors (*quid pro quo*); sexual advances, whether physical (groping) or verbal; and the creation of a *hostile environment*. **Hostile environments** are those where the culture is deliberately offensive to one group; for example, where there is the persistent use of sexual humor and/or employees' lockers or work spaces are decorated with obscene or pornographic imagery.

Each year the Equal Employment Opportunity Commission (EEOC) receives thousands of complaints of sexual harassment. Filed in 1988, *Jenson v. Eveleth Taconite* was the first successful class-action sexual harassment law suit. Portrayed by Charlize Theron is the movie *North Country*, Lois Jenson detailed years of harassment working in the iron mines of northern Minnesota; there, she and other women endured abusive and sexual language, stalking, and threats and intimidation. The court ruled that the harassment was intentional and motivated by the women's gender and that the company had a responsibility to prevent it. The case was finally resolved in 1998, when

Portrayed by Charlize Theron in the movie *North Country*, Lois Jenson was the lead plaintiff in the first successful class-action sexual harassment lawsuit.

Eveleth Taconite settled out of court, agreeing to pay $3.5 million to the 15 women who were part of the case.

How do discrimination and sexual harassment affect the gender gap in pay? Overt forms of discrimination tend to keep women in lower-level positions, where they are passed over for promotions. This clearly fuels the gender gap in pay, as workers are unable to break the glass ceiling and advance to more highly paid positions. Sexual harassment, especially, has both financial and psychological consequences. Women who are sexually harassed may experience high levels of stress, leading to absenteeism and lower levels of productivity. Lois Jenson, for example, was diagnosed with post-traumatic stress disorder (PTSD) after she left Eveleth Taconite in 1992. Workers who experience these psychological stresses may not perform at their best, leading to lower levels of pay and advancement.

In 2009, legislation was passed to address this source of the gender gap in pay. Signed into law by President Barack Obama, the **Lilly Ledbetter Fair Pay Act** provides a legal tool to those who feel they have experienced gender discrimination in pay. The law honors Lilly Ledbetter, a manager at the Goodyear Tire Company, who discovered after 20 years of employment that she was paid $3,727 per month, while the lowest paid male with similar seniority received $4,286 per month and the highest paid received $5,236. While paying workers different amounts based on performance and productivity is perfectly legal, paying workers different amounts based on gender is not. While the notion of "equal pay for equal work" was originally articulated in the Equal Pay

Signed into law in 2009, the Lilly Ledbetter Fair Pay Act provides greater flexibility in filing lawsuits over gender discrimination in pay.

Act of 1963, the Lilly Ledbetter Fair Pay Act updated one of its provisions, allowing more time for workers to initiate their complaint. While all of these laws apply to both men and women, it is women who have been historically most negatively affected and, therefore, most likely to initiate cases.

GENDER INEQUALITY AND THE CULTURAL ORGANIZATION OF WORK

Beyond overt forms of discrimination and harassment, men's and women's experiences at work—and the resulting gender gap in pay—are profoundly shaped by deeply embedded notions about gender. Socially constructed notions of a "good employee" are not gender-neutral. How an ideal employee speaks and negotiates, dresses, and behaves, as well as assumptions about his or her commitment to work, are often based on a male standard. At the macro-level, then, *male privilege* is a very real force in the workplace. It subtly permeates many workplace cultures, making it difficult for women—and men who do not adhere to traditional notions of masculinity—to excel.

The role of gender in scouting, tryouts, and promotions

In many professions, the first step in getting a job is applying and sending letters of recommendation. In a landmark study of letters of recommendation for medical faculty positions, researchers found that the language in these letters was highly gendered (Trix and Psenka 2003). Women candidates were more likely to be described as "hardworking," "conscientious," "dependable," "meticulous," "diligent," and "careful." Men, by contrast, were more likely to be described as "brilliant," "outstanding," "superb," or "exceptional." In addition, letters for women were more likely to mention their personal life and emphasize teaching accomplishments, while letters for men were more likely to emphasize research accomplishments. In writing these letters, recommenders unintentionally frame women as collaborative teachers and men as competitive researchers. Such language may have unintended consequences for hiring, especially in an environment where "competitive" functions as a shorthand for a desirable worker.

Researchers have discovered similar findings in studies of applications and résumés. These studies suggest that the gender-based assumptions may hinder women's ability to get hired and earn an appropriate salary. In a lab-based experiment, Shelly Correll and co-authors (2007) asked 188 undergraduate students to evaluate the résumés of fictitious male and female job applicants. These fictitious résumés controlled for parenthood status, work experience, and educational background. The goal was to see whether females are discriminated against when applying for jobs. The researchers found that there is, indeed, a **motherhood penalty**: even when applicants' objective qualifications were held constant, mothers were perceived as less competent and less committed to their careers than fathers. Mothers, in general, are perceived to be less reliable, more likely to take time off of work, more likely to attend to children on sick days, and so forth. This perception—which has been confirmed in separate studies of attorneys (Fuegen et al. 2004) and management consultants (Cuddy, Fiske, and Glick 2004)—then resulted in lower salary recommendations from evaluators.

The men in Correll et al.'s study—which included an audit study of actual employers—were not penalized for being parents. In fact, compared to childless men, fathers were "seen as more committed to paid work and [were] offered higher starting salaries" (2007:1332). Correll et al.'s research confirms that male workers experience a fatherhood or **marriage premium**: a pattern where married men with children are paid more than those without children—even after controlling for relevant human capital traits (qualifications, experience, etc.). While some economists believe the marriage premium reflects the fact that married men are more motivated to work and are actually more productive than those without children, other researchers believe it simply reflects a cultural preference and a belief that married men with children make the best workers.

The cultural preference for male workers has been called the glass escalator. Popularized by the sociologist Christine Williams (1992), the **glass escalator** refers to the invisible mechanisms by which men are promoted and move to higher levels in the workplace. In her research on men in traditionally female jobs, Williams found that men working in fields like nursing, education, and social work were rewarded for being progressive pathbreakers; women working in traditionally male fields, however, are often viewed as interlopers (Kanter 1977). Williams and others describe the glass escalator as the process by which men are effectively "kicked upstairs," often as a result of cultural beliefs about where their talents lie. In social work and education, for example, employers may have an unconscious belief that men's talents can best be utilized in supervisory roles, rather than boots-on-the-ground positions as caseworkers or classroom teachers. Other research finds that men actively seek out supervisory roles as a way to reassert their masculinity within female-dominated occupations and distance themselves from their "lowly" female co-workers (Cross and Bagilhole 2002).

Unconscious preferences for males seem to operate in many fields, including professional orchestras. Yet changes have taken place. During the 1970s, women made up less than 5 percent of the nation's top orchestras; today, they comprise at least 25 percent of these orchestras. What happened? Did women suddenly up their game and become better musicians? Actually, the rules of the game surrounding the hiring of musicians changed. In the late 1970s, orchestras began using blind auditions. By placing performers behind a screen, hiring panels were unable to rely on gender cues to evaluate those auditioning. By focusing more on what evaluators were hearing, hiring panels consequently hired more female musicians. This suggests that employers should make efforts to conceal the gender of applicants during the hiring process and that, in so doing, greater emphasis may be placed on ability than on gender stereotypes.

Ball hog or team player? Gender and workplace culture

According to researchers, many workplace cultures reflect a male standard, and workers in those settings are evaluated using a male standard of behavior. This suggests that male privilege operates in many work settings (sometimes even those where women dominate). Scientific professions provide an excellent illustration of this. To be a successful scientist, it should be enough to produce novel, relevant, and rigorous work. It appears, though, that scientific excellence is determined by more than simply the quality of one's work. Subtleties in language and self-presentation also contribute to the social construction of an excellent scientist. Even the simple decision to describe one's research using "I" or "we" can impact how a scientist is perceived. While men tend to use "I," which highlights their individual accomplishments, women tend to use the inclusive and communal "we;" this may lead to the impression that she is not the driving force in her lab.

The flip side of this dynamic is that when women do assert themselves (asking questions about lab space, research assistants, etc.), they risk being perceived as unlikeable. Quoted in a *New York Times* article on women in science, Columbia University professor Daniel R. Ames stated that "the band of acceptable behavior for women [in employment negotiations] is narrower than it is for men" (Dean 2006). Women who ask for multiple research assistants and new lab equipment may be viewed as pushy and, therefore, may not be rewarded with these resources. Such differential treatment in individual negotiations can, according to Ames, "'accumulate over a career [and] lead to significant differences in outcomes." In this context, male players are allowed to be "ball hogs" and are rewarded for selfish and self-aggrandizing behaviors, while women are expected to be team players and may be penalized if they deviate from this expectation.

Research conducted in other work settings similarly suggests that the traits of success and likeability are at odds for women: at work, women may have to choose between being successful *or* likeable. Social psychologists refer to this as **perceived role incongruity**, meaning that occupational success and femininity are seen as incompatible. Using experimental research designs, researchers find that assertive women who display masculine, "agentic" (active and self-serving) traits are viewed as violating prescriptions of feminine niceness (Heilman et al. 2004; Rudman and Glick 2001). Women who display these "masculine" traits may suffer bias in hiring and promotions, given the perception that while they may be highly competent, they are not especially likeable.

Such dynamics in the workplace are not individual acts of discrimination. Rather they are unconscious norms, operating at the macro-level. The irony of these preferences in gender behavior, though, is that they do not always serve a firm's best interests. Research suggests that businesses that have a strong record of promoting women to executive positions or to serve on corporate boards are more profitable than those with few women in leadership positions. In his analysis of 200 Fortune 500 companies over a 19-year period, Roy Adler (2008) found that firms that aggressively promoted women were more profitable, earning profits 34 percent higher than industry medians—even when controlling for other traits. The profitability of women executives has been confirmed by others, including Catalyst (Carter 2007), an organization that researches women in business.

So what do women bring to the table that benefits corporate performance? Some researchers speculate that simply bringing diverse voices into leadership positions is in a company's best interest. With more diverse points of view, companies are able to develop more innovative product development and marketing strategies. Similarly, companies with a higher percentage of black executives are more profitable than those lacking racial diversity (Herring 2009). A second explanation for the female advantage in the workplace is that women's traditional communication styles foster better teamwork, given the focus on consensus-building and deliberation (Dezsö and Ross 2012). This is another way of saying that women's "rapport-talk," which is an adult manifestation of childhood socialization centered on role playing and finding common ground, can be quite productive. As it turns out, promoting qualified women is not just equitable, it can also be profitable.

THE SOCIAL ORGANIZATION OF WORK: THE CHALLENGE OF PLAYING FOR TWO TEAMS

Finally, the social organization of work in the United States makes it difficult for both men and women to balance work and family roles. The **social organization of work** refers to the nearly invisible and taken-for-granted ways in which work is structured within a society. Elements of this structure include the scheduling of professional work between the hours of 9 to 5 (or 8 to 6); the fact that employees are asked to be most productive during their childbearing years; and the lack of policies that help employees play for two teams at once—their workplace and their home lives. While the social organization of work applies both to men and women, its consequences tend to be more deleterious for women, given that they are the ones who bear children (and that families typically make decisions about how to balance work and family life in the context of women's already lower wages). These decisions, in turn, tend to reinforce the same workplace structures that generate these inequalities in the first place.

Consider for a moment the fact that most professional jobs (doctors, lawyers, bankers, insurance agents, pharmaceutical sales, etc.) take place between the hours of 9 to 5. Why is this the case? Is there anything inherent in the nature of this work that requires it to be conducted during these hours? The fact is, there is no inherent need for these professions to operate during "regular business hours"; indeed, many professionals would like their doctors to have more flexible hours so that they do not have to take time off of work for their appointments. The fact that work is organized in this way is a holdover from earlier days; it reflects the assumption that families are nuclear in structure, and that while Dad goes off to work, Mom gets the kids off to school and takes care of the family business (banking, doctors' appointments, grocery shopping, etc.).

The social organization of work is shaped by gendered assumptions like the one above. Despite the fact that women now represent nearly 50 percent of the paid labor force, these gendered assumptions remain. Many young women who are planning their careers take into account the fact that they are the only sex that can give birth; that social norms still assume they will be the primary caregiver (especially early on); and that they should select a career that takes these factors into account. In practice, these gender ideologies mean that many women select careers that allow them to balance work and family life—like teaching, which conveniently takes place during the same hours that kids are in school. Young men are constrained as well, as they may be expected to take on careers that pay enough to support a family. The consequences of this macro-level reality is that women tend to select jobs that are flexible but lower paying, while men typically select jobs that are less flexible but offer greater earning potential. Note, again, that these assumptions are heteronormative—based on the assumption that young men and women will ultimately partner with someone of the other sex—and that they constrain the choices of both men and women.

A second aspect of the social organization of work that can hinder women is that many occupations require employees to be most productive during their early careers. Jobs in sales, for example, ask that employees be especially flexible during the beginning of their careers, where they can show commitment by their willingness to travel for meetings, conventions, etc. Within academia and law, the most significant work is done during the first 6 years (or so) on the job. At that point, professors go up for tenure and lawyers can be promoted to "partner." Similarly, doctors enroll in residency programs where they are asked to be both flexible and almost singularly devoted to their professional development. While these are, admittedly, high-level examples, the general principle applies to many jobs—especially those requiring a college degree.

This structural feature of employment has gendered consequences in the sense that workers are expected to be most productive during their reproductive years. Although some people do not aspire to become parents and others may have difficulty becoming parents, 80 percent of all people *do* become parents. Unless there are major scientific discoveries that cannot be anticipated, *all* of those who bear children will be women. The tensions that exist between the social organization of work and gendered expectations of family life (and the fact that only women can give birth) mean that many women (and their partners) must choose between work or family as their priority.

A reasonable solution to these tensions would be for employers to offer more part-time options or flexible scheduling arrangements. In some fields, these are increasingly common. Many jobs, however, maintain an *all-or-nothing* approach. While some professionals do successfully reduce their hours (or work from home), some who choose these options face a brick wall in terms of career advancement. A part-time lawyer can still take on cases, but it is unlikely they will be given the most interesting or demanding cases in their firm. College professors can also have a hard time cutting back. If I wanted to cut my course load from three classes to two classes per semester (thereby becoming an *adjunct*), my salary would drop from about $30,000 to $4,000 for that semester. In addition, I would likely lose my employment benefits, like health care and retirement savings. While the same is true for a man who chooses to reduce his workload, gender schemas, biological realities, and unequal paychecks mean that women are more likely to make these choices.

It is, of course, imperative to point out that while professionals may struggle to cut back at work, other families cannot get enough work. The fact that many employees in service occupations (retail, food service, etc.) are offered *only* part-time work is also problematic. While these employees may have time to devote to their families, the lower-paid nature of these jobs and the fact that workers typically do not receive affordable health insurance means they may not be able to provide for many of their family's basic needs.

Finally, the lack of **family leave policies** at the state and federal levels also makes it difficult to balance work and family life. Family leave policies include maternity and paternity leave, as well as leave to take care of a sick family member. The United States is the only Western industrialized country that does not offer paid maternity leave. While about 20 percent of workers are eligible for paid leave from their employer, there are no federal policies that grant paid leave. Instead, workers in the United States are covered by the **Family and Medical Leave Act** (FMLA). Passed in 1993 under President Bill Clinton, the Act provides 12 weeks of unpaid family leave annually; the leave is available to people working in firms with more than 50 employees. Because this policy is gender-neutral, both women and men have the option to take time off to care for a newborn or newly adopted child (or sick adult relative).

Since the passage of FMLA, the gender pay gap has narrowed. Prior to its passage, there was no guarantee that a woman's job would be waiting for her when she returned to work after a pregnancy. This resulted in a lot of stopping and starting in women's employment, which led to lower human capital accumulation and lower pay over time (Hofferth and Curtin 2006). Because FMLA offers job-secured leave, workers are now able to return to their jobs and continue building seniority in the same position. The ability of social policy to affect gender inequalities is also evident in the examples of family leave abroad, discussed below.

Despite these advances, problems remain in the organization of family leave. These lingering issues reinforce the gender gap in pay. One issue is that as many as 40 percent of workers are not covered by FMLA, whether because they work in small firms or because they have not worked long enough to be eligible for the leave. Another factor is that some workers cannot afford to take unpaid leave. FMLA, then, appears to be a policy that most benefits economically advantaged families. This insight illustrates the importance of looking at issues like the gender gap in pay from an intersectional perspective.

Taking a closer look at the gendered dimension of family leave, research shows that even when men have access to paternity (FMLA or employer-sponsored), they tend not to take it. Many men hesitate to take family leave, worried they may be sending the message they are not serious about their jobs and, therefore, unlikely candidates for promotion (Halverson 2003). When men perceive family leave as optional or unwise, this calculation—in heterosexual relationships—typically leads to the decision for women taking time off. These gendered perceptions about the meaning of work in men's and women's lives, combined with the existing gender gap in pay, establishe the macro-level context in which individuals make decisions—decisions that unwittingly perpetuate these unequal social arrangements.

EXPLORING INTERSECTIONALITY:
RACE, FAMILY, AND THE GENDER GAP IN PAY

While making generalizations in terms of race, class, and gender is the bread and butter of sociology, we know there are limits to drawing such broad generalizations. For that reason, sociologists often take an intersectional approach. When it comes to the gender gap in pay, this means telling a more nuanced story about men's fatherhood premium and women's motherhood penalty. Not all men experience a boost to their wages when they become fathers, and not all women experience a decrease when they become mothers. The benefits associated with marriage for men and the penalties for women seem to apply mostly to white parents, with different patterns applying to racial and ethnic minorities.

Sociologist Rebecca Glauber built her early career examining the intersection of race, gender, and work experiences. Using national data sets with thousands of respondents, Glauber has shown that gender inequalities in wages are more pronounced in married white and Latino families than in married black families (2007, 2008). Compared to married white and Latino men with children, black men experience less of an increase in wages when they become fathers; moreover, while white and Latino men experience a 15 percent increase in wages when they have three or more children, black men experience no increase. Similarly, motherhood is not associated with a wage penalty for Latino women or black women (unless they have more than two children), yet white women experience a reduction in wages when they become mothers.

Researchers like Rebecca Glauber speculate that structural realities of employment intersect with gender ideologies, shaping how members of different racial and ethnic groups balance work and family life. First, the gender gap in pay is larger among white workers than it is among minority workers. On average, white women earn 81 percent of what white men earn; by comparison, Hispanic women earn 88 percent of what Hispanic men earn and black women's earnings are 90 of their male counterparts. Because minority families earn less, on average, than white families, and—this is crucial—because of the smaller gender gap in pay, minority women may be less likely to reduce their work hours and minority men may be less likely to increase theirs when they become parents.

Second, researchers note that the gender division of household labor is less stark in black families than in other racial and ethnic groups. In general, black couples tend to divide housework and paid work more equally than other racial and ethnic groups (John and Shelton 1997; Orbuch and Eyster 1997). Another way of saying this is that black men do more household tasks than white men. These relationship dynamics among adults may reflect earlier experiences with childhood socialization. Research shows, for example, that young black males are socialized to take on a range of household tasks (Penha-Lopes 2006); meanwhile, young black females are socialized to be independent (Hale-Benson 1986). Historically, young black females have grown up witnessing their mothers and other female kin having high rates of labor force participation; black men, by contrast, have been less able to assert their masculinity through work compared to white men, given their lower earnings and rates of employment.

Ultimately, history, gender socialization, and continuing gender and racial inequalities in the workplace enter the equation of how men and women divide up household labor. These factors, then, seem to affect men and women's contributions to the paid labor force. Together, these findings show that gender and race intersect so that wage penalties and premiums play out differently, depending on race and ethnic identity.

EXPLORING INTERNATIONALLY: THE GENDER AND FAMILY POLICIES ABROAD

If the average woman in the United States earns 77 cents for every dollar earned by the average man, how does this stack up against other countries? Is the United States more or less unequal than other countries when it comes to gender? One feature of the sociological perspective is the belief that we can better understand social phenomena by looking at them historically and cross-culturally. Doing so can help us understand the degree to which gender differences and inequalities are socially constructed, rather than inherent (i.e., biologically determined).

While this chapter has focused on gender inequalities in employment, a more comprehensive understanding of men and women's positions in society requires a focus on educational opportunities, health and well-being, and political representation as well. Taking these factors into account, in 2014 the World Economic Forum ranked the United States 20th (up from 23rd the year before) among 142 countries in their **Global Gender Gap Report** (see Table 13.4). While the United States stands in 4th place for economic participation and opportunity, its ranking is pulled down by landing in 62nd place for "health and survival" and 54th for "political empowerment"— due to the small numbers of women represented in federal government.

So which nations score well for gender equality? A journey to find the most gender-egalitarian societies would take us to Europe's Nordic countries. Iceland, Finland, Norway, Sweden, and Denmark occupy the top five spots. What makes these countries unusual is the degree to which they have consciously enacted social policies to promote gender equality. For example, in the 1970s, several of these countries introduced voluntary gender quotas in political representation; this has led to high representation of women in politics. Sweden has one of the highest percentages of women in its parliament in the world, at nearly 45 percent. By contrast, women made up 19.4% of the representatives of the 114th U.S. Congress (2015). In Iceland, women won 41% of the seats in 2013 parliamentary elections. In 1980, Iceland was the first country to elect a woman, Vigdís Finnbogadóttir, to serve as its prime minister.

Table 13.4 **Gender Inequality in Global Perspective (Most to Less)**

Country

1. Iceland	11. Switzerland
2. Finland	12. Germany
3. Norway	13. New Zealand
4. Sweden	14. Netherlands
5. Denmark	15. Latvia
6. Nicaragua	16. France
7. Rwanda	17. Burundi
8. Ireland	18. South Africa
9. Philippines	19. Canada
10. Belgium	20. United States

Source: World Economic Forum, 2014.

One set of policies in the Nordic countries that seem to affect these other dimensions of gender inequality are family leave policies. Generally speaking, these nations offer parental leave that is paid and relatively lengthy. In Iceland, new mothers and fathers *each* receive 5 months' paid leave (80 percent of one's wages), with another 2 to be divided as the parents choose. In Sweden, parents are given a total of 16 months to divide up between them, where they are also paid at 80 percent of their wages (up to about $65,000 annually). Families are allowed 3 years during which they may use their leave. While their children are growing up, all families also receive a "child allowance" of approximately $100 per child per month.

In these Nordic countries, paid paternity leave is credited as one mechanism that has helped narrow the gender pay gap. Across these countries, women earn about 85 percent of what men earn. By giving men the chance to take paid time off, couples no longer have to decide whose job is worth more. Accordingly, men and women experience similar disruptions to their work trajectories and acquire similar levels of human capital (seniority, job skill, etc.) during their reproductive years. Although some families can handle the 20 percent cut in wages better than others, it is estimated that about 75 percent of new fathers end up taking family leave. In some European countries, it is not simply that new fathers are given the option of taking time off; in some cases, paternity leave is mandated.

The mandatory nature of paternity leave in many European countries and the imposition of gender quotas among elected politicians rubs many Americans the wrong way. For many Americans, these kinds of social policies involve excessively high levels of government involvement in the private lives of citizens. But especially in the Nordic countries, there is the belief that private lives and government policies are closely connected and mutually reinforcing. Accordingly, citizens generally support such government mandates and see them as tools for producing the greatest benefits for the greatest portion of the population.

THE FUTURE OF GENDER, WORK, AND FAMILY LIFE

What is the future of work and family life in the United States? Will the gender gap continue to close? Will women and men continue to make gendered choices when it comes to work and family life? Will employers or the government implement new strategies to help people balance work and family life?

Indeed, it is predicted that the gender gap in pay will close at some point in the future. While the Economic Policy Institute predicts it will close by 2024, the Institute for Women's Policy Research sets the date for 2058. These projections are based on patterns of college enrollment, choice of college majors, changes in family policy, and shrinkage (manufacturing) or growth (health care and social services) in many different occupational sectors.

Is the closing of the wage gap cause for celebration? Is this a victory for women? A closer look at the Economic Policy Institute's projections—which are based on U.S. Census data—tells a more complicated story. The gap is projected to close not so much because women "catch up" with men, but because women's wages stagnate and men's wages fall. In fact, these trends illustrate a long-term pattern, one with origins in the early 1970s, whereby men's economic fortunes have been eroded. This pattern is evident in the phenomenon dubbed the "mancession," where the global economic recession of 2008–2012 hit men more harshly than women. In the wake of the housing and banking crises that set off the recession, men's unemployment exceeded 10 percent, while women's hovered around 8 percent; some economists estimated that men—who make up slightly more than half of all workers—accounted for three-quarters of the job losses during the recession. Women were more buffered from these forces, given their concentration in fields that are less subject to economic fluctuation—education, health care, and social services.

How might men and women respond to these economic transformations? Hanna Rosin is concerned that men are not responding well. In her book *The End of Men*, she coins the term "cardboard men" to describe what she sees as men's rigidity and resistance to changing gender roles and shifting economic realities. Her concern is that many men are holding on to older notions of masculinity that emphasize profit, brawn, and competition while failing to adapt to changes in the job market that would channel them into growing fields, like education, health care, and social services. Women, by contrast, are flexible and adaptable; she calls them "plastic women." The things women have traditionally excelled at, Rosin says, cannot easily be outsourced and are increasingly important in many occupations. These skills include creativity and interpersonal skills (emotional intelligence, verbal ability, etc.). While women may need to "lean in"—as Sheryl Sandberg says—and take on more leadership roles at work, it appears that ongoing economic transformations are playing to their strengths and, thereby, elevating their professional value.

How will these transformations affect (heterosexual) men and women inside the home? If and when they have children, men and women will be faced with new calculations about who can or should take time off to care for their family. Sometime between 2024 and 2058, it will be a flip of the coin whether the new mother or the new father is the one whose job will take less of an economic hit if they choose to take unpaid time off. These projections suggest that from an economic standpoint, parents will have new flexibility in terms of determining which parent should stay home and whose earnings should be protected. Unfortunately, since projections show that in upcoming decades the average wages of women will stagnate and those of men will fall, taking time off to care for a child may increasingly become an option only for the highest paid workers. Most workers may not have the luxury of deciding which parent will stay home to care for a young child. When discussing this in class, one of my female students said she did not look forward to the closing of the gender gap in pay, worried it may mean she would not have the freedom to opt out of the labor force to take care of any children she may one day have.

These new strategies among the "players" assume that the "game" will remain unchanged. When it comes to gender inequalities in wages and work–family balance, it is clear that the player and the game are mutually reinforcing. In this case, it is difficult to determine whether new strategies among the players will force employers and the government to change the nature of the game or whether decisions by employers and the government will allow players (i.e., workers) the chance to make new decisions. It is reasonable to assume, however, that workplaces will have to respond to the possibility that more women will remain in the workforce and that more families will require dual earners. At that point, it may be in the economic best interest of the government and employers to offer flexible employment and paid family leave. These changes would allow for more gender-egalitarian families and workplaces, while also improving the productivity of many employers, given the possibility for workers to have more job security and more opportunity to enhance their human capital.

CHAPTER 13: REVIEW OF KEY POINTS

- This chapter explains the gender gap in pay by focusing on dynamics at the micro- and macro-levels. The fact that men earn more than women reflects both circumstances and decisions made by individual "players" and the structure of "the game" (cultural beliefs and policies that govern the workplace).
- Among full-time workers, women earn 81 cents for every dollar earned by a man. Over a worker's lifetime, a man with a college degree earns an average of $2.1 million, while a woman with a college degree earns $1.4 million.

- Reflecting historical patterns, continued inequalities, and differences in childhood gender socialization, the gender gap in pay is smaller in black and Latino households than it is in white and Asian American households.

- The gender gap in pay starts young, with research suggesting that even young girls do more housework and receive lower allowances than young boys. Similarly, there is a leisure gap among males and females from early on.

- At the micro-level, one reason that women earn less than men is that they select jobs and college majors with lower earnings; on the macro-level, this reflects broader patterns of childhood gender socialization.

- Women also earn less than men because they are more likely to take time off for the birth of a child or reduce their commitment to part-time; at the macro-level, these decisions reflect broader patterns in how the workplace is organized in the United States.

- Overt, explicit discrimination against women is part of the gender gap in pay; more significant, yet less visible, are the subtle cultural beliefs that shape our attitudes toward men and women in the workplace.

- Currently, the United States is unique among Western industrialized countries in not offering paid family leave. At the macro-level, this means that women are more likely than men to take time off of work to care for a child and, therefore, are more likely to experience fewer gains in human and economic capital.

- In countries that have a smaller wage gap between men and women, social policies typically play a role in advancing women's roles in the workforce and policies and encourage men to play more active roles at home.

- In order to ameliorate gender inequalities in pay, changes can be implemented at both the micro- and macro-levels. The former would involve changing individual players' occupational choices. The latter would involve changing workplace organization in the United States, offering paid family leave or flexible employment arrangements that would allow people to balance work and family life.

- The future of the gender gap in pay is uncertain; macro-level changes in the types of jobs available in the United States, how much those jobs are paid, and who takes those jobs all suggest that men's wages may fall in future decades, thereby closing the gender gap in pay.

CHAPTER 13: QUESTIONS FOR REVIEW

1. Statistically speaking, how large is the gender gap in pay? More important, how is the gender gap in pay expected to change over the next 30 years? What factors account for these predicted changes?

2. On the micro-level, it is individual circumstances that influence the gender gap in pay. What are the main micro-level factors involved in this process?

3. On the macro-level, larger structural factors, like policies and procedures governing the workplace, affect the gender gap in pay. What are the main macro-level factors involved?

4. When you look at these two sets of explanations, do you feel that one is more significant in shaping the gender gap in pay? Similarly, at which level do you think the most progress can be made in terms of narrowing the gender gap in pay and/or promoting greater gender equity in the workplace?

5. Considering your own situation, in what ways may your own micro-level circumstances contribute to a gender gap in pay between men and women? Shifting your focus to the macro-level, what factors do you think will (or already have) affect how much you earn?

6. More broadly speaking, taking into account the material presented in this chapter and in this textbook as a whole, to what extent do you feel that the gender gap in pay and gendered experiences in the workplace are problematic? Why or why not?

KEY TERMS

danger wage premium

Family and Medical Leave Act

family leave policies

FTYR

gender discrimination

gender gap in pay

gender parity

gender pay gap across occupational sectors

glass ceiling

glass escalator

Global Gender Gap Report

hostile environment

human capital

labor force participation rate

leisure gap

Lilly Ledbetter Fair Pay Act

mancession

marriage premium

mommy track

motherhood penalty

perceived role incongruity

rapport-talk

report-talk

sexual harassment

social organization of work

tyranny of nice

REFERENCES

Adler, Roy. 2008. "Women in the Executive Suite Correlate to High Profits." European Union Project on Equal Pay. Retrieved October 27, 2013 (http://www.w2t.se/se/filer/adler_web.pdf).

Babcock, Linda and Sara Laschever. 2003. *Women Don't Ask: Negotiation and the Gender Divide*. Princeton, NJ: Princeton University Press.

Belkin, Lisa. 2013. "The Opt-Out Revolution." *The New York Times Magazine*, August 7. Retrieved April 23, 2015 (http://www.nytimes.com/2013/08/11/magazine/the-opt-out-revolution.html?_r=0)

Bielby, William and James Baron. 1987. "Undoing Discrimination: Job Integration and Comparable Worth." Pp. 211–232 in *Ingredients for Women's Employment Policy*, edited by Christine E. Bose and Glenna D. Spitze. Albany, NY: SUNY Press.

Blau, Francine. 2012. "The Sources of the Gender Pay Gap." Pp. 189–219 in *The New Gilded Age: The Critical Inequality Debates of our Time*, edited by David B. Grusky and Tamar Kricheli-Katz. Stanford, CA: Stanford University Press.

Blau, Francine and Lawrence Kahn. 2008. "Women's Work and Wages." Pp. 762–772 in *The New Palgrave Dictionary of Economics*, 2nd ed., Vol. 8, edited by Steven Durlauf and Lawrence Blume. New York: Palgrave Macmillan.

Bowles, Hannah Riley, Linda Babcock, and Lei Lai. 2007. "Social Incentives for Gender Differences in the Propensity to Initiate Negotiations: Sometimes It Does Hurt to Ask." *Organizational Behavior and Human Decision Processes* 103(1):84–103.

Brown, Penelope and Stephen C. Levinson. 1987. *Politeness: Some Universals in Language Usage*. New York: Cambridge University Press.

Budig, Michele J. and Paula England. 2001. "The Wage Penalty for Motherhood." *American Sociological Review* 66(2):204–225.

Bureau of Labor Statistics. 2014. "Highlights of Women's Earnings in 2013." Washington, DC: U.S. Bureau of Labor Statistics/U.S. Census Bureau.

Carter, Nancy M. 2007. "The Bottom Line: Corporate Performance and Women's Representation on Boards." Catalyst. Retrieved October 27, 2013 (http://www.catalyst.org/knowledge/bottom-line-corporate-performance-and-womens-representation-boards).

Charles, Maria and David Grusky. 2004. *Occupational Ghettos: The Worldwide Segregation of Women and Men*. Palo Alto, CA: Stanford University Press.

Cohn, Samuel. 1985. *The Process of Occupational Sex-Typing: The Feminization of Clerical Labor in Great Britain*. Philadelphia: Temple University Press.

Correll, Shelley J. 2001. "Gender and the Career Choice Process: The Role of Biased Self-Assessments." *American Journal of Sociology* 106(6):1691–1730.

Correll, Shelley J., Stephen Benard, and In Paik. 2007. "Getting a Job: Is There a Motherhood Penalty?" *American Journal of Sociology* 112(5):1297–1339.

Cross, Simon and Barbara Bagilhole. 2002. "Girls' Jobs for the Boys? Men, Masculinity and Non-Traditional Occupations." *Gender, Work, and Organization* 9(2):204–226.

Crouter, Ann C., Melissa R. Head, Matthew F. Bumpus, and Susan M. McHale. 2011. "Household Chores: Under What Conditions Do Mothers Lean on Daughters?" *New Directions for Child and Adolescent Development* 94: 23–42.

Cuddy, Amy J. C., Susan T. Fiske, and Peter Glick. 2004. "When Professionals Become Mothers, Warmth Doesn't Cut the Ice." *Journal of Social Issues* 60(4):701–718.

Dean, Cornelia. 2006. "Women in Science: The Battle Moves to the Trenches." *New York Times*, December 19. Retrieved April 23, 2015 (http://www.nytimes.com/2006/12/19/science/19women.html?pagewanted=all)

Dezsö, Cristian L. and David Gaddis Ross. 2012. "Does Female Representation in Top Management Improve Firm Performance? A Panel Data Investigation." *Strategic Management Journal* 33(9):1072–1089.

Donato, Katharine. 1990. "Programming for Change? The Growing Demand among Computer Specialists." Pp. 167–182 in *Job Queues, Gender Queues*, edited by Barbara F. Reskin and Patricia A. Roos. Philadelphia: Temple University Press.

Dorman, Peter and Paul Hagstrom. 1998. "Wage Compensation for Dangerous Work Revisited." *Industrial and Labor Relations Review* 52(1):116–135.

Etaugh, Claire and Marsha B. Liss. 1992. "Home, School, and Playroom: Training Grounds for Adult Gender Roles." *Sex Roles* 26(3–4):129–147.

Fuegen, Kathleen, Monica Biernat, Elizabeth Haines, and Kay Deaux. 2004. "Mothers and Fathers in the Workplace: How Gender and Parental Status Influence Judgments of Job-Related Competence." *Journal of Social Issues* 60(4):737–754.

Glauber, Rebecca. 2007. "Marriage and the Motherhood Wage Penalty among African Americans, Hispanics, and Whites. *Journal of Marriage and Family* 69(4): 951–961.

Glauber, Rebecca. 2008. "Race and Gender in Families and at Work: The Fatherhood Wage Premium." *Gender and Society* 22(1):8–30.

Goldin, Claudia. 2014. "A Grand Gender Convergence: Its Last Chapter." *American Economic Review* 104(4):1091–1119.

Hale-Benson, Janice. 1986. *Black Children: Their Roots, Culture, and Learning Styles*. Annapolis, MD: Johns Hopkins University Press.

Halverson, Chuck. 2003. "From Here to Paternity: Why Men Are Not Taking Paternity Leave Under the Family and Medical Leave Act. *Wisconsin Law Journal* 18(2):257–279.

Heilman, Madeline E., Aaron S. Wallen, Daniella Fuchs, and Melinda M. Tamkins. 2004. "Penalties for Success: Reactions to Women Who Succeed at Male Gender-Typed Tasks." *Journal of Applied Psychology* 89(3):416–427.

Herman, Alexis M. 1999. *Report on the American Work Force*. Bureau of Labor Statistics. Washington, DC. Retrieved October 9, 2013 (http://www.bls.gov/opub/rtaw/pdf/rtaw1999.pdf).

Herring, Cedric. 2009. "Does Diversity Pay? Race, Gender, and the Business Case for Diversity." *American Sociological Review* 74(2):208–224.

Hofferth, Sandra S. and Sally C. Curtin. 2006. "Parental Leave Statutes and Maternal Return to Work after Childbirth in the United States." *Work and Occupations* 33(1):73–105.

John, Daphne and Beth Anne Shelton. 1997. "The Production of Gender among Black and White Women and Men: The Case of Household Labor." *Sex Roles* 36(3–4): 171–193.

Juster, Thomas F., Hiromi Ono, and Frank P. Stafford. 2004. "Changing Times of American Youth, 1981–2003." Ann Arbor, MI: Institute for Social Research, University of Michigan. Retrieved October 7, 2013 (http://www.ns.umich.edu/Releases/2004/Nov04/teen_time_report.pdf)

Kanter, Rosabeth Moss. 1977. *Men and Women of the Corporation*. New York: Basic Books.

Kimmel, Michael. 2009. *The Gendered Society*, 4th ed. New York: Oxford University Press.

Martin, Karin A. 2003. "Giving Birth Like a Girl." *Gender and Society* 17(1):54–72.

National Center for Education Statistics. 2012. "Digest of Education Statistics, 2012." Washington, D.C., U.S. Department of Education. Retrieved April 23, 2015 (http://nces.ed.gov/programs/digest/current_tables.asp)

Orbuch Terri L. and Sandra L. Eyster. 1997. "Division of Household Labor among Black Couples and White Couples." *Social Forces* 76(1):301–332.

Penha-Lopes, Vânia. 2006. "'To Cook, Sew, to Be a Man': The Socialization for Competence and Black Men's Involvement in Housework." *Sex Roles* 54(3–4):261–274.

Raley, Sara, and Suzanne Bianchi. 2006. "Sons, Daughters, and Family Processes: Does Gender of Children Matter?" *Annual Review of Sociology* (32): 401–421.

Reskin, Barbara F. and Patricia A. Roos. 1990. *Job Queues, Gender Queues: Explaining Women's Inroads into Male Occupations*. Philadelphia: Temple University Press.

Rosin, Hanna. 2012. *End of Men: And the Rise of Women*. New York: Riverhead Books.

Rudman, Laurie A. and Peter Glick. 2001. "Prescriptive Gender Stereotypes and Backlash towards Agentic Women." *Journal of Social Issues* 57(4):743–762.

Sandberg, Sheryl. 2013. *Lean In: Women, Work, and the Will to Lead*. New York: Knopf.

Small, Deborah A., Michele Gelfand, Linda Babcock, and Hilary Getman. 2007. "Who Goes to the Bargaining Table? The Influence of Gender and Framing on the Initiation of Negotiation." *Journal of Personality and Social Psychology* 93(4):600–613.

Strober, Myra H. and Carolyn L. Arnold. 1987. "The Dynamics of Occupational Segregation among Bank Tellers. Pp. 107–158 in *Gender in the Workplace*, edited by Clair Brown and Joseph A. Pechman. Washington, DC: The Brookings Institution.

Tannen, Deborah. 1996. *Gender and Discourse*. New York: Oxford University Press.

Trix, Frances and Carolyn Psenka. 2003. "Exploring the Color of Glass: Letters of Recommendation for Female and Male Medical Faculty." *Discourse and Society* 14(2):191–220.

Turner, Sarah E. and William G. Bowen. 1999. "Choice of Major: The Changing (Unchanging) Gender Gap." *Industrial and Labor Relations Review* 52(2):289–313.

U.S. Census Bureau. 2014. "Income, Poverty, and Health Insurance Coverage in the United States: 2012." Washington, D.C.: Current Population Reports/U.S. Census Bureau. Retrived April 23, 2015 (http://www.census.gov/prod/2013pubs/p60-245.pdf)

Williams, Christine. 1992. "The Glass Escalator: Hidden Advantages for Men in the 'Female' Professions." *Social Problems* 39(3):253–267.

World Economic Forum. 2014. "The Global Gender Gap and Its Implications: 2014" Geneva, Switzerland. Retrieved April 23, 2015 (http://www3.weforum.org/docs/GGGR14/GGGRMainChapterAppendices_2014.pdf)

Zafar, Basit. 2009. "College Major Choice and the Gender Gap." [Staff Report no. 364] New York: Federal Reserve Bank of New York. Retrieved October 12, 2013 (http://www.newyorkfed.org/research/staff_reports/sr364.pdf)

Living to a Ripe Old Age?

Understanding Inequalities in Health and Well-Being

How long do you expect to live? How old do you think you'll be when you "kick the bucket"? Since the 1800s, life expectancies in Western countries have increased dramatically. Today, people are living longer than ever before and are able to manage and mitigate the effects of diseases that were once fatal. Greater access to fresh food, more sanitary living conditions, and medical advancements all play a role in the improving life expectancies and qualities of life in modern societies. Some observers interpret these patterns as suggesting that life expectancies can be expected to increase indefinitely, so that living past 100 may become routine.

Yet beneath these aggregate trends of longer and healthier lives, more complicated patterns emerge. Patterns are complicated not just by high rates of malaria and HIV/AIDS in Africa and so-called developing countries, but by variations *within* modern societies like the United States. While it is true that Americans are living longer and healthier lives than ever before, it is also true that these patterns play out differently across race, class, and gender lines. The life expectancies of men and women differ, as do those of different races and ethnicities. Patterns of life expectancy across income and educational groups are especially complicated, illustrated dramatically by the fact that life expectancies for less educated white Americans have recently been on the decline.

This chapter explores social inequalities in health and well-being. It is organized around a central question: How are race, class, and gender related to a person's quality of life and how long they may live? As in all of the chapters in this unit, the question of health and well-being is approached from the micro- and macro-levels. A person's quality of life and how long he or she lives clearly reflects factors on the individual level. While genetics are certainly a part of this, that topic is best left to scholars in other fields. Instead, the sociological perspective focuses on individual choices and circumstances such as diet, exercise, and health care utilization. Yet because none of those individual choices and experiences occurs in a bubble, we add to our perspective the role of macro-level forces. We conceive, for example, of a person who aspires to live a healthy lifestyle but still faces health-related challenges and risks from the environment in which he or she is embedded. Ultimately, this chapter illustrates that both individual choices and circumstances and macro-level factors are structured so that a person's race, class, and gender are systematically related to their quality of life and life expectancy.

HOW LONG MIGHT YOU LIVE?: A STATISTICAL OVERVIEW OF HEALTH INEQUALITIES

When researchers in sociology, epidemiology, demography, and public health wish to describe how healthy a population is, they typically draw on a small set of indicators. The most prominent among them are life expectancy, death rate, and infant mortality. Each of these indicators serves as a proxy for a society's standard of living and quality of health care. In addition to comparing these indicators across countries or regions of the world, in a diverse country like the United States it is also possible to compare these rates across gender, race, and social class lines.

According to the Centers for Disease Control and Prevention (CDC), **life expectancy** at birth in the United States is approximately 78.7 years. This number represents a steady and dramatic increase: around 1890, the typical person born in the United States could expect to live only to about age 50. Compared to low-income countries, the typical American lives a long and healthy life. For example, life expectancies across most African countries hover around 50 years. Compared to other high-income countries, however, the United States falls toward the lower end (see Table 14.1). Organizations like the National Research Council and the Organization of Economic Cooperation and Development (OECD) rank the United States between 17 and 27, respectively, among peer nations. At the top of the list are Japan, Iceland, and Switzerland, where life expectancies top out around 82 years.

Comparing the life expectancies of women and men, we find that across the globe women live longer than men (the only exception seems to be some South Asian countries like Nepal and Bangladesh). As shown in Table 14.2, women live nearly five years longer than men (81 years vs. 76.2 years) across all American racial and ethnic groups. But why? Is this a biological artifact, or are the reasons social? In fact nature and nurture are both at work in extending the lives of women. Biologically speaking, researchers believe that mammalian species with larger bodies—like men—are simply at greater risk for degeneration, disease, and death. Others suggest that mitochondrial mutations that shorten life span are more likely to be passed to males compared to females (Innocenti, Morrow, and Dowling 2011).

With respect to social factors, men and women are socialized differently and occupy different positions in the social structure. In terms of gender socialization, men

Table 14.1 Life Expectancy in Select OECD Countries

Country	Life Expectancy at Birth (years)
Japan	83.7
Iceland	82.4
United Kingdom	81.1
Germany	80.8
United States	78.7
Hungary	75.0
Turkey	74.6
Mexico	74.2

Source: OECD 2014.

Table 14.2 Gender, Race, and Life Expectancy in the United States

Group	Total (Women and Men)	Women	Men
Overall	78.7	81	76.2
Asian Americans	—	85.8	—
Hispanic Americans	81.2	83.8	78.5
Whites	78.9	81.3	76.5
Blacks	75.1	78	71.8

Source: National Center for Health Statistics 2014.

simply partake in more risky behaviors. Compared to women, they are more likely to consume tobacco, alcohol, and addictive drugs. They are also more likely to die in car crashes and other types of accidents. The fact that they tend to hold more dangerous jobs—jobs that expose them to injury, like those in fishing and forestry, and those that expose them to toxins and carcinogens, like agriculture and mining—also accounts for their higher mortality rates. Socially, women may also have healthier ways of dealing with stress, especially in terms of utilizing social support. This may partially explain why men are more likely to suffer from health conditions associated with stress, such as heart disease and hypertension (high blood pressure). Finally, women are more inclined than men to utilize the health care system and even see that as an extension of their role as caretakers (Auerbach and Figert 1995). Further, the routine of the "annual exam" is a key form of preventative care and may result in detecting health problems before they become serious. Alas, most men do not perform a similar annual ritual and may only seek health care once problems have become severe.

Does social class also shape how long a person lives? It surely does, but it's also hard to measure: Is social class best represented by a person's education, income, or occupational position? Further, a person's social class can change over his or her lifetime; the class circumstance of one's childhood—not just one's adulthood—may influence one's health and well-being. Because of these difficulties, researchers usually focus on individual aspects of a person's socioeconomic status (SES) and then link them to mortality rates and morbidity rates for specific health conditions (cancer, heart disease, diabetes). Not surprisingly, income, education, and occupational status are all linked to good health: the higher a person is on each dimension, the less likely they are to experience negative health outcomes (Phelan et al. 2004; Warren and Hernandez 2007).

Although income, education, and occupational status are all linked, researchers increasingly believe that education is the single biggest predictor of how long a person will live and how healthy they will be (Goesling 2007; Mirowsky and Ross 2003; Schnittker 2004). What can education "buy" that money can't? While income can help a person afford the best quality of care, education can help a person understand what that means and where to obtain it. Controlling for other factors (like income), better-educated people are generally better-educated health consumers and may also have social connections that help them navigate the health care system. They may also feel more empowered to speak to health professionals as peers—knowing what kinds of questions to ask, asserting their right to a second opinion. Finally, better-educated people also tend to hold jobs that are more rewarding and provide them greater autonomy. These factors may help reduce job-related stresses and promote general well-being.

Finally, race and ethnicity are powerfully linked to health and well-being in the United States. Looking at Table 14.2, some surprising patterns emerge. Given that SES is closely linked to health and well-being, and given that whites have relatively high SES, it may be surprising that they rank third among major racial/ethnic groups in terms of life expectancy. Indeed, they rank third behind Hispanics, who generally have a lower SES. While it may be tempting to conclude that racial and ethnic differences in life expectancy and disease simply reflect genetic differences among racial and ethnic groups, this is likely *not* the case. Indeed, social differences are more likely the cause. The fact that Hispanics have relatively high-level expectancies *despite* their relatively low SES is referred to as the **Hispanic Paradox**: their good health is paradoxical given that they typically lack the social characteristics (e.g., income and education) that contribute to good health. So what are Latinos up to that promotes health and longevity? Researchers believe that a couple of factors are at work. One of these is *social support*. Many Hispanics in the United States live in an *ethnic enclave*; there, residents may experience kinship and social network ties that provide information about health behaviors, as well as social activities that promote trust, cohesion, and psychological well-being (Eschbach et al. 2004).

Yet researchers also speculate that health and well-being among Hispanics begins well before the backyard parties with family and neighbors. Although researchers don't entirely know why, Hispanic infants have lower mortality in the first hour, day, and week of life compared to children born to white women (Hummer et al. 2007) (Figure 14.1a). It is likely that healthy prenatal behaviors—including diet, lower rates of smoking and drinking, and stress reduction—rather than any biological advantage contribute to this pattern. Thereafter, breastfeeding may have a lifelong impact on health and well-being. As shown in Figure 14.1b, Hispanic women have higher rates of breastfeeding compared to women from other racial and ethnic groups. The health advantages of breastfeeding are well documented, especially its boost to immune function (Horta et al. 2007). Throughout the life course, early breastfeeding may allow people to fight off diseases of the intestinal tract and other types of infection; it is also associated with lower rates of respiratory infections and allergies. It turns out this low-cost practice may be associated with lifelong health benefits.

Infant Deaths Per 1,000 Live Births

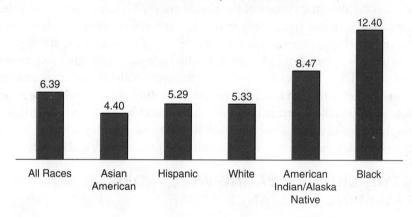

Percent "Ever" Breastfed (2011 Cohort)

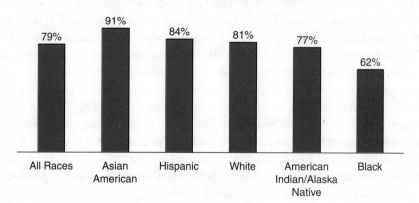

Figure 14.1 (a) Infant mortality rates by race/ethnicity. (*Source:* CDC/*Morbidity and Mortality Weekly Report*, 2009/2013b)

(b) Breastfeeding rates by race/ethnicity. (*Source:* CDC/National Immunization Study, 2012)

It is clear from these patterns that gender, socioeconomic status, and race are all related to how long a person lives. Moreover, it is equally clear that social factors are at least as important as biological factors in shaping these patterns. The remainder of this chapter explores the micro- and macro-level forces that contribute to these social inequalities in life expectancy and well-being. The overall theme guiding this chapter is that while individual choices and personal circumstances matter, the degree to which these choices "pay off" is strongly shaped by the broader social and environmental context in which a person is embedded.

EAT WELL, WORK OUT, AND VISIT THE "TRAINER": MICRO-LEVEL EXPLANATIONS FOR UNEQUAL HEALTH OUTCOMES

Within the individualistic culture of the United States, it is tempting to conclude that the recipe for a long and healthy life is simple: each player simply needs to eat well, work out, and make regular visits to the "trainer" (i.e., the doctor). From this perspective, health and well-being derive from individual decisions and other factors operating at the micro-level. The fact that health outcomes differ along race, class, and gender lines simply reflects the tendency for people with different race, class, and gender characteristics to make different decisions about health and well-being. This section explores the range of micro-level factors that affect health and well-being, as well as the degree to which these factors vary according to gender, race, and social class.

LIFESTYLE CHOICES: EATING WELL, WORKING OUT, AND AVOIDING SUBSTANCE ABUSE

According to medical sociologists, whether a person eats well, exercises, and enjoys an occasional glass of wine is not an individual choice or personal preference. According to medical sociologists, race, social class, and gender are predictably related to the degree to which individuals maximize healthy behaviors and minimize health risks.

Take smoking as an illustration. While smoking rates have steadily declined in the United States, the likelihood of being a regular smoker is strongly connected to a person's gender, race, and social class. It is also a great example because smoking is a predictor of participating in other unhealthy behaviors. According to data from the CDC (see Table 14.3), men are more likely to smoke than women; people with lower levels of education and income are also more likely to smoke. The patterns associated with race/ethnicity are more complicated. Eating a healthy diet (low in fat, high in fiber), drinking, and exercising regularly exhibit similar patterns across gender, race, and social class (Grzywacz and Marks 2001).

Together, medical sociologists refer to the bundle of everyday choices that contribute to one's risk for disease as a **health lifestyle**. In addition to diet, exercise, and substance abuse, health lifestyles also include participation in risky sexual behaviors, driving habits (speed, wearing a seat belt), and even personal hygiene (dental care,

Table 14.3 **Tobacco Use by Gender, Race, and Social Class**

Category	Percent Regular Smokers
Male	21
Female	15
High School	22
Bachelor's Degree	9
Post-Graduate Degree	6
Below Poverty	29
Above Poverty	16
Native American	26
White	19
Black	18
Hispanic	12
Asian American	9

Source: Centers for Disease Control and Prevention (2013)

flossing). The fact that participation in positive health lifestyles is associated with gender, race, and social class reflects several sociological principles. For one, exercising and preparing healthful foods requires time and money. According to sociologist K. A. S. Wickrama and co-authors (1999:260), members of socially disadvantaged groups "have less access to health information and health resources; they have less control over sleeping hours, and food choices; and they are more likely to live in a social environment where unhealthy eating, smoking and heavy drinking are normality, making the formation of risky lifestyles more probable."

In addition to focusing on constraints posed by money, time, and knowledge, sociologists also suggest that health lifestyles are influenced by broader cultural orientations. Pierre Bourdieu, the scholar who coined the term *cultural capital*, theorized that healthy lifestyles are part of a person's *habitus*—the durable set of dispositions, cultural attitudes, values, and ways of being that shape who we are and how we act. Members of the privileged classes, according to Bourdieu, have a habitus that reflects their freedom, stability, and sense of autonomy. This gives them a proclivity to experiment with new and exotic foods and new exercise methods and generally cultivate an identity as the type of person who cares about living a healthy life. The working classes, by contrast, live more constrained lives, characterized by lower levels of economic opportunity and personal freedom and choice. For men of the working class, in particular, the need for a strong body, combined with the physical toll taken by laboring in many blue-collar jobs, inclines men toward hearty and fortifying—yet fatty—foods, while also stimulating an appetite for items perceived to reduce their stress, like alcohol and smoking.

Ultimately, Pierre Bourdieu argued that a person's *distance from necessity* strongly shapes his or her health lifestyle. For those groups that have fewer economic resources and less autonomy in their lives, the short distance between themselves and necessity means that they live in the present moment, which means they are more likely to make unhealthy choices. Because members of privileged social classes and racial groups live further from necessity, they have more freedom of choice and more opportunity to orient their lives toward the future. Indeed, sociologist Josyln Brenton (2014) discovered that these habits begin very early, as middle-class mothers socialize their children to eat healthy foods—a strategy she calls "feeding for the future"—and justify it with the notion that their children are intended to live long, economically productive lives, while also having adventurous and refined tastes in food that will allow them to fit in with other members of the privileged classes.

RECOVERING AFTER A TOUGH "GAME": INEQUALITY, STRESS, AND WELL-BEING

How does stress, or the ability to recover from a "tough game," affect a "player's" health and well-being? Stress isn't simply the feeling of being under pressure or having a hard time meeting life's challenges (work, divorce, loss of a loved one). Physically, **stress** manifests as a fight-or-flight response—to life events, daily challenges, or chronic strains (Pearlin 1989; Thoits 1995)—that can erode the body over time. While it is possible to measure stress *subjectively* by asking a person how much stress they feel, there are also *objective* indicators of stress, such as blood cortisol levels and resting blood pressure. Early stress—both in fetal development and during childhood—can affect the body's ability to grow and thrive. It is also a phenomenon that is unequally distributed across the population, with some groups being more susceptible than others.

Consider for the moment the intriguing relationship between gender and stress. Using subjective measures, women report higher levels of stress than men. Yet they are also more likely to say they effectively manage their stress. Further, despite reporting lower levels of stress, men exhibit higher rates of chronic illnesses associated with stress, such as high blood pressure, diabetes, and heart disease, while women exhibit higher rates of anxiety and depression. When it comes to the physical manifestations of stress, underlying biological differences may play a role in women's lower rates of morbidity; yet social differences in how men and women manage stress also play a role. Access to social support, for example, may help women buffer the negative effects of stress. Rather than exhibiting a flight-or-fight response, women are more likely to respond to stress with a **tend-and-befriend response** (Taylor et al. 2000). They "tend" by engaging in nurturing activities that protect the self and "befriend" by reaching out to social networks that create a sense of safety and protection, thus buffering against stress.

Who do you imagine experiences more stress—an attorney or the person who cleans the attorney's law office at night? It is conceivable the patent attorney experiences more pressure and demands at work, yet she probably has more resources to deal with those stressors. Indeed, research is clear that people in the lower classes experience more stress and are at greater risk of stress-related illnesses compared to those in higher classes (Lantz et al. 2005; Pearlin et al. 2005; Turner and Avison 2003). They experience personal financial struggles and uncertainties, as well as environmental threats, such as exposure to crime. Lower-SES people also have less **social power** when dealing with these stresses. Social power is the power that allows one to feel a sense of control over his or her life—a sense of control that provides a sense of security (Link and Phelan 2001). When it comes to work-related stress, higher-class people also experience more **autonomy**: although their jobs may come with considerable pressures, they also have more freedom and control over where, when, and how they do their job. The lack of autonomy within lower-income and lower-class occupations means that work is repetitive, time-sensitive, subject to scrutiny, and lacking a creative outlet. These micro-level experiences with stress, then, illustrate one mechanism by which higher income and education promote health and longevity.

Some of the most innovative work on stress relates to its racial dimensions. While the lower life expectancies and greater exposure to stress among some minorities is partially explained by their lower socioeconomic status, among African Americans there appears to be an enduring impact of racial discrimination on health and well-being. Higher levels of education and income do not have the same health benefits for blacks that they do for other groups (Farmer and Ferraro 2005). One area in which this is especially apparent is in infant mortality rates. Not only do black women have the highest **infant mortality** rates of all groups—defined as infant death during childbirth through the first year—but data also indicate that black women with a college degree have infant mortality rates nearly three times higher than white women with a college degree.

Researchers have largely rejected the notion that underlying genetic differences can explain racial differences in infant mortality rates. Instead, they point to race-related stress as the cause. Using complicated epidemiological studies, researchers find that African Americans have a higher *allostatic load* than other groups: they are less able to recover from the prolonged bombardment by stressors over an extended period of time. Among pregnant women this results in poor fetal development and higher rates of illness and chronic disease among blacks overall. While the thesis remains controversial, there is growing consensus that the small but cumulative effects of "everyday racism"—subtle slights and ordinary disadvantages that are not part of white privilege—add up over time, so that by young adulthood many African Americans exhibit an acute stress response (Lu and Halfon 2003). Medical researcher Arline Geronimus (1992) calls this the **weathering hypothesis**—a dynamic in which everyday racism puts the body on high alert, never allowing for a period of rest, so that the stress response remains activated and eventually wears down the body's immune response. The significance of this research is that it shows that race, independent of low socioeconomic status, seems to affect the poor health outcomes of African Americans.

ACCESS TO HEALTH CARE: SEEKING A "TRAINER" TO SUPPORT GOOD HEALTH

Even the healthiest of players get sick sometimes. When they do—or in order to reduce the chance of that happening in the first place—they may seek medical care from a health care provider, in our metaphor, a "trainer." Access to health care is another factor that promotes health and well-being at the individual level. "Players" who have access to preventative care, or who seek attention to emerging health problems, generally have better health outcomes than those who don't. Yet access to health care and the utilization of that care are also unequally distributed across the population.

One reason many Americans do not seek preventative medical care, or medical care when they begin having symptoms, is that they lack health insurance. Paying out of pocket is expensive—even for routine checkups—so many people forgo or delay care. As of 2013, the U.S. Census Bureau reported that slightly more than 13 percent of all Americans were uninsured (this is down from 17 percent, prior to the passage of the Patient Protection and Affordable Care Act). Table 14.4 presents these data according to race, showing that Whites are the most likely to have health insurance, while Hispanics and Native Americans are least likely. Income is also associated with the likelihood of being uninsured—especially because in the United States most Americans get their health insurance from their employers, and those working stable, full-time jobs are most likely to be covered. Among those earning less than $25,000 per year, 22 percent are uninsured; among those earning more than $150,000 annually, less than 5 percent are uninsured.

Table 14.4 Uninsured Americans by Race/Ethnicity and Income

Category	Percent Uninsured
RACE/ETHNICITY	
White	10
Asian American	15
Black	16
Hispanic	24
Native American	31–35
ANNUAL INCOME	
Less than $25,000	22
$25,000–49,999	19
$50,000–74,999	13
More than $75,000	5

Source: U.S. Census Bureau 2014

The fact that uninsured Americans lack access to preventative care and tend to delay care in light of emerging symptoms means that by the time they do seek medical attention, they are typically sicker than those who seek treatment at earlier stages. Whether experiencing symptoms related to diabetes, heart disease, respiratory illness, or cancer, those lacking health insurance consequently exhibit higher morbidity and mortality rates. While lower-income individuals have high rates of utilization of hospital emergency rooms and outpatient clinics, they have low rates of visitation to private doctors. This means that they are more likely to seek care for emergencies or symptom management but not for preventative care or consistent treatment of chronic conditions. Because the lack of insurance is structured across social class and racial lines, this is one piece of the puzzle for understanding why minorities and lower-income people have lower life expectancies.

Thinking about this phenomenon from a broader social perspective, the fact that so many Americans lack health insurance is also a public concern. When those lacking health insurance do seek care, the delay in treatment means that their care is more expensive than it would have been had they sought earlier intervention. The costs of this care are absorbed by the system but are generally transferred to taxpayers and insurance companies. Reducing these costs is one goal of the **Patient Protection and Affordable Care Act**, also known as "ObamaCare." Passed in 2010 and gradually implemented through 2014, this new law has sought to extend care to more Americans—largely by requiring them to obtain health insurance—and provides greater incentives to seek preventative care. For example, the law eliminated co-pays—the direct cost to patients when visiting a health care provider—for preventative services such as "well woman" visits (Pap tests and breast exams), mammograms, colonoscopies, and gestational diabetes screenings. Although this law remains controversial, the hope is that health care costs for everyone will decline by providing incentives for patients to seek preventative care.

SOMEBODY CALL THE DOCTOR: DIFFERENCES AND INEQUALITIES IN HEALTH CARE UTILIZATION

Just because a person has health insurance doesn't mean he or she will use it. Going to the doctor can be tedious and scary, after all. Across gender, race, and social class lines, different groups appear to have different cultural orientations to health care utilization. That is, they have different beliefs about the importance and usefulness of seeking medical attention. This is a micro-level factor, given that it shapes whether and how a person goes about seeking health care; yet it is a factor that is patterned across social groups, thereby affecting physical well-being and life expectancies.

How do you respond when you're sick? Do you seek out a doctor at the first sign that something's wrong, or do you tend to ignore your symptoms or otherwise manage on your own? As it turns out, many ethnic groups in the United States—especially those of lower income—have tight social networks and typically turn inward when confronting an illness. Rather than seek professional medical attention, they tend to delay care and rely on folk knowledge and recommendations from within their social networks. Eliot Freidson (1960), a pioneering medical sociologist, called this the **lay-referral system**, distinguishing it from the tendency of higher-income, better educated persons to seek out information from and express trust in medical professionals.

Looking at social class, classic studies in medical sociology have found that regardless of race or ethnicity, lower-income people have lower rates of health care utilization (relative to their health needs) for several reasons. This may be due to financial constraints (having to take time off from work, incurring medical bills, etc.), along with a tendency to ignore or downplay symptoms in order keep putting food on the table and paying rent. Even more important in inhibiting health care utilization among lower-income people is the *alienation* they feel within the health care system: that is, they felt somewhat disrespected, but more generally ignored, by what they experience as a cold, impersonal, and confusing experience. Researchers have called this the **systems barrier explanation** (Dutton 1978; Rundall and Wheeler 1979), reflecting especially the experiences lower-income and minority patients may have within the public welfare system.

While black Americans exhibit higher rates of health care utilization compared to earlier generations, historical perspective explains why some have been reluctant to seek care. Indeed, several key historical incidents suggest that black Americans may have good reason to distrust the medical establishment. Begun in 1932, the **Tuskegee experiment** was a medical study conducted by the U.S. Public Health Service, the goal of which was to explore the impact of untreated syphilis—a sexually transmitted infection—on the human body. Nearly 400 subjects of the study were explicitly recruited from a community of poor black sharecroppers in rural Alabama. The 40-year-long study serves as an example of how ethical standards can be violated in the name of medical science. While these research subjects were provided free medical attention, they were generally treated only by doctors affiliated with the study. These doctors knowingly lied to them about the benefits of the study and failed to identify the risks associated with the study. While a viable treatment for syphilis was discovered in 1947, these largely illiterate patients were denied this information, as well as access to the treatment, since providing treatment would undermine the goals of the study.

By the time information about the study was leaked in 1972, at least 128 of the test subjects had died from syphilis or related causes. Many had also passed the disease to their wives, who passed it congenitally to their children. Following an investigation and lawsuit, the 74 remaining survivors were awarded $9 million in damages. In his 1997 apology, President Bill Clinton described the study as "clearly racist," adding, "The United States government did something that was wrong—deeply, profoundly, morally wrong. It was an outrage to our commitment to integrity and equality for all our citizens." In 2010, it was revealed that the U.S. government had conducted similar studies in Guatemala in the 1940s.

In addition to this experiment, the legacy of eugenics subjected Native American, black, and Puerto Rican women to forced sterilizations during the 1930s. Through a number of official state programs, medical officials forcibly sterilized tens of

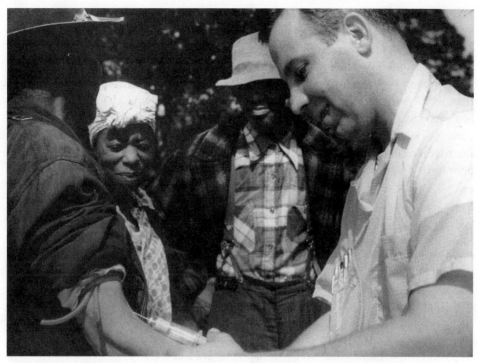

The Tuskegee experiment illustrates a case where researchers violated the dignity of study participants. It also shows why black Americans may mistrust the medical system.

thousands of women against their will. In the interest of producing a genetically "pure" and healthy population—essentially the goal of **eugenics**—government officials took it upon themselves to determine who was worthy of reproducing and who wasn't. While they entered the hospital to give birth to a child, many nonwhite women left without the ability to get pregnant ever again.

In 2011, author Rebecca Skloot published a highly acclaimed book about *The Immortal Life of Henrietta Lacks*. In it she documented the discoveries medical scientists were able to make after harvesting some unique cells from this woman suffering from cancer. Although she never consented to donate her cells to science, nor benefited from doing so, medical doctors have used her cells in studies on cancer, polio, HIV/AIDS, and genetic research. While her "contributions" have yielded positive discoveries for science, commentators argue that this instance further illustrates the racialized politics of medicine, in which some groups have been systematically exploited in the name of science. Lacks's daughter Deborah hits on this tension, noting: "Truth be told, I can't get mad at science, because it help people live, and I'd be a mess without it. I'm a walking drugstore! . . . But I won't lie, I would like some health insurance so I don't got to pay all that money every month for drugs my mother cells probably helped make" (Skloot 2010: 256).

Today, some speculate that these historical instances contribute to a general distrust of the medical establishment among some racial and ethnic minorities, causing them to delay treatment, question medical guidelines, or even reject doctors' recommendations. Black women tend to avoid mammograms and other diagnostics, which is one reason why they are twice as likely to die from breast cancer, once diagnosed, than white women (Silber et al. 2013). A history of exploitation and experimentation has even been linked to relatively low levels of organ and bone marrow donation among black Americans (Cohen 2007)—a factor that may unwittingly compromise their treatment options. Here, they illustrate a micro-level dynamic that shapes the poor health outcomes of African Americans.

JUST CUT IT OFF?: DIFFERENCES AND INEQUALITIES IN TREATMENT

Imagine that two patients visit the same doctor, each with similar access to health insurance, similar medical histories, presenting nearly identical symptoms. Given these similarities, one would expect that their doctors would provide roughly equivalent treatment protocols. This does not happen, however; in fact, researchers know that a person's demographic traits—their race, gender, and social class—influence the treatment protocols given by doctors. Indeed, minority patients, in particular, are less likely to receive kidney dialysis or transplants; are less likely to be given appropriate cardiac medications, cardiac catheterization, or to undergo bypass surgery; and are more likely to receive lower-limb amputations, as opposed to medications or lifestyle modifications, when being treated for diabetes (Smedly, Stith, and Nelson 2003). These disparities in treatment lead to measurably higher death rates among racial and ethnic minorities.

So why is it that two patients, different primarily in terms of race, receive different—and unequal—treatment recommendations? Many researchers believe that the root cause lies in the face-to-face interactions between doctors and patients. Because the majority of doctors in the United States are white, they may lack the necessary **cultural competencies** when interacting with minority patients. First, there may be literal language barriers that prevent doctors and patients from having fruitful conversations. Second, doctors and patients may have different understandings of an illness and may describe symptoms differently. Third, doctors may hesitate to ask minority patients about diet and exercise, fearful that their recommendations to change dietary habits—reducing consumption of meat, fried foods, and vegetables cooked with pork fat—may be interpreted as racially insensitive. Finally, doctors may hold stereotypes about their patients, some of which frame black patients as less inclined to follow detailed medical guidelines (changing diet and exercise or taking medications as prescribed); accordingly, doctors may elect simple procedures like foot amputations over more detailed protocols.

Scholars do not believe that doctors are simply acting on overt prejudices; rather, their decisions reflect subconscious judgments or differences in communication styles

(Balsa and McGuire 2003). This insight is further echoed in studies examining doctor–patient interactions across social class lines. Doctor and medical sociologist Howard Waitzkin (1991, 2004) found that physicians from higher social class backgrounds communicate more with their patients compared to physicians from more modest social class backgrounds, and that patients from higher social class positions receive more information than those holding more modest social class positions. Moreover, less educated patients are more likely to be treated impersonally and have their questions ignored, while better-educated patients receive more personalized, detailed, and responsive interactions. It is, perhaps, the cultural similarity in communication styles that leads to more detailed and positive medical encounters for those with higher class positions (Anspach 1993; Atkinson 1995). From a policy standpoint, researchers recommend that doctors take more time and practice active listening skills with their patients, while also acknowledging the need to educate and mentor more doctors from minority backgrounds.

All of the patterns described in this section operate at the micro-level. That is, they capture individual circumstances, decisions, cultural beliefs, or the outcomes of face-to-face interactions. The micro-level perspective assumes that the player is largely in control of his or her health and well-being. Yet these examples also show that individual circumstances, cultural beliefs, and social interactions are patterned along race, class, and gender lines. This patterning suggests that something larger is at play in shaping health and well-being; that how we live as individuals is also shaped by larger social forces. The next section amplifies this point, showing that even an individual who eats well, exercises, manages his or her stress, and seeks health care when needed may experience unequal and devastating health outcomes.

EXPLORING INTERSECTIONALITY: A CLOSER LOOK AT RACE, GENDER, AND MEDICAL SCIENCE

As mentioned above, demographic traits influence a person's experience in the medical system. Imagine again that two patients visit their doctors, complaining of troubling symptoms. Both describe chest pains. One describes the pain as a vice-like grip on the chest, with pain radiating through the arm; the other describes pain just under the breastbone, combined with abdominal discomfort. The first patient is given a stress test to detect a possible heart attack. The second is referred to a gastroenterologist to explore the possibility of gall bladder disease. That afternoon, the first patient begins taking a "clot-busting medicine," a routine treatment for early signs of a heart attack. Later that evening, the second suffers a mild heart attack.

The above scenario is all too common. Research shows that female patients are routinely misdiagnosed and fail to receive the treatment they need. Indeed, gender disparities exist in the signs, diagnosis, and treatment of many diseases, including heart disease. A landmark study published in the *New England Journal of Medicine* (Shulman et al. 1999) found that black patients and female patients were significantly less likely to be recommended for cardiac catheterization—a potentially life-saving surgery—compared to white patients and male patients. With studies such as these, doctors and researchers are increasingly aware that medical science, from diagnosis to treatment, contains gender and race biases. A majority of medical studies have been conducted using white male patients. This includes pharmaceutical studies on the efficacy of prescription drugs. Accordingly, doctors and researchers have assumed that what works for white men works for other patients. Unfortunately, this is not the case, as women and people of color may describe different symptoms at the outset of a disease; similarly, medications may work differently on their bodies, especially for women.

The increasing diversity of the U.S. population challenges the equitable and effective delivery of health care. New immigrants, for example, bring language barriers, and many doctors' offices and hospitals are not equipped to deal with these patients. In addition to the lack of translators, even subtle differences in *tense* (whether symptoms eased in the past, are ongoing, etc.) can lead to problematic differences in diagnosis and treatment. On a cultural level, members of different racial and ethnic groups may have fundamentally different understandings of similar medical symptoms and conditions. Anne Fadiman (1997) wrote about this famously in her book, *The Spirit Catches You and You Fall Down*, in which she details the culture clashes between a Hmong family and the medical establishment in dealing with a child, Lia, with epilepsy. The American doctors and Hmong parents had fundamentally different ways of understanding the illness—misfiring of her cerebral neurons versus the wandering of one's soul into the spirit realm—as well as different preferences for treatment. The frustrations and lack of respect that Lia's parents experienced with doctors led them to mistrust and defy their recommendations. At the age of four, a seizure then resulted in Lia slipping into a coma; for the next 26 years she lived in a persistent vegetative state.

In addressing their daughter's epilepsy, Lia's parents relied on a **folk healer.** Indeed, many cultures come to the United States with a tradition of using folk healers and folk remedies. In general, these practitioners take a more holistic approach, seeing greater connection between physical, mental, and spiritual well-being. By contrast, Western medicine tends to isolate and treat the body, relying on science while downplaying the role of religion or traditional knowledge. Whether the *curanderos* of the Mexican tradition, the *papaloi* and *mamaloi* of the African American tradition, or the *singers* and *diviners* of Native American tradition, these healers seek the underlying causes of an illness—usually thought to be spiritual in nature—rather than treat its symptoms. While many Westerners remain skeptical of some of these practices, **integrative medicine**—which combines scientific, biomedical approaches with spiritual and traditional (acupuncture, herbs, *homeopathy, naturopathy*, etc.) approaches—is increasingly common in the West.

It appears that progress is being made in ensuring that medical protocols more accurately address groups across racial, ethnic, and gender lines. Drug treatments and surgical interventions are being tested on a wider array of subjects, and medical doctors are increasingly provided with training in cultural diversity. Indeed, the medical establishment is so aware of the need for additional training in cultural diversity and cultural competency that they are increasingly requiring premed students to take more courses in fields like sociology and are even incorporating sociological knowledge into the MCAT, the primary admissions test for medical school

LOCATION, LOCATION, LOCATION: MACRO-LEVEL EXPLANATIONS FOR UNEQUAL HEALTH OUTCOMES

Let me introduce you to Bruce. Bruce strives to be a paragon of health: he tries to eat well and exercise; engages in stress reduction; has good health insurance provided by his employer; and seeks medical attention when needed (and follows doctors' orders). On the micro-level, Bruce has a positive *health lifestyle*; one that should promote health and well-being. Yet Bruce is at risk for many diseases—diseases that could compromise his quality of life and cut short his life expectancy. It's not that Bruce has an underlying genetic risk for health problems. Instead, dynamics at the macro-level—broader social patterns beyond his direct control—threaten his health and well-being. You see, Bruce was born to a lower-income family living in an old home in the former industrial city of Pittsburgh, Pennsylvania. After finishing high school, he moved to Ohio, where a relative connected him with a job in auto manufacturing. After that industry hit some rough times, Bruce moved his family to North Dakota to find a job in the newly emerging oil and gas industry. At each stage in his life, Bruce's health has been compromised.

Using Bruce as an example, the research in this section shows that environmental factors—whether in one's neighborhood, workplace, or community—can hinder one's health and well-being, regardless of their individual choice. These environmental risks, however, are not randomly distributed across the population. In addition to individual patterns and behaviors that structure health and well-being, location and context powerfully shape health inequalities across gender, race, and social class lines.

AN APPLE A DAY KEEPS THE DOCTOR AWAY: THE PROBLEM OF FOOD DESERTS

It is generally accepted that a healthy diet is one that is low in saturated fats and processed foods and high in vegetables and whole grains. While some people do not have a taste for lean meats, whole grains, and unadorned fruits and vegetables, others may have a hard time acquiring such food products. This is especially the case for those living in a *food desert*.

Although there is no universal definition of a **food desert**, the term generally refers to a geographic area where residents face physical and economic barriers to acquiring healthy foods. These barriers include the time it takes to travel to a full-service supermarket, the cost of such foods, and the quality or selection of foods. GIS (*geographic information systems*) data show that food deserts are especially prevalent in the urban core and, perhaps somewhat ironically, rural areas where farming takes place (see Figure 14.2). While those in rural areas face primarily a geographic barrier in acquiring

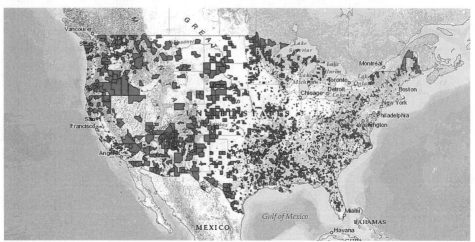

Figure 14.2 Rural food deserts.
(*Source:* USDA 2014)

healthy, affordable foods (residing more than 10 miles from such a store), those in the urban core live in a desert of plenty: one where relatively cheap but not especially nutritious foods are available at convenience stores, fast food outlets, and, increasingly, "dollar" stores. Residents of poor inner-city areas also experience a poverty tax or ghetto tax on many food items. Not a literal tax, a **poverty tax** refers to the higher prices for the exact same items that people in inner city neighborhoods pay for food, gas, and other daily needs. These higher costs partially reflect the fact that customers lack transportation and may not be able to comparison shop and that the smaller stores in low-income areas charge higher prices because they cannot buy in bulk (Fellowes 2006).

Connecting access to healthy and/or affordable foods to the question of health disparities, it appears that food deserts disproportionately impact lower-income Americans and minorities. Figure 14.3 shows the distribution of food deserts in Chicago and Baltimore, suggesting that food deserts closely map onto neighborhoods with higher concentrations of minorities. Data collected by the USDA (U.S. Department of Agriculture) echoes this point, showing that lower-income Americans spend more time traveling to do their grocery shopping. In terms of health consequences, greater "time costs" associated with acquiring and preparing healthier foods may be associated with lower demand for those foods (ERS 2009). Similarly, access to a supermarket or large grocery store may be associated with healthier food intakes (Larson, Story, and Nelson 2009). Looking at the relationship between food access and obesity, researchers find that proximity to fast food restaurants is associated with higher weights—as measured by BMI, an important indicator of weight and associated health problems—while proximity to a grocery store is associated with lower weights (Chen, Florax, and Snyder 2013).

When it comes to health issues like food access and obesity, it can be hard to sort out cause from effect: Do people eat poorly because they have no other options, or do people have no other options because they prefer to eat poorly? A number of studies have attempted to unravel this riddle. These studies suggest that when new full-service stores open, shoppers switch to them, and that when existing stores add healthier options, shoppers gravitate toward those options (Cummins et al. 2005; Wrigley, Warm, and Margetts 2003). Still, measured changes in consumer behaviors have been

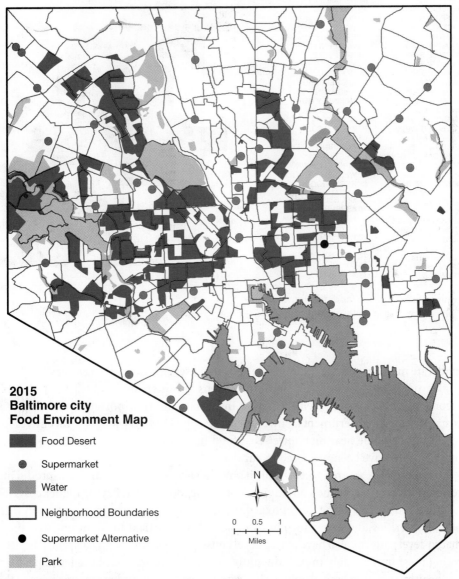

**2015
Baltimore city
Food Environment Map**

- ■ Food Desert
- ● Supermarket
- ▨ Water
- ▢ Neighborhood Boundaries
- ● Supermarket Alternative
- ▨ Park

N

0   0.5   1
Miles

Figure 14.3 (a) Urban food deserts, Baltimore. (Source: Baltimore Food Policy Initiative 2012)

(Continued)

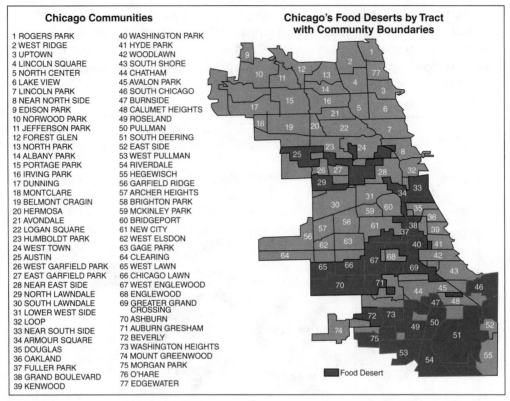

Figure 14.3 (b) Urban food deserts, Chicago.
(*Source:* Mari Gallagher Research & Consulting Group)

moderate in scale—on the order of one additional serving of vegetables per day (Ayala et al. 2013). Unfortunately, few national chains are interested in locating to lower-income neighborhoods, given the higher insurance and transportation and shipping costs. More local governments, however, have stepped in to try to create incentives for retailers to provide healthier, lower-cost food items in the inner city—though fewer interventions have been proposed in rural areas.

While Bruce aspires to eat well, it's not always easy: in a rural, oil-producing region of North Dakota, he's now living in a classic food desert. Paying higher costs for healthy food and traveling longer to acquire it is something he holds in common with other minorities and lower-income Americans. It is critical to point out that these macro-level patterns also have macro-level consequences. Although barriers to healthy eating most immediately impact the individual in question, their broader impact is a less healthy society, where people are less productive at work and more expensive to the medical system. The fact that so many Americans experience obesity, diabetes, and other related conditions both lowers their life expectancies and incurs significant costs to the health care system that are paid by all Americans.

"IS THERE A DOCTOR IN THE HOUSE—OR EVEN IN THE COUNTY?": THE PROBLEM OF MEDICAL DESERTS

Through his job in the oil fields, Bruce receives health insurance from his employer. So far, he's been lucky: as a 52-year-old man, his main medical needs are minimal—annual checkups, along with screenings for colon and prostate cancer. But what if one day he tested positive for one of these conditions or developed other medical problems? Like many lower-income Americans and minorities, his health might suffer due to the fact that he lives in a medical desert. Despite his health insurance and his goal of seeking preventative care, he may struggle due to limited access to health care services.

The technical term for a **medical desert** is a **medically underserved area**, or MUA. Like food deserts, medical deserts are not randomly distributed across the population: they are found in rural areas and inner cities—areas with higher concentrations of minorities and lower-income residents (see Figure 14.4a). Two of the simplest criteria used to determine whether an area is a medical desert are: (1) the ratio of primary care physicians for every 1,000 people in the population and (2) whether it takes longer than 30 minutes to travel to a primary care provider. Broader criteria include the number of hospital beds and access to advanced diagnostic and treatment facilities, like those used for dialysis and chemotherapy. As of 2013, the U.S. Department of

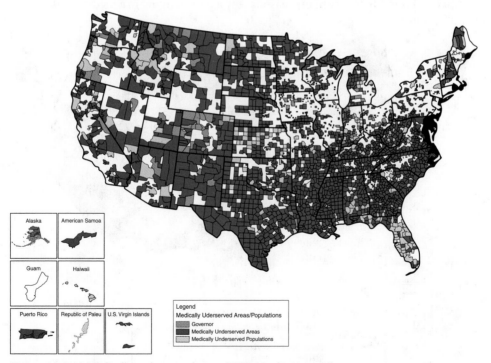

Figure 14.4 (a) Medically underserved areas (MUAs) in the United States. (*Source:* HRSA 2013)

(Continued)

Health and Human Services calculated that there are approximately 5,800 areas in the United States that lack access to primary care physicians, 4,600 that lack access to dental care, and 3,700 that lack access to mental health services (see Figure 14.4b).

So how does limited access to health care affect health and well-being? Imagine a scenario involving two people: James, a relatively affluent and educated man, living in a middle-class urban area, and Brad (Bruce's co-worker), less affluent and less educated, living in a rural medical desert. Both have developed some troubling symptoms—numbness and tingling, which may signal a pinched nerve. While Brad ignores his symptoms, James's wife urges him to visit an orthopedist. The orthopedist comes up short in the diagnostics, and James's symptoms disappear. When they reappear a few months later, his second visit is to a neurologist. Like the first doctor's visit, this specialist's office is just five minutes from James's home. Meanwhile, Brad is still ignoring his symptoms. Based on some preliminary findings, James's neurologist sends him for an MRI (magnetic resonance imaging) and then, based on those results, to a local hospital for a spinal tap. Like the other appointments, these took place in medical facilities within five minutes of his home. Four months later, James was diagnosed with multiple sclerosis; Brad, meanwhile, is still ignoring his symptoms.

Whether multiple sclerosis, Crohn's disease, chronic obstructive pulmonary disease (COPD), lupus, diabetes, Sjögren's disease, Parkinson's, or any number of chronic health conditions, there are many reasons why a person living in a medical desert may

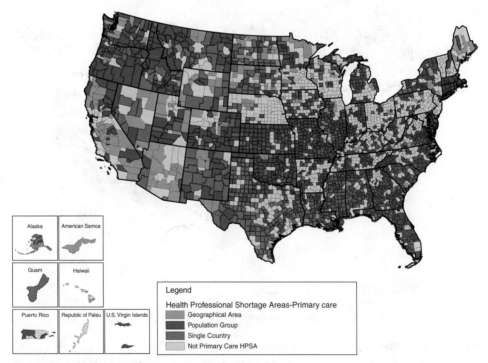

Figure 14.4 (b) Physician shortage areas in the United States.
(*Source:* HRSA 2013)

delay treatment. For lower-income folks, however, the primary reasons may be financial. In Brad's case, relevant medical offices are two hours from his home—that includes specialists, imaging centers, and infusion centers (where patients may receive radiation, chemotherapy, or steroid treatments). Not only are the appointments themselves costly, but gas for the round trip visit may cost $60; he would likely have to take an entire day off work for the trip, and he might need his wife to take off work to accompany him, as well. These are incredible expenses for a person to bear. Had he lived in an area like James's, he might not have experienced these barriers.

Living in a medical desert is a macro-level dynamic with consequences at both the micro- and macro-levels. On the micro-level, the fact that those living in medical deserts tend to delay care, combined with the fact that they are more likely to be less advantaged people, means that minorities and lower-income Americans are sicker when they do seek treatment. For conditions like cancer, diabetes, and heart disease, this delay can reduce quality of life and shorten one's life expectancy—partially explaining why blacks and lower-income Americans have worse health outcomes. At the macro-level, there are costs to the general public: delaying care results in disease progression, which typically increases the cost of treatment. These costs are distributed across society and the health care system, resulting in higher premiums for private insurance holders and higher taxes to fund programs like Medicaid. While Bruce's individual efforts are currently helping him live a healthy life, if he is diagnosed with an illness these barriers may play a role in reducing his well-being and life expectancy.

IS YOUR NEIGHBORHOOD MAKING YOU SICK?: THE PROBLEM OF UNSAFE HOUSING

Out in North Dakota, Bruce is thousands of miles from where he grew up. His childhood began in Pittsburgh, Pennsylvania, an area hemmed in by highways, littered with vacant lots where factories used to stand, and dotted by run-down homes built in the early 1900s. As a student in the public school system, Bruce's asthma made it difficult to get involved in athletics or join the school band; inside the classroom, he struggled, and his teachers suspected a mild cognitive impairment. He didn't do well enough to enter college but has managed to find steady work in "blue-collar" fields. Although these problems feel like a distant memory to Bruce, they are a reality to millions of children growing up in the United States today—and pose a legitimate threat to their health and well-being.

Many minorities and lower-income Americans live in homes and neighborhoods that are literally making them sick. Millions of Americans live in homes that expose them to **lead poisoning** (see Figure 14.5). In homes built prior to the 1970s, lead-based paint was considered a modern marvel—bright, glossy, and water resistant. We now know that lead exposure—whether through household paint, cheap toys, or lead pipes—can cause serious health problems. Chronic exposure can result in gastrointestinal issues, sleep problems and energy deficits, depression, aggression and hyperactivity, male infertility, and brain damage (resulting in lower IQs and cognitive difficulties). One study of the effects of lead exposure on academic performance found

Variable	Students, No.	BLL, µg/dL, Mean (SE)	F Statistic (P)
Mathematics			154.9 (< .001)
Advanced	4375	5.81 (0.14)	
Proficient	8699	6.47 (0.06)	
Partially proficient	6206	8.31 (0.10)	
Not proficient	1837	9.10 (0.18)	
Science			54.3 (< .001)
Advanced	1539	5.97 (0.13)	
Proficient	5113	7.48 (0.14)	
Partially proficient	4093	8.67 (0.11)	
Not proficient	1546	9.28 (0.19)	
Reading			124.3 (< .001)
Advanced	3709	5.41 (0.07)	
Proficient	10 585	6.96 (0.08)	
Partially proficient	5037	8.06 (0.10)	
Not proficient	1709	8.81 (0.18)	

Note: BLL = blood lead level. F statistic and P value are for testing null hypotheses of equal BLLs by level of proficiency

Figure 14.5 Lead exposure and academic achievement.
(*Source:* American Journal of Public Health)

that the odds of scoring "less than proficient" on major standardized exams were two times higher for children with higher levels of lead in their bloodstream (Zhang et al. 2013).

Despite being banned in 1978 and government-sponsored clean-up efforts, older, run-down homes still have layers of lead paint, paint that sometimes flakes off and is consumed by young children. Millions of still-growing children are vulnerable to these threats, especially children living in lower-income, inner-city areas with older rental properties. Although it's just one illustration, the map of Jacksonville, Florida, shows that the area of the city with the highest concentration of homes testing positive for lead and the area with the highest rate of asthma admissions to the hospital are also the poorest areas of the city with the highest concentration of black residents (see Figure 14.6).

Many of the areas afflicted by lead exposure also place residents at risk for asthma and other respiratory illnesses. **Asthma**—the prevalence of which has been increasing since the 1970s—is the leading health condition among young children, affecting about 10 percent of children in inner cities. Day-to-day physical, social, and educational activities can be compromised by asthma, which restricts the airways and can cause attacks of troubled breathing. Among children, it can mean long absences from school; it can also prove deadly. While this inflammatory condition can be controlled with medications, treatments are increasingly costly.

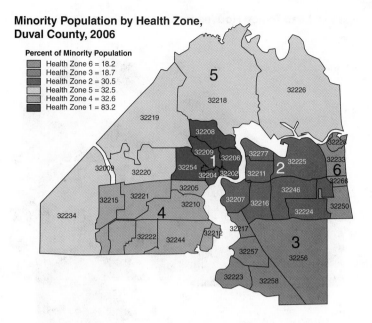

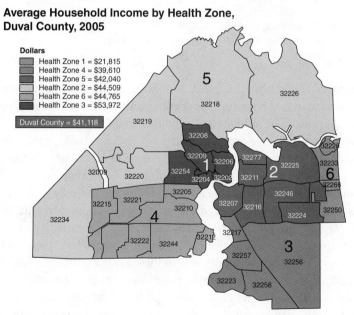

Figure 14.6 (a) Demographic profile of Duval County.
(*Source:* Claritas Data 2006)

(b) Socioeconomic profile of Duval County.
(*Source:* Demographics Now, 2005)

(*Continued*)

Positive Lead Tested Houses by Zip Code, Duval, 2006

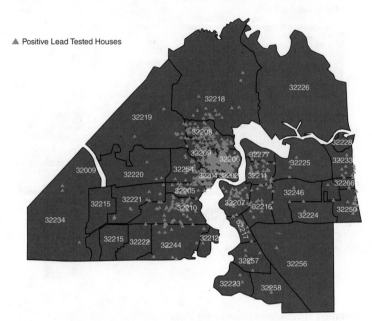

Figure 14.6 (c) Positive lead-tested houses by zip code, Duval, 2006. (*Source:* Environmental Division, Duval County Health Department)

At the macro-level, asthma has much to do with neighborhood context and the high prevalence of substandard housing in poor communities. While asthma is partially genetic in origin, it can also be brought on by environmental triggers. For children living in older homes in lower-income areas, these triggers include smoke, mold, dust and dust mites, rodents, and cockroach infestations. Exposure to cockroach "dander" (flaked-off skin, wings, legs, etc.) is much more harmful to children than other environmental irritants—making it the most prevalent trigger for asthma-related emergency room visits (Gruchalla et al. 2005) (see Figure 14.7). If this were an individual problem, the individual "players" could simply clean their homes and be done with it or move to a new rental unit without such nasty problems. Yet this is a macro-level problem in the sense that such a high proportion of homes within these areas are afflicted with infestations and substandard conditions. For example, poor inner-city children are exposed to cockroach dander at a rate four times greater than children in suburban areas (Sharfstein and Sandel 1998). This is not an isolated problem—it is one that affects many and is sustained by a "game" that permits weak enforcement of rental housing standards and provides limited access to safe and affordable housing options (Sharfstein et al. 2001).

Looking at the consequences of these patterns, children who grow up with lead exposure and asthma suffer in clear ways. With breathing compromised, it may be difficult to exercise; when exacerbated, it may result in absence from school. Lead exposure can similarly pose social and developmental problems to children. While

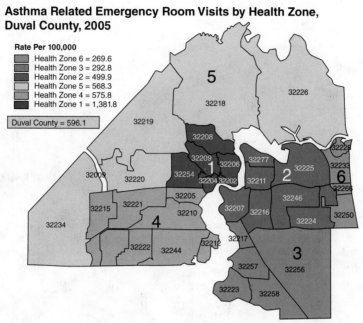

Asthma Related Emergency Room Visits by Health Zone, Duval County, 2005

Rate Per 100,000
- Health Zone 6 = 269.6
- Health Zone 3 = 292.8
- Health Zone 2 = 499.9
- Health Zone 5 = 568.3
- Health Zone 4 = 575.8
- Health Zone 1 = 1,381.8

Duval County = 596.1

Figure 14.7 Race, socioeconomic status, and asthma-related emergency room visits. (*Source:* Florida Agency for Health Care Administration Emergency Room Data, 2005)

Bruce has been only minimally impacted by his childhood exposure to these environmental pollutants, they likely have affected his cognitive function, academic success, and the types of jobs he can hold. Millions of children across the country are now growing up in similar conditions, ones that may compromise their health and their individual economic fates, as well as their costs to the health care system and contributions to the economy as a whole.

If it weren't bad enough that lower-income and minority Americans face environmental threats in their immediate dwellings, their health is also systematically compromised by toxic exposure and environmental threats outside of their front doors and in their places of employment. As discussed in Chapter 11, *environmental racism—* the placement of toxic waste sites and factories in predominantly minority areas—is a very real health threat, given its association with asthma and other respiratory illnesses, cancers, brain tumors, and miscarriage. Being hemmed in by highways and other transportation routes can pose additional health risks, especially in terms of air quality and respiratory distress.

In old industrial areas like the one in which Bruce grew up, brownfields are also a problem. **Brownfields** are areas where factories and industrial sites used to stand but which now have soil and groundwater contamination (usually by lead, asbestos, arsenic, chromium, or other toxins). They are prevalent in older industrial cities in the Northeast and Midwest, as well as mill towns of the South. While the land can typically be reused for housing and, in some cases, green space (open recreational land), cleanup

Typically located in close proximity to the neighborhoods of low-income and minority residents, industrial brownfields present a macro-level health threat. They also show why grassroots efforts, like community gardens and parks, may be doomed from the start.

is expensive, and underlying environmental threats can remain. Contaminated soil and groundwater, for example, make it difficult to use this land for urban or community gardening—a strategy that could otherwise be a partial solution to the problem of food deserts. These same threats may limit using the space for playgrounds or recreation—another macro-level initiative that could increase exercise among residents and provide a reprieve from their potentially dangerous homes. Had Bruce remained in Pittsburgh, he might not have been able to introduce his son and daughter to the joys of gardening or cultivated in them a love for biking and basketball.

Finally, many men, minorities, and lower-income Americans face systematic health threats at work. Despite Bruce's healthy lifestyle, his well-being has been chipped away by 30 years spent working in manufacturing and "fracking" (shale oil extraction). "Dangerous jobs" like these have high rates of fatalities and workplace injuries; they also wear the body down over time due to repetitive physical tasks or toxic exposure (coal dust, asbestos, pesticides). Before he left his job at the auto plant, Bruce suspected that the repetitive motion of operating machinery on the production line was leading to a case of carpal tunnel syndrome. In the shale oil fields, he is now at risk for silicosis—a respiratory infection brought on by silica dust, a byproduct of the sand that is pumped into the earth to extract the oil.

Looking at the "most dangerous jobs" (as measured by fatalities) presented in Figure 14.8, only one—aircraft pilots and flight engineers—can be considered a "white-collar" or "middle-class job." Somebody's got to do these dirty jobs, and it just so happens that these dirty jobs are more often held by men, minorities, and low-SES individuals. In some cases, the continued exposure to toxins and other risks reflects the fact that those doing these jobs are relatively powerless. Take, for example, the people who make "healthy eating" possible. Many agricultural workers are undocumented; even those who are documented and native-born may be denied the right to form labor unions or collectively bargain for workplace protections. Because of this, many go into the fields without gear that would protect them from pesticides and insecticides (gloves, eyewear, breathing masks) or other safeguards against workplace dangers. The CDC estimates there are 10,000–20,000 doctor-confirmed cases of pesticide poisoning annually among agricultural workers, which are associated with skin conditions, respiratory illnesses, cancers, and miscarriages. Generally speaking, farm workers face unusually high rates of leukemia, non-Hodgkin's lymphoma, and cancers of the skin, lip, stomach, brain, and prostate.

Yet another reason why those in "dirty jobs" experience health risks is the poor enforcement of workplace regulations. Several federal agencies are charged with overseeing worker safety, including the Occupational Safety and Health Administration, the Environmental Protection Agency, and the Mine Safety and Health Administration. Yet in the spring of 2010, 29 mine workers were killed by an explosion at the Upper Big Branch mine in West Virginia. Investigations found the mine owners, Massey Energy, and the Mine Safety and Health Administration responsible for the blast through their flagrant disregard of safety regulations. Factory owners sometimes disregard such regulations due to the belief that workplace protections are too costly, and enforcement agencies sometimes lack the resources to investigate alleged violations. In this case, the disregard of such regulations led to a fine for corporate criminal liabilities in the amount of $209 million.

Most Dangerous Jobs (Fatalities per 100,000 workers)

Job	Fatalities per 100,000 workers
Logging Workers	91.3
Fishers and Related Fishing Workers	75.0
Aircraft Pilots and Flight Engineers	50.6
Roofers	37.7
Refuse and Recyclable Materials Collectors	33.0
Mining Machine Operators	26.9
Driver/Sales Workers and Truck Drivers	22.0
Farmers, Ranchers, and Other Agricultural Workers	21.8
Electrical Power-line Installers and Repairers	21.5
Construction Laborers	17.7

Source: Bureau of Labor Statistics 2014

Figure 14.8 Most dangerous jobs (per capita fatalities). (Source: Bureau of Labor Statistics)

Many people in David's hometown have been excited about the growing shale oil and gas industry. It has been celebrated as part of a "clean energy" strategy, with hopes it will be safer for workers than coal mining. Still, others have environmental concerns. A 2012 study by the National Institute of Safety and Health found that 79 percent of air samples taken at 11 fracking sites in Arkansas, Colorado, North Dakota, Pennsylvania, and Texas contained silica levels beyond recommended limits.

Each year, hundreds of Americans die from illnesses related to silica exposure. Current workplace regulations, however, may be inadequate. Many environmental agencies and those representing workers have proposed significant changes to the allowable levels of exposure. They allege, however, that discussions of these proposed changes has stalled out in "backdoor talks" involving industry, corporate stakeholders, and government officials. Outside of the factory walls, others are concerned that the processes involved in shale oil extraction will lead to soil and water contamination. If true, this too would represent a macro-level health threat to the people living in and around these communities—many of whom have sold their farmland with the hope of earning oil revenues. Still in its early stages, fracking remains tremendously controversial, as industry stakeholders deny the environmental risks or insist that the risks can be easily managed.

Compared to Bruce, the manager at the auto plant and the one at the oil field experience relatively few occupational or environmental risks. As white-collar professionals who have lived all their lives in new, suburban homes, these men work relatively safe jobs and are unlikely to be exposed to lead or allergens in their home. Moreover, compared to other lower-income and minority workers, these managers live far away from food or medical deserts. Finally, minorities and lower-income men like Bruce tend to live in disordered neighborhoods—ones lacking basic safety, dotted with abandoned buildings, and people constantly moving in and out—while more advantaged Americans tend to live in orderly neighborhoods, ones where such risks are fewer and residents have the opportunity to build social capital. This factor, too, can exacerbate or relieve stress, and partially contributes to inequalities in health across race and social class lines (Ross 2000).

Throughout this section, Bruce has been used as a fictional character—one who strives to live a healthy lifestyle but experiences limitations due to broader gender, race, and social class patterns. Although his circumstances are plausible, they cover only a small portion of the macro- or environmental health threats that systematically compromise the well-being and life expectancies of men, (some) minorities, and lower-income people. The overarching point, though, is that despite variations across the United States, the **structural amplification** of macro-level conditions means that advantaged Americans systematically accumulate health advantages over their lives and across social domains (home, neighborhood, work), while less advantaged Americans systematically accumulate disadvantages, which adversely affect their health (Mirowsky and Ross 2003). This shows that while each individual has some control over his or her health, aspects of the "game" at the macro-level also matter and can either hinder or help those individual efforts.

EXPLORING INTERNATIONALLY: SOCIAL INEQUALITY AND HEALTH CARE POLICY

Compared to other Western industrialized countries, the United States spends considerably more on health care per capita but has worse health outcomes. More specifically, for what we spend on health care, we have surprisingly low life expectancies and surprisingly high infant mortality rates—two indicators consistently used to measure a country's health and well-being. Comparatively, countries like Iceland and Japan spend much less on health care (per person) but have substantially longer life expectancies, with fewer infant deaths. Researchers are locked in a debate over this question, focusing on the degree to which these differences reflect micro-level differences in health lifestyles versus macro-level differences in social inequality and health care policy.

Richard Wilkinson, a social epidemiologist, is a major voice in this debate. He finds that among developed countries, it's not the richest societies that have the best health; rather, it's those with the smallest gap between rich and poor. He argues that wealthy societies with lower levels of income inequality—like Japan and the Nordic countries—are more socially cohesive; the stronger sense of community provides a positive sense of connection and well-being, making these healthier societies. By contrast, in societies with higher levels of inequality—like the United States and Great Britain—those on the lower end of the economic ladder are continually reminded of their relative deprivation. To be poor in a rich society, Wilkinson writes, is "[t]o feel depressed, cheated, bitter, desperate, vulnerable, frightened, angry, worried about debts or job and housing insecurity; to feel devalued, useless, helpless, uncared for, hopeless, isolated, anxious and a failure: these feelings can dominate people's whole experience of life, colouring their experience of everything else. It is the chronic stress arising from feelings like these which does the damage" (2002:215). This stress and vulnerability weakens the social fabric and erodes the population's health and well-being.

Another reason that unequal societies are "sick societies" is that when one segment of society exceeds others in terms of riches, they have the capacity to monopolize access to the best medical resources. Called **opportunity hoarding**, this means that the wealthy and powerful can pay more for access to the best doctors, hospitals, diagnostics, and so forth and that providers of these services similarly prefer to work with more affluent clients. Accordingly, lower-income patients are left to receive care with doctors and hospitals of lesser quality—potentially compromising their health and well-being.

Another perspective is that health care policy significantly shapes health outcomes. Among Western industrialized countries, the United States is unique in that it does not have **universal health care**: a health care system where everyone is covered by insurance. This does not necessarily mean that the government is the single provider and payer of health care. That approach is called socialized medicine. It simply means that there is a mechanism by which all citizens are covered by insurance. In the United States, by contrast, people are covered by a combination of sources: employers, private health insurance, and government programs. Although the Patient Protection and Affordable Care Act requires everyone to buy health insurance or pay a penalty, it is not true universal health care.

The clear virtue of universal health care is that everyone has access to health care; this means there is greater access to preventative care as well as treatment for chronic conditions. Because of this, people are more likely to receive medical attention more consistently, and sooner, which increases their well-being and life expectancy. On the other hand, many Americans are concerned that universal health care comes with too many costs: poorer-quality care, less freedom of choice, and waiting lists for care are some of their concerns. A look at the many countries that provide health insurance suggests there are certainly pros and cons to such a system. In his acclaimed book *The Healing of America: A Global Quest for Better, Cheaper, and Fairer Health Care*, T. R. Reid (2010) shows that there are waiting lists for elective procedures—hip and knee replacements—in Canada and the United Kingdom, but access to primary care doctors and emergency services are readily available. In Japan, patients have access to a wide array of new technologies and use them enthusiastically. Despite their access to the latest technologies, the government has kept the prices for these services so low that the system has a problem controlling costs. The clearest takeaway when looking at countries that have universal systems of health care is that there are many different ways to provide health care to the entire population.

One of the great advantages of the U.S. health care system is that many patients do have access to the most cutting edge technologies. Yet those who lack health insurance are entirely cut off from these services. In addition, the United States does not have a comprehensive system of preventative care. Doctors in the United States have few economic incentives to keep their patients healthy, given that they are generally paid for each visit or test they run. This is a **fee-for-service** model, which some believe incentivizes doctors to keep seeing patients rather than get them healthy and out of the system. By contrast, the National Health Service in the United Kingdom gives doctors bonuses for keeping patients healthy; rewarding them, for example, for quitting smoking or maintaining healthy blood pressure. Thus, while the United States may be the best place for patients to be *once* they get sick, it may not be the ideal system for preventing people from becoming sick in the first place.

FROM HERE TO INFINITY?: THE FUTURE OF HEALTH AND HEALTH INEQUALITIES

Across the globe, life expectancies have been rising. Many life-improving and life-extending technologies are now available, especially to those living in wealthy, modern societies. The innovations of the last 100 years beg the question: Where are we headed in terms of well-being and life expectancy? Can we expect that Americans and others in Western industrialized societies will soon routinely live past 100?

Alongside this optimistic stream of thought, this chapter highlights a more pessimistic theme: both within the United States and across the globe, substantial inequalities remain in health and well-being. Five to six years, for example, separate the life expectancies of white and black Americans, just as approximately five years separates the life expectancies of men and women. Complicating these patterns, research shows that life expectancies have actually fallen for white women with less than a high school education (in large part due to prescription drug addiction and drug overdoses) and that high rates of HIV/AIDS along with gun violence have threatened the well-being of black Americans.

On the micro-level, many efforts have been made to improve health outcomes in the United States. Starting with macro-level policy interventions, some efforts aim to alter micro-level behaviors. For example, New York City under the leadership of then-mayor Michael Bloomberg saw the posting of calorie counts on menus and the attempted restriction of large-sized sugary beverages. The thought was that these efforts would encourage more people to adopt healthier lifestyles. Other areas have imposed higher taxes on cigarettes and sugary sodas, with the goal to both curb unhealthy behaviors and raise revenues to pay for the health costs associated with these behaviors. Understanding that unhealthy behaviors are costly to society and employers, health insurance companies and employers have introduced financial incentives to employees who purchase gym memberships or work out regularly.

Meanwhile, other efforts are being made to promote health and well-being from the macro-level. Although the micro- and macro-levels are, ultimately, linked, in this sense I refer to fundamental transformations in health care policy. Passed in 2010, the controversial Patient Protection and Affordable Care Act popularly known as "ObamaCare"—seeks to extend health and well-being, in the first instance by covering more Americans. In theory, this will provide more people with greater access to care, which will help treat illnesses before they become problematic. The law also provides greater access to preventative care services. Rather than deliberately targeting individual behaviors, the plan assumes that this approach will provide broad incentives for doctors to provide and patients to seek routine care.

Frankly, it is too soon to see how these strategies will affect the health and well-being of the American population as a whole, much less health disparities along race, class, and gender lines. The sociological perspective, however, will continue to be a key tool for understanding these trends, focusing as it does on the individual and cultural factors that shape the behavior of the player along with structural dynamics that shape the game itself.

CHAPTER 14: REVIEW OF KEY POINTS

- This chapter explains inequalities in health, well-being, and life expectancy by focusing on dynamics at the micro- and macro-levels. The fact that some people live longer, healthier lives reflects both circumstances and decisions made by individual "players" and the structure of "the game" (environmental factors that shape health and well-being).

- In the United States, women live longer than men; income and education improve health and life expectancy; and the relationship between race/ethnicity and well-being is complicated, as Asian Americans and Hispanics live longer than whites and blacks.

- At the micro-level, individuals influence their health and well-being by the lifestyle choices they make; even though these are micro-level choices, lifestyle choices are correlated with a person's gender, race/ethnicity, and social class.

- Whether and how people access the healthcare system and how health professionals engage them and provide treatment for their care are also structured by gender, race, and social class. These micro-level dynamics produce patterned inequalities.

- At the macro-level, location and environmental and workplace contexts powerfully shape health inequalities across gender, race, and social class lines.

- Lower-income Americans and racial and ethnic minorities are more likely to live in food deserts and medical deserts (medically underserved areas) than more affluent and white Americans. Food and medical deserts are more common in rural areas and the urban core.

- People living in the urban core are more likely to be exposed to health risks in their homes or through the surrounding areas; these health threats include asthma triggers, lead exposure, and exposure to other toxins in the soil, air, and water.

- Men, lower-income Americans, and racial/ethnic minorities are also more likely to experience health threats due to the type of work they do. This is also a macro-level factor, due to the fact that an individual may make excellent choices but still experience significant health risks. The fact that these risks apply to large numbers of people in a systematic way also illustrates its macro-level nature.

- In order to reduce health disparities and promote health and well-being for all, changes can be made at both the micro- and macro-levels. The former would involve changing individual players' health lifestyles and health-seeking behaviors. The latter would involve changing the broader social content—using public health measures, for example, to clean up unsafe neighborhoods and workplaces, or implementing access to health care aimed at disease prevention.

CHAPTER 14: QUESTIONS FOR REVIEW

1. Looking at the information presented in this chapter, what are the social reasons that some groups of people live longer and healthier lives? How can this information be used to ensure longer and healthier lives for more people?

2. On the micro-level, it is individual factors that affect health and well-being. What are the main micro-level factors involved in this process?

3. On the macro-level, larger structural or environmental factors impact health and well-being. What are the main macro-level factors involved?

4. When you look at these two sets of explanations, do you feel that one is more important than the other in shaping health and well-being? Similarly, at which level do you think the most progress can be made in terms of promoting longer and healthier lives for more people?

5. Considering your own life experiences, in what ways do your micro-level circumstances promote or inhibit your own health and well-being? Shifting your focus to the macro-level, what aspects of your job, neighborhood, and so forth may help or hinder your health and well-being?

6. According to Richard Wilkinson and others, what are the factors that make some societies "sicker" than others? What aspects of unequal societies contribute to poor health outcomes?

KEY TERMS

alienation

asthma

autonomy

brownfields

cultural competencies

eugenics

fee-for-service

folk healer

food desert
health lifestyle
Hispanic Paradox
infant mortality
integrative medicine
lay-referral system
lead poisoning
life expectancy
medical desert
medically underserved area
opportunity hoarding

Patient Protection and Affordable Care
   Act
poverty tax
social power
stress
structural amplification
systems barrier explanation
tend-and-befriend response
Tuskegee experiment
universal health care
weathering hypothesis

REFERENCES

Anspach, Renee. 1993. *Deciding Who Lives: Fateful Choices in the Intensive-Care Nursery.* Berkeley: University of California Press.

Atkinson, Paul. 1995. *Medical Talk and Medical Work.* London: Sage.

Auerbach, Judith and Anne Figert. 1995. "Women's Health Research: Public Policy and Sociology." *Journal of Health and Social Behavior* 36(9 Extra Issue):115–131.

Ayala, Guadalupe X., Barbara Baquero, Barbara Laraia, Ming Ji, and Laura Linnan. 2013. "Efficacy of a Store-Based Environmental Change Intervention Compared With a Delayed Treatment Control Condition on Store Customers' Intake of Fruits and Vegetables." *Public Health Nutrition* 16(11):1953–1960.

Balsa, Ana I. and Thomas G. McGuire. 2003. "Prejudice, Clinical Uncertainty and Stereotyping as Sources of Health Disparities." *Journal of Health Economics* 22(1):89–116.

Brenton, Joslyn. 2014. "In Pursuit of Health: Mothers, Children, and the Negotiation of an Elusive Ideal." PhD dissertation, Department of Sociology, North Carolina State University, Raleigh.

Bureau of Labor Statistics. 2014. "News Release: National Census of Fatal Occupational Injuries, Preliminary Results." Washington, D.C.: U.S. Department of Labor. Retrieved April 23, 2015 (http://www.bls.gov/news.release/pdf/cfoi.pdf)

Centers for Disease Control and Prevention. 2013. "Current Cigarette Smoking Among Adults in the United States." Atlanta, GA: Centers for Disease Control and Prevention. Retrieved April 23, 2015 (http://www.cdc.gov/tobacco/data_statistics/fact_sheets/adult_data/cig_smoking/index.htm#national)

Chen, Susan E., Raymond J. G. M. Florax, and Samantha D. Snyder. 2013. "Obesity and Fast Food in Urban Markets: A New Approach Using Geo-referenced Micro Data." *Health Economics* 22(7):835–856.

Cohen, Elizabeth. 2007. "Tuskegee's Ghost: Fear Hinders Black Marrow Donation." Retrieved December 20, 2013 (CNN.com).

Cummins Steven, Anne Findlay, Mark Petticrew, and Leigh Sparks. 2005. "Healthy Cities: The Impact of Food Retail-led Regeneration on Food Access, Choice and Retail Structure." *Built Environment* 31(4):288–301.

Dutton, Diana B. 1978. "Explaining the Low Use of Health Services by the Poor: Costs, Attitudes, or Delivery Systems." *American Sociological Review* 43(3):348–368.

Economic Research Service (ERS). 2009. "Access to Affordable and Nutritious Food: Measuring and Understanding Food Deserts and Their Consequences." Washington, DC: United States Department of Agriculture. Retrieved December 30, 2013 (http://www.ers.usda.gov/publications/ap-administrative-publication/ap-036.aspx).

Eschbach, Karl, Glenn V. Ostir, Kushang V. Patel, Kyriakos S. Markides, and James S. Goodwin. 2004. "Neighborhood Context and Mortality among Older Mexican Americans: Is There a Barrio Advantage?" *American Journal of Public Health* 94(10):1807–1812.

Fadiman, Ann. 1997. *The Spirit Catches You and You Fall Down.* New York: Farrar, Straus, and Giroux.

Farmer, Melissa and Kenneth F. Ferraro. 2005. "Are Racial Disparities in Health Conditional on Socioeconomic Status?" *Social Science and Medicine* 60(1):191–204.

Fellowes, Matt. 2006. "From Poverty, Opportunity: Putting the Market to Work for Lower Income Families." Washington, DC: The Brookings Institution. Retrieved December 31, 2013 (http://www.brookings.edu/research/reports/2006/07/poverty-fellowes).

Freidson, Eliot. 1960. "Client Control and Medical Practice." *American Journal of Sociology* 64(4):374–382.

Geronimus, Arline T. 1992. "The Weathering Hypothesis and the Health of African American Women and Infants." *Ethnicity and Disease* 2(3):207–221.

Goesling Brian. 2007. "The Rising Significance of Education for Health." *Social Forces* 85(4): 1621–1644.

Gruchalla, Rebecca S., Jacqueline Pongracic, Marshall Plaut, Richard Evans, Cynthia M. Visness, Michelle Walter, Ellen F. Crain, Meyer Kattan, Wayne J. Morgan, Suzanne Steinbach, James Stoud, George Malindzak, Ernestine Smartt, and Herman Mitchell. 2005. "Inner City Asthma Study: Relationships among Sensitivity, Allergen Exposure, and Asthma Morbidity." *The Journal of Allergy and Clinical Immunology* 115(3):478–485.

Grzywacz, Joseph G. and Nadine Marks. 2001. "Social Inequalities and Exercise during Adulthood: Toward an Ecological Perspective." *Journal of Health and Social Behavior* 42:202–220.

Horta, Bernardo L., Rajiv Bahl, Jose C. Martinez, and Cesar G. Victora. 2007. "Evidence of the Long-Term Effects of Breastfeeding: Systematic Reviews and Meta-Analysis." Geneva, Switzerland: World Health Organization. Retrieved November 27, 2013 (http://whqlibdoc.who.int/publications/2007/9789241595230_eng.pdf)

Hummer, Robert A., Daniel A. Powers, Starling G. Pullum, Ginger L. Gossman, and W. Parker Frisbie. 2007. "Paradox Found (Again): Infant Mortality among the Mexican-Origin Population in the United States." *Demography* 44(3):441–457.

Innocenti, Paolo, Edward H. Morrow, and Damian K. Dowling. 2011. "Experimental Evidence Supports a Sex-Specific Selective Sieve in Mitochondrial Genome Evolution." *Science* 332 (6031):845–848.

Lantz, Paula M., James S. House, Richard P. Mero, and David R. Williams. 2005. "Stress, Life Events, and Socioeconomic Disparities in Health: Results from the Americans Changing Lives Study." *Journal of Health and Social Behavior* 46(3):274–288.

Larson, Nicole I., Mary T. Story, and Melissa C. Nelson. 2009. "Neighborhood Environments: Disparities in Access to Healthy Foods in the U.S." *American Journal of Preventive Medicine* 36(1):74–81.e10.

Link, Bruce G. and Jo Phelan. 1995. "Social Conditions as Fundamental Causes of Disease." *Journal of Health and Social Behavior* 35(Extra Issue):80–94.

Link, Bruce and Jo Phelan. 2001. "Conceptualizing Stigma." *Annual Review of Sociology* (27) 363–385.

Lu, Michael C, and Neal Halfon. 2003. "Racial and Ethnic Disparities in Birth Outcomes: A Life-Course Perspective." *Maternal and Child Health Journal* 7(1):13–30.

Mari Gallagher Research & Consulting Group. 2006. "Examining the Impact of Food Deserts on Public Health in Chicago." Chicago, IL: Mari Gallagher Research and Consulting. Retrieved April 23, 2015 (http://www.marigallagher.com/site_media/dynamic/project_files/Chicago_Food_Desert_Report.pdf).

Mirowsky, John and Catherine E. Ross. 2003. *Education, Social Status, and Health.* New York: Aldine de Gruyter.

National Center for Health Statistics. 2014. "Health, United States, 2013: With Special Feature on Prescription Drugs." Hyattsville, MD: U.S. Department of Health and Human Services/Centers for Disease Control and Prevention. Retrieved April 23, 2015 (http://www.cdc.gov/nchs/data/hus/hus13.pdf#018)

OECD. 2014. *Society at a Glance 2014: OECD Social Indicators.* Paris, France: OECD Publishing.

Pearlin, Leonard I. 1989. "The Sociological Study of Stress." *Journal of Health and Social Behavior* 30:241–256.

Pearlin, Leonard I., Scott Schieman, Elena M. Fazio, and Stephen C. Meersman. 2005. "Stress, Health, and the Life Course: Some Conceptual Perspectives." *Journal of Health and Social Behavior* 46(2):205–219.

Phelan, Jo, Bruce G. Link, Ana Diez-Roux, Ichiro Kawachi, and Bruce Levin. 2004. "'Fundamental Causes' of Social Inequalities in Mortality: A Test of the Theory." *Journal of Health and Social Behavior* 45(3):265–285.

Reid, T.R., 2010. *The Healing of America: A Global Quest for Better, Cheaper, and Fairer Health Care.* New York: Penguin Books.

Ross, Catherine E. 2000. "Neighborhood Disadvantage and Adult Depression." *Journal of Health and Social Behavior* 41:177–187.

Rundall, Thomas G. and John R. C. Wheeler. 1979. "The Effect of Income on Use of Preventative Care: An Evaluation of Alternative Explanations." *Journal of Health and Social Behavior* 20(4):397–406.

Schnittker, Jason. 2004. "Education and the Changing Shape of the Income Gradient in Health." *Journal of Health and Social Behavior* 45(3):286–305.

Sharfstein, Joshua and Megan Sandel. 1998. "Inadequate Housing: A Health Crisis for the Children of the Poor." *Journal of Housing and Community Development* 55(1):14–24.

Sharfstein, Joshua, Megan Sandel, Robert Kahn, and Robert Bauchner. 2001. "Is Child Health at Risk While Families Wait for Housing Vouchers?" *American Journal of Public Health* 91(8): 1191–1192.

Shulman, Kevin A., Jesse A. Berlin, William Harless, Jon F. Kerner, Shyrl Sistrunk, Bernard J. Gersh, Ross Dubé, Christopher K. Taleghani, Jennifer E. Burke, Sankey Williams, John M. Eisenberg, William Ayers, and José J. Escarce. 1999. "The Effect of Race and Sex on Physicians' Recommendations for Cardiac Catheterization." *New England Journal of Medicine* 340:618–626.

Silber, Jeffrey H., Paul R. Rosenbaum, Amy S. Clark, Bruce J. Giantonio, Richard N. Ross, Yun Teng, Min Wang, Bijan A. Nikham, Justin M. Ludwig, Wei Wang, Orit Even-Shoshan, and Kevin R. Fox. 2013. "Characteristics Associated With Differences in Survival Among

Black and White Women With Breast Cancer." *Journal of the American Medical Association* 310(4):389–397.

Skloot, Rebecca. 2011. *The Immortal Life of Henrietta Lacks*. New York: Broadway Books.

Smedly, Brian D., Adrienne Y. Stith, and Alan R. Nelson. 2003. *Unequal Treatment: Confronting Racial and Ethnic Disparities in Health Care*. Washington, DC: Institute of Medicine/ The National Academies Press.

Taylor, Shelley E., Laura Cousino Klein, Brian P. Lewis, Tara L. Gruenewald, Regan A. R. Gurung, and John A. Updegraff. 2000. "Biobehavioral Responses to Stress in Females: Tend-and-Befriend, not Fight-or-Flight." *Psychological Review* 107(3):411–429.

Thoits, Peggy A. 1995. "Stress, Coping, and Social Support Processes: Where Are We? What Next?" *Journal of Health and Social Behavior* 35(Extra Issue):53–79.

Turner, R. Jay and William R. Avison. 2003. "Status Variations in Stress Exposure: Implications for the Interpretation of Research on Race, Socioeconomic Status, and Gender." *Journal of Health and Social Behavior* 44:488–505.

U.S. Census Bureau/Current Population Reports. 2014. "Health Insurance Coverage in the United States: 2013." Washington, D.C. Retrieved April 23, 2015 (http://www.census.gov/ content/dam/Census/library/publications/2014/demo/p60-250.pdf)

Waitzkin, Howard. 1991. *The Politics of Medical Encounters*. New Haven, CT: Yale University Press.

Waitzkin, Howard. 2001. *At the Front Lines of Medicine: How the Medical Care System Alienates Doctors and Mistreats Patients . . . and What We Can Do About It*. Lanham, MD: Rowman and Littlefield.

Warren, John Robert and Elaine M. Hernandez. 2007. "Did Socioeconomic Inequalities in Morbidity and Mortality Change in the United States Over the Course of the Twentieth Century?" *Journal of Health and Social Behavior* 48(4):335–351.

Wickrama, K.A.S., Rand G. Conger, Lora Ebert Wallace, and Glen H. Elder, Jr. 1999. "The Intergenerational Transmission of Health-Risk Behaviors: Adolescent Lifestyles and Gender Moderating Effects." *Journal of Health and Social Behavior* 40:258–272.

Wilkinson, Richard G. 2002. *Unhealthy Societies: The Afflictions of Inequality*. London: Routledge.

Wrigley, Neil, Daniel Warm, and Barrie Margetts. 2003. "Deprivation, Diet, and Food-Retail Access: Findings from the Leeds 'Food Deserts' Study." *Environment and Planning A* 35(1):151–188.

Zhang, Nanhua, Harolyn W. Baker, Margaret Tufts, Randall E. Raymond, Hamisu Salihu, and Michael R. Elliott. 2013. "Early Childhood Lead Exposure and Academic Achievement: Evidence from Detroit Public Schools, 2008–2010." *American Journal of Public Health* 103(3): e72–e77.

Credits